Object-Oriented Systems Analysis and Design

Noushin Ashrafi

Professor of Information System
University of Massachusetts–Boston

Hessam Ashrafi

Software Architect

Pearson Education International

VP, Editorial Director: Sally Yagan
AVP, Executive Editor: Bob Horan
Product Development Manager: Ashley Santora
Editorial Assistant: Kelly Loftus
Marketing Manager: Anne Fahlgren
Permissions Project Manager: Charles Morris
Senior Managing Editor: Judy Leale
Production Project Manager: Mike Lackey
Senior Operations Specialist: Arnold Vila

Operations Specialist: Carol O'Rourke
AV Project Manager: Rhonda Aversa
Manager, Rights and Permissions: Zina Arabia
Manager, Visual Research: Beth Brenzel
Composition: Integra Software Services
Full-Service Project Management: BookMasters, Inc.
Printer/Binder: Edwards Brothers
Cover Printer: Coral Graphics
Typeface: 10/12 Palatino

Credits and acknowledgments borrowed from other sources and reproduced, with permission, in this textbook appear on appropriate page within text.

If you purchased this book within the United States or Canada you should be aware that it has been wrongfully imported without the approval of the Publisher or the Author.

Pearson Prentice Hall™ is a trademark of Pearson Education, Inc.
Pearson® is a registered trademark of Pearson plc
Prentice Hall® is a registered trademark of Pearson Education, Inc.

Pearson Education Ltd., London
Pearson Education Singapore, Pte. Ltd
Pearson Education, Canada, Inc.
Pearson Education–Japan
Pearson Education Australia PTY, Limited

Pearson Education North Asia, Ltd., Hong Kong
Pearson Educación de Mexico, S.A. de C.V.
Pearson Education Malaysia, Pte. Ltd
Pearson Education Upper Saddle River, New Jersey

Prentice Hall
is an imprint of

www.pearsonhighered.com

10 9 8 7 6 5 4 3 2 1
ISBN-13: 978-0-13-135479-1
ISBN-10:   0-13-135479-5

BRIEF CONTENTS

CONTENTS

iv

PART II: ANALYSIS   101

PREFACE

Building information systems requires a highly abstract way of thinking that has very practical consequences. This dual nature of software development makes it both intensely satisfying and highly challenging. An architectural framework is an indispensible necessity but is useless or, worse, counterproductive unless it is supported by a good grasp of engineering principles and tools. In turn, the best engineering tools and techniques, by themselves, do not lead to the development of a successful information system.

Between the extremes of practice and theory, we have chosen to follow an approach that can be best described as **pragmatism**: We have not suggested theories and methodologies just because they appear logical or are fashionable, but because they can work in practice; we have not proposed tools and techniques only because they shine in solving a subset of problems posed by the development challenge, but because they complement each other within the broader framework of theory.

Software development is a kind of product development—a very special kind, but many of its basic concepts would remain valid even within the ongoing technological whirlwind. More than anything else, we have tried to indentify and clarify these concepts.

The approach of this book is to present the tools within the context of modeling and modeling within the context of system development, not the other way around. To learn modeling or Unified Modeling Language (UML) is not an end into itself but a means toward an end. We learn UML because it is an effective and flexible modeling language, and we promote a model-driven approach because we believe it to be the best way, or perhaps the only way, to create complex but reliable software through teamwork.

The technology and acceptance of object-oriented development have moved far faster in the marketplace than in the classroom. The theory has been tempered and enriched by experience and by experiments. From modeling to analysis and from design to programming, object-oriented methods and tools have proven to be winners.

WHY THIS BOOK?

Textbooks on object-oriented software development, like books in any other field, are of varying quality. Quite a few of them have very worthwhile elements, but the main reason that persuaded us to write this book is that they all fall short in one aspect or another. Some have a strong theoretical core, but cannot succeed in the classroom because their language is too inaccessible to the students or they have ignored the need for case studies and practical examples.

Altogether, existing textbooks fall into three categories:

❶ "Legacy" textbooks that use process modeling with data-flow diagrams and/or data modeling with entity-relationship diagrams. These books have grafted some object-oriented analysis and design topics to retain their presence, but mostly as an afterthought, not as an integral part. Some of them are indeed very good at their original intent: to teach traditional system analysis and design. But the teachers will most likely skip the object-oriented topics, either because they run out of time, or it is too difficult to convince the student of their relevance.

❷ Textbooks that do focus on object-oriented system analysis and design, but in one way or another fail to show the advantages of object orientation. They are either too technical, concerned with "in" arguments, or are not able to exactly show how to apply object orientation to an actual development undertaking. Although they have been in the market for a while, none have succeeded as textbooks on object-oriented system analysis and design.

❸ Textbooks that do apply object-oriented system analysis and design to the development lifecycle, but have other shortcomings: (I) the integration is uneven—for example, object-oriented concepts are introduced in the first chapter but then disappear until many chapters afterwards; (II) the concepts are over-simplified; or (III) from the first chapter, the exercises and the case studies pose problems that sometimes even veterans would need a good amount of time to analyze and solve with a minimum degree of satisfaction.

We also have to mention non-textbooks—written by gurus and experts such as Booch and Jacobson—which are, justifiably, the most celebrated books on object orientation and UML. However, they are written for software architects and engineers in a highly technical language and are not suitable for teaching information system students. Without their books, a book such as ours would not be possible, but they are not performing the same function.

OUR OBJECTIVES

Object-oriented software development is now mature, and the student who hopes to become a player in the field needs, and deserves, a mature book. To prepare for the challenge, the student needs a textbook that:

- provides a firm grounding in the theory of object orientation through a narrative that is **comprehensive but appealing and clear**. It must converse *with* the students instead of talking *over* their heads by stringing together important-sounding but insufficiently explained terms, talking *at* them by a **dogmatic approach** to concepts, or talking *down* to them by **over-simplifying**.
- provides a **balance between theory and hands-on experience**. It must illustrate the relevance and the significance of the object-oriented approach toward development by examples and case studies that are interesting and relevant but are not dumbed down to fit the most simple-minded interpretation of the theory.
- takes a fresh look at the subject and liberates it from the baggage of mantras that textbooks often repeat because *other* textbooks have invoked them but are now out-of-date or were never really relevant.
- takes into account the most recent developments in concepts and tools such as **patterns**, **component-based development**, and **service-oriented architecture**.
- helps the teacher to help the students. It provides the instructor with case studies, tests, and up-to-date extra materials that pick their interests, encourage their independent thinking, and allow the teacher to be more than a book reader.

THE IMPORTANT FEATURES

We believe that the following features enhance the value of our book:

- **Business Relevance.** Software development has to produce working products, and producing actual products, unlike making models, does not follow a clear-cut path nor take place in a clean laboratory. How can a textbook help the student in the transition from schoolroom to the workroom? A textbook certainly needs examples and case studies that fit the theory (and we have included many of them), but it also needs to illustrate what to do when situations do not fit the theory, the people with whom one works do not follow the expected game plan, resources are inadequate, the established practices are short-sighted or counter-productive, etc. No book can replace experience, but most examples in this book (and on its companion Web site) aim to illustrate not only the concepts, but also the *context* in which the concepts must be realized. Our main ongoing case study (the development of an information system for a fictional "Walden Hospital") was selected not because it was easy but, on the contrary, because it posed challenges that are frequently encountered in a business setting.

- **Technological Relevance.** In software development, as we said, the object-oriented technology is now mature: It is no longer an academic ideal or a research laboratory project. *Every* chapter in this book has the following fact in its sight, explicitly or implicitly: The result of all analysis and design must be implemented in code, and this code is object-oriented (except in a few islands that "Time Forgot"). To put it another way, if it does not work for the object-orientated technology, it is not there. What is more, technologies are embodied in products but teaching the principles and the basic concepts of a technology must go beyond studying specific products (although both are necessary). This book remembers the distinction by teaching about analysis and design modeling tools that apply to existing products but, in all likelihood, will outlive them.

- **The Wide View.** For any textbook such as this, technology is both a boon and a bane. Detachment from the ever-changing technological landscape will consign the book to irrelevance. On the other hand, tying it too tightly to a set of technologies will condemn the education that it provides to inevitable obsolescence. Our approach to walking this tightrope has been to (I) introduce the concept in broad terms, (II) illustrate it by presenting readily understandable examples which are not limited to software development, and only then (III) apply it to existing or emerging technologies. We present object orientation in its wider context, both in time and in place. We provide the students with the background, the analysis, the examples, and the comparisons so they can observe the concepts as they relate to their broader surroundings.

- **Clear Narrative.** A textbook can have only so many pages and cover only so many topics. Within this limited physical and intellectual space, any author (including us) is liable to present a jumbled narrative and, in the process, lose the student's interest and concentration. Or a technically correct discourse might turn into a disappointing lesson in pedagogy. We have exerted a considerable effort to keep the narrative clear and flowing. Everybody likes a good story, even if it is about object orientation.

- **Forthrightness.** We have been clear on what object orientation *does* and *does not*. Creating an information system needs many ingredients besides any model of analysis and design, be it object-oriented or otherwise. We will not make excessive claims for object orientation, by commission *or* by omission.

SPECIAL CHAPTERS

A major goal of this book is to teach concepts that are vital to the real development process but have been partially or totally missing from the classroom. Among them are the following chapters:

- **Domain Analysis** (chapter 5). Domain analysis should be called the "missing link" in system development. Requirements are meaningful only if they are studied *in context*, and no product can be successful if analysis ignores the context in which it has to work.
- **Patterns** (chapter 14). Patterns are increasingly important to the industry but, perhaps, perceived as too difficult to teach in an introductory course. We believe that this chapter will prove that this is not the case.
- **Components & Reuse** (chapter 15). Software has become too complex for each development project to reinvent the wheel. Components and their virtual siblings, Web services, are the most important vehicles for reuse and are now a established presence in the industry.
- **Architecture** (chapter 16). The construction of a house cannot start without some sort of an architectural plan and yet many—including practitioners—behave as though an information system can be built without one.

THE STRUCTURE OF THE BOOK

The book has three sections:

- Part I, **The Foundations**, presents the basic concepts for understanding information systems, object orientation, methodology, and project management.
- Part II, **Analysis**, explores how to discover and gather requirements, how to analyze the "problem space" to put requirements in context, and how to arrive at a conceptual model of the solution.
- Part III, **Design**, focuses on the "solution space" or how to design a solution from the conceptual model.

Each chapter is *relatively* independent. Sometimes a concept has been repeated, but from a new viewpoint. However, no chapter is completely self-contained: It is a constituent part of a narrative that can be fully understood only within the context of previous and subsequent chapters. This approach is *intentional* since software development and object orientation rely on complex and interrelated concepts that cannot be introduced or concluded within a single chapter.

In each chapter of the book:

- An **Introduction** lays out the purpose of what is to come. In most chapters, the introduction also covers the logical connection with the topics and the concepts in the previous chapter.
- A **Wrap-Up** fulfills the **Objectives** laid out at the beginning of the chapter and rounds up the topics discussed. It is more than a simple summary as it aims to present the content from a slightly different point of view.
- **Key Concepts** provides a short description for the concepts discussed in the chapter, including—but not limited to—technical terms.

- Instead of asking the students to repeat what they have memorized, **Review Questions** poses problems that the students can answer by *applying* the concepts learned in the chapter.
- **Suggested Readings** is not limited to a list but discusses how the students can benefit from the suggested literature in the context of the chapter.
- **References** honors the sources, whether quotation marks are used or not. If the reference is a book, we have consistently identified the page number and have not left the reader wondering how to find the context.

CASE STUDIES AND EXERCISES

Besides examples that clarify and illustrate each concept or tool, the book follows one case, the **Walden Medical Center**, from gathering requirements to architecture and implementation. The first three chapters lay the theoretical groundwork for what the rest of the book aims at: a pragmatic roadmap to system analysis and design.

In addition, we have provided four more ongoing cases: marketing and subscriptions for a sports magazines, a car dealership, a pizza shop, and a real estate agency. Guided by the teacher, the students can apply what they have learned to cases that focus on the "real world."

RESEARCH PROJECTS AND TEAMWORK

The development of any complex product depends *equally* on how well individuals can perform and how well individual accomplishments can be integrated into a *working* whole. No book can teach this vital skill, but it can (and must) supply the raw material for the exercise. The "practical" chapters in this book provide students with five more ongoing case studies for both individual research and teamwork.

THE WEB SITE

Nobody is ignorant of the fact that everything about software development changes with lightning speed. Some "innovations" prove to be passing fashions or marketing buzzwords, but even these cannot be ignored because they raise questions from an increasingly computer-savvy student body that cannot be instructed to leave them at the classroom door. A printed book has its advantages, but the ability to update itself on short notice is not one them. Plus, it cannot be easily adapted to various backgrounds, expectations, and preferences of different teachers or students.

The World Wide Web has already replaced the "teacher's manual," but it can do much more in keeping both the teachers and the students up-to-date and satisfy their diverse approaches. The Web site for this book, of course, offers the full range of what the teachers require:

- **Answers** to review questions or examples when the question asks for examples.
- **PowerPoint slides** for each chapter.
- Solutions—text and diagrams—for **case studies**.

- **Test banks**, with enough variety for the teacher to design tests that do not repeat themselves easily.

We do, however, aim higher. The **supplements** on the Web provides both the teacher and the student with:

- **Topic discussions**, short essays, or stories that expand on the topics covered in the book.
- **Reference material** and **examples** that supply an extra layer of detail when needed.
- **Ideas** for teaching, or studying, each chapter.
- **Updates** to printed topics, when the occasion demands it.
- **New discussions** that the teachers or the students may suggest to authors.

The printed book stands by itself, but the Web site is not an afterthought: They were conceived together and complement each other.

ILLUSTRATIONS AS NARRATIVES

The illustrations in this book are not decorative. They were designed to narrate a topic or a chapter visually. Often, they serve as a visual index or overview of the whole chapter. (Full-color versions of many illustrations are included in the PowerPoint slides.)

Diagrams follow what we preach throughout the book: They must ❶ be understandable and ❷ serve a purpose. We have avoided diagrams that might impress the layperson by their complexity, but are utterly useless in practice.

THE MARKETPLACE FACTOR

Software development is a practical field. A college-level course should rise above purely practical or market considerations, but it cannot be irrelevant to them. Unfortunately, "irrelevant" is precisely how many topics in system analysis and design courses have gradually become—in spite of the dedication and enthusiasm of most teachers. A graduate armed with the best knowledge in Structural Analysis would be very lucky to find any job in the industry. To continue to hold on to obsolete concepts is a disservice both to the students and to their teachers.

The globalization of software development—"outsourcing" or "off-shoring" as it is often called—is not a subject of a course on system development, but it is a factor that must be seriously taken into account. Among other things, it results from the increasing complexity of software which, in turn, forces **specialization**. Crudely put, to succeed in the global market, one has to climb higher in the "food chain." Gaps in the classroom would become holes in the armor of graduates when they have to face the global competition in the marketplace.

This book, however, is not about how academia can catch up with the industry. On the contrary, it is written in the belief that academia can enrich the industry by giving the students what they seek and what they deserve: **knowledge without compromise**.

ACKNOWLEDGMENTS

We would like to thank the many colleagues who reviewed the manuscript and offered valuable feedback. Their comments were pivotal in the development of this text:

Nenad Jukic, *Loyola University Chicago*
Makoto Nakayama, *DePaul University*
Solomon Negash, *Kennesaw State University*
Sridhar Nerur, *University of Texas, Arlington*
Sarah Pulimood, *The College of New Jersey*
Srinivasan Raghunathan, *University of Texas at Dallas*
Eliot Rich, *University at Albany, SUNY*
Larry Seligman, *University of Georgia*

The authors especially wish to thank **David Carroll, Ph.D.,** for his invaluable contribution to this book. His depth of knowledge, his breadth of experience, and—not least—his critical eye and patience were there when we needed them. The authors also wish to thank Jen Welsch, Nancy Ahr, and Rebecca Roby of BookMasters, Inc., for their highly professional and caring assistance with the production of this volume.

All shortcomings in this book, however, are entirely ours. We just hope they are not many.

ABOUT THE AUTHORS

Noushin Ashrafi, Ph.D., is a full professor of Management Information Systems (MIS) at the University of Massachusetts in Boston. She has been an active teacher and scholar in the Information Systems discipline since 1989. She has conducted seminars and workshops in the United States, Europe, Mexico, Russia, and China. Her research fields include application of operations research and management science tools to measuring, controlling, and predicting the reliability of conventional software and expert systems; software process improvement; and security and privacy issues in e-Business. Her most recent research focuses on IT capabilities for business agility.

Dr. Ashrafi has developed and taught courses both in information systems and production operation management disciplines. She has taught object-oriented system analysis and design for the last four years at both graduate and undergraduate levels. During this time, she has carefully tested the concepts presented in this book in her classes and implemented the feedback from her students in the book. Her publications have appeared both in technical journals such as *IEEE Transactions* and IT management periodicals such as *Information and Management, Journal of Database Management,* and *The Journal of Information Technology Management.*

Hessam Ashrafi is a New York-based software architect and consultant who has experienced first-hand the good, the bad, and the ugly of actual system development for nearly three decades. In this time, he has developed a diverse set of applications and information systems for a diverse set of industries, including financial applications for oil industry and Wall Street firms, package tracking and purchasing for an international cosmetics company, distribution and project management for a film studio, stock trading and portfolio management, inventory management, and cargo transportation. In between, he also taught corporate developers and ran user groups.

He has lived through the transition of software from punch cards to time-sharing, from mainframes to personal computers, from primitive networks to the Web, from machine and assembly languages to the object-oriented ones. Many of the stories, insights, and practical conclusions in this book result from his personal experience and observations.

Chapter

1

Information Systems

1. OVERVIEW

Information systems are systems that process data into information. We can view an information system from various perspectives: its goals, its processes or its components, that is, applications, information technology, people, and procedures.

Information systems are also products, and like other products they must satisfy their consumers and be developed by following a methodology that ensures the best possible quality and the best possible use of resources.

Chapter Topics

➤ Information and its components.

➤ System and its components.

➤ An overview of information systems.

➤ An introduction to information technology.

➤ The core building blocks of information technology.

➤ The concept of "application."

➤ Information systems as products.

➤ The business of developing information system products.

➤ Information system as the infrastructure of the business.

➤ The enterprise of software development.

Introduction

To develop a modern information system, we must start with a clear understanding that an information system is primarily a *commercial product*. All products such as cars, houses, or computers might be built to satisfy demands or wishes that fall outside the domain of the marketplace, but it is the marketplace that defines their center of gravity and shapes their overall features.

Furthermore, we cannot arrive at an effective understanding of information systems unless we comprehend their **components**—what they do, how they relate to each other, and how they work together. Developing information systems and software applications involves highly *abstract* concepts that have very *concrete* outcomes and sometimes very serious consequences.

The term "information system" is relatively recent, but the concept is as old as history. As many historians have concluded, writing appeared with the need for accounting, the first application of information systems. Accounting has always exemplified the everlasting components of the information systems: data as *input*, statements and balances as *output*, arithmetic as the application of **logic** (processing), some sort of *storage* or data management system, **security** to prevent unauthorized access, and *communication* through oral and written symbols.

Information automation, however, has changed both the reach and role of information systems within the human civilization. Information automation means that a nonhuman device can apply information logic to data through a set of stored instructions or a "program." This, in turn, means that information processing can become more capital-intensive and less labor-intensive. Another consequence has been the increasing *commoditization* of information systems. By packaging information logic into software, automation has allowed information systems and applications to become *market* products.

All commercial products have three basic traits in common: ❶ they must satisfy certain requirements or take advantage of opportunities, ❷ they are human artifacts and, therefore, must be built, and ❸ their development must follow a methodology that helps to lower costs, raise quality, and make success more likely.

To say, however, that the development of a product must follow a methodology is not to say all products must be developed following the *same* methodology. Even with the same product, methodology changes with technology, experience, theory, scale, and context.

Figure 1.1
Information System and Its Components

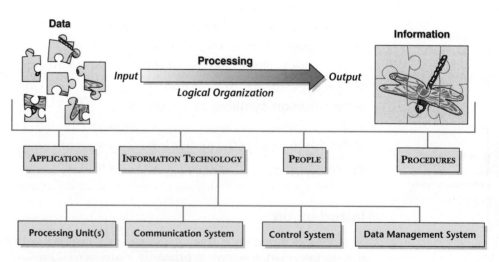

An information system can be viewed from two angles: what requirements it must satisfy and how it satisfies those requirements.

A concise but separate review of both "information" and "system" is necessary before we can effectively introduce information systems. The reach of both terms is very wide, but each one constraints the other: An information system is *not* concerned with every kind of information, but only those that can be obtained by processing data through a system; it is *not* any system, but an open system that accepts input, produces output, and has understandable logic.

Any information system requires an information technology, but the information technology is not the same as the information system. The latter is not one technology, but an interrelated and often rapidly changing *collection* of technologies and subsystems.

Information

> Information is an organized collection of data that allows its recipient to ❶ gain knowledge, ❷ draw meaning, ❸ arrive at conclusions, or ❹ execute a set of actions to reach an objective.

From this definition, it follows that the term "information" covers a very vast ground:

☞ A broad definition of "information" would also include works of art and entertainment—novels, poems, movies, etc.—even though their data are not "real." These works, however, are outside the scope of this book, which is information systems, not information in general.

👆 Any information also relies on a **cultural context** to be meaningful.

- A news report in the paper, on the radio, or on TV.
- The itinerary of your upcoming trip.
- The year-end balance sheet of a company.
- A business report.
- A fire alarm.
- A bank statement.
- A book on system analysis and design.

These items are all information—regardless of whether the data consists of words, sounds, numbers, images, or other symbols. Some, like alarms and traffic signs, are designed to communicate their intentions immediately, with a minimum amount of data and a minimal need for interpretation. At the other end of the spectrum, news reports, books, and documentaries paint a complex picture by offering a large amount of data within a narrative composed of numerous logical packages (sentences, paragraphs, pictures, dialogues, and scenes).

In practice, how we characterize "information" depends on our judgment and on our expectations. However, regardless of how we designate it, any information has three main constituents: **data,** *purpose, and logical organization*.

Data

> Data are the building blocks of information.

☞ Properly speaking, *data* is the plural form of Latin *datum* and many insist that the separation between the plural and the singular should be maintained. But, for better or for worse, it seems that "data" will play both roles in the English language. Therefore, it is the verb that must distinguish between "data" as a single item and "data" as plural.

The original meaning of *datum* in English was "assumption." And "fact," at some point in the past, meant "crime" (a meaning which still applies to "accessory after the fact.")

Data are the facts *or* assumptions that are structured within a logical framework to convey information. In other words, data are the ***raw material*** for information:

Data	Information
Deposits, withdrawals, interest, and service charges for a certain month, plus the forwarding balance from the previous month.	Bank Statement
Moving images, dialog, music, and commentary.	Television Report
Titles, subtitles, words, paragraphs, quotations, and pictures.	Newspaper Report
The red outline of a circle bisected by a red line.	No Entry!
Weigh, height, cholesterol, sugar level, age, symptoms, etc.	Patient Profile

It is often said that data are meaningless by themselves until they are turned into information. (Hence the modifier "raw," which is frequently added to "data.") This is true in many cases, especially when the data consists of numbers, but the relationship between data and information is usually multileveled and subtle: A deposit to your bank account is meaningful by itself, even though it must be placed in the context of other data to present the monthly activity and the state of your bank account. (See *Data Hierarchy* later in this chapter.)

"Unfounded" is the usual term for the information that lacks data or is based on wrong or incomplete assumptions.

Goal

Information has an objective.

Any information must have a ***purpose***, a meaning that it wants to impart or a goal that it wants to achieve. Some goals are simple, some are ambitious, and some are open to multiple interpretations:

☞ A logical conclusion (or information) would prove incorrect if the data are wrong or unrelated. **Logic is a matter of form, not of content**. In other

Information	Purpose
Bank Statement	Reports how much money you had in your account at the beginning of the month, the amounts that you deposited or withdrew during the month, bank charges, and how much you have now.
Television Report	Communicates (or tries to communicate) the what, when, where, how, and (perhaps) why of an event to its audience.
Year-End Corporate Report	Attempts to tell shareholders (or anybody else who might be interested) how well the corporation did in the previous year (and why) and what to expect for the next year.

If the information lacks an understandable purpose, we call it "pointless," "rambling," or a similar term.

Logic

> The objective of information is achieved through logic.

To arrive from data to meaning, information must follow a logic—simple or complex, apparent or not readily apparent. ("Nonsense" is the term we apply to information if it lacks logic, and "misleading" or "sophistry" is applied if it follows an unacceptable logic.)

The purpose and the logical organization of information may be combined into an infinite number of packages. The only constant is that without either, data does *not* become information.

Figure 1.2 is an easy-to-understand chart. Acme International enjoyed a rapid growth from 1995 to 2002, but witnessed its fortunes reversed in the 2003–2004 period. Left to themselves, the underlying data would not enlighten us as to the fortunes of the company. By correlating the sales figures (the Y axis) and the years (the X axis) we arrive at certain conclusions (or knowledge).

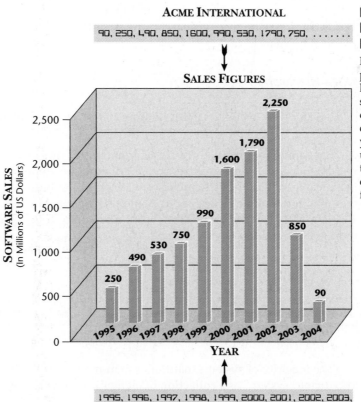

Figure 1.2
From Data to Information

Information results from providing data with a logical organization that serves a purpose. In this chart, it is the logical correlation between the years and the sales figures for 10-year periods that allows us to conclude that Acme has fallen on hard times.

Two points are crucial for understanding how data is processed into information:

❶ *Information uses data selectively.*   Since the process has a purpose, the data that underlies the information is always selective *because it must relate to the purpose.* For example, our chart does not represent *all* data about Acme International (which is not possible, in any case); nor does it even show *all* sales figures, but only *software* sales and only *yearly* totals for a specific period.

❷ *Information is only as valid as the logic that produces it.*   Since the process organizes data based on a certain logic, if the logic is wrong, distorted, or incomplete, the resulting knowledge will be wrong, distorted, or incomplete as well, even if *every* assumption is an undisputable fact. The chart about Acme International suggests a company in trouble, but what if Acme has a thriving *hardware* business and is actually dismantling its software division by selling it off piece by piece? If the answer to this question is affirmative, then the logic of presenting *only* the software sales as a reference to the overall fortunes of Acme is misleading.

Symbols

> Both data and information are expressed as symbols.

The bulk of information that we send or receive is expressed through verbal symbols. But information is by no means limited to verbal messages. (The chart in Figure 1.2 is a hybrid message: Its verbal and visual elements reinforce each other.) Information can be delivered by sound, pictures, or multimedia as well: traffic signs, smoke signals, the sound of a bugle instructing soldiers what to do, skulls and crossbones (which can mean both "pirate" or "this is a dangerous place: stay clear").

Data Hierarchy

> The relationship between data and information is hierarchical.

Something that is considered "information" at one level may be used as "data" in a higher level, and vice versa. The distinction depends on the purpose. For instance, the chart about Acme's software sales can become "data" if we intend to merge it into a fuller report about Acme International or industrial trends between 1995 and 2004. (Each yearly sales figure or column in the chart, in turn, consists of many sales figures *within* each year.)

System

> A system is a set of interrelated elements organized into an identifiable whole.

[Van Gigch 1991, 30–31]

The majority of systems, natural or man-made, fulfill a function. Hence, we may also define "system" as **a collection of elements that work together to perform a task.**

Figure 1.3 Data Hierarchy: One Person's Information Is Another Person's Data

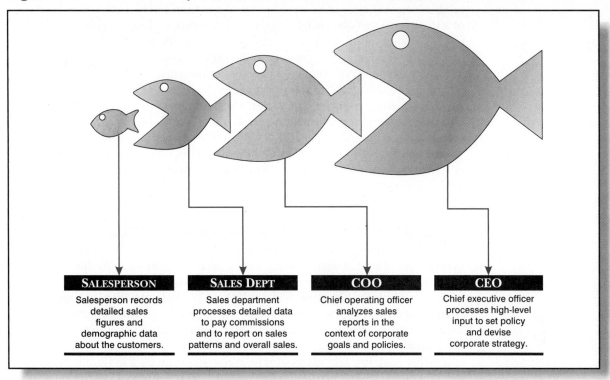

SALESPERSON	SALES DEPT	COO	CEO
Salesperson records detailed sales figures and demographic data about the customers.	Sales department processes detailed data to pay commissions and to report on sales patterns and overall sales.	Chief operating officer analyzes sales reports in the context of corporate goals and policies.	Chief executive officer processes high-level input to set policy and devise corporate strategy.

Information at one level often becomes input data for a higher level.

The elements may be few or many, they may be very similar or extremely different, the collection may be tightly knit or loosely connected, and the function may be simple or complex. Examples are plentiful:

Elements	System
Locomotives, wagons, tunnels, railroads, switches, engineers, conductors, etc.	Railroad System
Microprocessor(s), printed circuitry, keyboard, monitor, mouse, operating system, storage, etc.	Computer
Receipts, canceled checks, correspondence, folders, file cabinets, etc.	Filing System
Canals, ditches, dams, sprinklers, etc.	Irrigation System
Organs, such as the lungs, that deliver oxygen to the circulatory system.	Respiratory System

To correctly understand *information* systems, we must achieve a clear understanding of the parts that constitute the definition of *system*: elements, interrelationships, organization, and the "identifiable whole" (or the *distinct identity* of the system).

❶ *Elements of the System: A system is **not** monolithic, but consists of a* **set** *of elements.*   The constituent elements of a system can be real objects (parts of a watch), virtual objects (characters in a computer game), concepts (words in a sentence), or a combination of all (an automated factory). The constituent elements of a system are also called **components**. A component, in turn, may consist of other elements or components.

❷ *Interrelated Elements: The elements making up a system must be both related* **and** *interrelated.*   An element within a system must interact with at least one other element and the interactions must, directly or indirectly, link all elements. A fruit basket does not qualify as a system even through it consists of a set of related entities packaged as "an identifiable whole"; a class of students, on the other hand, is a system even if no word passes among the students because the teacher provides a focal point of interaction.

[American Heritage 1996]

❸ *Organization: Elements within a system must have a formal structure.*   Organized means "functioning with a *formal structure*, as in the coordination and direction of activities." No formal structure means no system. In other words, we do not consider a random assembly of entities as a "system."

❹ *Identifiable Whole: A system must have a distinct identity.*   We have heard, often enough, that "a whole is greater than the sum of its parts." If we cannot identify a whole that is more than a collection of elements, then, at best, we have identified a *set* of related elements, not a "whole." Prime numbers (those divisible only by one and themselves) do not constitute a system, but a set.

❺ *Subsystems: A subsystem is a system that functions as a component of another system.*   An element within a system can be a system in its own right, in which case it is called a **subsystem**. In fact, any system can be a subsystem of a bigger system. The human body consists of several subsystems—respiratory, alimentary, nervous, etc.—while, in turn, a human is a component of the society.

❻ *Open and Closed Systems:*   The relationship of a system to the outside is identified by its place on a spectrum from open to closed. An perfect open system is one that ❶ accepts input, ❷ the logic of its internal workings can be understood and/or changed, ❸ can change as a result of interaction with the outside world, and ❹ produces output. A closed system is the opposite of an open system. No system, however, is "perfect."

Networks vs. Systems

> A network is a cooperating set of relatively independent elements.

The terms "network" and "system" are often used interchangeably and, indeed, they overlap in many aspects: Like systems, networks consist of a set of interrelated elements. The differences appear when we move towards stricter definitions of both terms:

❶ While the elements within a system *cannot* function the same way if they are taken out of the system, elements within a network are more or less able to function independently. (The circulatory system of the human body is a typical example of the "system," whereas workstations connected to the Internet are members of a "network.")

❷ A network has a less sharply defined identity as a "whole" than a system.

These differences, however, depend on the nature and the organization of the system or the network in question. In a network of roads, individual elements (roads) are less dependent on each other than the components within a computer system. In addition, elements within a network are not necessarily of equal importance: in a computer network, the failure of a server can effectively halt the operation of the network.

A system or network in which the constituent elements are highly dependent on each other is described as *tightly coupled* (which, of course, is a relative term). The Internet is an example of a *loosely coupled* network in which the failure of a part does not bring the whole "system" to a halt.

In general, the more loosely coupled a system or a network is, the less it is prone to failure. As a result, however, as the coupling is loosened the role of a central authority is diminished—for good or for bad.

The Information System

> An information system is a system that processes data into information according to a predictable set of logical assumptions.

☞ As we shall see immediately below, any information system is *vitally* dependent on storage and communication systems, and *vice versa*.

☞ Our purpose here is not to split hairs between information systems and information technology. But too many people involved in developing and using information *systems* are waylaid by the siren of technology. And, too often, technological solutions are offered as information system solutions.

So, if you are told that a company's information system consists of so many servers, such and such networks, etc., do not object to the term: After all, the usage is very widespread, easy to understand, and not entirely wrong as no information system exists *without* an information technology. But keep the question open: What does this system actually *do* (or *should it* do) for the information needs of the company?

As you would expect, our assertions about information and systems apply to information systems as well, but with qualifications that partly arise from the act of combining the two:

- An information system is an **open system**: It takes input and produces output based on a logic that is comprehensible. A **closed system**—with no definable input, output, and/or logic—is *not* an information system.
- An information system *processes* data (or input) *into* information (or output). A system that manages data is a **data management system** and a system that sends and receives data or information is a **communication system**. The two are components of an information system but neither is the information system itself.
- Since information has a *goal* and is *selective* regarding data, an information system must have goals and be selective as well.
- Information systems are *man-made*. Therefore, information systems share many properties with other human products: They serve a range of social and economic needs; they are built by using available methodologies, processes, and tools; and they are subject to rational and irrational forces (such as theorizing, experience, fashion trends, and prejudices).

Even though numerous sources of information exist, not all can be deemed "information systems."

The major components of any information system are:

- **Applications** that perform specific tasks.
- **Information technology** that consists of processing and control units, and communication and data management systems.
- *People* who use the system or who provide it with services.
- *Procedures* that decide how the information system is operated and by whom.

The Information Technology

> Information technology is the know-how, methods, tools, and material used to support information systems.

Data and, as a result, information are always *virtual*. Anything virtual needs a *real* vehicle to be sent, received, stored, or manipulated. Therefore, any information system is shaped by, and is dependent on, an information technology or technologies that carry and maintain it. (As we mentioned, information systems and information technology are so intertwined that they are often used interchangeably, and distinguishing them in certain areas is rather difficult.)

As the definition indicates, information technology is not one thing, but a set of interrelated components:

- *Know-how* is the knowledge and the skill required to do something correctly. The technology would go to waste if the developers of a product do not know how to shape and exploit its material base.
- **Method** is a systematic way of accomplishing something. Methods result from both experience and the theoretical interpretation of experience. Methods function as guidelines to people with know-how to accomplish a task. In turn, new experiences must refine existing methods, or else methods lose their relevance.
- *Material* has a complex and varied relation to the technology that uses it. Increasingly, the invention of new material and methods is not left to chance, but is *targeted.* Modern research labs systematically experiment and search for material and solutions that are required by the expressed needs of the business or the marketplace.

Usually, a technology is not used to its full potential when it emerges. The Internet, the foundations of which were laid by DARPA (Defense Advanced Research Projects Agency) in 1973, was more than anything else an imaginative use of *existing* computer technology. In turn, the impact of the Internet would have been minor without improvements to the computer technology and the availability of rather inexpensive but reliable personal computers.

The technology to support an information system is, itself, composed of one or more **processing units** and three systems: **communication, data management,** and *control*. These systems are conceptually distinct but are intertwined in actuality. Furthermore, each system, in its own way, has a foot in the real world and another in the virtual world of the information system, bridging the gap between the two.

Processing Unit(s)

> A processing unit is an entity that applies the logical rules of the information system to data.

Until the invention of mechanical calculators and then electronic CPUs (central processing units), the processing units were humans employed to process data into information: mainly accountants (as information systems mostly performed bookkeeping functions), but also surveyors, mapmakers, census takers, tax estimators, etc.

As previously mentioned, an information system is a system that processes data into information based on a set of logical rules. Processing units play a vital role in information systems, but they are not the whole story. Let us explain.

Banks, and the concepts of "bank account" and "double-entry bookkeeping," predate modern computers by many centuries. But the logical rules are essentially the same: When a bank customer deposits money in the bank, the amount (**data**) is credited to the customer's account (**processing**) and the balance of both the customer's account and the overall bank's debts and assets is adjusted accordingly (**information**). Before the advent of computers, bank clerks performed the required processing (with the help of abacuses and calculators). With the adoption of computers, the CPU applies the same logic and performs the calculations. But the processing units merely apply the logical rules with varying degrees of speed and accuracy: They do not set the rules by which the information system operates.

The *technology* of processing data, of course, is not irrelevant to the functioning of information systems. Far from it: The speed and the accuracy of electronic processing units have radically changed expectations and, consequently, the logical complexity of information systems has reached a point where resorting to any previous technology has become inconceivable. Modern businesses, governments, factories, and airlines (to name only a few) would grind to a halt without computers, even if they can employ thousands of clerks equipped with the best abacuses.

Still, it is crucial to remember that it is the creators of information systems who set the logic (simple or complex) that the technology executes.

The Communication System

> The communication system transmits data to the information system and carries information back to its users.

Without incoming data and outgoing information, a processing unit (and, as a result, the whole information system) would be useless. It is the task of a communication system to carry messages to and from an information system.

Communication systems (or networks) are many and varied: the telephone system, the postal service, the network of geocentric satellites, the telegraph network (that quietly passed away quite recently). But, regardless of technological sophistication, any communication system consists of communication devices, protocols, and the connections between those devices:

- *Devices.* A phone set, a fax machine, a modem, an envelope, a computer keyboard, and a monitor are all communication devices. The task of a communication device is to *encode* messages (data or information) into packages that can be carried by the system to another device that will *decode* the message for the benefit of the recipient. (The *content* of the message is irrelevant to the communication device or the communication system.)
- *Protocols.* Protocols are a set of rules or standards that allow two devices to communicate. Like data and information, the protocols are *virtual*, even though they are carried by real mediums: electrical current for the telephone and the computer, written symbols on the back of envelopes, or hand signals in the communication between the hearing-impaired.

- *Connections.* Communication devices cannot exchange messages unless they are connected through some medium: electrical current over copper wires, light waves over optical fibers, radio waves, visual spectrum, voice, etc.

Information systems are so intertwined with communication systems that often it is very difficult to distinguish where one ends and the other starts. The most important distinction is not technological but conceptual: If a system processes data into information, it is an information system; if it carries messages with disregard to their contents, it is a communication system.

The Data Management System

> A data management system is a set of rules, procedures, material, and tools that stores, organizes, protects, and retrieves data needed by the information system.

✍ The data that is stored "for keeps" is called **persistent** and the act of storing such data is **persistence**. Remember these terms, as they are used extensively in object-oriented theory and in this book.

All information systems need data management systems to safe-keep data—before processing and after, temporarily or permanently. But a data management system is more than just a cellar for storing data. It must also:

- *organize* the stored data in a manner that can be retrieved as needed;
- establish connections between *related* data;
- ensure the *integrity* of data against decay, misplacement, and erroneous identification; and
- *secure* data against unauthorized access and manipulation.

☞ A **database** is a collection of related data, while a data management system includes not just data, but also rules, procedures, the material on which the data is stored, and, depending on the technology, people in one capacity or another.

Modern database management systems have gone far beyond the mere management of data. Though conceptually we should still distinguish them from information systems in the strict sense of the term, they have incorporated many information system functions such as the enforcement of business rules (or logic). In effect, there is no longer a distinct and *actual* border between the two systems.

The Control System

> The control system ❶ directs and facilitates the interactions between the building blocks of the information technology, and ❷ provides the information system with the services of information technology.

Information systems have goals that are usually reflected in the names of their applications: accounts payable, college registration, stock trading, supply chain management, and so on. But, as we have said, information systems must use a set of technologies to connect to the real world. This requirement presents two challenges:

- how to achieve the connection between the virtual world of the information system and the real world, and
- how to maintain and manage the technology that supports such connections.

Answering these challenges is the task of the control system. For computer technology, the most important (and the best-known) component of the control system is the *operating system*, nowadays known as a "brand name" software product (such as Linux, Windows, Unix, etc.) that controls the operations of a computer and network.

But the control system goes beyond the operating system. First, even in computers, the control system is not all software: Every computer has a hardware "control bus"—a set of lines or conductors that carry signals and instructions between the CPU and various devices. Second, no operating system can function without utilities (programs that carry out specific housekeeping tasks) and drivers (software that allows communication between the general-purpose operating system and specific devices).

In other words, a control system is an interconnected *collection* of subsystems and entities—hardware *and* software—that caters to the specific needs of the technology on which that information system operates. For non-automated technologies, the control system also includes people, actions that they must take, and procedures that they must follow to ensure the successful operation of the technology.

Information Automation

Information automation is the application of information logic to data by a device that executes a program.

The term "automation" applies to numerous areas in which labor-saving machines that can (more or less) operate on their own have replaced (or nearly replaced) humans: manufacturing, telephone switches, military drones, automatic controls, and so on. In fact, automation has found its way into common household items as well: TV sets, video recorders, radios, and personal computers.

By now electronic computers are so common that conceiving any other automated device for processing data is difficult. Indeed, the terms "information system" and "computer" have become near synonyms.

In the past fifty years the progress in the automation of information technology has been impressive but the trend does not show any signs of slowing down. On the contrary, the existing technology is overhauled constantly and new areas appear continuously. One of the latest is *interoperability*, driven by strong market demand: Producers and consumers of information are searching for standards and technologies that would allow exchange of information free from the current obstacles resulting from incompatibilities among systems and lack of standards.

In the blizzard of new tools, standards and protocols for the technology of information automation, one important rule must not be overlooked:

The task of the information technology is to support information systems; the task of information systems is to support human enterprises.

As we shall explain later, the problems of information systems and the issues of the information technology belong to two different (although related) spheres: the "problem space" and the "solution space."

Applications and Systems

An application is a set of programs that performs a specific task.

☞ It is interesting to know that early electronic computers—circa 1940s—did *not* have operating systems. It was with the introduction of IBM's System 360 in 1964 that a well-defined concept for "operating system" was established.

☞ Even though this book is not about technology per se, without the automation of information systems it would not have existed. The emergence of each significant technology allows (or forces) us to view many non-technological concepts in a new perspective. Without the need to program machines to process data, we would not have been required to examine information concepts under a microscope.

☞ Two of the most important and promising technologies in the effort to achieve interoperability are **Web services** and **XML**, which we will discuss later in this book.

Applications are software programs that help their users perform well-defined jobs: word processing, photo editing, contact management, accounting, etc. However, we started this chapter by introducing information *systems*, not applications. So what is the difference?

At one time, no great difference existed. Very early electronic computers were capable of solving only individual functions. Later, they grew to handle more complex tasks, from processing payroll to analyzing sales. The structure of the applications, however, remained the same: a **monolithic** piece of software that performed a task, from the beginning to the end, by itself. And these monolithic pieces were usually called applications.

☞ It is difficult to declare, with any certainty, when the awareness of the shortcomings of monolithic software became clear. The first major *practical* steps to remedy the situation, however, can be attributed to the late 1970s and early 1980s.

At a certain point in time, the combination of rising expectations and increasingly powerful computing platforms resulted in monolithic applications that were more capable and complex but also more fragile and prone to failure. (Imagine, if possible, a modern passenger jet made up of one piece, not thousands of parts.)

The early efforts to address the issue of **complexity** in software were focused on the *inside* of the application: how to structure various functions within the application to facilitate its construction and maintenance. Next came the idea of **modularity**: the concept that an application can be constructed from a set of modules, conceived around a certain functionality—database module, calculation module, reporting module, etc., so that the code would become more reusable and reliable, teams of programmers could work on different parts of the application, and redundancy would decrease. This approach also resulted in the acceptance of general-purpose **libraries**: pieces of independent software that could be used by unrelated applications that, nevertheless, share certain common needs.

The realization that managing complexity needs a new vision appeared only gradually (and under the fire of failures). This vision holds that, to be successful, applications cannot be conceived as islands unto themselves.

> Applications must be viewed and developed as integral parts of an information system.

In other words, applications can no longer remain as monolithic "pieces" of software, but must be constructed as components of a system (even if the system supports only one application). The "system" approach allows software to absorb complexity without falling victim to it.

Two other trends have supported this approach: **object orientation** and software development as an **architectural enterprise**. (We will discuss both, extensively, in the coming chapters.)

3. THE INFORMATION SYSTEM AS PRODUCT

Before information automation, the term "information system" was not applied to what we now associate with it. Companies had "accounting" (the oldest type of information system, undoubtedly), surveyors gathered geographical data, mapmakers made maps, spies gathered intelligence, and so on. Even after computers first appeared in the workplace, software was not considered as **merchandise**, a product that you build for selling in the marketplace and buy from the marketplace.

General-purpose software such as word processors, building blocks of information systems such as databases and development tools, and operating systems are already products in the marketplace. But, for better or for worse, all software—regardless of purpose—is being transformed into market products. As a result, to succeed, software must be conceived, designed, and marketed as a product.

Business and Information Systems

> Information systems started as tools of business, trade, and the administration of political and economic enterprises. Today, information systems are becoming less tools and more the backbone of an enterprise.

Today, information is becoming an asset equal in importance to others such as expertise, organization, equipment, property, labor, and capital. Information, like other assets, is stored, bought, and sold (and sometimes stolen). Any enterprise must track its resources: An accounting system monitors cash flow and financial transactions, an inventory control system keeps track of the inflow and the outflow of products, and a human resources system manages tasks related to employees such as hiring, firing, and promotion.

Information is different from other resources but it must be managed—collected, stored, maintained, and distributed—like others. This task has evolved to a level of complexity that it now requires a functional division of its own within the organization. Such a functional division, in turn, requires information systems that are much more integrated and "enterprise-wide" than a collection of applications that manage the individual needs of separate divisions.

The outcome is that the earlier modes of production for software are no longer adequate. **The craft of programming must now become the industrial production of software.** Market trends confirm this observation.

The Business of Information Systems

> The production of software and the management of information has increasingly become a business in its own right.

☞ In the more recent business jargon, information systems were considered "cost centers," not "profit centers."

[Campbell-Kelly 2003, 1–27]

Until the advent of automated information technology, the production of information systems was rarely a business in its own right. The development of an information system was usually contained within a bigger entity such as a company or a government agency that used the system strictly for its own purposes.

The first information merchants to assume distinct identities in the marketplace were accounting firms. The rise of shareholder capitalism made independent auditing of publicly held firms a necessity. Income taxes provided another incentive to the general population to seek accounting services.

The takeoff velocity for the information *business* happened with the take off of market demand for software that would allow computers (capital-intensive) to replace human data processing (labor-intensive and, therefore, usually more expensive). Within about sixty years—a very short time in historical terms—the sales of software have gone from negligible to hundreds of billion of dollars.

Today, we can distinguish several sectors in the software industry. Even though these sectors differ in their target markets, it is not uncommon for one company to be active in more than one sector. Undoubtedly, as the industry and the market change, so will the boundaries between the sectors and their modes of operation and production.

❶ **System software** consists of operating systems, utilities, and other basic components of information technologies.

❷ **Software components** are reusable parts that are assembled with other components to create complete systems and applications.

❸ **Software contractors** build custom software for enterprises that need very specialized solutions.

❹ **ERP vendors** provide ERP (Enterprise Resource Planning) software that aims to supply the enterprise-wide information needs of a business within an integrated system.

❺ **Mass-market software** consists of general-purpose products that are targeted at end users.

Infrastructural Information Systems

> Infrastructural information systems are a set of systems and applications that support the basic functions of an enterprise.

Information systems that serve as the foundations of an enterprise can be classified into several broad categories. These categories are usually intertwined and need each other. (Their names and their definitions are frequently at the mercy of market fashions and trends.)

❶ *Transaction Processing Systems (TPS).* Transaction processing systems record and process data about the routine activities of an enterprise. Transaction processing systems, such as accounting, payroll, inventory, order processing, and invoicing, were the first systems in the enterprise to be automated. The main reason for this precedence was that ❶ they were the most obvious candidates for replacing labor-intensive work with capital-intensive machinery and ❷ their automation did not challenge the established organizations or the prevailing fundamentals of doing business.

☞ B2B systems have their origins in EDI (Electronic Data Interchange). EDI, however, is not a "live" transaction system, but a set of standards for the exchange of business documents, such as invoices and orders.

❷ *Business-to-Business (B2B) Systems.* Business-to-business systems allow businesses to conduct transactions or exchange of information online. By providing secure, cheap, and nonproprietary communications, the Internet has made business-to-business systems practical. By relying on B2B systems, businesses are able to buy and sell products and services *online* and in *real-time*. Thus far, the most successful area of B2B has been *supply-chain management* (SCM): procurement of material and parts from suppliers and the distribution of finished products and/or parts to corporate customers.

A B2B system is fundamentally a transaction processing system with one crucial difference: Since it must communicate with the outside world, it must obey standards and protocols that go beyond an individual enterprise.

❸ *Business-to-Consumer (B2C) Systems.* Business-to-consumer systems allow consumers to buy products and services directly from businesses online. Both B2B and B2C are often called **e-commerce**: conducting business electronically (or online). Oftentimes, the distinction between them is blurred. In general, however, B2C systems are the better-known of the two. Purely e-commerce companies such as Amazon.com and eBay are frequently front-page news and famous for their success. In fact, B2C systems have been so successful that no consumer-oriented company can afford to be without a Web site that allows the customers to order products or, at the very least, receive information that they seek. (You may not be able to actually buy a Boeing passenger jet online, but if you decide to order one, the Boeing Web site would provide you with a complete information package—including prices.)

One business sector that has benefited greatly from B2C systems does not relate to old and established businesses or new e-commerce giants, but consists of small (sometimes very small) businesses with unique products: Irish monks who handcraft a limited number of pottery and Andes craftsmen, in addition to an assortment of less exotic enterprising entities. (Such entities usually do not have the means to have their own systems but use a commercial "host" that manages the technology and/or credit card transactions.)

❹ *Business Intelligence (BI) Systems.* A business intelligence system consists of a set of subsystems and applications that allow management to analyze operational and market data, create models, make forecasts, and virtually test business decisions. By recording day-to-day business operations and transactions, transaction processing systems produce massive amounts of data. Analyzed intelligently, these accumulated data show not only how the business *is* run, but could indicate how it *should* be run. The mission of a BI system is to provide a variety of analysis, modeling, and "what-if" tools to management so that it can make *strategic* decisions.

Transaction processing systems provide the foundations for BI systems, but the latter has its own technological and informational needs. Data, such as those about the performance of competitors and general market trends, cannot be gathered from a TPS. Oftentimes, the business of the company is run on disparate and incompatible systems and, as a result, a metadata (data about data) database and/or a data-mapping database (to match data across systems) is required to provide the necessary depth and breadth for business intelligence.

❺ *Artificial Intelligence (AI) and Robotics.* Artificial intelligence systems ❶ enable machines to automatically perform tasks that otherwise would require human intelligence *and* intervention, ❷ solve complex problems by using non-mathematical algorithms, ❸ simulate real or imaginary environments, and ❹ provide expert opinion by using available information, heuristic, and inference.

The Enterprise of Software Development

> Software development must follow the discipline of product development.

Information systems are not like other products. The underlying reason is that information system products are the automation of **logic**. They are faster than the human thought process, more accurate if built correctly, and can handle an immensely vaster amount of data but, all the same, they are logical "machines," not mechanical ones.

Nevertheless, information systems are products and their development must follow the path of product development. This is not to say that a single set of rules applies to the development of all products: The manufacture and the marketing

☞ It seems that the systems we now call "business intelligence" are doomed to be renamed every decade. First, they were called **MIS** (Management Information Systems). Then, **DSS** (Decision Support Systems) came along. Though the emphasis on each successive name is slightly different, the mission is really the same.

☞ An **algorithm** is a step-by-step procedure for solving a problem in a finite number of steps.
  Heuristic, in this context, has two related definitions: ❶ a problem-solving technique in which a solution is selected by weighing alternatives; ❷ an algorithm for solving problems by learning from the results of previous attempts to solve the same problem.

of garments differ from those of cars or airplanes, as do the production, distribution, and the sale of food from those of steel. However, if the features of software production and distribution are taken individually, most (but not all) are shared with one product or another. For example:

- *Reproduction.* Like music and video, but unlike manufactured products such as cars and TV sets, the cost of reproducing software is negligible when compared to the cost of production. Therefore, per-unit cost is also negligible.
- *Testing.* Like manufactured products, but unlike music and video, software must be tested—extensively—before release. (We do not mean *market* testing, but testing for reliability and conformance to requirements.)
- *Modeling.* Like garments and architecture, but unlike farm production, each product needs a certain amount of modeling before the development can start.
- *Prototyping.* Unlike manufactured products, but like music, a software product does not require a prototype. (Some visual techniques for software modeling are called "prototyping," but such a designation must not confuse us: A prototype must do everything that the final product does.)
- *Installation.* Cars and soft drinks do not need installation (i.e., setting the product in a specific position and/or environment). Like large entertainment systems, software must be installed.
- *Support.* Potato chips and, nowadays, radio sets do not need support. (If a radio set breaks, you have to buy a new one.) Support for software is a normal part of the business.

Software products (even in the stricter sense of "information systems") cover a vast ground: They are different in size, mission, target market, required reliability, price, innovation, capacity, etc. Depending on the particulars of the product, the specifics of one aspect of production might become less or more important. The constant is that *any serious software is a product.*

Requirements

Requirements identify the objectives of the product.

Before anything is done to develop a product, we must identify what the product must do. This proposition seems reasonable and obvious, but in reality, inadequate or wrong identification of requirements is a major cause of failure in software development. Therefore, understanding what requirements are, what they are not, and how best to identify them is crucial to the success of the product:

- *Requirements identify the specific objectives that the product must help its users to achieve.* The objectives may include anything: productivity, security, bookkeeping, entertainment, sales, training, etc. These are, of course, general objectives and rather easy to comprehend. The difficulty lies in details: You want an accounts receivable system, but what *is* accounts receivable? What is an invoice? Who is the customer? When do you send out invoices? How are the customers supposed to pay you? Do you accept credit cards? What if customers do not pay you on time? And so on into the lower depths. In this descent into details, what you do *not* know can, and will, hurt you.
- *Requirements are **not** product specifications.* The objectives of a shelf-top radio set include the following: must receive radio signals (AM and FM) broadcast by radio stations, must convert the radio signal into sounds within the

hearing range of humans, must allow users to change stations, must allow users to adjust the sound level, must not be deeper than 12 inches (to fit on a shelf). The requirements do *not* include the following, even though they are of paramount importance in building the *actual* radio set: the configuration of circuits boards and their components, the length of the wire that connects the speaker to the amplifier unit, the drill holes for screws that keep the components attached to the box, the model of the converter that must transform alternating current to the correct direct current used by the components.

A finished product has two set of features: One set satisfies the objectives of the product (**business requirements**); the other set includes those features that are necessary to make the first set possible (**solution features**). For example, a radio set must allow the user to select a station and a display panel to display the selection. In older radio sets, these two objectives were achieved by a knob and a relatively wide panel with a moving pointer that indicated the selected station on a pre-marked location. On some newer digital sets, station selection is achieved by pressing one of the two buttons marked as Up and Down, and the display is a smaller LCD or LED readout that identifies the station by the exact frequency. In both cases, the first set of features (business **requirements**) are the same, while the second set (**solution** features) have changed.

☞ Often, both sets of product features are called "requirements." Such a use should not trigger a scholastic debate. Just remember that the two sets of features are not the same.

The role of technology in product development is overwhelming. New technologies either create new alternatives for satisfying requirements or replace the previous technology. (Today, a tube-based radio would not have a market, even though it satisfies the given requirements.) But, regardless of technology, the product must first satisfy business requirements.

Unfortunately, there are no checklists for deciding, *beforehand*, what is a requirement and what is a product feature. The color and the aesthetic design of the casing for the radio has no bearing on its functionality, but if the business decides a certain set of colors and designs would give the product a marketing advantage, then these features become part of the requirements—which makes the correct identification of requirements more difficult, but also more crucial.

Methodology

> Development of a product must follow a set of practices, procedures, rules, and techniques.

**Figure 1.4
Requirements
Versus Features
of the Product:
Same
Requirements,
Two Solutions**

A product has two sets of features: one set satisfies requirements while the other makes the product possible. The radio on the left lets the user select stations by a turning a knob. The radio on the right uses buttons for the same purpose.

Each kind of product needs its own methodology of production. Compared to other fields of production, the development of automated information systems is a relative newcomer. Ad hoc, the improvised manner of writing software, is theoretically extinct (although it is very much alive in practice, sometimes under clever new names). But the battle over methodology for information system development is still a heated one.

Methodologies for software development have come a long way, but still have some way to go: They suffer from blind spots; offer concepts that are not well-defined or easy to understand; are not integrated enough with development tools; sometimes cannot keep up with technological advances; and are not very flexible in regards to the scope, the nature, or the size of the project.

Nevertheless, with the rise in the complexity of software, methodology has become indispensable. Besides, methodology is not a set of dogmas, but a system of lessons learned from past experiences and theoretical speculations. If the conclusions are wrong, they can be corrected; if theories prove to be mistaken or incomplete, they can be set right or improved. We must remember that a methodology itself is an artifact.

☞ See Chapter 3, Methodology, for a more detailed discussion of methodology in general and software development methodologies in particular.

In plain terms, the more complex a product is, the less we can rely on purely personal experiences and preferences, word of mouth, arbitrary conclusions, and half-learned lessons. Product development needs a methodology, one that is relevant to the task at hand, is flexible, and can accommodate new experiences. Information system development is different from construction of ships, manufacture of cards, construction of buildings, or growing of crops. Still, it is a development process.

Project Management

> Project management is planning, monitoring, and controlling the course of the development process and the resources used by that process.

The development of any product that must meet deadlines and/or budgetary constraints is in need of project management. Project management describes and prescribes the sequence of events that must take place from the conception to the completion of a project.

Project management has general principles, practices, and guidelines, but must be adapted to ❶ the goal of the project, ❷ the resources available to a specific project, and ❸ the methodology used to achieve the goal.

• *General Principles.* A project has a *goal* and a *life cycle*: It starts when the decision is made to launch the project (or inception), and ends when the goal is achieved (or completion). Not every goal-oriented enterprise is a project. Developing an information system is a project; the ongoing maintenance of an information system is not: Maintenance has a goal but not a well-defined life cycle. (A specific maintenance task, however, may be organized as a project.) The advertising campaign to launch a product is a project; the marketing department is not.

Achieving the goal of a project is a function of *time* and *resources*. (Time itself must be considered a finite resource.) The task of project management is to plan the best use of resources within the required timeframe.

A project is rarely a monolithic task, but consists of sub-tasks that, combined together, will achieve the ultimate goal. To build a house, one must buy the land, acquire architectural plans, obtain permits, and engage a contractor; in turn, the contractor must prepare estimates, hire workers, order material, prepare the land, lay the foundations, etc.

The achievement of a sub-goal is called a **milestone** that results in a **deliverable**. The deliverable must be *measurable* and verifiable (the building permits have been obtained, for example). The health of each milestone indicates the health of the overall project.

Project plans for managing time and resources are always estimates and, of course, do not carry themselves out. Hence the need for monitoring and controlling the process, receiving *feedback*, and *adjusting* plans by taking into account the feedbacks and the success or the failure of milestones.

• *The Goal.* The particulars of a project—planning of time and milestones, and the resources needed—are decided by its ultimate goal. In manufacturing a car model, after ideas are developed, feasibility is ascertained, and prototypes are built and tested, comes retooling (or building) a factory for the reproduction of the car, which is a project by itself with many milestones. In the development of a computer game, on the other hand, reproduction (burning the program on CDs or DVDs and packaging them for distribution) is relatively simple and has few milestones.

• *Resources.* Resources consist of whatever contributes to the achievement of milestones: people, the quality of their expertise, money, etc. Sometimes choosing resources is within the power of project management: One may be able to fire a person with deficient expertise, hire a better expert, or ask for more money. Other resources or their availability, however, may lie outside management's control. All the same, project management must take into account any factor that affects the project. More importantly, starting a project without some sort of a feasibility study is comparable to jumping from an airplane without a tested parachute.

Different goals, of course, demand different types of resources, but it is almost impossible to obtain the same resources for the same goal when the conditions of the project are different. As we said, a project is a function of time and resources. If resources are scarce, then the time must suffer.

☞ See Chapter 3, Methodology, for a more detailed discussion of project management and its relationship to software development.

• *Methodology.* Arguments about competing methodologies aside, sometimes the same goal (or almost the same goal) must be achieved under very different conditions, and different conditions often require different methodologies, even if each methodology is solidly valid under another set of conditions.

In the battlefield, soldiers must often build pontoon bridges under dangerous conditions and within a very short timeframe. Although these bridges may have to carry a weight equal to the strongest bridges built under peaceful conditions, the methodology is different: They must be built from prefabricated, reusable, and well-tested units that can be assembled and disbanded quickly.

The differences in methodology result in differences in the particulars of the project and its milestones: In building a pontoon bridge, military engineers must limit the feasibility study to a quick survey of the river, bids and permits are unnecessary, parts must be flexible but cannot be customized, and testing—if possible at all—must be very limited.

Quality Control

> To achieve the maximum possible quality in a product, quality control must be built into the process of its production.

Quality control often sounds like an oxymoron: Quality is not quantity, so how can it be measured in a convincing manner? We will attempt an answer, but an important premise must be stated first: Quality is not quantity, but the two are not opposites in the manner of "good" and "evil," "tall" and "short," or "dead" and "alive." An entity, such as a product, consists both of quantity (or quantities), and quality (or qualities).

The first point about quality control is that, often, the judgment about quality is a direct result of quantitative measurement or judgment: A car is perceived as high-quality if it needs a tune-up only after so many thousands of miles, and a shirt is high-quality if it does not lose its color or does not come apart at the seams after so many washes. To measure the efficiency of two programs that perform the *same* tasks, we can assign one group to use one first and the other second, and compare the results.

At other times, the quality is really in the eyes on the beholder. In such cases, we must ask (or occasionally observe) the beholder and thus measure the quality. If you conduct a survey with a scientifically correct sampling, and discover that 90 percent of users are generally satisfied with a certain software product, then the "quality satisfaction indicator" for the product is 90 percent: a translation of quality into quantity.

Furthermore, the quality of a product is rarely decided by one factor only. The quality of an information system is often decided by weighing several factors, including:

☞ *Quality* is always expressed in values that are measurable against each other: "low" might be part of a set of values that may include high, average, excellent, and poor.

To gain a measure of uniformity (if not objectivity) in the quantification of qualitative values, questionnaires often impose their own value system. For example: "In a scale of 1 to 10, in which 1 is the lowest and 10 is the highest, how do you evaluate your job satisfaction."

There are objects, such as works of art or relationships, that cannot be quantified in a meaningful way. Therefore, spending "quality time" with your family is outside the realm of industrial quality control.

- *Correctness.* An information system will be accepted by the users only if it meets their needs and requirements correctly.
- *Reliability.* An information system is more reliable if its output is predictable within a acceptable range.
- *Availability.* An information system should be available to the users when they need it.
- *Security.* An information system must be secure against unauthorized access.
- *Robustness.* An information system must resist mishandling and negligent operation.
- *Efficiency.* An information system must carry its tasks with the maximum speed and a minimum amount of resources.
- *Flexibility.* Within predictable parameters, an information system must accommodate changes in its environment and in business needs.
- *Maintainability.* When an existing system cannot cope with changes or displays a behavior that was wrong to start with, then it must be repaired. The easier it is to repair a system, the higher are the marks for maintainability.
- *Testability.* An information system processes data into information based on a set of logical assumptions. If the logic cannot be tested thoroughly, the information that it produces will not be reliable.

The weight given to each factor depends on the mission of the specific product, technological constraints, and the budget: You must pay for what you want in a product. (Sometimes one quality may work against another: A rugged laptop computer that can survive a severe shock is inevitably heavier than a normal laptop, though both may belong to the same technological generation.)

Within and without the information system industry, the field of quality control is lively and dynamic. One rule that enjoys broad support is that the quality of the final product depends on the *quality of the process*. And the process consists of two things: methodology and project management.

☞ *W. Edwards Deming* (1900–1993) is a pioneer of quality control. He is credited with helping the revival of the post-WWII Japanese economy by advising Japanese manufacturers on the issues of quality control and efficiency.

From extensive surveys and statistical analyses, he concluded that many failures in business result from defective systems of production, *not* from the inefficacy of workers.

American manufacturers paid scant attention to him, until the success of Japanese manufacturers in the 1970s and 1980s forced them to take his ideas seriously.

A methodology that allows project management to enforce quality control at meaningful milestones has a far better chance of producing a quality product than one in which *only* the final product can be measured for quality. The quality of a car is decided both by the quality of its individual components and the quality of the assembly at each stage in the assembly line. A poor-quality final product is either very expensive to fix, or impossible to correct.

Problem Space and Solution Space

> Problem space is the environment in which the product must operate; solution space contains issues related to the product itself.

Any product divides the space around it into two overlapping and connected spaces: problem space and solution space. (Often the term "*domain*" is used interchangeably with "space.")

In the problem space we find problems that the product must solve and the issues that the product must confront when it becomes available. A car solves the problem of fast ground transportation, but it must also contend with dust, heat, rough roads, slippery roads, etc. An accounts receivable system must solve accounting problems, and those who use it are accountants with their own concepts of what the problems of accounting are and what their solutions must be.

The issues in the solution space are relevant to the product itself. How a car turns fuel into motion or what alloys must be used to prevent the pistons from melting when this conversion takes place relate to the product itself. In the accounting system, how the database stores invoices and payments, how it retrieves them, and how the integrity of data is ensured are of no concern to the accountants and the clerks who use the system, as long as they are done satisfactorily.

We will discuss the two spaces extensively later. What is important to remember is their distinction: Understanding the problem space is the job of **analysis**, whereas in the solution space we **design** the product.

As we said, these two spaces are connected and overlap. *Implementation* of the product—that is, its actual construction and final testing—takes place somewhere in this area of overlap: Will the car climb the hill, or will the accounts payable system correctly apply the payments?

4. WRAP UP

☑ **Information and its components**

Information is a set of data organized in a way that conveys a knowledge or enables its recipient to execute a set of actions to reach an objective. Information has three main constituents:

- Data are the building blocks of information. Data is any *fact* or *assumption* that is combined with other data to constitute a meaningful message.
- Goal is the purpose of information. A message that has no "point" is not information.

- Logic gives data the organization that is needed to achieve the goal.

If any one of the elements above is missing, then data does not become information.

Information uses data selectively. Therefore, if data are wrong or incomplete, the information would be incomplete or wrong as well. What is more, information is only as valid as the logic that produces it. Correct logical *form* does not produce correct *content*. As a result, the outcome of wrong or distorted views can only be wrong or distorted information.

Both data and information are expressed as **symbols**. A symbol is anything to which we attach a meaning. If symbols are misunderstood, the information carried by them will be misunderstood as well.

The relationship between data and information is *hierarchical*: What is information at one level can become data at a higher level that strives for a larger meaning.

☑ **System and its components**

A system is an assembly of interrelated elements or **components** that together make the system a distinct "whole." The components of a system must have a *formal structure* and the system as a whole must have a recognizable *identity*. Therefore, a monolithic entity is not a system; neither is an entity without a distinct identity.

A system may consist of other systems or it may be a **subsystem** of a larger system. As a result, the relationship between systems can become hierarchical.

Systems may be designated as more **open** or more **closed**. A "perfect" open system is one that accepts input, the logic of its internal workings can be understood and/or changed, can change through interaction with the outside world, and produces some type of output. A perfect closed system is the opposite (but a perfect closed system is unknowable).

Networks are similar to systems, but the constituent elements of a network are more independent than those within a system and, consequently, the identity of a network is more diffused.

The dependency among the elements of a system or a network on each other or on the whole is called **coupling**: Within a system, the components are more tightly coupled, whereas a network has more loosely coupled elements. In reality, networks and systems are not always distinct from each other. Some systems are looser than other systems and some networks are tighter than other networks.

☑ **Information systems**

An information system is an **open system** that processes data into information according to a set of clear and unambiguous logical assumptions.

Features that an information system inherits from information *and* systems constrain each other. An archive stores data systematically, but it does not produce information; therefore an archive is not an information system by itself (even though it is very likely to be a part of information technology).

Like information itself, an information system *selects* the data that it processes. Consequently, no one information system can satisfy every need.

Information systems consist of applications, information technology, people, processes, and procedures.

☑ **Information technology**

Information is *virtual* and, consequently, needs a medium with *physical* presence to make it tangible. This vehicle is provided by information technology, a collection of methods, tools, material, and know-how that support an information system.

The identity of an information system is separate from the identity of the technology that it rides: A taxation system is essentially a system for collecting taxes, regardless of whether the taxpayer files electronically or "files" with the tax agents of Attila the Hun. (But the information technology and the information systems are so organically connected that keeping them separate conceptually is often a challenge.)

Information technology is not one entity, but a set of interrelated components:

- **Know-how** is the knowledge and the skill required to do something correctly. Without know-how, other components of technology are wasted.
- **Methods** are a systematic way of reaching objectives. Methods function as guideline to people with know-how to accomplish a task. In turn, new experiences must refine existing methods.
- **Materials** are frequently seen as the only components of technology, perhaps because they are tangible whereas know-how and methods are not. But even though no technological revolution is possible without them (consider paper and printing), they constitute only one side of the technology triangle. (Consider that paper and printing: paper, lead and the wine press were available to Europeans long before Johannes Gutenberg invented moveable type printing in the 15th century.)

☑ **The building blocks of information technology**

Information technology is composed of one or more processing units and three systems:

- **The Processing Unit.** An entity that applies logical rules to processing data. Processing units may be human (as was the exclusive case before automation) or circuit boards (as is the case with computers).
- **The Communication System.** Transmits data to the information system and fetches

information for the users. A communication system consists of ❶ communication **devices** that send and receive messages, ❷ **protocols** that ensure communication devices understand each other, and ❸ **connections** that carry messages between devices.

- **The Data Management System.** A set of rules, procedures, material, and tools for organizing, protecting, and retrieving data used or produced by the information system. Modern database management systems, however, go well beyond this definition and provide services that must be considered part of the information system.
- **The Control System.** Directs the interactions among the building blocks of the information technology and provides their services to the information system. In computer technology, the most prominent part of the control system is the operating system (or OS). But any control system also includes utilities and drivers (for both horses or video cards).

Information automation, largely the gift of computer technology, is the application of information logic by a device that executes a program. Information automation has touched every aspect of the material life, even though it is fairly recent. However, we must never belittle the fact that the task of information technology is to support information systems; the task of information systems is to support human enterprises.

☑ **Information systems and applications**

An application is a set of one or more programs that performs a specific task. At the early stages of the software revolution, when automation requirements were modest, applications were seen as independent entities and were created as *monoliths*. As the *complexity* of software products has become overwhelming, however, applications must be viewed and developed as integral parts of information *systems*. Fortunately, the technology to build systems instead of monoliths is now mostly mature.

☑ **Information systems as products**

At the beginning of information automation, information systems were not viewed or constructed as products—things that you buy and sell in the marketplace. But a change in perception and in the marketplace has been taking place for a couple of decades and is gaining momentum. Companies that produce software for the market now equal or surpass many big manufacturing corporations. Plus, the increasing complexity of information systems is driving software development out of in-house shops and into companies that specialize in the various fields of software development. As a result, to be successful, software must be conceived, designed, and marketed as a product.

At the same time, information systems are turning from tools of business, trade, and administration into an integral part of an enterprise. Today, information is becoming an asset equal in importance to others such as expertise, organization, equipment, property, labor, and capital. Information, like other assets, must be managed, stored, bought, and sold (and is sometimes stolen). Managing information systems has evolved to a level of complexity that it now requires a functional division of its own within most organizations.

☑ **The business of making information systems**

Production of information systems and/or their components is increasingly becoming a business in its own right. Today, we can distinguish several sectors in the software industry:

- **System Software:** operating systems, utilities, and other basic components of information technologies.
- **Software Components:** parts that are assembled and combined by their buyers to create complete systems and applications.
- **Software Contractors:** build custom software for enterprises that need very specialized solutions.
- **ERP:** Enterprise Resource Planning software products aim at satisfying the enterprise-wide information needs of a corporation within a unified system.
- **Mass-Market Software:** general-purpose products that are targeted at end users.

☑ **Information systems as infrastructure**

Infrastructural information systems are a set of systems and applications that support the basic functions of an enterprise. They can be classified into several broad categories:

- **Transaction Processing Systems (TPS):** record and process data about the routine activities of an enterprise.
- **Business-to-Business (B2B) Systems:** allow businesses to conduct transactions or exchange of information online.
- **Business-to-Consumer (B2C) Systems:** allow consumers to buy products and services directly from businesses online. Both B2B and B2C are often called e-commerce.
- **Business Intelligence (BI) Systems:** a set of subsystems and applications that allow management to analyze operational and market

data, create models, make forecasts, and test business decisions virtually. Whereas previous systems provide *tactical* advantages, BI must provide a *strategic* view.

- **Artificial Intelligence (AI) and Robotics:** enable machines to automatically perform tasks that otherwise would require human intelligence, solve complex problems by using non-mathematical algorithms, simulate real or imaginary environments, and provide expert opinion by using available information, heuristic, and inference. AI is used in a vast and expanding array of products: robotics, forecasting, virtual reality (games and simulations), and expert systems.

☑ **The enterprise of making information systems**

Software is product, and software development must follow the discipline of product development. Products are not developed in the exact same manner, but certain general guidelines apply to all.

The first is to identify **requirements**. Requirements describe the objectives of the product. But they are not the same as product specifications. A finished product has two sets of features: One set satisfies business requirements, whereas the second set makes the first set possible. A bicycle must have two wheels and be light (requirements), but the wheels must be sturdy enough not to bend. By using spokes (a solution feature) the requirements are met, but spokes are not part of requirements.

Product development must follow a **methodology**, a set of practices, procedures, rules, and techniques. Methodology results from abstracting and organizing experience within a theoretical framework. In simpler times, when demands on software were modest, methodology did not play a role. The ever-increasing complexity of information systems, however, makes methodology indispensable.

The development of any product by a team under time and financial constraints is in need of **project management**: planning, monitoring, and controlling the course of the development process and the resources used by that process. Project management has general principles, practices, and guidelines, but must be adopted to the goal of the project, to the resources available to a specific project, and to the methodology used to achieve the goal.

A product must achieve an expected level of *quality*. To achieve the maximum possible quality in a product, quality control must be built into the process of its production. This means a partnership between methodology and project management is necessary: A good methodology allows project management to verify the quality of the product at critical **milestones** during the development process, not just at the completion of the project.

In product development, it is prudent to distinguish between **problem space** and **solution space**. Problem space is the source of requirements; it is the environment in which the final product must work and solve problems. The solution space, on the other hand, contains issues that are related to the product (solution) itself, not the problems addressed by the product. In problem space we **analyze** business problems and their related concepts; in solution space we **design** the product. The two spaces, however, overlap and affect each other.

5. KEY CONCEPTS

Algorithm. A step-by-step procedure for solving a problem in a finite number of steps, each of which is simpler than the problem itself. Long division is an example of algorithm.

Analysis. The process of identifying problems, conceptual solutions, and their related concepts in the **problem space** (or problem domain).

Application. A set of programs that performs a specific task. Even though the users often see applications as independent entities, they must be viewed and developed as integral parts of an information system.

Artificial Intelligence (AI) Systems. A vast and varied area of software industry that includes robotics, forecasting of complex systems, virtual reality (games and simulations), and expert systems. AI systems ❶ enable machines to automatically perform tasks that otherwise would require human intelligence, ❷ solve complex problems by using non-mathematical algorithms, ❸ simulate real or imaginary environments, and ❹ provide expert opinion by using available information, heuristic, and inference.

Business Intelligence System. A set of subsystems and applications that allows management to analyze operational and market data, create models, make forecasts, and virtually test business decisions. BI systems help the **strategic** direction of the business.

Business-to-Business (B2B) System. An information system that allows a business to conduct transactions or exchange information with other businesses online. A type of **e-commerce**.

Business-to-Consumer (B2C) System. An information system that allows consumers to buy products and services from a business online. A type of **e-commerce**.

Communication System. Transmits data to the information system and brings information to its users. A communication system consists of communication **devices**, **protocols**, and the **connections** between those devices.

Component. A constituent element of a system. A component can be a system in its own right.

Connections. In communication systems, the medium that connects two devices together and allows them to communicate.

Control System. Directs and facilitates the interactions between the building blocks of the information technology, and provides the information system with the services of information technology. In computerized systems, the most important component of the control system is the **operating system** (**OS**). But a control system also consists of utilities and drivers (control programs for the hardware).

Coupling. The degree of interdependence among the elements within a system or a network or between the individual elements and the whole. **Tight coupling** denotes high interdependence, while **loose coupling** means the opposite.

Data. Facts or assumption that are the building blocks of information.

Data Hierarchy. The relationship between data and information at various levels. Something that is considered "information" at one level may be used as "data" in a higher level, and *vice versa*.

Data Management System. A set of rules, procedures, material, and tools that stores, organizes, protects, and retrieves data needed by the information system. Modern database management systems have incorporated many information system functions such as the enforcement of business rules.

Deliverable. The measurable and verifiable outcome of a **milestone** in a project.

Design. The process of finding and modeling *concrete* solutions for the problems discovered and conceptually modeled by **analysis**.

Device, Communication. An input and/or output device that receives and/or sends data. The task of a communication device is to *encode* messages (data or information) into packages that can be carried by the system to another device that will *decode* the message for the benefit of the recipient. To communicate, devices must rely on a **protocol**.

e-commerce. An information system that allows an entity to conduct business online, either with other businesses or with consumers.

ERP. Enterprise Resource Planning. An information system that aims at satisfying the enterprise-wide information needs of a business within an integrated system.

Heuristic. ❶ A problem-solving technique in which a solution is found by weighing alternatives; ❷ an algorithm for solving problems by learning from the results of previous attempts to solve the same problem. Heuristic is instrumental in the functioning of artificial intelligence (AI) systems.

Information. An organized collection of data that allows its recipient to ❶ gain knowledge, ❷ draw meaning, ❸ arrive at conclusions, or ❹ execute a set of actions to reach an objective. Information has three main constituents: data, purpose, and logical organization.

Information Automation. The application of information logic to data by a device that executes a program.

Information System. A system that processes data into information according to a predictable set of logical assumptions. Information systems are **open** systems.

Information Technology. The know-how, methods, tools, and material used to support information systems. Information technology is not one entity, but a set of related components: know-how, methods, and material. What is collectively called information technology is actually composed of one or more **processing units** and three systems: **communication**, **data management,** and **control**.

Infrastructural Information System. A set of systems and applications that supports the basic functions of an enterprise. This category includes **transaction processing** systems, **business-to-business** systems, **business-to-consumer** systems and **business intelligence** systems.

Logic. A *form* of reasoning that proves a proposition by starting from stated premises (assumptions or data). The objective of information is achieved through logic. Logic by itself, however, is not about the *content* of the information, but about its *formal structure*.

Mass-Market Software. General-purpose products that are targeted at end users.

Method. A systematic way of accomplishing something. It results from both experience and the theoretical interpretation of experience.

Methodology. A set of practices, procedures, rules, and techniques used to achieve an objective or build a product. (Methodology *includes* methods.)

Milestone. An important event in the course of a project, resulting in a **deliverable**.

Network. A cooperating set of relatively independent elements. Networks and systems are similar entities and sometimes cannot be distinguished.

Problem Space. A space (or domain) the problems of which are addressed by the product (solution) and in which the product must operate. (*See also* **Solution Space**.)

Processing Unit. An entity that applies the logical rules of the information system to data. In traditional information systems, humans function as "processing units." In computerized systems, the CPU (Central Processing Unit) and its associated circuitry apply the logical rules.

Product Specifications. Features that the finished product must have. A finished product has two sets of features: One set satisfies the objectives of the product (business requirements); the other set are those features that are necessary to make the first set possible (solution features).

Project Management. Planning, monitoring, and controlling the course of the development process and the resources used by that process. Project management is a function of time and resources. It must have an identifiable goal that completes (and ends) the project. A project is composed of **milestones** that must achieve sub-goals and result in **deliverables**.

Protocols, Communications. A set of rules or standards that allow two devices to communicate. Like data and information, the protocols are *virtual*, even though they are carried by real mediums.

Quality Control. A methodology to ensure that the final product meets the expected quality standards. To achieve the maximum possible quality in a product, quality control must be built into the process of its production.

Requirements. Identify the objectives of a product. Requirements are not the same as product specifications. The former express business needs and problems, whereas the latter include features that relate to the solution itself.

Software Components. Reusable software parts that are assembled with other components to create complete systems and applications.

Software Contractor. An entity—individual or corporation—that builds custom software for enterprises that need very specialized solutions.

Solution Space. The space that contains issues related to the product itself. Must be distinguished from the **problem space**.

Subsystem. A system that functions as a component of another system.

Symbol. Something that represents something else by association, resemblance, or convention; a sign that represents an operation, a quantity, a quality, or a relationship. Both data and information are communicated through symbols.

System. A system is a set of interrelated elements organized into an identifiable whole with a distinct *identity*. A system is *not* monolithic, but consists of a *set* of elements (or **components**).

System, Open and Closed. Identifies the accessibility of a system to the outside world. A "perfect" open system is one that accepts *input*, the **logic** of its internal workings can be understood and/or changed, can *change* as a result of interaction with the outside world, and produces *output*. A closed system lacks one or more of the qualities described. Most systems fall somewhere between the perfect types. (A perfect closed system is unknowable.)

System Software. Operating systems, utilities, and other basic components of information technologies such as large-scale databases.

Transaction Processing System (TPS). An information system that records and processes data about the routine activities of an enterprise.

6. REVIEW QUESTIONS

1. Explain the difference between data and information. Give two examples for each.
2. Explain why your university is considered a system. Give examples of other systems that you know.
3. Comment on the phrase "information system is an open system."
4. What is the difference between an information system and information technology?
5. How does a data management system differ from a communication system?
6. Give examples of information systems and automated information systems. How do they differ from each other?
7. Define "business intelligence."
8. What is the difference between business intelligence and artificial intelligence?

7. RESEARCH PROJECTS & TEAMWORK

The first three chapters of this book provide a theoretical framework for the more practical chapters that follow. "Theoretical," however, does not mean "passive." On the contrary, one has to apply one's critical faculties *actively* to really understand the strengths, and the shortcomings, of any theory.

In each chapter, under this topic, you will find ideas on how to do so—individually or in cooperation with each other.

❶ Create a study group and schedule a discussion session for your group. Select one group member as the leader for this week. The leader must divide the work and determine who does what. The leader is also responsible for putting the final report together and submitting it to the instructor. The first project is to conduct research on Enterprise Resource Planning (or ERP) systems. Find the most popular ERP software, the most prominent enterprises that have adopted such software, and "pro" or "con" reviews. Note the pricing: Has a lower price helped the vendor?

❷ Following the same process and organization as above, conduct research to find the major differences between business-to-business (B2B) and business-to-consumer (B2C) systems. For each system, provide some examples and identify its potential users. If you can, provide your own critique and suggest ways for improving the systems.

❸ Conduct research about artificial intelligence (AI) and robotics. For quite some time, robots have been used in the exploration of the Moon and the planets. Can you find other areas in which robots have become indispensable?

❹ There are many service companies that develop systems to support enterprise activities. PriceWaterhouseCoopers and Electronic Data Service (EDS) are just two examples. In fact, conduct a Web search with the key word "business systems integrators" to find a long list of companies that provide such services. Find who the customers of these service providers are and what kind of information systems they develop. (You may want to look at prices as well.) Summarize the results of your research and submit it to the instructor.

❺ Business Intelligence (BI): You cannot escape the term if you are in the information systems business. Do research to find out how it helps (or is supposed to help) the business.

8. SUGGESTED READINGS

Subjects introduced in this chapter will be explored in more detail in the following chapters. At the end of each chapter, we will suggest books and literature that relate to the topic(s) under discussion. One subject, though, will not be covered: the history of information systems. A concise and well-rounded book on this topic is yet to be written. To be sure, a vast amount of knowledge can be found in books on general history and on information technology (such as paper and printing), but a narrative that focuses on the evolution and the revolutions of the information system as a distinct concept is lacking.

One book, *From Gutenberg to the Internet: A Sourcebook on the History of Information Technology*, by **Jeremy M. Norman** (historyofscience.com, 2005) tells the story in the framework of technology, but also provides a good narrative on the role of information in the period that it covers.

Software industry is a moving target. Many products and companies appear with fanfare but are quietly forgotten after only a short time. *From Airline Reservations to Sonic The Hedgehog: A History of the Software Industry*, by **Martin Campbell-Kelly** (Massachusetts Institute of Technology, 2003) is a good and readable roundup and taxonomy of software as business from its inception to the date of writing. We hope that the author would continue to follow this moving target.

For the latest in software history, visit the Web site of the Software History Center (http://www.software history.org). It offers a selective but very useful bibliography for writings on the history of software industry.

Chapter 2

The Concept of Object Orientation

1. OVERVIEW

An object-oriented information system consists of objects, and an object-oriented approach to software development models objects, their relationships, and their interactions. This chapter presents the basic concepts that apply to objects.

Chapter Topics

➤ Real-world objects.

➤ The meaning of object *identity*.

➤ Object's attributes and operations.

➤ The *state* of an object.

➤ Classes and the process by which classification is achieved.

➤ Superclasses, subclasses, and class hierarchy.

➤ The similarities and the differences between real and virtual objects.

➤ Encapsulation and information hiding and their significance.

➤ Object interface.

➤ Aggregate and composite objects.

➤ The concepts of inheritance and polymorphism.

➤ An overview of the emergence of object-oriented technology.

➤ An introduction to object-oriented modeling and the Unified Modeling Language (UML).

Introduction

In the previous chapter we discussed the nature of information systems and their components. We also argued that, despite the wide variety of what they do and how they do it, information systems and applications must be viewed as products and, as products, their development must follow a certain methodology that is the most suitable for the product, available technologies, and available resources.

So far, object-oriented analysis and design, coupled with object-oriented technology, has proven itself as the most effective methodology to build software and information systems. An object-oriented approach, however, requires an understanding of what objects are, how they relate to each other, and how they behave and interact. In this chapter, we lay the groundwork for object-oriented analysis and design by exploring their most basic concept: object. In later chapters, we will review all concepts introduced here in much greater detail.

We will also briefly discuss the Unified Modeling Language (UML), a widely used modeling tool that we will use in the process of analysis and design.

2. INTRODUCING OBJECTS

To understand object-oriented technology, methodology, and modeling, we must first understand what objects are. With minor variations, real and virtual objects share most of their characteristics, but some features are easier to understand in the context of the real world, while others are more significant in a virtual system.

Below, we briefly explore the most important and relevant concepts that shape our understanding of objects in the real world. Then we revisit some of the same concepts in the context of virtual objects and introduce new ones that have special significance for information systems.

Real Objects

> An object is ❶ something that is perceived as an entity and referred to by name; ❷ something perceptible by one or more of the senses; ❸ something intelligible or perceptible by the mind.

In sum, an object is a *thing*: animate or inanimate, human or nonhuman, tangible or intangible. As "things," objects do not appear to require elaborate definitions or introductions: After all, they are the basic units of our *perception* of the world. Nevertheless, this apparent simplicity hides several concepts that are not so readily apparent, even though they lie at the foundation of how we grasp the significance of objects.

Identity

> The identity of an object is what distinguishes it from all other objects.

☞ Whenever we fail to identify the exact identity of an object with a name, we first try a generic term instead. And if we fail at all levels of generalization, we resort to the term "thing" as the most generic, identity-less term for the concept we are trying to communicate.

Let us repeat one of the definitions at the beginning of this section: An object is something that is perceived as an *entity* and referred to by *name*. Name is a *symbol* that communicates the identity of an object both to ourselves and to others. Without such an identity symbol, we cannot be sure what "thing" we are thinking about and we cannot communicate our concepts to others.

What is more, we also believe that an object not only has an identity, but that its identity is both *unique* and *unchanging*:

- *Unique:* We admit that, sometimes, we may assign the wrong symbol to an object—mistaking one twin for the other, for example—but we never doubt that

☞ When we state that somebody has changed so much that he or she no longer "seems like the same person," we are relying on the shock value of everybody's underlying belief in a constant identity to express the magnitude of the change.

the object's identity remains solid and inviolable, regardless of errors or deliberate attempts by one entity to fake the identity of another.

- *Unchanging:* An object may change superficially or profoundly, but our perception of its unique identity does not change. During a person's lifetime, neither the person's character nor the molecules that constitute his or her body remain the same; our firm belief, however, that the person's identity has not changed remains unshaken.

Attributes

> Attributes are features, properties, qualities, or characteristics that are associated with an object.

Names and other symbols are actually tokens for the *totality* of an entity. The totality of an object consists of *everything* that the object *is* and everything that the object *does*. We merely use symbols as a shorthand method to communicate a much more complex mental image to ourselves and to each other.

☞ As can be expected, the same symbol can—and often does—mean different things to different people. The resulting misunderstandings can lead to massive failures in information system development. (For a discussion on how to reduce the risk, see Chapter 5, Domain Analysis).

Attributes are what an object is. But even the simplest object in the real world has numerous properties and characteristics. Our *perception* of an object, however, is often limited to a selected or subjective set of attributes: *selected*, because neither we nor the people with whom we communicate can possibly hope to grasp the full complexity of all the likely attributes that an object can possess; and *subjective*, because we assign properties (such as beauty) that are not inherent to the object.

Attributes are usually *paired* with *values* that qualify or quantify the attribute. The employment record of an object called **John Doe** could contain a list of attributes such as the ones illustrated in Figure 2.1.

Operations

> An operation is what an object does or is capable of doing.

We easily recognize actions performed by animate objects: dogs bark, humans talk, birds fly, plants breath and grow. We can even concede that automobiles move and planes fly. But what operations could we possibly assign to a ball, a rock, or a piece of metal?

**Figure 2.1
Object: John Doe**

Attributes	Operations
■ **Name**: John Doe	■ Order
■ **Born**: 1972	■ Approve Order
■ **Sex**: Male	■ Get Bids
■ **Marital Status**: Single	■ Evaluate Bids
■ **Citizenship**: USA	■ Report to President
■ **Degree**: MBA	■ Report to Board
■ **Current Position**: VP of Purchasing	■ Notify Inventory
■ **Years with Company**: 5	■ Hire
■ **Starting Salary**: $70,000	■ Fire
■ **Current Salary**: ...	■ Evaluate Employees
	■ Approve Vacations
	■ ...

Attributes and Operations As Perceived By His Employer

Attributes constitute what an object is; operations describe what an object does or can do.

The answer lies in the second part of the given definition: An operation is not only what an object does—with or without a trigger from outside—but also what it is *capable* of doing. A ball bounces if dropped because it is capable of doing so. Exposed to oxygen, a piece of iron will eventually oxidize, but gold will not corrode and, therefore, lacks the "oxidize" operation. A rock, exposed to extreme hot and cold, turns to sand (or performs "break up").

State

> State is the condition of an object at a certain stage in its lifetime.

An object has a set of attributes and these attributes accept a range of values. The combination of these attributes and their associated values constitutes the state of an object: an infant boy grows to be an 80-year-old man; a sapling becomes a tree; a student becomes a graduate. While the **identity** of the object remains the same, its **state** might change.

The concept of "state" needs three further clarifications.

❶ The condition of an object changes because of **objective** changes to the values of its attributes; however, how we *name* the state is **subjective** and **selective**. For example, is the state of an 80-year-old man *old*, *grandfather*, *wise*, or, if things have gone well, *wealthy*?

❷ Since state is selective, then the *same* object can be described by several states *simultaneously*, even though the condition of the object has not changed in its totality. For example, John Doe can be employed, married, and happy at the same time. (But multiple state names cannot be contradictory: John Doe cannot be employed and unemployed at the same time.)

❸ An object may have **secondary** states that require a **primary** state, but can change without any changes in the primary state. For example, a car must be in working order (the primary state) before it can move but, even with a good engine and enough fuel, it might be either stationary or moving (secondary states) or change from one to the other.

In the real world, most states result from incremental changes and do not happen suddenly (although some do), but we tend to perceive or acknowledge them as abrupt: While a student works for years towards a college degree, it is only with the graduation ceremony that we grant him or her the graduate state.

Class

> Class is a set of objects that share the same attributes and operations.

The simplest way to describe a class is to say that it results from **classification**. But what is classification? It is the result of two *simultaneous* mental activities: abstraction and generalization.

❶ Abstraction

> Abstraction is identifying those characteristics of an entity that distinguish it from other *kinds* of entities.

When classifying objects, we *select* those attributes and operations that we consider to be *significant* or *relevant* to the concept. For instance, to classify telephones, we choose a set of attributes and operations that we believe will exemplify the essence of a telephone:

- Has a numeric keypad for dialing.
- Has an earpiece (separate or integrated).
- Has a microphone (separate or integrated).
- Can connect to the telephone network, wired or wireless.
- Can dial a number.
- Can transmit voice by modulating it into electrical current.
- Can receive voice by unmodulating it from electrical current.

To arrive at the `Telephone` class, we ignore attributes that we consider inconsequential—properties such as size, color, or price. (We may qualify *actual* phone sets with terms such as "big" or "small," "white" or "black," "cheap" or "expensive," but we would not consider either the size or the color as essential to the definition of the class `Telephone`.)

This process of selection is called abstraction, which means separating certain attributes and operations from a concrete object.

❷ Generalization

> To generalize is to conclude that characteristics of a particular entity apply to a broader range of entities.

☞ To say that somebody is "in a class of his own" really means that a person, for better or for worse, is so unique that he cannot be generalized into a class.

If we cannot apply what we have abstracted to more objects than one, we do not have a class. If there were only one telephone set in the entire world, it would be not only useless, but also unclassifiable: A class must apply to a set of objects that share a set of selected attributes and/or operations.

As in the case of state, it follows that classification is based on *perception* of reality and is, therefore, *subjective*.

Figure 2.1 illustrates the object `John Doe` from the viewpoint of his employer. But among all the objects in the real world, humans can perhaps posses the longest list of attributes, for they are not just physical or biological objects, but exist within a web of social and economic relationships that confers upon them many tangible or intangible characteristics. Therefore, a hospital would see John Doe's attributes differently than his employer.

- **Name**: John Doe.
- **Born**: 1972.
- **Symptoms**: acute pain and cramps on the lower right side of the abdomen, fever, nausea, vomiting, and diarrhea. A punctured appendix is the most likely cause.
- **Blood**: A+.
- **Reaction to Penicillin**: none.
- **White Blood Cell Count**: high.
- **Sugar Level**: normal.
- **Health Insurance Provider**: TUC (Taurus Universal Care).
- **History of Major Surgery**: . . .

Instance

An instance is the concrete manifestation of a class.

Put in plainer language, an instance is a synonym for an object when we intend to emphasize the fact that it belongs to a class. For example, **John Doe** is an "instance" of the class **Human**.

An object can be an instance of numerous classes that have *parallel* or *hierarchical* relationships to each other. **John Doe** can be viewed as an instance of **Employee** or **Patient** classes (parallel abstractions) or an instance of **Human**, **Primate**, **Mammal**, or **Vertebrate** classes (hierarchical abstractions).

Superclass & Subclass

A superclass results from *generalizing* a set of classes. A subclass results from *specializing* a superclass. The relationship among superclasses and subclasses is called class hierarchy.

By following the arguments about classification, we are likely to arrive at the logical conclusion that some classes can be more generalized than others. And this, indeed, is the case: The **Mammal** class is more generalized than the **Primate** class, but it is less generalized than the **Vertebrate** class. A class that results from a higher level of generalization is called a **superclass**.

The reverse of generalization is *specialization* and results in a **subclass**: **Passenger Car** is a subclass of **Automobile**; both **Truck** and **Bicycle** are specializations of the **Vehicle** class.

Usually the higher the generalization is, the more abstract the class becomes. The reason is that we can select fewer attributes and operations that are shared among objects belonging to the more generalized class. (The most generalized class, **Thing** or **Object**, is so abstract that it does not have any attributes—except perhaps "is" or "exists.")

The relationship between less generalized and more generalized classes is called **class hierarchy**. A superclass is called the *parent* of the subclasses that belong to it. In turn, subclasses that belong to a superclass are considered its *children* and are *siblings* to each other.

Virtual Objects

> Information systems are composed of virtual objects that embody the same concepts as real objects, but are created *from* concepts instead of giving rise *to* them.

Regardless of technology, information systems have always relied on **virtual objects**: A widely accepted view is that written language evolved from the efforts to virtualize real, everyday objects such as goats or cows. Babylonians wrote on clay tablets to transform oral contracts and transactions into more enduring and binding virtual objects. Medieval and renaissance bankers would issue letters of credit—virtual money—that could be converted back to "real" cash in distant places, in essentially the same way that a modern ATM accepts your card, dispenses cash, and changes the state of a virtual object—your bank account.

All characteristics of real objects apply to virtual objects, but since by definition virtual objects are not real, certain concepts have to be discussed from a slightly different viewpoint. Other concepts, such as encapsulation (discussed later in this chapter), legitimately apply to real objects as well, but their significance to information systems is better understood if viewed in the context of virtual objects.

Class

> For a virtual object, class is both an abstraction and a template.

When a hospital treats a patient, it attends to a real object, even though the attributes and the behavior of the real patient are abstracted and generalized into the class **Patient**. But when the hospital wants to track the patient's medical history, it is no longer concerned with a real object, but with a virtual object that has only—and only—those attributes that the hospital considers relevant to an instance of the **Patient** class. In other words, the real **John Doe** object can be classified in a myriad of foreseen *and* unforeseen ways—an employee, a citizen, a brother, a member of a sports club, etc.—but the hospital's virtual **John Doe** object is created from a *preconceived* idea about a patient. The hospital may keep the patient's medical history on paper forms, in a computerized database, or use a mix of both, but it uses a *template* to fill in the attributes of **John Doe** or any other patient.

☞ It is important to distinguish between information itself and information *technology*: While an information technology must have "real" components to interact with real people and keep permanent data, information is always virtual, whether the technology consists of clay tablets, paper, or computers.

This is true of all virtual objects. When you enroll in a college, you become a student by virtue of the fact that the college agrees to abstract certain attributes from you (the real object), place them in a template, and instantiate a virtual **Student** object (or "register" you, to use a more conventional term). To open an account, a bank must use a **Customer** template and one or more **Account** templates.

We do not abstract or generalize virtual objects into classes, but create them from templates or classes that are already abstract and general. A bank must first decide what attributes the **Borrower** class must have before it can accept or reject loans. Almost anywhere that you fill a form with personal information (or a form is filled *for* you), your attributes are abstracted and fed into a predefined class to emerge as a virtual object.

Classes that mold virtual objects fall into two broad categories that result from their different origins: business classes and utility classes.

❶ Business Classes   "Business" classes are those that have a counterpart in the real world: tree, student, contract, office, poet, shirt, patient, etc. We arrive at these classes through the normal route: abstraction and generalization. In fact, by the time we are entrusted with building an information system, such classes are usually already defined. (Perhaps not *well-defined*, but a general idea exists.) The discovery of business classes and their relationships is the main task of *analysis*.

❷ Utility Classes   Utility classes are those that lack a *direct* counterpart in the real world and are used to create objects that manage the responsibilities of the information system: to interact with the outside world, to make communication among business objects possible, and to save information when required. Command buttons, menus, and dropdown lists are a few such classes (though the majority are not visual or visible). Utility classes are either *de facto* standards (very similar to hanging folders, letter-sized paper, or ruled notebooks) or are conceived by analyzing the *specific* needs of an application or a system and by generalizing those needs into classes. The discovery and definition of utility classes and their relationships is the task of *design*.

☞ In object-oriented vocabulary, business class are usually called **entity** classes.

Utility classes are further grouped into subcategories: **control** (those that act as traffic cops), **boundary** (those that interact with the outside world), **life cycle** (those that manage other objects), etc. We will discuss utility classes under the section for design.

Attributes & Operations

Attributes and operations of virtual objects are defined, not discovered.

Even though the properties of virtual "business" objects may result from a process of discovery in the real world, a virtual object can possess *only* those attributes and operations that its class defines. For example, the real John Doe may or may not have a cell phone or an email address, but the `John Doe` object as an employee (that represents only those attributes that relate to his job) *cannot* have a cell phone or an email address unless the `Employee` class in his company's information system has those attributes. Therefore, the definition of attributes for virtual objects (or rather, their template classes) cannot be left to chance but must be carefully researched and designed.

☞ An attributes may accept an "unknown" value as part of its domain. This is not a contradiction: "**unknown**" is not ambiguous, but clearly declares that we do not know the answer. This argument holds true for both real and virtual objects.

As previously mentioned, the attributes of an object and the values assigned to those attributes are *paired*. For virtual objects, the characteristics of values must be clearly defined because ambiguity can wreak havoc with the mission of the information system. The range of values that can be assigned to an attribute is called the attribute's *domain*. This range is constrained by the nature of the attribute and other limiting factors. For example, a birthday *must* be a date (not an amount, for example) and, for a living person, cannot be a thousand years in the past.

Encapsulation

Encapsulation is the packaging of data and processes within one single unit.

Being a unit, of course, is the prerequisite for being an object: Half a tree is not a `Tree` object, neither do scattered bits and pieces of a car constitute a `Car` object. You might ask, therefore, what is so important about encapsulation? What are the practical benefits of emphasizing encapsulation as an object-oriented concept?

The significance of encapsulation to software development is best revealed when we compare encapsulation to any other mechanism for managing data and processes that handle data.

Objects in the real world, natural or man-made, *do* things. When you run, you do not micromanage your muscles, your bone structure, and the general flow of blood in your body, even though running is a very complicated operation: Witness the fact that we are still having problems with creating robots that can mimic the agility and the flexibility of a human being who walks over an uncharted or uneven territory. Nevertheless, you do it as an *encapsulated unit* that displays a certain behavior *without* revealing how the behavior is achieved and what is involved in achieving that behavior. If you have to attend to every detail of how your body accomplishes the task of running, you would not be able to run normally.

This, in short, is a description of encapsulation: Objects do things that they do without distracting us with *how* they do it. Driving a car needs a minimum amount of skill and attention; you may serenely ignore how the engine works and how the wheels of the car respond to the signal of the steering wheel to turn left or right. In other words, encapsulation makes **complexity** manageable and safe. Without it, we would be overwhelmed with many details that we cannot hope to control.

But how else could it be? Like most other object-oriented concepts, the problem of explaining the significance of encapsulation lies not in its difficulty, but in its simplicity and familiarity: The real world is object-oriented. But imagine a different world in which you had to assemble your TV set every time you want to watch a program, or had to know, in detail, what should be done (*inside* the TV set) to change channels or adjust the volume. In the real world, such situations do not occur frequently or, when they do, somebody finds a way to encapsulate the process (as a TV set or a car does). But in the virtual world of software, such was the state of affairs before the adoption of object-oriented technology.

Information Hiding

> Information hiding conceals and protects what goes on inside an object from the outside world.

The concept of information hiding is closely related to encapsulation and, like encapsulation, is central to the object-oriented concept.

Information hiding not only conceals the complexity of the inner workings of objects, but also protects them from careless, malicious, or unauthorized interference. When you use an ATM, encapsulation and information hiding ensure that you ❶ are not burdened with the complexity of how the machine works, ❷ cannot perform operations that you are not allowed to, and ❸ cannot change the way the machine operates.

☞ Often, the term "interface" is reinforced by the qualifier "public," even though, by definition, an interface is the boundary *between* entities, not *inside* them. In other words, a "private interface" is an oxymoron.

Together, encapsulation and information hiding turn an object into a **black box** (Figure 2.2). A black box divides the space in which the object lives into *inside* and *outside*: What is inside is *private* to the object and cannot be accessed or change without the object's permission; what is outside is *public*.

Interface

> An object's interface consists of operations that are available to the public.

If encapsulation packages data and processes into one unit and information hiding conceals them, then how can objects interact? The answer is the interface—one or more **services** or operations that the object offers to the entities outside it, the public.

**Figure 2.2
Encapsulation
and Information
Hiding: Object
as "Black Box"**

A TV set conceals its inner workings and is operated only through its interface.

In everyday life, we are constantly communicating and interacting with other entities through their interfaces. In the case of some objects, using the term "interface" is easy to accept: The interface of a car—steering wheel; gas pedal; brake; and gauges for gas, speed, etc.—allows the driver to operate and monitor the car.

In other cases—such as humans—the term seems amusingly out of place (and inevitably results in a range of somehow funny to mostly boring puns). But a friendly chat *is* an exchange of messages between the public interfaces of two friends, even if both sides are revealing their innermost private thoughts. After all, what a person knows and feels is hidden in his or her mind and using language (including gestures or body language) to communicate is not a private process but a public "operation."

The interface of an object is composed not only of the services that it offers, but also of how those services are arranged and ordered. In other words, an interface consists of both **content** and **form**. Figure 2.3 illustrates the importance of the form. The picture shows a common battery of the kind normally used to power flashlights. How it provides the power (its "service") is encapsulated and well-hidden. (Without a label we cannot readily identify its type.) But the battery must follow a predefined

**Figure 2.3
Interface: Form
and Substance**

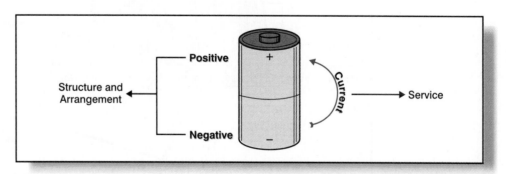

The interface of an object is both the services that it offers and how those services are arranged. A battery that offers the right current but with the wrong arrangement of negative and positive poles is unusable.

form—standard size, standard current, placement and shape of negative and positive poles—or it would be useless as a battery.

Aggregation & Composition

> An object may consist of other objects.

Objects are not monolithic. We do not have to descend deep into the strange territory of subatomic particles to recognize this fact. A car is made up of an engine, a chassis, a transmission system, etc.; a car's engine, in turn, consists of combustion, lubricating, electrical and cooling (sub-)systems. Higher forms of living beings consist of numerous cells; a monocellular bacterium is composed of complex proteins.

In object-oriented terminology, the relationship of one object to its component objects is called **aggregation**. A strong form of aggregation in which the life of components relies on the life of the whole is called **composition**. A school class is a simple aggregation: Students who make up the class can participate in other classes. The human body is a composition: The components cannot function without the whole.

A book is both a real object *and* a virtual object. (See Figure 2.4.) We buy the *physical* object because we are interested in the *virtual* object (the same way that we buy CDs because we want to listen to music, not because we want to collect shiny disks). As a physical object, a book is *composed* of pages, a cover, and the material used for binding. Separated from the book, neither the cover nor single pages fulfill their functions. As a virtual object—a detective story, a history, a textbook—a book is composed of letters, words, sentences, paragraphs, chapters, and maybe pictures, all of which are necessary to enable the book to reach its objectives. (Imagine a detective novel in which the last pages are physically present, but are left blank.)

A library, on the other hand, is an aggregation: It must have a certain number of books to be called a library, but the identity of individual books might change. A library may lend out books to individuals or other libraries and still remain a complete library, while a book with missing pages cannot be called a complete book.

Figure 2.4
Aggregation and Composition

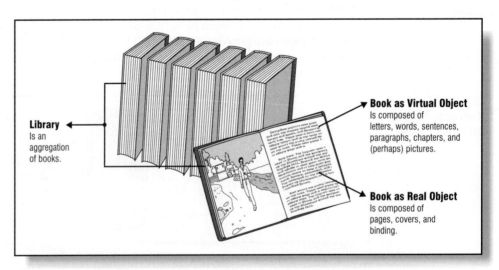

Library
Is an aggregation of books.

Book as Virtual Object
Is composed of letters, words, sentences, paragraphs, chapters, and (perhaps) pictures.

Book as Real Object
Is composed of pages, covers, and binding.

Aggregation defines the relationships of individual components to the whole object. Composition is an aggregation in which components cannot be separated and remain meaningful objects.

Abstract & Concrete Classes

> An abstract class is one that cannot have instances, whereas a concrete class can.

Object-oriented terminology gives you many chances to become confused, and the distinction between abstract and concrete classes is one such chance. We stated that classes result from classification, which is a process of abstraction and generalization. How, then, can a class be concrete?

We have pointed out that some classes are more abstract than others. (See "Superclass & Subclass.") In the hierarchy of superclasses and subclasses, some classes can be instantiated into actual (real *or* virtual) objects, while others cannot. Those that can be instantiated are called **concrete classes**; those that cannot be are **abstract classes**.

What are the criteria for distinguishing a concrete class from an abstract class? The answer is our judgment on the adequacy of a class to represent a specific object. In other words, if a class has all the required attributes and operations that we expect from an object, then it is concrete. If it has only a subset, then it is abstract and we need a more specialized class.

Figure 2.5 is a simple illustration of the concept. (The actual situation is more complex and nuanced, even for a simple example such as this.) **Art** is an *abstract* class because we have found it to be too general to satisfactorily represent a specific work of art. Saying that somebody is interested in "art" does not explain enough. At best, it prompts a question: What *kind* of art? The answer might be music, literature, painting, theatre, etc.

If it turns out that the person is interested in music, we may have to search still deeper: What kind of music? Classical, perhaps. If we are satisfied here, we decide to go no further. (If not, we can proceed down the *hierarchy* and identify Renaissance, Baroque, Romantic, and other classical subclasses.)

☞ Maybe the definers of object-oriented terminology should have chosen other terms to distinguish classes that can and cannot be instantiated—such as "instantiable" and "uninstantiable" (as unwieldy as they are). But the deed is done and we are left with the results.

**Figure 2.5
Abstract
and Concrete
Classes**

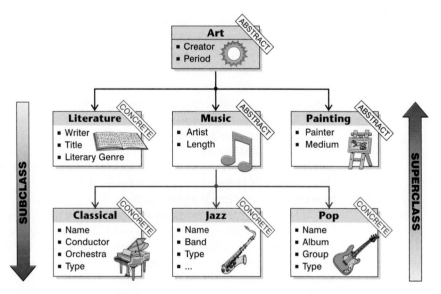

Concrete classes can have "instances" whereas abstract classes cannot. Whether a class is concrete or abstract, however, is a subjective decision.

This illustration is also an example of inheritance, the mechanism by which a subclass inherits the features of one or more superclasses.

☞ We will explain the relationship between the **Creator** attribute of the **Art** class and the **Writer**, **Artist**, and **Painter** attributes of its subclasses in the upcoming "Inheritance" section.

Any of these subclasses inherit the properties of their superclasses. Every work of **Art** has a **Creator** (even if the creator is unknown) and belongs to a certain **Period**. Any **Painting** has a **Painter** and a **Medium** (oil, watercolor, pencil, and so on). While **Period** applies to all works of art, **Medium** applies only to certain subclasses.

Literature, **Music**, and **Painting** are subclasses of the superclass **Art**. We have decided that the **Literature** class has enough attributes to be "concrete." That is, we believe it can properly represent an actual literary work. But we have left **Music** and **Painting** as *abstract* classes because in our judgment they lack enough properties to present specific works in their own categories. The three subclasses of **Music**, on the other hand, have the right properties to represent musical "objects" and are, therefore, "concrete."

In considering abstract and concrete classes, two points are important to remember.

❶ Any classification is a result of selection and judgment. Therefore, you can create another level of hierarchy under the **Classical** subclass for different categories of classical music (in which case the **Type** attribute should be removed). Or you may decide that all works of art must have a name and a type and, as a result, **Name** and **Type** belong to the superclass **Art**. The objective is to create a *family tree* that serves your purposes with a minimum amount of redundancy.

❷ Do not be misled into believing that only the lowest level of subclasses can be concrete classes. **Human** is a superclass to **Patient**, but both can have instances. As we just said, any abstraction is a matter of judgment (and context).

Inheritance

> Inheritance is the mechanism by which a subclass incorporates the behavior of a superclass.

Inheritance in the natural world has always been fascinating—and until recent times, it was also very mysterious—but not surprising. We expect a child to resemble his or her parents and, in general features, all other human beings. We expect the same from an oak tree, a deer, or a fish: that it should, first, inherit most (if not all) of the characteristics of its parent or parents and, second, resemble other members of its kind. We also expect living creatures to carry some of the features of their biological lines: Trees have trunks and leaves and fish have gills and live in water.

Inheritance also applies to virtual objects. Figure 2.5, which we presented as an example for abstract and concrete classes, illustrates inheritance as well. It shows a *family tree* of classes in which **Art** is the *ancestor* and other classes are its *descendants*: A symphony is an instance of **Classical Music** that descends from **Music**, which in turn is a child of **Art**.

Whether the object is real or virtual, inheritance is a *mechanism*, *not* an idea or an abstraction. For living objects, the mechanism consists of blueprints that the DNA carries. For virtual objects in an information system, the mechanism depends on the specific technology used. (Fortunately, object-oriented tools do not require you to know their inner workings.)

In both cases, children resemble their parents in essentials, but are *not* clones or replicas of the parents: A tree can grow to be taller or shorter than its parent and can have a different arrangement or number of branches; a human being is rarely a carbon copy of a parent and definitely does not have to follow the family profession.

(In object-oriented vocabulary, *override* is the term used when a child changes the value of an attribute or the workings of an operation that it has inherited from its parent or parents.)

Descendants may also specialize in what they inherit. All mammals have two eyes, but in primates the eyes have been rearranged to the front of the head for three-dimensional vision. In Figure 2.5, every work of art has a creator, but in the case of descendants, the same general attribute has been specialized: **Literature** has **Writer**, **Classical Music** has **Composer**, and **Painting** has **Painter**.

There is one *crucial difference* between living and virtual objects regarding the inheritance mechanism. In nature, when a new object is born its relationship with its parents is severed and, as a result, changes in a parent no longer have any effect on the children. If a cosmic ray or a nuclear accident causes a mutation in a frog, the mutation is not retroactive and would not alter the tadpoles born earlier. If your father learns to speak Italian, either before you were born or afterwards, it would not teach you Italian.

In object-oriented software, however, inheritance is *live* and *continuous* (within certain logical and technological limitations). If the parent "learns" to finish an operation five seconds faster, the child becomes five seconds more efficient as well.

In nature, living objects have one or two parents. Man-made objects, including virtual ones, can have many. Figure 2.6 represents a good example of multiple inheritance (and illustrates the challenge of forcing too many functionalities into one object). Portable devices such as cell phones and personal digital assistants are the modern rivals to Swiss army knives in the race to implement multiple inheritance.

Polymorphism

Polymorphism is the ability of objects belonging to different classes to perform the same operation differently.

Figure 2.6
Multiple
Inheritance

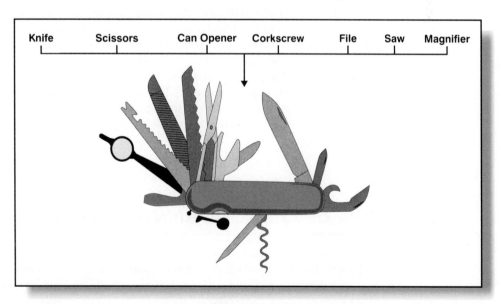

A Swiss army knife is an example of multiple inheritance in the real world. In object-oriented technology, but not in the real world, if the regular (the ancestor) is sharpened, the Swiss army knife (the descendant) will become sharper as well.

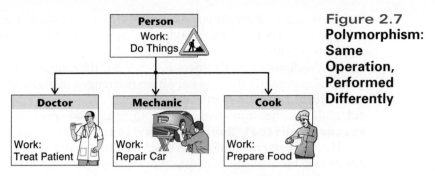

Figure 2.7 Polymorphism: Same Operation, Performed Differently

A doctor, a mechanic, and a cook all share the **Work** responsibility that they inherit from their parent, **Person**. But the work that they actually do is completely different.

☞ "Polymorphism" literally means "many shapes." It might not be the most appropriate term for the concept of "one operation, different implementations," but it has to do.

Polymorphism is closely related to inheritance and we effectively described it (as "override" and "specialization") under the previous topic. But since inheritance for virtual objects is an ongoing process and not a one-time occurrence, polymorphism must receive some extra emphasis.

In Figure 2.7, **Person** is a superclass with a **Work** responsibility. **Person** can have numerous subclasses, including **Doctor**, **Mechanic**, and **Cook**. Instances of all subclasses must **Work**, but the work that they actually *do* is very different from each other: When objects belonging to **Person** subclasses are told to work, the doctor treats patients, while the mechanic fixes cars and the cook prepares food. In other words, the same message, "**Work**," is implemented differently depending on the nature of the object, *not* the nature of the message.

Why is this important? We know if we ask people to sing and they do sing, we will get very different results depending on the talent, the musical education, the voice, and the taste of the person whom we have requested to sing.

In an object-oriented information system, polymorphism is an effective tool for managing complexity and increasing efficiency by promoting *reuse*. For example, we might decide to add another subclass, **Teacher**, to the **Person** hierarchy. The new subclass would inherit every attribute and operation from the **Person** class. (Besides **Work**, we have not listed any attributes and operations for the **Person** class but, in a split second, we can come up with many: name, salary, education, work experience, etc.) The developer of **Teacher** has only to provide for what the teacher has to do for **Work**. And if the inner workings of **Person** have to be fixed or enhanced, its descendants would benefit from the improvements at no cost.

3. THE ORIGINS OF OBJECT-ORIENTED TECHNOLOGY

> Object-oriented technology is a response to the ever-increasing demand for complex information systems. It has become possible by the immense leaps achieved by information technology.

If, from the start, we take an object-oriented approach towards learning about information systems, we may be puzzled as to why certain concepts, such as encapsulation, are emphasized (or overemphasized). The notion that an information system must emulate the workings of the world that it mirrors seems self-evident. But such was not always the case: Like other human artifacts, information technology goes through a process of evolution before cumulative changes bring it to the threshold of a revolutionary change.

Early computers, true to their names, were purely *computing* machines. Operators used switches and (later) punched cards to program the computer to perform a specific function; data was supplied the same way as the instructions, and when the answer appeared, the task was done and nothing remained—no operating system, no storage, no trace. In essence, computers were still a type of "super calculator."

The evolution of computers into an information technology, capable of supporting complex information systems and software, happened only gradually. Even before disk drives were invented, businesses discovered that they could use punched cards for input, output, *and* storage of data. Why not create a punched card for each employee with his or her salary encoded on the card and, when the time comes, feed the cards to the computer and have it print the checks? Very soon utility companies were mailing out punched cards instead of typed bills. (As late as the early 1980s, many people still received their electricity bills in the form of punched cards.)

☞ *Simula* itself evolved from another programming language, *Algol*. As Simula's name implies, it was meant as a tool for creating simulations.

Smalltalk was created by the Learning Research group at Xerox. Both languages still enjoy a loyal following, especially at universities and research centers.

But the technology gained momentum very fast. Soon computers were used to manipulate not only numbers, but also other symbols. Their processing power and storage capacity increased exponentially, as did the sophistication of the input and output devices attached to them. But expectations also increased. Performing simple tasks such as printing monthly checks was no longer enough. Computers were now expected to become information systems and support an ever-increasing array of complex functions.

The legacies of the early days, however, dragged on. Data were kept as separate entities and programs remained a collection of functions that hunted for data that they needed. The tangled web of data and processes created formidable barriers to the adoption of a methodology that could cope with the complexity of demands and the complexity of solutions. Increasingly, "software crisis" became a topic of discussion among experts in information systems.

Object-Oriented Languages

Quite evidently, a more effective and radical approach was needed. The first object-oriented language, called *Simula*, appeared as early as 1967. It was followed in the 1970s by *Smalltalk*, a more successful technology due to its forward-looking adoption of a graphical user interface.

☞ "*Data center*" and "*data processing*" were the common terms for what we call "information systems." The terms suggest the worldview behind the methodology: Data is what counts and the rest is just manipulation of data or "processes."

But the story of object-oriented technology is a perfect example of how revolutionary technologies cannot overthrow entrenched competitors in one fell swoop. Modern transportation technologies have followed a similar storyline: Before automobiles could replace the horse-and-buggy technology, a capital-intensive infrastructure of roads, fuel stations, and repair shops had to evolve and, last but not least, people had to learn how to drive cars.

While object-oriented technology was being argued over and streamlined, languages such as **Fortran** and **Cobol** established themselves in business and in government data centers. They were easy to learn and did not put undue resource pressures on the hardware. What is more, information systems were seen as primarily programming tasks and programming was considered an exercise in problem-solving, similar to solving mathematical problems. Programmers—who had yet to learn how to drive an object-oriented "car"—had an easier time adapting their problem-solving expertise to writing functions that manipulated (or "processed") a small set of data.

The mainstream adoption of object-oriented technology only started in the mid-1980s with the emergence of C++, a derivative of C, a low-level procedural language. Since C had found a secure base in business computer departments, adopting the object-oriented concepts and features of C++ did not require a *disruptive* change in the existing business technology and know-how. Programmers were able to mix procedural and object-oriented modules and make a gradual transition from the former to the latter in small steps. (To this day, most implementations of C++ remain a mixed language.)

In the early and mid-1990s, the threshold of adopting object-oriented technology by software developers was reached. **PowerBuilder**, an object-oriented language for building business applications, was introduced shortly after information technology departments started to officially recognize PCs and the Windows operating system as legitimate platforms. Later, **Visual Basic**—though not fully object-oriented; among other things, it lacked inheritance—provided a bridge to object orientation for a vast number of programmers. **Java**, a streamlined adaptation of C++, found a willing and eager audience in IT departments who were searching for ❶ a powerful tool for handling the complexity of products that they were asked to create and ❷ a common language for the Web that had just made its presence felt. (The first goal had been realized more than the second, however.)

The success of Java was followed by the adoption of object-oriented concepts and features by other language merchants, including Microsoft, which around the turn of the millennium introduced **C#** and **.Net** as object-oriented development tools. Today, finding a language or development platform that is *not* object-oriented (or does not *claim* to be) is as difficult as finding a newly manufactured mechanical typewriter. Even Cobol has been turned into an object-oriented language.

☞ In *procedural* languages, the basic building blocks of a program are not objects but named procedures or functions that—theoretically, at least—perform simple tasks and/or invoke each other.

☞ *C* was developed by the Bell Labs along with its successful operating system, Unix. *Java* was created by Sun Microsystems, which had been doing a brisk business in providing Unix-based servers to businesses.

4. OBJECT-ORIENTED MODELING

> Object-oriented analysis and design is using an object-oriented approach to building conceptual and logical models of the system.

The real world consists of objects, and development tools have now become object-oriented as well. But what about the process that takes us from the requirements of the real world to the features of the information system?

This process consists of two activities: *analysis*, which discovers the concepts of the real world and builds a conceptual model of the product, and *design*, which develops the results of analysis into a concrete model for building the system.

The main motive for adopting an object-oriented approach to analysis and design is the challenge of complexity, both the complexity of requirements and the complexity of the product that must satisfy those requirements.

> Complex products, regardless of the field to which they belong, need modeling.

Unlike object-oriented technology, however, object-oriented analysis and design—and, as a result, object-oriented modeling—have been behind in gaining momentum or acceptance.

Part of the reason is due to inertia: Information technology organizations, like all human organizations, are reluctant to adopt *any* methodology that mandates or produces a radical change in their structures. The rest results from the fact that the object-oriented approach needs tools that satisfy its more complex and demanding requirements, and such tools have been slow in coming, are sometimes difficult to learn or to use, and are usually works in progress.

Nevertheless, without modeling, systems analysis and design is distorted into a multilayered guessing game. The systems analyst tries to understand what the client wants, interprets the requirements to the best of his or her abilities, and communicates his or her interpretations to the programmer. The programmer, in turn, uses his or her judgment to understand the analyst and build the actual system. The result is like the "telephone game" that children play: The first child starts by whispering a phrase or a sentence to the second child who, in turn, transmits the message to the third. By the time the last child in line receives the sentence and utters it loudly, the message has been distorted beyond recognition.

The main modeling tool for procedural programming languages was the **flowchart**. By using a limited set of boxes, diamonds, and lines, a flowchart was able to present the logical flow of a function clearly and effectively. (In the object-oriented toolbox, the flowchart has evolved into the **activity diagram** that we will introduce in the next section.)

Object-oriented concepts, however, need a much more powerful tool than a diagram that presents the flow of a procedure, however clearly. What object-oriented analysis and design requires is a *language* that can model objects, classes, encapsulation, inheritance, and other object-oriented concepts. Enter UML.

5. The Unified Modeling Language (UML)

> UML is a *modeling language* for object-oriented system analysis, design, and deployment. UML is *not* a product, nor is it a process or a methodology.

☞ To be exact, UML is a "meta-modeling" language. What this means is that UML "models the models," those object-oriented concepts such as classes, objects, and their interactions that are the *actual* models of the system—the same way that words and sentences are "meta-models" that describe our concepts of the world.

This book uses UML as a modeling language for analysis and design. It will explore UML tools as the need arises. But before all that, it is necessary to point out what UML is and is *not*.

UML is a language for object-oriented modeling. UML's notation—its system of figures and symbols—is designed to represent object-oriented concepts. It is *not* a product that you have to buy (a sharp pencil and a blank sheet of paper will do fine), although an increasing number of development and modeling tools support it. (Some of the modeling tools are even free.) It is *not* a process that your development project must go through, even though different stages of the development process use different tools in its toolbox. And it is *not* a methodology, even though it favors a model-driven approach that affects any methodology that you may use.

UML supports multiple views of same system, with varying degrees of detail or generalization as needed.

- *Owner's View:*   what the owner (or business) wants, or the *conceptual* view of the system.
- *Architect's View:*   how the architect conceives the solution, or the *logical* view of the system.
- *Builder's View:*   the blueprints for building the product, or the *physical* view of the system.

To achieve these tasks, UML embodies four properties.

❶ Visualization

UML diagrams visualize system components, their relationships, and their interactions.

UML provides of a set of graphical elements that are combined to form diagrams. Each diagram is a visual presentation or *view* of the system and satisfies one or *more* broad but overlapping types of modeling:

- **Behavioral** modeling represents the interaction of the system with the outside world.
- **Structural** modeling represents the components of the system and their interrelationships.
- **Dynamic** modeling represents how the components of the system interact with the outside world and with each other to satisfy the behavioral requirements of the system.

Figure 2.8 is a sample of a *structural* UML diagram that illustrates five classes and their relationships. In subsequent chapters, we will discuss each UML diagram in detail and *in the context* of their roles in modeling.

❷ Specification

UML provides precise and complete models for the three major activities of system development: analysis, design, and implementation.

The three types of modeling—behavioral, structural, and dynamic—are used *iteratively* throughout the development of the system. Analysis starts with modeling the behavioral requirements of the system in *conceptual* terms; that is, it models the product as the *business* wants it to behave, regardless of *how* this behavior is achieved. This behavioral model is then transformed into a conceptual model of the system's structure and, finally, into an interactive model.

Design and implementation use the same types of modeling (with a few new ones), but with different priorities and details. UML supports the required views and the priorities of all three development activities with the same set of basic building blocks.

❸ Construction

UML models are compatible with object-oriented languages.

Figure 2.8
A UML Diagram:
Modeling
Object-Oriented
Concepts

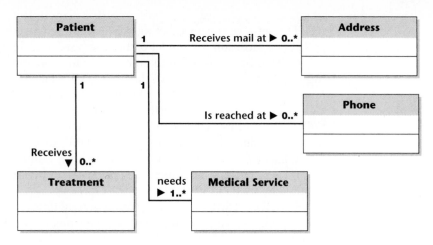

This is a simple UML diagram that illustrates the relationships of five classes. Most of the diagram should be understandable at first glance. We will explain this kind of diagram in Chapter 8, Structural Modeling. But if you are curious about the numbers over the connections between the boxes, here is a short preview. The "0..*" next to **Phone** means that one **Patient** may have no telephone numbers or many; the "1..*" next to **Medical Services** indicates the one Patient must at least one medical service (otherwise he or she would not be a patient), but may need more.

While UML is *not* a programming language, its models can be mapped to object-oriented programming languages. With varying degrees of effectiveness and ease, UML-based modeling and development tools allow both forward-engineering (generating code from models) and backward-engineering (generating or modifying models from code). The result is that any changes to the visual model can be traced back to code, and vice versa.

❹ Documentation

> UML modeling tracks major development activities throughout the system life cycle.

The advantage of UML for documenting system development is that UML modeling is not a *separate* activity, but an organic part of the development project. In other words, documentation, modeling, and specification are one and the same. As a result, the problems of inconsistency in documentation are significantly reduced.

The Origins of UML

UML did not emerge fully formed. It is still a work in progress, but has succeeded in easing the "Tower of Babel" symptom that for years plagued the communications between, and among, object-oriented theoreticians and developers.

UML originated from the work of three pioneers in object-oriented modeling: ❶ **Grady Booch**, one of the first to introduce an effective notation for modeling; ❷ **Jim Rumbaugh**, who (at General Electric) developed the Object Modeling Technique

(OMT), a set of complementary models for representing objects and their interactions; and ❸ **Ivar Jacobson**, the framer of the "use case" modeling concept.

In 1994, Booch and Rumbaugh decide to cooperate and "unify" their modeling notations. (Hence, the "unified" in UML.) Jacobson joined them a year later (and ever since, they have been known as "The Three Amigos").

To succeed, however, UML needed more than the cooperation and the goodwill of its creators. Their company, Rational Software (which was later merged into IBM), submitted their proposals on UML to the Object Management Group (OMG), a *de facto* standards organization with hundreds of member companies. Thus, UML became an "open" (as opposed to proprietary) standard and was adopted by OMG in 1997.

Since then, UML has been updated several times to incorporate concepts such as component-based development. The last major revision, UML 2.0, was adopted in 2003.

6. Wrap Up

☑ **Object**

Before we can proceed with object-oriented analysis and design, we must understand what objects are. An object is a "thing," an entity with clear boundaries and a unique identity. If a "thing" is intelligible or perceptible by the mind, it is an object, regardless of whether it is tangible or intangible.

☑ **Identity**

Objects have a unique identity even if they are cloned. The identity of an object is what distinguishes it from all other entities and objects. This identity is both unique and unchanging, even if everything else about the object changes.

☑ **Attributes & operations**

We associate objects with their characteristics and, often, with what they do. Properties that make an object what it is are called attributes, and what they do are called operations. Attributes are paired with values that quantify or qualify them. We see "age" and "wealth" as quantities, and assign qualities such as "beautiful" or "ugly" to the "looks" attribute of a person.

It is important to remember that even though objects have an "objective" existence outside us, our perceptions of them are *subjective*; therefore, although an object may have a myriad of attributes and operations, our perception is necessarily limited to a selected subset.

☑ **State**

Objects change or, to put it somewhat differently, the values that their attributes hold are changed: a child becomes a grown woman, a sapling grows into a mighty oak, and an ugly duckling becomes a swan. Sometimes even the attributes themselves (or our selective perceptions of them) change.

State is our perception of the condition of an object at a certain stage of its life. State is based on the values that an object's attributes hold, but since our perception of an object is selective, its state can be simultaneously described in many ways: a car may be "luxury" and "moving" at the same time.

☑ **Classes**

Classes are concepts that result from classification, and, in our everyday lives, we are in a constant process of classification. Classification is to define, rightly or wrongly, what attributes a set of objects shares. It results from two related mental processes: **abstraction**, which selects the set of attributes that we find relevant or significant, and **generalization**, which broadens the reach of selected attributes to more than one object.

An **instance** is a member or manifestation of a class. Therefore, when we intend to imply the relevance of a class to an object, we call the object an instance of that class: John Doe is an instance of the class **Human**, and Spotty is an instance of **Dog**.

☑ **Superclasses, subclasses & class hierarchy**

Some classes are more abstract or generalized than others and some are less. The class **Bird** is more abstract than the class **Eagle**, and the class **Lion** is less abstract than the class **Cat**. The more abstract classes are called superclasses, which own a set of less abstract subclasses.

The relationship among superclasses and subclasses is called **class hierarchy.** The superclass is the *parent*; its subclasses are *children* to their parent and *siblings* to each other.

☑ **Virtual objects**

Objects that constitute an information system are called virtual objects. They are generally similar to real-world objects with one significant difference: In a *virtual* world, classes are both abstracts of objects and templates for creating them. In a banking system, a new bank account is created from a class from which all other accounts are created as well.

Virtual classes fall into two broad categories: **business** or "entity" classes that reflect business concepts, and **utility** classes that manage the responsibilities of the information system and do not, usually, have counterparts in the real world.

☑ **Encapsulation & information hiding**

Objects, real or virtual, are encapsulated. That is, attributes and the operations of an object exist within a "capsule," an enclosed area or a *black box*, that divides their living space into two areas: *public*, exposed to the outside world, and *private*, known only to the object itself.

Information hiding is a result (and an advantage) of encapsulation: How an object does something, and the data that it holds, are concealed within the object, secure from abuse or misuse.

☑ **Object interface**

Since outside entities cannot interfere with the internal workings of an object as a result of encapsulation and information hiding, they must work with its interface—operations that the object provides to the public. These public operations are also called *responsibilities* since by exposing an interface, the object promises to perform certain services.

An interface, however, is more than the services that it provides. An interface is equal parts *form* and *content*.

☑ **Aggregate & composite objects**

Whether the fact is relevant to us or not, almost all objects are made up of other objects. When this whole-part relationship *is* significant to us, we define it as an aggregation relationship: classrooms consist of students and teachers; cars are made up of engines, wheels, etc.; and living organisms are composed of cells.

Composition is a strict form of aggregation in which the part belongs to one, and only one, whole. Whereas a student may participate in many classes, a cell can belong to only one living organism (even if, like blood cells, it can be transferred).

☑ **Inheritance & polymorphism**

Like DNA and genetics in the living world, inheritance is a mechanism by which virtual objects that belong to a *subclass* inherit the characteristics of the *superclass*. How this is done *in actuality* is within the realm of specific technologies, but all mechanisms of virtual inheritance have one important feature in common: Whereas inheritance in the real world is cast in stone when a living organism is born, virtual inheritance is *live* and ongoing. If the superclass learns to do something better, so do all the instances of the subclass.

Polymorphism is a result of specialization, and is closely tied to inheritance: All mammals move, but while deer move on four legs, humans walk on two legs, monkeys swing from tree to tree, and bats fly.

☑ **Origins of object-oriented technology**

In the early days, computer programs treated data and processes as separate entities. With the emergence of more powerful computers and the increasing complexity of information systems, a technology that could handle the complexity by adopting an object-oriented approach became both a necessity *and* a possibility.

The adoption of object-oriented technology has been a gradual process, but has now gained a critical mass and has established itself in the majority of development shops.

☑ **Object-oriented modeling & the Unified Modeling Language (UML)**

Object-oriented technology will yield the maximum profit only with object-oriented analysis and design. But such an approach requires modeling tools that generally lagged behind object-oriented technology. The Unified Modeling Language is a language that provides the "primitives" (or the basic elements) for building object-oriented *conceptual* (analysis) and *concrete* (design) models.

UML is not a specific product, process, or methodology, but a *notational* system that allows analysts, designers, and developers to adopt its diagrams to the task at hand, detailed or general, conceptual or concrete. UML has been adopted by a *de facto* standard body (OGM) and has been implemented in a large number of modeling tools, many of which are capable of round-engineering between the code and the models.

7. KEY CONCEPTS

Abstract Class. A class that cannot be instantiated.

Abstraction. Identifying those characteristics of an object that distinguish it from other *kinds* of objects.

Aggregation. The relationship of a "whole" to its parts when an object consists of other objects.

Attribute. A property, quality, or characteristic that is associated with an object. Attributes are usually paired with their corresponding values and define what an object *is*.

Business Class. A virtual class that reflects a class of objects (or concepts) in the real world.

Class. A group of objects that share the same set of attributes and operations. In the real world, class is the result of abstraction and generalization. In a virtual world, class also works as a template for creating objects.

Class Hierarchy. The relationship between a **superclass** and its **subclasses**.

Composition. A strict form of **aggregation** where the life of the part is tied to the life of the whole.

Concrete Class. A class that can have **instances**.

Encapsulation. Packaging of data and processes within one single unit.

Generalization. Applying the characteristics of a particular entity to a broader range of entities.

Identity. The quality that distinguishes one object from all other objects. The identity of an object is unique and unchangeable, even if everything else about the object changes.

Information Hiding. Conceals the inner workings of the object from the outside world. Is made possible by **encapsulation**.

Inheritance. The mechanism by which a **subclass** incorporates the behavior of a **superclass**.

Instance. The concrete manifestation of the attributes and the operations of a class. Is used instead of the term "object" when the purpose is to emphasize the relationship between the object and the class.

Instantiation. The creation of a virtual object from a class template.

Interface. The services and the operations that the object makes available to the outside world. An interface is made up of both the form *and* the content of the services provided to the public.

Object. A "thing," but more specifically ❶ something that is perceived as an entity and referred to by name; ❷ something perceptible by one or more of the senses; ❸ something intelligible or perceptible by the mind.

Object-Oriented Analysis. The process by which a *conceptual* model of the system is built based on transforming business requirements into object-oriented concepts such as classes and units of behavior.

Object-Oriented Design. The process by which a *logical* model of the system is created based on developing and refining artifacts from an object-oriented analysis.

Operation. What an object does or is capable of doing.

Polymorphism. The ability of objects belonging to different classes to perform the *same* behavior differently.

State. The condition of an object at a certain stage in its lifetime. An object may be described simultaneously by more than one state.

Subclass. A class that is less abstract than another class. A subclass is also called a "child" to its superclass and a "sibling" to other classes in the same level of hierarchy.

Superclass. A class that is more abstract than other classes. A superclass is a "parent" to subclasses that belong to it.

UML. Unified Modeling Language. A *modeling* language for object-oriented system analysis, design, and deployment.

Utility Class. A virtual class that serves the information system as a whole and, usually, does not reflect an object in the real world.

Virtual Object. An entity in a virtual system similar to objects in the real world. Virtual objects are created from classes that act as templates.

8. REVIEW QUESTIONS

1. What is the difference between real objects and virtual objects? Give an example for each.
2. Give three specialized subclasses for the `Student` class.
3. Give a superclass for the following three classes: car, airplane, tank.
4. How do business classes differ from utility classes? Provide one example for each.
5. What is the difference between the operations of a class and its attributes?
6. How does encapsulation protect the object from an intruder?

7. Explain the difference between multiple and simple inheritance and provide one example of each.
8. What is object-oriented modeling? How does it differ from Unified Modeling Language (UML)?
9. What is the difference between object-oriented languages and UML?
10. Where is the place of UML in the process of software development?

9. Research Projects & Teamwork

❶ Conduct group research on various modeling languages for object-oriented software development. Why is UML the most popular?

❷ Find out, through group research, what percentage of software developers are using object-oriented technology. What percentage use object-oriented development?

❸ Research object-oriented languages and create a table to compare their characteristics and popularity.

❹ Identify large and influential high-tech companies that use the object-oriented approach to systems development.

❺ Research job opportunities for systems analysts that specialize in the object-oriented approach to systems development. What is the average salary for such analysts?

10. Suggested Readings

Introductions to the concept of object orientation are typically included in more comprehensive books on software development (such as the present book). An exception is *Object Technology: A Manager's Guide, Second Edition* by **David A. Taylor** (Addison-Wesley, 1998), a concise book that aims to familiarize nonprofessionals with object-oriented concepts. Even as professionals, you can benefit from it by learning how to convey the ideas that it covers in a simple and down-to-earth manner.

The Object-Oriented Thought Process: The Authoritative Solution by **Matt Weisfeld** (Sams Publishing, 2000) aims at a different audience: people who are starting out to become professionals in software development, or programmers who might be experienced otherwise but need a systematic introduction to object orientation. Programming examples (in Java) are provided but, fortunately, they are not necessary for understanding the concepts. The book illustrates its examples in UML.

James Martin and **James J. Odell** are not part of the "UML Gang," and therefore their modeling notations may look unfamiliar, but their two-book set, *Object-Oriented Methods: A Foundation* (Prentice Hall, 1995)

and *Object-Oriented Methods: Pragmatic Considerations* (Prentice Hall, 1996), explores the foundations of the object-oriented worldview with a depth and breadth that is difficult to find elsewhere. The books are in no way introductory, though, and require concentration and time.

Among many books on UML, two deserve attention. The first, *UML Distilled: A Brief Guide to the Standard Object Modeling Language, Third Edition* by **Martin Fowler** and Kendal Scott (Addison-Wesley, 2003), provides a short course on the Unified Modeling Language, as well as concise introductions to other elements of an object-oriented approach. The second, *UML In Nutshell: A Desktop Quick Reference* by **Sinan Si Alhir** (O'Reilly, 1998), is *not* for reading from cover to cover, but a well-organized reference book that will serve you well when you need it.

Mindware: An Introduction to the Philosophy of Cognitive Science by **Andy Clark** (Oxford University Press, 2001) is not about software development (although it refers to software in its discussions) but is very useful if you feel the need to gain a more in-depth knowledge of topics that we briefly touched on: concepts, symbols, mental representations, etc.

Chapter 3

Methodology

1. OVERVIEW

What is methodology and why is it needed? This chapter starts with exploring the answers. It then presents an overview of the most common concepts in software development methodologies. The discussion is followed by a brief summary of project management concepts and tools.

Chapter Topics

➤ Methodology, its fundamental concepts & its building blocks.

➤ Benefits & risks of methodology.

➤ What software development methodologies address.

➤ The most common concepts in software development methodologies.

➤ Modeling concepts & software development.

➤ Project management concepts & tools.

Introduction

In developing software, programming is just one activity among many. Programming is preceded by a set of crucial and often time-consuming and labor-intensive activities: gathering and analyzing requirements; analysis that results in a conceptual model of the product; design that goes from logical modeling to physical modeling; architecture that determines the overall structure of the system; and modeling for each activity so that the participants in the development can understand, communicate, and verify the features of the product.

If the software is small or simple, some activities may be skipped and all activities may be performed by one person or a team whose members play similar rules. However, as software grows more complex and demands more resources, both activities and roles must become more specialized.

The *quantitative* change in *complexity* calls for *qualitative* changes to the development process. Financing and budgeting become an issue because the stakes are now high. Specialization becomes necessary and communication, or miscommunication,

Figure 3.1 Methodology: The "How" of Building Solutions

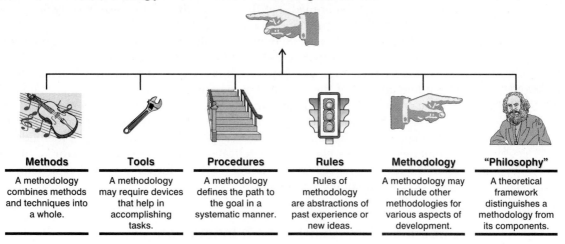

Methods	Tools	Procedures	Rules	Methodology	"Philosophy"
A methodology combines methods and techniques into a whole.	A methodology may require devices that help in accomplishing tasks.	A methodology defines the path to the goal in a systematic manner.	Rules of methodology are abstractions of past experience or new ideas.	A methodology may include other methodologies for various aspects of development.	A theoretical framework distinguishes a methodology from its components.

No methodology is prefect, but "no methodology" means "no strategy."

☞ A major shortcoming of comparing software development to car manufacturing is this: Manufacturing is not development. A more appropriate comparison would be to the development of a revolutionary car design—one that, for example, uses fuel cells instead of gasoline.

among team members and between the team and its clients can make or break the whole undertaking. Organization of the people and coordination of their activities becomes a vast challenge.

Software development has often been compared to the production of cars (and judged to be less efficient by an order of magnitude). The analogy has many shortcomings, but it does help to illustrate some points. The first cars were handmade. The manufacturing process—if it can be called that—was haphazard and wasteful. Henry Ford streamlined the process by employing the logic of assembly line.

Any area of human production begins in a disorderly manner. At a certain point, however, the process needs to be streamlined. This is when a revolution happens and the first methodologies appear. A period then follows in which the fundamental methodology remains the same, but its particulars, its constituent methods, are refined. Then comes another revolutionary shift. In the car industry, it has been—among other things—the application of robotics and computer technology. In software development, it is the object-oriented approach and its logical extensions, including component-based software and service-oriented architecture.

2. INTRODUCING METHODOLOGY

To understand software development methodologies, we first need to know certain things about the essence of methodology itself: what it is, where it comes from, what it addresses, what its benefits are, and what risks it involves. We start with a short definition.

Defining Methodology

Methodology is ❶ a set of methods, rules, practices, procedures, techniques, and tools used to achieve a goal; or ❷ the theoretical understating of the principles that determine how such methods, practices, tools, etc., are used.

[Avison 1995, 419]

The debate over the exact meaning of methodology appears to be an unending one. Some have even argued that the term itself has no place in software development and that the less pretentious word "method"—meaning a "systematic or regular way of accomplishing something"—would suffice. After all, "scientific method" is a good enough term for scientists and the way they work.

In the strict confines of etymology, this is true. "Methodology" means the study or understanding of method(s). The meaning of words, however, changes. For instance, "technology" no longer simply means an understanding of techniques but refers to the vast landscape of applying scientific knowledge to practical use. In the same manner, "methodology" has been expanded to mean a *body* of methods, rules, techniques, and tools, *plus* their theoretical underpinnings. In other words, "method" defines a **tactic**, whereas "methodology" defines the **strategy**. Often, a tactic makes sense only in the context of strategy.

Generalization, Abstraction & Innovation

Methodology is a variable blend of two sources: a systematic generalization and abstraction of lessons learned from the past and ideas for improving on the past.

☞ This position, of course, does not justify elevating every method, technique, or card trick to "methodology" to sound important.

What guides us in *consciously* doing something? We rely mostly on the following, individually or in combination.

- *Cookbook.* We take steps identified in a recipe, an ordered set of steps. This "cookbook" approach is easy and can be very successful if all the assumptions are predictable and the recipe is correct.
- *Observation.* We can learn something by observing others do it. Observation can teach even an experienced person a thing or two. Like the recipe, it tells us *how* to do something, but not *why* it is done in a certain way. Of course, we can always draw our own (right or wrong) conclusions.
- *Anecdotes.* We might hear or read stories about how somebody has done something—for example, "when confronted with a bear, play dead"—and hope that it is right.
- *Trial & Error.* Lacking any reliable guidelines, we *imagine* some method that would work, and try it. If it does not work, we try another approach, if we can.
- *Experience.* Clearly, if we have done something similar in the past, we rely on the experience. If the results are not satisfactory, then we adjust the "experience."
- *Patterns.* Patterns are problems, and the solutions to them, that occur repeatedly in a certain context. Patterns result from *collective* experience. For example, the deterioration of agricultural land due to monoculture (cultivation of a single crop such as wheat) is a pattern. The answer, learned through the experience of many generations, is crop rotation: alternate wheat with, for instance, beans.
- *Methodology.* Methodology is both the most abstract and the most systematic guide to action. It evolves from the above but cannot be reduced to any of them.

☞ Studying **patterns** in order to build better solutions has emerged as a serious area in software development (even though it views patterns from a different point than the one we mention here). See Chapter 14, Patterns.

Experience does not abruptly turn into methodology, but goes through an evolutionary process that involves many steps, from trial and error to patterns, before it finds a theoretical framework.

Since, unlike recipes, methodology is applied to solving problems that are either partially new or that occur in different contexts, revisions and new ideas are always

☞ One attitude that dooms any methodology to failure is to treat it, or present it, as a set of recipes or **dogma**. Like a scientific theory, a methodology must be "falsifiable" to be valid: If experience does not support it, it must be changed or even discarded. Applied blindly and without a healthy skepticism, methodology is more likely to lead to failure. Unfortunately, time and again, this is what happens.

required. In addition, sometimes we find out that we have derived the *wrong* lessons from the experience.

Complexity is the primary source behind the emergence or the change of methodology. When either understanding the problem or building the solution (or both) goes beyond the capabilities of small groups, improvised techniques, and informal coordination, the need for methodology slowly dawns. This observation applies equally to software, architecture, manufacturing, or any other complex undertaking.

Revolutionary methods or methodologies are often inspired by *cross-fertilization*— the application of the lessons, the principles, or the theories from one field to another. For example, the relational model for data management (discussed in Chapter 13, Application Design III: Database & Persistence) is rooted in the *set theory*, a mathematical theory that deals with collections of abstract objects.

Challenges of Methodology

> Methodology is needed not only in creating the solution but also in understanding the problem, organizing the production, assuring quality, and managing the consequences of the solution.

We buy a product or a service because we think it will solve a problem or satisfy a need, regardless of whether the product is a philosophy book, a detective story, a car, food, a train ride, a pair of shoes, or something else. As long as we are acting as consumers, this problem-solution pair is almost all we need to know. When, however, we are the ones who must provide the service or build the product, this binary concept proves inadequate: In addition to *what* is needed, we must also decide *how* to build the solution. As creators, we have to confront *three* elements: the problem, the solution as method or methodology (or "how"), and the solution as answer (or "what").

This argument seems self-evident but, depending on the complexity of the problem or the solution, the surrounding issues can become highly challenging.

☞ For a more detailed discussion of the relationship between the problem and the solution, or between the problem and the solution domains, see Chapter 5, Domain Analysis.

• *The Problem Domain.* The problem that is to be solved, or the need that is to be satisfied, does not exist in a vacuum but in a *context*. This context, called the "problem domain" (or the "problem *space*"), can be relatively simple or complex, but deeply affects the understanding and the diagnosis of the problem regardless of complexity.

Medicine provides a ready example. To a patient, a headache is a problem, but the doctor must treat it as a *symptom* of the real problem. The doctor would be negligent to prescribe aspirin for every headache, regardless of whether the root cause is listening to loud music or something less benign or even life-threatening. In other words, understanding the problem and its context requires its own methods or methodology.

• *The Solution Domain.* In building a solution, we also create a *new* and distinct *context* called the "solution domain" (or the "solution *space*"). This context contains elements that can be unrelated to the problem but that are needed to support the purpose and the functionality of the solution: Most cars have fans to cool down the engine, even though the heat produced by the engine has no connection to transportation for which the car is built. (Similarly, the fans in computers are not related to "computing.")

- *Quality Assurance.* Regardless of the methodology used for building a product, in the end the product itself must be **tested** to verify that it complies with requirements and expectations. To do this, we need a methodology to assure the **quality** of the product.

Such a methodology, however, cannot be exclusively concerned with the "end product." What is developed is always affected by the process of development, and the more complex the process, the deeper the effects.

☞ This quotation is from **William Edwards Deming** (1900–1993), a pioneer of building product quality into the development process. His advice was mostly disregarded in the United States before Japanese automakers adopted his philosophy and proved him right in the 1980s.

> Inspection with the aim of finding the bad ones and throwing them out is too late, ineffective, costly. Quality comes not from inspection but from improvement of the process.

The methodology to assure the quality of the product must be integrated with the methodology for its development. Undoubtedly, a car must be tested as a whole once it is assembled, but such a final test is too late for the components of the car.

- *Multiple Solutions for the Same Problem.* Sometimes multiple solutions can solve the same problem: trains, planes, and automobiles are all viable choices for traveling between many cities. In such a situation, selecting the "answer" requires its own analysis and, since analysis is a part of problem solving, the process of selection requires its own method or methodology.

- *Multiple Methodologies for the Same Solution.* If the same solution can be provided with different methods, techniques, and methodologies, then selection among them might not be straightforward. Without a doubt, some methodologies have proven to be superior to others. In software development, however, no methodology has gained such a dominance.

As far back as 1994, according to one source, there were over 1,000 "brand name methodologies world-wide" for software development. Although this number may be an exaggeration,

[Avison 1995, 417]

> . . . there is no doubt that methodologies have continued to proliferate. Many of these are of course similar and are differentiated only for marketing purposes. Others are internal to individual companies and have been developed in-house. Nevertheless, there is a large and confusing variety of methodologies in existence.

We might be exaggerating as well, but it seems that, in software development, selecting among methodologies presents a real problem all by itself.

- *Resources & Other Constraints.* Even if the problem and the solution are the same, **different contexts** may require different methodologies (which presents a strong argument for analyzing the problem domain). By building a bridge, for example, we solve the problem of moving people and vehicles over a body of water. The conditions under which we build the bridge, however, may force a completely different approach. The successful methodology that built the magnificent Golden Gate Bridge could never be applied to pontoon bridges that soldiers must build under battlefield conditions and, often, in locations that are decided with little or no forewarning.

Furthermore, while certain components of any methodology are tightly related to the problem-solution pair, others are unrelated, either partially or totally. If the quality is the same, it makes no difference to the *mission* of the car whether its body parts are welded together by robots or by humans.

The *size* of a project is often a deciding factor in selecting or shaping the methodology. Note that the size and the *availability of resources* are not necessarily the same.

☞ Chapter 5, Domain Analysis, focuses on analyzing the **problem domain** as the starting point for building software solutions.

    • *Consequences of the Solution.* The solution, once implemented, creates a new reality, a new *problem domain*. Solutions have consequences, intended and unintended, foreseeable and unforeseeable, positive and negative. By revolutionizing transportation, automobiles revolutionized most aspects of human interaction, but also led to pollution, damage to the environment, and the aesthetic wastelands of car parks.

In dealing with unintended consequences, two complementary approaches are available: predict the consequences, and design the solution in a way that it can adapt both to the results of its own presence and changes in the problem domain.

The first approach sounds like an oxymoron: How can we have methodologies that produce solid cost-benefit analyses of *unintended* consequences? Reliable methodologies are based on experience, not speculation. Such methodologies, however, need not be based on *pure* speculation. Often, we can derive theoretical methodologies from *patterns* (which we previously described) and from an extensive analysis of the *existing* problem domain. Environmental scientists take this approach in assessing the effects of dams, highways, oil pipelines, and so on. Predictably, their conclusions are sometimes right, sometimes wrong, and always controversial. Predicting the future will never be an exact science.

The second approach, building a flexible solution, is also dependent on an understanding of the context and issues that may arise once the solution is introduced: Nothing can be *totally* flexible, even if we had the resources to try it. Fortunately, making software more flexible is comparatively less expensive than doing the same for real-life products—provided the right methodology is used.

Methodologies in Parallel

☞ We should exclude organic and agricultural products from the "complexity" argument. A bean is a complex product but practically grows itself with minimal requirements. (The storage, the packaging, and the distribution of agricultural products is another story.)

> The process of building a solution may require more than one methodology to succeed.

Somehow the illusion persists that when you want to build something, you select *one* good methodology and build it. (This illusion may not benefit you but most certainly would benefit those who sell the methodology or the tools that it requires.) An unfortunate outcome of this illusion is the aversion to methodology that spreads among enterprises and developers when things do not work out as advertised. After a few tries, most will conclude that methodology is a costly confidence game.

Besides the golden rule that *any* methodology should be applied prudently, the fact is that one methodology cannot handle *every* aspect of a complex undertaking, even if that methodology is the best and the most appropriate one.

☞ A methodology can be **hierarchical**, meaning that it is composed of **sub-methodologies** which, in turn, might consist of other methodologies.

The reasons should not be difficult to see. Any product results from a **process** of development and production, and the complexity of the process usually corresponds to the complexity of the product.

Inevitably, some components of a methodology do come into conflict with the components of another methodology to which they are running parallel. Not all conflicts are easy to notice or easy to settle. In many cases, true ingenuity is needed. Nevertheless, this is how methodologies evolve or are replaced—when they come into conflict with each other or with the task for which they are used.

Methodology & Technology

> A technology needs an appropriate methodology, but the two are not the same.

In the previous discussion of methodology, it might seem in many places that we are talking about technology. This is inevitable since the two—certainly in product development—have an organic relationship. The two, however, must not be confused. Multiple methodologies may target the same technology—as we discussed before—and the same methodology (or at least methods) may apply to multiple technologies. The same architectural modeling, for example, can accommodate various building technologies.

Methodology and technology constantly interact: Methodology is needed for the effective use of technology, but technology also sharpens and transforms methodology continuously. Consider all the methodologies for analyzing financial markets and then imagine them without tools such as spreadsheets or databases.

In software development, thanks to ever-improving modeling and programming tools, methodology and technology overlap so extensively that one might not notice the distinction between the two.

Variations on a Theme

> Methodologies with the same goal do not necessarily cover the same ground.

We said that a relatively complex undertaking requires not one but a set of methodologies. A closely related issue is that even methodologies that proclaim the same goal(s) may not address the same issues. The following is how a writer on methodology describes the scene.

[Avison 1995, 430]

- *A methodology can range from being a fully fledged product detailing every stage and task to be undertaken to being a vague outline of the basic principles in a short pamphlet.*
- *A methodology can cover widely differing areas of development process, from high-level strategic and organizational problem solving to the detail of implementing a small computer system.*
- *A methodology can cover conceptual issues or physical design procedures or the whole range of intermediate stages.*
- *A methodology can range from being designed to be applicable to specific types of environments or industries to an all-encompassing general-purpose methodology.*
- *A methodology may be potentially usable by anybody or only by highly trained specialists or be designed for users to develop their own applications.*
- *A methodology may require an army of people to perform all specified tasks or it may not even have any specified tasks.*
- *A methodology may or may not include CASE [Computer-Aided Software Engineering] tools.*

Furthermore, the components of a methodology might be *tightly coupled*, meaning that if a tool, technique, or procedure is not used exactly where, when, or how the methodology prescribes, it will not work properly (or will not work at all). Some methodologies, on the other hand, are more *loosely coupled*, which makes them more flexible: You can use their techniques (or their "sub-methodologies") outside their general flow or modify them to take into account different circumstances.

Obviously, a loosely coupled methodology is more flexible and more flexible is better, but it might prove to be more expensive and also more confusing because it requires good judgment as to what should be modified and why.

Organization as Methodology

> Companies, factories, government agencies, and the like represent organized methodologies.

When we talk about development, we are usually thinking of a project, a finite process that is terminated after its goal is achieved or discarded. Many undertakings, however, are ongoing and must perform the same tasks repeatedly. In such an enterprise—be it a manufacturing company, a software vendor, a business, or a government agency—the organization itself embodies a methodology. A patient goes to a hospital for a specific goal: to receive surgery, for example. The staff of the hospital, however, is selected, trained, and organized to follow a methodology that governs how patient after patient is treated: Receptionists manage how the patient is received and directed, clerks follow specified procedures to register the patient and handle the financial side, nurses take predefined steps to prepare the patient for surgery, and so on.

☞ We are not using the term "**bureaucracy**" in a disparaging sense, but as the administrative machinery of an enterprise. Like any other human grouping, of course, bureaucracy can become counterproductive and self-serving.

Most software is developed within an ongoing enterprise. In such an enterprise, the organization is optimized for an ongoing operation, even if it is a software company. Consequently, there is always a tension between a one-time project and the organization of its parent. The bureaucracy is interested in accountability, standards, approved procedures, chain of command, and (often) self-preservation; therefore, it prefers methodologies that reflect its interests by producing comprehensive, detailed, and (sometimes) excessive documentation.

A one-time project, on the other hand, is *explicitly* results-oriented. Developers tend to react to most organizational requirements (sometimes even those that are genuinely justified) as counterproductive to *their* project; they prefer methods or methodologies that facilitate *their* work and keep the bureaucracy at bay.

The two sides usually talk past each other. The gap between the two is sometimes too great to be bridged by *any* methodology. Organizations continue to buy methodologies that give them documentation, while programmers champion methods that require none or very little. What is needed to confront this issue—empathy, wisdom, and leadership—cannot be packaged as a methodology.

Methodology as Product

> In choosing a methodology product, flexibility and training costs must be weighed against each other. No methodology product, however, can ensure success by itself.

The abstract theoretical framework is what distinguishes a methodology from its individual building blocks. Certain components of methodology, however, have been marketed commercially as products or services (such as consulting or auditing). One of the more successful and comprehensive methodology products, for example, has been the Rational Unified Process (RUP) created by the authors of the Unified Modeling Language. Moreover, most development environments (such as those by Microsoft, IBM, and Oracle) offer integrated modeling tools. Such tools are sometimes different from each other and may fall short of a comprehensive methodology, but reduce or eliminate the cost of keeping the code and the models in sync.

Because the term "software development" covers a wide variety of products, development resources, and organizational contexts, methodology products face a dilemma: offer a strict approach that allows little deviation from the prescribed path, or provide great flexibility and risk a steep learning curve.

Consumers face a similar dilemma. Some of the comprehensive methodology products are expensive and also need expensive training to be useful, but the turnaround in software development jobs is still so high and so fast that return on investment in training may seem like a waste of money, especially when consumers discover, sooner or later, that even a good methodology tool, by itself, is unable to ensure a high-quality, on-time, and on-the-budget software.

Benefits & Risks

| Methodology is indispensable, but no methodology is perfect, sacred, or infallible. |

☞ The question "Why is methodology needed?" is likely to be asked more by the software industry than by a car maker or any other manufacturer. Long experience has shown manufacturers that they cannot succeed without methodology.

Methodology is an intangible, but it has tangible costs. These costs are often for tools but, more importantly, also for training and for what can best be described as "compliance," which means following the prescribed path by the enterprise and by the participants in the development process. Understandably, when an enterprise must spend money, it has the right to ask the question: Why? The enterprise believes that it hires the best people that it can find, so does methodology make them any better?

The answer is yes, it *would* make them better, provided that the methodology is moderately good. The following is a short list as to why.

[Avison 1995, 421–424]

- *A Well-Rounded Approach.*   Methodology is not a mysterious concept. We may use different terms—method, framework, approach, etc.—but the essence is the same: It is a systematized interpretation of the past experience and new ideas for improving on the past. Since a methodology is formalized and systematic, it is open to public critical review, whereas private thoughts, at best, have limited exposure to public inspection.
- *Standardizing the Development Process.*   People who are involved in a development process, from managers and architects to designers and programmers, should have *at least* a minimal understanding of what is to be expected from them and what they can expect from others. Methodology frames and formalizes these expectations.
- *Higher Productivity.*   Two teams can follow the exact same methodology and arrive at very different results in terms of quality. Even in performing completely repetitive tasks, people are not completely interchangeable. The more intellectually challenging a task is, the more the result depends on who performs the task.

   Nevertheless, whatever the inherent possibilities of the human "raw material," methodology can enhance those traits that are desirable for a certain task.

(Or it can suffocate them, if the methodology is ill-chosen.) Furthermore, within an enterprise, methodology can reduce the amount of resources that must be devoted to training or retraining.

If methodology can perform near-miracles, then why it is so underappreciated by the software industry? The primary reason is that existing software development methodologies have some distance to go before they can be considered truly mature.

[Avison 2003]

[Existing] methodologies are overly complex, usually designed for the largest and most complex development projects. They may lead to developing requirements to the ultimate degree, often over and above what is legitimately required, sometimes encouraging users to create unrealistic wish lists. They also require highly technical skills that can be difficult and expensive for developers and end users to learn or acquire. Moreover, the tools advocated by methodology proponents can be costly, difficult to use, yet still not deliver enough benefit.

Methodologies are often not contingent on the type or size of a project, nor upon the technology environment and organizational context. A methodology is often said to be one-dimensional, that is, it adopts only one approach to the development of projects that may well not address a particular organization's underlying issues or problems. Few recognize or address the critically important social, political, and organizational dimensions of development.

A methodology may be inflexible, not allowing changes to requirements during development. Most methodologies make a number of simplifying yet invalid assumptions (such as a stable environment, a well-documented business strategy, users knowledgeable about their own requirements, or that a consensus of requirements can be achieved). Rarely do such conditions exist in practice. The use of a methodology in an organization may lead to its rote implementation and to a focus on following the procedures of the methodology rather than on addressing the real implementation and business issues. Strict adherence to the methodology rule book has been described as slavish adherence to the methodology and the fetish of technique, that is, the methodology is allowed to inhibit creative thinking. . . . Some organizations have found it difficult to adopt methodologies in practice, confronting resistance from both developers and users. . . .

Another reason, until recently, was the relatively low level of competition among individual developers. Before the new millennium, there was an insatiable demand for anybody who could write computer code. As always, when demand far exceeds supply, scruples about the quality of supply are few and far between. In the frenzy to finish software as soon as possible, luxuries such as methodology were *not* given high priority.

It is said that no battle plan survives contact with the enemy. Pity the commander, however, that enters a battle *without* a plan. Software development methodologies are works in progress (and will remain so for the foreseeable future), but discarding them is no cure for pervasive failures. Even in industries more mature than software, no methodology can be considered perfect and no methodology should be applied (or discarded) uncritically.

If we were to provide even a short summary of each software development methodology that has appeared in the past few decades, this book would run out of space. Here, we present a brief review of the most basic, useful, well-known, or controversial concepts that underlie most methodologies in this field. As the overall picture emerges, we shall see that software development methodologies still have some ways to go.

What Do Methodologies Address?

> Software development consists of a wide spectrum of activities that individual methodologies cover selectively and from different viewpoints.

Many activities must be carried out to turn the *idea* of software into *actual* software. A set of factors such as size, complexity, and the availability of resources affect the particulars. Taken together, however, the following list specifies the most important of them.

- *Requirements Gathering.*   Called requirements *discovery* in initial stages, this activity determines the requirements that the product must address: the problems that it must solve, desires that it must satisfy, or opportunities of which it must take advantage.
- *Feasibility Study.*   Determines whether it is possible—technically, economically, legally, or organizationally—to build a certain software. If the software is a commercial product, it also evaluates the viability of the product in the marketplace.
- *Domain Analysis.*   Discovers ❶ the meaning of requirements within the context, ❷ concepts within the domain that are related to the problem and which can affect the solution, and possibly ❸ the consequences of the solution on the problem domain.
- *Analysis.*   Analyzes the requirements to build a **conceptual** model of the solution (the product). Such a model represents *what* the solution must do, without identifying *how*.
- *Design.*   Transforms the "what" into "how." Design itself consists of several distinct activities, the most important of which are **logical design**, which represents the solution without reference to a specific technology; **physical design**, which maps the logical modeling to specific technologies; and *architectural design*, which determines the high-level structure of the product.
- *Implementation.*   Turns the blueprints of design into an actual product. Programming is usually the most important component of this activity, but it is not the only one.
- *Testing & Quality Control.*   Verifies that the product functions according to specifications *and* does not produce unacceptable consequences.
- *Deployment & Training.*   Depending on whether the software is in-house or commercial, this activity consists of ensuring the correct installation on the target platform (without breaking other things), user training, creating help files and user manuals, setting up Web sites to guide users, packaging, etc.
- *Maintenance.*   Consists of solving problems that may emerge after the deployment of the software due to faulty requirements, insufficient analysis, defective design, or changes in the environment, whether in the business context or in the technological framework.

Notice that we have used the term "*activity*," not "stage," "phase," or "step." Whether these activities take place sequentially, iteratively, in parallel (when possible), or even without a clear pattern depends on the methodology (or the lack of it). Furthermore, a methodology may not agree that a certain activity can, or should, be formalized. And some methodologies, consciously and explicitly, cover only one activity or a selected set.

The *Ad Hoc* Approach

> The *ad hoc* approach is development without an overall theoretical framework.

[American Heritage 1996]

The *ad hoc* approach is a "non-methodology" or an impromptu methodology. It is "the tendency to establish temporary, chiefly improvisational policies and procedures to deal with specific problems and tasks." What distinguishes an *ad hoc* approach from a formal methodology is that the general flow of the process is not defined by an overall "philosophy," even though it might borrow individual tools, methods, techniques, and procedures from formal methodologies (and often does).

To succeed, the *ad hoc* approach must rely overwhelmingly on ❶ the ingenuity of participants to improvise solutions for unforeseen problems; ❷ the ability of the participants to coordinate and communicate with each other to merge small solutions into bigger solutions that contribute to the ultimate goal; and ❸ what can be conveniently described as "luck," meaning that the right people hit the right targets under the right circumstances. As should be expected, *ad hoc* is a high-risk approach.

☞ At the programming level, the *ad hoc* approach is sometimes referred to as *cowboy coding*. Humorous as this might be, it is not a very accurate comparison since most cowboys have infinitely more discipline than some programmers.

Whenever we want to achieve something that is largely new, the *ad hoc* approach is inevitable for we have little or no precedents. An *ad hoc* approach is also inevitable when something completely unexpected happens.

☞ **SDLC** has been used as an acronym for various terms, including "Software Development Life Cycle" and "System Design Life Cycle." The concepts are very close, however.

In books on methodology (including this book), you will read strong objections to an *ad hoc* approach to developing software. The objections are not against improvising *per se*: Any complex undertaking involves new problems that require creativity and improvisation. (Furthermore, as we mentioned, no single software methodology has proven to be sufficient.) What is inexcusable is, first, ignoring the collective experience of the past every time a new project is undertaken and, second, giving up the chance to add the new experience to the collective pool.

System Development Life Cycle (SDLC)

> SDLC methodologies view software development as primarily a project management process rather than a technical one.

☞ For a brief discussion of project management, see "Project Management Concepts" later in this chapter.

A project is an undertaking that starts with a concept and ends with achieving a goal or a set of goals. SDLC methodologies focus on software development as a business project, most aspects of which are independent of coding or technology. Hence the term "life," which indicates a beginning and an end. "Cycle" means that the process, in part or in whole, can be repeated. Beyond this basic similarity, the numerous SDLC methodologies part ways from each other.

The Waterfall Model

> The Waterfall Model specifies a set of sequential phases for software development.

The Waterfall Model is often called "the traditional SDLC" because it was the first of its kind to appear, around the early 1970s. It was also one of the first methodologies to be heavily and extensively criticized.

The Waterfall Method views development activities as strictly defined *steps* or stages:

[Avison 1995, 23]

- Feasibility study.
- System investigation (generally the same as gathering requirements).
- System analysis. This system analysis, however, does not correspond to the activity that we described earlier (under "What Do Methodologies Address?"). Instead, it has elements of domain analysis, and is basically "an attempt to understand all aspects of the present system and why it developed as it did, and eventually indicate how things might be improved by any new system."
- System design.
- Implementation.
- Review and maintenance.

Each step cannot begin until the previous step has been completed *and* documented. In fact, most SDLC methodologies and their derivatives are *document-driven*: No phase is considered complete until its documentation is approved. Formally, the documents are technology-neutral but, in practice, design is conceived as *processes and data*, not as objects. (Considering the technology of the time, this is to be expected.)

☞ See "Project Management Concepts" for terms such as "milestone" and "deliverable."

The Waterfall Model is tightly tied to project management: Each phase is a "milestone" and the resulting documents are the "deliverables." In such a framework, software development can be managed as a well-ordered, predictable undertaking—in theory, at least.

Experience, however, has generally proved otherwise. The Waterfall Model deserves some consideration and some praise: It identified some of the basic concepts and issues pertinent to software development and pioneered the proposition that creating software does not have to be a chaotic undertaking. On the other hand, it has shown the following shortcomings when applied in the field:

- *Inflexibility.*   There is a reason the approach is called "waterfall": You cannot easily swim upstream. It assumes that the results of each phase, after they are approved, are as perfect as possible. Since each phase relies on the correctness of the previous one, errors and misunderstandings may continue undetected until the product is implemented, by which time any noncosmetic change to the software would require another full cycle.
- *Overreliance on Documentation.*   Documentation is good, but its usefulness, obviously, depends on what is documented, how it is documented, when it is documented, and why it is documented. The Waterfall Model makes a few assumptions that are problematic: ❶ businesspeople can express their requirements unambiguously, clearly, and completely in a textual narrative; ❷ documents produced by each stage, technical or nontechnical, are equally comprehensible to all stakeholders; ❸ documentations accurately reflect the

actual product and are kept in sync with all changes; ❹ all communication can occur through textual documentation; and ❺ documentation becomes the yardstick by which management measures the productivity and the success of the development team (while programmers, justifiably or not, usually treat documentation as an unnecessary burden).

- *Detachment from Technology.*   It is tempting to believe that a "one size" methodology can fit all technologies. It cannot, unfortunately. The relationship between the nature of the product and how it is built is always an interactive one. A product composed of objects and components has different requirements than those conceived as procedures that handle data.

- *Detachment from Marketplace.*   In the early 1970s, when the Waterfall Model emerged, most software was developed either in-house by major corporations or by mainframe vendors such as IBM, with little or no competition. The situation has changed radically and the change is gaining momentum. Most software products must now compete in the marketplace. As a result, "when" a product gets to the market is as important as "what" (if, sometimes, not more important). A slow-paced methodology is not fast enough.

- *Detachment from the Profession.*   Production of all human artifacts have certain things in common, but they are not interchangeable. Programming is not the same as assembly of cars or baking breads, nor do programmers work the same way as manufacturing workers or bakers. Nevertheless, the Waterfall Model (like many similar methodologies) treats the programming profession like any other.

To be fair, some of these objections apply to other approaches as well. Furthermore, changes in the environment affect any methodology, no matter how sophisticated it is.

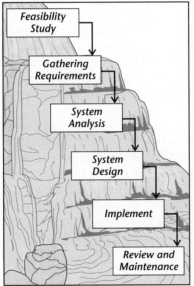

Figure 3.2
The Waterfall Model

The Waterfall Model is the classic life cycle methodology and is closely tied to project management. This methodology was one of the earliest attempts to bring order to the chaos of software development, but it has been widely criticized for its inflexible approach to an undertaking that is extremely iterative.

Prototyping

> Prototyping is the creation of a working model with the essential features of the final product for testing and verification of requirements.

Prototyping aims to remedy one of the main problems of the Waterfall Model: Textual communication falls short of capturing complete requirements.

Software prototyping addresses this issue by creating a working model after gathering the basic requirements and performing a quick design. The prototype is then refined iteratively through feedback and additional rounds of gathering requirements, design, and implementation.

The idea of prototyping has wide applications in other industries, such as in manufacturing where design errors can find their way into millions of units, and in architecture and civil engineering where correcting errors can be impossible or enormously costly.

There are two types of prototyping: *incremental* or *evolutionary* and *throwaway*. In the incremental approach, the initial prototype is revised and refined repeatedly until it becomes the final product. In the throwaway approach, the prototype is discarded after the stakeholders in the development are confident that they have arrived at the correct specifications and the development on the "real" product can start. Sometimes, only areas that are problematic are prototyped.

Prototyping may seem like an ideal way to overcome the shortcomings of "traditional" SDLC methods, but it has the *high potential* (not certainty) of creating its own serious problems as a result of common work habits, time constraints, prejudices of the clients, and so on. Some of these are as follows:

- *Unbalanced Architecture.* Since the main thrust of prototyping is towards the user interface, developers tend to include more and more functionality in the outer layers of the information system, creating a distorted architecture. (We will clarify this statement in the design section, especially the chapters on the user interface and architecture.) If the prototype is really and truly throwaway, then this issue can be avoided.
- *The Illusion of Completeness.* The real power of an application is "under the hood" (even if the application is a picture editor). For most users, however, the interface is what the application is all about. As a result, clients might not understand why developers insist that a lot more is to be done, especially if the prototype is of the throwaway variety. On the other hand, the prototype may successfully present the user interface for a complex functionality, the feasibility of which is far from certain.
- *Diminishing Changeability.* If the prototype is incremental, changing it becomes more costly with each iteration as the application becomes more complex. Even if the prototype is a throwaway, however, the problem is not solved but delayed: No application or information system can remain unchanged until it is *completely* discarded. Since prototyping can leave little trace of how the development evolved, modifying the application can resemble an archeological undertaking to piece together a lost civilization. If the Waterfall Model relies too much on documentation, prototyping can result in too little documentation or, more importantly, too little modeling.

☞ A more detailed discussion of prototyping and its alternatives appears in Chapter 12, Application Design II: The User Interface. By then, you will be more familiar with the concepts mentioned here.

Like most other methodologies, the usefulness of prototyping depends on how it is used and *who* uses it. Prototyping, used prudently, can be very helpful.

Incremental & Iterative Approach

> In incremental development, the product is built through successive versions that are refined and expanded with each iteration.

☞ Incremental development is also known as **staged delivery** or **evolutionary delivery**.

At first glance, the incremental approach may appear the same as prototyping. It is not, however. Whereas prototyping aims to build a model that implements *all* major requirements (in theory, at least), in the incremental development each version of the product *fully* implements a *selected* set of requirements.

The incremental approach groups the requirements into **layers**. The requirements in the innermost layer, considered most essential to the mission of the software, are implemented first. In each successive iteration, the defects of the previous version are corrected, the design is adjusted accordingly, and the requirements in the next layer are undertaken.

Three concepts underlie the incremental approach.

- *The Initialization Step.* A "base" version of the software is created and presented to users to elicit critical response.
- *The Control List.* A list specifying necessary changes to design as well as new requirements. This list is not static but changes continuously as a result of user interaction with successive versions and new analysis.
- *The Iteration Step.* New versions are built from the most recent control list. The goal of each iteration is to be clear-cut and modular to allow for redesign. Furthermore, in each iteration, the development goes through a complete life cycle: requirements analysis, analysis, design, and implementation. Unlike the Waterfall Model, however, each iteration is relatively short. When the control list becomes empty, the product is complete. (Some authors argue that only when the product is discarded and replaced by another can the list can go empty.)

The incremental approach considers the code, and the control list, as the main *development* documentation. Since the users interact with versions that fully implement a set of requirements, so the argument goes, most other system documentation would be superfluous.

One of the strongest objections to the incremental approach is its overoptimistic assumption that the architecture of the platform, the information system, or the application can gracefully accommodate changes that each iteration requires. Architecture, as the highest view of a system's structure, is a design decision that cannot be done piecemeal, cheaply, or easily. Imagine constantly changing the structure of a building while we are building it.

The Spiral Model

[McConnel 1996, 141]

> "The spiral model is a risk-oriented life cycle model that breaks a software project up into mini-projects."

The Spiral Model combines the Waterfall Model with prototyping and iteration. It can also accommodate alternate life cycle methodologies. The result is a complicated approach that has nevertheless been very popular with government projects since its focus is on **risk management**: any kind of risk including, but not limited to, risks associated with quality, performance, architecture, cost, and so on.

(Risk management is important for any mission-critical and/or expensive undertaking but it is not difficult to understand why it appeals especially to government agencies that have to justify their decisions and expenditures to bodies and authorities that oversee them.)

The Spiral Model starts as a small project that spawns other small projects as it moves forward through a *spiral* iteration. Each iteration has six steps:

[McConnel 1996, 141]

1. Determine objectives, alternatives, and constraints
2. Identify and resolve risks
3. Evaluate alternatives
4. Develop the deliverables for that iteration, and verify that they are correct
5. Plan the next iteration
6. Commit to an approach for the next iteration (if you decide to have one)

> In the spiral model, the early iterations are the cheapest. You spend less developing the concept of operation than you do developing requirements than you do developing the design, implementing the product, and testing it. . . .

☞ See Chapter 12, Application Design II: The User Interface for discussions on *prototyping*, *simulation*, and *storyboarding*.

Depending on the risks identified, you can combine the Spiral Model with other approaches and methods. For example, if performance is important to the goal of the iteration, then you can plan for benchmarking, or if the flow of the user interface is of concern, then you can employ some kind of prototyping, simulation, or storyboarding.

Besides the complexity of the concept, the Spiral Model has been criticized in that it largely ignores specifications, milestones, reviews, and scheduling (things that the traditional Waterfall Model has been criticized for *over*emphasizing).

Rapid Application Development (RAD)

> Rapid Application Development is selecting techniques, methods, practices, and procedures that result in faster development and shorter schedules.

The RAD definition begs the question: Who would *not* want "faster development" and "shorter schedules"? The answer is that RAD is a triple-functionality concept. First, it functions as a mostly advertising enticement: Buy this product and you will develop your software faster. Second, as a general concept (not capitalized), it is a pragmatic approach, not a product or a step-by-step methodology: Select the fastest and most effective methods and practices and discard the ineffective and slow ones. In other words, do not become a slave to everything that this or that methodology prescribes or proscribes. In this sense, any kind of rational and well-scheduled development plan is RAD. The third function is when RAD is offered as a "named" and formal methodology (this time capitalized). As such, it has its own characteristics and guidelines, the most important of which are the following four phases.

- *Requirements Planning.* Aims at eliciting information and requirements from the senior people and verifying the goals. RAD's preferred method for doing so is Joint Requirements Planning (JRP), a workshop for the managers from different functional areas who must ❶ be knowledgeable and ❷ have the authority to make decisions. The purpose of this workshop is to ensure that the proposed information system will satisfy a range of requirements from *across* the enterprise.

☞ See Chapter 4, Gathering Requirements, for an introduction to **JAD** and other requirements gathering techniques.

- *Design.*   The design phase begins once the *top-level* requirements of the system are identified. To discover more detailed requirements, RAD relies on **Joint Application Development** (JAD) workshops. JAD is based on the belief that traditional approaches to gathering information, such as interviews, observation, and documentation analysis, are too slow and problematic; they do not allow users from one functional grouping to exchange ideas with people from other groupings and (sometimes) compromise so that the system can serve as wide a range of users as possible.

  If necessary, prototyping is used to verify requirements and invite comments and criticism from users. (RAD is a vigorous proponent of CASE, or Computer-Aided Software Engineering, tools.)

  RAD is rather specific on the shape and composition of JAD workshops. There is a "facilitator" who acts as a coordinator and an interpreter between business and technical people. The optimal environment is a U-shaped room as far away from the work area as possible to prevent disruption or distraction. The room is equipped with conferencing paraphernalia and computers on which CASE tools are installed.

- *Implementation.*   Once the users approve the preliminary design, a detailed design of the system is created and code is generated. The implementation phase is heavily dependent upon CASE tools and on a series of prototypes that are viewed and reviewed by the key users and that go through a number of iterations by a small but skilled team.

- *Enhancements & Maintenance.*   In the framework of RAD, a software is never completed until it is retired. Therefore, past the initial stage, all modifications and updates to the software are equal and there is no significant difference between development and maintenance. (This position is in opposition to most SDLC methodologies.)

The scheduling framework for RAD development is the **timebox**, a definitive period of time, often 90 days, during which a version of the application must be completed:

> The Timebox Development practice produces its schedule savings through redefining the product to fit the schedule rather than redefining the schedule to fit the project. . . . The success of timeboxing depends on using it only on appropriate kinds of projects and on management's and end-users' willingness to cut features rather than stretch the schedule.

[McConnel 1996, 575]

Given the current state of software development methodologies, RAD as a *non*formal approach offers excellent advice: Choose the most appropriate tools and practices. Even as a nonformal approach, however, we encounter three issues. First, selecting the best requires **strategists** who are reasonably familiar with various methodologies, either through direct experience and/or careful analysis of case studies. (In this field, however, reliable case studies are very difficult to come by.) Second, absorbing multiple new methodologies is difficult and time-consuming, both for a team and an individual. (Like bicycle riding, after you learn a methodology and work with it for a while, a considerable part of the work is carried out by the subconscious.) Third, matching techniques and procedures to the tasks at hand consumes resources and has its own risks. In essence, you would be constructing your own methodology from prefabricated components. You might have to do it, but beware of the costs and risks.

☞ See Chapter 4, Gathering Requirements.

As a *formal* methodology, some rather predictable objections can be raised. The first is that JRD and JAP are very good tools for the resolution of problems, conflicting views, and clarifying concepts, but they cannot replace other tools for gathering requirements. Furthermore, the effectiveness of a workshop depends on factors that vary greatly from situation to situation: the willingness and the ability of participants to spend extended periods of time away from their daily activities, the expertise level of those who *do* attend, their effectiveness in communication in an environment with inevitable political undercurrents, their goodwill, etc.

Timeboxing can be problematic, as well. The idea that development should focus on necessary features—not on wish lists—and that developers should feel a sense of obligation by meeting deadlines must be taken seriously. However, *abstract* ways of implementing this idea would be counterproductive. A realistic timeframe for achieving milestones depends on the nature and the complexity of software and available resources—human, financial, and otherwise. (Also, developers can easily "cheat" in meeting unreasonable deadlines by playing up the importance of trivial features.)

Agile Methodologies

☞ Agile methods are sometimes referred to as "***light***" or "lightweight" methodologies. Some believers in agile methods, however, prefer to stay away from this label.

Agile methodologies aim at being adaptive rather than predictive.

Arriving at an exact definition for agile methodologies is impossible. The reason lies in their very worldview that holds that software development must be "adaptive"; that is, development should not follow a "predictive" path in which every step is planned in advance. Proponents of agile methodologies (or "methods," as they prefer to call it) usually point to the Waterfall Model as the most "predictive" of all methodologies and to its failures as proof that strictly planned processes do not work.

The theoretical framework of agile methods is best expressed by the *Manifesto for Agile Software Development*, published in 2001.

☞ Authors of the manifesto require the following notification:

This declaration may be freely copied in any form, but only in its entirety through this notice.

Kent Beck, James Grenning, Robert C. Martin, Mike Beedle, Jim Highsmith, Steve Mellor, Arie van Bennekum, Andrew Hunt, Ken Schwaber, Alistair Cockburn, Ron Jeffries, Jeff Sutherland, Ward Cunningham, Jon Kern, Dave Thomas, Martin Fowler, Brian Marick.

© 2001, the above authors.

See http:// agilemanifesto.org

> *We are uncovering better ways of developing software by doing it and helping others do it. Through this work we have come to value:*
>
> ***Individuals and interactions*** *over processes and tools*
>
> ***Working software*** *over comprehensive documentation*
>
> ***Customer collaboration*** *over contract negotiation*
>
> ***Responding to change*** *over following a plan*
>
> *That is, while there is value in the items on the right, we value the items on the left more.*

How is this vision applied to the actual development? It depends on the specific agile method. (Like RAD, "agile" has become an advertising enticement and is applied to many, sometimes incompatible, products and approaches.) Attempting to summarize them all would do justice to none. Nevertheless, there are "themes" that many of them share. Some of the themes, or methods, should be familiar from previous discussions in this chapter, such as evolutionary **prototyping** and *iterative* development (with very short iterations).

A better-known example of agile methods, and one of the earliest, is ***Extreme Programming*** (XP). "Adaptive" claims notwithstanding, XP has a set of clear-cut practices and rules (twelve of them, to be exact) that must be implemented. These practices can be grouped into four categories, as follows:

☞ For a more detailed, but still brief, introduction to XP concepts, go to http://www.extreme programming.org.

- *Planning.* Planning for development starts with *user stories*. User stories are similar to the "use cases" that we will discuss later in this book, but are very short and informal, no more than a few sentences, that are written by the customers, in the customers' terminology, and that identify something that the system must do. (XP authors emphasize that user stories are *not* detailed requirements documents, but just enough to make "low-risk" estimates of how long it would take to implement them.)

Developers then estimate the time necessary to implement the user story. If the implementation takes longer than three weeks, then the story must be broken down into chunks, each of which can be implemented in three weeks or less. If there are about 80 such user stories (give or take 20), then a *release plan* is created through a *release planning meeting* that works out the course of the project and individual *iterations*.

Release planning is based on the idea that four variables shape the project: scope (how much is to be done), resources (people), time, and quality. Management can choose three out of the *four variables* and the developers decide on the remaining one.

The organization of developers is based on *pair programming* and "moving people around." XP takes pair programming literally: Two programmers use *one* workstation. When one of them is engaged with the workstation, the other observes or communicates with the first programmer. The rationale for pair programming is that ❶ no knowledge can remain in the sole possession of an individual whose departure would disrupt the project and ❷ programmers must learn from each other. "Moving around" means that no programmers should be consigned to working on only one area of the software, exciting *or* boring.

Every day the whole team gathers, in a circle, for a *stand-up meeting*. (They "stand up" rather than sit, so the meeting will not drag on unnecessarily.) The purpose of the meeting is to exchange ideas about problems and solutions and the "revival" of the project's vision and spirit by keeping the developers focused.

- *Designing.* "*No* big upfront design" is XP's motto. Design must be kept simple and no functionality should be added before it is scheduled. Developers should use *CRC cards* to represent objects. (CRC stands for **C**lass, **R**esponsibilities, and **C**ollaboration. See "Topic Discussions" in Chapter 8, Structural Modeling, for a description of CRC cards.) The objects take shape in *CRC meetings* where the cards are passed around to the participants.

Spike solutions are part of the design. A spike solution is a very simple piece of software, often a throwaway, that explores only (and only) the potential solution(s) to a problem.

An integral part of XP design is *refactoring*, removing redundancy in code and increasing its efficiency *without* changing its functionality. XP advises that refactoring must be done regularly and "mercilessly."

- *Coding.* XP requires that the "customer" always be available to the development team to clarify, explain, and answer questions. This is why both XP's requirements gathering (user stories) and "upfront" design are so light. The customer is supposed to supply the details whenever the developers call for them.

Code must be simple to understand and should be written to standards upon which the development team agrees. One of the functions of pair programming and stand-up meetings is to criticize and self-criticize nonstandard and "clever" coding. (Some advocate ridiculing those who write "clever" code.)

For every "unit" of code, developers must devise a **unit test**, a small program that verifies the correct functionality of the unit. Unit tests *must* be written before the code that they test, and the process is iterative: the simplest unit test for the simplest functionality, a more sophisticated one for a more sophisticated functionality, and so on.

Any code that goes into production must result from pair programming. Furthermore, the **collective ownership** of the code ensures that any programmer has the power to change any code to improve it. But whereas development of "units" is parallel and the code belongs to everybody, the integration of the code to a collective pool is a **sequential integration**. This means that programming pairs must take turns to release their code into the common code repository. In case this practice may appear as encouraging idleness, XP specifies that integration must be done frequently—every few hours in fact, never past a day.

Regardless of the demands, **no overtime** is allowed for developers, because it discourages people. Instead, if the workload cannot be managed within normal working hours, convene a release planning meeting and come up with a new plan.

• *Testing.* As we said, all code, without exception, must go through unit testing. No code can be "passed on" without unit testing. When a user story has been developed to a reasonable level, an **acceptance test** in which the customers participate is performed. A "story" may have multiple acceptance tests, each verifying a set of requirements.

Acceptance tests are automated so the test can be repeated. Each test has a **test score** that is published to the whole team.

We gave more space to Extreme Programming than to other methodologies because its components and its focus are very different from other approaches. This difference may account for the wide-ranging controversy over agile methods. (Some of the harshest critics of XP are champions of other agile methods and would not approve of being included in the same category.) Proponents of Extreme Programming point towards the failures (real or perceived) of "predictive" methods; opponents point out XP's shortcomings (real or perceived) and its ideological aspects: manifestos, collective ownership, group criticisms, and "educational" meetings.

Many of the symptoms that agile methods, especially XP, try to address are real enough. Among them are:

- Projects that are often planned with no regard to the particular nature of software development or the task at hand.
- Managers who have unreasonable, counterproductive, or wasteful expectations from the development team.
- Analysts who imagine they can "document" the last bit of detail before design.
- Designers who believe they produce a *perfect* design before coding starts.
- The isolation of programmers in their limited spheres of activity that prevents them from learning or contributing to the collective knowledge and, consequently,
- The widely incompatible coding styles and coding solutions that result in chaos and create roadblocks to improving the code by different programmers.

It is not certain, however, that such symptoms can be treated by methods that XP prescribes. Proponents of agile methods tend to make straw men out of "predictive" methodologies so they can set fire to them. Using any methodology without flexibility, adaptation, or (some) imagination equals failure.

Our fundamental reservation about XP (and some of the other agile methods) is not so much its rituals, but something else. As a writer in the field of information technology comments:

☞ Andrew Binstock, "Not So Extreme Programming," *SD Times*, May 1, 2004. © 2006 BZ Media.

The foundation of XP, in my view, is part of the problem: It is a radical embrace of an approach that goes *from particular to universal*. You never design more that what is immediately needed, you write the least amount of code that will fulfill your next test, and you design the test to provide the least amount of incremental change. After you've written lots of tests (frequently thousands), you clean up your code by using one of 72 refactorings which are specifically analyzed techniques for cleaning code without changing its functionality.

The fundamental problem with this approach is that software today is complex and large, so it cannot be designed properly by using the least-increment approach and hoping that a sound product will eventuate through the organic accretion of lots of small design decisions (followed up by code cleaning).

Large, complex projects have to be designed top-down and the code must be developed to that design, regardless of its complexity. . . . Some projects cannot be fully tested except at deployment, at which point it is too late to perform hundreds of small revisions. . . .

The Capability Maturity Model (CMM)

> CMM aims to measure the maturity of the software development *process* within an organization.

☞ CMM has now been changed to CMMI (Capability Maturity Model Integration). The basic concepts of both, however, are the same.

The Capability Maturity Model is different from most other methodologies in that its focus is not on the product or the techniques used to build the product, but on the organization and the processes for developing software. Therefore, CMM does *not* claim that following its guidelines will ensure the production of quality software, but maintains that its guidelines *will* enable the enterprise to do so or, failing that, recognize *why* it has failed.

The Capability Maturity Model was developed in the late 1980s and early 1990s by the Software Engineering Institute (SEI) at Carnegie Mellon University in response to the concerns of the U.S. Department of Defense (DOD), specifically the United States Air Force, about the capabilities of software contractors.

CMM is essentially a *rating and auditing framework of standards*. In this framework, an organization fits into one of five "maturity levels" and each level has a "focus."

❶ *Initial (or ad hoc).* *Focus: Individual Effort.* At this level, the organization lacks a stable environment for developing products. The successes and the failures depend on the capabilities of the people, not on processes. As a result, the successes are not repeatable, budgets are often exceeded, and schedules are frequently missed.

❷ *Repeatable.* *Focus: Project Management.* At this level, processes are repeatable and the organization has adopted basic project management principles and practices to control costs and manage schedules. To attain this level, processes must be institutionalized and documented and must lend themselves to training, evaluation, and verification. The requirements and the design documents are "controlled." If the development is for a contract, the development team must establish clear communication channels with the client.

❸ *Defined.* *Focus: Engineering Process.* Processes are "defined" as standard procedures, tools, techniques, etc. Through training programs, the standards are established *across* the organization to ensure that everybody, managers and staff alike, have the required knowledge and training to fulfill the standards. Roles and responsibilities are clear. Costs and schedules are firmly controlled through project management.

❹ *Managed.* *Focus: Product & Process Quality.* By establishing precise measurement criteria, management has effective control of the development process, can improve the processes, and can tailor them to fit new technologies or specific projects. The major difference between levels 3 and 4 relates to *predictability*; whereas in level 3 *quality* is predictable, level 4 can predict *quantitative* variables thanks to statistics and other measuring techniques.

❺ *Optimizing.* *Focus: Continuous Process Improvement.* The organization as a whole is focused on improving the processes continually through both incremental and radical improvements. The organization gathers data on the development process and performs cost-benefit analyses.

How does an organization prove that it belongs to a certain level and not any lower? By the certification that auditors, from inside or outside the organization, grant it. In fact, CMM certification and auditing has emerged as a considerable business in its own right.

More than anything else, CMM reflects the concerns of clients with the **outsourcing** of software development. (For this reason, Indian software companies have eagerly sought CMM certification.) Packaged software, available in the marketplace, is itself the proof, or the disproof, of the quality. When a large corporation or a government agency wants to award a contract worth tens or hundreds of millions of dollars, it wants to ensure that the developer of the software meets certain standards.

Has it worked? Regardless of the answer, if you are doing contract development for large public corporations or government agencies in the United States, this question is likely to be rhetorical: You are required to have CMM certification for a certain level. If you are seeking such a contract, then nobody has to certify or audit your operation, even if you decide that CMM guidelines are worth following.

CMM has been a strong incentive for the emergence, acceptance, and improvement of document management and version control software. It has also helped to drive home the necessity of following transparent and verifiable guidelines. Critics, however, argue that despite good intentions and justified concerns, CMM has degenerated from "good practices" into a wasteful, bureaucratic "paper factory" that has had little effect on the quality of the *product* (which must be the *paramount* concern) and has effectively shut out small developers who cannot afford the huge expense of auditing and certification. They also argue that empirical and scientific evidence to support the contention of qualitative and quantitative "predictability" in higher levels of CMM is still lacking.

The European counterpart to CMM is **ISO-9000-3**, developed by the International Standards Organization. Presented as guidelines for software quality, it views software development mainly as a relationship between the client and the contractor, who must be certified by a recognized "registrar" for compliance with the standards. Whereas CMM does not require yearly certification, ISO-9000-3 does, and whereas CMM has five levels, ISO-9000-3 certification is only "fail" or "pass."

Again, if your company does not have ISO certification it is unlikely to get a software development contract with European governments or large European corporations (which tend to emulate their governments more than their American counterparts do). As a result, any software contractor with international ambitions is wise to seek *both* certifications.

Undoubtedly, standards are good and necessary but

[Ashrafi 1995]

ISO guidelines . . . are vague in outline, confused in expression, and sometimes remotely linked to the software industry. Registrars are few and far between, and [their] experience in software development is of necessity limited and short-lived.

Modeling

> Modeling, as a methodology, is the systematic representation of the relevant features of a product or a system from particular perspectives.

☞ Very few methodologies reject modeling explicitly. Extreme Programming, for example, does not prohibit models, but leaves little room for systematic modeling, basically bundling it with "upfront documentation" and "upfront design" that are to be avoided as much as possible.

Modeling is a *super-methodology* because the methods, techniques, and practices of modeling can be adapted and "inherited" by most other methodologies, even if these methodologies are otherwise incompatible. Some methodologies are essentially based on modeling, while others are silent on modeling but do not exclude it.

Interrelated Concepts

> Modeling is not a single concept but refers to a set of interrelated concepts.

In the context of methodology, the terms "modeling" and "model" apply to different concepts that should not be confused with each other:

- *Artifact.* An individual model, in the shape of a drawing or a plaster cast, is an artifact.
- *Techniques & Methods.* Modeling can refer to individual techniques, methods, activities, or practices, performed with modeling tools.
- *Language.* Modeling often uses *specialized notations* that consist of shapes, lines, labels, and symbols. A roadmap with symbols for gas stations, rest stops, etc., is a typical example. Notations can form a modeling language. For instance, the UML that we presented in the previous chapter (and which we will use throughout this book) is a modeling language, not a methodology.
- *Methodology.* Modeling as methodology conforms to the definition that we provided early in this chapter. The implementations may differ, but it is a systematic approach for achieving a goal.

Characteristics

> The same entity can be represented with numerous models by selecting different characteristics.

Models can be categorized by a number of characteristics. These characteristics are not merely "fine points" of theory, but factors that affect the effectiveness of any model.

- *Level of Abstraction.*   In certain contexts, a model represents every detail that there is: in making a statue from a cast, in "stamping" automobile parts, or in making replicas. Otherwise, a model represents an abstraction, a *selected* set of features. That is to say, the *same* entity can be modeled with a *different* level of abstractions.

    In system development and architecture, the abstraction level of a model depends on the specific activity within the development process. (See "What Do Methodologies Address?") Analysis leads to *conceptual* models that represent *what* is required, without specifying how the product would satisfy these requirements. In design, we must transform conceptual models into *concrete* ones. This process of transformation starts with *logical* models that show *how* the product works *without* reference to specific technologies and leads to *physical* models, or *blueprints*, with exact specifications. (The transition among these abstraction levels is *not* sudden and final, but incremental and iterative.)

- *Point of View.*   As with abstraction, the same entity can be modeled from different viewpoints (or perspectives) by selecting a different set of features. A roadmap for driving represents features that are different from a geological map of the same terrain. Maps that an architect presents to the client are necessarily different from those provided to the builders. In software development, understanding and satisfying various viewpoints, from businesspeople to programmers and database designers, is one of the most challenging and critical tasks.

- *Scope.*   Models can cover different ranges, from a small part of an entity to the relationship among numerous entities. The scope of a model must be meaningful in the context of the selected point of view. That is to say, the modeler must be able to justify why a specific range has to be depicted by the model.

- *Scale.*   Scale is the proportion used to decide how the dimensions of a model relate to the dimensions of what it represents. In software development, scale is usually not a factor (unless we are modeling how much space a virtual entity consumes on the disk or in the memory). In information *technology* modeling, however, scale becomes a factor since networks and workstations are real products as well as virtual.

- *Medium.*   Most of us are accustomed to think of models as *visual* artifacts and, indeed, a great many models *are* visual. We can, however, exploit almost any communication medium for modeling. A model can be *textual*, like the use cases that we will discuss later in this book. (An address is a textual model that represents a place in relation to other places.) A model can be *mathematical*: The famous $E = MC^2$ is a model of the relationship between mass and energy. And a model, like many simulations, can be *multimedia*.

The Mission

A model for construction must first be effective at communication.

Modeling has a primary function and a secondary function. The effectiveness of the second depends on the success of the first.

- ❶ *Communication.*   As a tool for understanding and communication, a model cannot be complex beyond comprehension *even if the entity that it represents is extremely complex.* Clearly, this is a real challenge for many reasons. The clarity of communication depends on both the message itself and the *audience* who receives it: Most of us would not grasp the meaning of models for a nuclear power plant. To understand a model, we must be familiar with both the modeling language (notations) and the concepts behind the language. If the audience for the model is reasonably familiar with both and still has difficulty grasping it, then the modeler has to go back to the drawing board.

❷ *Construction & Maintenance Guide.* Some models have no function beyond representing something, while others define how that something must be built. What is often overlooked, much more widely in software development than in any other field, is that when the construction is complete the life of the product is just beginning. During its lifetime, any product that is not meant for one-time use needs maintenance—be it a building, a car, or a software that manages a company's finances. Without construction models (or *blueprints*, if they are detailed enough), maintenance becomes costly and difficult, if not impossible: original builders leave, or forget gradually, and nobody has a clue about what makes the product work. **A complex product without good construction models is never good enough.**

Modeling for Software Development

> Software modeling is shaped by four interweaved factors: ❶ how the real world is seen, ❷ how software is defined, ❸ the process of development, and ❹ the modeling language.

As we make our way through this book, we will come across many examples of how these four factors shape modeling. Following is a brief introduction to each.

• *How the Real World Is Seen.* Development of most software must incorporate an interpretation of the real world: its building blocks, their relationships, and their interactions. Business software, from simple accounting to eCommerce and Supply Chain Management, reflect real-world workflows as they exist or as they should be when the software becomes operational. Simulations—for training, scientific purposes, or as games—must account for numerous forces that affect actions in a certain context.

On many occasions, prior to the development of an information system, *business process modeling* (BPM) is performed to identify how the business works, to locate shortcomings and inefficiencies, and to decide what processes can be or should be automated. As the name indicates, the world of BPM is primarily a world of processes and everything else is represented only in relation to the logical flow of the process.

Domain analysis should also precede development but, unlike BPM, it is not interested in the details or the logical flow of processes, but in the overall *concepts* of the problem domain. These concepts, of course, include processes as well, but domain analysis aims to discover what the concepts really mean, how they interrelate, and in what *context* they exist and operate.

The models that result from the two viewpoints are inevitably different. Whereas BPM models graphically show the process flow, domain analysis models are classified as textual items.

• *How Software Is Defined.* As an artifact, the definition of software depends as much on technology as on utility. Before the emergence of object-oriented technology, software was defined *and built* as a collection of procedures and data: A procedure received data as input, processed the data, and returned it as output. Consequently,

☞ **Activity diagram** is the tool that UML provides for business process modeling. This diagram is introduced in Chapter 7, Behavioral Modeling II: Developing Use Cases, and explained further in Chapter 9, Dynamic Modeling. **Domain analysis** is the subject of Chapter 5.

and logically, the business unit responsible for automation was often called the "Data Processing Department" (or DP, for short) and the modeling (done only if absolutely necessary) represented how software was seen: a *flowchart* for the internal logic of a procedure or the external interaction among functions, and a *data flow diagram* for how data is affected by processing.

Since a procedure was viewed as the basic building block of software, **functional decomposition** was used to discover the most atomic procedures from large-grain functions through a process of successive breakdowns. (Functional decomposition is a *method*, not a model, but various modeling notations have been used to represent its findings. See Chapter 14, Patterns, for an example.)

Obviously, if software is not defined as procedures and data, these models become misleading or irrelevant. An object-oriented software still has procedures (under a different name) and data, but a data flow diagram does not match either its worldview or its technology.

- *The Process of Development.* We stated that modeling is, first, for understanding and communication and, second, for guiding construction. *How* something is built, and *who* builds it, therefore, is bound to impact modeling. The same product, with exactly the same features, can be built through a different process and by a different combination of people. To repeat, different development methodologies require different kinds of modeling (and some do not require *any* modeling).

- *The Modeling Language.* The same worldview, the same definition of software, and the same development process can be represented by different modeling languages that might not exactly match each other but which can overlap to a significant degree. The "unified" in Unified Modeling Language (UML) means that it replaces other object-oriented languages. (Some authors still use other notations for presenting object-oriented concepts.)

These factors, as we have said, are "interweaved": A change in one factor can have a domino effect on others and the whole. The concept of object-orientation was at first just a concept, without technology. It was deduced from reexamining the real world. For a while *after* the technology became available, however, the procedural modeling continued unchallenged, until object-oriented notations started to appear. Then, interestingly enough, the process came back full circle: If we are building software as a collection of objects and interactions among them, why not take the same object-oriented approach to analyzing and modeling the real world?

Object-Oriented Development

A full object-oriented development requires three things: ❶ an object-oriented technology, ❷ an object-oriented analysis and design, and ❸ a project plan adapted to an object-oriented approach.

Object-oriented *technology* is mature and rules the market, while object-oriented *methodology* for system analysis and design is still controversial and far from universally adopted. The difference between the two is the following.

Object-oriented *technology* means that the **product** is composed of objects. *How* you get to this product does not affect its composition. Object-oriented *methodology*, on the other hand, is about *how*: how to analyze the problem domain in terms of objects *and* their interactions, how to discover classes from this analysis, how to refine classes into a conceptual model of the product, how to discover and define design objects that must manage the working of the solution, and so on.

The structure of this book is self-explanatory as to how we view object-oriented software development. The activities that we cover are generally the same that we described before: gathering requirements, domain analysis, system analysis, etc. (See "What Do Methodologies Address?") A few observations here, however, are necessary.

☞ The term "*iterative*" here does *not* refer to formal methodologies that use it as a part of their names, but simply signifies that the same activities or artifacts are revisited in the course of development. (The same qualification applies to other terms that might be confused with named methodologies.)

- Object-oriented software development is *iterative*. Activities such as design do not start *only* if analysis is complete and, in turn, the start of analysis is not dependent on having *every* requirement in hand. During the process of development, the *baseline* of activities changes. We *start* with requirements discovery, but gathering requirements tapers off only gradually. At some point, depending on the project, we might be engaged in both analysis and design. The structure of the book is necessarily sequential; the flow of development is not.

- Since its inception, object-oriented development has expanded to absorb and adapt concepts and approaches that, strictly speaking, are not object-oriented but are highly compatible with the concept. They greatly benefit from an object-oriented approach and, in turn, make software development much more reliable and productive. The following are the most notable of these concepts.

  ❶ **Component-based** development, the idea that software should be constructed *as*—and *from*—components. (Discussed in Chapter 15, Components & Reuse.)

  ❷ The **architectural** approach, the practice of designing the software's structure from a high-level point of view *before* attending to details. (Discussed in Chapter 16, Architecture.)

  ❸ Learning from **patterns**. A pattern is the *core* of the solution to a problem that occurs repeatedly in an environment. (Discussed in Chapter 14, Patterns.)

  ❹ A **model-driven** approach to software development to manage complexity and facilitate communication both inside the development team and between the team and other stakeholders. (Discussed throughout the book.)

- As we argued earlier, no existing methodology covers every aspect of development. Object-oriented software development is no exception. For instance, it does not address the organization of labor or resources in the project. Neither does it offer any opinion on how coding must be managed. It takes more than one methodology—established or improvised, formal or informal—to guide a project to its goal.

4. PROJECT MANAGEMENT CONCEPTS

Developing software is predominantly done through projects, even if the primary business of the business is developing software. The main reason is that developing a new product always involves factors that do not fit into the routine.

Since a project is a one-time "thing," it always involves unknown elements, and unknown always means *risk*: Is the project realistic? Can it be completed on time and on budget? Have we selected the right people and the right tools? Have we organized the people and the process correctly? How can we be sure that, once it is under way, the project is going in the right direction? If something goes wrong, how can we correct it?

Project management is the **methodology** for coping with risk by answering the previous questions. Like in any other field, there is no single methodology for managing projects, but many overlapping and complementary methodologies compete with each other. Furthermore, project management is an independent discipline in its own right, explored through numerous books and taught as college courses. Here, we introduce the basic concepts of project management because we must be familiar with them before we can proceed to software development.

Defining Project

> A project is a collection of related tasks that must be completed in a particular order and within a certain timeframe to achieve a specific goal.

A project is an organized *process* through which:

- *An idea is realized:*   painting of the ceiling of the Sistine Chapel by Michelangelo, writing a midterm paper by a student, landscaping of the garden by the proud owners of a new house.
- *A real-world problem is solved:*   building of the Channel Tunnel between England and France, organizing personal papers after an extended period of neglect, developing an information system for an online bookseller.
- *An opportunity is exploited:*   founding of the Plymouth Colony by the Pilgrims sailing on the Mayflower, building a parking garage in the shopping district of a big city, writing an essay for a national competition.
- *A mission is accomplished:*   landing of the Allied forces on the Normandy beaches on D-Day (June 6, 1944); painting the rooms in one's home; arranging a wedding by finding space, engaging caterers, and sending out invitations.
- *A quest is fulfilled:*   reaching the North Pole by Robert E. Peary, finding the perfect gift for a friend's birthday, landing of astronauts on the Moon.

A project may be complex or simple, difficult or easy, mundane or noble, more likely to succeed or more likely to fail, but as different as projects are from each other, each project can be studied from somewhere between two distinct views:

- ***What***, or the *goal* of the project.
- ***How***, or the *process* by which the goal is accomplished.

☞ The "*why*" is undoubtedly as important to the project as the "what" and the "how," if not more. Usually, however, a project starts where the "why" has been established— correctly or incorrectly, wisely or unwisely.

We must not confuse the two but, equally important, we must not emphasize one at the expense of the other. The goal dictates the components of the process, but it is the process that decides the outcome.

No simple definition of the term "project" would be able to fully express the intricacies of the relationship between the "what" and the "how." To better grasp this relationship, we must explore the explicit and the implicit concepts underlying the definition.

The Goal

> The goal of a project must be verifiable.

☞ A project's process is shaped by its goal but, at the same time, a project is *not* undertaken and a goal is *not* defined unless we have a minimum amount of confidence in existing tools, existing resources, or existing know-how. As late as in the early 20th century, "Mission to Mars" would have been the obvious title for a work of science fiction, not a project by the U.S. government.

The goal dictates what types of tasks, resources, planning, and methodologies are required for the projects. A project to send astronauts to Mars would have components very different from one that is undertaken to organize a wedding.

In all projects, however, we must be able to verify the goal. *"Improving the Quality of Human Life"* is a worthwhile goal and can result from many scientific, charitable, and industrial projects but, as the goal for one project, cannot be readily verified to our satisfaction. (It is also a never-ending quest whereas, as we shall see, projects must have boundaries in time.) *"Manned Mission to Mars"* is complex and ambitious, but once an astronaut lands on Mars, all can agree that the mission has been accomplished.

The Scope

> The scope of the project defines the boundaries of the goal.

The fact that the project's goal must be verifiable seems self-evident but, in reality, many projects, especially software projects, fail because either their goals are too vague, their boundaries are not clear-cut, or they change continuously.

"Developing an Enterprise-Wide Information System" may seem like a clear goal but it is, at best, a starting point for defining the *scope* of the project. Since an ever-increasing array of activities can be automated, what does an "enterprise-wide information system" exactly entail? If the enterprise is a manufacturing company, does the system include automation of the manufacturing process? What about customer relations? Considering that the information technology usually changes faster than the **life cycle** (discussed in a following section) of a large project, how can we ensure that the final product is not obsolete even before it comes online?

Obsolete Goals

The question of technological obsolescence may seem unrelated to the "goal." But the goal of many projects is embodied in one or more products that cannot survive technological obsolescence. An air-conditioner is the embodiment of a goal that can be described as "the cooling of indoor spaces," but if by the time the air-conditioner reaches the market its efficiency is substandard, the project has failed. Software is even more sensitive to technological obsolescence because ❶ its survival is dependent on platforms whose availability and support is not under the control of consumers and ❷ inter-operability with other systems is fast becoming more an absolute business necessity rather than a luxury.

Frequently, a project might start with a verifiable goal and a well-defined scope but at some point it might fall prey to *scope-creep*—requests for additional features that overstep the original scope, invalidate previous project planning, and strain all budgetary estimates.

Not every type of revision to the goals and the scope of the project is "scope-creep." Business requirements do change legitimately and some complications can be understood only when a project—especially a project with an unprecedented goal—is well under way. But the following two situations are likely to produce disruptive requests for features outside the original scope.

☞ See Chapter 4, Gathering Requirements, for a detailed discussion of defining the scope through requirements discovery.

- *Incorrect or Inadequate Requirements Discovery.* The scope of the project may be ill-defined as a result of carelessness, sheer ignorance, or the dedication of insufficient resources to the requirements discovery, the most important phase of the project *before* the actual development process begins. Consequently, the real requirements "creep up" when their absence becomes noticeable: in other words, when the project has to be "retrofitted" with additional features at higher cost.

- *Opportunism.* In nature, scavengers are usually attracted to carrion; in development projects—especially in software development projects—the reverse is sometimes true: The rate of project failures is usually so high that when a project appears to be progressing well, the temptation to exploit it for far-flung and new goals is irresistible.

For example, a small team might be given the task of developing a small application meant to record individual expenses while the employee is traveling. When the first test version is ready and proves to be successful, the client makes a reasonable request: The application should be able to export data to the corporate accounting system so that duplicate entry is avoided.

Trying to accommodate this request, the development team discovers that since the corporate information system relies on a set of codes for employee identification and accounts, their application must now incorporate those as well. When the conclusion is presented to the client, the client has another brilliant (and reasonable) idea: Shouldn't the application be able to "synchronize" its data with the corporate system when the employee's notebook is reconnected to the corporate network? In the meantime, it would be helpful if the employee (and management) could produce reports and charts that analyze his or her patterns of expenditure. (All, needless to say, within the same general timeframe and budget.) Somewhere along the line there appears the straw that breaks the camel's back.

The Timeframe

> A project's lifetime is finite.

A project is not a continuous undertaking but has a beginning and an end. Designing a new car model and retooling the assembly line to manufacture it is a project, but the day-to-day affairs of the production are not. Developing a software application is a project, but its daily operations and its regular maintenance (such as monitoring the size and the integrity of the database, or authorizing new users) are not.

After a project is finished—successfully or not—it ceases to exist as a unique entity, whereas an automobile assembly line or a commercial enterprise continues to function. In fact, the timeframe may be the most distinguishing identifier for projects that are similar in almost every other aspect. Every year, sometime before April 15th, most American wage earners engage in a disliked but widespread "project": organizing their financial documents and filling out their tax returns. Or a construction company might dispatch the same team for consecutive projects of tract housing development.

A project has a limited lifetime but **the completion date of a project is not necessarily fixed**. Besides the inevitable miscalculations in time estimates and delays in implementations, some projects are either not time-sensitive or are considered so important that they are granted all the time that they need. For example, to develop a long-lasting incandescent lamp, Thomas Edison (or rather Edison *and* his laboratory) spent a year testing every conceivable material for the lamp's filament. The result was a carbon-thread filament that could burn for more than forty hours. They certainly wanted a solution as soon as possible, but when the project started, neither he nor his colleagues had a fixed target in time. They would have continued even after a year if the solution had eluded them.

The Life Cycle

> The life cycle identifies the phases of the project from its inception to its completion.

The ending date for a project might be predictable or not, but the project has a life cycle. That is, the project goes through *different* phases between its inception and its completion. The project life cycle can be summarized as "*5 times 5*"—five phases with five steps within each phase.

[Wysocki 2000, 80–85]

☞ Other writers may characterize the life cycle somehow differently from our source but the general outline remains similar. (Five phases, each with five steps, seems a little contrived.)

❶ *Scope the project:* ❶ state the problem and/or opportunity; ❷ establish the project goal; ❸ define the project objectives; ❹ identify the success criteria; and ❺ list assumptions, risks, and obstacles.

❷ *Develop the plan:* ❶ identify project activities; ❷ estimate duration for activities; ❸ determine required resources; ❹ create and analyze the project network diagram, a visual model of the sequence of activities (see Figure 3.3); and ❺ prepare the project proposal.

❸ *Launch the plan:* ❶ organize the project team, ❷ establish how the team operates, ❸ marshal project resources, ❹ schedule work "packages," and ❺ document work packages.

❹ *Monitor progress:* ❶ establish how progress reporting is to be done, ❷ install processes and tools to manage change, ❸ define procedures to handle problems, ❹ monitor the correlation between the project plan and the actual progress, and ❺ revise plans when necessary.

Figure 3.3
The Network Diagram: The Visual Layout of the Project Workflow

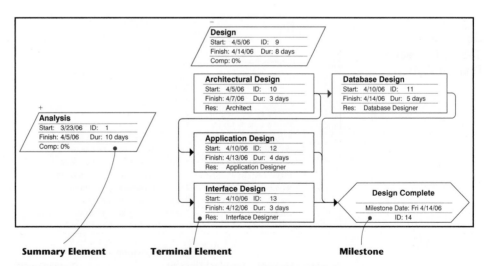

Summary Element   **Terminal Element**   **Milestone**

The constituent elements of this diagram, such as summary element and terminal element, are explained in the *Tasks & Activity Threads* section. This is a partial view; the full network diagram for a project would span many pages.

❺ *Close the project:* ❶ get client acceptance, ❷ deploy the deliverables, ❸ complete project documents, ❹ perform the post-deployment audit, and ❺ issue the final report.

These phases are abstract. In theory, they should apply to any project, regardless of the content or the goal: developing software, building a bridge, creating an advertising campaign, etc. In practice, however, the picture is more complicated. We have more to say about this topic later in this chapter. (See "Project Management & Software Development.")

Tasks & Activity Threads

> A project is composed of related tasks that take place on one or more activity threads or paths.

A project is a collection of tasks. The most atomic task is called a ***terminal element***, an undertaking that must be completed within a clearly specified timeframe. (See Figure 3.4.) A ***summary element*** is a task that is composed of terminal elements or other summary elements.

Tasks have certain features in common.

- *Name.* A very short label for the task. The name is usually prescriptive: "Review Functional Requirements," for example.
- *Start & Finish Dates and Duration.* A task *must* have a start date and a finish date. Except for milestones and events (described in the next section), the task must have a duration which is commonly specified in days.
- *Resources.* People who carry out tasks are the project's primary resources, though anything that the project needs, from a meeting room to a cargo plane, falls into this category as well. A resource can be a job description such as "analyst" or a specific person. The same resource can work on multiple tasks at the *same* time. In such a case, the percentage of the time that the resource

**Figure 3.4
Scheduling
Tasks: Project's
Plan of Action**

	Task Name	Duration	Start	Finish	Predecessors	Resource Names
1	⊟ **Analysis**	**10 days**	**Thu 3/23/06**	**Wed 4/5/06**		
2	Organize Requirements	2 days	Thu 3/23/06	Fri 3/24/06		Business Analyst
3	Domain Analysis	3 days	Tue 3/28/06	Thu 3/30/06	2	Business Analyst
4	Discover Use Cases	3 days	Mon 3/27/06	Wed 3/29/06	2	Business Analyst, System Analyst
5	Elaborate Use Cases	2 days	Thu 3/30/06	Fri 3/31/06	4	System Analyst, Business Analyst
6	Develop Structural Models	3 days	Mon 4/3/06	Wed 4/5/06	3,5	System Analyst
7	Develop Dynamic Models	2 days	Mon 4/3/06	Tue 4/4/06	5	System Analyst
8	Analysis Complete	0 days	Tue 4/4/06	Tue 4/4/06	7	
9	⊟ **Design**	**8 days**	**Wed 4/5/06**	**Fri 4/14/06**		
10	Architectural Design	3 days	Wed 4/5/06	Fri 4/7/06	8	Architect
11	Database Design	5 days	Mon 4/10/06	Fri 4/14/06	10	Database Designer
12	Application Design	4 days	Mon 4/10/06	Thu 4/13/06	10	Application Designer
13	Interface Design	3 days	Mon 4/10/06	Wed 4/12/06	10	Interface Designer
14	Design Complete	0 days	Fri 4/14/06	Fri 4/14/06	11,12,13	
15	⊞ **Implementation**	**3 days**	**Mon 4/17/06**	**Wed 4/19/06**		

Milestone

Summary Element   Terminal Element   Dependencies

This schedule is simplified for illustration. A real development project has many more detailed tasks. The timeline would be much more expansive as well.

must devote to each task must be identified. (Project management applications warn you if the total time of a particular resource for a specific period exceeds 100 percent.) Note that *one* resource is not necessarily *one* person. If we have a group of ten programmers, 60 percent of the group (or six programmers) might work on one task while the remaining 40 percent are assigned to another task.

- *Dependencies.*   A task may be dependent on the completion of other tasks, called its *predecessors*, before it can start.

Tasks can be identified by other attributes such as budget and cost and, as the project proceeds, by actual start and finish dates, percentages done, actual costs, and other metrics.

Tasks are not necessarily sequential. A project has a fixed starting point and (hopefully) a fixed ending but, between the two points, tasks can branch out and run parallel to each other. Theses branches, called **activity threads** or **paths**, may be composed of one task or a set of sequential tasks. For example, database design and interface design can proceed (relatively) in parallel.

The longest path in a project is the **critical path**, which determines the *shortest* time required to complete the project. (See Figure 3.5.) In other words, if a task on the critical path takes longer to complete than planned, then the completion of the whole project will be delayed as well. This does not mean that each task on the critical path is necessarily longer than other tasks, but simply that *total* time for all the tasks on the path is the longest.

A task may have a **slack time** (or **float**) that allows it to start or finish later than planned, provided that it does not overstep the timeframe restrictions imposed by the tasks in the critical path. One of the challenges of project scheduling is how to prevent the idleness of *resources* as a result of *task* slack times.

Milestones & Deliverables

Milestones are significant events in the life of the project. Deliverables are the verifiable results of tasks.

It would be too late if we have to wait for the project to end before we know whether it has been successful. To ensure that the project is on the right track, or to correct its course if it has gone astray, we must use a "divide and conquer" strategy and organize the project as *mini-projects*, each with its own verifiable outcome. A milestone is a significant event that marks the completion of a mini-project.

In scheduling a project, a milestone appears as a task, with one crucial difference: A milestone happens at a specific time but its duration is *zero*, meaning that it happens *in* time but does not *take* time. In Figure 3.4 **Design Complete** is a milestone that sends a clear-cut message when it occurs: *All* tasks for the **Design** mini-project have been completed *and* their results have been verified.

[Wysocki 2000, 145]

A deliverable is the verifiable result of a task—any task, be it a milestone or not. (The deliverable for a milestone, however, must leave less room for doubt.) The deliverable is a *visible sign* that an activity is complete. This can be any sign, from the foundation of a building or a set of UML diagrams to the signature of the client.

One of the greater challenges in software development is how to avoid the discrepancy between what we *think* the product should do and what the product must *really* do to meet the requirements. By defining an intelligent and practical set of milestones and deliverables, we can go a long way towards answering this challenge.

After a milestone, we must compare the *actual* deliverables with the *planned* deliverables. If they match, we move on; otherwise we ❶ analyze the reasons for the discrepancy to discover whether the projection was erroneous or something in the implementation went wrong, and ❷ determine the effects of the mismatch on the whole project (resources, budget, timeframe, etc.), adjust the plan, and take corrective action.

Note, however, that having *too many* milestones is as destructive to the project as having too few. The nature and the number of milestones and deliverables is absolutely tied to the nature of the specific project, but expecting accountability every few hours, as some methodologies do, is counterproductive: Developers would constantly think of how to *look* good instead of how to *do* good.

Tools & Techniques

> Project management tools are primarily focused on modeling the components and the flow of the project from various perspectives and with different levels of detail.

Scheduling and tracking of tasks for a complex project is a daunting task by itself—if done manually. Fortunately, project management applications are mature enough to make both tasks relatively painless. This does not mean that that the techniques are beyond pencil-and-paper technology, but that ❶ automated tools for project management have gone through a few generations of evolution and are no longer experimental, ❷ the tasks that they perform are tailor-made for what computers do best (i.e., computing), and ❸ manual modeling of the project takes too much time without adding any value.

☞ Unfortunately, as mature as they are, project management applications cannot make an unrealistic project plan more realistic, or a defective understanding of software development less defective.

Most of the tools and techniques for project management are concerned with the *same* concepts: modeling the schedule, tasks, activity threads, and critical path. The differences, like in any kind of modeling, lie with the viewpoint, the detail, and the language. (See "Modeling.")

We briefly describe the most established tools and techniques next.

☞ "Gantt" is not an acronym but refers to **Henry Laurence Gantt** (1861–1919), the American engineer. He developed his namesake chart in 1910s.

Gantt Chart   One of the most popular and easiest tools for both scheduling and tracking the project flow is the Gantt chart. In its most basic form, a Gantt chart is a timeline or a calendar along which tasks are shown as horizontal bars. The length of the bar indicates the duration of the task while the vertical arrangement represents the sequencing of the tasks. Arrows stand for dependencies and identify activity threads or paths. Usually, the critical path is distinguished from other paths by a different color. (Figure 3.5 is a Gantt chart for the same tasks that are shown in Figure 3.4.)

Labels on the task bars can show a range of information: resources (and the share of their time devoted to the task), actual percentage of the progress, or any other task-related data.

The simplicity of the Gantt chart is both an advantage and a disadvantage. It is effective in presenting a snapshot of the project but can only show details selectively before it becomes overcrowded.

Network Diagram   The network diagram (Figure 3.3) displays tasks as networked boxes that contain a set of data about each task. Like the Gantt chart, the positioning

Figure 3.5
Gantt Chart:
Tracking the
Project

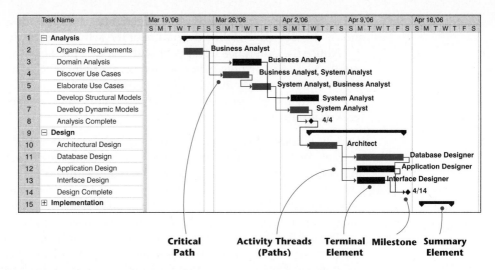

The critical path is rendered in blue and arrows indicate dependencies.

of boxes indicates the sequence of tasks. Unlike the Gantt chart, however, the size of the box has no relation to the duration of the task and the tasks are not necessarily arranged horizontally.

Since each task on the diagram occupies a fixed-sized box with several lines of text, the network diagram cannot offer a bird's-eye view of a complex project or even significant portions of it. Most likely, you will have to switch between the Gantt chart and the network diagram as the need arises—a task that, with project management applications, is as easy as a few clicks of the mouse.

PERT Chart   The schedule table, Gantt chart, and the network diagram are the most popular tools for managing and tracking projects, but many other tools are available. A notable one is the **PERT chart**. (PERT stands for Program Evaluation and Review Technique.) It was invented in 1958 by the U.S. Department of Defense, Navy's Special Project Office, to manage the development of the Polaris submarine defense program. (See Figure 3.6.) The effectiveness of the PERT chart results from its extreme simplicity: nodes, in the shape of circles or boxes, represent events or

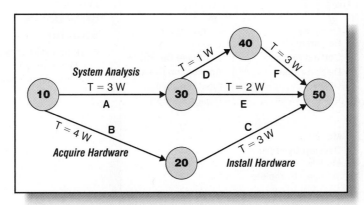

**Figure 3.6
PERT Chart**

Each node on the chart (such as 10 or 20) represents an event or a milestone. A relatively small chart can provide an effective snapshot of the project.

You will encounter PERT charts that are slightly different from this version. This basic idea, however, is the same.

milestones. The activities are represented as arrows that flow from event to event and can be labeled to define the nature of the activity or the duration.

Notice the difference in concept with the two previous tools where boxes represent the tasks and arrows indicate the flow. With the PERT chart, an activity is identified by the two events that define its boundaries, such as "task 20–30." (Some tools, however, define and produce PERT charts that closely resemble Gantt charts or network diagrams.)

Work Breakdown Structure   Work Breakdown Structure (WBS) is not a tool but a method. As the term indicates, it starts with breaking the project into smaller activities and continues with breaking down the results until it arrives at the most atomic activities (or "terminal" elements.) In effect, WBS *decomposes* the project into a *hierarchy* with different levels for activities. The tasks on the lowest level of a branch that cannot be reasonably subdivided into other tasks are called a *work package*.

The WBS technique can be presented by a variety of models: an *organizational chart*, an indented *table* of activities similar to Figure 3.4, or a *tree-view* such as the one in Figure 3.7. (We have illustrated the simplest tree-view. Each node on the tree, the so-called "branches" and "leaves," can contain detailed data on the activity or the task.)

The main advantage of the WBS view is that, by removing the element of time, it allows us to better see the activities *in relation to each other*. It can also provides an alternate view of the project's structure by consolidating lower-level tasks into higher ones as those tasks are completed.

Feasibility Studies & Risk Management

☞ Graham Winch, "Thirty Years Of Project Management What Have We Learned?" © Revised August 1997. http://intl-oss. sagepub.com/cgi/content/citation/25/9/1475.

Feasibility studies aim to discover whether the expectations are realistic. Risk management guards against the unexpected.

It seems self-evident that a project that cannot possibly succeed must not be undertaken. Many failed projects, however, are started with the honest belief that they *will* succeed. To reduce the chances of failure, a two-pronged approach is required: study the feasibility of the project *before* it starts, and provide for what can go wrong *after* it gets under way.

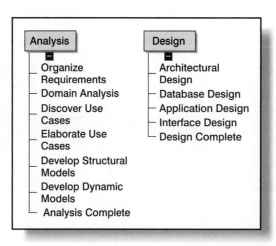

Figure 3.7
Work Breakdown Structure

Work Breakdown Structure (WBS) represents the project as a hierarchical organization of tasks.

The nature of a project usually falls somewhere between two theoretical extremes: *development* projects and *implementation* projects. Development projects create something that is basically new: a new car model or a new software for managing customer relations, for example. Implementation projects essentially repeat the same process: for instance, the building of another tract house. No project is completely new and no project is completely devoid of new elements, but the closer a project is to the "development" extreme, the more difficult it is to determine the chances of its success and the risks associated with it. Software development projects, by and large, belong to this category.

Note that in this section heading, we have used the plural "studies" because a single feasibility study is not sufficient to determine the chances of success. Depending on the project, a set of questions must be answered: Is the goal of the project possible at all? If possible, do we have the resources—financial, human, organization, etc.—to achieve it? If so, what are the legal ramifications? If the project is time-sensitive, can it be done on time? And so on.

One of the most intractable issues in development projects is *cost estimation*. Software development has proved to be especially resistant to cost predictions. Numerous methods have been proposed to solve this problem, but none has proved to be acceptably accurate. Despite repeated failures in this regard, however, we must do our best to arrive at a reasonable cost estimate, without promising that it will be 100 percent accurate. First, *no* business would sign a blank check for an open-ended expenditure. (Government agencies have even tighter requirements.) Second, it is through experience and comparing projected and actual costs that we can arrive at more accurate models for the future.

How about managing risk in general? At the very least, certain questions must be answered *before* the project starts:

- *What are the risks?*
- *What is the probability of loss that results from them?*
- *How much are the losses likely to cost?*
- *What might the losses be if the worst happens?*
- *What are the alternatives?*
- *How can the losses be reduced or eliminated?*
- *Will the alternatives produce other risks?*

The small space given here to feasibility studies, cost estimation, and risk management do not correspond to the importance of these topics. There is a vast literature (and vast controversies) where they are concerned. The literature might not solve all project management problems, but if you are not armed with an adequate knowledge, your project can only succeed by luck.

☞ The argument has also been put forward that there is a theoretical (and mathematical) limit to the accuracy of cost estimation for large and complex software developments. See: J.P. Lewis, "Large Limits to Software Estimation," *ACM Software Engineering Notes*, Volume 26, Number 4 (July 2001).

[Wysocki 2000, 95]

The Project Manager

The job of the project manager depends on how "management" is defined.

The position of the project manager is problematical. Managing a development project requires such a vast range of skills, knowledge, and competencies that finding them in one person would almost amount to a miracle. The following is a (very brief) summary of how one author would rate a candidate for project manager.

- *Business Awareness.* Ensures that the project is in harmony with the organization's business plan; evaluates the impact of industry and technological developments; balances technical issues with business priorities; quickly adapts to changing business conditions.

[Wysocki 2000, 39–41]

- *Business Partnership.* Ensures full understanding of business stakeholders' needs and concerns; structures the activities of the project team so that system staff work closely with business stakeholders.
- *Commitment to Quality.* Pushes for more efficient ways to do things; sets and enforces high standards of quality for self and others; coordinates the project plan with a quality plan.
- *Initiative.* Develops innovative and creative approaches to problems; takes calculated risks; puts in whatever effort is needed to get the job done.
- *Information Gathering.* Actively solicits input from all stakeholders in the project; gets enough information to support design and implementation decisions.
- *Analytic Thinking.* Develops an overall project plan including resources, budget, and time; translates business goals into project goals and goals into a detailed plan; generates and presents logical and clear alternatives.
- *Conceptual Thinking.* Considers the project within the context of future changes in both business and technology; understands both business and technical objectives to prioritize effectively; plans proactively for the impact of the project on other systems; develops a clear vision for the deliverables.
- *Self Confidence.* Sets an example for the whole team by presenting a confident and positive attitude; confronts problems quickly and directly; has good self-control and functions well under stress.
- *Concern for Credibility.* Consistently delivers what has been promised; can answer all detailed questions about the project; answers honestly even if the answers are embarrassing; reports problems immediately.
- *Flexibility.* Adjusts readily to changes in the work environment; adjusts managerial style, depending on the people and on the situation; delegates tasks and activities to others.

Though this list downplays the importance of technical expertise, the criteria that it offers are appropriate for the job. (A frequent complaint of software developers is that project managers are mostly "enforcement agents" who do not understand technological issues well enough.) The problem is that organizations, perhaps hoping for a miracle, expect everything from *one* person on whom they bestow the title of "Project Manager." This is where management by committee actually makes sense. The composition of such a committee would depend on the actual people who are available, not on titles or predefined templates.

Project Management & Software Development

> A project plan is sequential in concept. Software development is iterative in practice.

The methodologies for project management are highly abstract. They should apply to any project, regardless of the content or the goal—developing software, building a bridge, conducting an advertising campaign, and so on. This abstractness is what makes project management a field independent from software development, civil engineering, advertising, etc., but it can be problematic as well.

Organizations, including the organization of projects, tend to be more or less hierarchical and *vertical*. What organizations do—and this is reflected in project planning as well—is conceived as *sequential*. On the other hand, development of new things, especially software development, tends to be *iterative* and *horizontal*.

We stated that projects are located somewhere between two extremes: development and implementation. The concepts of project management favor the latter. For example, building a bridge by using known and well-tested civil engineering techniques and know-how fits comfortably within the framework of project management. As the proportion of newness increases, project management loses its effectiveness. Witness the Channel Tunnel between England and France: It had huge cost overruns (some sources put it as high as 80 percent) and pushed its private investors to the edge of bankruptcy.

Can the iterative undertaking of software development fit into a sequential plan of action? The answer is that it can, but not readily. Both the project plan and the development methodology need to adapt to each other. Project planning must take into account the fact that software development is composed of activities—requirements gathering, analysis, logical design, physical design, architectural design, coding, testing, and deployment—that *cannot* start and stop as clear-cut phases, but are "phased in" and "phased out" only gradually. On the other hand, software development (with some help from technology) must produce artifacts that have distinct identities and clear, verifiable attributes.

We believe that object-oriented development and its logical extensions, including component-based development and architecture, can provide the most effective *possible* answer to the question above.

5. WRAP UP

Programming is just one activity among many that must be carried out to develop an information system. Developing software is a multifaceted undertaking that is shaped by *what* we are building, the *complexity* of what we want to build, the availability of *resources*, and *how* the process of development is organized. In other words, ❶ developing software is different from the development of other products and goods, ❷ a complex software poses challenges that are qualitatively different from those presented by a simple one, ❸ all projects cannot enjoy the same resources, and ❹ the plan of action and the organization of resources have a crucial impact on the outcome. Software development needs a **methodology** to define and guide its process, and it needs *project management* to implement the methodology.

☑ **Methodology, its fundamental concepts & its building blocks**

Methodology is a systematized interpretation of the past experience, and often new ideas for improving on the past, that provides a set of methods, rules, procedures, and tools to achieve a goal. What distinguishes the methodology from its components is a "philosophy" or a *theoretical framework*. Methods and techniques may be used *across* methodologies, but it is the methodology that defines the significance of each method or technique. In other words, "method" defines a *tactic*, whereas "methodology" defines the *strategy*.

The need for methodology is not limited to the journey from the problem to the solution. Depending on the complexity of the problem or the solution, various challenges call for methodology: understanding the **problem domain** or the *context* in which the problem occurs and the solution must work; creating the **solution domain** that contains elements which can be unrelated to the problem but must be built to support the solution; *assuring quality*, which means making certain that the product works as expected; selecting among *multiple solutions* for the *same* problem; selecting from *multiple methodologies* for the *same* solution; coping with *available resources* and different contexts; and preparing for the *consequences of the solution*.

One methodology usually does not cover every aspect of development. A methodology may address the stages of the development but be silent on the responsibilities and the organization of developers. Another may address quality assurance but not model the requirements on which the quality depends. Therefore, development often depends on employing methodologies *in parallel*. When the theoretical frameworks of parallel methodologies prove to be incompatible, we have to resolve the resulting conflicts by bending or modifying one methodology or the other.

In fields such as software development, methodology and *technology* are closely related and move each other forward. The two, however, should not be confused: Multiple methodologies often target the same technology and the same methodology is sometimes applied to different technologies.

Even methodologies that aim at the same goal might not cover the same grounds. One methodology can cover every detail and every step, while another may offer a very general framework. One methodology may be proper only for a specific context, while another might not address the context at all.

Most software development takes place through projects, and a project is an undertaking that has a limited lifetime. Most undertakings, however, are ongoing and repetitive. The methodology of such an undertaking is embodied in an *organization*: a company, a hospital, a government agency, or an army. Since most projects are owned by ongoing enterprises, the friction and sometimes the conflict between the two is inescapable: whereas bureaucracy is interested in accountability, standards, approved procedures, and the chain of command, the project is results-oriented and assigns the priority to its goal.

☑ **Benefits & risks of methodology**

Some methodologies are offered as *products*, packages of tools, development frameworks, training, auditing, etc. Even as pure theories, however, methodologies can be costly. At the very least, the enterprise must "comply" with the methodology; that is, people must be trained to follow the proper procedures and guidelines. Therefore, an enterprise has every right to ask this question: If we spend money on methodology, what do we get in return?

If methodology is moderately well-chosen, it can ❶ *offer a well-rounded approach* to development because any methodology, unlike private experience, is open to public scrutiny and public discussion on its weakness and strengths; ❷ *standardize the development process* and thereby make the communication among

participants in the development more effective and more reliable; and ❸ *increase productivity* and quality by promoting and fostering those personal traits that are most favorable to the task at hand.

Unfortunately, no methodology is ideal or ever will be. Existing methodologies often overlook the size of the project, the available resources, or the context in which development must take place. Most are too complex and target very large or complex projects. Some are more flexible and can be adapted to the context (an undertaking that incurs its own costs and risks) and some are less inflexible.

Nevertheless, undertaking a project *without* a methodology is much riskier than adopting a methodology that might be less than ideal.

☑ **What software development methodologies address**

Software development consists of *a wide spectrum of activities* that individual methodologies cover selectively and from different viewpoints. These activities can be broadly classified as follows: ❶ gathering requirements, ❷ feasibility study, ❸ domain analysis, ❹ system analysis, ❺ design, ❻ implementation, ❼ quality assurance and testing, ❽ deployment and training, and ❾ maintenance.

Whether these activities take place sequentially, iteratively, in parallel (when possible), or even without a clear pattern depends on the methodology. What is more, a methodology may not recognize a certain activity as a distinct entity. Some methodologies, consciously and explicitly, cover only one activity or a selected set.

☑ **The most common concepts in software development methodologies**

There are too many software development methodologies for a meaningful summary. Certain concepts, however, recur through most of them.

Ad hoc is an approach to development *without* an overall theoretical framework. What distinguishes an *ad hoc* approach from a formal methodology is that the general flow of the process is not defined by an overall "philosophy," even though it might borrow individual tools, methods, techniques, and procedures from formal methodologies. *Ad hoc* relies heavily on the ingenuity and the experience of developers in improvising and communicating.

System Development Life Cycle (SDLC) methodologies view development primarily as a project management challenge, rather than a technical one. The "classic" SDLC methodology is the **Waterfall Model** that specifies a set of *sequential* *phases* for software development: feasibility study, system analysis, design, etc.

Prototyping proceeds on the basis of creating a working model of the essential features of the final product for testing and verification of requirements. There are two types of prototyping: incremental or *evolutionary*, in which the same prototype is refined successively to arrive at the final product, and the *throwaway*, which discards the prototype after verification of its features.

In the **incremental** or **iterative approach**, the product is built through successive versions that are refined and expanded with each iteration. The **Spiral Model** combines the life cycle approach with prototyping and iteration. The result is a complicated approach that has nevertheless been very popular with government projects since its focus is on *risk management*.

Rapid Application Development (RAD) is selecting techniques, methods, practices, and procedures that result in faster development and shorter schedules. Nevertheless, the *formal* RAD methodology has its own characteristics and guidelines. It views development as four distinct phases: requirements planning, design (which includes prototyping if necessary), implementation, and maintenance (including enhancements).

Agile methodologies form a distinct but diverse category. Their common goal is being "adaptive" rather than "predictive." Furthermore, they generally (but not universally) consider "upfront" documentation, "upfront" modeling, and "upfront" design as a waste of time. *Extreme Programming* (XP) is the best-known agile method.

The **Capability Maturity Model** (CMM) aims to measure the maturity of the software development *process* within an organization. For CMM, an organization fits into one of five maturity models: ❶ "initial" (or *ad hoc*), where the organization lacks a stable environment and relies on the capabilities of the individuals; ❷ "repeatable," where the organization has adopted project management principles; ❸ "defined," where the workflow has been shaped into an engineering process; ❹ "managed," where product and process quality are *quantitatively* predictable; and ❺ "optimizing," where the focus of the organization is continuous process improvement.

Like CMM, **ISO-9000-3**, developed by the International Standards Organization, focuses on the quality of the organization, not the product. Unlike CMM, an organization can belong to only one of the two categories: those that pass its criteria, and those that fail them. It also requires yearly certification.

Object-oriented development is not directly concerned with the organization of the project but with the product itself, from conceptual to physical. It has three requirements: ❶ an object-oriented technology, ❷ an object-oriented analysis and design, and ❸ a project plan that is friendly to an object-oriented approach. Object-oriented development is highly iterative. An *expanded* object-oriented development also includes the following concepts: *component-based* development, *architectural design*, learning from *patterns*, and a *model-driven* approach.

☑ **Modeling concepts & software development**

As a methodology, modeling is the systematic representation of the relevant features of a product or a system from particular viewpoints. Modeling is a *super-methodology* because the methods, techniques, and practices of modeling can be adapted and "inherited" by most other methodologies, even if these methodologies are otherwise incompatible.

Modeling is not a *single* concept but refers to a set of interrelated concepts: an individual model is an *artifact*; modeling can mean individual *techniques*, methods, or practices; modeling often uses a *language* composed of specialized *notations*; and, last but not least, modeling is a methodology that can have numerous implementations.

We can represent the same entity with very different models by choosing a set of characteristics: abstraction, point of view, scope, scale, and medium (visual, textual, mathematical, etc.).

Models are primarily for *communication* and understanding. The secondary function of modeling is for *construction* and maintenance. The second function, however, cannot work without the first. Furthermore, a product might work as expected, but **a complex product without good construction models is never good enough**.

Software modeling is shaped by four interweaved factors: ❶ how the real world is viewed, ❷ how software is defined, ❸ the process of development, and ❹ the modeling language. These factors are "interweaved": A change in one factor can have a domino effect on others and on the whole.

☑ **Project management concepts & tools**

Project management is the **methodology** for coping with *risk* by ensuring that ❶ the goal of the project is feasible, ❷ the project has a realistic plan for reaching its goal, ❸ we can track how the project is proceeding, and ❹ we can correct the course of the project if it deviates from the plan. There is no single methodology for managing projects, but many overlapping and complementary methodologies compete with each other.

We can define the project as a collection of related tasks that must be completed in a particular order and within a certain timeframe to achieve a specific goal. The *goal* of a project must be verifiable and the **scope** of the project defines the boundaries of the goal.

A project's lifetime is *finite*: It is not a continuous undertaking but has a beginning and an end. A project's **life cycle** is composed of five "umbrella" phases that in turn cover other steps or activities: ❶ scope the project, ❷ develop the project plan, ❸ launch the plan, ❹ monitor the project's progress, and ❺ bring the project to a conclusion.

A project is composed of related tasks that take place on one or more **activity threads** or **paths**. The most atomic task is called a *terminal element*, an undertaking that must be completed within a clearly specified timeframe. A *summary element* is a task that is composed of terminal elements or other summary elements. The longest path in a project is the **critical path**, which determines the *shortest* time required to complete the project.

The sequence (or the calendar) of a project's tasks is called its **schedule**. **Milestones** are significant events in the schedule. **Deliverables** are the verifiable results of tasks.

Project management tools are primarily focused on **modeling** the components and the flow of the project from various perspectives and with different levels of detail. One of the most popular and easiest tools for both scheduling and tracking the project flow is the **Gantt chart**. In its most basic form, the Gantt chart is a timeline or a calendar along which tasks are shown as horizontal bars.

Another popular tool is the **network diagram**, which displays tasks as networked boxes that contain a set of data about each task. Like the Gantt chart, the positioning of boxes indicates the sequence of tasks. Unlike the Gantt chart, however, the size of the box has no relation to the duration of the task and the tasks are not necessarily arranged horizontally.

One major challenge in applying project management to software development is that a project plan is *sequential* in concept, whereas software development is *iterative* in practice. Organizations, including the organization of projects, tend to be more or less *hierarchical* and *vertical*. On the other hand, development of new things, especially software development, tends to be *iterative* and *horizontal*.

6. Key Concepts

Activity Thread. Also called a **path**, a set of sequential tasks that may run parallel to other threads.

Ad Hoc. An approach to development without an overall theoretical framework.

Agile Methodologies. Methodologies that aim at being "adaptive" rather than "predictive." The best-known agile methodology is XP (Extreme Programming).

Architecture. The high-level structure of the product.

Capability Maturity Model (CMM). An approach that aims to ensure the maturity of the software development *process* within the organization. Essentially a rating and auditing framework that assigns an organization to one of five levels of maturity: initial (or *ad hoc*), repeatable, defined, managed, and optimizing.

CMM. See **Capability Maturity Model**.

Critical Path. The longest path (*see* **Activity Thread**) in a project that determines the shortest time required to complete the project.

Deliverable. In project management, the verifiable result of a task. A deliverable is a visible sign that a task is complete—any sign, be it the foundation of a building, a set of models, or a signature on a contract.

Dependency. In project management, the relationship of one task to another that must be completed before the task can start. The latter task is called the *predecessor*. A task might be dependent on multiple predecessors.

Deployment. Consists of ensuring the correct installation of the software, user training, creating help files and user manuals, packaging, etc.

Design. See **System Design**.

Design, Logical. Represents the solution (the product) without reference to specific technologies.

Design, Physical. Maps *logical modeling* to specific technologies.

Domain Analysis. Discovers ❶ the meaning of requirements within the context, ❷ concepts within the domain that are related to the problem and which can affect the solution, and possibly ❸ the consequences of the solution on the problem domain.

Duration. The amount of time between the start and the end of a task.

Feasibility Study. A study that determines whether it is possible—technically, financially, legally, or otherwise—to build a product.

Float. The amount of time that a task may be delayed in starting or completing without adversely affecting the project's schedule. Float is also called **slack time**. Tasks on the **critical path** cannot have float.

Functional Decomposition. A technique to discover the most atomic procedures from large-grain functions through a process of successive breakdowns.

Gantt Chart. A modeling tool for managing projects. A Gantt chart is a timeline or calendar along which tasks are shown as horizontal bars.

Implementation. Turns design into an actual product. In software development, programming is the most important component of this activity, but it is not the only one.

Incremental Approach. See **Iterative Approach**.

ISO-9000–3. A set of standards, similar to the **Capability Maturity Model** (CMM), that define the quality of the software development *organization*, rather than its products. Developed by the International Standards Organization.

Iterative Approach. A methodology to build the product through successive versions that are refined and expanded with each iteration. This approach is also known as **incremental**.

Life Cycle. Identifies the phases of the project from its inception to its completion. Development has a "life cycle" because its life is limited: It starts at a certain time and is completed or abandoned within a certain timeframe.

Maintenance. Solving problems that may emerge after the deployment of the software due to faulty requirements, insufficient analysis, defective design, or changes in the environment, whether in the business context or in the technological framework.

Methodology. ❶ A set of methods, rules, practices, procedures, techniques, and tools used to achieve a goal or ❷ the theoretical understating of the principles that determine how such methods, practices, tools, etc., are used. Methodology is a variable blend of two sources: a systematic generalization and abstraction of lessons learned from the past and ideas for improving on the past.

Milestone. A significant event in the life of the project. In project scheduling, a milestone appears as a task of *zero duration*.

Modeling. As a methodology, modeling is the systematic representation of the relevant features of a product or a system from particular perspectives. Modeling uses a set of techniques and methods and a language of specialized notations to produce artifacts in a variety of media.

Network Diagram. A modeling tool for project management that displays tasks as networked boxes that contain a set of data about each task. Unlike the Gantt chart, the size of the box has no relation to the duration of the task and the tasks are not necessarily arranged horizontally.

Object-Oriented Development. A methodology that is focused on developing software through analyzing and designing objects. It relies on object-oriented technology for building the actual product.

Path. See **Activity Thread**.

PERT Chart. A modeling tool for project management that displays the activities as the flow between events. (PERT stands for Program Evaluation and Review Technique.)

Problem Domain. The context in which the problem occurs and in which the solution must work.

Project. A collection of related tasks that must be completed in a particular order and within a certain timeframe to achieve a specific goal. A project is an organized process through which an idea is realized, a real-world problem is solved, an opportunity is exploited, a mission is accomplished, or a quest is fulfilled.

Prototyping. The creation of a working model of the essential features of the final product for testing and verification of requirements. *Evolutionary* prototyping is one in which the final product evolves from the successive refinement of the prototype. In *throwaway* prototyping, the prototype is discarded after verification of feasibility and/or its features.

Quality Assurance. The methodology to ensure that the product accurately satisfies requirements.

RAD. See **Rapid Application Development**.

Rapid Application Development (RAD). A development methodology based on selecting techniques, methods, practices, and procedures that result in faster development and shorter schedules.

Requirements Gathering. The activity that must arrive at a comprehensive and accurate set of functions that the product must perform and features that it must have to solve problems.

Resource. Anything—human, financial, material, etc.—that is needed or is employed by the project to achieve its goal.

Schedule. In project management, the organization and the sequencing of tasks.

Scope. The boundaries that define the goal of the project.

SDLC. See **System Development Life Cycle**.

Slack Time. See **Float**.

Solution Domain. The "space" containing elements that can be unrelated to the problem but which are needed to support the purpose and the functionality of the solution.

Spiral Model. A risk-oriented development approach that breaks a software project into mini-projects.

System Analysis. Analyzing the requirements to build a *conceptual* model of the solution (the product). Such a model represents *what* the solution must do, without identifying *how.*

System Design. Transforms the conceptual model of the product into a *concrete* one. Design itself consists of several activities, the most important of which are architecture, logical design, and physical design.

System Development Life Cycle (SDLC). Methodologies that view software development as primarily a project management process rather than a technical one.

Task. The basic building block of a project plan or schedule. The most atomic task is called a *terminal element*. A *summary element* is a task composed of terminal elements or other summary elements.

Waterfall Model. The oldest of SDLC methodologies, it specifies a set of sequential phases for software development: feasibility study, system investigation, system analysis, system design, implementation, and review and maintenance.

Work Breakdown Structure (WBS). A project management technique that starts with breaking the project into smaller activities and continues with breaking down the results until it arrives at the most atomic activities (or "terminal" elements). WBS decomposes the project into a hierarchy with different levels for activities. WBS can be modeled both textually or graphically.

7. REVIEW QUESTIONS

1. Differentiate technology from methodology and from method. Can you come up with an example that differentiates these concepts in a specific context, perhaps software development?
2. Name activities in software development covered by various methodologies. Can you explain why more than one methodology is needed in developing a piece of software?
3. Name a major difference between software development life cycle methodologies and *ad hoc* approaches to developing a software product.
4. In using an *ad hoc* approach, do we apply project management principles to software development? Elaborate on your answer.
5. Using the software development life cycle approach, do we apply project management principles to software development? Elaborate on your answer.
6. Compare and contrast prototyping and the incremental and iterative approach to software development.
7. How do you manage risk in the Spiral Model?
8. Explain the four phases of the Rapid Application Development (RAD) methodology. How do they differ from the "traditional" SDLC approach?
9. Name the strongest benefit and the greatest weakness of "agile" development methodologies.
10. What are the advantages and weaknesses of the CMM (Capability Maturity Model) approach?
11. What are the factors that shape software modeling?
12. What are the four concepts that are essential to the *extended* object-oriented approach to software development?
13. Define project management principles in the context of software development.
14. What are the deliverables and milestones of a software development project?
15. Can the project manager and the systems analyst be the same? Explain your answer.

8. RESEARCH PROJECTS & TEAMWORK

❶ By using the college library or the Web, have the team conduct research on various software development methodologies. Choose three methodologies: one structured (such as Waterfall), one object-oriented, and one agile. Answer the following questions.

- To what extent does each methodology cover the full project life cycle?
- Which methodology is the most robust? In other words, how well can it be adapted to suit different projects or circumstances?

- What is the underlying philosophy for each methodology?

❷ Find out why the Waterfall Model is being used *despite* its shortcomings. Who is using it?

❸ Agile methodologies stand in the opposite corner from the Waterfall methodology. Investigate various agile methodologies used by software development companies. Search the Web for reviews of these methodologies. Determine which one is the most popular, and identify some of its pros and cons.

❹ Do research on the Capability Maturity Model (CMM) and examine its different levels. How many companies in the United States have reached level 5?

Compare the numbers in the United States to those abroad, especially in India.

❺ There are more than 250 project management software packages available in the market. Find the top ten, evaluate the top five, and recommend one of them. The criteria for selecting the best product should include performance, ease of use, price, maintenance support, etc.

❻ Interview a project manager and find out about his or her detailed responsibilities. In other words, find out what a project manager does "day in and day out."

❼ Select a methodology. Write a short team paper describing its advantages and disadvantages.

9. SUGGESTED READINGS

While books on specific methodologies are many, books on methodology itself, even confined to one field, are few. An exception is *Information Systems Development: Methodologies, Techniques and Tools* (2nd Edition) by **D. E. Avison** and G. Fitzgerald (McGraw-Hill, 1998). The book offers a comprehensive and insightful view of software development methodologies. It is clearly laid out and highly readable. We hope new editions appear as methodologies keep piling up.

There is no "*the*" object-oriented approach to software development, even though concepts put forward by various authors are similar and often overlap. Therefore, you must pick the best of the breed. *The United Software Development Process* by **Ivar Jacobson**, Grady Booch, and James Rumbaugh (Addison-Wesley, 1999) describes an object-oriented approach and what we called in this chapter "methodology as product." The authors are the creators of the Unified Modeling Language (UML), and the product that implements their approach is Rational Rose. (Their company was later sold to IBM.) Note that the book is not for casual reading, but is an in-depth discussion of the Rational Unified Process (RUP).

Rapid Development: Taming Wild Software Schedules by **Steve McConnell** (Microsoft Press, 1996) is the best-known reference for Rapid Application Development, and it examines the approach extensively and with patience. It is not, however, limited to RAD. Many of the various concepts introduced in this chapter (and some that we would have introduced, had we more space) are discussed in the book, which is also very well-organized.

If you have become curious about agile methods and want more than what you can find on the Web, then you should read *Extreme Programming Explained* by

Kent Beck (Addison-Wesley, 2000), who is credited with creating Extreme Programming (XP) and is a signatory to the *Agile Manifesto.* Another book by Beck is *Planning Extreme Planning* (Addison-Wesley, 2000), co-authored with **Martin Fowler**, which aims to guide project managers in planning a development project based on XP.

As we said, XP is extremely controversial. *Extreme Programming Refactored: The Case Against XP* by **Matt Stephens** and Doug Rosenberg (APress, 20003) illustrates this point by its energetic arguments, summarized on the cover by promising that the book "cuts through the hype and tells 'the other side of the story' about XP."

The literature on project management is vast, even for specific contexts, but an effective and popular introductory book is *Effective Project Management* by **Robert K. Wysocki**, Robert Beck Jr., and David B. Crane (Wiley, 2000, 2nd Edition). If you are new to project management, a book like this a where you should start.

A book that aims to address the specific issues of an object-oriented approach to software development, including its iterative nature, is *Software Project Management: A Unified Framework* by **Walker Royce** (Addison-Wesley, 1998). It is most useful, however, *after* you have gained a rather good understanding of object-oriented analysis and design.

Writings that do not follow an expected formal structure are sometimes more powerful in conveying the lessons of experience than books that lay out theoretical arguments in an orderly manner. *The Mythical Man-Month: Essays on Software Engineering* by **Frederick P. Brooks, Jr.** (Addison-Wesley, 1995) has achieved an almost mythical place in this genre. The book is based on the experience of the author as the project manager for developing the IBM System/360 computer and OS/360, the first truly modern operating system. It might seem like an experience that belongs to prehistory, but the issues that he and his team encountered in developing a complex software system are as relevant today as they were then.

Software Craftsmanship: The New Imperative by **Pete McBreen** (Addison-Wesley, 2002) takes a view of software development that is almost opposite to ours. Nevertheless, we recommend reading it. The book is well-argued and eloquent. (At around 180 pages, it is also rather short, which these days is a virtue by itself.) A well-rounded knowledge in any field requires serious attention to *all* serious viewpoints.

Chapter 4

Gathering Requirements

1. OVERVIEW

Requirements identify the objectives that the information system must help its users to achieve. Gathering requirements is an ongoing process that provides system development with features and rules that it must implement to satisfy its objectives. The reliability and the correctness of requirements is dependent on their sources, the techniques that we employ to elicit and verify them, and their effective management.

▪□ Inception

▪□ **Requirements Discovery**

▪□ Development

Chapter Topics

➤ Define requirements.

➤ Requirements discovery vs. requirements gathering in general.

➤ Classifying requirements.

➤ Techniques for eliciting requirements.

➤ Sources of requirements.

➤ Managing requirements.

➤ Walden Medical Center case history, the main source for examples in this book.

Introduction

An information system is a product, and a product must have features that its customer wants in order to achieve specific objectives. Some features represent the functionality of the product, while others are required by the customer, by law, by standards, or by a number of other considerations or rules.

The task of requirements gathering is to collect and define all features that the information system must have in order to fulfill the objectives that the customer has set. Thus, even though it is not a glamorous task, requirements gathering must be done *thoroughly* and *correctly*; otherwise, we will build a product that might be stylish and impressive, but will not be what the customer wants.

Gathering requirements starts when the development project starts, but it is an ongoing activity, not a phase that is completed at a certain point in time. (See Figure 4.1.) During the process of development, the role of requirements gathering changes, both in quantity and in nature, but it does not entirely fade away until the information system is deployed, tested, and accepted by the customer.

Requirements discovery sets the boundaries of requirements gathering by defining its **scope**. Without clear boundaries, gathering requirements would be in danger of missing its destination: It would end up with either irrelevant or insufficient information. Requirements discovery is a finite activity that is conducted on the surface of requirements, unlike requirements gathering that must go increasingly deeper as development goes forward.

To arrive at the correct and relevant requirements, we must choose the right **sources** and employ relevant **elicitation techniques**. Talent and experience are, without a doubt, very important to the gathering requirements, but they must be sharpened by learning about techniques and by paying attention to detail.

Finally, requirements are useless to the development of the information system if they are not correctly documented or cannot be traced, identified, or verified. The task of *requirements management* is to ensure that requirements are well-organized, easy-to-locate, reliable, and consistent. Since it supports an ongoing activity, requirements management is an ongoing task as well.

Figure 4.1   Requirements Gathering: An Ongoing Activity

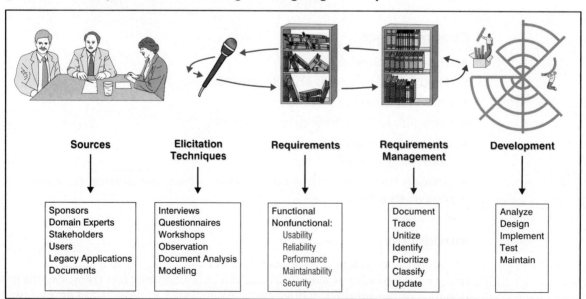

During the later stages of development the role of gathering requirements diminishes, but it never disappears.

2. Defining Requirements

> Requirements express those features of a product that enable its users to achieve specific objectives.

To gather requirements, we must first define what a requirement is. In the widely accepted meaning of the word, the task is easy: A requirement is whatever is required or necessary. In the context of software development, however, the term has a more specific meaning.

Requirements are whatever a product *does* and whatever a product *has* that its users need to reach their goals.

- The ATM system must allow the customer to withdraw cash from his or her account. (Among other things, the system must have cash and must be able to dispense it to achieve this goal.)
- The billing system must allow the account manager to inspect the billing activities of a client for the prior six months. (The system must have at least six month's worth of transactions at its disposal and must be able to report it.)
- The online registration system must allow the student to register for desired classes.

However, requirements specify not only what the users *can* do with the product, but also what they *cannot* do. In other words, requirements define specific **objectives** and **constraints** on those objectives.

- The user must be able to change his or her password (objective), but no password can be less than 6 characters or more than 15 characters long (constraint).
- The customer must be able to use a credit card to order books (objective), but the credit card must be in the customer's name (constraint).
- The student must be able to register for courses online (objective), but for each course the student must have passed prerequisite courses (constraint).

Requirements can be complex or simple in relative terms. That is, one requirement may translate into more than one requirement upon analysis. For example, to state that a student must be able to register online is to imply other requirements:

- The student must be able to find and select the desired course.
- The student must be able to drop a selected course.
- The system must verify the student's identity and refuse access to imposters.

Requirements can belong to two major categories: **functional** (what the product *does*) and **nonfunctional** (what attributes the product *has*). We will discuss the classification of requirements later in this chapter.

3. Requirements Discovery

> Requirements discovery identifies the scope and the major objectives of the system. Requirements gathering defines what is needed to reach those objectives.

A business expresses its need for a software system by declaring the **mission** of the system: sell merchandise online, manage inventory, track medical records, etc. To build an actual system, however, we have to go through a process of *drilling down* from the stated mission to what is actually needed to accomplish that mission.

In a model-driven and object-oriented approach to software development, we use models to capture, define, and represent requirements. But we need a "critical mass," a minimum amount of relevant concepts to start the process. We find this critical mass right below the mission but above the detailed and precise definitions that drive analysis and modeling.

The task of requirement discovery is to identify the *chief objectives* or the general outlines of what the system is expected to do and to be. Since this task lays the foundation for everything that follows, it decides the fate of the product and the development process.

Requirements discovery must be distinguished from requirements gathering in general.

- Requirements discovery is a *phase* that takes place at the start of the development process. Requirements gathering, on the other hand, is an *ongoing* pursuit that accompanies *every* analysis activity and, although its level usually drops as the system nears completion, it never disappears.
- Requirements discovery is very *wide but shallow* as it tries to identify the **scope** of the system. Requirements gathering goes *deep* within the boundaries that requirements discovery has identified. In other words, requirements discovery locates where we must "drill," while requirements gathering is the act of drilling down.
- Requirements discovery aims to elicit the *objectives* of a vast group of stakeholders and then verify them with business decision makers to separate "wish lists" from actual business goals. Requirements gathering acts on the belief that the goals are defined and we must identify *what is needed* to achieve the goals.
- Requirements discovery is more *chaotic* than requirements gathering because we have yet to ascertain what we are seeking. Requirements gathering is more *ordered* as we know what we are searching for.

If the mission of the project is to travel to the moon, requirements discovery identifies the major elements that are necessary for such a mission: a rocket that can carry astronauts to the moon and bring them back, a vehicle that will land on the moon and take off later, astronauts that we send to the moon, facilities for training the astronauts, etc. Requirements gathering then identifies what is necessary for each element within the mission. If our understanding of the objectives of the mission is incorrect—for example, if we are merely sending an unmanned vehicle—then gathering requirements about the training of the astronauts is a misguided effort and a costly failure.

Requirements discovery is crucial but rather simple provided you focus on the task at hand: Identify *only* the basic requirements and the scope of the system.

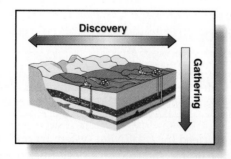

**Figure 4.2
Requirements:
Discovery Versus
Gathering**

To hit "pay dirt," you must first "prospect" the field before drilling down.

Once you have identified the boundaries, you have a real chance of finding and gathering relevant requirements.

4. CLASSIFYING REQUIREMENTS

Requirements fall into two broad categories: functional (or behavioral) and nonfunctional. Since both relate to the same product, they are interrelated and affect each other.

Functional Requirements

> Functional requirements specify the behavior of the system and the constraints on that behavior.

The most top-level requirements express the **mission** of the system. An information system, however, must provide specific services that helps it users to achieve specific goals. The sum of these services is called the *behavior* of the system, specified by a set of functional requirements.

> A mission specifies a strategic goal; functional requirements specify how the mission is to be accomplished by achieving tactical goals.

To accomplish each tactical goal, the system and its users must interact in a set of clearly defined steps. For example, the mission of an ATM system is to allow customers to perform many banking transactions through automated teller machines. The mission consists of several individual goals including, for example, `Get Cash`, `Deposit Check`, `Transfer Money`, `Get Account Balance`, etc. In turn, each goal requires a set of interactions between the customer and the system. For instance, to deposit a check, the ATM and the customer must perform the following steps.

☞ In the listing of functional requirements for ATM, certain customer responses are implicit in system actions. For example, we have not specified every button that the customer presses.

1. Customer swipes his/her banking card.
2. System asks for password.
3. Customer enters password.
4. If the password is correct, the system displays a menu of options from which a customer may pick one. (If the password is wrong, the system requests the password again. After three failures, the system blocks the account and asks the customer to contact the bank.)
5. Customer selects the `Deposit Check` option.
6. System displays a list of customer's accounts and requests the customer to select one account for deposit. (If customer has only one account, this step is skipped.)
7. System asks the customer to enter the amount of the check that is to be deposited.
8. System asks the customer to verify that the check and the deposit slip are in the deposit envelope and are ready for deposit.
9. After the customer's verification, the system turns on the rollers to reel in the deposit envelope into the deposit bin.
10. The system turns off the rollers after receiving the envelope.
11. The system asks the customer if a receipt is required. . . .

In these statements, any action performed by the system is a **functional requirement**. The main device for capturing functional requirements and modeling them is the *use case*, which we will discuss extensively in the chapters on behavioral modeling. (The previous statements illustrate the essence of a use case.)

Nonfunctional Requirements

[Leffingwell 2000, 237–242], [Armour 2001, 185–187], [Robertson 1999, 112–136], [Kulak 2000, 96–97]

> Nonfunctional requirements specify nonbehavioral properties of the system and the constraints on those properties.

Categories of nonfunctional requirements vary from product to product. For a software system, the following categories are the most common.

Usability

> Usability defines how the behavior of the system must be shaped to fit the users and their work environment.

Usability is *about* the behavior of the system, but it is *not* the behavior itself. It specifies how the behavior of the system must be tailored to the level of its users' expertise, the environment in which a system operates, the volume of input and output, etc.

☞ Video stores are rapidly disappearing. This example, however, applies to any store that wants to provide its customers with automated means to search its inventory.

One might argue that any system or any interface must be as "usable" as possible. But as noble as the idea is, it is both impractical and counterproductive. Consider the case of a video store that wants to install one or more terminals so its customers can find the movies they are looking for and verify that a copy is available. The scenario would have functional requirements such as the ability to search by name, director, actors, and/or the genre. But since the user is a customer and the customer cannot be trained and must interact with the system under less than optimal conditions, usability becomes an especially important issue.

- The interface must be designed for a touch-sensitive screen, not a keyboard.
- Icons and letters must be large enough for the customer to recognize without having to get too close.
- An online image of the keyboard would allow the customer to type by touching the screen.

Under normal circumstances, that is, working on a keyboard while sitting behind a desk, such an interface would annoy us. But it is the right one for its intended use.

To define the required usability of a system (or its subsystems), some of the common questions that must be addressed are as follows:

- Is the user expected to be an expert, a novice, or somewhere in between?
- Is training necessary (or possible) to use the system? If so, how much training is required?
- If users have been using a legacy system, should the new application follow the navigation of the existing one to save training costs and reduce disruption? (Or is it possible to do so?)
- Would the interface need help features? If so, to what level of expertise should the help be tailored?

Reliability

> Reliability requirements define the dependability of the system both in time and in the fulfillment of its functions.

In a perfect world, everything would be reliable. In this world, reliability—or as much of it as we can possibly get—costs money. The customer terminal in the video store example is a convenience; it is not essential to the business of the store. But for the same video store, renting movies and the system that tracks the rentals is essential: Without it the business stops. If the system administrator has to shut down the system for maintenance and upgrades, then it has to be done when the store is closed for business.

For an international airline, however, even a temporary suspension of ticket reservation is unacceptable. (It happens of course, but not according to an accepted plan.) Airline agents around the world must be able to reserve seats for flights from any origin to any destination. Even if the human resources subsystem of the airline is unavailable for a few hours and cannot print salary checks, ticket reservation must somehow work. As a result, we are talking about a distributed *and* fail-safe system—which means a very large investment. Such an investment is feasible and necessary for an international airline, but not for a supermarket.

Reliability requirements generally relate to issues such as availability (in terms of time), mean time between failures (MTBF), and accuracy. If such issues are raised *beyond* a commonly accepted level, then the analyst must define them *exactly*. For a financial system, two digits of accuracy to the right of the decimal point is usually enough; for guiding a rocket that lands a robot on the surface of Mars, accuracy must be higher.

Performance

> Performance requirements specify the response time and the input-output volume that the system can handle within a particular timeframe.

☞ **Capacity** is a nonfunctional category that is related to performance. For example, how many users can a system handle before its response time becomes unacceptable? How many transactions?

The faster any system performs, the better. But, again, it costs money to make a system go *faster*. For a telephone company, printing telephone bills may take hours or days. But for our video store example, even minutes would try the patience of the customer who is trying to find a movie.

It might seem that performance is simply a hardware issue: Install faster computers or faster networks and performance will improve. True, but this is irrelevant to improving the performance of one system or subsystem. If an application is to run faster compared to others, then programmers and database designers have to work hard and long to make it happen.

And again, when "good" performance is required, the analyst must make sure that the requirement is defined in quantitative terms.

Maintainability

> Maintainability requirements specify the ability of the software to be modified and enhanced.

Some applications are more prone to change than others. Often this is due to future plans—a wish list, if you will. A car dealership may have many branches, but wants to install the pilot project in just one store—either as a result of budgetary constraints or to debug the system, or both. But the plan is that the system will eventually find cars in other branches as well. Better yet, perhaps the system would connect with other dealerships in a network so they can exchange customers—to their mutual benefit—by finding the car they are looking for.

At other times, changes to a software system are required as a result of what it does. Any application that handles taxes is subject to changes beyond the control of the programmer, the designer, the analyst, the business, or even a single government. If a company is operating in the United States, sales taxes are a familiar pattern; therefore, we can provide for changes in the sales tax rates by looking up the rates in tables that are maintained by the users. If the sales happen in Europe, then we have to provide for VAT (Value-Added Tax). But governments are notorious for finding creative ways to tax that no designer can foresee or provide for.

On the whole, it is difficult to judge how helpful specifying maintainability will be. In some cases, we can make certain allowances for change, like relying on tables instead of hard-coded values (which is a good practice anywhere, anytime). In other cases, knowing about possible future issues can be of value.

☞ *Components* are discussed in Chapter 15, Components & Reuse. *Coupling* is discussed in Chapter 16, Architecture.

One *architectural* approach to better maintainability is to construct the software system from components with distinct responsibilities and relative independence (or *loosely coupled* components). This approach is an important outgrowth of the object-oriented idea.

Security

> Security requirements specify the rights of access to the services of a system, the manner of access to those services, and the tracing of interaction with the system.

☞ We will discuss behavioral modeling in Chapters 6 and 7.

In its most basic level, security requirements specify who can access a system or, to be more precise, the services of the system. Behavioral modeling (or *use cases*) that describes the interaction between user *types* and the system is a reliable source for specifying *role* security.

There is, however, a wide range of nonfunctional requirements that are related to security. They include:

- **Does data need to be encrypted?** We do not want to send or receive unencrypted data for a credit card transaction.
- **Do we need to log certain events?** If a patient's appointment with a hospital is cancelled, most likely management would want to know the reason. Did the patient cancel the appointment? Was the medical staff absent? Did lab equipment break down?
- **Do we need an audit trail?** While logs record an event, audit trails record changes to the value of one attribute or a set of attributes. If the price of merchandise in a supermarket is changed, we may want to see what the price was before it was changed and who changed it.

Requirements are not self-evident. They must be captured by a set of tools and techniques that have varying degrees of effectiveness and must be wielded differently depending on the situation. Some tools need more skills than others, but some skills in eliciting requirements can be sharpened by learning and experience.

Interviews

> The interview is the most flexible and direct tool for eliciting requirements. It also is more prone to misunderstanding and failure than any other technique.

Interview with stakeholders of the system—users, sponsors, and domain experts—is an indispensable tool not only for its verbal responses but also because it allows one to observe and learn from nonverbal reactions: attitudes, body language, and emotional overtones. These nonverbal connotations put the requirements into a human context that must be taken into account to build a successful information system.

The interview is also a sensitive tool: It is very flexible but exactly because of its flexibility it can lead us to blind alleys. Since an interview is limited by a timeframe it is also a precious commodity, the use of which must be planned with great care.

Interviewing needs a great amount of "people skill" and experience, but there are things that we must know and actions that we must take to increase its chances of success.

Scope vs. Detail

> Early interviews in the requirements gathering process have a broad scope, while later ones are defined by more focus on detail.

Adopting a wide scope in early interviews—the discovery phase—is both necessary and advantageous: necessary because we are yet to acquire enough knowledge to ask probing questions; advantageous because when we *are* able to ask questions that go deep, we can place the responses in a context that renders them meaningful beyond the confines of their literal meaning.

As Figure 4.3 illustrates, a wider scope means that the interview must be more "structured," whereas to arrive at useful details the interview must be more "focused." These two terms need explanation because "structured" does not mean that the interview can lose its focus and "focused" does not signify that the interview is completely freeform. Rather, they are the two extremes of a spectrum.

- *Structured.* An interview is structured when the flow of an interview can be planned according to a script. In a structured interview, **we generally know what types of responses we are going to receive**. Therefore, we can categorize the questions and follow a script.

During the *discovery* of requirements, the scope is unknown; we do not know the nature of the project, except in the broadest and most general terms. Paradoxically, this ignorance allows us to structure the interview and control its

**Figure 4.3
Interview:
Scope Versus
Detail**

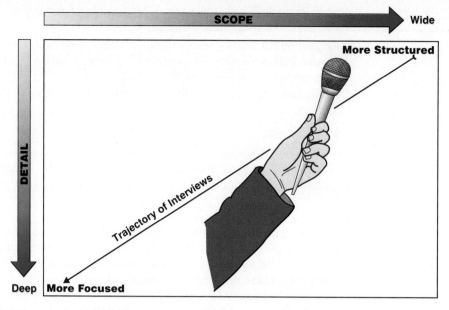

The trajectory of interviews generally matches the passage from requirements discovery to requirements gathering in general.
[Graham 2001, 456–457]

flow: Who is the interviewee? What is the environment in which the information system must work? What are the expectations of the interviewee from the product? What problems does the solution hope to solve? And so on. (See "Building Blocks of an Interview.")

• *Focused.*   An interview is focused when the questions center around one topic or a few related topics. In a focused interview, **we know the direction but not the exact responses that we will find by following that direction**. The only thing we have is the beginning of a thread that we intend to follow. What transpires afterwards is the result of roughly *unscripted* interactions between the interviewer and interviewee. As a result, a focused interview needs an interviewer who can compensate for the shortage of structure by his or her skill in directing the flow of discussions.

When we have discovered and verified a broad outline of requirements, we must gather specific and detailed requirements—detailed enough so we can actually build a product by following them. Such an undertaking is only possible if we ask *focused* questions: How exactly is a function to be achieved? What is the unambiguous definition of a term or a concept?

Building Blocks of an Interview

> To maximize the benefits of an interview and control its flow, the interviewer must construct the interview from building blocks with predefined scope and identifiable goals.

In an interview, the initiative is always with the interviewer. Unquantifiable skills such as fast reaction time and the ability to detect and follow unpredictable leads are priceless in some situations, but nothing can save an interview if the interviewer is not prepared.

Interviews for gathering requirements follow certain outlines that can be more or less categorized into building blocks with identifiable features and goals. By planning the interview around a selected set of these building blocks, the analyst can ensure the best possible use of time and arrive at the best possible outcome.

Figure 4.4 illustrates the most distinguishable building blocks for gathering requirements about an information system product. It is unlikely that a single interview will consist of all building blocks. Moreover, this view of building blocks is illustrative of their scope rather than their depth. For example, questions about the current environment and general expectations would stop at a certain stage, while closed question and "probes" would dwarf every other category as requirements gathering moves forward.

One important point to remember is that the actual building blocks are much finer and more intertwined than a listing of the categories can illustrate. For instance,

Figure 4.4   Interview: The Building Blocks

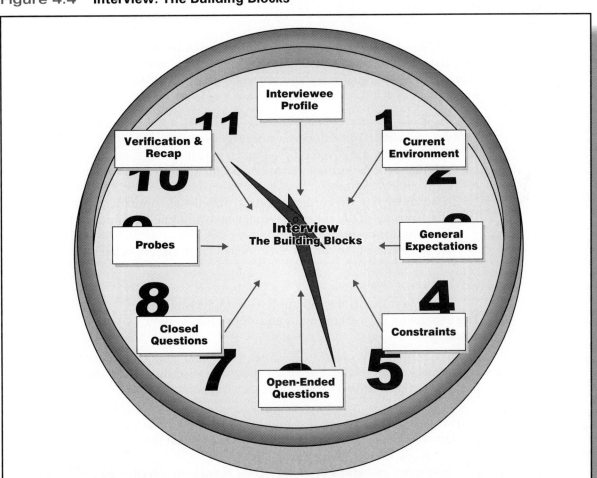

An interview may consist of any number of building blocks. Notice, however, that time is a constraint on any interview.

a question about constraints might need to be followed by probes and closed questions to arrive at a satisfactory conclusion.

❶ *Interviewee Profile.* By establishing a profile of the interviewee, the analyst can better evaluate his or her responses on other topics. Usually the answers to most of the following questions are available *before* the interview, and time would be saved by gathering them beforehand.

- Name.
- Position.
- Department.
- How long with the company.
- How long in the current position.
- Supervisor.
- **Responsibilities**, including what is produced by the interviewee, co-workers, department, or company.
- Extent of the interviewee's **expertise** in working with information systems.
- Other **personal data** that may be relevant, such as experience in previous positions or with previous employers, education, etc.

---

❷ *Current Environment.* The existing conditions are our starting point, even if the plan is to discard or replace parts of it. Unless an enterprise is to be established along with its information system, understanding how it functions *now* is essential for the success of any future plans.

- What software and hardware is **currently used**.
- What **activities** are covered by system(s) in place.
- **Advantages** of the current system(s), including both functional and nonfunctional features.
- **Disadvantages** of the current system(s), functional or nonfunctional.
- What elements of the current environment (including hardware and software platforms) are **necessary to keep**.
- What elements of the current environment are **desirable to keep**.

Some questions in this set apply only to decision makers (or their delegates). The experience of working with an information system, however, applies to all users.

❸ *General Expectations.* Responses to this set of inquiries must provide a general framework for the features of the product—what they should be and what purpose they would serve.

- The areas of business activities (or "**domains**") that the new information system, or its subsystems, must cover.
- Description and **scope** of each business domain involved. ("Scope" is the sum total of a domain's activities, although sometimes it is necessary to define scope in the negative, meaning what the domain does *not* do.)

- **Scope** of the planned system, or its subsystems: what it must do for what business domains (and what it must *not* do).
- Expectations about **legacy system**(s)—if any: replacement and migration or cooperation. In simpler terms, does the new software have to live with the old software (in whole or in part), or would it replace the old (in whole or in part)?
- **Required** features in the new (software) product.
- **Desired**, but not required, features of the new software.
- **Description of** *each* **feature**, required or desired.
- **Problems and/or opportunities** that demand each feature. In other words, why the new software is necessary.
- The **priority** of implementation for each component and each feature.

To formulate effective questions for this set, one must be familiar with the relationship between problems and solutions, between problem space and solution space, and between product specifications and requirements. The next chapter, Domain Analysis, explores these issues.

❹ *Constraints.* Asking questions about limitations must not be an afterthought: Constraints separate fantasies from actual products. Moreover, questions about constraints cannot be limited to any list. They are not about requirements in a narrow sense. They do not concern "features" but explore those issues of the environment (both for the development of the product and for the product itself) that most people would rather avoid, but must not be allowed to. Essentially, you must ask: What can derail the development? What can hurt the product even if every requested feature is implemented? In what kind of "real world" must the product operate?

- What are the **legal** or **regulatory** constraints on the features of the product?
- What are the **security** constraints?
- What are the **time** constraints?
- What are the **budgetary** constraints?
- What compromises in **performance** and **quality** are acceptable?
- What difficulties will the **users** have in adjusting to the (new) system?
- What level of **user support** is required or desired?
- What level of **operational support** is required or desired?
- What level of **maintenance support** is required or desired?

❺ *Open-Ended Questions.* A question is open-ended when, generally, the response is not expected to follow a strict boundary. Examples include:

- How can a new system help you in your work?
- What do you think about the current system?
- What problems do you think deployment of the new system would create?

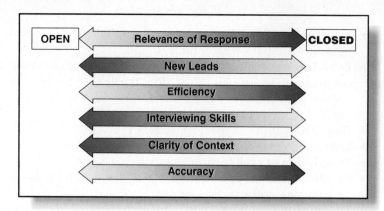

Figure 4.5 Questions: Open-Ended Versus Closed

Open-ended question are better at finding new leads and clarifying the context but require better interviewing skills. Closed question elicit more relevant responses, are more efficient, and provide more accurate responses.

Source: Kendall, Kenneth E.; Kendall, Julie E., *Systems Analysis And Design*, 4th, © 1999. Electronically reproduced by permission of Pearson Education, Inc., Upper Saddle River, New Jersey.

Compared to closed questions (discussed next), open-ended questions have certain **advantages**:

- *Provide leads.* They can provide us with leads to issues and concepts of which we have been unaware.
- *Clarify context.* Both the interviewer and the interviewee can place other questions in a context familiar to the interviewee. As a result, the interviewer can understand the interviewee better, while the interviewee can relate more to the purpose of the interview.
- *Provide new openings.* When prepared questions are not producing the desired results, open-ended questions can provide the interviewer with a second chance.

And of course there are **disadvantages**:

- *Are time-consuming.* By asking open-ended questions, we are effectively giving the control of the response to the interviewee and the interviewee can take any direction that he or she prefers. (Interrupting the interviewee is never a good practice.)
- *Need high skills.* To control the flow and to spot useful leads, the interviewer must be highly skilled and swift in deduction.
- *Result in unfocused detail.* The relevance of detail to the development of an information system is not decided only by the scope of the project, but also by *when* the detail is useful. The interviewee, of course, cannot be expected to see the world through the eyes of a systems analyst.

⑥ *Closed Questions.* Unlike open-ended questions, closed questions require the interviewee to give answers that fall within a predictable range. Examples include:

- How many employees use the current system?
- What is the definition of "registration"?
- How many days can the customer keep a rented DVD?
- How is the penalty for late payment calculated?

Compared to open-ended questions, closed questions have certain **advantages**:

- *Save time.* The interviewee may or may not have the answer to a closed question but, in either case, we do not have to waste time looking for clues.
- *Do not need high skills.* The interviewer must recognize the sufficiency of the response, but does not have to react fast to the unknown. The danger of losing control over the flow of the interview is also minimal.
- *Serve a specific purpose.* Behind a closed question there is usually a task to be done: a business rule must be defined, a model has to built, a feature must be coded. In other words, we usually have a clear and present need for the response to a closed question.

The disadvantages of closed questions are generally the reverse of the advantages for open-ended questions:

- *Provide a limited scope of detail.* A closed question, by nature, seeks specific detail. In response, the interviewee is not free to roam into details that do not seem related to the question.
- *Do not engage the interviewee.* As seen by the interviewer, closed questions are to the point. The interviewee, however, might miss the point since he or she cannot place the question in a comprehensible context.
- *May put undue pressure on the interviewee.* In an interview, a closed question means "answer correctly and answer now!" An accumulation of failures to answer is likely to stupefy and/or embarrass the interviewee. If there are too many questions that require exact answers or prior research, consider using a questionnaire instead of an interview.

❼ *Probes.* Probes are requests that the interviewer poses to clarify, expand, or deepen concepts expressed by the interviewee. Also called "follow-ups," they generally require the interviewer to be knowledgeable about the subject and fast in making deductions, even though the probe itself might be simple. (Repeating "why" indiscriminately after every response might be effective in a comedy, but it is bound to exasperate the interviewee.) Examples include:

- Specify each step in registration.
- Why? (Or why [the assertion by the interviewee]?)
- Who is included in "medical staff"?
- You said that if a customer has a "special checking" account, deposited checks are cleared immediately. Is there a limit to the amount that is cleared?
- Would you give some examples of how returned merchandise is processed?

Probes are often used when the interviews are focused, that is, when specific facts and rules are required.

❽ *Verification & Recap.* Time permitting, it is always a good practice to end an interview by verifying the responses of the interviewee and the conclusions of the interviewer. This practice is especially helpful when there is a semantic gap between the interviewer and the interviewee: Either the business concepts are unfamiliar to the interviewer or the questions demand the interviewee to think in unfamiliar contexts. (The analyst must do his or her best to speak the language that the business speaks. But the problem is *not* always terminology: As we go from business territory towards system territory, even familiar terms tend to acquire unfamiliar implications.)

If time is short, then the next best thing is to summarize the interview and send it to the interviewee as a questionnaire. All requirements and business rules eventually must be verified by *all* relevant stakeholders. The difference is that we save a round-trip by performing the verification at the end of interview (or during the course of it).

Verification has a simple format. Ask the interviewee to reply with a simple "yes" or "no" to your conclusions:

> • When a customer with a "special checking" account deposits a check, the amount that is immediately cleared will be less than or equal to the amount of revolving credit. (Yes/No.)

Of course, if the answer is "no," the interviewee must offer a correction or an explanation, and the interviewer must correct the conclusion. (The "no" reply may trigger another round of discussion and ripple through other conclusions.)

Planning

> Interviews constitute a limited resource; therefore, they must be carefully planned to achieve maximum gain.

Even if the analyst has unlimited time at his or her disposal, the interviewees certainly do not. The more valuable a source of knowledge is, the more likely it is that the source's time is in high demand by the daily operations of the *business*. Moreover, the value of the interviewee to the process of requirements specification varies with the timing: A wider scope of knowledge is more useful at the start of requirements gathering (or discovery), while a more focused expertise becomes more valuable as the scope of requirements becomes clearer.

The tasks that must be performed prior to an interview are generally what you would expect them to be:

> • Learn as much as possible about the subject by reading background material and asking prudent questions in informal meetings with knowledgeable sources.
> • Learn as much as possible about the interviewee.
> • Outline the general structure of the interview, as far as possible, by selecting the building blocks that fit the purpose of the interview.
> • Create as many closed questions as possible. Closed questions expect precise answers and are the best way to use limited time.
> • Roughly estimate the time necessary to conduct the interview. (Do not forget to allocate time for recap and verification.) If you have more questions than time, then prioritize questions.

The point is to do them. To reiterate:

> Before an interview, learn as much as possible about both the interviewee and the subject of the interview.

The need to know about the subject of a dialogue is rather obvious, but knowing about the person whom we are going to interview is equally important. Who the interviewee is decides what questions to ask and how to evaluate the answers given:

- *The Depth and the Breadth of Knowledge.*   Is the experience of the interviewee focused on one subject or does it encompass a wide variety of areas within the enterprise? A limited scope of experience does not automatically devaluate the interviewee's answers. As we previously argued (see "Scope vs. Detail"), we start the discovery process with a general but shallow view of the requirements but must narrow our focus and delve into details as the process goes forward. Interviewing a person with a narrow but detailed knowledge is more productive as we go deeper into requirements than when we start.
- *Relevance.*   Does the interviewee have direct experience with the subject under discussion? Responses of a person who is *not* directly involved in an area of activity are a double-edged sword: On the one hand, it might be an inaccurate opinion; on the other hand, an outsider can sometimes make shrewd observations that has escaped those who are directly involved in a job. So wait for the actual interview before you decide to ask questions that are removed from the interviewee's area of expertise. (You may write down some questions to ask if the interviewee proves to be sound in mind and judgment.)
- *Commitment.*   A committed person would go the extra mile to be helpful, accurate, and honest. This quality is, however, difficult to gauge beforehand. The length of the interviewee's employment may be a positive indication. (On the other hand, the person might be what is unkindly called "dead wood.") Usually you can get an impression by paying attention to the feelings of co-workers towards the interviewee. But reserve judgment: Negative impressions are easy to form and can doom an interview even before it starts. (Also, a person's sense of loyalty will be harshly tested if the person believes—rightly or wrongly—that his or her job is in danger because of *your* work.)
- *Overlooked Needs.*   There are humble workers that perform the same humble routines day in and day out. Their knowledge is not considered to be either wide or deep. They might prove to be the most resistant to changes that an information system would bring. Nevertheless, understanding what they do and improving their performance (and their lot) may prove enormously beneficial to the business. Listen to them carefully and make allowances for their wordings. More often than not, they express needs that are important.

Questionnaires

Questionnaires are the second choice for requirements elicitation and the first choice for requirements verification.

In gathering requirements, questionnaires can play two roles: *elicitation* and *verification*. As a tool for requirements elicitation, questionnaires are a poor replacement for interviews. As a verification tool, however, they are superior.

Questionnaire as Elicitation Tool

> The building blocks of a questionnaire as an elicitation tool are generally the same as in interviews, but the flow is inflexible.

For various reasons—lack of availability, time difference due to geographic location, number of stakeholders—you may not be able to use interviews for elicitation. As a result, questionnaires become the only choice at your disposal.

Questionnaires, however, have disadvantages. Because they do not happen in real time and lack direct interaction, even via voice, they are inflexible, open to misunderstanding, and cannot easily provide new leads. (See Figure 4.6.) Therefore, if you *have* to elicit requirements through questionnaires, you must take certain steps to compensate for some of their shortcomings.

❶ *Make the assumptions that underlie the questions as clear as possible.* Your next chance to clarify any misunderstanding is another questionnaire away. If assumptions apply to a set of questions, clarify them in the preamble to the questionnaire or its sections and subsections. If it applies to one question, then clarify it in the body of the question itself.

❷ *Craft your questions carefully.* In an interview, you may adjust your wording in response to the reactions of the interviewee. In a questionnaire, such an adjustment is impossible.

❸ *Avoid questions of dubious relevance.* If you are not certain that the question is relevant to the stakeholder, or the question might become irrelevant by a preceding response, then ensure that the respondent is aware of your understanding. (The general format for formulating such a question is: If [the assumption applies], then [the question]?)

❹ *Avoid super-questionnaires.* The interval between sending questionnaires and receiving responses may seem painfully slow. Besides, free from the pressure of the interview, respondents may be lax in meeting deadlines. Thus there is the temptation to load the questionnaire with every question that comes to mind. Avoid this temptation with all your power. It would certainly

**Figure 4.6
Questionnaires:
Weaknesses and
Strengths**

Weaknesses

Inflexibility
The flow cannot be changed based on responses.

Misunderstanding
If the question is misleading, there is no chance for immediate clarification.

Limited Interaction
Neither side can learn from the other side's non-verbal or implied responses.

Difficulty of Expression
Talking is easier for most people than writing.

Strengths

Verification
Is the most exact tool for verification.

Traceability
The source of the requirement can be accurately identified.

Relevancy
The respondent is more likely to remain in the boundaries defined by the question.

Structure of Expression
The respondent has more time to ponder the question and prepare the answer.

Questionnaires are most useful when questions are focused.

dishearten the respondents. More importantly, it is counterproductive: Regardless of the tools, the *right* way to gather requirements is iterative and cumulative. Wide-scope requirements must be analyzed before any attempt is made to find more detailed and focused requirements. In other words, each round of gathering requirements is dependent on the preceding round. Therefore, first send out a relatively small questionnaire. Then, when the responses are back, put together a second one that takes those responses into account. Continue with further questionnaires until the job is done. An additional benefit to this version of the "divide and conquer" method is the next consideration.

❺ *Build up the respondent's trust.* By introducing yourself to the respondents with a small but relevant questionnaire, you give them a chance to build confidence in you and in themselves. They will have a more positive outlook towards your later inquiries if they find your first questionnaire relevant and convenient to answer. (Never underestimate first impressions, even if you are physically absent.)

Questionnaires have one important advantage over interviews: The respondent can ponder the answers carefully. Not everyone is comfortable with interviews and, even among those who are, not everyone is able to produce facts and details on demand. With a questionnaire, the respondent does not have to worry about looking good, talking eloquently, or appearing to be in command of the situation.

Questionnaire as Verification Tool

> The questionnaire is the most traceable tool for the verification of requirements.

The questions that we include in a questionnaire for the verification of a requirement must follow a rather rigid format: ❶ a unique ID for the requirement, ❷ a concise definition of one—and only one—requirement, ❸ a space for a True or False answer, ❹ a field for comments by the respondent, and perhaps ❺ a multiple-choice field for assigning priority.

A questionnaire may be a blunt tool for gathering requirements, but it is the most reliable one for *verification* of requirements. The reasons are as follows:

❶ *The definition of requirements are mature.* By the time you need to verify a requirement, a valuable amount of requirements gathering has already been done. By providing a written, "black-and-white" definition that can be accepted or rejected, you concentrate the mind of the respondent. The vagueness and the blind alleys of oral discussions will not intrude.

❷ *The flow of verification is the most traceable* The stakeholders and development team can point to an exact answer to an exact definition as the source of their conclusions and decisions.

❸ *Questionnaires are politically convenient.* Finger pointing (or perhaps a real or an expedient loss of memory) is an unfortunate fact of any group undertaking. When things go wrong, members of the development team must be able to show that their decisions have been well-founded.

A verification questionnaire often initiates another round of requirements gathering. "False" answers and/or comments by the respondents indicate that the definitions involved are in need of revision.

Elicitation Workshops

> Elicitation workshops are the most powerful but also the most expensive tool for requirements elicitation.

Elicitation workshops are commonly referred to as *Joint Application Development* (JAD) workshops. This technique brings together all the stakeholders in one room and, through a series of intense but focused interactions, attempts to get a consensus on the requirements. Depending on the size and the complexity of the information system and the number of stakeholders involved, the process could last from one or two days to a week or more. It may require a professional facilitator or it may be conducted by a skilled employee.

The primary objective of the elicitation workshop is to give all stakeholders a chance to participate in achieving a common goal: building an information system that meets the requirements of the enterprise.

The major benefits of elicitation workshops are as follows:

❶ *Time Efficiency.* The potential disagreements on requirements are discussed and ironed out within a minimum timeframe and without multiple round-trips.

❷ *Dispute Settlement.* Political issues and legitimate disagreements are brought into the open and dealt with in the most beneficial manner to the development team and the organization.

❸ *Positive Attitude.* By participating in the workshop and expressing their opinions, the stakeholders will form a positive ownership attitude towards the upcoming product. Later, this attitude will be a great help in adopting the system by the enterprise.

But the benefits materialize only if the workshop is well-planned and well conducted.

Planning the Workshop

> Select participants carefully and help them to help the workshop.

[Leffingwell 2000, 103–111]

Planning a workshop is hard work. It needs teamwork and assistance from professionals in organizing events. The following pointers are not complete, but can point you in the right direction.

❶ *Educate stakeholders.* Make sure that stakeholders understand the benefits of the workshop, are willing to spend the required time, and are prepared to participate in discussions.

❷ *Select the right participants.* Depending on the scope of the information system—whether it is enterprise-wide or more limited—request the participation of *both* decision makers and knowledgeable employees. If only decision makers participate, they might not get the right information to make the right decisions. And if only knowledgeable employees are present, the crucial decisions are left unmade. (And, of course, choose a qualified facilitator who can work with both groups, will not be intimidated by the bosses, and is sympathetic towards lower-level participants. Note that this is not easy.)

❸ *Do not overlook logistics.* It is preferable that the workshop be convened outside the workplace to minimize distractions. Find a room with proper lighting and adequate equipment and facilities: computers, flip charts, etc. A U-shaped seating arrangement is better than rows as it helps to give an impression (or useful illusion) of equality and openness to the participants. (And do not forget travel arrangements and accommodations, if necessary.)

❹ *Help participants to prepare.* Send the participants "warm-up" materials in advance of the workshop. These materials fall into two categories: ❶ information on the specific project (which can include the preliminary results of requirements gathering), and ❷ encouragement to bring new ideas to the workshop.

Conducting the Workshop

> The conductor of the workshop must encourage free discussion of ideas without losing control of its goal.

Running an elicitation workshop requires an exceptional combination: a politician with good intentions, patience, persistence, and decisiveness. Political tensions, power struggles, and conflicts of interest among stakeholders often create a highly charged atmosphere in the workshop. But if the workshop goes well, the results are worth the trouble.

The most important feature of the workshop is the *brainstorming* process. Done correctly, it fosters a creative and positive environment and could entice valuable input from all stakeholders. The major benefits of brainstorming are as follows:

- It encourages "out-of-the-box" thinking; that is, by challenging and inspiring each other, the participants are likely to go beyond conventional boundaries.
- Full solutions can emerge from the accumulation of ideas: One participant may build upon another's proposal or streamline it.
- The scope of the solutions will go beyond the narrow interests of individual groups.

The conductor (or the "facilitator") of the workshop must have truly professional skills. Among the responsibilities of the conductor, the following are the most important.

- Establish a professional and objective tone for the meetings.
- Establish and enforce the rules.
- Introduce the meeting's goals and agenda.
- Manage the meeting and keep the participants focused.
- Facilitate the process of decision making and accord building, but avoid taking sides in the arguments.
- Make certain that all stakeholders have an equal chance in voicing their opinions.
- Control disruptive and unproductive behavior with subtlety but decisiveness.

Field Trips & Observation

> Field trips provide valuable requirements where workflow is rich in action and interaction.

Professionals in software development must develop software for a wide range of human activities in which they are not professionals, cannot be professionals, and cannot hope to be professionals. Nevertheless, they must provide software that either automates or facilitates at least some aspects of those activities. Therefore, they must pry from others the information they need.

In most elicitation techniques, we ask the stakeholders to interpret the world in which they work. Field trips and observation of the workflow afford us a chance to interpret that world by ourselves.

Seldom do we encounter a stakeholder who can describe a complex workflow and its requirements in a narrative that is rich enough for a comprehensive analysis. This should not be unexpected since the stakeholder must generalize his or her own everyday tasks and experiences, and express them in abstract terms. But performing tasks and expressing them through abstract concepts are not the same thing.

The value of the field trip depends on the goal of the observation, the nature of what is observed, and the qualifications of the observer.

The Goal of the Observation

> The value of observing a workflow depends on the goal of the observation.

A surgical team is about to perform a complicated heart surgery and you are invited to observe and learn. But observe what and learn what? The goal decides what must be observed.

- A novice nurse must observe what surgical equipment the nurses prepare, how they arrange it, and how they cooperate with surgeons.
- A lab technician must observe how the technicians operate monitoring equipment and how and when they communicate with doctors.
- A student of anesthesiology must observe how the anesthesiologist administers the proper doses and keeps the patient stable.
- A resident must observe the surgeons.
- A medical efficiency expert must observe the combined flow to make recommendations for the shape and the arrangement of the operation room.

In these cases the goals are different, but in each case the observer is aware of his or her goal. Without a goal, the value of observation drops precipitously. And, as we saw, "how a heart surgery is done" does not provide an unambiguous goal.

How, then, is the analyst to define a goal that maximizes the value of observation? The answer is what we mentioned under "Functional Requirements" and will discuss extensively in Chapters 6 and 7 on *use cases*. A use case identifies a *goal* that is of value to a particular user class (called the *actor*) and the exact steps (called the *scenario*) that are required to reach that goal.

Armed with a use case, the analyst can observe with a *purpose*. The observation may add to the "scenario," change it, or invalidate it. But that is the function of observation.

The Observed

> The more evident the elements of a workflow are, the more useful is the observation.

Observation needs something that can be observed. If you are hired to automate all or part of an automobile assembly line, observation will yield a treasure trove of requirements. On the other extreme, watching a writer at work would not help you in writing a software application that analyzes writing styles. (Such software applications are not hypothetical; they exist and, once in a while, make the news by identifying a writer who had hoped to remain anonymous.)

In between the two extremes, observation will provide a varying degree of useful requirements. The rule is: The more a workflow is based on concepts and thinking, the less is the value of observation (and *vice versa*.)

The Observer

> The observation is wasted if the observer is unqualified.

If we are not a surgeon and we try to learn heart surgery by observing an operation, we won't. Certainly, a systems analyst does not observe the workflow to take the job of a surgeon, a stockbroker, or even a mail clerk, but some aspects of "qualifications" still apply to observation for analysis.

The chief qualification is that the analyst must be prepared *before* the observation. The observation itself must confirm, reject, or modify the prior knowledge, but it must not be the first encounter between the analyst and the concepts behind the actions that are to be observed.

The second qualification, which has a strong bond to the first, is the observer must not disrupt what he or she is observing. To ask for clarification is justified; to ask questions that preparation should have answered beforehand is not.

The third qualification is a negative one: The observer must not allow preconceptions to distort the observation. Prior experience helps, but it can have counterproductive effects as well. Enterprises work differently, define concepts differently, and have different expectations, *even if everything appears the same*. In short, a good observer does not take anything for granted.

Modeling

> Models for elicitation and verification of requirements must be understandable to stakeholders.

A model-driven approach to software development is becoming increasingly popular. But besides acting as blueprints for the developers, models can also be used as powerful tools for the verification of requirements. And verification, by nature, is elicitation by another name: It invites comments and criticisms that, in turn, give birth to new requirements.

[Zachman 1987]

A large part of this book is about modeling, but the kind of modeling that is more for software developers and less for business stakeholders. The stakeholders, on the other hand, need models that have become known as "owner's view."

An owner's view, in short, is a drawing or a word chart that is primarily aimed at *business* stakeholders. Since it generally illustrates concepts, it should be called "conceptual," but it is not necessarily a type of conceptual model that we will introduce later in this section (though some of the formal models may be useful to "owners" as well). And such a model should not be expected to provide an "engineering

**Figure 4.7
An Owner's
View of Patient
Treatment**

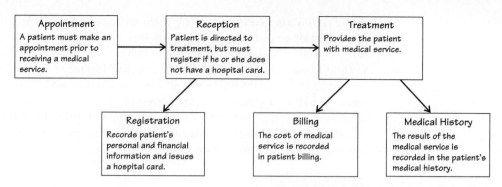

The model presents a (preliminary) version of the workflow for treating patients, understandable to business stakeholders.

blueprint" for the actual building of the system (although system builders could benefit from any clear model).

Figure 4.7 is one example of an owner's view. It models the major concepts in the workflow of treating patients by a hospital.

No technical training is required to understand this model. Stakeholders can easily correct its shortcomings or verify the concepts.

The briefness of this topic should not lead you to believe that your choices in creating "owner's view" models are few. On the contrary, the choices are limited only by your imagination. (All you need is a pencil and a paper.) However:

- First try formal models that are discussed in later chapters. Some, like the activity diagram, can be made to represent an "owner's view" and still be useful as construction blueprints. (We will introduce the activity diagram in Chapter 7, Behavioral Modeling II: Developing Use Cases.)
- Avoid any ornamentation as ornaments go against the main purpose of the undertaking, which is the ease of understanding. As analysts, you will not be judged by your aesthetic abilities but by your prowess in gathering requirements.

Mock-Ups

Mock-ups are approximations of the system's user interface to elicit comments and requirements.

Users are usually impatient with the pace of development and they cannot be blamed. If you heed the advice of this book (and countless others) and go through iterations of analysis and design, it will be a long time before the users can see any functioning "screen." And for most users, the user interface *is* the system, regardless of your protestations to the contrary.

In response to this impatience, developers have adopted the tactic of constructing a mock-up that imitates the user interface or the navigation through the interface.

Mock-ups can be constructed by writing words and drawing boxes and arrows on a piece of paper. Or they can be actual screen shots from forms created by using

☞ As it happens, this model also represents part of our main case history in this book. You can read the story under "Case History: Walden Medical Center" later in this chapter. But to understand this model, you really don't have to.

☞ Frequently and inaccurately this technique is called **prototyping**. This designation is dreadfully misleading. In product development, a prototype is "an original used as a model," a "full-size functional model," or a "model for testing and debugging." You can drive a prototype car and you can fly a prototype plane, but a mock-up of an information system cannot do what a complete information system does. (And if it does, then it is not a prototype.) A mock-up is simply another model, and even though a prototype is a model not every model is a prototype.

increasingly easy-to-use and rich development tools. In either case, they present a dilemma to the developer.

- Mock-ups are not merely a tactic to hold off the horde of impetuous users, but are a legitimate and powerful technique to elicit requirements. However,
- Mock-ups can put the developer in a difficult situation, because the users may see them as the final user interface. (And they may even get *more* impatient: "We saw the screens. What is holding you up?") You can also count on a predictable reaction: countless discussions on the aesthetics of the mock-ups. These discussions have a time and place—when you are designing the user interface—but they must not be allowed to steal time and resources from discovering, gathering, and analyzing requirements.

Do mock-ups—as we have said they are powerful tools—but also do your best to convince users that they are *not* the final user interface (let alone the finished system). Any development that starts with the user interface is doomed to failure.

6. Sources & Authorities

In discussing elicitation techniques, we mentioned stakeholders, domain experts, and users as almost synonyms. But they must be distinguished more clearly because they play different roles in making decisions about the product, defining its features, and gathering requirements. Sponsors form an important group that must be added to the list.

Sponsors

> Sponsors are those who launch the project and decide its fate.

Sponsors are usually a small but influential group within the enterprise who launch the project, support it, and have the authority to make decisions about its crucial aspects such as budget and resources. Since different groups within the enterprise may have different and conflicting expectations from the product, it is the sponsors who must resolve the issues and prevent waste of money and time.

The sponsors also determine the most high-level requirement, its **scope**, from which all other requirements flow.

Domain Experts

> Domain experts are those who are the most knowledgeable about the areas of business activity within the project scope.

☞ We will explore the significance of domains more fully in the next chapter, Domain Analysis.

A business domain is an area within an enterprise with similar activities and concepts. To build a system that serves a business domain, you need domain experts. If you are building an accounting system, you need expert accountants. If you are building an ATM system, you need expert bankers.

Domain experts may come from inside the enterprise or, if the enterprise is seeking to streamline its operations or engage in new activities, from outside. Often called a "business analyst," a domain expert must have three qualifications:

- Must know the ins and the outs of the business domain.
- Must be able to communicate with stakeholders (*see below*) to capture and express their needs.
- Must be able to communicate business knowledge and needs to the systems analyst. This function requires that the business analyst understand the general constraints of building an information system.

The given portrait is rather an ideal one. In real situations, one of the qualifications is usually missing. Usually it is the systems analyst who must learn to speak the language of the business.

Stakeholders

Stakeholders are those whose interests are affected by the operation of the system.

A stakeholder may or may not use the system, but how the system operates will affect his or her interests. Therefore, the stakeholder's primary interest is not the user interface, but the accurate adherence of the system to business concepts and rules and the integrity of data.

Stakeholders do not belong to one group. Their relationship to the system is defined by two different associations: what business domain they belong to, and their level of interest in the system. (See Figure 4.8.) For example, an inventory system would involve multiple business domains: *inventory* that must keep track of stock, *ordering* that must replenish the stock, *sales* that must rely on the inventory, and *accounting* that must monitor financial transactions. Among them, employees who directly monitor, order, pay for, or sell the merchandise have the highest interest in how the system works. A mover in the warehouse has the least interest. And the decorator for a showroom has none. (They all have interest in the *business*, of course, but not necessarily in a software application that serves the business.)

Any enterprise-wide or cross-domain information system must take into account the interests—and the requirements—of the business domains that it affects. Therefore, stakeholders are the most important source of *business* requirements. The analyst, however, must take two precautions:

- Stakeholders may present their "wish list" as requirements.
- Business domains and/or stakeholders may have conflicting interests or incompatible interpretations of the requirements.

The most important stakeholder is the enterprise, represented by the sponsors. When other stakeholders take flights of fancy or engage in conflicts with their peers, the sponsors must step in and hand down final judgments on scope, budget, features,

**Figure 4.8
Circles of
Interest:
Stakeholders
and Domains**

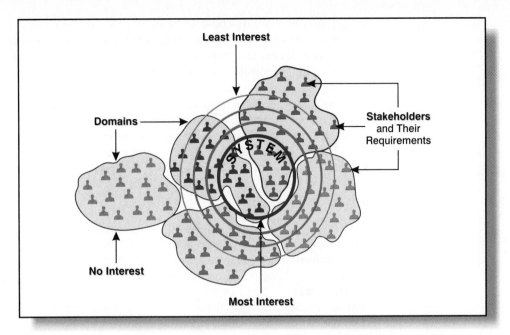

Stakeholders are identified by two affiliations: their interest in the system and the business domain to which they belong.

interpretations, business rules, and everything else that the development team is powerless to decide.

Users

Users are those who directly interact with the system.

☞ This separation between principals and operators is true only in extremes. Furthermore, it does not imply that "operators" are robots or drones or that they have an easy life. Neither does it mean that "principals" are knowledgeable in every case.

Stakeholders do not necessarily interact with the system. Those who do are called users. But even though all users are stakeholders in a very generic sense, the analyst must distinguish between two groups: *principals* and *operators*. Principals are participants in the business process and are expected to be knowledgeable about not only *what* they do but also why they do it, whereas operators act as assistants to the principals and usually perform a routine job.

Like all stakeholders that we discussed in the previous topics, principals are the primary sources for business knowledge, but the analyst must consult both the principals and the operators for user interface requirements. While the stakeholders are interested in business objectives, the users are concerned with the efficiency of day-to-day interaction with the system.

Reverse Engineering

Legacy applications and existing documents are rich sources of requirements and business rules, but they must be rigorously evaluated and verified.

Enterprises that have been in business for a while normally accumulate a varying mix of software applications and documents, procedures, rule books, manuals, etc. As a result, new development is often expected to upgrade, replace, or collaborate with existing applications. In many such cases, the business would ask you to mine legacy applications and documentation for rules and concepts to save time and resources. (How much of the savings are real and how much are perceived is another story.)

To discover the business concepts—rules, processes, people, objects—from legacy applications, you must resort to "reverse engineering": observing and analyzing *what* they do—especially to data—to discover *why* they do it.

A very simple example, written in "pseudo-code," is the following ATM example.

```
Requested Cash = Amount entered by the customer.
Withdrawn Cash = Retrieve from database the amount of cash
  withdrawn by the customer for today.
Cash Limit = Retrieve cash limit per day from the database.
Total Cash = Requested Cash + Withdrawn Cash for today.
If Total Cash > Cash Limit then
      Display Message "Sorry: you cannot withdraw more than
      " + Cash Limit + " dollars per day."
Else
    Dispense Requested Cash.
    Account Balance = Account Balance - RequestedCash
    Save Account Balance to the Database.
End If
. . .
```

The actual code would be longer and more convoluted, and it would include other conditions (relating, for example, to the account balance), but the business rule that we should extract from the code is the following:

- The total cash that the customer can withdraw during the day cannot be greater than an amount set by the bank.

[Robertson 1999, 99–100] For documents, you should verify the following by consulting domain experts, stakeholders, and users.

- **Who** uses the document?
- To what **purpose** is the document used?
- How **valid** is the document?
- How are the document's concepts and rules **processed** or **enforced**?
- How **intelligible** is the document to its intended audience (users and stakeholders)?

All requirements derived from reverse engineering must be verified *at least* as forcefully as requirements from other sources, but perhaps even more persistently: Many legacy applications are full of rules that are difficult to understand from code, not complete, obsolete, or just plain wrong. And keeping documents current and valid is an expensive undertaking that usually receives the lowest priority.

7. Managing Requirements

Managing requirements is as crucial to system development as is gathering requirements itself.

You might gather the best requirements but it would do nobody any good if you cannot find them or trace their sources. Regardless of the tools you may use, the following tasks must be performed to ensure success in requirements management.

❶ *Document & update requirements.* Documenting requirements seems like the most obvious task to perform but, unfortunately, it is often neglected. Not at the beginning, because when the project starts people usually remember that there is such a thing as requirements gathering. It is as the development moves forward and time for delivery becomes more pressing that the process becomes rather chaotic. During design and implementation, when the product is seriously taking shape, we discover many missing or conflicting requirements. Usually short conversations clear the issues away, but leave no trace for the future. Avoid this. To wit, an oral requirement is not worth the paper it is written on.

❷ *Document sources.* As accurate as a requirement may be, we must be able to *trace* the sources. First, sources allow us to verify the requirements. Second, referring to sources is the *only* way to resolve inconsistencies—both for the current project and future changes (or maintenance).

❸ *Separate requirements into distinct units.* Requirement statements must be "atomic." In other words, each requirement must be written in such a way that a simple True or False can verify the essence of it. (Constraints and explanations must merely qualify this "essence.") If a requirement depends on other requirements for its clarity or validity, then add references (a "see also"), but never combine them.

❹ *Uniquely identify each requirement.* Assign a unique number to each requirement. This is the only way to make references unambiguous. Assign numbers sequentially; do not build any meanings in them and do not reuse them if a requirement is dropped.

❺ *Verify requirements & document verifications.* A requirement must be verified by at least one (human) source. A second verification is highly recommended, and more verifications are better. Questionnaires are the best tool for verification. If there are inconsistencies in verifications (and there is no chance of a roundtable), then in the next questionnaires for the same requirements cite all responses and ask the verifiers to sort it out.

❻ *Prioritize requirements.* Assigning priorities is not an exact science, even though designations may appear to be exact. For example, the stakeholders might assign a priority of "High" to a requirement whose implementation is dependent on the fulfillment of another requirement designated as "Low." Nevertheless, assigning priority gives a general idea of the requirement's importance to the business.

❼ *Classify requirements meaningfully.* Government agencies and many companies have their own mandatory standards and formats for SRS (Software Requirements Specifications) documents. If you can *choose* a format, a number of popular templates for organizing requirements are available.

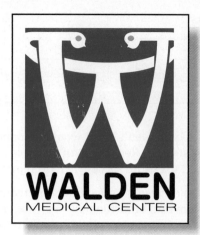

Figure 4.9
**Walden Medical
Center Logo**
We will use Walden's case history
in the following chapters as our
main example.

Most templates, however, are rigid and cater to the least common denominator, whereas in the course of a development project you have presented the *same* requirements to various groups with different interests and different priorities who want to see a classification that is relevant to *them*. (And let us not forget the models that accompany requirements and sometimes are the *sole* representations of requirements.) Therefore, at least for large projects, automated requirements management tools can be of great help. (The automated tools may not be very flexible for specific purposes, but if they can export requirements to popular text and image formats, your range of presentation is increased without losing the integrity of the requirements.)

8. CASE HISTORY: WALDEN MEDICAL CENTER

We argued that a well-rounded effort at gathering requirements is essential to the success of building an information system. We also introduced the basic techniques for doing so. But where to go from here? The distance between requirements and the final product is a long one. Abstract guidelines are necessary but not enough. Best-case examples illustrate the theory—and we will resort to them whenever clarity mandates it—but only a lucky few will actually work with best-case scenarios. To get a better sense of the obstacles and opportunities that lie ahead, we need a story that challenges us, if not with the untidiness of the real world, then at least with its complexity.

A hospital is a small world unto itself. Treating patients is its prime objective, but a full-service hospital must provide a great variety of services to succeed in its mission. And it must provide them expeditiously, often under emergency conditions, and often for profit.

Transportation, laundry, document management, research, inventory, feeding staff and patients, accounting, managing dormitories for doctors and nurses, buying supplies, buying pharmaceuticals, legal affairs—these and more are needed in addition to strictly medical services. Modeling the business and the operation of a hospital is certain be a fond dream for one analyst and a nightmare for another.

This challenge also makes a hospital a hospitable ground for discovery, for the variety of examples and for dealing with complexity at different, selected levels.

Thus we have chosen the story of Walden Medical Center as our main narrative for illustrating the concepts of modeling and building an information system.

We take time to recount the tale at some length before taking the first steps towards analysis and modeling. The story, as presented here, is in some aspects a simplified version and in others an exaggerated one (as healthcare professionals would undoubtedly recognize). Clarity of illustration, however, demands such an approach. But as we shall see, even this simplified version is complex enough when it comes to building an information system. In later chapters, we focus on only one point in the story: patient management. But we should first put that point in its complex perspective.

The Rise

In 1910, a group of New England physicians, philanthropists, and businessmen agreed to pool their resources together and establish a hospital that would offer excellent treatment for the well-off, affordable care for the expanding middle-class, and a healing haven of last resort for the impoverished. Being men of culture as well as means, they christened the hospital as Walden to honor the native son, Henry David Thoreau. Like him believers in Nature, they situated the hospital on a hilltop with woods in the back, a sloping view towards a lake, and a good supply of sunshine during the day.

It was a fortunate convergence: The eminence of the founding physicians appealed to the wealthy, even beyond New England, and the charity work attracted not only the more idealistic doctors but also the goodwill of the community, which translated into donations and tax breaks. The grounds, which originally recommended itself for its natural charms, provided ample space for the growth of the hospital.

And grow it did, thanks to the business acumen of its stockholders and executives and the vision of its medical leadership. When a new medical technology or practice emerged, Walden Hospital did not allow inertia to dictate its choices. By extending into research and preventive medicine it attracted funds and expertise, which helped it to keep its reputation and its contributions to the community.

Walden Hospital reached its zenith in the 1970s, with more than 500 licensed beds and departments in most areas of hospital medicine. But even then the picture was about to change. The financial success and the change of generations was bringing in stockholders and executives who had a different idea on how a hospital should be run. For them, and the prevalent culture of the day, a hospital was a business like any other, and the return on investment had to be as good, and as predictable, as any other business.

The Decline

The next cyclical downturn in the hospital's revenue came in the early 1980s and coincided with the enthusiasm of all industries, including managed healthcare organizations, for increasing efficiency by cutting costs. Against the objections of its medical leaders, the business managers wholeheartedly joined the trend. Going beyond traditional cost-cutting measures such as finding the lowest bids for hospital supplies and prescribing cheaper generic drugs when appropriate, they discarded services that had distinguished Walden Hospital during its lifetime. Research was out.

So were most outpatient visits and the treatment of charity cases. Some lab work that depended on expensive human expertise and equipment was outsourced as well.

Some doctors resigned in protest. The end of research also ended the mutually beneficial relationship between the hospital and drug companies, which in turn dissuaded a new generation of medical researchers and doctors from joining the organization. Reduction in charity work dried up tax breaks and donations. And outsourcing of lab work hindered the efficiency of medical diagnosis and treatment. The intangible capital of the hospital was reduced along with its tangible expenses.

Towards the end of the millennium, Walden Hospital was no longer profitable. The medical staff was still dedicated and effective. Compared to the industry's average, the number of malpractice suits against the hospital was very low and, as a consequence, insurance rates were favorable. But nothing else was. Well-to-do patients who could afford elective surgery and medical care outside managed healthcare organizations were not charmed by Walden's bargain-basement environment and outdated equipment. Outsourced lab work ended up being expensive when the bills had to be paid. And the hospital was not able to fully staff its medical team. Year-round, a considerable number of hospital beds went unoccupied.

The Revival

With the boom market of the late 1990s, the private corporation that owned Walden decided to herd its capital towards the greener pastures of dot-coms and put the hospital on the block. The medical leadership concluded that they must take an active part in the hospital's destiny. By putting together a document about the past and the potential future of the hospital, they set out to find a group of venture capitalists who would be willing to take the risk that Walden could regain its past reputation and profitability. Their prospectus was not the most professional of its kind, but the arguments were convincing enough to succeed. The Walden Medical Corporation, a privately-held company, was born.

Inception of the Project

The first act of the new corporation was, of course, to change the name: Walden Hospital became Walden Medical Center. The second was to engage a business consultant to turn the doctors' wish list into a concrete business plan (or to modify the list when not practical).

In his final report, the consultant advised the owners that the hospital needs a capital project to upgrade both its tangible and intangible assets. According to the consultant's report, the project has to address four broad, separate, but *interrelated* areas.

Business & Finance

- *Patient Care.*   Any and all improvements must have patient care at their sights. It is the mainstay of the hospital's business.
- *Service Cuts.*   Walden Medical Center has to reduce costs for its present and future operations not by cutting services that provide its revenue and reputation, but by increasing efficiency.
- *Charity.*   Charity treatments and community outpatient visits must be reinstated to enhance Walden's prestige, to attract donations, to win tax breaks, and, last but not least, to attract research grants and projects.

☞ We have summarized the consultant's report but have kept many points that might seem, at best, of distant relation to the development of an electronic information system. But:

❶ The project managers and the analysts must do their best to overcome the technical tunnel vision and grasp the *business* requirements that make the whole enterprise necessary and possible.

❷ As we shall see later, the outlines of an information systems emerge from a *business* context.

☞ Creating a cooperative Web site for vendor bidding is not a negligible undertaking. If the business decision makers approve of the idea, it would probably have to be a joint venture with other hospitals.

☞ An effective JIT system requires a large-scale automation of the hospital's operation. The analyst must make this point very clear to managers.

☞ In terms of security and access, a public Web site has to be isolated from other applications. However, in analysis and system design it should not stand alone.

- *Bidding.* Purchase of consumables, from disinfectants to food items to linen, should be done through bidding to get the lowest price and the highest quality and service. The medical center should look at establishing a joint bidding Web site with other hospitals, following the example of the auto industry. (However, the legal parameters of such a joint venture are very sensitive and must be researched thoroughly.)

- *Inventory.* Though availability of consumables are more critical to a hospital than most other businesses, the medical center is well-advised to implement the essence of just-in-time (JIT) inventory, so that ❶ cash will not be bound in items that are not going to be consumed within a projected duration, and ❷ the pressure on the hospital's resources for keeping inventory—especially for perishables—will be eased.

- *Drugs.* Drugs, of course, cannot be treated as just another category of consumables. However, when possible, the hospital must find a reasonable balance between name-brand and generic drugs. Research projects would allow Walden to get experimental and other drugs at low cost or for free.

- *HMOs.* Some Health Maintenance Organizations (HMOs) are transferring their own inefficiencies onto the doctors and hospitals in their network. For example, one HMO's defective billing system has prompted it to pass on its losses by curtailing allowable patients' visits and tests. Even though one single hospital has limited bargaining power against a big HMO, it should try group bargaining and, as the last resort, cut the ties if the *medical* logic demands it. HMOs may be the major source of business for clinics and hospitals, but without the latter they cannot function.

- *Subscription Plans.* Gaining popularity recently, subscription plans would allow the hospital to win back a measure of independence from HMOs. If tailored properly to various income levels in the community, such plans would allow Walden to become a mini-HMO itself. Subscription plans, if they prove to be successful, would also allow networks of hospitals to support each other.

- *Web Services.* The hospital's current Web site is little more than an ID card. Walden Medical Center must burnish its image—and provide a valuable service—by creating a Web site that advises the general population about preventive medicine and health issues. The site should be updated regularly and should address current issues. As an additional feature, subject to the availability of volunteer medical staff, the site can reply to visitors' health questions (pending legal clearance). In other words, Walden should get into publishing, which may not provide a direct source of income, but would buy it mind-share and goodwill.

- *Incentives.* At the present, hospital administration and staff do not consider themselves as stakeholders and, except in a very general concern about their jobs, nothing binds them closely to its financial performance. Walden Medical Corporation is not a public entity, so the stock options used by public corporations are not really an option. Other—perhaps innovative—methods should be devised to reward good performance. And it is critical that the incentives should not be limited to the management (medical and administrative), but be extended to the most low-level employees.

Organization & Staff

- *Hierarchy.* The present organization of the administration is too hierarchal. There are four reasons for this: ❶ No one has attempted to reengineer the structure; ❷ the flow of tasks and information is mostly based on paper and is inefficient; ❸ the neglect of the business leadership has prompted the individual managers to protect their own turfs; and ❹ there have been no incentives to change.

- *Alienation.*   As was previously mentioned, the staff does not consider themselves as partners.
- *Inertia.*   The new Walden would not be to the liking of some of the old-timers who are set in their ways. But no hasty action should be taken to replace or dismiss anybody before they have a chance to adapt. Loyalty of the staff is an essential part of the renovation.

Infrastructure

- *Neglect.*   The hospital infrastructure suffers from almost two decades of neglect. The lack of investment and planning has had an inverse impact on buildings, elevators, garbage disposal, air ventilation, food preparation, labs, surgical equipment, operating rooms, patient waiting areas, and nurses' and doctors' quarters.
- *Inadequacy of IS.*   Information systems, such as they are, are islands in the administrative turfs. For example, the admissions and appointments program, a commercial software, is more suited to a small office than a big hospital. It does not communicate with any other application in the hospital such as accounting, let alone with outside systems like HMOs and doctors.

Medical

The medical services and the medical staff of Walden are adversely affected by most of the previous shortcomings, plus:

- *Outsourcing.*   Some lab work has been outsourced, hampering prompt and convenient diagnosis. These labs must be reinstated and staffed. If there is excess capacity, the hospital should try to sell the services *to* other consumers instead of buying *from* outside.
- *Obsolescence.*   Existing labs rely on mostly antiquated equipment, like recording X-rays directly onto film. They must be modernized and—again—excess capacity should be sold outside.
- *Archives.*   Patient records are still in paper form. Even the basic information gathered in the admissions process is not available in electronic form, since that application is not part of a system.
- *Drug Inventory.*   Lack of a drug inventory system leads to confusion in administering medication. Making their rounds, the doctors often prescribe out-of-stock drugs that have their almost-equivalents in the hospital's pharmacy, but the nurses are not authorized to make the decision to use the available ones because the slight variations may have harmful side effects on a particular patient. Instead, they have to call on a doctor who might not be the same one who administered the drug originally. And most probably the doctor has to pay a visit to the patient in question.
- *Cost Predicament.*   The slavish cost-cutting, following every whim of HMOs, often puts the doctors in an awkward position: cut tests and

☞ For Walden's information system to be successful, it needs to not only replace its existing paper flow and archives, but to provide a decision support system to the business so that the hierarchy may be flattened more effectively.

☞ Modern lab equipment creates digital output. This output, saved in a digital library, must be integrated with the rest of the information system to be useful for medical history, accounting, research, and legal.

☞ Like just-in-time inventory for nonmedical supplies, a real-time drug inventory requires a considerable infusion of technology into medical workflow. Ingredients of mobile automation such as tablet computers and wireless networks are either mature or close to it. The question is organizational feasibility: Would doctors and nurses resist such an intrusion in the way they work?

treatments they find absolutely necessary, or incur the wrath of the management for overspending. Since giving a completely free hand to doctors is also impossible for an entity that is after all a business, the hospital must create a committee of doctors and executives to examine points of contention. The hospital's board of directors must have the final authority to arbitrate unresolved differences.

- *Research (Lack of).*   Absence of research has dissuaded promising young doctors from joining the hospital.
- *Accreditations.*   Loss of a number of accreditations, like CAP (College of American Pathologists), has depressed the morale. The process of receiving accreditations must be taken seriously and speeded up.

Initial Requirements

☞ We will discuss the actual gathering and analysis of the requirements for Walden Medical Center in the next chapter, Domain Analysis. Since a book is inevitably sequential, it might appear that analysis is a separate stage that follows the gathering of requirements. They are in fact an integrated process, as we shall illustrate.

The consultant concluded that to achieve the goals of the capital improvement project, an integrated, comprehensive electronic information system was indispensable. Moreover, the report argued, an enterprise-wide information system would give the hospital a competitive edge by increasing efficiency and reducing costs. It warned, however, that even though the complete information system must cover the whole enterprise, it must not be developed in an "isolation chamber," nor should it be presented to the staff as a *fait accompli*, but must take shape in step with other tasks in the capital project. This way, the information system would absorb the lessons of the hospital's real workflow, and the hospital would be able to absorb the requirements of working with an automated system.

9. DELIVERABLES

Even though requirements *discovery* takes place at the start of the project, requirements *gathering* is an ongoing process that surges with analysis and design and ebbs with implementation and testing. (Or should, if the project is done correctly.) Many of analysis artifacts, such as use cases, are in fact requirements gathering tools as well as models for development. Therefore, even though we may gather our definitions, rules, and models in a single document, **there is no single "end product" for gathering requirements because requirements gathering is not a single phase**.

Nevertheless, requirements *discovery* must yield some results so that we can start analysis. We have already discussed elicitation questionnaires, verification questionnaires, and SRS (software requirements specifications) documents. Before defining requirements, however, you must define the **scope** of the product. (Scope of the product is its reach: its major features and functions and limits *to* those functions—what it must do and what it cannot do.)

Table 4.1 illustrates an example for our sample case, Walden Medical Center. The document's title, *Scope: Candidate Requirements*, signifies that the requirements listed are those discovered by the analyst and have yet to be verified by the business. If and when they are verified, then the analyst will start gathering *detailed* requirements that, together, amount to the major functions of the system.

Table 4.1
Patient Management
Scope: Candidate
Requirements

☞ The reference to
the context diagram in
row 4 illustrates how
questionnaires can
refer to other
documents and
models for
clarification. (We will
discuss the context
diagram in Chapter 6,
Behavioral Modeling I:
Use Cases, The
Basics.)

Walden Medical Center
Patient Management Scope: Candidate Requirements

ID	REQUIREMENT	TRUE/FALSE		COMMENT
001	The product shall replace all current legacy systems.	☐	☐	
001	The product shall automate all clerical functions of patient management in an integrated system.	☐	☐	
003	The architecture of the patient management subsystem must be compatible with the architecture of future subsystems within the enterprise-wide system.	☐	☐	
004	Major functions of the system will be: • Scheduling appointment to receive a medical service. • Registration of the patient. • Recording of medical services. • Recording of costs incurred by the medical service. • Patient billing See the attached **context diagram** for patient management.	☐	☐	
005	. . .			

10. WRAP UP

☑ **Define requirements**

Businesses build information systems to do something for them. Requirements express those features of a product that enable its users to achieve specific objectives. Requirements are whatever a product *does* and whatever a product *has* that its users need in order to reach their goals.

☑ **Requirements discovery vs. requirements gathering**

Requirements discovery is a finite phase in the development process. It identifies the scope and the major objectives of the product. Requirements gathering is an ongoing activity throughout most of the project that defines what is needed to achieve the objectives identified by the discovery of requirements.

☑ **Classifying requirements**

Requirements are classified into two broad categories: functional (or behavioral) and nonfunctional.

Functional requirements specify the behavior of the system and the constraints on that behavior. They specify how the mission of the system is to be accomplished by achieving tactical goals. Functional requirements are captured through use case modeling that will be discussed in later chapters.

Nonfunctional requirements specify nonbehavioral properties of the system and the constraints on those properties. The major

subcategories of nonfunctional requirements are as follows:

- *Usability* defines how the behavior of the system must be shaped to fit the users and their work environment.
- *Reliability* requirements define the dependability of the system both in time and in the fulfillment of its functions.
- *Performance* requirements specify the response time and the input-output volume that the system can handle within a particular timeframe.
- *Maintainability* requirements specify the ability of the software to be modified and enhanced.
- *Security* requirements specify the rights of access to the services of a system, the manner of access to those services, and the tracing of interaction with the system.

☑ **Techniques for eliciting requirements**

Techniques for eliciting requirements have varying degrees of effectiveness and must be wielded differently depending on the situation.

- **Interviews** are the most flexible and direct tool for eliciting requirements. They are also more prone to misunderstanding and failure than any other technique. Early interviews in the requirements gathering process have a broad scope, while later ones are defined by more focus on detail. Interviews fall between two extremes:

structured, where we can control the flow, and focused, where we must go deeper with the flow. Since interviews are a finite and expensive resource, they must be planned carefully in advance to derive maximum benefit.

- **Questionnaires** are the second choice for requirements elicitation and the first choice for requirements verification. The structure of questionnaires as *elicitation* tools is generally the same as in interviews, but the flow is inflexible. As a *verification* tool, questionnaires are the most traceable.
- **Elicitation workshops** are the most powerful but also the most expensive tool for requirements elicitation. Since they are very expensive, you must select participants carefully and help them to help the workshop.
- **Field trips and observation** provide valuable requirements where workflow is rich in action and interaction. But you must be aware that the value of observing a workflow also depends on the goal of the observation.
- **Models** can be used to verify requirements. These models need not be formal blueprints for the construction of the system, but can be any drawing or word chart that the stakeholders can understand. **Mock-ups** are one such modeling technique; they are approximations of the system's user interface to elicit comments and requirements.

☑ **Sources of requirements**

The relevance and the reliability of the requirements are strongly influenced by their sources.

- **Sponsors** are those who launch the project and decide its fate. They also set the scope and the major goals of the product.
- **Domain experts** are those who are the most knowledgeable about the areas of business activity within the project scope. Domain experts may come from inside or outside the enterprise.
- **Stakeholders** are those whose interests are affected by the operation of the system. A stakeholder may or may not use the system, but how the system operates affects his or her interests. Therefore, the stakeholders' primary interest is not the user interface, but the accurate adherence of the system to business concepts and rules and the integrity of data. Stakeholders are the most important source of *business* requirements.

- **Users** are those who directly interact with the system. They can be classified into two groups: principals who participate in the business process, and operators who act as assistants to the principals and usually perform a routine job. The analyst must consult both the principals and the operators for user interface requirements.
- *Legacy application* and existing **documents** are a rich source of requirements and business rules, but they must be evaluated vigorously.

☑ **Managing requirements**

Managing requirements is as crucial to system development as gathering requirements itself. To manage requirements effectively, certain tasks must be performed conscientiously and accurately:

- Document and update requirements.
- Document sources.
- Separate requirements into distinct units.
- Uniquely identify each requirement.
- Verify requirements and document verifications.
- Prioritize requirements.
- Classify requirements meaningfully.

☑ **Walden Medical Center case history**

Walden, a once thriving hospital, has fallen on hard times. A new management takes over and, to turn around the fortunes of the hospital, hires a business consultant to analyze the problems and to draw a recovery plan. Among other things, the analyst makes a strong recommendation for deploying an enterprise-wide information system to cut costs, streamline operations, and gain a competitive edge. (This case history will be used throughout the rest of this book as the main source of examples and models.)

11. Key Concepts

Closed Question. A question that asks the interviewee for a specific and unambiguous response. It saves time, does not require high interviewing skills, and is focused, but provides a limited scope of detail and might put undue pressure on the interviewee. (Compare to **Open-Ended Question**.)

Constraint. ❶ A rule that limits a feature of the information system, dictated by law, regulations, business guidelines, security, etc. ❷ Limitations imposed on the development project by budget, time, operational support, user expertise, etc.

Domain Expert. A person, from inside or outside the enterprise, who is an expert in an area of business activity within the scope of the development project.

Elicitation Techniques. Techniques used to collect relevant requirements from relevant sources. They include interviews, questionnaires, workshops, field trips and observation, document analysis, and modeling for elicitation.

Field Trip. Observation of workflow and business activities in real time in order to collect and/or verify requirements.

Focused Interview. An interview that explores business concepts and requirements in depth. Its flow cannot be accurately planned in advance, since we cannot determine beforehand where the interview will take us. Most useful when the general outlines of requirements are known. (Compare with **Structured Interview**.)

Functional Requirement. Specifies the behavior of the system and the constraints on that behavior. While the mission of the information specifies a strategic goal, functional requirements specify how the mission is to be accomplished by achieving tactical goals.

Interview. Elicitation of requirements through direct conversations with the sources. Is the most flexible and direct tool for eliciting requirements, but is limited by resources and time and must be planned carefully.

Maintainability. Specifies the ability of the software to be modified and enhanced.

Mission. The strategic goal that the information system must achieve.

Mock-Up. An approximation of the system's user interface to elicit comments and requirements. (A mock-up is sometimes called a "prototype.")

Model for Elicitation. A model whose primary purpose to elicit and/or verify requirements. It can be formal or informal, but it must be understandable to target stakeholders.

Nonfunctional Requirements. Specify the nonbehavioral properties of the system and the constraints on those properties. They include usability, reliability, performance, maintainability, and security.

Open-Ended Question. A question to which the answer is not expected to follow a strict boundary. For gathering requirements, it provides new leads and openings and clarifies the context, but is time-consuming, needs high interviewing skills, and the resulting details are unfocused. (Compare to **Closed Question**.)

Performance. Specifies the response time and the input-output volume that the system can handle within a particular timeframe.

Probe. A request to an interviewee to clarify, expand, or deepen concepts expressed in a previous response. Also called a *"follow-up."*

Questionnaire. A written set of questions that ask the source to provide requirements or to verify them in writing. Less useful than an interview for eliciting requirements, but more useful for verification.

Reliability. Defines the dependability of the system both in time and in the fulfillment of its functions.

Requirement. Defines a feature—or a constraint on a feature—of the information system that enables its users to achieve specific objectives.

Requirements Discovery. Identifies the scope and the major objectives of the system. Is a task that precedes **Requirements Gathering.** Uses the same sources and techniques as requirements gathering but is less ordered and more chaotic.

Requirements Gathering. An ongoing activity during the development process that identifies and defines the features that the information system must have to fulfill its mission.

Reverse Engineering. The process by which legacy applications and their supporting documents are analyzed to discover business rules and requirements.

Scope. Defines the boundaries of **requirements gathering.** The scope is defined through **requirements discovery**.

Security. Specifies the right of access to the services of a system, the manner of access to those services, and the tracing of interaction with the system.

Sources. People, software, and documents from which requirements are gathered. They include sponsors of the project, domain experts, stakeholders, users of the information system, legacy applications and business guidelines, rule-books, manuals, etc.

Sponsor. A member of the group that initiates the development project and provides the project with its mission and resources.

Stakeholder. A person whose interests are affected by the operation of the information system.

Structured Interview. An interview in which the flow is more or less predictable because its structure can be planned in advance. More suited to discovering the context and the scope of requirements than exploring their depth. (Compare to **Focused Interview**.)

User. A person who directly interacts with the system.

Workshop. A planned and structured forum to elicit requirements from selected stakeholders. Is the most powerful but also the most expensive tool for requirements elicitation.

12. CONFUSING CONCEPTS

Requirements. Requirements are often used to identify *anything* that is needed or necessary to perform the task. In product development (including the development of information systems), requirements specify those features and rules that the product must have in order to achieve its objectives. As we shall discuss in the next chapter, Domain Analysis, requirements should also be distinguished from "product specifications" that must satisfy requirements but are not the same as requirements.

Gathering vs. Discovery. Requirements gathering is similar to most mining activities, including gold and oil. Before spending capital and resources, we must identify (or "prospect") the reserves in the ground. For requirements gathering, requirements discovery (and "domain definition," which we will discuss in the next chapter) is equivalent to prospecting. While prospecting is completed at a certain point, mining will go on until the reserves are fully exploited or the operation is no longer profitable. The same is true for the discovering and gathering of requirements.

Structured and Focused Interviews. An interview is "structured" when you have a scenario for the interview: You do not know the answers, but you know most of the questions. On the other hand, an interview is "focused" when you know a few question but you do not know where the exchange with the interviewee will take you. "Structured" is useful for defining the scope, while "focused" reveals the depth by relinquishing some control to the interviewee. "Structured" and "focused" are actually two ends of a spectrum: an interview usually falls somewhere in between.

13. REVIEW QUESTIONS

1. Why do we need to gather requirements?
2. Explain the difference between requirements discovery and requirements gathering in general. Provide an example that clarifies the distinction between the two.
3. Comment on the following: An information system is a product.
4. When is the best time to gather requirements about a product?
5. Define requirements.
6. Give some examples of requirements where they define both objectives and constraints.
7. Provide examples of simple and complex requirements.
8. Explain the difference between functional and non-functional requirements.
9. Identify requirement categories.
10. Provide three examples for open-ended and closed questions.

14. CASE STUDIES

The first three chapters laid the theoretical groundwork for what the rest of the book aims at: a pragmatic roadmap to system analysis and design. As we stated, we will follow the case of Walden Medical Center to provide an uninterrupted stream of examples for each chapter.

Under this topic, however, we present cases that *you* must follow and for which *you* must provide solutions. The narratives are presented here, but the questions and exercises will continue in subsequent chapters.

Remember: A problem usually has more than one solution. In fact, it is very likely that one of your most interesting challenges will prove to be choosing among alternatives, especially when alternatives are presented by others.

The *Sportz* Magazine

Michael has two passions: sports and computers. After a few years working as a software developer for a company that he has not been even remotely passionate about, his dream of combining the two was about to come true.

He noticed a "wanted" ad in *Sportz* magazine, one of his favorite publications. The magazine was looking for a project leader to develop an information system for supporting a set of business activities: subscriptions, advertising, editorial (managing contributions), distribution, payables, receivables, etc. In the usual language of "want" ads, the requirements included the following:

- Must have project management and team coordination skills.

- Must be able to communicate equally well with both the "business" and the development team members.
- Must have excellent analytical skills in translating business needs to clear guidelines for the developers.
- Must be able to create clear and "actionable" documents.
- Must have a bachelor's degree in information systems, or equivalent experience.

Despite his youth, Michael was not lacking in self-confidence. He knew not only that he *wanted* the job, but that he could *do* it as well. He sent his resume, along with a cover letter that emphasized his strong interest in both sports and *Sports*.

This got him an interview with the chief information officer (CIO) of the magazine, and the interview convinced the CIO to give Michael a chance. He decided that his intelligence, communication abilities, eagerness, and analytical mind far outweighed his limited experience.

Shortly after settling into his new job, he participated in the "kick-off" meeting for the project. To provide the upcoming team members with a snapshot of the business and the mission of the project, Michael put together a short "report" by taking notes and asking questions in the meeting. The essence of his report is as follows:

Sportz magazine is published **quarterly**. Each issue has a summary of the sports news for the preceding quarter, commentaries by well-known and respected sports writers, interviews with athletes, health and nutrition information provided by sports physicians, and reviews of the latest athletic products from wardrobes to equipment.

The magazine is known for its in-depth coverage, but it also prides itself on its "high production values": glossy paper and stunning photos. Indeed, *Sportz* is often proudly displayed on the coffee tables of many of its readers.

Like some other "elite" (and high-priced) publications, *Sportz* magazine is sold mainly through **subscriptions** and, up to now, it has not been interested in anything other than one-year subscriptions: long enough to convince advertisers but short enough to increase the subscription price at year-end to compensate for the ever-increasing cost of paper, ink, and print.

Recently, however, **competition** from the Web has taken a bite of the magazine's circulation. *Sportz* has a Web site but its popularity has been lackluster. The publisher is seriously thinking about revamping the Web site, but believes that the "core business" must come first.

Subscribers to *Sportz* include both **individuals** and **corporate** customers. The individual subscriptions are based on single-copy orders and are delivered to the individual's address directly. The corporate orders are usually multiple copies, for which they receive a 5 to 10 percent discount and are delivered to designated unit heads.

The publisher wants to take promotional measures to stimulate circulation: a money-back guarantee for first-time subscribes who want to cancel, and a free, six-month extension to anybody who pays for three full years.

The **renewal** system works very simply: Two months before the subscription expires, the subscriber receives a notice for renewal. No more than three notices are sent to each subscriber, be it an individual or a corporation. Subscribers can pay by **check** or **credit card**.

Contributors receive a complimentary one-year subscription to the magazine. But all are not treated the same. The sports physician receives the subscription for one article per year. Athletic stars are not paid for their interviews, but receive a one-year subscription for one interview per year. Each extra interview per year means a one-year additional subscription. (The magazine's preference is not to interview the same person more than twice a year.) A sports writer receives a one-year complimentary subscription for two contributions a year.

The new system must enable subscribers to use the magazine's Web site for renewals. Needless to say, it must be both secure and easy to use. For contributors, the system must provide the following (among other things):

- Maintain the name, the address, and the contact detail for each contributor.
- Maintain the details for each contribution, including the type of the contribution, the dates, the payments, and the complimentary subscription type.
- Record which staff is working with which contributor.
- Track the status of each contribution.

The Car Dealership

Jeanne is a graduate with an IS degree and is looking for a job as a systems analyst. Every potential employer, however, asks for job experience and particularly if she has worked through at least one full product life cycle.

Finally, desperate for any kind of employment, Jeanne met with Mr. Tucker, the owner of a car dealership, and asked for a summer job. Responding to his questions about her qualifications, she mentioned her degree and, almost in passing, brought up the notion of automating the information flow of the car dealership.

This suggestion caught the owner by surprise. He thought for a few minutes and eventually answered the nervous Jeanne. "Why not," he said. "Can you help me?" Jeanne wanted to know what the system should do. "I will tell you in a nutshell how we operate," Mr. Tucker replied, "and you tell me how we can improve our efficiency by using a new information system."

He continued:

> We have eight salespeople. As the customers come in, they greet them and ask them what kind of car they are looking for. We also buy and sell used cars. The customer has three options: buy a car in stock, order (through us) from the car manufacturer, or get a car transferred from another dealer (e.g., when the customer wants a car similar to one in stock but in blue instead of in red).
>
> We have three lots for three categories: family cars, sport cars, and recreational vehicles. We also have "weekly specials" where a number of cars are offered with discount prices. For those whose purchase exceeds 50k, we offer them a coupon that gives them a discount for a full year of monthly car washes.
>
> Some customers are interested in used cars and some want to trade in their old cars for new ones. Each buyer can trade in only one old car, but of course can buy as many new cars as they wish. In fact, we have had customers that come in and want to buy new small cars for two kids going off to college and a new sports car for the spouse.
>
> The salespeople work on a small salary, but most of their income is from the commission that they earn by selling cars. There is an incentive program that awards salespeople by higher commission percentages as they sell more: 5% commission for sales up to 100K per month, 7% for sales between 100K–200K, and 10% above that. The commission is calculated weekly and is a percentage of their total sales including additional features, extended warranties, etc. We like to keep track of our salespeople's performance and we choose a "salesperson of the year" who receives a bonus.

Jeanne asked to be given an hour. She sat behind the desk of a salesperson on vacation and, before the hour was over, presented Mr. Tucker with a list of what the system should do. Among her suggestions were the following:

- Record customer information.
- Record car information, for both new and used cars.
- Record information for traded-in cars.
- Create invoices.
- Calculate salesperson's commission.
- Calculate discounts.

The Pizza Shop

Fatima's dream has finally come true and she is the proud owner of a new (small) pizzeria in her neighborhood. She has hired two cooks, one waitress, and one delivery person. She is anticipating mostly takeouts, some in-house customers, and a lesser number of deliveries.

To minimize her costs, she prefers (or wishes) to receive cash for all sales to avoid credit card processing fees. Nevertheless, she has made arrangements with her bank to process credit cards. In-house customers are charged a 5% service charge. Delivery orders are accepted only when the credit card has been validated. (She also adds a $3 delivery charge. Whether this is a good idea or not is to be seen.)

Take-out customers can order in the shop or call to place their order and pick it up within 20 to 30 minutes at no additional charge. Those who call need to have their credit card validated. Fatima has heard horror stories about people who call in huge orders and never pick them up.

She believes that the success of her pizza shop depends on good planning and a growth direction that will satisfy the customers. Fatima is sure that the neighborhood will provide enough business for her to make a good living, but is not quite sure where the bulk of the business will come from: in-house customers, takeouts, or deliveries? She wants to be ready for expansion and has three choices: enlarge the seating area and hire more waitstaff, hire more delivery people and buy (or lease) delivery cars, or just hire more cooks and kitchen aids.

To decide where the expansion should take place, she needs a simple accounting system that calculates revenue from in-house customers, takeouts, and deliveries separately. Luckily, her husband just got his degree in information systems and has been bragging that systems analysis and design is his *forte*. He has offered to develop a simple system for accounting and told Fatima that "if my system works for your pizza shop, I can expand it and turn it into a commercial system. I am sure there are other pizza shops that have the same need for a system that keeps track of their sales."

The Real Estate Agency

Elizabeth (who likes to be called Elisa) has just inherited her father's real estate company. The company is financially in good shape because of the good reputation of her father and a number of faithful customers who return to buy or sell.

Elisa just graduated from a reputable university with a degree in real estate and has big dreams for the growth of the company. She wants to keep the old faithful customers, but attract new ones as well. She is very familiar with services that the Web can perform and has taken courses on using technology in real estate business. To automate the business and establish a Web presence, she wants to develop an information system that lists available houses, condos, and rentals. All information on the number of rooms, bathrooms, footage, garage, parking space, price, tax (for buyers of a property), etc., must be available to prospective customers. Condos require information on condo fees and rentals require the terms of the contract such as duration, required deposit, and so on.

The system should also collect buyer information such as preferences, the price range that they can afford, and personal information (name, address, etc.). Preferences include location, size, condo or house, number of rooms and bathrooms, garage and parking space, and the like.

The system should be able to match buyers' preferences with the sellers' offerings and, if it cannot find an exact match, should offer the closest matches.

The system should be able to assist buyers and sellers alike. **Buyers** might need help in choosing an agent and, as a result, the system must provide a list of agents complete with personal information such as name, phone number, and credentials. They might also need help with getting a mortgage, choosing a home, making an offer, getting insurance, and closing the deal. **Sellers** would need advice on choosing an agent, setting the price, marketing the house, selling the property, and closing the sale.

Considering the expectations, the system should satisfy three major requirements:

- Collect information from buyers and sellers.
- Match buyers and sellers.
- Help and advise buyers and sellers.

15. EXERCISES

The following exercises relate to *all* case scenarios presented.

❶ Create an "owner's view" for the narrative. Use Figure 4.7 as your guideline.
❷ Identify the users of the system.
❸ What are the major functions and their related tasks?
❹ Is any information missing? If you were gathering data, what additional information would you like to have?
❺ Complete the requirements list.

16. RESEARCH PROJECTS & TEAMWORK

❶ The new owners and managers of Walden Medical Center are certainly an ambitious lot. When you have a full-service, established, and reputable hospital, they ask themselves, why not train doctors, nurses, and paramedics? So, soon after embarking on the development of a comprehensive information system for the hospital, they decide to expand their domain by starting **Walden Medical School**.

The new school can rely on the hospital for many of its services, labs, and facilities, but it must have its own (cutting edge) information system—not only for the staff and the faculty, but also for the student body. As management envisions it, in addition to educational services the system would offer administrative services to the students as well: for registration, constructing schedules, viewing assignments and grades, etc.

Your team has been assigned the task of identifying requirements for this system. The following steps should be helpful to determine the features of the system and enable the stakeholders to achieve their objectives.

- Identify sources that you will contact to gather information on the required features.
- Decide which techniques you will use to elicit information. (You may want to use a combination of techniques.)
- Collect information and identify requirements.
- List functional and nonfunctional requirements for the system.
- Document your requirements. Don't forget to prioritize them.

- Check and revise your document—if necessary. (It is *always* necessary.)
- Submit the document and be prepared to present your work to the class.

❷ One of the annoying challenges that students face in writing term papers is organizing references and keeping track of them. Describing and identifying references as well as editions, dates of issue, and authorship is tedious and time-consuming, but absolutely necessary for research. Needless to say, an application that can automate this task (as much as possible) would make many college students very happy.

Briefly, such a "**reference engine**" should be able to do the following:

- Display a list of references.
- Allow sorting and grouping of lists by author, publication date, subject, etc.
- Allow editing and addition of bibliographical items and fields.
- Allow attachment and editing of notes with page numbers and keywords for each bibliographical item.
- Display notes for each item sorted by page number or keyword.
- Allow for upload, storage, and retrieval of digital copies of references.
- Allow for field-specific and full-text searches.

If you were to develop such a system, how would you modify the list? Start with your own requirement discovery: identify the scope and the major objectives of the system.

- What are the possible sources for gathering information on required features for this system? How would you elicit information?
- Organize requirements, or a related group of them, in a "scope" document.
- Identify the type of the requirement: functional or nonfunctional (reliability, performance, etc.).
- Check and revise your requirements document—if necessary.
- Submit the document and be prepared to present your work in the classroom.

❸ E-commerce has changed the shopping habits of consumers and has created an opportunity for anyone who is interested in creating an online business.

You and a group of your friends have decided on selling an exotic product online. Use your imagination to come up with a product that you feel has a market and can generate a small fortune for you. Your goal is to create a cyberstore according to the material you have learned in this chapter.

In other words, you want to test the practicality of your textbook and put the theory to practice.

Refer to this chapter as many times as you wish and create a document that describes a step-by-step procedure to gather requirements for developing your cyberstore. For example, identify sources of information, methods for eliciting information, functional and nonfunctional requirements, etc. (Remember: For this project, the nonfunctional requirements are as important as the functional ones.) Start your efforts by creating a template. Feel free to deviate from the book and introduce a more creative way of managing your requirements.

❹ Conduct team research to find the most popular method(s) actually used for gathering information. Start with a Web search and see if you can find papers and publications on the subject. You can also gather information by interviewing people in the software development departments of some organizations that you know.

- Is there a correlation between the size and the type of organization and the methods that they use to elicit requirements?
- Is there a correlation between the type of information system being developed and the methods used?
- Which method provides the *fastest* results?
- Which method is the most *reliable*?
- What would you consider the best practices?

Create a matrix that matches different methods of information gathering—for example, interview, observation, questionnaire, etc.—with the characteristics of the organization, and with the type of the information system to be developed.

❺ Which requirements gathering approach is the more suitable when you are upgrading a legacy system versus a completely new system? Give a thorough explanation for your answer.

❻ You have just received your degree and have been hired as a junior systems analyst to help develop an information system that will automate the process of employee promotions. The CEO believes that seniority must be an important factor but wants to know every other criteria that could be essential to the decisions for promotion. The company has put you in charge of this project: You must decide the source, the requirements gathering methods, and the documentation of the requirements. Create a one-page work plan that answers the questions of "who," "what," and "how."

17. Suggested Readings

No matter how hard we might try, gathering requirements remains an activity with a high component of chaos. Therefore, we must equip ourselves with available knowledge and tools to confront various contingencies. Only we should not expect that every tool is necessary for every project or that a certain tool would be useful to all projects.

A book that provides an accessible discussion of requirement gathering techniques is *Software Requirements: 2nd Edition* by **Karl E. Wiegers** (Microsoft Press, 2003). Gathering requirements cannot remain unaffected by the development methodology (explicit or implicit), and this book is no exception. Regardless of methodology, however, the book is a highly useful guide to the issues and the concepts that you will inevitably come across.

Methodology explicitly shapes *Managing Software Requirements: A Unified Approach* by **Dean Leffingwell** and Don Widrig (Addison-Wesley, 2000). The "Unified Approach" is the theoretical framework developed by the creators of UML and embodied in Rational Rose. Many of the topics discussed later in this book are discussed by the authors in the context of gathering requirements.

In *Mastering the Requirements Process*, **Suzanne Robertson** and James Robertson (Addison-Wesley, 1999) propose their own methodology (labeled *Volere*). They offer a general-purpose template for managing requirements, but their main focus is on the *process* of gathering requirements. Whether you subscribe to their methodology in its entirety or not, the book provides many valuable techniques and insights.

Domain Analysis

1. OVERVIEW

Domain analysis identifies business concepts that will be refined into the building blocks of an analysis model for the information system. Domain definition sets the boundaries of domain analysis and a domain dictionary organizes its findings.

- ▜☑ Inception
- ▜☑ Requirements Discovery
- ▜☐ Development
  - ▜☐ Analysis
    - ☐ **Domain Analysis** ⬅
    - ▜☐ Behavioral Modeling
    - ☐ Structural Modeling
    - ☐ Dynamic Modeling
  - ▜☐ Design
  - ▜☐ Implementation

Chapter Topics

➤ The three components of problem solving.

➤ The problem space vs. the solution space.

➤ Requirements vs. product specifications.

➤ Domains and their boundaries.

➤ Identifying domain concepts for analysis and modeling.

➤ Domain dictionaries and domain catalog.

➤ Identifying and organizing business rules.

Introduction

To build a software system—a product—we must understand the problem. We must also understand *what* is required to solve the problem *before* we can decide *how* to solve it. But equally important is *where*: where the problem resides and where the solution—the product—must work. In other words, we must understand the *context*.

We studied requirements, requirement types, and methods to elicit requirements in the previous chapter. To sum, requirements specify a set of objectives that a product, software or otherwise, must meet. A requirement can be functional or nonfunctional, simple or complex. Requirements express goals and limits to those goals. But the failure to understand *where* requirements come from will most likely lead to failure in building the solution.

The task of **domain analysis** is to help us understand the context of requirements and discover the related concepts that the product must incorporate, or take into account, to fulfill its objective. The boundaries of context, however, may not be self-evident. Therefore, we must first identify the scope of the context through **domain definition**.

Depending on the complexity of the context and/or the requirements, domain analysis results in one or more **domain dictionaries** that organize domain concepts, explain them, and categorize them for further analysis and modeling. A **domain catalog** is a directory of supporting domain documents.

One set of concepts discovered through domain analysis is **business rules**. Business rules are *technology-independent* guidelines under which an enterprise operates. They need special handling because a product that does not incorporate business rules will fail even if all other requirements are satisfied.

Building information systems includes solving problems. The concepts and issues that relate to the problems are situated in a "space" that is commonly called the **problem space** or *problem domain*. Those that relate to the solution reside in the **solution space** or *system space*. Domain analysis is primarily concerned with the problem domain, but its justification is provided by requirements and the objectives that the solution must meet. Therefore, understanding the relationship among problems, solutions, and requirements should be the first step for system analysis in general and domain analysis in particular.

Domain analysis is iterative. High-level requirements are its starting point, but it is an ongoing task that demands round-trips to gather further requirements and knowledge from all relevant sources including—but not limited to—the users of the final product. (See Figure 5.1.) Domain analysis is the foundation for all analysis modeling.

Along the way, we will use Walden's case history, introduced in the last chapter, both to illustrate the concepts and lay the groundwork for other models of the system down the road.

Figure 5.1 Domain Analysis: Understanding the Context

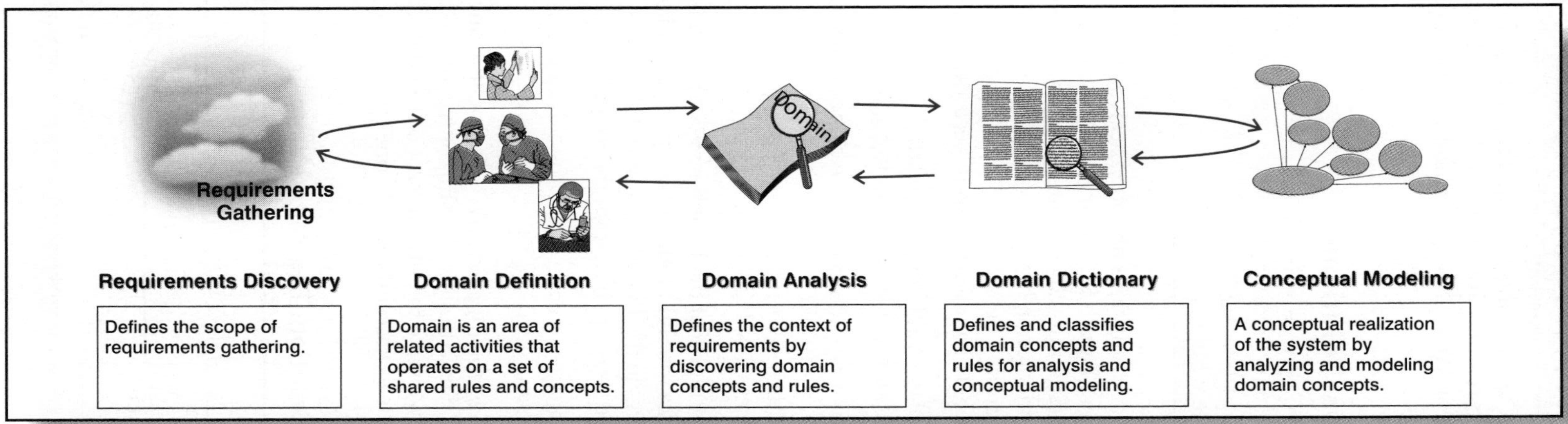

Requirements Gathering
Domain
Requirements Discovery
Defines the scope of requirements gathering.
Domain Definition
Domain is an area of related activities that operates on a set of shared rules and concepts.
Domain Analysis
Defines the context of requirements by discovering domain concepts and rules.
Domain Dictionary
Defines and classifies domain concepts and rules for analysis and conceptual modeling.
Conceptual Modeling
A conceptual realization of the system by analyzing and modeling domain concepts.

By discovering and organizing domain concepts, domain analysis puts requirements back into the context.

Requirements express the features that a product must have to solve one or more problems. The relationship between these elements is not as straightforward as it may first appear. We will next discuss the *same* components of problem solving from *different* angles.

Problems vs. Solutions

> Solving problems involves not a pair but a trio of components: problem, solution as method or process, and solution as answer. Each can be understood only in relation to the whole.

Problems and solutions are often seen as pairs. While not wrong, this perception is too simplified. Figure 5.2 illustrates a problem, a knotted rope, and a solution, the rope untied, neither of which seem too complicated.

Even as a metaphor, however, the knot is not always easy to untie. First of all, the arrow between the "before" and "after" pictures is not a small matter. The arrow should be labeled "solution" as well, because the term has two meanings:

☞ The distinction between the two meanings of solution is not mere hair-splitting. Confusing the two is confusing the process of building a product with the product itself.

❶ The *answer* to a problem, or "*what.*"
❷ The *method* or the *process* of solving a problem, or "*how.*"

So instead of two, we now have three components: the problem that we want to solve, the answer to the problem, and the method to arrive at the answer. By becoming aware of the third element, we might imagine that we know how to fill the gap and propose a process (see Figure 5.3):

> Take the left loop of the knot between the left index finger and the left thumb, take the right loop between the right index finger and the right thumb, wiggle the loops apart until the knot is loosened, and pull until the ends of the rope are free from the loops.

> Unfortunately, we have made the following assumptions that may not hold up under further scrutiny.

- *Both ends of the rope are free.*   A rope that anchors a ship to the shore is tied at both ends. Since pulling the ship or the shore through the loops is out of the question, we have to untie at least one end of the rope (and revise the proposed instructions to account for only one free end).

Figure 5.2   Problem Versus Solution: The Paired View

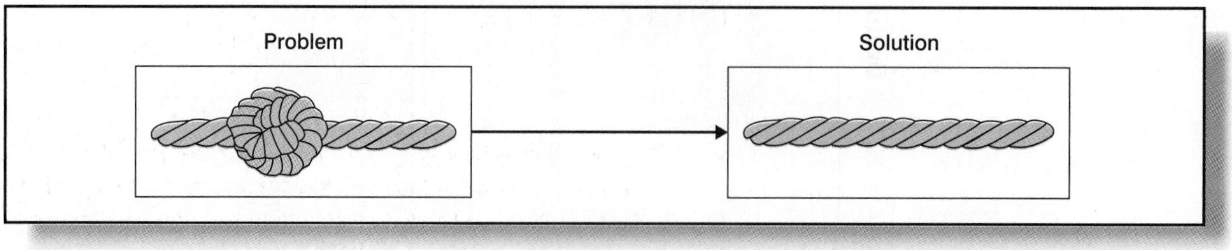

In this view, solution is a single concept.

Figure 5.3 Solution as Two Concepts: Method Versus Answer

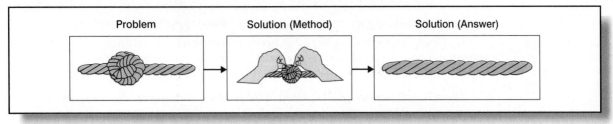

Without analyzing the context, we might choose the wrong method *and* the wrong answer.

- *The rope is thin enough to fit in a human hand.* The same rope between the ship and the shore could not possibly be handled by a normal hand.
- *The knot and/or the rope are accessible.* This is not easy if the rope is fifty feet above the water.
- *The knot is really a knot and not how the rope was made in the first place.* Far-fetched perhaps, but we would not know until we verify. (After all, barbed wire is not a regular wire with a "problem.")

These are not frivolous exercises in speculation. We have to put the problem in the right *context* to work out the right solution as *method* to arrive at the right solution as *answer*.

Complications, however, do not stop here. In practice, especially in the practice of building information systems, things are more complicated than this. Imagine the last illustration without the problem and, consequently, without a method to solve the problem. (See Figure 5.4.) In other words, we are given the *requirements*—a straight rope of indeterminate length—but not *why* it is needed or *where* it is needed.

Even if we put the knotted rope back into the picture, we need to address three issues before we can allow ourselves to proceed with building a solution.

❶ *What is the* **real** *problem?* Often we are given part of a problem or a simplified perception of it. Is the knot on the rope itself the problem? (It could be, at least aesthetically.) If the problem is that the knot prevents us from using the rope for a certain purpose, what is that purpose? Why cannot the knotted rope work? What would the straightened rope do that the knotted one does not?

❷ *What are the* **alternative** *solutions?* We rightly rely on experience, knowledge, and judgment to find solutions. (What other choices do we have?) But the same factors also create an envelope around us that may limit our ability to see beyond it. But we do

Figure 5.4 Requirements as the Answer: "What" Needs "Why," "Where," and "How"

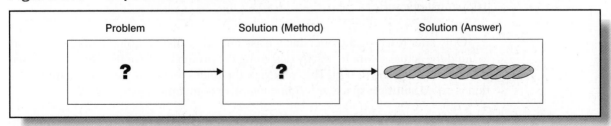

Merely knowing the features of the solution is inadequate for building it correctly. We must understand the context to ❶ find the proper method(s) and ❷ design a solution that takes the context into account.

have to ask: Is there an alternative to using a rope for the same purpose? Can we cut the rope—as Alexander the Great did with the famous Gordian knot—instead of trying to untie it? As some people are fond of saying, we have to "push the envelope."

☝ By no means are we suggesting that every problem is this complex. Fortunately for us, it is not. Developing software, however, has a tendency to get that way.

❸ *Does the answer satisfy the needs* in context? A solution might answer a specific problem quite effectively but fail in context. An untreated rope may be used to pull a car by another car, but it will not last long through a fire: It will burn.

These issues are not independent of each other. A change to our perception of the problem might change the answer, which in turn would affect the method for building the solution.

Problem Space vs. Solution Space

> The three components of problem solving reside in two organically related spaces: the problem space and the solution space. Changing an element within one space has a ripple effect across both.

It seems obvious that any product is designed to address problems—or opportunities—within a certain context. Change or ignore the context and the product becomes irrelevant, less useful, cumbersome and annoying, wasteful, or outright dangerous and destructive.

☞ The relationship of software to its surroundings is more abstract than most human artifacts. Therefore, conceptualizing the requirements is more difficult and error-prone. This is nothing to be ashamed of, but we must compensate with more effective analysis and modeling.

- A car designed for inhospitable country roads must be squat and wide so that it will not overturn in tight turns. Its size, weight, and fuel consumption does not recommend it for an urban environment.
- A shelf-top audio system is a good fit for a small apartment, but useless for a great hall. On the other hand, a sound system for a great hall would overwhelm a small apartment (and annoy neighbors).
- A billing system for a utility company most probably would not serve the needs of a hospital for billing patients.

Obvious? Maybe. Well-heeded? Not always, at least as far as software development is concerned. One reason is that we fill in the blanks in the requirements with assumptions that often turn out to be incomplete or wrong. (There are *always* blanks in the requirements.)

To reduce incomplete and wrong assumptions we must model the solutions within the **problem space** or *problem domain*. (See Figure 5.5.) For this to become possible, we must first analyze and model this space.

> Problem space is the context from which the problem arises and in which the solution must operate.

Only after reaching a model that we assume will satisfy requirements can we start to build the actual solution, first by designing the product and/or its components, then by implementing the design. The context of the issues related to design and implantation is called **solution space**, *solution domain*, or sometimes *system space*.

> Solution space defines the territory in which concrete decisions about the information system—as opposed to its features—are made.

Figure 5.5 Solution Must Fit the Context

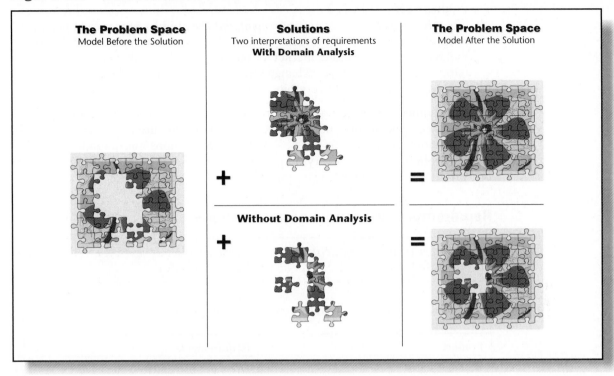

To model solutions within the problem space we must model the problem space as well. As in a jigsaw puzzle, each piece must not only be correct itself, but must fit within the context that is composed of many other pieces.

Boundaries of the solution space are decided by the analysis model. In solution space we do not question the requirements or discover them, but try to realize them. The "what" is solved and the "how" now becomes the problem.

- How can we build the wide chassis for the rugged-terrain car? Do existing alloys work or should we go back to the lab?
- How can we fit high-quality electronic components inside the required size of the shelf-top audio system without overheating and interference?
- How can we keep track of medical expenses the moment that a medical service is rendered?

Of course, one should not be misled into believing that the problem space and the solution space are located in separate planets. What happens in one affects the other, for three reasons:

☞ Sometimes, of course, the requirements prove to be unrealistic. In the 1980s, the Japanese launched a "Fifth-Generation" computer project that they hoped would result in a very advanced AI (artificial intelligence) technology. At the time, it alarmed many American computer makers, but the project eventually fizzled out.

❶ *Requirements are usually made with a reasonable awareness of what is available or what is possible.* New electronic gadgets are more often than not a repackaging of available components. President John F. Kennedy's promise in the early 1960s "to put a man on the Moon before the decade is out" was in the realm of possibility. (He should serve as a model to analysts, because he was careful enough to add: "and bring him back.")

❷ *Against all expectations, we might fail to find an answer for the requirements.* We might not be able to squeeze the electronic components in the specified space without overheating. (More on this in the next topic, "Requirements vs. Product Specifications,")

❸ *The solution satisfies every requirement, but the product proves to be partially or totally unsuitable to the task.* After testing the prototype, we might find that the roads in the target market for our new rough-terrain vehicle are too narrow for a wide chassis. (Change the requirements: make the chassis heavier instead of wider; adjust everything else to accommodate the change.)

There is another twist to reason number three: The "wide body" requirement is actually a product specification, not a requirement. What is required is that the car should navigate mountainous roads, not how. Often, specifications masquerade as requirements. Though in the end everything may work out well, we must be able to separate product specifications from requirements.

Requirements vs. Product Specifications

> Requirements specify the *desired* features of the product or service. Product specifications define the product that must realize those features.

Products are solutions to real, perceived, or hoped-for problems.

☞ Throughout this book, we will use **products** and **services** interchangeably, unless otherwise indicated. In many cases, they are indistinguishable.

Product	Requirements
Hammer	Drive in a nail and pull out a nail.
Watch	Tell time and attach to wrist.
Telephone System	Enable people to talk to others across vast distances in real time.
Movie	Entertain with sound, music, and moving pictures.
Plane	Fly people from location to location.
Rocket	Carry people into space.

Products, however, do not mechanically flow from requirements, nor are the requirements enough to define a specific product.

Take the simple case of a food distribution company that wants to deliver shellfish from coastal fishing grounds to inland population centers. Shellfish are notorious for spoiling fast. And when they spoil, the poisoning can be lethal. (Hence the old adage: Do not eat shellfish in months that lack an "R.") As a result, the requirements for building a shellfish distribution system must include one imperative item:

☞ Some shellfish can also be transported in a container of seawater, but the load would be very heavy and after a relatively short while the water would become polluted.

• Get the catch to the consumers before it goes bad.

Satisfaction of this requirement is not optional: Either we find a way to satisfy it or there is no business to start with. But the imperative does not give us a clue about how to devise a solution.

If we are living in the early 1800s or before, our choices are not many. We understand that ice would keep the shellfish from rotting. But roads are bad and the speed is capped by (real) horsepower. We can store natural ice in underground vaults for use in

Figure 5.6   Alternate Solutions for the Same Requirements

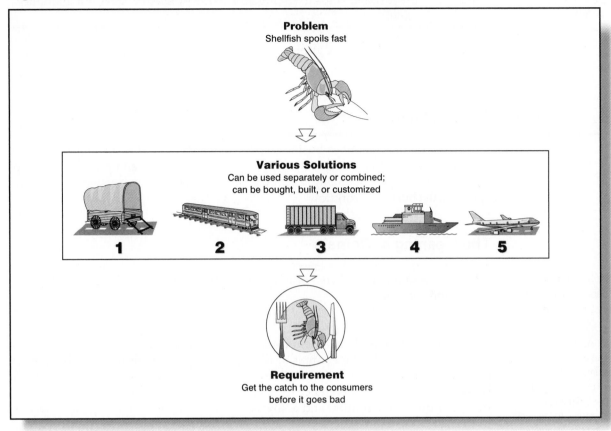

Sometimes more than one product or service can satisfy a requirement. The choice depends on many factors. The covered wagon was one of the few choices available before railroads. Though still a choice, we doubt that it will be used.

☞ It was only in 1877 that Gustavus F. Swift, a Chicago meatpacker, perfected a practical refrigerator car that made it possible for farmers in California to send their fresh produce to the East Coast of the United States. (It was, incidentally, also the beginning of the end for large-scale cattle drives that have proven a treasure trove for many Western movies and TV series.)

the summertime. All in all, we can add a limited range to our marketing reach. However, creating and maintaining a far-flung distribution channel is out of the question.

We have to jump to the latter half of the twentieth century to find viable, alternative solutions. Then we can pick and choose among various products and services that the market offers (*buy*), that we can create ourselves (*build*), or mix both (*customize*). (See Figure 5.6.)

We can use refrigerated trucks to carry the catch to refrigerated railroad cars which then carry it to main distribution centers from where we can reload it on trucks and dispatch it to restaurants and retail stores. If the rates that trucking and railroad companies charge seem unreasonable, we can even dare to plan a truck or railroad fleet of our own if we are big enough. If there is enough demand, we may consider delivery by plane. (It has been done.) And we may establish sizeable cold storage facilities in major distribution hubs to compensate for fluctuations in supply and demand.

Had we lived a few hundred years ago, of course, we could *not* have jumped to the late twentieth century. Since the 1870s when carrying fresh food by railroads became a possibility, various solutions have appeared only gradually. Each solution, or each set of solutions, has demanded a different set of specifications while the business requirement itself has remained constant.

[Graham 2001, 384–391]

> Analyzing the problem helps us to understand the problem; it does not guarantee or specify a solution.

The previous argument applies as much to software development as to food distribution.

3. DOMAIN DEFINITION

Domain definition identifies business spheres of activity and their boundaries. The boundaries of a domain decide the scope of domain analysis and provide a conceptual framework for organizing the information system into subsystems that correspond to the business workflow.

The Meaning of Domain

☞ See "Domain as a Concept" under "Topic Discussions."

> A business domain is an area of related activities that operate on a set of shared rules and concepts.

☞ As we have mentioned before, by business we mean any organized, goal-oriented human enterprise. It does not have to make a penny to qualify as a "business."

We have discussed "problem domain" and "solution domain" in relation to solving problems. In the context of distinguishing problem-related issues from solution-related concerns, "domain" simply refers to a space or an area in a general sense. (Hence we gave preference to "space" even though "domain" is equally popular.) For domain definition and analysis, however, the term holds a more specific meaning.

To arrive at this more specific application, we must start at the basic meaning of the term: **Domain is a territory where kindred rules reign**. The Roman Empire was a domain, so is a school, the world of the subatomic particle, and the ecosystem of the Amazon rainforest.

In any business enterprise with a minimum of complexity, we can readily recognize some domains: inventory, purchasing, sales, accounting, etc. Each has its own set of similar activities, common rules, and shared concepts—distinct from other sets in other domains.

Business domains have three significant properties.

❶ *Business domains are organized domains.*   Whereas in a natural domain the activities and the fate of one member does not necessarily affect another member, in a business domain the members interact and this interaction affects the domain and its members as a whole.

❷ *Business domains are goal-oriented.*   In a natural domain, individual members may have goals, but the domain usually does not. On the contrary, business domains are formed with a mission: purchasing exists to purchase goods and services with the most advantageous terms, inventory exists to stock needed goods and retrieve them correctly and on time, and a maternity ward in a hospital exists to deliver babies as healthy as possible.

❸ *Business domains can change fast.*   Natural domains change over a long stretch of time, in response to evolution and the environment. Business domains can appear, change, or disappear overnight as a result of a human decision, arbitrary or not: outsource shipping, restructure the sales on functional lines instead of geographic ones, restructure the corporation on geographic lines instead of functional ones, take down inventory and rebuild it as JIT (just-in-time) inventory, create a division for online sales, etc.

The Domain Scope

> Domain scope defines the boundaries that separate shared activities, rules, and concepts within a domain from those on the outside.

☞ We use the terms "domain" and "sub-domain" interchangeably. But, as we shall see in "Domain Analysis," it is important to remember the hierarchy: A business itself is one domain that contains other domains.

We argued that to meet requirements we must find the problems that the requirements aim to solve and analyze those problems within their context or "domain." But in the world we call "real," everything flows to and from everything else, so a real-world "context" has no boundaries. Even the most insignificant object is situated in a context that is situated in a bigger context or is related to another context, and so on.

For domain analysis, which is a finite and practical endeavor, we must draw lines to identify the scope of our interests. These lines are, of course, human artifacts. They are not, however, completely arbitrary but show a commonality of interests, goals, or functions.

❶ Domain definition must discover and define the boundary between one sphere of interest and another.

❷ Domain definition must *impose* such boundaries if the complexity of the context or the requirements threatens to overwhelm us.

Usually, a business enterprise makes the first objective relatively easy. By tradition, experience, necessity, or otherwise, a business is already organized into domains and sub-domains: sales, accounting, inventory, human resources, and so on. (They may call them departments or divisions or some other name, but for us they are all domains.)

☞ Many information system projects do not require such an enterprise-wide analysis. But they often accompany some form of overt or covert **Business Process Re-Engineering** (BPR) project that aims to restructure the entire business or large portions of it to increase efficiency. Therefore, even though many IS projects will succeed without formal domain definition, it is useful to have a notion of it.

The second objective—*imposing* domains—requires a broad analysis of the enterprise to find commonalities that are not readily apparent. To put it differently, we must **derive** new domains from existing ones. An obvious example is accounting. Even though accounting itself is an ancient discipline, it was primarily the Industrial Revolution that catapulted accounting to its prominent position. With the scale of mass production and the invention of publicly held corporations, accounting could no longer be treated as something incidental to the main functions of a business.

Except for accounting and audit firms, however, accounting is not "the business of the business": an airline flies planes, transports people and goods, buys fuel for its planes and food for its passengers, maintains the planes, etc. Accounting is a by-product of other functions, but no modern corporation can effectively or legally function without accounting as a distinct domain. (See Figure 5.7.)

Some other derived domains, such as "human resources," also seem obvious because they have already been discovered by the business. We may need, however, to discover and define others if

❶ we find that a pattern of **redundancy** across domains contributes to an unnecessary complexity, and

❷ it is practical and **desirable**—in terms of both technology *and* business—to do so.

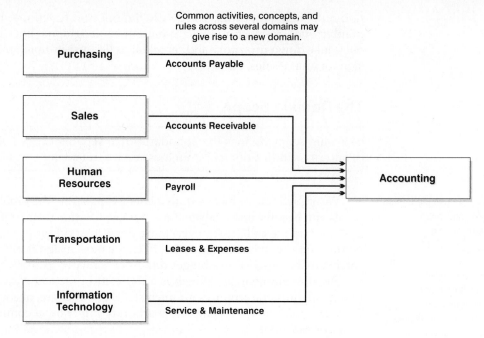

Figure 5.7 Derivative Domains: The Case of Accounting

A derived domain is arrived at by discovering similar activities, concepts, and rules in other domains.

For example, each domain in a business might have its own archiving system and its own personnel to manage the archive. If we are given the task of building a subsystem for keeping digital records instead of paper ones, scoping a "document management" domain—with its own rules and concepts—for the whole enterprise instead of producing one for each domain could result in a more robust information system and lower costs for the business.

Domains and Subsystems

> Domain definition provides a framework for the conceptual subsystems within the information system.

Domains and systems or subsystems are not the same thing. Components of a system are connected together in an organized way. They affect each other and the behavior of the system as a whole. In a domain, the members are subject to the same or similar rules and display the same or similar attributes and behavior, but do not necessarily interact. All mammals belong to a domain, but they do not make a mammalian "system."

[Booch 1994, 155]

Domains and systems come closer when we are dealing with a human enterprise. In this case, we have to narrow the definition of these two broad concepts and make them more specific to our goal of building an information system: A domain is "an area of knowledge or activity characterized by a set of concepts and terminology understood by practitioners in that area." A system becomes "a set of elements organized to accomplish a specific purpose and described by a set of models, possibly from different viewpoints."

In such an enterprise, if we determine the domains then we are very close to establishing subsystems from a *conceptual* point of view. By "conceptual" we mean how an information system is *perceived*, not its logical design and certainly not its physical architecture. In a hospital information system, doctors and nurses should see a view of the enterprise that is streamlined for performing medical services and patient care, while accounting is not concerned with the specifics of medical care but requires a commanding view of all financial transactions.

Walden's Domain Definitions

☞ See Chapter 4, Gathering Requirements, for the beginning of Walden Medical Center's case history.

In his report, the business analyst employed by Walden Medical Center to analyze the needs of the hospital both as a business and as a medical enterprise identified the domains that must be considered for inclusion in the future information system. (See Table 5.1.)

The report went to great length to make it clear that:

- These domains (and sub-domains) are interdependent. Each feeds into several others and in turn is fed by other domains.
- Management must assign an order of priority to the development and implementation of the subsystems. Otherwise, the development and the deployment would overwhelm the center financially and the staff mentally.
- Not all domains need to be automated—at least not immediately.

The Information System Strategy for Walden

To fulfill this mission, Walden Medical Corporation hired a CIO (chief information officer) with a strong background in designing and integrating systems for the pharmaceutical industry.

Instead of rushing to buy computers and hire programmers, she asked the CEO to provide her with a snapshot of what the medical center would look like in three years.

Table 5.1
Walden Medical Center: Domain Definitions (Partial Listing).
For a complete listing see Appendix A, "Walden Medical Center's Domain Definitions."

Walden Medical Center
Domain Definitions
Version 1.0—July 19, 2006
(Partial Listing)

DOMAIN	SCOPE OUTLINE
Patient Management:	All activities that directly come into contact with patients fall within this domain, including • Referrals • Scheduling • Registration, Admissions • Treatments • Patient Billing Issues
Drug Inventory & Purchasing:	• Pharmaceutical Inventory • Drug Supply Chain
Medical & Lab Technology:	• Medical Equipment Purchasing • Medical Equipment Inventory • Medical Equipment Maintenance
House Services:	• Laundry • Cleaning • Food Preparation & Diets

Table 5.2
Capital Project:
Snapshot of Medical
Goals for Walden
Medical Center.
Walden Hospital's
capacity and work-
force in three years, as
projected in the mis-
sion statement of the
capital project.
(This document
should be included in
the domain catalog,
discussed below.)

☞ "Licensed beds"
are the number of
beds that the U.S.
Department of Health
Services has licensed
a medical facility to
have in a given
treatment category.
(The National Guard &
Reserve Web site
offers a useful
glossary of hospital
care terms: http://
www.tricare.osd.mil/
mhsophsc/mhs_
supportcenter/
Glossary/
glossary.htm.)

Walden Medical Center *Capital Project: Snapshot of Medical Goals* Version 1.0—July 25, 2004	
Beds:	800 licensed beds
Doctors:	Close to 300 fulltime and 150 participating
Nurses:	More than 1,600
Labs:	30
Lab Technicians:	150
Nonmedical Staff:	400
Permanent Research Projects:	5
Referral Admissions:	5,000
Outpatient Visits:	10,000
Emergency Admissions:	200 per day

As it happens, such a statement of mission was just put together to guide all those responsible for the capital improvement project. (See Table 5.2.) By analyzing this statement, she concluded that the strategy to satisfy Walden's information system requirements must be two-pronged: bring mission-critical applications online first but build the foundations for an enterprise-wise system in parallel, with strong emphasis on upfront analysis and modeling.

In her first-draft proposal to the CEO, she took the position that the medical center should not turn itself into a software company: it lacks the know-how and the resources to develop an information system on such a scale. Instead, it should rely on the following entities to build and maintain an enterprise-wide information system.

- *A software consulting company,* preferably experienced in medical fields, to build the system in cooperation with a small number of employees who would coordinate the communication between the consultants and the knowledgeable hospital staff.
- *A system integrator company* that would work, through the same staff as above, to provide the infrastructure—networking, workstations, servers, etc.— to deploy the software as it becomes available.
- *A Help Desk staff,* which would really be the same employees who would work with the software and hardware consultants to implement the system. Both consulting companies would be required to train the Help Desk. In turn, these employees would be responsible for training users, reporting problems, and requesting services and enhancements.
- *System maintenance staff,* mostly for hardware and the operating system support. They will be trained by the system integration consultants.

The CIO also warned management that not everybody would accept the changes with open arms. She reported that during her research she has found that:

- Most doctors in the center consider using a computer when making their rounds a waste of time. "We are doctors, not computer operators," one had said. "If we have any spare time, we prefer to use it to update our knowledge in our own field. If you need to computerize the information, hire somebody to enter it after we do our job."

- The nurses are more receptive, but likewise they are afraid that they would become more and more clerical workers.
- Clerical workers are afraid that they will lose their jobs. "Downsizing by any other name!" according to a veteran who remembered the first round.

Therefore, she advised, the users must become stakeholders in the development. They should consider the product as something of their own and root for it.

Walden accepted her recommendations and, wisely, decided on giving **Patient Management**, the core of hospital's business, the first priority.

The Scope of Walden's Patient Management

At each and every phase of analyzing and designing a system, another round of information gathering becomes necessary. It is neither desirable nor possible to gather every requirement in one attempt, no matter how many resources we throw at it, for the following reasons:

- *Not desirable,* because if the information gathered is not shaped into various models that—separately or combined—make a system intelligible, then the avalanche of data will bury the most agile and sophisticated mind.
- *Not possible,* because only by digging into one level of information may we uncover another layer or discover inconsistencies that are not apparent at the first glance.

In defining the scope of a domain, gathering information becomes more focused. To create a conceptual model of **Patient Management**, we need to go one layer down and outline its boundaries. When the analyst concludes that sufficient data for *this* level of analysis has been unearthed, a *scope* document is created that outlines the topmost functions of the target domain. (See Table 5.3.) Supporting documents—interviews, existing documentations, notes, etc.—are either included or referenced.

The scope document is written in a language understandable to all the interested parties in the domain. It is revised as many times as needed until stakeholders agree that it is accurate. More often than not, somewhere in the process that follows the overview, the analyst has to revisit the outline to reflect new discoveries that escaped attention before.

4. DOMAIN ANALYSIS

Domain analysis is analyzing the context of requirements. It has a twofold task:

❶ Define the context in which the information system will operate.
❷ Discover and define concepts that the product must incorporate or take into account in order to meet its objectives.

[Booch 1994, 155]

By augmenting these concepts through elaboration and the discovery of new concepts, system analysis will build a *conceptual* model of the system, a template from which we will design the product.

Table 5.3
Domain Scope for
Walden's **Patient
Management**.

☞ While domain
definition provides an
outline of domain
boundaries (see
"Walden's Domain
Definitions"), domain
scope explains what
each item means.

> **Walden Medical Center**
> *Domain Scope: Patient Management*
> Version 1.0—August 5, 2006
>
> ---
>
> - **Referral.** A referral source refers a patient to Walden Medical Center for using its medical services. The referral source can be a doctor, an emergency medical worker, another hospital, or the patient.
> - **Appointment.** A hospital clerk makes an appointment for the patient, consulting the referral source and the hospital schedule for the availability and the suitability of the service. If this is the first time that the patient has been referred to the hospital, the hospital clerk records the basic information about the patient.
> - **Registration.** On the first visit to the hospital, before providing the service, a hospital clerk registers the patient by entering or updating the patient profile and payment information along with demographic information. If the patient is new to the hospital, a hospital ID card is issued to the patient at the end of registration. An ID card is also issued if the old card is lost.
> - **Medical Service.** Depending on the nature of the medical service, doctors, nurses, and lab technicians provide the patient with appropriate service(s) for which the appointment has been made.
> - **Hospitalization.** Either as a result of the original referral or the decision of in-house medical staff, a patient may be hospitalized. (Hospitalization, commonly called "admission," is a service that needs an appointment: The bed must be available when it is needed.) If a patient is hospitalized, some services, like monitoring the patient's progress or the administering of prescribed drugs, are provided without appointment. Other services still need appointment, but the appointments are initiated by medical staff.
> - **Cost & Record Keeping.** After providing each service, the cost and the results of each service are recorded in detail, for medical history *and* billing.
> - **Discharge.** When the hospital decides that there are no more services that can be offered to the patient—either because the services are not necessary or not available—the patient is discharged.
> - **Patient Billing.** Regular patient billing is done on a monthly cycle. However, billing for a particular patient may be done on demand. Sources of payment are the insurance company and/or the patient (credit card, cash, or subscription). If the amount is small, usually for co-payments, the patient is asked to pay before or after the service to save billing costs. Charity cases are not billed but recorded.

Finding Domain Concepts

> Domain concepts are objects, processes, people, and rules that constitute the goals, behavior, and structure of a domain.

An enterprise needs a common vocabulary. For information system development this is all the more important: Once the final product is deployed, misconceptions will be even more expensive to correct than errors cast in stone. The upfront effort to find the right definitions for a common vocabulary is not negligible, but it is worth every penny.

A business, however, is awash with concepts, even within a single domain. In this sea of concepts, which ones should we look for? Domain analysis has more than one use, including business process modeling (BPM) that models existing business processes, and business process reengineering (BPR) that models a business as it should be. They may or may not involve information systems. For an information system in the strict sense, we must do what we prescribed earlier in this chapter.

❶ *Discover the essence of the requirements.*   We argued that requirements are not the same as product specifications. But in many instances they are offered as a package. Sometimes this packaging is done inadvertently and can lead us in the wrong direction: The *real* requirement for the car that we mentioned before is that it must be safe to drive in mountainous roads, not that it must be wide and low—even though that is how the requirement was expressed.

❷ *Discover problems that the requirements are supposed to solve.*   Keep in mind that, in the context of product development, the term "problem" expresses opportunity and desire as well. In our example of the food distribution company, the problem can be expressed in a typical form:

- Shellfish decays fast in normal temperatures.

For Walden Medical Center, it is the opportunity that primarily drives the development of an information system:

- The automation of **Patient Management** should make referrals, appointments, registrations, recording of medical services, cost tracking, and patient billing easier, faster, cheaper, and more reliable.

❸ *Discover the components of the problem.*   The components of the problem are the first concepts that we must discover in domain analysis. For the food distribution company, we can identify these *intertwined* concepts from the previous problem statement.

- *Shellfish.*   The definition of "shellfish" seems obvious, but we should not take our own ideas for granted. Are all shellfish created equal? Do all decay at the same rate? Do we ship them separately or together?
- *Decay.*   What do we mean by "decay"? When must a shellfish be judged as spoiled?
- *Temperature.*   What is "normal temperature"? What temperature is required to keep the shellfish from spoiling? Would freezing reduce the value of the shellfish?

❹ *Discover related domain concepts.*   This is the core of the detective work that we call "domain analysis." Its success depends not only on what we discover, but also on what we leave out. Only concepts that directly or indirectly affect our planned product should be captured—no matter how close or how far they may be. Domain definition is necessary because it defines the scope of our search in general outlines. But even with the best domain scope, finding the relevant concepts is an iterative task. (We may even be forced to revise our domain definition or definitions as a consequence.)

In the **Shellfish Distribution** domain, we can only begin to scratch the surface.

- *Container.*   When caught, shellfish are stored in some kind of a container to be distributed—locally or otherwise. Define the container. Does it matter what kind of containers are used? The size? The price range?
- *Market.*   What does the business mean by "market"? A wholesaler in a city? Individual restaurants?
- *Fishing Source.*   Does the company catch the shellfish itself? Does it buy from individual and geographically dispersed fishers? Are there middlemen who buy the catch in one area and then sell it to the company?
- *Volume.*   How much shellfish does the company have at its disposal—now or in the future? Does the volume change depending on the season?

☞ The requirements that we are discussing here are rather high-level and preliminary. The foremost tool for modeling requirements is the use case, the subject of the next chapter.

And so on. We have not even touched on the related financial issues. Neither have we given a hint of *how* we are going to solve the problem. (At this point, we are still trying to understand the "problem domain.") But the concepts are essential to the design of a solution.

In a nutshell, through domain analysis we discover concepts that are relevant to *both* the business domain *and* the information system. Figure 5.8 illustrates the place of domain analysis in system development.

On the *left* are concepts that do not affect the product (the information system). For example, in a restaurant, the concept of `Service`—how the patrons are treated and served—is of extreme importance to the business (or should be) if it wants to attract a loyal clientele. But it does not concern an information system for the restaurant (except that it makes the waiters more efficient).

On the *right* are issues related to *design*: concepts that are purely concerned with the product or the solution we intend to build. If we decide to run a fleet of refrigerated cars for the food distribution company, every concept, every issue having to do with putting together, operating, and maintaining the fleet belong to this branch of the "M." For an information system, this is the **solution space**: hardware and software architecture, interface design, application flow, databases, platforms, etc.

It is the concepts in the *middle*, where the problem space and the solution space overlap, that domain analysis for an information system must discover and define. These concepts are the source of *analysis*, which aims to build a *conceptual model* of the system. (Note, however, that "source" means the origins or the raw material for the model, not the model itself.)

☞ When a solution is built and deployed, it moves to the left of the "M"; that is, it becomes part of the problem space. Therefore, when building a system that includes or interacts with legacy systems, we must include them in domain analysis, but only as "black boxes": We must not entangle ourselves in the inner workings of anything that does not concern us.

Figure 5.8
"M" for Model: The Passage from the Problem Domain to the Solution Domain

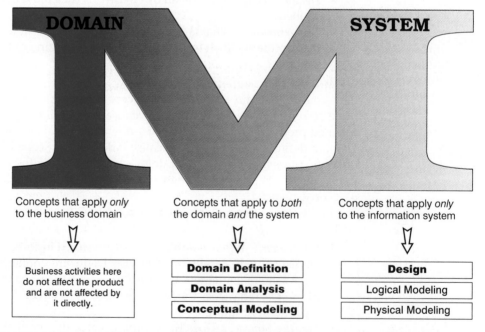

By "domain" we mean the business domain. "System" means an information system, a product, or a service that satisfies the requirements of the business. In building a product, depending on the complexity and the number of components, there would be a series of "M"s that overlap.
[Jackson 1995, 125]

Source: Jackson, *Software Requirements & Specifications*, © 1995 Pearson Education, Inc. Reprinted by permission of Pearson Education, Inc. All rights reserved.

☞ Legacy systems, even if we are replacing them, are usually rich sources for concepts. But they must be treated with caution: The underlying assumptions might be wrong or outdated. Verify each and every concept derived from such sources.

Walden's Patient Management: An Interview

To discover the right concepts, we must gather information from any source at our disposal: interviews, documents, observations, and existing workflows (if they exist). The task is very much that of detective work: gaps exist, and people are embarrassed to admit to certain practices and may not be able to narrate in a way that we would find clear and logical. Sometimes, it is not easy to describe a job that one does everyday. (That is why being an analyst is as much a matter of aptitude and attitude as it is of theoretical knowledge and experience.)

The following interview, provided in part, was conducted between the analyst who wants to build a scenario for treating patients at Walden and a *domain expert* (DE). The analyst has to go back and forth within the narrative and grab at hints to round up the concepts.

☞ The analyst is not taking any important concepts for granted. We may know what a patient is, but we must establish the hospital's definition.

Analyst:	*You treat patients. Who is a patient?*
DE:	A patient is someone who suffers from a medical condition. (Or thinks he does.) We treat them, give them a medical service—if we can.
Analyst:	*How do they come to you?*
DE:	They are referred to us by a doctor, usually a primary care physician.
Analyst:	*Is this the only source?*
DE:	No. They can walk in or they can come in through the emergency room. Sometimes another hospital sends them—if they cannot do what is needed.
Analyst:	*What is the first thing you do for the patient or about the patient?*
DE:	We make an appointment for them.
Analyst:	*Appointment to do what?*
DE:	Appointment for any of the hospital's services—like examination by a specialist, CAT scan, or X-ray.
Analyst:	*Even hospitalization?*
DE:	Even hospitalization (except that we call it "admission"). There must be an empty bed when we want it and it must be of the right kind for what the patient needs. And you just don't give them a bed: You also need the right doctor, an operating room perhaps—all kinds of resources. Yes, especially hospitalization.
Analyst:	*What do you do when you make an appointment?*
DE:	We verify the patient's name, who has referred them to the hospital, and the medical reason. We also ask them if they have ever been to the hospital.
Analyst:	*And then the patient can go for the service?*
DE:	Yes. But of course the clerk has to find an open spot in the hospital schedule and arrange an available date and time and agree with the patient about it.
	(Continued)

☞ When the "hospital ID card" is mentioned, the analyst concludes that a step has been overlooked. By posing a question about "when," we find that the missed step is registration, which involves much more than the ID card.

☞ Many hospitals issue an ID bracelet instead of, or in addition to, an ID card. This is especially useful when a procedure or an operation is to be performed as the chances of losing a bracelet is less. Most probably the analyst would discover this during a **field trip**.

Analyst:	*When the patient shows up for the service, how does the medical staff know what there is to know about the patient?*
DE:	Oh, we issue a hospital ID card to the patient. They use it to identify the patient, record service, and look up the case history.
Analyst:	*When do you issue the card?*
DE:	Just before they go in for the service. When they come to the hospital, we register them and if they do not have a hospital card, we issue one.
Analyst:	*What does registration involve?*
DE:	We get all the information we need about the patient: name, address, sex, date of birth, and so on. And the payment information, of course: insurance provider and the policy.
. . .	
Analyst:	*If the doctor sends medical documents—diagnosis, X-rays, etc.—to the hospital, how do you manage them?*
DE:	If the patient brings them along, they are entered in the patient's file right after the registration. If the documents are sent beforehand, then we take care of them before the patient comes for the appointment.
Analyst:	*What if the patient walks in without prior appointment but has every qualification to be considered a patient by the hospital (has been referred by a doctor, has necessary documents, and has a medical need that the hospital can attend to)?*
DE:	Then the same clerk would combine appointment and registration. Appointment would be done on an emergency basis, if necessary.
. . .	
Analyst:	*And when the service is done—CAT scan is finished, doctor is visited—then what happens?*
DE:	It depends.
Analyst:	*On what?*
DE:	On whether they have to have more tests, examinations, procedures, and so on. And if the patient has to be admitted, we are not finished with the patient until the medical staff says we can discharge him.

Domain Dictionary

☞ The more commonly used word is **glossary**. Since we attach more attributes to terms than just definitions, we decided on **dictionary**. But there is no fundamental difference.

> The domain dictionary organizes and brands domain concepts. It is the link between stakeholders who must verify the concepts and the analysts who would use them as the foundation for building a conceptual model of the system.

The outcome of domain analysis is a set of concepts. Concepts are expressed as words and words are, by nature, subject to interpretation. For system development, however, we need clarity of definition. Therefore, concepts must be shepherded and branded: free-roaming concepts tend to get lost. A domain dictionary supplies a good shelter.

The dictionary, which will change shape after the initial stage, organizes domain concepts (the **problem space**) pertinent to the system (the **solution space**). Each entry has a concise definition which serves as *the* authority whenever the term is used.

To populate the dictionary, we turn to all the products of information gathering: requirements, interviews, manuals, and so on. To keep a fruitful focus, however, we *start* from the product of domain definition: the **domain scope**.

☝ Some enterprises do have a glossary of their business terms, with varying degrees of quality. Such a glossary is a good start, but do not accept them at face value. Trust but verify!

We are interested in *any* concept expressed through sentences, phrases, and titles. (We will explain why we are doing this, so be patient.) The most promising ones are as follows:

- **Subjects**, in the grammatical sense: "The noun, noun phrase, or pronoun in a sentence or clause that denotes the ***doer of the action***."
- **Objects**, again as in grammar: "**a.** A noun or substantive that receives or is affected by the action of a verb within a sentence. **b.** A noun or substantive following and governed by a preposition." These nouns are candidates for becoming objects in an ***object-oriented*** sense.
- **Verbs** are interesting: they can indicate processes, but they can also hide nouns or grammatical objects: "ordering a book" is a variant of "placing *an order* for book." The object "order" is hidden in the verb "order."

[American Heritage 1996]

We highlight, extract, and organize the concepts we find as we parse the document(s), as is illustrated by this passage from Walden's **`Patient Management`** domain scope:

> **Medical Service.** Depending on the nature of the medical service, doctors, nurses, and lab technicians provide the patient with appropriate service(s) for which the appointment has been made.

We are now in possession of several concepts: **`Medical Service`**, **`Doctor`**, **`Nurse`**, **`Lab Technician`**, **`Patient`**, **`Appointment`**. We can deduce from the passage that a "doctor" is somebody who provides a "medical service" to a "patient." About **`patient`** we are likely to have our own idea, but what counts is how the *hospital* defines the term. We find our definition in the interview of the analyst with the domain expert:

> Analyst: *You treat patients. Who is a patient?*
>
> **Expert:** A patient is someone who suffers from a medical condition. (Or thinks he does.) We treat them, give them a medical service—if we can.

The definition is very close to how we define a patient, but what fine-tunes it from the viewpoint of the hospital is the concept of **`Medical Service`**: **`Patient`** is somebody who suffers from a medical condition *and* comes to the hospital for a medical service.

Now we have to chase after a definition for the term "Medical Service." And so on. Creating a system dictionary leads us from one trail to another.

Patient Management: A Domain Dictionary

Iterative does not mean "without end," so at a certain point we must publish the first draft of a domain dictionary for comments and verification on one hand, and to continue to the next phase of analysis on the other. Table 5.4 is the preliminary results of analyzing Walden's **`Patient Management`**.

Table 5.4
**Patient
Management**:
Domain Dictionary
(Partial Listing).

Walden Medical Center
Patient Management: Domain Dictionary
Version 1.0—August 15, 2004
(Partial Listing)

NAME	TYPE	DESCRIPTION
Appointment	Process	Scheduling of a <u>patient</u> to receive <u>medical service</u>(s). Performed by the <u>appointment clerk.</u>
Appointment	Object	The scheduled date and time for providing a <u>medical service</u> to a <u>patient</u>.
Appointment Clerk	Role	Makes <u>appointments</u> for the <u>patient</u>.
Medical Service	Object	Any service of medical nature provided by <u>medical staff</u> to a <u>patient</u>: diagnosis, prescription, administration of drugs, lab tests, etc.
Medical Service	Function	The act of providing a <u>medical service</u> to the <u>patient</u> by the <u>medical staff</u>.
. . .	. . .	. . .
Referral Source	Role	A <u>primary care physician</u>, an <u>emergency medical worker</u>, or an <u>outside hospital</u> that refers a <u>patient</u> for an <u>appointment</u> to receive a <u>medical service</u>. <u>Patient</u> himself or herself can be a referral source.
Registration	Process	Carried out before a set of <u>medical services</u> are performed. The process gathers new or changed personal and insurance information for a new or an existing <u>patient</u>. A hospital <u>ID card</u> may be issued as part of this process. Performed by the <u>registration clerk</u>.
Registration Clerk	Role	Performs <u>registration</u>.

The Dictionary Template

During its lifetime, the domain dictionary will metamorphose into other analysis artifacts such as use cases, use case diagrams, class models, etc. The *preliminary* template, as used for Walden's **Patient Management**, has three fields.

• *Name.* An identifier for a concept. The name must be (eventually) unique. When a group has to agree on a concept, its signifier—the name—must be *unambiguous*. For now, we enforce the uniqueness by constraining the name with the type.

- *Type.*   The type of entry. All entries, of course, are domain concepts, but we are aiming at an *object-oriented view* of the system that needs a set of richer concepts: use cases, actors, classes, relationships, associations, business rules, etc. Domain concepts are yet to become more sophisticated, but somehow we have to distinguish among them.

At the same time, not all the project stakeholders are privy to the specialized language of object-oriented modeling. We need to select a more common set of words (for now) to keep the lines of communication open.

There are no officially approved or industry-standard set of terms to describe the type in this context. At first contact with a business domain, there is a chance that you will be overwhelmed with *domain-speak*, terms and categories of terms that are only understandable to an insider. (No profession is immune to domain-speak.) Or, conversely, many objects might be described to you as "widgets" or an equally general or ambiguous term.

The point is that the type should reflect how the business domain sees the concept, but should also provide us with an opening towards object-oriented modeling. Following are a set of terms that can be applied to many contexts.

[American Heritage 1996]

- *Process.*   ❶ A series of actions, changes, or functions bringing about a result. ❷ A series of operations performed in the making or treatment of a product.
- *Function.*   The purpose or the result of one action or a set of actions.
- *Role.*   A grouping of any entity—be it a person, rank, position, job function, corporation, or system—that performs the same action or takes part in it.
- *Object.*   ❶ Something perceptible by one or more of the senses, especially by vision or touch. ❷ Something intelligible or perceptible by the mind. Or we can use **Entity** instead. The advantage of **Object** is that it is readily understood by the nontechnical members of the development team as a "thing." The disadvantage is that it is easily *mis*understood by the technical people as an instance of a virtual class in the information system.
- *Business Rule.*   A rule, independent of technology, that the system must observe in its transactions. For example: "*A checking account with less than $500 in deposit will be charged 50 cents for each check.*" It is crucial that business rules be defined very distinctly. As we shall argue later, business rules should be organized differently from the previous examples, especially since they normally cannot have meaningful names and are instead labeled, for instance, **BR-10**, **BR-44**, and so on.
- *Formula.*   ❶ A statement, especially an equation, of a fact, rule, principle, or other logical relation. ❷ A method of doing or treating something that relies on an established model or approach.
- *Identifier.*   A symbol—textual or otherwise—that identifies an object: Social Security Number, Universal Product Code, customer number, etc.

☞ We did not present a business rule or a formula in our example of the domain dictionary. In the initial phase, these two types are usually hidden in other concepts, especially processes. We will come back to them later.

No matter what terms we use in identifying types, eventually we have to evolve them into concepts employed by object-oriented modeling. As a result, we have some explaining to do to the business side of the development effort. We should, however, start from *their* world.

☞ For a more evolved version of the dictionary, you may also use **hypertext** to jump from a reference to the definition. But beware: It is a very time-consuming task. If you have organized your dictionary effectively, then finding an entry should not be very difficult even without hypertext. Do not start an effort that you may leave unfinished due to exhaustion or lack of resources. Consistency is more important than showing off.

- *Description.* A concise description of the entry, as precise and as short as possible. (The underlined words in the example *cross-reference* other entries in the dictionary. Highlighting references are nice to have but not essential, especially not in the draft dictionary.)

Though not included in our example, other highly recommended fields are:

- *Source.* The source of the concept: an interview, workshop, existing document or manual, etc. It provides two benefits: ease of verification and material for further analysis and expansion of the concept.

- *Notes.* Ideas are fleeting. An insight can light up the sky one moment and be gone the next. The ghost of a good question that we let go and forget about at this point will come back to haunt us later. However, one should be on guard against too many notes: Conciseness is the virtue of a dictionary.

Beyond Application Boundaries

> No domain is an island. Domain concepts must be viewed from the broad perspective of the whole business and not just one angle.

We define domains so that domain analysis can discover concepts required for building a solution within a *finite* context. In other words, we attempt to manage complexity by voluntarily putting on blinders.

If we stop here, however, our task would not be complete. A major aim of domain analysis is to find well-rounded, **multi-polar** concepts: concepts that apply across the enterprise, are not limited to the immediate task at hand, and can be **reused** readily.

This strategy is the exact opposite of creating self-sufficient application islands within the enterprise that serve the narrow interests of one group or another. Concepts that result from such a narrow analysis of domains resemble the observations that are offered in the old Indian parable of *Blind Men and the Elephant* (Figure 5.9). Each account of the elephant is more or less correct, but the combined image is wrong.

We must also emphasize that categorizing something differently does not change its nature. The boundaries of domains are porous. For a doctor, a patient may be of interest only as far as the process of diagnosis and treatment is concerned. For accountants, the interest in the patient concerns his or her account balance, while lawyers prefer *not* to see the patient in court. The hospital, as a whole, needs a more comprehensive profile. Health insurance companies and regulatory agencies have their own additional requirements.

Another risk in domain analysis is to mistake technological concepts with business concepts. Business problems are always solved with available technologies but, as we illustrated in the scenario about shellfish distribution, solution as method must not be confused with solution as answer.

[Coplien 1997]

> Domain analysis should avoid, as much as possible, abstractions that are biased towards a specific technology or a specific application.

Figure 5.9
Blind Men and the Elephant: Seeing the Parts, But Not the Whole

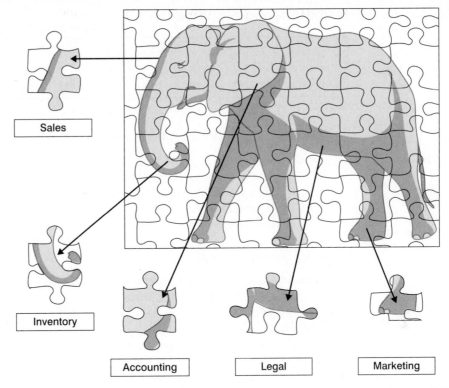

Sales

Inventory

Accounting

Legal

Marketing

Disjointed definitions of a concept distort the big picture, as in the parable of *Blind Men and the Elephant*:

It was six men of Indostan
To learning much inclined,
Who went to see the Elephant
Though all of them were blind,
That each by observation
Might satisfy his mind.

The First approached the Elephant
And, happening to fall
Against his broad and sturdy side,
At once began to bawl:
"God bless me, but the Elephant
Is very like a wall!"

 . . .
The Third approached the animal
And, happening to take
The squirming trunk within his hands,
Thus boldly up he spake:

"I see," quoth he, "The Elephant
Is very like a snake!"

 . . .
The Sixth no sooner had begun
About the beast to grope
Than, seizing on the swinging tall
That fell within his scope,
"I see," quoth he, "the Elephant
Is very like a rope!"

And so these men of Indostan
Disputed loud and long,
Each in his own opinion
Exceeding stiff and strong.
Though each was partly in the right,
They all were in the wrong!
        John Godfrey Saxe (1816–1887)

5. BUSINESS RULES

One set of concepts that we discover through domain analysis are business rules. All systems have rules but, depending on the nature of the system we are creating, the set of *business* rules may be small or large. *If* it is large, we need methods and procedures to find, document, present, implement, and maintain these rules.

Definition and Significance

> Business rules are a set of detailed policies, laws, procedures, guidelines, and standards under which an enterprise operates. A business rule is a statement that defines or demands adherence to a unit in the set.

Business rules are not the same as rules in general.

[Chapin 2002]

*If rules are about the logical design of the system, then they're "system design" rules. . . . If they're rules required to deal with a specific information technology, then they are "technology" rules. If rules are specific to a particular vendor's implementation of a technology, then they are "vendor specific" rules. . . . Only rules about business activities whose **content & purpose** are independent of the knowledge/information system that will enforce them should be called "business" rules.*

Domain analysis does not yield the key to all business rules. We cannot ask one simple question—"what are your business rules?"—and expect to be provided with a comprehensive catalogue. Like anything else in the system development, it is iterative and requires detective work.

Business rules require special handling because:

☞ Unfamiliar terms used here include use case, actor, and stored procedure. We will discuss them in upcoming chapters. The only thing we have to know about them at this point is that they are rather clearly defined concepts for modeling, design, and implementation.

❶ In an enterprise, business rules must be correctly applied to any workflow, automated or not. Their significance overshadows all other issues, including those related to analysis and design of an information system.

❷ Unlike other concepts discovered by domain analysis, business rules do not necessarily evolve into object-oriented concepts and modeling artifacts. (Some do, some do not.) While processes and functions can turn into use cases, objects are likely classes, and people are candidates to become actors, many business rules have to be enforced across different layers of a system, including database stored procedures.

Classification

> Classification helps us to correctly incorporate business rules in the design and implementation of an information system.

An image editing program has many rules but few business rules. An accounts payable subsystem or tax-calculation application, on the other hand, has many. If we have to handle many, we should also be able to classify them, since their classification will affect how they are implemented and managed.

[Wiegers 2003, 153–164]

Like use cases, business rules are made up of statements. And when language is involved—as you would expect—many different taxonomies (classification schemes) are proposed, argued, disputed, and repudiated. Following is one such taxonomy which we believe would satisfy most requirements.

- *Facts.* Facts are business rules that state how things are.
  - A patient is anybody who suffers from a medical condition and is referred to the hospital by a referral source—a doctor, a medical emergency worker, or another hospital.
  - A medical service is any service for diagnosis, test, and treatment provided by the medical staff—doctors, nurses, and lab technicians—for the patient.
  - An inventory code identifies all grocery items.
  - A billing clerk is a clerk who resolves billing issues, accepts payments, produces patient statements, and mails them.
  - Payment is by cash, credit card, or personal check.

☞ Some authors propose that another category, **Terms**, should apply to words, definitions, and abbreviations that are important to the business but are not policies. With such a category, our definition of "patient" would belong to *Terms* while the entry about "inventory code" will remain with **Facts**.

Another term for facts is *invariants*, since they are not supposed to change. (Or at least we do not expect them to.) Facts are likely to end up as classes (`Medical Service`) or attributes (`Inventory Code`).

- *Inferences.* An inference is a business rule that we derive from a condition that we know to be true. In other words, an inference is a fact concluded from another fact. It is often expressed in an " `if/then[/else]` " construct.
  - If the customer is less than 21 years old, then the customer is ineligible to buy alcoholic beverages.
  - If the employee has worked for more than 5 years, then his or her vacation days are 21 days, else the vacation days are 15.
  - If the patient bill is not paid within 30 days, then the bill is considered overdue.

- *Action Enablers.* Action enablers are triggers for action if a certain condition is met. Like inferences, they are expressed in an " `if/then[/else]` " construct, but the result is an action rather than a fact.
  - If the patient has an appointment but has not been registered, then the reception clerk directs the patient to the registration.
  - If the patient billing cycle terminates abnormally, then send notification to billing clerk.
  - If a CD is out of stock, then disable overnight delivery option.

☞ With some of the examples for business rules, we are actually jumping ahead of ourselves. Many of the rules are discovered through use case and class modeling that are just ahead. We will refer to them again when the context requires it.

- *Constraints.* Constraints are business rules that put restrictions on the actions that the system or the actors may perform or must not perform. The statements expressing constraints are imperative: must, may not, can, cannot, etc.
  - A patient less than 18 years old must be accompanied by a related adult or an emergency medical worker.
  - Only the billing clerk may accept cash payments from the patients.
  - A bank customer with less than $500 dollars in the checking account must be charged 10 cents per check.
  - A patient may not be removed from records after receiving the first medical service.

- *Computations.* Computations include formulas and algorithms.
  - The line item total for books ordered is the number of copies multiplied by the price for each copy.

- The employee overtime rate for weekdays and non-holidays is the normal rate multiplied by 1.6.

Among the business rule types, computations have the least dependency on the natural language. If possible, they should be written as formulas to enhance clarity.

- Line Item Total = Number of Copies × Book Price.

Frequently, one computation is based on a set of variables that must eventually be maintained in a database lookup table. Tax tables and volume discounts are two examples. (See "Managing Business Rules" later in this chapter.)

In implementation, constraints are mostly hidden in classes, in constraints on database tables, in referential integrity rules, in triggers, and in stored procedures. (We will discuss such topics as referential integrity in later chapters.)

Automation Rules

[Lin 2002]

The preceding categories apply to business structure and operations with or *without* an automated system. The following categories include rules that the business may require from an application. They would not exist outside an information system but are, nevertheless, business-related.

- *Presentation Rules.* Presentation rules are about *what* should or should not be presented, not about *how* (which is technology-dependent). For example:

  - When the shipping clerk fulfills an order, the credit card information must not be displayed.

- *Workflow Rules.* Workflow rules define how a user goes through a process.

  - An unregistered patient must be registered before receiving medical service.

As we shall see in the next chapter, workflow rules are normally part of a use case.

Restatement of Rules

Often one business rule can be easily rephrased as another type, especially inferences and action enablers. For example, the inference rule that

- If the customer is less than 21 years old, then the customer is ineligible to buy alcoholic beverages.

can be restated as an action enabler:

- The customer must be refused the sale of alcoholic beverages if he or she is less than 21 years old.

Such is the magic of the language, but the magic would become a curse if it compels us to waste time by arguing the merits of assigning a rule to one type rather than another. (Some, of course, would enjoy the long arguments—excluding our clients.) Business rules we must discover. Rule types guide us in how to express and organize them clearly and where (roughly) to implement them (as we shall see later).

Managing Business Rules

> Business rules must be organized, maintained, and verified for the life of a business, not for the duration an application.

Discovering business rules is an iterative effort to glean the DNA of the business we are modeling. This is challenging enough, but equally challenging is how to manage them: The significance of business rules does not stop with one phase of development but is felt even after the final product is deployed. To discuss the *maintenance* of a system is, to a considerable degree, to discuss how the business rules in the system are to be corrected or changed.

Besides discovery through successive requirements gathering and analysis, management of business rules must ensure:

- *Origin Traceability.* Not only the current development team, but also those who might come afterwards should be able to trace business rules to their origins.
- *Integrity.* Competing or obsolete business rules must be weeded out.
- *Flexibility of Presentation.* Business rules may crisscross multiple domains and, as a result, systems and subsystem. What is more, a single business rule may be related to multiple other rules. We must be able to reorganize and cross-reference them for presentation and verification.
- *Implementation Traceability.* As we previously hinted, a great many business rules are implemented as "black boxes" and then fade from living memory: gradually what rules the system follows to do what it does become a mystery. The idea of "information hiding" is one of the success stories of object-oriented software development, but if we cannot trace business rules, they are not *hidden*, but effectively *lost*.
- *Flexibility of Maintenance.* This is important for any product but, as we mentioned, a great part of a software product's maintenance consists of corrections and changes to business rules.

Can we ensure all these? We must try our best, even though we may lack tools that work, tools that integrate with other development tools at our disposal, tools that the development team knows how to use, or tools that the development team is willing to use. Like many other elements that we derive from domain dictionaries, we can organize business rules within a customized dictionary.

Rules Dictionary

There is a fine line between requirements and business rules.

> Requirements specify features of the product, while business rules apply beyond any single solution.

In practice, however, it is often impossible to distinguish between the two. We discussed managing requirements in the last chapter. You may use the same template(s) for business rules as for requirements. But if there is a pressing need for (and a realistic possibility of) separating them, you may tailor a template dedicated to rules. Table 5.5 is a sample dictionary for Walden's **Patient Management** business rules.

Table 5.5
Sample business rules
dictionary for
Walden's **Patient
Management**
business rules.

	Walden Medical Center		
	Patient Management: Business Rules Dictionary		
	Version 1.0—August 15, 2004		
ID	DEFINITION	TYPE	SOURCE
001	A **patient** is anybody who suffers from a medical condition and is referred to the hospital by a referral source—a doctor, a medical emergency worker, or another hospital.	Fact	Domain dictionary
002	A **referral source** is a medical authority—a primary care physician, another hospital, or an emergency medical worker—qualified by the hospital or an accepted health maintenance organization to refer patients.	Fact	Hospital policy
003	A **patient** less than 18 years old must be accompanied by a related adult or an emergency medical worker.	Constraint	Hospital policy
004	Before **appointment**, patient's contact and referral data must be recorded: **ID** **Data** 004–01 Last Name 004–02 First Name 004–03 Middle Initial 004–04 Contact Address 004–05 Phone 1 004–06 Phone 2 004–07 Social Security Number (Optional) 004–08 Contact ID	Constraint	Interview with domain expert (attached)
005	A **registration clerk** is one who enters or updates a patient's personal and payment data and issues a hospital card, if necessary.	Fact	Domain dictionary
006	If the **patient bill** is not paid within 30 days of due date, then the bill is considered overdue.	Inference	Hospital policy

Do not be misled that an advanced business rule dictionary will be such a simple affair. Even the smallest business can have a very long list of business rules. After a certain point, we may want to reorganize our business rules in categories that are relevant to business: **Patient Management**, **Accounting**, etc.

The Template

The template that we used as an example is almost the least common denominator. Other authors have suggested additional fields (not necessarily the same ones) and you might find that you must add your own fields to satisfy specific requirements.

- *ID.* A *unique* identifier for the business rule. It must hide no meaning and is assigned sequentially. In the majority of cases, it is difficult to assign a concise name to a business rule, therefore ID is all we have. Nevertheless, if possible, we can make IDs somehow more meaningful. For example, rule number 1 in the example can become **Patient-001**, or number 4 can be relabeled **Appt-001**. What is important is to assign a unique reference ID across the dictionary. (If the ID is not combined, it is customary to add a **BR-** prefix to the number to distinguish it from other entries in the "system document"—whatever its format—such as **UC-100**, which should be a use case.)

- *Definition.* As we can see from rule **004** in the example, a definition may comprise a set of sub-rules. We have identified each sub-rule with a compound ID: the ID from the parent rule, plus a unique identifier within the namespace. If sub-rules become too unruly for the space granted them, they may be enumerated somewhere else and just referenced here.

- *Type.* Type is the classification of the rule as we discussed before. It is primarily useful as a hint for design and implementation.

- *Source.* Source is a reference to a document or documents from which the rule originates.

We may add other attributes to the business rules. For example, a **Dynamic/Static** column would show whether we expect the rule to change over time or to remain as it is for eternity (i.e., when we are finished with the project).

[Reeder 2001]

A template for business rules does not have to be in tabular format. You may even use separate templates for different categories because each category can be reduced to a well-defined syntax. For example, an action enabler rule can be abstracted as:

```
IF <rule phrase>
 [AND <rule phrase>
 AND <rule phrase>  . . . ]
 THEN <inferred knowledge>
```

However, we suggest simplicity graced with consistency as far as it is practical. And if you are using an automated rules management tool (or you have to), then your flexibility is defined by the flexibility of the tool.

Verification

A critical purpose of organizing business rules is verification by business stakeholders. The importance of this task cannot be exaggerated. In the soft light of early requirements gathering, inconsistencies do not stand out sharply. Experts from two different domains in a bank would tell you that a customer can do this or the customer cannot do that, and we would be left with the impression that by "customer" they have meant the same thing. It is only when we present them with a compact definition of **Customer**—in black and white, so to speak—that we find how deep the chasm has been: one expert was talking about *corporate* customers, while the other meant individual consumers. (The situation is even less pretty when experts in the *same* domain mean different things by the same term.)

Depending on the volume and the complexity of our business rules, we may have to reorganize them for the *explicit* purpose of verification. If so, after verification, after we are reasonably sure that the rules have been captured correctly, we must reintegrate them within our dictionary to ensure integrity. (We may keep our verification documents as an audit trail.) Table 5.6 is a sample verification questionnaire for Walden's **Patient Management** business rules. We should not encumber the questionnaire with nonbusiness attributes such as the type of the rule.

Table 5.6

Sample verification questionnaire for Walden's **Patient Management** business rules. As you can see, there is no significant difference between this questionnaire and the one for verifying requirements in the previous chapter. (Instead of descriptive names we have used numeric IDs.)

Walden Medical Center
Patient Management: Business Rules Questionnaire
September 2, 2004

ID	DEFINITION	TRUE / FALSE		COMMENT
001	A **patient** is anybody who suffers from a medical condition and is referred to the hospital by a referral source—a doctor, a medical emergency worker, or another hospital.	☐	☐	
	. . .			
003	A **patient** less than 18 years old must be accompanied by a related adult or an emergency medical worker.	☐	☐	
	. . .			
006	If the **patient bill** is not paid within 30 days, then the bill is considered overdue	☐	☐	

6. DELIVERABLES

The products of domain definition and domain analysis must be adequate, not perfect. They will be refined through analysis in subsequent steps, and will be transformed into other models.

- *Domain Scope.* The definition of domain boundaries and major functions. It must be concise and understandable to both the business and the development stakeholders.

- *Domain Dictionary.* A dictionary of concepts discovered through domain analysis within the boundaries identified by the domain definition. If the scope of the system is enterprise-wide, then definitions from multiple domain dictionaries must be consolidated into one. The definitions must be concise and clear to all stakeholders.

- *Rules Dictionary.* Depending on the nature and quantity of the business rules, they can be included in requirements, incorporated in the domain dictionary, or granted a dictionary of their own. Find a solution that corresponds to the scope, needs, and resource limitations of your project. But, in whatever shape or form, rules *must* be documented, traced, and verified.

- *Domain Catalog.* A directory of domain documents. The catalog serves as a reference *and* a referee for all issues surrounding definitions of concepts.

7. WRAP UP

Between the statement of high-level requirements and the conceptual modeling of the information system, a crucial task must be accomplished: discovering the business concepts that ❶ constitute the context of the problem or ❷ are expected from the solution.

The mission of domain analysis is to explore, define, organize, and verify this set of concepts: processes, rules, people, objects—existing or planned, across the enterprise or limited to a more modest scope.

Domain analysis itself, however, requires an understanding of the concepts that relate to the nature of problem solving. It also requires its own context, provided by domain definition.

☑ **The three components of problem solving**

Developing an information system is building a solution in answer to a problem, an opportunity, or a desire. While problem solving is often viewed as having a pair of components—the problem and the solution—in reality it consists of three elements: the problem, the solution as method, and the solution as answer. Requirements, in the strict sense of the word, express the features that the solution as answer must have. It remains to us to discover or verify the first two components.

☑ **The problem space vs. the solution space**

The problem, the method (or the process) for solving the problem, and the answer to the problem operate in two distinct but dialectically related spaces: the problem space and the solution space. To build the solution, we must discover the concepts within the problem space (or the problem domain). But the two spheres interact and affect each other. Therefore, we must also understand how the solution will operate within the domain that gave rise to the problem in the first place.

☑ **Requirements vs. product specifications**

Products (or solutions as answer) are not the same as requirements. Requirements are the features that a product must have, while many products can satisfy the same requirements. The factors that decide in favor of one product against other are many: technology, preferences, cost, experience, time, resources, etc. Without a comprehensive domain analysis, a product may satisfy all requirements but fail nevertheless.

☑ **Domains and their boundaries**

In search for business concepts, a well-defined and finite context is required so that domain analysis will not spin out of control. Domain analysis identifies the boundaries of business domains. A business domain is a sphere of related business activities that have shared rules and concepts and are organized to achieve a goal or set of goals.

By identifying the scope of domains—their major functions—domain definition also provides a framework for partitioning a complex system into conceptual subsystems.

☑ **Identifying domain concepts for analysis and modeling**

Domain analysis is the process of discovering and organizing domain concepts. But domain analysis for building an information system is not concerned with just *any* concept, and certainly not with *all* concepts.

First, if necessary, it must analyze the requirements to distinguish them from accidental or intentional product specification. Second, it must identify problems that these requirements are supposed to solve. Third, it must identify the concepts within the problem. Last, but not least, it must discover concepts that may not be apparent by the requirements or the analysis of the problem, but will affect the product nevertheless.

If the information system goes across domains, or will at some point, then concepts must be expanded as well. An advantage of domain analysis is that it permits an application to be local while the perspective of the whole system can remain enterprise-wide.

☑ **Domain dictionaries and domain catalog**

The findings of domain analysis must be organized as a dictionary. This dictionary, or its subsets, allows the business stakeholders to verify the concepts and provides the development team with building blocks for modeling.

The domain catalog is a consolidation of business documents (or references to them) that support the domain dictionary. It serves as an authority for settling issues related to the definition of domain concepts.

☑ **Identifying and organizing business rules**

A set of business concepts that do not readily fit within one model or another are business rules. As the name signifies, business rules are the guidelines and rules under which a business must operate, *regardless of technology*. So a product must abide by these rules, whether analyzing the requirements and the problems directly point towards them or not.

Whereas requirements are features that a product must have, business rules serve as constraints to those features. Without a thorough and correct implementation of these constraints, the product will be a failure. And since the implementation of business rules often travels across individual models, they must be rigorously managed and verified.

8. KEY CONCEPTS

Business Rule.   A guideline, procedure, policy, law, standard, or constraint under which an enterprise operates. Business rules are independent of information technology and its applications.

Business Rules Dictionary.   A document that defines and categorizes business rules. The dictionary is updated through questionnaires that allow stakeholders to verify individual rules.

Domain.   A territory with shared concepts and rules. A *business domain* is an organized, goal-oriented domain. The term may be applied to an entire enterprise, its sub-domains, or the context in which the enterprise or the product or the service operates.

Domain, Derived.   A domain that results from discovering a set of common concepts across various domains or sub-domains.

Domain Analysis.   An iterative activity to discover and define domain concepts within the scope of an enterprise and/or its sub-domains.

Domain Catalog.   A directory of documents (or references) that support domain concepts and rules. The documents may include business policies, guidelines, manuals, interviews, etc.

Domain Concept.   An abstraction of a process, function, object, or role within a domain.

Domain Definition.   Identifying the scope and the boundaries of a domain or sub-domain.

Domain Dictionary.   An ordered repository for domain concepts, concept definitions, and concept types.

Domain Expert.   A person with a high degree of knowledge about a domain or sub-domain.

Domain Scope.   ❶ Definition of boundaries that separate shared activities, rules, and concepts within a domain from those outside. ❷ A document that establishes domain boundaries by describing its identifying features.

Problem Space.   The context from which the problem originates and in which the solution must operate. Also called *problem domain* (usually shortened to just "domain").

Product.   A product (or service) is the realization of features specified by requirements. A product is also the solution as answer to the problem that the requirements seek to solve or the opportunity of which they hope to take advantage.

Solution.   ❶ Answer to a problem. (See **Product**.) ❷ Method or process to build a product or service that aims to solve a problem.

Solution Space.   Where concrete decisions about the design and the implementation of the solution as a product or service are made. Solution space defines the scope of *how* a product is made, not *what* features it must have. Also called *solution domain* or *system domain*.

Sub-Domain.   A domain within a larger domain. (See **Domain**.)

Subsystem, Conceptual.   A unit within an information system that correlates to a business domain; integrates with its processes, rules, and its goals; and is used by the people in that domain (actors).

9. CONFUSING TERMS

Domain.   The term "domain" has more than one application, even in the context of information systems. For example, in database design, it determines the range of acceptable values. In networking, it is a collection of computers that share the same management and security database. And more. Even though all meanings are related, they should not be confused.

Requirements.   Strictly speaking, requirements should only identify the features that a product must have. In practice, however, descriptions of the problem, guidelines for solving the problem, and product specifications are also thrown into the mix. While we have emphasized that you must discover the "true" requirements, do not disregard the non-pure elements. Also, "requirements" often are used in a general sense: what is necessary to do something or a prerequisite. We must rely on the context to distinguish between the two meanings.

Solution.   The method to solve a problem and the answer to a problem are both called "solution." Sometimes the distinction is not important. Most of the time the context will guide us. When the context does *not* help, we must make the distinction clear.

10. Topic Discussions

Emergence of Domain Analysis

The idea of domain analysis was introduced in the 1980s in response to the "software crisis." But it has not been long since it has shown signs of becoming popular and mainstream. The perception of "crisis," of course, has not changed. What has changed is that **[Neighbors 1981]**

- first, business is learning, very slowly and in its own good time, that reinventing the wheel every time is expensive and wasteful; and
- second, the building blocks of an enterprise-oriented approach to software development are falling into place, in terms of both technology (powerful computers, storage, networks, etc.) and methodology (object-oriented tools, languages, and modeling).

Still, you can read many chapters and papers on domain analysis and not recognize that the authors are talking about the same concept (like many other subjects in system analysis and design). Evidently, a lot more needs to be done and, fortunately, is being done.

Domain as a Concept

Domain is a *concept*, which means it is a perception of reality, not the reality itself—even though the perception might come very close to reality. Nevertheless, domains do display an inherent logical coherence—once we discover the rules or, perhaps, once we select and organize them based on our preferences and our aims. Animal Kingdom is a recognizable domain: We do distinguish between the rules that apply to a bear and those that bear upon a rose which belongs to the Plant Kingdom.

Domains, however, are *not* mutually exclusive. Within one domain, we can distinguish other domains and sub-domains: birds and mammals within the Animal Kingdom, for example. They may also overlap: We can take elements from one domain, combine it with elements from another one, and come up with a new domain that is equally valid. Take a fly from the insects domain, a finch from the birds, and a bat from the mammals and we are likely to "discover" a domain in which the rules of aerodynamics apply because they all fly. The new domain has an internal coherence and an objective reality, but we arrive at it by an act of selection.

☞ In building an information system, the point that domain is a perception is important to remember since we have a wide latitude in how we interpret the reality of a business.

11. Review Questions

1. What is the difference between domain definition and domain dictionary? Give an example for each.
2. Define business roles and give three examples for a bank.
3. Write requirements for the following products and services:

   a. Computer.
   b. Airplane.
   c. Food Processor.
   d. Online Banking.
   e. Life Insurance.
   f. Party Planning.

4. What are the characteristics of business domains? Explain them in the context of a specific business.
5. Define "derived" domain. Could an information system be a derived domain? Explain.
6. Distinguish between logical and physical models.

   a. Which one comes first?
   b. Where do conceptual models fit?

7. Create a domain dictionary for an ATM system.
8. Identify three business rules for an ATM system.
9. Identify three objects for an ATM system.
10. Identify three functions for an ATM system.

12. Exercises

The following exercises apply to each of the four narratives introduced in Chapter 4: *The* Sportz *Magazine, The Car Dealership, The Pizza Shop,* and *The Real Estate Agency.*

❶ What are the business concepts in the scenario?
❷ Categorize the business concepts into processes, functions, roles, objects, and business roles.
❸ What would you name the system and its subsystems?
❹ Write domain definitions and, from there, proceed to establish the domain scope for the system and each subsystem.
❺ Create a domain dictionary for the proposed information system.

13. Research Projects & Teamwork

❶ Refer to the narrative for Walden Medical College in Chapter 4. All team members should read this chapter thoroughly before meeting to discuss how the following questions should be answered.

- Create a domain dictionary for the online registration subsystem. Identify concepts, their types, and descriptions. Use Table 5.4 as a guide.
- Identify business rules for the subsystem and create a "rules dictionary," complete with definition, types, and sources. Use Table 5.5 as a guide.
- Create a business rules questionnaire similar to Table 5.6. Each definition should be formulated in a way that can be verified by a simple **True** or **False**.
- Select a group member as group leader and let the leader prepare a report addressing the questions above with an appendix that indicates the contribution of each member as the percentage of total work.

❷ Refer to the *automated research system* (the "reference engine") in Chapter 4 and select one team member as the leader for this project. The team leader should decide how the team proceeds to answer the following questions. (One way is that each team member answers the two questions individually and hands them over to the leader, who then combines them to arrive at the most comprehensive answers and submits them to the instructor.) The team leader should also evaluate each member's contribution and write a short memo describing how the team worked together.

- Create a domain scope for the reference engine. Make sure to define domain boundaries and functions clearly. Use Table 5.3 as a guide.
- Create a domain dictionary for the application. identify concepts and their types and provide descriptions. Use Table 5.4 as a guide.

❸ Refer to the *online shopping system* in Chapter 4 and answer the following questions. (Follow the same process described for the previous project, but with a different project leader.)

- Create a domain scope for the online shopping system. Make sure to define domain boundaries and functions thoroughly.
- Identify business rules for the system and create a rules dictionary complete with definitions, types, and sources. Use Table 5.5 as a guide.
- Create a business rules questionnaire similar to Table 5.6. Each definition should be formulated in a way that can be verified by a simple **True** or **False**.

❹ Alberto is a new graduate and has been hired by a doctor to automate his patient scheduling system. He is your best friend and has no clue where to start. Use all you have learned from this chapter and help him by conducting a domain analysis. (If you do not have access to a real doctor's office, there is always the Web.) Identify domain boundaries, functions, tasks in each function, and business rules.

14. Suggested Readings

Despite the growing acceptance of domain analysis, the volume of writings on the subject in the context of object-oriented software development is still rather limited. Many valuable contributions are published as academic papers or articles, not as books. The good news is that more than a few are available on university Web sites.

Some of the books cited in our References discuss domains (if not domain analysis) at some length. But for a basic and clear introduction to domain analysis, see "Domain Analysis: An Introduction" by **Rubén Prieto-Diaz** in *Software Engineering Notes*, 15–2 (April 1990, http://www.cs.jmu.edu).

If you are interested in the origins of the idea and its relationship to components, read *Software Construction Using Components* by **J. Neighbors** (Ph.D. Thesis, Department of Information and Computer Science, University of California, 1981).

For an advanced discussion of problems within the context of software development, consult *Problem Frames: Analyzing and Structuring Software* by **Michael Jackson** (Addison-Wesley, 20001).

Our discussion of business rules barely scratches the surface. There are a number of comprehensive Web sites dedicated to business rules, including:

- The Business Rules Community (http://www.brcommunity.com).
- The Business Rules Group (http://www.businessrulesgroup.org).

6

Behavioral Modeling I
Use Cases: The Basics

1. OVERVIEW

Use case modeling represents the behavior of a system. A use case details the interaction of entities outside a system, called actors, with the system to achieve a specific goal by following a set of steps called a scenario.

- ☑ Inception
- ☑ Requirements Discovery
- ☐ Development
    - ☐ Analysis
        - ☑ **Domain Analysis**
        - ☐ Behavioral Modeling
            - ☐ **Use Cases: The Basics** ◀
            - ☐ Developing Use Cases
        - ☐ Structural Modeling
        - ☐ Dynamic Modeling
    - ☐ Design
    - ☐ Implementation

Chapter Topics

➤ What use case modeling is and is not.

➤ The four components of a use case.

➤ The basic elements of use case diagram.

➤ Various flows in the narrative of a use case.

➤ How to transform concepts from domain analysis into use cases.

➤ Identifying prominent actors.

➤ Identifying major use cases.

➤ The context diagram.

Introduction

In the previous chapter on domain definition and domain analysis, we argued that to build a solution we must first understand the problem and, second, distinguish between the method for solving a problem and the answer to the problem. We also identified two spaces: *problem space* where the problems arise and solutions must operate in, and *solution space* where issues relating to the product itself are encountered.

The task of *domain analysis* is to put requirements back into context and discover and define *business concepts* that are shared between the problem space and the solution space. *Domain definition* is needed to establish the *domain scope* for analysis and provide the conceptual framework for subsystems.

Domain analysis, however, does not produce a model but the concepts that we must use for modeling. The main gateway between domain analysis and the modeling of the information system—be it dynamic or structural, conceptual or logical—is **use case** modeling (Figure 6.1), which represents a *behavioral model* of the system.

Use case modeling is the foremost tool in taming the complexity of developing systems. It is also the most sensitive stage in gathering requirements. Gathering requirements, of course, does not start with use cases: The project starts with the initial requirements, and domain analysis must carry a heavy load of it. Nor does it end with use cases: We have a mass of detail to work out before the structure of an information system really takes shape.

Figure 6.1   Discovery of Use Cases: Transforming Domain Concepts into Behavioral Models

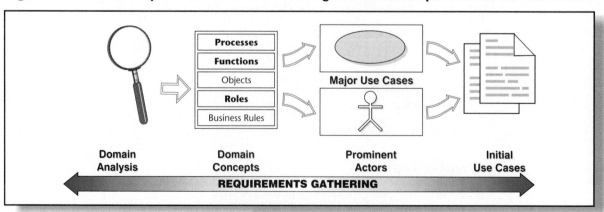

Use case are discovered by analyzing and expanding domain concepts, discovered through domain analysis.

The significance of use case modeling is that it provides the *framework* for the most important building blocks of modeling and beyond. Use cases are the indispensable guideposts from one end of system development to the other: from gathering requirements and communicating upstream with stakeholders to exchanging information downstream with designers and programmers to testing the product and training the users.

As we shall show, the essence of a use case is simple. However, use case modeling extends beyond use cases themselves. It is not limited to the components of the use cases but also originates a diverse set of documents that shapes both the means and the goal of system development.

The formal definition of use case is straightforward. Grasping its significance and depth, however, takes some effort. In this chapter we first present a *definition* of use case modeling and the *four components* of a use case. Next, we draw a map for arriving at *major use cases* from domain concepts. Later, we discuss how the findings of this *initial stage* of use case modeling should be organized and presented.

2. INTRODUCING USE CASES

A use case is a compound entity. Understanding it requires a good understanding of its components and how they affect each other. It also requires a clear understanding of what use case modeling is *not*. Without this negative definition, use cases are liable to miss their mission and turn into a grab bag of irrelevant and misguiding details.

What Use Case Modeling Is

☞ A *unit* is "a group regarded as a distinct entity within a larger group." [American Heritage 1996]

> Use cases model the behavior of a system.

A use case is a unit of system behavior. This definition needs a description to clarify it.

✍ By *behavior* we mean exactly that— and no more: A use case describes *what* a system does as viewed from outside, not *how* it does it inside it own boundaries.

> A use case details the interaction of an actor with a system to accomplish a goal of value to the actor.

The description, in turn, needs a story to illustrate what a use case actually is.

A customer enters the supermarket. The customer takes a shopping cart or basket and strolls through the supermarket. The customer selects items from the shelves and puts them in the shopping cart or the basket. When finished, the customer brings the items to the cash register. The cashier calculates the total price of the merchandise. The customer pays for the merchandise. The cashier bags the items, issues a receipt to the customer, and, if necessary, returns the change. The customer picks up the bags and leaves the supermarket.

If we add a name to this story—**Purchase Groceries,** for instance—the example will represent the *core* of a use case. (The name, we shall see, is very important.)

Use cases are technology-independent. They are not limited to information systems, computerized or otherwise. Use case analysis can be applied to master the behavior of any "open" system, from a supermarket to shipping operations to a mission to Mars, from a small system to a gigantic one, from a simple system to a complex one, from an existing system to one that is yet to be realized.

In developing a system, a use case may also be described as a contract.

> A use case is a contract that formalizes the interaction between stakeholders and the system.

As a contract, a use case binds all parties—the system as well as the stakeholders—to observe all obligations specified in the use case. In other words, if a system behaves exactly as promised in the use cases that describe its behavior, then the requirements for the system are fulfilled and the job is done.

What Use Case Modeling Is Not

> Use case modeling is limited to a system's external behavior.

To better understand what use case modeling *is,* it is imperative to be aware of what it is *not.*

- *Use cases do not model the system from inside.* What goes inside a machine—the information system—to satisfy a requirement does not concern a use case and must not be part of its story.
- *Use cases are not effective in capturing the nonfunctional requirements.* Even though, intentionally or not, nonfunctional requirements find their way into use cases, use case modeling was not created, and should not be used, as a vehicle for nonfunctional requirements.
- *Use case modeling is not the same as functional decomposition.* Methods based on functional decomposition break down the functionality of a system into successively smaller tasks and subtasks until they reach the most atomic functions. Use cases, on the other hand, are *units* of behavior that must accomplish a "meaningful result" (as we will describe in detail).
- *Use cases are not inherently object-oriented.* Object-oriented analysis and design would be seriously handicapped without use case modeling. But use cases can be used in methodologies that are completely alien to object-orientation.
- *Use cases describe what a system accomplishes, not how.* Even though a "pure" use case is near to impossible, use case modeling is a tool of analysis, not of design (even though design flows from analysis).

We will expound on these points—what use case modeling is and what it is not—throughout this chapter.

An **open** system is one which interacts with the outside world.

A job done is not the same as a job done *right.* The industry is littered with information systems that conform to somebody's idea of requirements, but are total or partial wastes. Regardless of who is the culprit, if use cases are wrong, incomplete, or obsolete, the resulting system will also be wrong, incomplete, or obsolete. The quality of the final product begins from the beginning.

See the chapter on Gathering Requirements for a definition of nonfunctional requirements.

Components of a Use Case

A use case has four components: a goal, stakeholders, a system, and a scenario.

Not every story that describes a system's behavior is a use case. A use case must consist of four well-defined components (Figure 6.2) to qualify as such:

- A **goal,** the outcome of a successful use case.
- **Stakeholders** whose interests are affected by the outcome of the use case, including **actors** who interact with the system to accomplish the goal.
- A **system** that provides the services that the actors need to reach the objective.
- A **scenario** that the actors *and* the system follow to accomplish the goal.

We examine each component before returning to discuss the use case as a whole.

❶ *A Goal.*

A goal is what the successful completion of a use case achieves.

A use case itemizes the interaction between a system and the actor(s) to achieve a goal. This goal

- must be meaningful,
- must be a logically complete function, and
- must be of measurable value.

All of the above mean essentially the same thing. But what exactly is this "same thing"? It is a concept that can be clarified more by examples than semantic analysis.

✍ Components of a use case are tightly integrated and cannot be understood properly without each other.

[Jacobson 1995, 105]

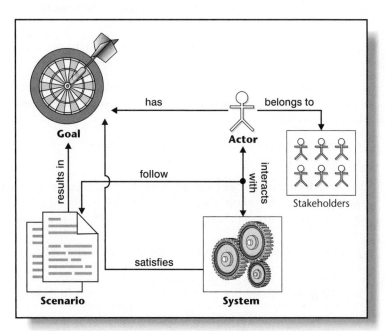

**Figure 6.2
Components
of a Use Case:
Actor(s), System,
Goal, Scenario**
The goal must result in measurable value, but the value is a matter of judgment.

Consider the use case, **Purchase Groceries,** that we previously described. If the customer does not select any item to buy and leaves the store, nothing useful is accomplished. Consider another example: If a bank customer inserts a bank card into an ATM and then retrieves the card and simply walks away, the goal of the use case—call it **Conduct ATM Transaction**—is logically incomplete.

☞ Rarely does anybody go to an ATM thinking that "I am going to conduct a transaction." We think about getting cash, making a deposit, checking an account balance, etc. What we just described is a *generalization*, a type of use case which will be explored later.

> A use case is successful only if its stated goal is completely achieved.

A goal is also shaped to a large degree by judgment. Suppose the supermarket customer picks up items and then leaves the supermarket without paying for them. It is undoubtedly of some "measurable value" to the customer, but the supermarket management would not be amused. Without payment for the groceries, the use case is *not* successful.

Development is not started from neatly delineated use cases with clearly identified goals and names. What we have is a mixed bag of clear to utterly cloudy ideas about how the end product should work. Buying groceries is a fairly common experience (which is why we chose it as an example), but our mission is to venture into unknown territory even if, in the end, we find more of the same: that things are exactly what we had imagined them to be. Relying only on experience, how many analysts can write a set of accurate use cases for putting a passenger airliner together? Or for operating it?

Things can and do go wrong if the goals are defined *out of context*, especially in respect to the other components of the use case, which influence and constrain the goal (and each other).

Reaching the goal can be simple or complex but the *name* of the use case, which declares the goal, must be clear, active, and simple. If the name is muddied, chances are that either the goal is not clearly understood or we are trying to squeeze more than one goal into the use case. (It may happen that the goal is clear but we are unable to express it clearly: "*Go to Supermarket, Get a Basket, Put Groceries Into the Basket . . .* " is a failed equivalent to **Purchase Groceries**).

> A use case's name is its goal. The name must be active, concise, and decisive.

A use case's name must show action. It must have one transitive verb, simple or compound, and one grammatical object, simple or compound. The following examples are acceptable:

☞ For the customer's convenience, the video store may register you as a member the first time you rent a DVD. In other words, the **Rent A DVD** use case may *include* another use case, **Register Member.** This is a type of dependency that we will study later.

- **Verify Credit Card:** compound object.
- **Set Up Tent:** compound verb.

However, **Become a Member of the Video Store & Rent A DVD** is not: registering at the video shop is a precondition for renting a DVD, but it is not required each time you rent a DVD they are separate activities even if they are done in one session.

To accomplish a goal, a set of steps must be taken, but:

> It is the goal that decides the relevance of activities in a use case.

We previously stated that simply swiping your card at an ATM without performing a transaction is meaningless. Consider a different scenario: **Verify Transit Card** in the context of a mass transit system. Many mass transit systems offer their passengers prepaid cards for weekly or monthly travel or a preset number of trips. These cards are often anonymous, come with discounts, and can be refilled. The passenger swipes the card through a turnstile, goes through the gate, and boards the train.

For a **Ride Train** use case, simply swiping the card is a cumulative step, far short of the final goal. But if the passenger is at the gate and discovers that the card has expired or has run out of funds, it is inconvenient to go back to the ticket area and perhaps stand in line to refill the card or buy a new one. To save the passenger this annoyance, some mass transit systems have installed small machines whose only function is to show the status of the card. Swiping the card is the only action necessary and achieves the goal. The same action, with a different goal, has a different relevance.

❷ *Stakeholders and Actors.*

> Stakeholders are those entities whose interests are affected by the success or the failure of the use case.

A use case needs at least one stakeholder. (Otherwise, there is no point in having a use case.) In turn, at least one stakeholder must be an actor.

> An actor is an entity outside the system that interacts with the system to achieve a specific goal.

☞ What happened to the "user"? Isn't the customer a user of the supermarket system? As a specific person, an actor is a *user type.* "Actors define roles that users can play." [Jacobson 1992, 157]

Among the actors identified in a use case, one, and only one, is the **primary actor.** In the **Purchase Groceries** use case, the primary actor is the customer who wants to buy groceries. The services that the system provides in a use case are *primarily* for the benefit of the primary actor, although not *exclusively.*

> The goal of the primary actor is specified by the name of the use case.

An actor is in fact not a specific person or group of persons, but a **role.** The same person may appear in different roles. That is to say, a person may play one role in one

Figure 6.3
Circle of Stakeholders

Actors are stakeholders who interact with the system. The primary actor is an actor whose goal is accomplished by the use case.

use case and a different role in another use case. Even in the same use case, the same person can play multiple roles. In **Purchase Groceries,** the cashier can also play the customer.

Other actors are **supporting** (or **secondary**) actors. They support the primary actor in reaching the goal of the use case. In primary or supporting guises, the same actor may feature in multiple use cases.

An actor is *any* entity that interacts with the system. (See the following "A System" section.) It can be a person; it can also be another system or subsystem, a device, an organization, or even time.

In the **Purchase Groceries** use case, identification of the primary actor is simple: it is the customer. It is the customer whose goal is to buy groceries; other elements in the story provide a service to facilitate the customer including (for the moment) the lone supporting actor, the cashier.

☞ The term "actor" includes any entity outside a system that interacts with it, including another system.

> An actor is a role that any user who has been given the part can play.

☞ Within the confines of one use case, there is a boundary beyond which we should stop doing detective work for finding further, and farther, stakeholders. In purchasing groceries, we may be tempted to include market analyst because selling items affects analysis results. Or, in a use case about treating patients, we may think that listing society at large is relevant because a healthy person benefits everybody, but we should resist it. Having more stakeholders does not mean a better or more accurate use case.

We will emphasize repeatedly that an actor is a role. If the cashier decides to buy some groceries and ring them up, we would still have two actors, even though the same person plays both parts.

The story of **Purchase Groceries,** by itself, does not explicitly identify other stakeholders in the use case, but a close reading *within the context of the whole system* gives us some idea of who the other stakeholders might be.

We said that a use case *primarily* serves the interests of a primary actor. But that is not the only thing that it does or should do. A use case, as we have stated, is also a contract, which means that

> A use case must enforce the interests of all stakeholders.

To protect the interests of the business, the customer *must* pay before departing with groceries. Another interest is that of the supermarket's inventory system: Even if the transaction is part of a going-out-of-business sale, the business must know what items have left the building. If it is business as usual, merchandise sold must be reordered and replaced on the shelves.

Discovery of stakeholders is an iterative work. We must ask the stakeholders to review use cases more than once and tell us whose interests are *not* included.

> An actor is identified by a unique name that describes a unique role.

☞ Often, but not always, the disputed concepts are close enough that they can be resolved through **generalization,** which is discussed in the next chapter.

The name must be unique across the whole enterprise, across the whole system, and not just within the scope of one use case, a set of use cases, or one domain or subsystem. The commercial division of a bank may believe that a **Customer** is a corporation *only*, while the consumer division may consider only an individual as such. Both are correct within their own spheres of activity. However, an enterprise-wide information system for the bank cannot abide by double meanings. One actor must become **Commercial Customer,** the other **Individual Customer.**

❸ *A System.*

> The system defines the boundaries of a use case.

In other words, the scope of the system constrains the scope of the use case. This constraint has a more profound effect than appears at first glance. In order to have the correct actors and the right scenario (see the "A Scenario" section) we must identify the correct system. Precise as the goal of a use case is, more than one system can satisfy the same goal. We may go to a bookstore and buy a book, or we may order it through the bookstore's Web site. We have the same result, but two *different* use cases because we have interacted with two different subsystems of the enterprise: the physical bookstore and the virtual one.

The example of **Purchase Groceries** relates to the supermarket as a *real* system—"bricks-and-mortar," as some would say. As *information system* analysts, we are more likely to write a use case for the supermarket's point-of-sales (POS) system that belongs to the supermarket but is virtual and distinct from the physical supermarket.

Consider the following scenario for an information system that we would call **Checkout Groceries:**

The customer deposits groceries on the checkout counter. The cashier scans each item and deposits the item on the bagging counter. When the last item is scanned, the cashier reads the total amount from the system and announces it to the customer. The cashier then receives payment from the customer and prints the receipt. The cashier hands the receipt and the change (if any) to the customer.

By selecting a different system, we have created a use case different from **Purchase Groceries:** The customer is still there, but the primary actor is now the cashier. (See Figure 6.4.) In **Purchase Groceries,** we were not concerned with detailing the actions of the cashier; in **Checkout Groceries,** we are. In the latter use case, the actions that the customer takes to get the groceries to the checkout counter are ignored; in the previous one, they are detailed.

One can raise the commonsense objection that the "measurable value" still goes to the customer; that the cashier is providing a service to the customer. This is valid on both counts, but misses the point: We are dealing with two *different* systems. One, the supermarket itself, is a *real* system that primarily serves the customer. The second, the information system, is a *virtual* one that primarily serves the supermarket.

In **Checkout Groceries,** what is useful, what is of measurable value, is that the cashier seeks to do a cashier's job, which is making sure that the customer pays for every item and that the information system records the transaction. (This use case has some distance to go to become a truly usable one, but it illustrates the point.)

☞ For an example, see the **Refer Patient** use case in the next chapter.

This is not to say that **Purchase Groceries** should be discarded. At the least, it contributes to a better understanding of the context for **Checkout Groceries** and, if the supermarket business were a completely novel idea, we might not be able to conceive the second without the first.

> In developing an information system, some use cases may remain unautomated. They are required only so that the whole picture makes sense.

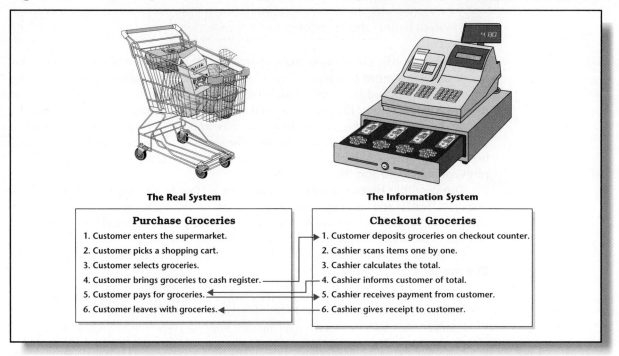

The Real System

Purchase Groceries

1. Customer enters the supermarket.
2. Customer picks a shopping cart.
3. Customer selects groceries.
4. Customer brings groceries to cash register.
5. Customer pays for groceries.
6. Customer leaves with groceries.

The Information System

Checkout Groceries

1. Customer deposits groceries on checkout counter.
2. Cashier scans items one by one.
3. Cashier calculates the total.
4. Cashier informs customer of total.
5. Cashier receives payment from customer.
6. Cashier gives receipt to customer.

The two systems come into contact (see blue arrows), but the use cases are not the same.

So the system defines the boundaries of use cases. Does this mean that there is an insurmountable wall between them, that one use case cannot call on the services of other systems outside its scope? Use cases are bound but not boxed in. To a use case inside a system, another system appears as a *supporting* actor, an outside entity. It is through interaction with this supporting actor that a use case can benefit from the services of another system.

> A use case cannot leave a system, but it can reach across its boundaries.

By expanding **Checkout Groceries** just slightly, we can illustrate the concept:

The customer deposits groceries on the checkout counter. The cashier scans each item and deposits the item on the bagging counter. When the last item is scanned, the cashier reads the total amount from the system and announces it to the customer. **If the customer pays by credit card, the cashier swipes the card through the cash register to charge the amount. The customer then signs the printout. If the customer pays by cash, the cashier returns the change, if any. The cashier then gives a receipt to the customer.**

☞ Don't be misled into believing that all supporting actors present another system.

The bank (or more accurately, a service by a subsystem inside the bank's information system) is responsible for verifying the credit card, for authorizing the supermarket to make the sale, and for deducting the amount from the customer's credit.

The same way that the cashier interacts with the supermarket's **Point-of-Sale** system by sending and receiving "messages," the **Point-of-Sale** system in turn interacts with the bank by exchanging a series of messages.

**Figure 6.5
Use Case
Diagram: The
Interaction
Between the
Actors and the
System**

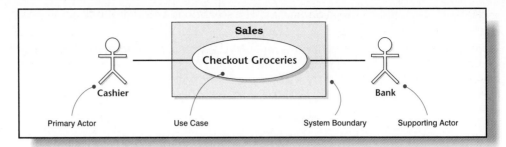

In this diagram Cashier is the primary actor and Bank the supporting actor. (When you are finished with this chapter, you can come back and criticize this diagram. It is missing something.)

In our use case, we have summarized this set of actions as:

- the cashier swipes the card through the cash register to charge the amount.

Disregard for implementation details at this point is intentional: It keeps the focus on the main task of **Checkout Groceries.**

Here a picture is worth more than words. Figure 6.5 is a use case diagram that illustrates an outside system as an actor. (We will concentrate on use case diagram later, but we introduce its elements as related topics are discussed.)

The constituent elements of this diagram are shown in Table 6.1. The **Checkout Groceries** use case is bound by the subsystem **Sales** (or **Point-of-Sale**). The primary actor, **Cashier,** communicates with the use case through an interface, the cash register. When the use case reaches the step where the credit card comes into action, it communicates with **Bank,** the supporting actor on the right.

Table 6.1
The Basic Elements
of the Use Case
Diagram.
We will introduce
other building blocks
of the use case dia-
gram in the next
chapter.

The Basic Elements of the Use Case Diagram	
Actor	The stick figure identifies an **actor.** It is the same for any actor, be it a person or a system. More than one actor can be associated with a use case, and one actor can be associated with more than one use case.
System Boundary	The rectangle is the *system boundary* or the *scope.* For the use case, any entity outside this boundary can exist only as an actor.
Use case	The ellipse (the oval) represents the **use case.** It resides inside the system boundary. In the diagram, the only textual information about the use case is its name.
Association	The simple line on the left represents *association.* It shows the communication between an actor and a use case.

❹ *A Scenario.* The scenario is a story but not *any* story:

> The scenario is an *ordered* sequence of interactions between the actor(s) and the system to accomplish a goal.

☞ The premise is that use cases should stay away from implementation details. But a "pure" use case is difficult to understand, if not impossible to write. Here cash register is just an interface, but "swiping the credit card through the interface" is ludicrous.

Therefore, the steps in the scenario must be sketched out carefully.

Use case modeling captures the *behavioral* requirements of a system in terms that must be readily understood by all stakeholders, from the business side to the development team. To do so, it tries to steer clear from details and nonbehavioral requirements as much as possible, or as much as is reasonable.

A formal use case, as we shall see in the next chapter, will have many parts, but all use cases start with concise stories such as our examples from the supermarket. If we parse a "good" story, we find that the steps fall into four categories. (See Figure 6.6.)

☞ For each category, you might see a slightly different term in other books. For example, **Normal Flow** might be designated as **Basic Course of Events.**

• *Normal Flow.* Normal flow is the best-case scenario, the ideal flow of events. If every step in the normal flow goes smoothly, the goal of the use case is accomplished. In **Purchase Groceries,** the customer finds all desired items, brings them to the checkout counter, pays for them, and carries them out.

Normal flow is the only category that a use case *must* have, at least explicitly. (It is difficult to imagine a use case that will never go wrong.)

• *Alternate Flow.* Alternate flow is composed of steps that are conditional: When a step is not part of the normal flow and is needed only if a condition is **true** or **false,** then it belongs to the alternate flow.

**Figure 6.6
Use Case Flows:
Classifying the
Steps**

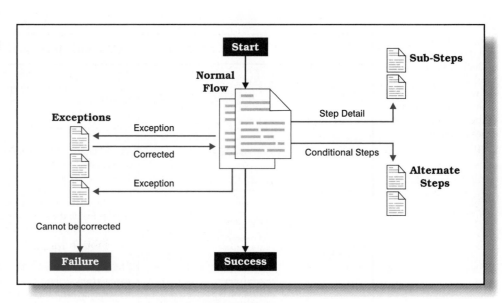

Normal flow is the only flow that a use case *must* have.

Let us expand **Checkout Groceries** again:

The customer deposits groceries on the checkout counter. The cashier scans each item and deposits the item on the bagging counter. **If an item is an alcoholic beverage, the cashier may ask for identification to verify that the customer meets age requirements. If an item does not have a label to scan, the cashier asks a sales manager to identify the code.**

When the last item is scanned, the cashier reads the total amount from the system and announces it to the customer. If the customer pays by credit card, the cashier swipes the card through the cash register to charge the amount. The customer then signs the printout. If the customer pays by cash, the cashier returns the change, if any. The cashier then gives a receipt to the customer.

In this story, if an item lacks a label then—and only then—the cashier calls for the manager's assistance. Similarly, when a customer wants to buy alcoholic beverages, the cashier may ask for identification. If the cashier decides that the customer looks old enough, the ID step is not taken.

- *Sub-Flows.*   Sub-flows detail steps in the normal flow that consist of discrete sub-steps. For example, when we want to buy a CD from a Web merchant, the site usually allows us to conduct a search and then select the CD from a list. A partial use case could resemble the following:

> . . . The customer selects the CD category. The customer adds CDs to the shopping cart:
> - Customer selects a music category.
> - Customer conducts a search.
> - Customer selects a CD from the search result.
>
> The customer then proceeds to checkout . . .

In their nature, sub-steps are not any different from normal steps. We merely decide they do not belong to the same order of importance as the normal steps. We separate them to keep the clarity of the basic course of events. (In our case we used bullets to mark them. In a formal use case, which segregates different elements, sub-steps might have their own section—depending on the preferences of the analyst.)

- *Exceptions.*   Exceptions are those events that prevent certain steps, or the entire use case, from completing successfully. In **Checkout Groceries,** if the customer's credit card is not accepted by the bank, then the customer has to pay by another valid credit card or by cash. If the customer cannot produce acceptable payment, then the "pay" step is canceled, which aborts the whole use case.

Many exceptions are not made explicit in a use case, because they seem obvious. The customer might have left his wallet at home, in which case no sale would take place. We should be on guard, however: An exception might be missing from the use case, but it does not follow that it can be ignored in design or implementation. If the customer discovers that the wallet is missing *before* the groceries are scanned, our information system can safely ignore it. But if the items are already scanned, then the system must allow the cashier to cancel the purchase.

☞ Often, as we will do, **Alternate Flow** and **Exceptions** are combined into one category. The events in these categories are sometimes so similar that theoretical hair-splitting could continue indefinitely.

Regardless of category, steps in a use case scenario share some features:

- *Steps can be repeated.* One step or a set of steps can be repeated until a certain condition is met. In **Checkout Groceries,** the cashier scans purchase items until there are no more groceries left to scan.

☞ See
"Dependencies:
Include and Extend"
in the next chapter.

[Jacobson 1995, 106],
[Cockburn 2001, 93]

- *A step can call on another use case.* Each step may call on another use case to complete its function. If the cashier calls on the manager to find the code and/or price for an item, most probably **Checkout Groceries** will call on another use case called, for example, **Find Price**.

- *A step is a transaction.* Each step appears as just an interaction, but it is really a transaction between the actor and the system. That means that in each step:

- the actor sends a request to the system,
- the system validates the request,
- the system changes its state as a result of validation, and then
- the system responds.

As the cashier ❶ scans each purchase, ❷ the sales system verifies that the scanned code is in the database, ❸ retrieves the price, adds the price to the total, and ❹ displays the price of the item and the new total.(In a use case, however, we do not get *inside* the system.)

Use Cases in the Modeling Spectrum

> Use cases reside near the dynamic edge of the modeling spectrum.

☞ Sometimes
"static" is used
instead of
"structural." We
believe that
"structural" describes
the type of modeling
more accurately, even
though "static" is still
appropriate for
elements within a
structure.

We construct a model by viewing the system from a certain point between two extremes: *dynamic* and *structural.* By describing the external behavior of a system, use case is more dynamic than structural. We use "more" because no model is purely one or the other, even though it may appear so:

- The architect who produces a floor plan for a building must take into account all the forces above and below that push and pull ceilings and floors, beams and pillars.
- Verbal directions for driving to a hard-to-find address—for an appointment or for a party—are really a model that lets you navigate an unknown terrain. It is a dynamic model since it guides your movements through time and space. Nevertheless, it is full of references to static objects: "the second traffic light," "the 5th exit," "building number 233." (Come to think of it, it is some kind of a use case: **Find Address.** It might even have an alternate flow: "If you take the train, then . . . ")

An information system's utility resides almost entirely in its dynamism, even though it must have a structure as solid and as reliable as a bridge spanning a wide river. Whereas we can take shelter in a car that is not moving, getting data out of a database, the most static component of an information system, needs interaction.

What makes use case modeling the first among equals is that by analyzing the behavior of a system into well-defined units, it provides a *measurable* framework for both the structural and the dynamic models of the system. By "measurable" we mean that if the components of a system are constructed, assembled, and behave in a manner that satisfies the demands of each use case, then the system satisfies the requirements as a whole.

3. DEVELOP INITIAL USE CASES

Before arriving at a fully formed use case model of the system, we must discover major use cases and actors. Developing initial use cases requires parsing, verifying, and expanding the business concepts discovered through domain analysis. In most cases, we have to engage in a new round of knowledge gathering by going deeper into the requirements.

From Domain Analysis to Use Cases

> Components of use case modeling are provided by analyzing and expanding concepts that result from domain analysis.

A use case model of a system is a set of use cases that describe the system. A use case, however, is not like other models that mostly consist of visual elements and/or exact symbols. A use case is both a model and a textual narrative.

> Use cases straddle two worlds: the language-driven world of requirements and the structured world of models.

This dual nature makes the use case powerful but also vulnerable because language is inexact and open to conflicting interpretations.

Use cases clarify language by giving it structure but need well-defined concepts to make the structure reliable. We previously argued that to create a conceptual model we need *domain analysis* to discover and organize business concepts. In turn, domain analysis needs *domain definition* to define the scope of those concepts and the system that we are asked to build.

As we explained in this chapter, a use case has four components. Before going into details, we should summarize the relationship of these components with the concepts that result from domain analysis:

- *A System.* The most reliable guidelines for defining the boundaries of a system (or subsystem) are provided by domain definitions.
- *Stakeholders.* The full range of stakeholders will not become clear until a few iterations of the use case development have taken place. However, among stakeholders, actors—or at least primary actors—can be deduced from entries in the domain dictionary classified as "**role.**"
- *A Goal.* Goal does not have a direct correspondence in the domain dictionary, but by parsing entries marked as "*process*" or "*function*" we can discover goals. (If we are not sure, we might have to back up and review requirements. Our task, after all, is iterative.)
- *A Scenario.* Constructing a scenario is the bulk of the work in use case modeling. The general outline of the scenario can be discovered by analyzing the definition of the concepts classified as "process" or "function." Frequently, however, we have to split or, conversely, combine processes and functions to arrive at viable use cases.

Other domain concepts, marked as "*object*" and "*rule,*" are used in constructing use cases *as needed.*

Walden Hospital: Milestones Achieved

To illustrate how domain concepts are transformed into use cases, we need concrete examples. Let us, then, recap the milestones that our main case history, the Walden project, has achieved up to this point:

☞ See Chapters 4 and 5, Gathering Requirements and Domain Analysis, for details.

- *Business Analysis.* The business analyst conducted a broad-based study of Walden Medical Center's business and presented his conclusions in a report to the management.
- *Problem Definition.* In his report, the business analyst identified and scoped the problems that the hospital must solve to save its sagging business.
- *Propose Solutions.* The analyst proposed a capital project for improving all aspects of Walden's operations and infrastructure. He highlighted the need for an enterprise-wide information system as a crucial piece of the hospital's infrastructure.
- *Project Initiation.* The hospital charged its newly hired *CIO* with the task of planning an IS strategy for the medical center. She concluded that the hospital's information system must be developed in stages, in an order based on the priority for the business, but with a broad, upfront analysis so that the pieces, when in place, would form an enterprise-wide system instead of application islands.
- *Domain Definition.* By conducting research into the hospital's current and projected operations, business domains that need the services of an information system were identified: Patient Management, Medical Records Management, Legal, Drug Inventory & Purchasing, Transportation, Accounting, and many more.
- *Domain Scoping.* The hospital decided that the `Patient Management` domain must have the highest priority. Therefore, with a new round of gathering information, the scope of the domain was identified and documented.
- *Domain Analysis & Domain Dictionary.* Within the scope of `Patient Management`, business concepts were explored, defined, and organized into a preliminary domain dictionary. Then, a "best effort" was made to give the concepts an enterprise-wide definition.

Identify Prominent Actors

☞ The term "user" must never be used as an actor because actor is a user *type*. A "user" is *anybody* who uses the system and is not specialized enough to express *roles*. However, we would use "user" whenever we *do* mean anybody who uses the system.

> The primary candidates for becoming actors are domain concepts classified as "role."

The task of identifying prominent actors is sometimes simple, and sometimes anything but. The most important point to remember in this detective work is that an actor is a *role*, not anybody specific. In the context of domain analysis, we asserted that a **role** is

> A **grouping** of any entity—be it a person, a rank, a position, a job function, a corporation, or a system—that performs the same function or takes part in it.

This is where our search for actors starts. But not every domain "role" is eligible to become an actor. Only a positive answer to the following question qualifies an entity to be an actor:

- Would the entity *directly* interact with the information system?

To find the answer, we begin with the definition of the entity in the domain dictionary but—unless it is patently obvious—we must verify it by examining other entries, original requirements, and supporting documents.

In Walden's case some actors such as **Doctor** are easily detectable. In other cases, we have to put more effort into it.

> Discovering actors is a process of consecutive abstraction.

A specific person is not an actor, but if we find that a person interacts with the system to do a job, we must analyze what he or she does to the point that we can generalize it. In the real hospital, people who register patients might not have a job title that refers to "registration." If, however, we discover that "registration" is a well-defined function or process within the hospital, then we must conclude that there is such an actor as **Registration Clerk**.

We might have to generalize even more: If, from the viewpoint of the hospital management, there is no difference between the person who makes an appointment for the patient and the person who registers the patient—that is, the *same type* of employees may do both jobs—then both of them can be designated as **Clerical Staff**. (However, if the hospital believes that these two functions need different qualifications or job descriptions, then we have two actors: **Registration Clerk** *and* **Appointment Clerk**.)

☞ As we shall see in the next chapter, we can combine and separate actors at the same time through *generalization*.

What about nurses and doctors? Do they play the same role? Yes if they interact with our system in the same capacity, with the same privileges and the same duties; no if they don't. In the first case we would identify **Medical Staff** as one actor; in the second case **Nurse** and **Doctor** would become separate actors.

**Figure 6.7
Finding Actors:
Does the Entity
Interact with the
Information
System?**

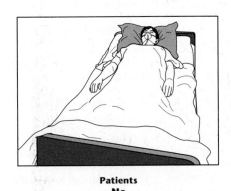

**Patients
No**

**Doctors and Nurses
Yes**

Only domain roles that interact with the information system would become actors. Patient is a stakeholder, but not an actor.

The process of abstraction is one in which we select certain characteristics and/or certain behaviors and cast off what does not concern us. Therefore, when we identify **Doctor** as an actor, we discard name, height, gender, or anything else that is unrelated to being a doctor.

Identifying "prominent" actors implies that there are *other* actors to be identified. Many supporting actors will be discovered through development of "base" use cases. (See the next chapter.)

Each use case is a distinct unit; therefore, we shall identify Walden's prominent actors along with its major use cases in the next topic. However, since in the last chapter we argued that it might be necessary to reorganize the domain dictionary for various purposes, including verification, we illustrate the point here and present a subset of the dictionary for entries classified as "role." (See Table 6.2.) Chances are that when the need for reorganization arrives, new discoveries will add or remove entries and change the definition of the rest as well.

Table 6.2
Subset of Walden's **Patient Management** domain dictionary.
Since all entries are roles, the column for *Type* has been dropped.

Walden Medical Center
Patient Management: Domain Dictionary
Type: Roles
Version 1.1—September 9, 2006

NAME	DESCRIPTION
Appointment Clerk	Makes appointments for the patient.
Billing Clerk	Produces individual patient bills on request; records payments; resolves billing issues.
Doctor	Provides a specialized level of medical services to the patient: diagnosis, procedures and operations, prescriptions, and monitoring of medical conditions.
Emergency Medical Worker	Refers the patient to the emergency room. Performs emergency medical services before emergency room.
Lab Technician	Performs a test medical service: X-ray, blood test, MRI, etc.
Medical Staff	Any person who provides a medical service to a patient: a doctor, a nurse, a lab technician, or an emergency medical worker.
Nurse	Helps the doctor in providing medical services. Administers drugs and monitors the patient.
Outside Hospital	Refers patient for an appointment and medical service.
Primary Care Physician	Refers the patient to the hospital to receive medical services.
Referral Source	A primary care physician, an emergency medical worker, or an outside hospital that refers a patient for an appointment to receive a medical service. Patient himself or herself can be a referral source.
Registration Clerk	Performs registration.

Identify Major Use Cases

> Major use cases are identified by analyzing business processes and functions.

☞ Some authors recommend that use cases be identified *before* actors, instead of the other way around. We believe both approaches to be equally valid. Most typically, you would go back and forth.

Domain analysis discovers concepts that are classified as *"process"* or *"function."* These concepts are use case candidates, but the conversion ratio from domain analysis is not necessarily one-to-one: Some "process concepts" and functions may have enough material for more than one use case; others might not have enough.

If the "process concept" cannot be mapped directly to a use case, then we must use one of the two following techniques.

❶ *Take Apart.* From a strictly business point of view, the following scenario, **Sell Groceries,** is correct enough.

> *A customer enters the supermarket. The customer takes a shopping cart or basket and strolls through the supermarket. The customer selects items from the shelves and puts them in the shopping cart or the basket. When finished, The customer deposits groceries on the checkout counter.*
>
> *The cashier scans each item and deposits the item on the bagging counter. If the cashier cannot identify the item for pricing, he or she asks a manager for help and enters the information manually.*
>
> *When the last item is scanned, the cashier gets the total amount from the system and informs the customer. The customers pays by cash or credit card. If the customer wants to pay by credit card, the cashier slides the card through the cash register to deduct the amount from the credit card. The cashier then prints the receipt. The cashier hands the receipt and the change (if any) to the customer.*
>
> *The cashier bags the purchased items. The customer picks up the bags and leaves the supermarket.*

As we have demonstrated, however, the story really consists of two use cases in two systems: **Purchase Groceries** and **Checkout Groceries**. We see two different *systems*: the supermarket system and the information system for the supermarket. We see two different *primary* actors with different goals: the customer who wants to get desired groceries but *has to pay* for them, and the cashier who *wants* the customer to pay and is not overly concerned with the nature of purchases. Further, the customer is not concerned with how the purchase items are scanned, or what steps are required for charging a credit card.

❷ *Join.* Sometimes the process described in the domain dictionary may be just a *subset* of a bigger scenario: **Bag Groceries** may be described as follows:

☞ Another example, closer to the supermarket's information system, would be **Charge Credit Card**, divorced from the context of **Checkout Groceries**.

> *The cashier estimates the number of bags required to hold purchases. The cashier then separates purchases into sturdy items like cans and fragile ones such as eggs. The cashier fills the bags with sturdy items at the bottom and fragile ones at the top.*

The cashier's role, however, is more than this, as successive iterations of **Checkout Groceries** demonstrate. Therefore, to arrive at a complete use case, we must combine the previous scenario with other steps that the cashier must take in order.

As we said, the components of a use case constrain and shape each other: the system offers a service, an actor desires the benefit that the service provides, and the system and the actor interact to complete the service. As a result:

> Any change in one component of a use case might result in a different use case.

In the mundane case of **Bag Groceries,** if the actor changes to **Bagging Assistant,** the story becomes a genuine use case. **Bagging Assistant** is the primary actor whose goal is to bag purchases and nothing else (in this scenario at least). It is not the scenario by itself, but all the components, taken together, that make a use case valid or invalid.

Identifying even the *major* use cases has twists and turn. But they *are* initial: They are the first cut and the goal is to create a model that will elicit comments and criticisms to set right what is wrong.

Walden's Major Use Cases

By analyzing Walden's **Patient Management**—its domain outline, its domain dictionary, and its supporting documents—we arrive at a set of initial use cases (Table 6.3).

There are five use cases in all. This seems anti-climactic for so much discussion and effort, but it will not stay that way. For starters, we may note that **Track**

Table 6.3
Walden's Patient Management: Use Case Summary.

		Walden Medical Center *Patient Management: Use Case Summary* Version 1.0—September 20, 2006		
	NAME	DESCRIPTION	ACTORS
100	**Refer Patient**	A referral source refers the patient to the hospital for an appointment to receive a medical service.	Primary Care Physician, Emergency Medical Worker, Another Hospital, Patient.
120	**Make Appointment**	On referral, the appointment clerk schedules a medical service for the patient.	Appointment Clerk
140	**Register Patient**	Before a medical service, the registration clerk updates personal and insurance information if the patient is new or the relevant information has changed. A hospital ID card is issued if the patient is new or has lost the card.	Registration Clerk
160	**Track Medical Service**	The hospital renders a medical service to a patient. A medical service covers all activities performed by the medical staff that relate to a patient, from a visit to a doctor to a lab test to hospitalization and discharge. Medical staff records each service along with its cost.	Doctor, Nurse, Lab Technician, Emergency Medical Worker
180	**Manage Patient Billing**	On request, the billing clerk produces a bill for the patient. The clerk also reconciles the patient's account and accepts payments.	Billing Clerk

Medical Service is an umbrella for two distinct processes: **Document Medical Service** and **Track Service Expense**. However, they are done in parallel. By leaving the two processes in one (initial) use case, we are asking for confirmation that our assumption is correct.

But there is more. Recording the results and recording the costs of medical services do not follow the same steps because each service has different requirements. A prescription needs a form, for the service *and* the cost, that is different from the form required by an X-ray. Later, we will need to break down the use case even further.

Summary or Initial?

After declaring that we are going to create a set of *initial* use cases, we titled the document "Summary of Use Cases." Why the discrepancy? Shouldn't we call it "Initial Use Cases"?

It depends on what we want to do with the document afterwards. Very soon we will arrive at fully developed use cases, but we may still need a summary, an index that provides us with a reliable outline in short order. However, it must be synchronized with full-length use cases. If we judge the effort to be worthwhile, we will call it "summary." If we decide to throw it away when we are done with it, then "initial" would do.

The less redundancy, the better. But sometimes redundancy serves a purpose.

Develop Context Diagram

A context diagram represents the interaction of outside entities with a system as a whole.

A context diagram is composed of three elements:

- **A system** or subsystem.
- **Entities outside** the system that interact with it.
- **Interactions** between outside entities and the system.

It is a quick sketch of the system boundaries and entities that interact with it. What happens inside the system and the steps and the variables that make up the interaction are *intentionally* ignored, as the initial context diagram for Walden's **Patient Management** subsystem illustrates. (See Figure 6.8.)

The oval represents the system, rectangles the entities that interact with the system, and arrows the interaction. Major interactions are listed under the actor. The outside entities normally would become actors, depending on our findings in the process of developing use cases.

The context diagram is a tool that may be used at any point in the development of use cases. In the initial phase, it helps to scope the system and verify its boundaries. In an advanced phase, it can serve as a visual summary. At any phase, it should be kept simple and clear.

Figure 6.8 Context Diagram for Walden's Patient Management

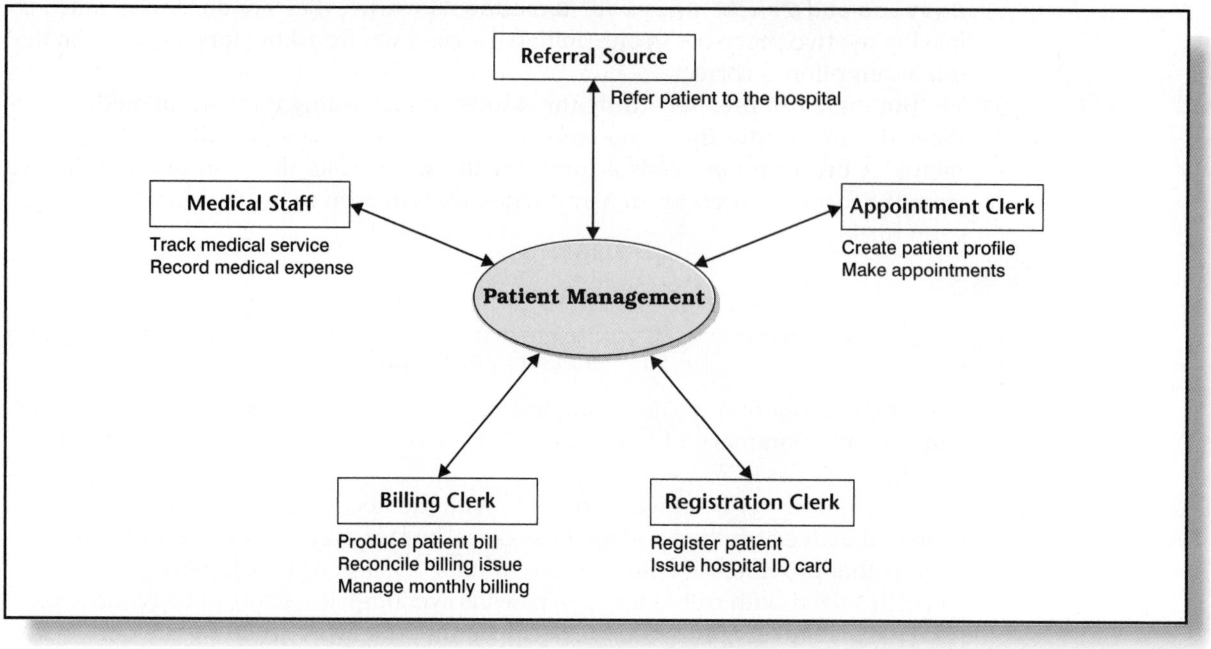

This is an initial view of the subsystem. More complex views may become necessary later on.

4. DELIVERABLES

The initial use case modeling has a modest output, disproportionate to its importance and the effort that it may involve.

- *Use Case Summary.*   The main product of the effort is a summary of use cases that identifies major use cases and their actors. Each use case should have a simple definition and no more. It is not possible to put a limit to the number of use cases that a subsystem is allowed, but if the use case summary exceeds a few pages, then something has gone wrong. As you shall see in the following chapters, even one use case can expand to a great volume of modeling and a still greater volume of design and implementation. In such a case, you may have to revise your domain definition to make the complexity more manageable.

- *Context Diagram.*   Along with discovering major use cases, you may also create a context diagram as a visual summary and verification tool. A context diagram is simple and does not go into detail, but its simplicity is its strength: At this stage, a correct bird's eye view is more important than details.

☞ In the next chapter, we will expand our coverage of use case diagram.

- *Use Case Diagram.*   Though we will broaden the discussion of the use case diagram in the next chapter, you have been introduced to its basics in this chapter. It can be used alongside, or instead of, a context diagram to show a little more detail by identifying individual use cases. Actually, it is not unusual to see an initial use case diagram labeled as a "context diagram."

5. WRAP UP

Use case modeling is the first step for *transforming domain concepts* into models for building a solution. A use case is a textual narrative that details how one or more entities called actors interact with a system to achieve a result that is primarily of value to one of them, the primary actor.

☑ **What the use case modeling is and is not**

Use case modeling is a set of use cases that, together, describe the *behavior of a system*. A use case is a *unit* of this model. It can also be defined as a contract between entities that have a stake in the outcome of a use case, that is, stakeholders, and the system.

Use cases do *not* model the internal workings of the system. They describe *what* the system does but not *how*. They are *not* effective tools for capturing nonfunctional requirements. They are *not* derived from successive divisions of a system's functions (functional decomposition). And they are not inherently object-oriented.

☑ **The four components of a use case**

A use case is a textual narrative, but it must have four well-defined components to qualify as a use case: ❶ a **goal** as the successful outcome of the use case; ❷ **stakeholders** whose interests are affected by the outcome, including **actor**(s) who interact with the system to achieve the goal; ❸ a **system** that provides the required services for the actors; and ❹ a step-by-step **scenario** that guides both the actor(s) and the system towards the finish line.

☑ **The basic elements of use case diagram**

Use case diagram is a *"meta-model,"* an abstraction of use cases. In its basic form, it displays the boundaries of the system, the name of the use cases, and the actors who interact with each use case.

☑ **Various flows in the narrative of a use case**

The narrative of a use case is made up of one or more flows: ❶ **normal flow** is the best-case scenario that results in the successful completion of the use case; ❷ **alternate flow** is present only if conditional steps are needed; ❸ **sub-flows** if steps in the normal flow contain sub-steps; ❹ **exceptions** that describe what may prevent the completion of one step or the entire use case.

☑ **How to transform concepts from domain analysis into use cases**

Domain analysis discovers and defines business concepts within the context of the *problem space.* Use case modeling channels, transforms, and expands these concepts into a model of *system behavior.*

☑ **Identifying prominent actors**

Domain analysis discovers entities that perform the same functions within the enterprise. These entities are classified as a **"role"** and are the prime candidates for designation as **"actors"** in use case modeling. They qualify as actors if they interact with the information system that we plan to build.

☑ **Identifying major use cases**

We arrive at major use cases by analyzing domain concepts marked as *"process"* or *"function."* But the conversion ratio is not one-to-one. A use case has features—four required components—that a function or a process may lack. Sometimes we have to break up a process into more than one use case; at other times we might have to combine pieces of multiple processes or functions to arrive at one use case. Other domain concepts, such as *objects* or *business rules*, might find their way into use cases if the context requires it.

☑ **The context diagram**

The context diagram describes the *interaction* of outside entities with a system, or subsystem, as a *whole.* It is simple: It does not elaborate on the system behavior as use cases do. And it must be kept simple to serve its purpose: verification of *functions* that the system provides and *for whom* it provides.

6. KEY CONCEPTS

Actor. An entity *outside* the **system** that interacts with the system to achieve a specific goal. An actor can be a person, another system or subsystem, a device, or an organization. It is a **role**, a user *type,* not a specific person or entity. Actors are a class of **stakeholders**.

Actor, Primary. An **actor** whose **goal** is expressed by the name of the use case. The services that the **system** provides through a use case are *primarily* for the benefit of the primary actor, although not *exclusively.*

Actor, Secondary. *See* **Actor, Supporting**.

Actor, Supporting. An **actor** who supports the **primary actor** to reach the **goal** of the use case.

Context Diagram. A diagram that represents the interaction of outside entities with a system as a whole.

Exceptions. Those events that prevent certain steps, or the entire use case, from completing successfully.

Flow, Alternate. Conditional steps in the **scenario** of a use case. If a step is not part of the **normal flow** and is needed only if a condition is *true* or *false*, then it belongs to the alternate flow.

Flow, Normal. The best-case **scenario** in a use case. If every step in the normal flow goes smoothly, the **goal** of the use case is accomplished.

Goal. A goal is what a successful completion of a use case achieves. The goal must be meaningful and must be of measurable value to the **primary actor**.

Role. ❶ In the context of use case modeling, a synonym for **actor**. ❷ In the context of domain analysis, a grouping of any entity—be it a person, a rank, a position, a job function, a corporation, or a system—that perform the same function or take part in it.

Scenario. An *ordered* sequence of interactions between the **actor**(s) and the **system** to accomplish the **goal** identified by the use case.

Stakeholder. Any entity, human or otherwise, whose interests are affected by the outcome of a use case. **Actors** are those stakeholders who interact with the system.

Sub-Flow. Detail steps in the **normal flow** that consist of discrete sub-steps.

System. In the context of use case modeling, defines the scope of a use case. (For a definition of "system" and "subsystem," see Chapter 1.)

Use Case. A unit of **system** behavior. A use case describes the interaction of an **actor** to accomplish a **goal** of value to the actor.

Use Case Components. The elements that make up a use case: a **goal, stakeholders,** a **system,** and a **scenario**. A change in one may redefine the other three.

Use Case Modeling. ❶ A set of use cases that, together, represent the behavior of a system or subsystem. ❷ The process of creating this set of use cases.

7. REVIEW QUESTIONS

1. Define what use case modeling is and is not.
2. Explain the steps for the discovery of use cases.
3. Define the difference between process and function and provide an example.
4. Identify the four components of a use case and how they affect each other.
5. Explain the difference between

   a. Actors and stakeholders.
   b. Primary and supporting actors.

6. Match the following concepts: goal, process, function, scenario, business system, information system, grocery store, check-out system, actors, role.
7. What are the basic elements of a use case diagram?
8. Describe normal flow, sub-flow, and alternate flow. How do they differ?
9. What is the difference between alternate and exception flows?
10. What is the use of a context diagram?

8. CASE STUDIES & EXERCISES

Four narratives were introduced in Chapter 4: *The* Sportz *Magazine, The Car Dealership, The Pizza Shop,* and *The Real Estate Agency*. The following exercises apply to all cases.

❶ Identify the stakeholders and the actors. Create a table similar to Table 6.2.

❷ Make a list of all the use cases for this scenario.

❸ Identify the scope of each use case.

❹ Identify a goal for each use case. Remember that identifying goals will help you name your use cases

in a meaningful way. (You may want to revisit exercise 2 and rename the use cases.)

❺ Write a short scenario for each use case. Include not only the normal flow, but alternates, exceptions, and sub-flows as well. (Hint: Do this only where applicable—do not force it.)

❻ Create a use case summary similar to Table 6.3.

❼ Create a **context diagram** for the system and/or each subsystem.

9. Research Projects & Teamwork

❶ Have all the team members participate in conducting research (online and offline) to prepare a one-page summary for the following: the origins of use case, when it started to be considered as the first step in system development, the pioneer who invented it, and those who first used it. Find out what types of information systems are best suited to development by employing use cases and what types are least suited to it.

❷ After all members of your team have read the chapter carefully on their own, set up a discussion session and, by using everybody's input, create a table with two columns. The first column should list " to dos" and the second column should list " not to dos" in discovering use cases. It is likely that the first attempt will not be very successful. Therefore, revise the table as many times as necessary.

❸ Writing good use cases is time-consuming, even though it is extremely useful. Most software shops recognize the necessity of use cases, but shy away from it in practice.

Conduct research to find out what the software development industry thinks about use cases: Are they useful? Are they a waste of time? A simple Web search will tell you a lot. You may also look at development journals. You will find many articles on the subject. Let the team members do their research individually, then form a discussion session and prepare a short document with full references and examples that summarizes each finding.

❹ Refer to the online registration system for Walden Medical College (in Chapter 4) and answer the following questions.

- Identify major use cases for the registration system and create a use case summary. Use Table 6.3 as a guide. Remember: If the use case summary exceeds a few pages, then something has gone wrong. If this happens, you may have to revise your domain definition.
- Create a context diagram as a visual summary and verification tool. Your context diagram should be as simple as possible.

Consider what you did for the same narrative in Chapter 5. The purpose of this exercise is to demonstrate the usefulness of the domain dictionary and business rules dictionary.

Consider the two sets of answers and write a short report that argues for or against the usefulness of domain dictionaries.

❺ Refer to the automated research application (the "reference engine") in Chapter 4 for the following exercises.

- Identify major use cases and create a use case summary for the application.
- Create a context diagram.

❻ Refer to the online shopping system in Chapter 4 for the following exercises.

- Identify primary and secondary actors.
- Identify major use cases and create a use case summary.
- Create a context diagram for the system.

10. Suggested Readings

See the next chapter for suggested readings on use case modeling.

Chapter 7

Behavioral Modeling II
Developing Use Cases

1. OVERVIEW

By defining the behavior that the users expect from the information system, use cases form the foundation of conceptual modeling. To serve as such a foundation, use cases must be fully developed, rigorously structured, and precisely refined into the building blocks of a reliable behavioral model. Use case templates provide the tool for structuring the flow and the attributes of use cases, and use case diagram creates a visual index for the model.

- ☑ Inception
- ☑ Requirements Discovery
- ☐ Development
  - ☐ Analysis
    - ☑ **Domain Analysis**
    - ☐ Behavioral Modeling
      - ☑ **Use Cases: The Basics**
      - ☐ **Developing Use Cases** ⬅
    - ☐ Structural Modeling
    - ☐ Dynamic Modeling
  - ☐ Design
  - ☐ Implementation

Chapter Topics

➤ Structuring and developing use cases through templates.

➤ Generalizing actors.

➤ Extending use cases.

➤ Reusing use cases.

➤ Use case generalization.

➤ Use case diagram.

➤ Dividing and joining use cases.

➤ Activity diagram.

➤ Use case modeling as a framework for development and deployment.

➤ Use case supplements.

Introduction

To discover use cases, we must first discover business activities—processes and functions—through domain definition and domain analysis. The previous chapter explored the process for turning business concepts into *initial* use cases and prominent actors.

Initial use cases possess all the *necessary* components of the use case but only in a rudimentary form: the *goal* of the use case is defined but we may notice that sometimes the goal is really an umbrella for other distinct goals; the various *flows* of the *scenario* are in summary form and are not organized into distinguishable *steps*; among the *stakeholders* we have only the most visible *actors*. The only component that is (almost) well-defined is the *system*, whose **scope** was decided by domain definition.

To summarize, initial use cases provide only the seeds that we must grow into a full model of the system behavior, the main objective of this chapter (Figure 7.1).

The first step after the discovery phase is to develop **base use cases**. Through further requirements gathering and analysis, we construct base use cases from the results of the discovery phase. Base use cases are structured in **templates** that lay out the scenario in distinct steps and flows, but also specify the conditions that must exist before a use case can start and the conditions that its completion creates, what triggers the interaction, and any nonbehavioral requirements that the use case might have.

Next comes consolidation and *reorganization*. By analyzing and reorganizing base use cases, we arrive at new use cases. Sometimes, we break apart and recombine flows into new use cases to eliminate redundancy or to make the model more comprehensible. Likewise, through actor and **use case generalization**, we attempt to streamline our model.

Use case modeling provides a framework for many analysis, design, implementation, and deployment activities that are not limited to the behavior of the system. By relying on the mature model that we derive from the consolidation and the reorganization of use cases, we start *elaborating* use cases into *supplemental documents*. These documents extend the logical thread of use cases into details that are required for the later phases of development.

Use case development is an iterative activity. Each step may reveal requirements and inconsistencies that would make it necessary to retrace our steps. One activity is shared across all phases: gathering of requirements and knowledge about requirements. And across all phases we can use other tools to help us in the process. **Activity diagram** is a tool that assists us in navigating complicated logical flows.

Figure 7.1   Use Case Modeling: Links in a Chain

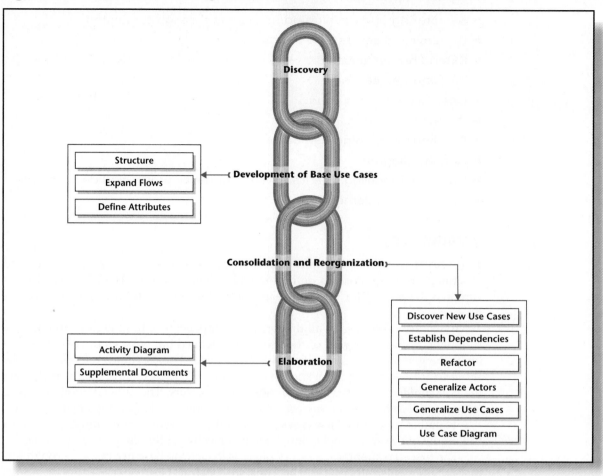

To provide a framework for the development, we must rigorously structure and develop use cases.

2. DEVELOP BASE USE CASES

Base use cases are the result of structuring and expanding initial use cases. The modifier "base" is used for two reasons. First, by analyzing them we arrive at other use cases that are often dependent on base use cases. Second, they provide a framework for other artifacts of analysis, design, and testing.

What a "Base" Use Case Is

> A base use case is a fully formed, structured use case that serves as a *base* to develop other analysis and design artifacts.

Initial use cases are minimal on purpose. We must not attempt to expand them *before* we are confident that they are correct in their broad outlines. To use them as models, however, we must provide them with structure and particulars.

❶ *Structure.*   A narrative can be written in many different ways. Without a structure, we cannot ensure that everything we need in a use case is present. Formal structure also facilitates communications: We know where to find something that we are looking for.

❷ *Particulars.*   The narrative for the use case must have *enough* details to enable us to model the system's behavior. "Enough," of course, varies with the context: As we shall argue, it must not be every possible detail, but it should not be too little, either.

☞ From now on, we will drop the ***"base"*** modifier, unless it is necessary to distinguish a base use case from an initial one.

The Template

> The template structures use cases by providing well-defined and ordered fields.

☞ "General format" because certain fields will go away once open issues are resolved. Other entries might be *too* specific to a use case.

No two use case templates are necessarily alike: The requirements of each project are different from another, as are the requirements of each system and the preferences of each development team. But it is prudent that we should continue with the same general format once we have settled on one.

Table 7.1 presents an empty template with the most common fields for a structured use case. We will take the template apart and discuss it field by field. The existence of a field, however, does not mean that every use case needs it. Since there are no perfect use cases, we will draw upon various examples if a point needs to be illustrated or clarified. (Three topics will be discussed separately to give them their due attention: **dependencies**, **actor generalization**, and **use case generalization.**)

Template Fields

> Template fields represent the building blocks of the use cases, joined in a predefined, orderly manner.

Use Case Name

[Armour 2001, 89]

> The name embodies the goal that the use case wants to accomplish.

In introducing use cases we emphasized two points:

- The use case name must clearly identify the goal from the *primary actor's viewpoint*. **Purchase Groceries** expresses what the customer wants; **Checkout Groceries** is what the cashier needs to do.
- The use case name must be an active verb–noun combination. Both **Register Patient** and **Registering Patient** are correct (though we prefer the first). **Patient Registration** is not.

To the last point we should add that **Patient Registration** is a process name (and we can picture the label on the door to a room in which this process occurs). But even though we should look at the processes (and functions) in a business domain to discover use cases, and even though they are related concepts, the distinction should remain clear: Use cases are **units** of system behavior; a use case fulfills a function or

Table 7.1
The Use Case
Template.

The Use Case Template	
Use Case:	A name that defines the goal of the use case. Required.
ID:	A numeric identifier that must be unique among all use cases for the system. Required.
Scope:	The system or the subsystem, the behavior of which is described by the use case. Required.
Priority:	The priority of the use case.
Summary:	A minimal description of the scenario. Required.
Primary Actor:	The actor whose goal is identified by the name of the use case. Required (except for extending use cases).
Supporting Actors:	The actors who assist the primary actor in achieving the goal of the use case, if applicable.
Stakeholders:	Those whose interests are affected by the outcome of the use case, if applicable.
Generalization:	Name of the parent use case, if applicable.
Include:	The names of the "included" use cases, if applicable.
Extend:	The names of "extending" use cases, if applicable.
Precondition:	Required state of the system *before* the use case can start, if applicable.
Trigger:	The event that starts the use case, if applicable.
Normal Flow:	Steps that normally lead to the successful completion of the use case. Required.
Sub-Flows:	Sub-steps of steps in the normal flow, if applicable.
Alternate Flow/ Exceptions:	Steps to remedy the failure of the normal flow, or steps triggered by the failure of the normal flow, if applicable.
Post-Condition:	The state of the system resulting from the successful completion of the use case.
Open Issues:	Unanswered questions about the use case, if applicable.
Source:	Reference to the requirements and domain concepts that are the basis of the use case.
Author:	Author(s) of the use case.
Revision &Date:	Revision number and the date of the revision.

☞ The weakness of certain verbs is a plus for naming domains and subsystems. ***Accounting*** implies everything that accounting does—past, present, or future. So does ***Patient Management***, which would include patient treatment, patient billing, public relations vis-à-vis patients, etc.

embodies a process but must be seen as a set of interactions between the actor(s) and the system. So we come to yet another, very slightly different, description of use case:

> A use case outlines a set of well-ordered interactions between actor(s) and the system that embodies a process and performs a function with a useful result.

Among active verbs, some are strong and some are weak: `Register Patient` has a strong verb; `Manage Patient Registration` has a weak one. A strong verb has the advantage that it leaves no doubt as to what it aims at, while a weak verb is usually vague: with its diplomatic ambiguity it leaves room for evasion.

A weak verb should be considered suspect until it is proven otherwise: It might be trying to hide too many things in one use case. Our initial use case `Manage`

☞ Use case dependencies are described later in this chapter.

Patient Billing is such a guilty party. It handles both billing on request *and* reconciles billing issues *and* accepts/records payments—it is a use case that embraces three separate goals (or more).

Sometimes, however, weak verbs are innocent: **Manage Customer Complaints** is a reasonable name, though it is likely to be an umbrella for many *dependent* use cases.

ID

> The ID is a *unique* numeric identifier for the use case.

☞ To present the relationship between use cases and the order of events, we must rely on the use case diagram.

ID has no meaning; it does *not* signify the importance of a use case and it does *not* show the relationship between use cases or the order in which they happen. Its only function is to make the use case unique across the board.

ID seems redundant. We said that object names must *eventually* be unique; we must qualify that now. As we shall see in the "Use Case Generalization" section later in this chapter, the name of the use case may change during analysis. Furthermore, to be exact:

> A name must be unique within a given *namespace*.

A *namespace* is a *hierarchical* scheme of naming in which each name is unique within the sphere of the one above it. A postal address is a good illustration: name, apartment, building, street, city, state and/or postal region, country. **Apartment 65** is unique for building **No. 15** in **Cedar Street** in. . . . Taken out of this hierarchy, **Apt. 65** loses its uniqueness.

☞ It is not uncommon to prefix the number with an identifier— **UC-120**, for instance—to readily separate it from, say, **BR-120**, which would be a business rule. Select a labeling convention that you find useful.

The same rule applies to naming a use case. The name has to be unique, but only within a domain (namespace). Other domains might have a use case with exactly the same name. **Bill Patient** (within the domain of **Patient Management**) is likely to have the same name as one in the **Accounting** domain that will produce monthly statements.

ID does not have a meaning and does not enforce an order *but* being humans we tend to enforce order and impart meaning even where it does not exist or is not required. That is why we have assigned IDs that start from 100 and are incremented by 20: so that we can "steal in" a subsequent use case that we want to appear above or below another one.

☞ An honest soul, with no illusions, would number the first use case "1" and continue with increments of one, putting faith instead in the power of use case diagrams to clarify the picture.

Scope

> The scope of a use case—its boundaries—is defined by the system or the subsystem to which it belongs.

☞ See "A System" in "Introducing Use Cases" in the last chapter.

Register Patient is bounded by the **Patient Management** subsystem. In other words, if an interaction between the actors and the system occurs *outside* the scope of **Patient Management**, the **Register Patient** use case cannot include it. This does not mean that a use case cannot use the services of another system or subsystem: it can, but the other system is considered a *supporting actor*, an *outside entity*. (We will discuss using other use cases later in this chapter.)

Priority

> Priority decides the order of design and implementation for use cases.

☞ See the next chapter to see how we refer to use cases to discover classes.

We derive most of our ideas for other models of the system from use cases. Therefore, priority becomes essential once we want to go beyond use cases. In design and implementation, we have to know in what order use cases must be developed.

The priority scheme is a matter of choice. We can categorize priorities by words: **High**, **Low**, **Medium**. Or we might assign numbers. Whatever the scheme, the significance of the priority must be clear and consistent across all use cases. (We have given **Register Patient** the priority of **1/5**. That is, on the scale of one to five, it has the first priority. Without the scale, we would not know where a use case with the priority of **4** would stand.)

Priority is decided by both the requirements of the project and the logic of system modeling and implementation.

Summary

☞ A business and an information system for the business do not exist in separate worlds: The information system serves the business and the business relies on the information system. Activities flow between the two and do not stop at an artificial border: In **Checkout Groceries**, the cashier will not take any action if the customer does not bring groceries to the counter.

By a minimal attempt at reasoning we may conclude, correctly, that these actor types are really terms of convenience; they are true only in extremes: **Patient** is a business actor, but **Reception Clerk** and **Registration Clerk** are not in an isolation chamber and interact both with the business and the information system.

> A summary is a long version of the use case name and a short version of the scenario.

The summary describes what the name of the use case means and what the *concrete* results of the scenario are. It must *not* include details that the scenario includes. Otherwise, a change in scenario would create a discrepancy between the two.

Consider the *summary of use cases* as a quick reference. If you maintain a summary of use cases as we discussed in the previous chapter, the descriptions should be interchangeable.

Primary Actor

> A primary actor is the actor whose goal identifies and drives the use case.

In an ATM use case, the bank customer is clearly the primary actor because the customer ❶ initiates the action; ❷ interacts, step by step, with the system; and ❸ achieves the desired goal if things go right.

But in two cases it might not be easy to distinguish the primary actor:

❶ When the **initiator** of the use case is not the primary actor. In the use case **Receive Patient**, patient is the entity who initiates the use case but is not listed as an actor, let alone the primary actor.

❷ When the primary actor functions as a **proxy** for another entity. A proxy is a facilitator for some other entity whose goal the use case satisfies. A clerk in a mail order company who records phone orders is acting on the customer's behalf.

To identify the primary actor in these two cases, we must also distinguish between two *actor types*:

❶ A **business actor** is one who interacts with the business. In **Purchase Groceries**, **Customer** is a business actor.

❷ A **system actor** is one who *directly* interacts with the information system. In **Checkout Groceries**, **Cashier** is a system actor.

In a use case for the *information system*, if the choice is between a business actor and a system actor, we choose the system actor. In fact, the business actor seldom appears as an *actor* in the information system use case—unless the business actor interacts with the system directly.

If both actors are system actors, then we are back to what we emphasized before: The primary actor is the actor whose goal is identified by the use case name.

If, after all, you cannot decide on the primary actor, then you must follow a guideline that we will explore more in the "Separating and Joining Use Cases" section later in this chapter:

> If there is more than one strong candidate for the role of primary actor, it is likely that we are dealing with more than one use case.

Supporting Actors

☞ Supporting actors are also called **secondary** or **auxiliary** actors.

> Supporting actors assist the primary actor in achieving the goal of the use case.

In **Register Patient**, the use case calls on another use case to verify the insurance plan for the patient. It is a small use case (in analysis only) that asks the health insurance company to verify the patient's insurance plan. For convenience sake, we assume that all insurance companies require the same information and work the same way.

Health Insurance Provider is the supporting actor for this **Verify Insurance Plan**. The diagram (Figure 7.2) illustrates the relationship of the two use cases and their actors. The arrow from **Register Patient** to **Verify Insurance Plan** signifies that the first use case "includes" the services of the second one. (According to this diagram, the registration clerk can also verify the patient's insurance plan outside the scope of **Register Patient**. Therefore, the clerk is the primary actor for both use cases.)

Stakeholders

> A stakeholder is any entity, human or otherwise, who has an interest in the outcome of the use case.

Figure 7.2
The Supporting Actor: Helping the Primary Actor to Reach the Goal

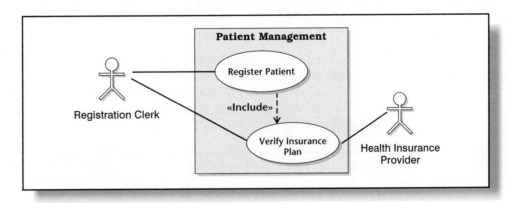

Use case diagram for **Health Insurance Provider** as a supporting actor.

A very short description is enough to explain the relevance of a stakeholder to the use case. From this field we usually exclude two types of stakeholders:

- *Primary Actor.* The goal of the use case *primarily* serves the interests of this stakeholder; therefore, there is no reason to repeat it. If the name of the use case does *not* identify the goal of the primary actor, then the name of the use case is wrong.
- *Supporting Actor(s).* Supporting actors are also given a prominent place in the template, so there is no need to include them in this field *unless* the role that they play as actors does not fully explain their interests. In **Verify Insurance Plan**, **Health Insurance Provider** is a secondary actor because it interacts with the system. However, by verifying the insurance plan, it also accepts the responsibility for paying the cost of medical services provided to the patient. Therefore, it merits a separate entry.

Precondition and Post-Condition

> Precondition defines the state of the system *before* a use case can start; post-condition defines the state of the system *after* a use case is complete.

By "state of the system" we mean those elements of the system that relate to the use case.

> State is "the cumulative results of the behavior of an object; one of the possible conditions in which an object may exist, characterized by definite quantities that are distinct from other quantities."

In other words, an object's state changes if the value of at least one of its attributes changes: a 70-year-old man is the same person, the same object, as when he was 7 years old, but is now in a different state.

By the "state of the system" we do not mean only the information system, but also the enterprise, or the business "system," that the information system serves: An information system, its services, and its application can be properly understood only in the context of a human enterprise.

[Booch 1994, 518]

> The relationship between an information system and its business context is organic: only together, not separately, do the two make a meaningful whole.

It is the responsibility of both systems to prevent the use case from starting if the precondition is not met. In **Register Patient**, the *reception* clerk is an entity *inside* the hospital system who does *not* directly participate in registration. Nevertheless, both the business system and the information system must interact to ensure that the precondition is enforced:

Register Patient	Precondition:	The reception clerk has verified that the patient has an appointment but must register.

On the other hand, the information system must also ensure that the *post-condition* of a preceding use case, **Make Appointment**, is available to the reception clerk so that the patient's appointment can be verified.

When registration is complete, the state of the system is changed again. Now the post-condition of **Register Patient** satisfies the precondition of providing the patient with medical services:

Register Patient	Post-Condition:	The patient is registered and is provided with a hospital ID card.

[Cockburn 2001, 211]

The existence of the precondition is an indication that another use case has previously changed the state: **Make Appointment** must succeed before **Receive Patient** can start; **Receive Patient** must start before **Register Patient** takes place.

We do not specify preconditions, or post-conditions, for steps *inside* the use case: They must be clear from the various flows of the use case. However, since the precondition for the use case itself falls outside the use case's scope, it must be made clear.

☞ Notice that we did not say that a use case must be *completed* to set a condition. If a use case is called from within another use case, even the first step of the calling use case can set the condition for starting another use case.

Post-condition should be clear from reading the use case. It is simply a more detailed version of the name—the *goal*—set to convey the state of the system *after* the use case completes.

There is one **exception** to the rule that another use case sets the state for the next one: when the precondition falls outside our (business *or* information) system. In **Refer Patient**, which is not to be automated, we identified a precondition to clarify a chain of events: "A patient suffers from a medical condition." The result of **Refer Patient** is a trigger for our system, not a precondition. That is why in **Make Appointment** the precondition has been left blank.

It is not always easy to find a unique and unambiguous description for the precondition. But we must not "invent" preconditions to fill the field. In an ATM case, a customer may simply decide to get cash. The reasons do not concern us.

Trigger

[Kulak 2000, 91]

A trigger is the event that starts the use case.

The trigger occurs, or can occur, only if the preconditions to the use case are met. A use case may have more than one trigger.

In **Make Appointment**, the use case does not start unless the referral source calls the hospital:

Make Appointment	Trigger:	The referral source calls the hospital for an appointment.

A template is *not* the use case itself, but a tool for presenting the use case in a structured format. Even within a template, the use case retains its dual nature: It is a *flow* of discrete steps. We wish to see a clear-cut precondition, an obvious trigger, explicitly enumerated steps, and a solid post-condition. But this convergence of clearly identifiable components does not always happen. The trigger is especially susceptible to uncertainty:

- *The trigger can overlap with the precondition.* In **Receive Patient**, the precondition is defined as "The patient has an appointment for a medical service," while the trigger reads: "The patient arrives at the hospital and is directed to the reception desk." Since both the appointment and the presence of the patient are required *before* the use case can begin, the precondition could have included both. We chose, however, to view the arrival of the patient as an *event*—something that happens—rather than a condition—something that *is*— and specify it as the trigger.
- *The trigger can overlap with the first step of the normal flow.* An example is when a customer inserts a bank card into an ATM. This action clearly triggers the **Conduct ATM Transaction** use case, but the first step of the normal flow *must* include the action as well because the information system must verify the card. Whether specified in detail or not, what takes place in the normal flow of this use case is not just one single action but an *interaction* between the actor and the bank's information system. Remember what we said before: A step in the flow of a use case is actually a transaction. A trigger, on the other hand, is an event.
- *The trigger can be elusive.* In a use case called **Climb Mountain**, what exactly triggers the use case—the actor's decision to climb a mountain, the first step out of the door, reaching the foot of the mountain, or the first vertical climb? In **Verify Insurance Plan**, we left the trigger blank and specified the precondition as

Verify Insurance Plan	Precondition:	Hospital needs valid health insurance plan for the patient.

There is no way to have an ironclad trigger in each and every use case. To expand on a point we made a little earlier:

> A use case has a dual nature: From one viewpoint it is a narrative that flows smoothly; from another viewpoint it has a structure that is composed of distinct steps within a territory marked by a precondition at one end and a post-condition at the other.

If this duality sometimes overburdens our logic, so be it. We should not invest an inordinate amount of time to fit a square peg in a round hole.

The following two guidelines can help us in placing the trigger within the context of the use case.

- If a recognizable precondition exists, **the trigger can occur only if the precondition has been met**. The tail end of the precondition may overlap with the trigger.
- **The trigger must come before the main action of the normal flow**, but it might overlap with the first step.

Flows

[Armour 2001, 24]

> A flow is an ordered set of activities that occur as the actors and the system attempt to reach a goal.

In introducing the components of a use case, we classified the actions within a scenario into four flows. Before discussing each flow in detail and within the context of the use case template, we explore the points that apply to all.

- *Steps are abstractions.*

Like the use case itself, steps in a use case are abstractions.

In presenting flows, we select those attributes of the behavior that we find relevant and discard the rest. For example, when we rule that the customer may pay by cash, we do not specify denominations ($5 or $20). Even if we do need to specify such a limitation—for instance "cashier may not accept denominations higher than $50"—we usually specify them as nonbehavioral requirements or organize them separately under business rules.

A patient may need an appointment for a variety of medical services. Therefore, in **Make Appointment**, we abstract and generalize the medical service and do not specify each one. In our version of how appointments are made, it is not important which medical service is required.

- *System's response must be limited to "what."*

Avoid design and implementation features in system responses.

In most examples in this chapter, the system's response to the actor has been primarily presented as implicit. The first reason, of course, is that we want to avoid implementation detail. We are focused on *what*, not *how*, and we do not probe into design features. For example, when we declare that the reception clerk verifies that the appointment exists, we leave the following issues open.

- How does the clerk tell the system of the intention to search for an appointment? A menu item, a button, a hyperlink, or any of these?
- Which options does the system present for searching—**Search Appointments by Name**, **Search Appointments by Date**, **Search Appointments by Social Security Number**, **Search Appointments by Medical Service**, or a combination?
- If the clerk searches the appointments by name, is the exact full name required? Or can the clerk enter a number of characters and ask the system for a list of all matches, from which the clerk then selects one?
- If the search is done by date, does the clerk enter the date longhand, or does the system provide a calendar? Or does the system assume that today's date is the default?

We have barely scratched the surface of possible variations. Even if we include a minimum, the reader would become hopelessly lost.

The argument is not that design and implementation details are not important. On the contrary, they are truly important: A sloppy or user-unfriendly interface can doom an application to the loss of honor and reputation. The point is that a use case is a *base*, not a *vehicle* for design and implementation. Use cases provide the behavioral model. We can only hope (and pray) that design would realize them effectively.

The second reason is that anything that clouds the clarity of the flow should be avoided. Otherwise, if the system response clarifies the interaction, it must be included. In **Conduct ATM Transaction**, the normal flow could start as follows:

Conduct ATM Transaction
_____

Normal Flow: 1. Customer inserts the bank card.
                   2. Customer enters password.
                   3. System verifies password.
                   4. System presents a list of transaction types that the customer may conduct.
                   5. Customer selects a type of transaction.
                      . . .

In step 2, we did not specify that after the customer inserts the card, the system responds by asking for the password. We just assumed that it would be inferred. In steps 3 to 5, however, we separated the system response from the actions by the actor.

The proper amount of the system's response in a use case depends on what point needs clarification.

- *Steps can be repeated.*

In any type of flow, one or more steps can be repeated until a predefined condition is met.

☞ The arrow (➜) has no significance except for attracting attention. You may replace it with another icon or remove it altogether.

In **Make Appointment**, the clerk tries to match the availability of a medical service to the availability of the patient by repeating two steps. And if more than one appointment needs to be made, another step is added to the loop:

Make Appointment
_____

Normal Flow: . . .

                   4. Appointment clerk consults hospital's schedule to find a free slot for the required medical service.
                   5. Appointment clerk verifies that the patient is available for the appointment.
                   ➜ Loop 1: **Repeat** steps 4–5 until hospital's schedule matches patient's availability.
                   6. Appointment clerk makes the appointment.
                   ➜ Loop 2: **Repeat** steps 4–6 for each appointment.

Normal Flow

Normal flow is the best-case scenario.

If the actors and the system interact successfully through each step of the normal flow, the goal of the use case is achieved.

In **Receive Patient**, the normal flow distinctly lays out what the reception clerk must do to send a patient for a medical service:

Receive Patient	
Normal Flow:	1. Patient informs reception clerk of the appointment.
	2. Reception clerk verifies that the appointment exists.
	3. Reception clerk verifies that patient has been registered and registration is valid.
	4. Reception clerks directs patient to the appropriate medical service.

In a template, steps in the normal flow are numbered consecutively. Completion of one step is the precondition for starting the next step: If the hospital does not possess valid data on the patient (step 3), the reception clerk cannot send the patient to the medical service (step 4).

☞ Some verbs, such as "verify," are strong indications that an alternate exists, even though we have not used a conditional construct.

Steps, however, are *never* expressed in a conditional format: alternate (or conditional) means of arriving at the objective of a step should be listed in the *alternate* section of the template. Similarly, handling failures is assigned to **exceptions**. Nevertheless, when stepping through the normal flow, we should inquire: What if the step fails? Is there another way to achieve the same goal (alternate) or not (exception)?

In specifying each step, we must use an active voice: "**Patient informs reception clerk of the appointment,**" *not* "**Reception clerk is informed of the appointment (by the patient).**" We should leave no doubt as to who is doing what. Even when finding an active voice seems hopeless, we should try and try again.

- *Number of Steps.*

There are no commonly accepted limits on the number of steps in the normal flow of a use case.

Some use cases need more steps, others need less. On the *less* side, we stated that the use case must provide "a result of measurable value" to the primary actor. If three steps are enough to get this result, then three steps are what the use case needs.

On the *more* side, however, there can be a problem if the normal flow approaches a size that cannot be grasped with ease. In this case, one of the following is the likely culprit.

❶ **The use case is really more than one use case** and we are trying to force them into one. The name of the use case is usually an indication: **Manage Patient Billing** is a case in point. We should review our packaging and divide the scenario into different use cases.

❷ The use case is legitimately one use case, but **too much detail has polluted the normal flow**. If the details are about design and implementation, then we should remove them. If the details are sub-steps, then they should go to the *Sub-Flow* field.

❸ The use case is legitimately one use case, but **steps can be combined**. In the previous ATM use case, steps 4 and 5 can be combined into one: "**Customer selects the type of transaction [from a list provided by the system].**"

❹ The use case is legitimately one use case, but **there are just too many steps**. Consider breaking apart this use case through "extends" or "includes." (See the "Dependencies: Include and Extend" section later in this chapter.)

Sub-Flows

> Sub-flows identify the details of the steps in the normal flow.

Steps in the sub-flow are *subordinate* steps. A use case is not necessarily a more accurate use case because it has many sub-steps. Sub-flows should be used only when details are required.

In a template, two styles may be used for presenting sub-flows. The first style is to place sub-steps in a separate field and identify their affiliation by numbering, as we did in **Register Patient**:

Register Patient	
Normal Flow:	1. Registration clerk enters or updates personal data. . . .
Sub-Flows:	1.1 Registration clerk enters the Social Security Number of the new patient.
	1.2 Registration clerk enters or updates the patient's address.
	1.3 Registration clerk enters or updates the patient's phone number.
	1.4 Registration clerk enters or updates the name, the address, and the phone number of the patient's closest relative.

The advantage of this style is that it does not clutter the normal flow. The disadvantage is that if understanding the normal step requires grasping its detail, the details are once removed.

The second style is to list sub-steps immediately after the main step:

Register Patient	
Normal Flow:	1. Registration clerk enters or updates personal data.
	• Registration clerk enters the Social Security Number of the new patient.
	• Registration clerk enters or updates the patient's address.
	• Registration clerk enters or updates the patient's phone number.
	. . .

The advantage is that by using this style the reader does not have to jump back and forth to understand what a step involves. The disadvantage is that if there are too many sub-steps for too many steps, the coherence of the flow is damaged.

Alternate Flow & Exceptions

> Alternate steps identify remedies; exceptions signify failure.

Alternate steps and exceptions are related: They specify what steps are to be taken if a step in the normal flow does not go according to plan.

In **Checkout Groceries**, if the customer pays by cash, the payment step in the normal flow is successful. If the customer pays by credit card instead of cash, the step is a remedy. If the customer cannot pay at all, it is a failure. In other words, if the normal flow goes well, there is no need for alternates or exceptions.

We can present alternates and exceptions in separate sections of the template, or combine them into one—as we have done. The argument for combining them is that they are related, sometimes even indistinguishable. If the ATM customer enters the wrong password, the system may give the customer two more chances to enter the correct one, and then refuses to recognize the card for a predefined period. In this example, it is the number of failures to enter the correct password that results in the overall failure of the use case, not the nature or the failure of a single step by itself.

In the use case template, the "*if*" is implicit in the label of **Alternate Flow & Exceptions**. Therefore, there is no need to repeat it. Better to express the condition in unconditional terms than to weaken the impact of the stated rule. In **Receive Patient**, just after the reception clerk has verified the appointment, we do *not* say "*If* patient is new or *If* patient has lost the hospital ID card," but:

☞ Sometimes alternate steps are alternates of each other, *not* of the normal step. In **Checkout Groceries**, if the normal steps simply declare that "the customer pays" then the alternates for payment—by cash, by credit card, etc.—become **specializations** of the **parent** step in the normal flow.

☞ As well as defining interactions, many steps in a use case establish **business rules**. See "Business Rules" in the chapter on Domain Analysis.

Receive Patient	
Alternate Flow/ Exceptions:	**3.a** Patient is new. Reception clerk directs the patient to registration . . .
	3.b Patient is not new but personal or insurance data has changed. Reception clerk directs the patient to registration . . .
	3.c Patient has lost the hospital ID card. Reception clerk directs the patient to registration . . .

As this example shows, conditions can be compound: "Patient is not new *but* personal or insurance data has changed."

Nonbehavioral Requirements

> When a nonbehavioral requirement applies to a specific use case, the requirement is specified in the template.

Use cases describe system behavior, but the context in which the actors interact with the system and the outcome of a use case may have requirements that are nonbehavioral or design-centered.

☞ See Chapter 4, Gathering Requirements. The term "nonbehavioral" applies to features of design and navigation as well.

We discussed nonbehavioral (or nonfunctional) requirements before. These requirements include categories such as usability, reliability, security, and performance that usually do not apply to a specific use case. But there are exceptions. For example, in the category of "*usability*," the needs and the qualifications of the actor may decide not only "*what*" the actor does, but also "*how*":

- Is the actor expected to be a novice?
- Is extensive training necessary to use the implementation of a use case?
- If users have been using a legacy system, should the new application follow the navigation of the existing one to save training costs and reduce disruption?
- Would the interface require help features specific to the use case?

A video store may want to install a terminal so that its customers can find the movies they are looking for and verify that a copy is available. **Find Favorite Movie** would have functional requirements such as the ability to search by name, director, actors, and/or the genre. But since the actor of the use case is the customer and the customer cannot be trained and must interact with the system under less than optimal conditions, usability becomes an especially important issue:

- The interface must be designed for a touch-sensitive screen. No keyboard.
- Icons and labels must be large enough for the customer to recognize without forcing the customer to move to normal reading distance.
- An online image of the keyboard would allow the customer to type by touching the screen.

Under normal circumstances, such an interface would annoy us. But it is the right one for its intended use.

Open Issues

> Open issues are questions that must be resolved before the use case can be judged as complete.

This field identifies issues that the client has intentionally left open or that an analysis of the use case has discovered. When the issues are resolved, or dismissed, there would be no need for the field. (However, you may keep it for consistency's sake and represent the lack of open issues with an "N/A.")

Audit Fields

> Audit fields help us to keep track of the evolution of the use case.

☞ Except for **Register Patient**, we have not included the audit fields in our examples. This is to save space, not a reflection on their importance.

Audit fields do not tell us anything about the use case itself, but are essential to keep development on track.

- *Author.* Besides taking responsibility (and pride), author identifies the person who should know about the use case and can answer questions.

- *Revision.* If we have two versions of the same use case, revision indicates which one is more recent.

- *Date.* Date reinforces revision. Even if we have the latest revision, we might be aware that something has changed that affects the use case and we must verify that the change has been taken into account.

- *Source.* During development, a considerable part of gathering requirements is informal: short conversations, short telephone calls, or short electronic exchanges. However, if we have identifiable sources—interviews, publications, documents, etc.— we should reference them here. The references not only help to verify the particulars of a use case, but provide a base for later phases of development.

Custom Fields

> A custom field in the template specifies an attribute or requirement that is specific to one use case or a set of use cases within the system.

You may add custom fields to the use case template to reflect special attributes. For example, in a system that has many automatic jobs, "frequency" or "cycle" becomes an important feature for use cases that must function without a trigger external to the system.

Prudence is the better part of originality, though: We should make sure that the new field is not due to the whim of the moment, and that it is a pattern that needs specific attention throughout the system or across a set of use cases.

3. ACTOR GENERALIZATION

> Actors are generalizations of real users. If necessary, we can generalize actors into even more abstract roles.

☞ Hospital managements usually, and fortunately, guard the financial data of their patients tightly. It is unlikely that the receptionist would be given access to such data. So consider this scenario as mostly hypothetical, intended to "reuse" actors with whom you are already familiar.

In analyzing Walden's domain concept, we identified **Appointment Clerk**, **Registration Clerk**, **Reception Clerk**, and **Billing Clerk** as actors. Each role was attached to a specific use case. However, the hospital may inform us that all these actors should be able to resolve (certain) patient billing issues.

A use case, however, has only *one* primary actor. Therefore, we need one actor who represents the new role and, at the same time, encompasses the existing ones. The new role is more abstract than the appointment, registration, reception, or billing clerks: it *generalizes* all four. For a new use case that resolves billing issues, we will call the new actor **Hospital Clerk**.

To illustrate generalization, let us view a diagram of this use case (Figure 7.3) and others that involve the actors in question. (To keep the picture clear, we have included only the base use cases.)

**Figure 7.3
Actor
Generalization:
Creating a
"Super-Role"**

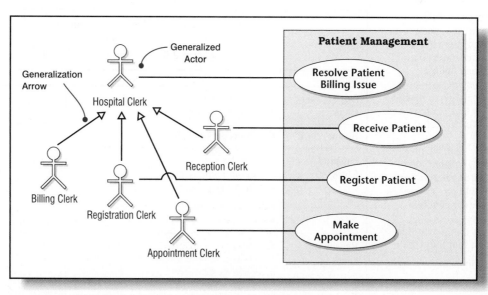

Billing Clerk has no other role in **Patient Management**, but would be a busy actor in the **Accounting** subsystem.

As we can conclude from the nonbehavioral requirements field, even though **Hospital Clerk** is the primary actor, **Billing Clerk** keeps the identity of an independent, distinct actor.

- The actor that is the outcome of generalization is called an *abstract* actor.
- Actors that are the source of generalization are *concrete* actors.
- The abstract actor is a *super-role*, the capabilities of which are *inherited* by concrete actors who play *sub-roles*.

Generalization may be multi-level: Were it necessary, we could have generalized the appointment, reception, and registration clerks into one super-role, **Administrative Clerk**. Then this abstract actor could have been generalized further, along with **Billing Clerk**, into **Hospital Clerk**. Furthermore, a concrete actor may participate in more than one generalization. For example **Billing Clerk**, along with **Payables Clerk** and others, could be generalized into **Accounting Clerk**.

Except for encapsulating more than one role, an abstract actor behaves exactly like a concrete one: the actor interacts with the system to achieve a goal. This stands in contrast to the generalization of use cases: An abstract use case is not "instantiated" except through its children. (See the "Use Case Generalization" section later in this chapter.)

We may arrive at abstract and concrete actors from two different directions:

❶ *Generalization:* abstracting actors into one higher level. This is what we just described.
❷ *Specialization:* the reverse of generalization, when we discover that one role, even though it is valid, needs to be differentiated into more than one. For example, even though for many purposes **Customer** is an acceptable actor for a bank, in some cases it is necessary to distinguish between **Private Customer** and **Corporate Customer**.

We have argued that as analysis goes forward, we should reorganize our findings, add new entries, and drop some old ones. We now know enough about actors to place them in a specialized dictionary. (See Table 7.2.)

Table 7.2
Walden's Actor Dictionary. We have not introduced an **Enter Bulk Payment** use case. We just want to show that **Billing Clerk** has other duties as well.

Also, we have not repeated the **Resolve Patient Billing Issue** use case for concrete actors since it is through generalization that they relate to it.

Walden Medical Center *Actor Dictionary* Version 2.0—September 20, 2004			
ACTOR	DESCRIPTION	ABSTRACT	USE CASE(S)
Appointment Clerk	Makes appointment for the patient to receive medical service.		Make Appointment
Billing Clerk	Maintains patient billing.		Enter Bulk Payment
Hospital Clerk	Generalizes: • Appointment Clerk • Billing Clerk • Reception Clerk • Registration Clerk	✔	Resolve Patient Billing Issue
Reception Clerk	Receives patient on arrival at the hospital. Verifies registration. Arranges for the patient to receive medical service.		Receive Patient
Registration Clerk	Enters or updates patient's personal and payment data. Issues a hospital card, if necessary.		Register Patient

4. DEPENDENCIES: INCLUDE AND EXTEND

Use cases, taken together, make up the *public* face of a system. As such, a use case must be cohesive and concise; it must make reaching its goal as intelligible as possible. Consequently, its facile façade often hides operations that are far more complex that the appearance implies.

To keep simplicity and perform complex actions at the same time, the use case might need to *delegate* one or more of its functions to other use cases. In other words, one use case becomes dependent on another. The relationships that express and model this dependency are two: include and extend.

Extend Relationship

> An extend relationship is one in which a use case is created to extend the functionality of a base use case.

☞ Besides the reasons discussed under "Dependencies," another element might be the driving force behind creating extend and include relationships: **refactoring**. See "Separating and Joining Use Cases."

As use cases mature through iteration, we may find that their behavior must be extended. This extension is needed in a manner that does not affect the normal functionality of the base use case, but enhances its features. If we add a sunroom to a house, we have not changed how it is used, but have simply *extended* it.

In **Register Patient**, we left a number of issues open, including one about patients who do not have health insurance:

Register Patient	Open Issues:	1.1	If the patient has no health insurance, what should be done?
			. . .

To resolve the issue, the analyst conducts a new interview with the domain expert:

Analyst:	What if a patient has no medical insurance?
DE:	We need a credit card or just bill them later. Actually, there is a lot of variety and we have to make a judgment on payments. There are charity cases. There is the emergency room—we have to take the patient in, regardless. It is the emergency room, mind you, and the patient may be in a coma. Even if the patient does have insurance, the insurance does not pay for everything in every case. You have the "deductible." You have the "coinsurance rate." Some patients come from HMOs. Some belong to a PPO. (You *are* aware that we are exploring subscription plans?)
	(Continued)

Analyst:	Would you explain the terms you just used?
DE:	"Deductible" is the minimum payment that the patient pays for a service. "Coinsurance Rate" is the percentage that the patient pays for anything above the deductible. HMO is—I am sure you know—a "Health Maintenance Organization." PPO stands for "Preferred Provider Organization." Subscription plans are new to us. As of now, we have made no decisions regarding them. But they are coming.
Analyst:	Seems like a tangle. How do you keep it straight?
DE:	We keep detailed records for each service and each service has a pre-defined cost. The form has room for all variations. Basically, there are two sources of payment: an insurance provider and the patient. That does not mean that we get paid in the end. (We don't bill a charity case, but we still need to know how much it costs us. It is tax deductible.)

So we get more than we bargained for. Among them: `Register Patient` needs to be enhanced to handle credit cards. We conclude that the normal scenario of the use case is just fine and need not to be changed. We only need to extend it through its alternate flow by delegating the functionality to another use case:

Register Patient	
Alternate Flow/ Exceptions:	. . .
	2.a Patient is not new and insurance data has not changed. Registration clerk does not update the insurance data by default.
	2.b Patient wants to pay the entire bill or the co-payments by a credit card. Registration clerk verifies the credit card (Extend: 142 – Verify Credit Card) and records credit card information.

`Verify Credit Card` is an *extending* use case. The *base* use case, `Register Patient`, calls on the extending use case through an *extension point*, alternate step 2.b. The template for an extended use case is different from the template for a normal one.

Like the sunroom that we previously cited as an example, an *extending* use case shares its "plumbing" with the *extended* (base) use case. Therefore, some fields have been removed:

- *Primary Actor.* The primary actor of an extending use case must be the same as the primary actor of the base use case. If the primary actor is different, then we are looking at an independent use case, not an extension. The owner of the sunroom is the owner of the house. If the ownership is different, we have two different properties. The **Supporting Actors** field, however, remains because the new use case might need extra help.

- *Scope.* The scope is the same as the extended use case.
- *Trigger.* An extending use case does not need an independent trigger.

☞ An extending use case can serve more than one "base" use case (the same way that two neighbors can build a greenhouse that straddles both their properties). Therefore, each of the three fields can contain more than one entry, each pointing to a different use case. In such cases, we should consider the alternative: the **include relationship**.

An extending use case must be as simple as possible. Instead of a sunroom, we can build another house or an apartment complex on our property, but then we are stretching the concept of "extension."

The *name* label of the use case identifies it as an "extend" rather than a normal use case. Three new fields describe where the extending use case comes from:

- *Base Use Case & Base Use Case ID.* Identifies the use case that *this* use case extends.
- *Extension Point.* Identifies the point where the extending use case is inserted into the extended one.

An extending use case is not instantiated independently. Though it is possible to build a sunroom somewhere in the middle of nowhere, it would be rather unusual unless, of course, the purpose is different: A bathhouse in a location with "miracle" mineral waters is a business unto itself; it does not "extend" your house.

Include Relationship

> An include relationship is one in which one use case uses the functionality of another, independent, use case.

A use case is built on the idea that a primary actor interacts with the system to achieve a single useful goal. But what if the success of a use case depends on the success of *another* use case—with the same primary actor or a different one—that must reach its goal before the first use case can reach *its* goal? The answer is the **include relationship**.

In **Receive Patient**, the reception clerk must ensure that the system has the right **state** about the patient *before* dispatching the patient to the medical service, but *after* verifying that the patient has an appointment:

Receive Patient	
Normal Flow:	. . .
	3. Reception clerk verifies that patient has been registered and registration is valid.
	. . .
Alternate Flow/ Exceptions:	**3.a** Patient is new. Reception clerk directs the patient to registration. (Include: 140 – Register Patient.)
	. . .

☞ An "include" relationship need not be conditional. An extending use case, however, must be referenced *only* in the alternate flow because "extension" must not affect the normal flow in any way.

The reception clerk cannot complete **Receive Patient** without **Register Patient** if registration is necessary. The latter use case is an *independent* use case that was modeled with a separate set of requirements: In the preliminary set of use cases for Walden Medical Center, **Register Patient** was sketched out, while **Receive Patient** was discovered only later. Besides, the primary actors are different—even though this difference, by itself, is not a condition for an include relationship. Here, unlike the **extend relationship**, it is the "base" use case that is dependent on the use case that it calls.

We compared the "extend" relationship to adding a sunroom to a house. The include relationship brings another image to mind: a military barracks, with the compound as a system. Soldiers live in quarters assigned to them, but the soldiers' daily routine *includes* the mess hall, the training ground, and the learning center. (The enlisted men have more colorful terms for these facilities.) Though each facility serves the whole system, they are independent of each other. Their "plumbing" and "wiring" is not an extension of another building.

As we shall see later in this chapter, independent conception is not the only reason to use the include relationship. It might also be dictated by the need to *reuse* common functionality, to manage complexity, and to set development priorities.

Use Case Diagram for Dependencies

> In a use case diagram, dependency type is indicated by the direction of an arrow.

In a use case diagram, dependencies are presented by an arrow. (See Figure 7.4.)

An *extending* use case is dependent on the extended use case, while an *included* use case is independent of the use case that *includes* it.

> The base use case is independent of an extending use case but dependent on an including one.

Figure 7.4   Use Case Dependencies: Include and Extend

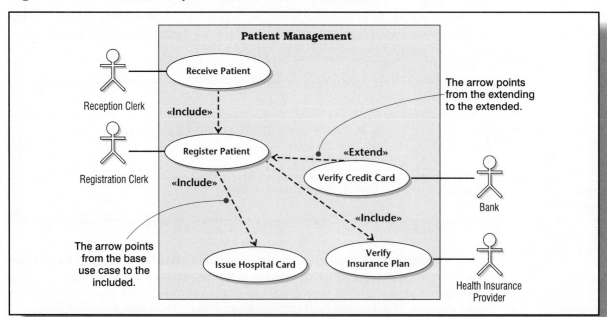

Therefore, the arrows expressing these two relationships are the reverse of each other:

- In an **extend** relationship, the arrow points from the extending use case to the extended one.
- In an **include** relationship, the arrow is from the including use case to the included one.

Base UC	Arrow's Direction	Referenced UC
Extended UC	←	**Extending UC**
Register Patient		Verify Credit Card
Including UC	→	**Included UC**
Receive Patient		Register Patient

5. USE CASE GENERALIZATION

> We generalize use cases when they achieve the same goal by different means.

Some use cases turn out to share the same goals, different only in minor details or in actors. Even this early in development, we are conscious that if we could somehow model the common ground between them, we would have a more robust design and a less costly implementation by ridding ourselves of redundancies. We want to abstract the behavior that is common to them and package it into one unit. To sum, we want generalization.

Use cases are not objects but units of behavior. Things—objects, systems, subsystems—have behavior but they are not the same as their behavior. Nevertheless, we can apply certain object-oriented concepts such as *abstraction*, *generalization*, and *inheritance* to use cases.

Make Appointment: New Requirement

☞ The requirements about the browser and the secure Web site are not business requirements in the strict sense and should not be included in the use case. Nevertheless, they are requirements and create the setting for the concrete system design. In this case, technical requirements have a business purpose.

In Walden's **Make Appointment**, it is a hospital employee who makes appointments for the patient. The hospital, however, may decide that after the first cut of the **Patient Management** subsystem goes online, it would like to allow a select group of outside doctors and hospitals—referral sources—to make appointments for their patients. The only limitations are:

- The patient must be *already registered* with the hospital. (The management is apparently hesitant to accept appointments for unknown entities.)
- The patient must "belong" to the *same referral source* who wants to make the appointment. The doctor cannot search through, or view, patients who come from a different source.

Also, since these doctors and hospitals are *outside* our system:

- They must be able to use a *Web browser* to make appointments. We do not want to install our applications on their computers—were it possible—and it is unlikely that they want us to do it, either.
- The Web interface must be served through a *secure site*.

Thankfully, we get this requirement before we are too deep into the labyrinth of implementation. "Thankfully" because it is a tall order: It may sound simple, but a considerable amount of investment in the infrastructure is needed for a secure, Web-based system. (The management is not hesitant here: It wants a forward-looking system; this is a capital improvement project and they are in for the long haul.)

☞ That is why a penny spent on gathering requirements and design can save a fortune on maintenance and implementation.

Furthermore, a patient may have more than one referral source: a primary care physician and several specialists. Theoretically at least, they all must be able to make appointments. This requirement impacts our class structure: We must accumulate referral sources for the patient and distinguish between active and inactive ones. An innocent-looking requirement can trigger a chain reaction.

One Goal, Two Use Cases

Implementation, however, is in the future. Therefore, first things first. We are in the midst of use case modeling and have to account for the new requirement in *this* phase of development: We have two use cases that have the same goal—make an appointment for the patient.

The same goal? Yes. The same primary actors? No. The same steps? Most, but not all. Altogether enough to make abstraction reasonable, logical, and possible.

After parsing the original **Make Appointment**, we come up with a new *abstract* use case with two "children." The relationship can be best understood by a diagram (Figure 7.5).

☞ Remember that we emphasized the need for assigning unique *numerical* identifiers to use cases. The name change here illustrates the need rather well.

The arrows pointing from **Make Appointment by Hospital** (our original **Make Appointment**) and the new **Make Appointment by Referral Source** use case) to the generalized **Make Appointment** identify the first two uses cases as children of the third: They inherit its behavior.

Since the two children use cases have separate primary actors, we have created an abstract actor, **Appointment Agent**, for the abstract use case. Theoretically, like all actors, this one can be instantiated (i.e., it can be a concrete user), but it would not be in reality because the one use case with which it interacts is an abstract use case, and abstract use cases cannot be instantiated.

Figure 7.5 Use Case Generalization: When the Same Goal Is Achieved by Different Means

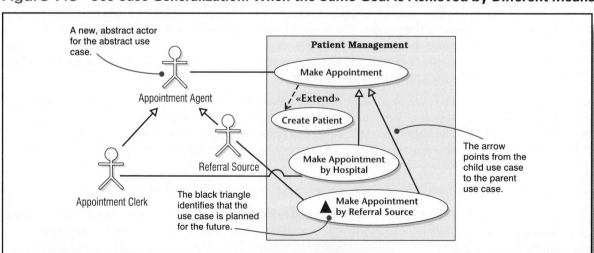

A new icon appears in the diagram, a black triangle that marks **Make Appointment by Referral Source** as a use case to be implemented in the future. (The triangle is an example of *stereotyping*—the extension of UML notation by adding our own building blocks. We will discuss stereotyping in Chapter 10.)

The diagrams looks comprehensible and convincing enough. How do we transform this sparkling vision to the structured text of use cases? With labor, patience, care, and a heavy heart: The clarity of the diagram does not translate well into a clear textual flow.

The Parent

The template for the abstract use case, the generalized **Make Appointment**, is familiar enough. The **Name** label is different and some fields have been left out to be handled by the child use cases. Four other fields need clarification.

- *Generalization.* Like a concrete use case, an abstract one can be generalized further. But this is only theoretical: After finishing this topic, you have to decide for yourself whether having multiple levels of use case generalization is practical.
- *Precondition & Post-Condition.* If precondition defines the system's state and is not a condition *outside* the system (such as this one), then it would usually be the same for both the parent and the children. Post-condition is more likely to be about the system's state after the use case completes. If you sense that either cannot apply to children, then leave them blank.
- *Trigger.* Trigger is usually specific to the concrete use case.

The Children

Use cases for children are more complicated. We have to show distinctively what is inherited from the parent, what is inherited and specialized, and what is new. For our example, we take the new **Make Appointment by Referral Source** use case.

The **Generalization** field in the template shows that this use case is a child of **Make Appointment**. Theoretically again, a concrete use case may have more than one parent (multiple inheritance).

Those fields that are affected by generalization are annotated to show how they associate with the parent use case(s). The first part of the annotation is a letter that indicates the type of inheritance:

- *I: inherited with no change.* Step 4 states that the referral source makes the appointment. Even though the primary actor is different, the step is exactly the same as in the parent, because the primary actor in this use case is the child of the primary actor in the generalized use case.
- *S: inherited but specialized.* Step 1 shows that, unlike the hospital's appointment clerk, the referral source cannot change the patient's personal data: "Referral source records patient's contact data." To use a different term, step 1 *overrides* the step that it inherits.
- *N: new.* Does not exist in the parent(s). For example, **Make Appointment by Hospital** would have a step that the parent use case lacks:

Make Appointment by Hospital		
Alternate Flow/ Exceptions:	**2.a**	Patient is not on file. Create new patient. (Extend: 141 – Create Patient.)
	(N)	

The second part of the annotation is the source in the parent use case. A child may have more, or less, steps than the parent. In **Make Appointment by Referral Source**, the system allows the actor to view only the patients who already belong the referral source, so there is no need for step 2 in the parent: "Appointment agent records information about the referral source." Now step 2 in the child matches step 3 of the parent. (The new inheritance cannot have such a reference and fields like **Precondition** do not need it.)

The third part is the unique identifier for the parent. As we said, a child may have more than one parent and the unique identifier tells us which. (If, like our example, a concrete use case has only one parent, you do not have to specify the ID of the parent.)

Replacing Alternates

Generalization can replace a set of alternate steps.

In **Resolve Patient Billing Issue**, the payment step in the normal flow is extended by three alternate steps: payment by cash, credit card, or check. "Payment" is already an abstraction, so we can transform it into a generalized use case with three children. The downside would be that, in most cases, maintaining use case generalization is very labor-intensive and the symbolic references widen the communication distance between use cases and business stakeholders.

6. USE CASE DIAGRAM

A use case diagram is a meta-model that portrays associations among actors, use cases, and the system.

As we have gone through topics in this chapter, we have introduced the components of the use case diagram one by one. By now it should be very familiar to us. What remains is to discuss it as a whole rather than as the sum of its constituent parts.

A use case diagram is a "meta-model," which means it represents another model—the use case model. As a result, it does not reveal a lot about the use cases themselves. While a use case models one unit of a system's behavior, a use case diagram illustrates how these units relate to each other within the system and to the actors outside the system. By hiding the *temporal* flow of use cases, it presents a *spatial* view of them: the place of each use case and each actor within the whole.

A broad spatial view is what use case modeling lacks by itself. Taken individually, use cases portray scenes that are more or less self-contained. It is as if they live in full-service apartments: They may "extend" their activities to a basement storeroom or "include" the common lobby in their daily activities, but are unable to convey a sense of the whole. As a meta-model, the use case diagram helps us grasp the web woven by actors and use cases that might be removed from each other by several degrees of separation.

Our first draft of "Use Case Summary" for Walden's **Patient Management** (see the last chapter) contained just five use cases. One, **Refer Patient**, falls outside the hospital's information system. Another, **Track Medical Service**, has yet to be explored. Through iterations in gathering requirements and analysis, the remaining three have grown to 14 use cases—some detailed, some just identified as "includes" and "extends." It is possible to mentally picture the relationships among a few use cases and actors; 14 use cases (and counting) need a map, a diagram, to make the perspective meaningful. (See Figure 7.6.)

What else does this grand view of use cases give us besides the grand view?

- *A Graphical Table of Contents.* No matter how many documents we create and how faithfully we maintain them, a graphical confirmation conveys an understanding that words and numbers alone cannot convey. Some of us need more visual input to understand something, others need less. But we all need it to one degree or another.
- *Dependency Management.* When a team works on a project, the chances are that each member will focus on certain use cases (good) while completely ignoring others (bad). The diagram provides a fast method for verifying whether changes to one use case will affect others.
- *Refactoring.* Use cases should not repeat each other's *major* functionality. Since the diagram treats use cases as black boxes and does not reveal their inner workings, it is not the principal laboratory for deciding what should be refactored. But if we notice that one use case is named **Verify Credit Card** and the other **Charge Credit Card**, we may wonder: Don't they have something in common?

- *Prioritizing.* It becomes easier to assign priority when we see all use cases under one roof, whether the priority is placed inside-out or outside-in.

7. SEPARATING AND JOINING USE CASES

The primary purpose of use case modeling is to channel the unruly requirements of a system into disciplined behavioral units with distinct boundaries. The task is not often easy. There are no visual markers, natural or man-made, to tell us when a use case stops and another starts. It is *we* who create use cases by transforming chaos into order. It is *we* who are entrusted with giving them shape.

We do not shape use cases based on mere whim. We use judgment, rely on experience, and, above all, follow the prime directive: Use cases are to make complexity comprehensible and manageable. The rest must serve the prime directive.

We apply three processes to shape use cases through iteration: ❶ We delineate them, ❷ we divide them into more use cases, and then—sometimes—❸ we combine them. The guidelines for these operations are closer to patterns than to strict formal rules; that is, in every situation we may find exceptions. Finding exceptions does not of necessity mean that the guidelines are wrong, just that we must use judgment and wisdom. As you create use cases, you also contribute to the shared knowledge about them.

Delineating Use Cases

One use case must have *one* primary actor, *one* useful goal, and *one* system.

Figure 7.6   Use Case Diagram: A Meta-Model for the "Big Picture"

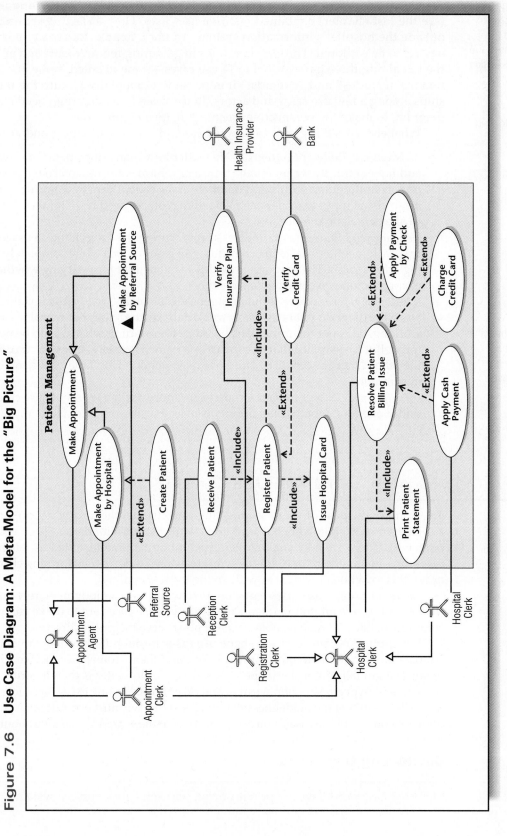

A meta-model is a model of other models. We use meta-models when models themselves cannot convey the grand view.

☞ Before concluding that the use case must be dismembered because the primary actor does not stand out, ensure that the *proxy* or the *initiator* is not the culprit. See "Primary Actor" under "Template Fields" in this chapter.

☞ By "invasion" we mean going *inside* another system. As we have discussed, a use case is allowed to interact with another system.

When do we know that a use case is really one use case and no more? By verifying three attributes:

❶ *One Primary Actor.*   If we have identified the actors but cannot distinguish the primary actor, most likely we are looking at more than one use case. Like in a play or a movie, an actor plays a role and it is the *role* that identifies the actor in a use case. Unlike in the movies, however, a use case has a *primary* actor, not a *leading* actor or actors. In the scenario that a use case illustrates, the primary actor is the only star.

❷ *One Useful Goal.*   The goal of a use case is to achieve "a result of measurable value" to the primary actor. Just how we decide the "measurable value" depends on the context, but if we can argue logically that components of the goal *can* be accomplished separately and—what is more significant—should be accomplished separately, then one use case is not enough. On the other hand, if the goal does not provide the primary actor with a meaningful result, then we do not have a complete use case. (For a more extensive discussion of this attribute, see "A Goal" under the "Components of a Use Case" section in the previous chapter.)

❸ *One System (or Subsystem).*   Whether we reach use cases by breaking down the behavior of a system into units or group use cases to reach a system, one system is the scope of a use case. If a use case "invades" the boundaries of another system, then it is not one use case. (See "A System" under the "Components of a Use Case" section in the previous chapter for a more comprehensive treatment of "system.")

Dividing Use Cases

> New requirements or the challenge of complexity may demand that a use case be divided.

[Armour 2001, 130–131]

Sometimes a perfectly good use case has to be broken apart, either because new requirements are introduced or because the use case embodies a long sequence of events with many actors. Depending on the reason, we can divide the use case vertically or horizontally.

Vertical Division

> Vertical division is necessary if the use case has too many parallel steps.

We may find that a use case, either in normal flow or in alternates, is trying to accommodate too many steps that are mostly parallel. That is, the majority of steps are *essentially* the same but are not *exactly* the same.

Let us revisit the **Make Appointment** use case, and let us assume that right from the beginning we knew that appointments could be made both by the appointment clerk at the hospital and by authorized doctors and hospitals from outside. Our scenario could have been written as follows:

A patient needs to receive medical service(s) from the hospital. The appointment agent (the appointment clerk at the hospital or an authorized outside referral source) matches the availability of the patient and the medical service(s) and makes the appointment(s).

Table 7.3

Parallel Steps in a Use Case.

We have not included the looping constructs required for matching availability and multiple appointments. They are not steps by themselves and are the same for both actors.

☞ Recall what we did in "Use Case Generalization": exactly what we did here, except that we abstracted the common and parallel steps into a generalized use case, **Make Appointment**. But, as we argued there, use case generalization is a work in progress and has its shortcomings. You might decide to simply divide the use case and forego generalization, especially if there are more parallel steps and their differences are more pronounced. Commonality among resulting use cases could be then managed through *include* and *extend*.

Let us emphasize that this approach (dividing the use case) does *not* invalidate the earlier approach (generalization). This is merely another way of solving the same problem.

Parallel Steps in a Use Case	
THE APPOINTMENT CLERK	THE REFERRAL SOURCE
The referral source contacts the hospital to make an appointment.	The referral source logs on to make an appointment.
The appointment clerk searches among all hospital patients to find the patient profile.	The referral source searches among patients that belong to the source to find the patient profile.
If the patient is new, the appointment clerk creates a new patient profile.	
The appointment clerk updates the referral source.	
The appointment clerk updates the contact information.	The referral source updates the contact information.
The appointment clerk matches the availability of the patient and the medical service.	The referral source matches the availability of the patient and the medical service.
The appointment clerk makes an appointment for the patient to receive a medical service.	The referral source makes an appointment for the patient to receive a medical service.

If the patient is new to the hospital, the appointment clerk (but not the outside referral source) creates a new patient profile and records basic information about the patient: name, contact information, and the referral source.

The outside referral source cannot select a patient who does not belong to that specific source, but can update contact information.

This use case is quite an acceptable one: It has one actor (the generalized **Appointment Agent**), one goal (make an appointment), and one subsystem (Walden's **Patient Management**). Let us, however, compare the actions that the two *concrete* actors perform. (See Table 7.3.)

The four gray rows identify the steps that are very similar but are not exactly the same. (We have also overlooked the fact that one actor is inside the "firewall," while the other is outside.) While we can write four generalized steps for the normal flow and modify each step with alternates, it is better to divide them vertically: the left side becomes **Make Appointment by Hospital**, the right side is turned into **Make Appointment by Referral Source**.

In the example, the differences in the steps were dictated by the differences between roles. But a use case might also have too many alternate steps for the *same* actor.

Horizontal Division

Horizontal division is necessary if the flow is too complex or the building blocks of the use case lack unity.

When we cut a set of steps out of the normal or the alternate flow of a use case into a new use case, we have divided it horizontally. There might be a few reasons to do so:

☝ If you do make strict rules about the number of steps, funny things start to happen: The use case that your colleague writes would either break the logical unity of steps to meet the minimum requirements or would force more than one transaction into one step to avoid exceeding the maximum. Human nature can come up with ingenious responses to irrational rules.

☞ At this point we do have two use cases, but imagine the world before that, when all we had was a story: the patient arrives at the hospital, the hospital clerk at the reception desk verifies that the patient needs registration, the patient is registered and sent to the medical service. It appears—quite plausibly—as one use.

☞ One potential negative result of refactoring use cases is **obsession**. We may turn refactoring into a (paid) version of solving crossword puzzles: "What can we refactor today?" In programming, one can indulge more in writing faster, smaller code. But the prime directive of use case modeling is different: Use cases are to make complexity comprehensible and manageable.

❶ *The flow is too long.*   What "too long" means depends on what you and your audience consider as too long. We *cannot* make rules such as "A use case shall have no less than three normal steps and no more than twenty." But if the use case *seems* too long, it probably is.

❷ *The scenario lacks unity of time.*   We might create a **Manage Patient Profile** use case and call it from both **Make Appointment** and **Register Patient** to record data about the patient. This is not a bad idea, but it does not take business requirements into account. When making an appointment, the hospital clerk needs certain data but not others. When the patient arrives at the hospital for a medical service, then some other data is required and not before. The two set of actions are separated by time. (There are also security considerations: Different actors might not have the clearance to see the same data.)

❸ *The role hides more than one actual user.*   We said that an actor is a *user type*, but a process may require more than one actual user. Think of a ping pong game: The role **Player** applies to both players, but one that serves the ball is not the same as the one who returns it. Had we abstracted the reception and the registration clerks at Walden into one abstract actor, **Hospital Clerk**, and had we joined **Receive Patient** and **Register Patient** into one use case, it would appear that the same *user* is the sole actor for the use case. This would not be true, since the hospital does not want the user who is "playing" the hospital clerk at the reception desk to be the same one who does the registration.

❹ *Some transactions are much more important or sensitive than others.*   In a well-written use case, all steps should have roughly the same level of importance or sensitivity. (Sub-flows were conceived with this purpose in mind: to keep details out of the normal flow.) But, as our examples show, we have created a separate use case whenever a credit card transaction is involved, not because the steps are that numerous, but because it is sensitive and must be implemented according to strict rules required by banks and credit card companies. (In practice, we usually buy a component certified by credit card agencies.)

Whatever the reasons, the resulting use case should follow the guidelines laid out earlier in the "Delineating Use Cases" section.

Refactoring

> Refactoring abstracts and reorganizes common behavior among use cases into new use cases.

Refactoring is a special case of horizontal division particularly useful for a large system in which ❶ certain behaviors are repeated and ❷ analysis is assigned to a team rather than one person.

In Walden's **Patient Management** subsystem, further requirements gathering might reveal that scheduling a medical service is not the exclusive behavior of the **Make Appointment** use case, but the medical staff might also need to make, change, or cancel appointments. Though our original use case does more than just setting the schedule, we should create a new use case, **Schedule Medical Service** perhaps, that encapsulates all actions related to scheduling and which is then *reused* by any use case that might need it. The mechanisms for such reuse are, of course, *include* and *extend*, which we discussed before.

8. ACTIVITY DIAGRAM

[Booch 1999, 271, 457]

> An activity diagram depicts the flow from activity to activity. It presents a visual, dynamic view of the system and its components.

☞ UML's activity diagram is based on a **flow chart** that has been around for a long time. Its longevity is a testament to its effectiveness.

☞ A use case diagram, contrary to the expectations that its name raises, does nothing to help us in visualizing what goes inside a use case. Its strong point is to provide a view from *outside*, between actors and a set of use cases and between use cases themselves.

☞ A use case has to make assumptions. If it does not, the explanations and the descriptions would overwhelm the flow. The question is: How safe is an assumption?

A use case is a *flow of activity in words*. If the flow is simple and linear, it can be understood on its own. If the flow is complex and iterative, words will not suffice.

In a model-driven development process, however, no one model has to stand alone. Where words fail us, an activity diagram can paint a clearer picture. Activity diagram is a flexible tool and its application is not limited to use cases. It can be attached to any dynamic model or to any operation whose flow needs clarification. The level of detail that an activity diagram reveals or hides is mostly up to us. To keep the diagram clear, we can conceal a set of activities in a placeholder and expand it in another diagram if and when the need arises.

Since the activity diagram requires an unambiguous logical flow, it may also help us to identify steps that the use case either missed or took for granted, as the activity diagram for Walden's **Make Appointment** (Figure 7.7) illustrates. (The building blocks of activity diagrams are explained in Table 7.4. We will discuss the remaining element, the synchronization bar which presents concurrency of activities, later in this book.)

The example has one activity, labeled **Find Patient**, that the use case *assumed* would be understood as a part of the process. However, we have made it explicit in the activity diagram to clarify the decision point that follows it: Is the patient a new one or an old one? To *keep* it clear, we have avoided exposing the logic inside the activity. (We may need an activity diagram for **Find Patient** at a later stage.)

In the same manner, the activity **Create Patient** hides an extending use case with the same name, called from an alternate step in **Make Appointment**.

If the flow of a use case is too complex for one clear activity diagram, we may use the technique of hiding a set of activities under a label and expanding it in another diagram. Before we do this, however, we should ask whether the flow is not too complex *by* itself.

The activity diagram has few elements. With a little care in *what* to show and the careful labeling of what *is* shown, it can be an effective means of communication between development stakeholders, technical or nontechnical alike.

9. USES OF USE CASES

> Use cases provide a crucial framework for analysis, design, implementation, and deployment activities.

We have discussed extensively what the use cases are. However, as we shall see in the following chapters, their usefulness does not stop with defining the interaction between an actor and the system. Following are the major uses of use cases. (See Figure 7.8.) Note that we do not argue that for each item the use case is the only source, nor that it is even the major source. Rather, we can arrive at them by keeping an eye on use cases as signposts.

Figure 7.7
**Activity
Diagram: The
Logical Flow of**
`Make`
`Appointment`

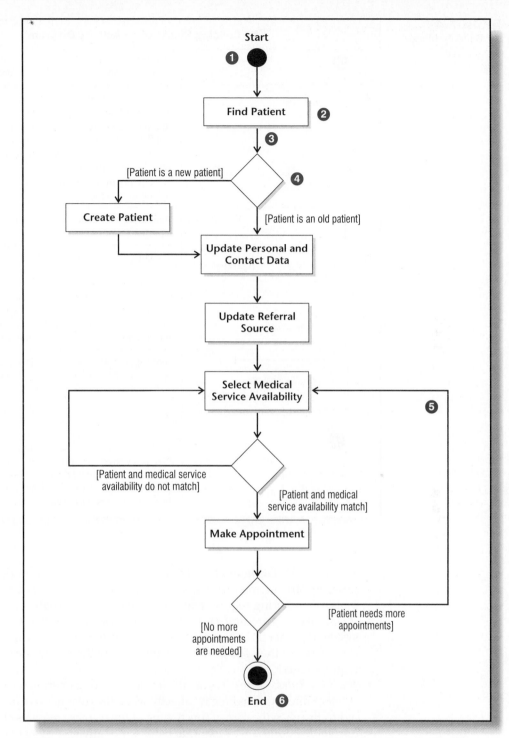

There is more to an activity diagram than you see here. We will expand on it in the following chapters.

Table 7.4

The Building Blocks
of an Activity
Diagram.

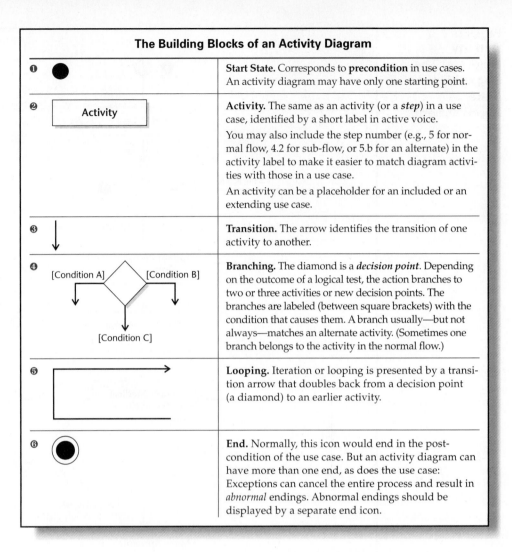

	The Building Blocks of an Activity Diagram	
❶	●	**Start State.** Corresponds to **precondition** in use cases. An activity diagram may have only one starting point.
❷	Activity	**Activity.** The same as an activity (or a *step*) in a use case, identified by a short label in active voice. You may also include the step number (e.g., 5 for normal flow, 4.2 for sub-flow, or 5.b for an alternate) in the activity label to make it easier to match diagram activities with those in a use case. An activity can be a placeholder for an included or an extending use case.
❸	↓	**Transition.** The arrow identifies the transition of one activity to another.
❹	[Condition A] / [Condition B] ... [Condition C]	**Branching.** The diamond is a *decision point*. Depending on the outcome of a logical test, the action branches to two or three activities or new decision points. The branches are labeled (between square brackets) with the condition that causes them. A branch usually—but not always—matches an alternate activity. (Sometimes one branch belongs to the activity in the normal flow.)
❺		**Looping.** Iteration or looping is presented by a transition arrow that doubles back from a decision point (a diamond) to an earlier activity.
❻	◉	**End.** Normally, this icon would end in the post-condition of the use case. But an activity diagram can have more than one end, as does the use case: Exceptions can cancel the entire process and result in *abnormal* endings. Abnormal endings should be displayed by a separate end icon.

- *Requirements Gathering.* A business is made of processes. But to what purpose? By structuring processes into purposeful units, use cases provide the base tools for gathering requirements *within a meaningful context.*
- *Requirements Traceability.* Why does a system do what it does? Why does a system do what it does in a certain way? Well-constructed and well-maintained use cases and their supporting documents are the prime sources for tracing requirements.
- *Business Rules.* Use cases are the framework for gathering business rules, whether directly or indirectly: directly when the rules are specified in a use case; indirectly when the correct functioning of the use case requires clarification of rules.
- *System Behavior.* The external behavior of any *open* system can be captured effectively through use case modeling by analyzing the behavior into intelligible logical units. Conversely, if we compose a system by implementing all use cases that define it, the system would have the overall expected behavior.
- *Object Derivation.* By launching a cycle of gathering requirements from the use cases, we can arrive at many of the objects that would form the structure of the system.

Figure 7.8
**Uses of Use
Case Modeling:
A Framework
for Development**

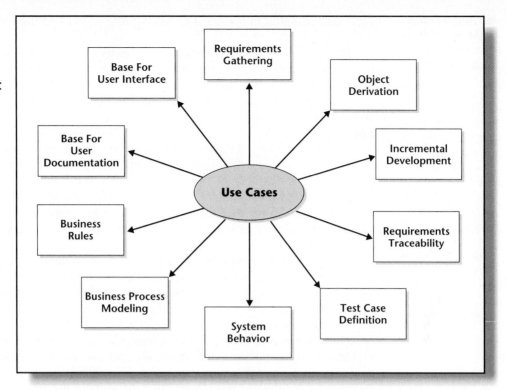

- *Incremental Development.* By prioritizing use cases and their dependencies, we can build a system incrementally. The incremental development allows us to allocate resources effectively and to facilitate later development by testing common components.
- *Base for User Interface.* Use cases describe the basic messages that the actor and the system must exchange to achieve a goal. User interface is a mapping of these messages and their flow to technology-specific visual components.
- *Test Case Definition.* Use cases are the conceptual blueprints for functional test cases.
- *Base for User Documentation.* From ground up, use cases are built to describe the interaction between a user type and a system. User documentation must combine this abstract interaction with implementation-specific components and navigation.
- *Business Process Modeling.* Since use cases are abstractions of behavior, they can be used to model business processes prior to, after, or independent from an information system.

10. USE CASE SUPPLEMENTS

Details that distract from the narrative of the use case must be placed in supplementary documents.

Nothing stops us from writing use cases as long as *War and Peace*. But even authors who would not agree with our minimalist approach do not go that far. Right or wrong, if challenged, we would all argue that our use cases are just the

☞ There is a risk in keeping use cases short and simple. If one is inexperienced, or if one does not pay attention to the complexity of tasks that the use cases express in simple terms, one might decide that it is *so* easy: "There are only 10 use cases. What do you mean that it is going to take so long?" (Sometimes producing a high volume of paper to counter such arguments does not look so bad. Not that we are suggesting it.)

right size: less, and they would be incomplete; more, and they would distract from the essentials.

By observing a voluntary limit—as subjective as it may be—we all agree that we have excluded some details from the use case, details that we may need but should not expect to find in the use case.

It is a good limitation to keep. But how can we capture those details? One answer is to place the details in supplementary documents. In the **Make Appointment** use case, we stated that the appointment clerk must record the patient's personal data and contact information before an appointment can be made. However, we intentionally did not specify exactly what must be recorded. Table 7.5 is an example of how we can capture detailed requirements through supplements to the use case. (It also illustrates an alternate way to document some business rules, though not all.) With this approach, we keep the flow of the use case clear but maintain a tight association between the use case and needed data.

Supplements are not limited to steps. We can accommodate detailed nonfunctional requirements as well. But opening the floodgates of "supplementals" carries a risk: We might be tempted into *functional decomposition* of the system. That is, we might try to explain the behavior of the system by progressively breaking it down into functions and sub-functions.

There is nothing wrong with decomposing a long function into sub-functions that are easier to write, easier to maintain, and easier to understand. However, if we do it at the system or the component level, we will be throwing away a major advantage of object-oriented development: *information hiding*. (See the next chapter, Structural Modeling.)

Table 7.5
A Supplemental Document for Walden's **Make Appointment** Use Case.

Supplement to Make Appointment	
Use Case Supplement:	120: Make Appointment
Step:	1. Record patient's personal and contact information.
Detailed Description:	The system must ensure that all required personal and contact information is recorded before an appointment is made: • First name • Last name • Middle initial (optional) • Sex • Date of birth • Phone number 1 • Phone number 2 (optional) • Street address • City • State • Zip code • Social Security Number (optional) • Full name of the next of kin if the patient is not of legal age or is incapacitated.

• *Use Cases.*   A set of developed, structured use cases for the system or the subsystems that you are developing. It is likely that you will have to revise the use cases later on, but this set must be good enough to sustain the next step of development: dynamic and structural modeling of the conceptual system.

• *Use Case Diagram(s).*   At least one diagram for the subsystem is necessary to summarize the use cases and the relationships with the actors and each other. If a use case has too many "extend" and/or "include" relationships, you may create diagrams for the subset. But never—never—feel that it is a good idea to create one diagram per use case. A use case diagram does not show what goes on *inside* the use case.

☞ Discovering correct information about the requirements is always difficult. So never discard details that a domain expert or a business stakeholder may give up voluntarily. Just do not clutter the use case.

• *Activity Diagram(s).*   If the alternate flow of a use case is difficult to understand by reading the textual narrative, then create an activity diagram and attach it to the use case. Activity diagrams, however, are not a *required* deliverable.

• *Use Case Supplements.*   If you have details that you judge to be necessary for development but that do not belong to the use case proper, then place them in supplementary documents. In design, where we elaborate the behavior of the system, we will need such supplements. In conceptual modeling, the need for them depends on the context.

12. Wrap Up

To be effective as a behavioral model of the system, use cases must be formalized and expanded. An unstructured textual narrative is prone to misunderstanding and cannot guarantee that the use case has all the required elements. For use cases to work as guidelines to development, they must be structured.

☑ **Structuring & developing use cases through templates**

A formal template ensures that ❶ a use case has the necessary building blocks and ❷ it can communicate its scenario and attributes clearly. The use case template is composed of a set of fields, one for each building block: name of the use case (its goals), a summary, primary actor, supporting actors, stakeholders, state of the system before the use case can start and after it completes, flow of events in discrete steps, etc.

Some fields are common to all use cases, some are optional, while others are customized for the needs of a specific system or a set of use cases within a specific system.

☑ **Generalizing actors**

An actor is an abstraction of real users. **Customer** generalizes selected attributes of real people who purchase goods and/or services from a business. But even these abstract entities may need to be generalized further if they share the same *role* with other actors in a use case: In conducting the affairs

of an airplane, **Chief Pilot** (the captain) and **Assistant Pilot** have distinct roles, but when one of them has the controls and actually flies the plane, it is *one* primary actor, **Pilot**, who follows the script of a **Fly Boeing 747** use case.

Sometimes, however, we end up with generalized actors through a reverse process: *specialization*. Through expanding use cases and gathering requirements, we may find that an existing role is appropriate for certain use cases, but not others: during the pre-flight check of the airplane, **Pilot** is not enough; **Chief Pilot** is needed to read off the checklist and **Assistant Pilot** is needed to check off the items.

☑ **Extending use cases**

When developing use cases, we may discover that some functionality has been left out: We expected the customer to pay by cash, but we find out that the business accepts credit cards as well. Instead of rewriting the use case, we can create an "extending" use case and add a conditional step to the "base" use case that branches to the new one if the customer decides to pay by credit card.

This type of **dependency** is called an **extend relationship** and adds flexibility to maintaining use cases. The catch is that the normal outcome of the base use case must not depend on the success or failure of the "extending" use case.

☑ **Reusing use cases**

To reach its goal, a use case may need to call on the services of another *independent* use case, either because the latter already exists, or because it qualifies as a full-fledged use case by itself and cannot be merged with the first one. This type of dependency is called an **include relationship**, and allows a use case to remain concise and focused without relinquishing any of its function.

The "include" dependency does not have the limitation of the "extend" relationship: It may be used conditionally or unconditionally, but it adds to the burden of maintenance because changing one use case may affect many others.

☑ **Use case generalization**

If two or more use cases achieve the same goal through different means but share most activities, we may consider abstracting their common features into a generalized *super-use case* (also called the *parent*). The *children* use cases are then recomposed to show where they *inherit* features from the parent, where they *override* (or *specialize*) them, or where they add new features.

Since use case generalization is maintenance-intensive, we may instead consider other techniques such as **include**, **extend**, and **refactoring**.

☑ **Use case diagram**

The use case diagram is a visual meta-model: It does not model the use case itself, but the associations between actors, use cases, and the system. It also depicts "extend" and "include" relationships between use cases and provides us with a visual table of contents.

☑ **Dividing & joining use cases**

A use case is defined by *one* primary actor, *one* useful goal, and *one* system. In other words, if a use case has more than one strong candidate for primary actor, aims at more than one (complete) useful goal, or models the behavior of more than one system or subsystem, it must be broken into more than one use case.

There are, however, other reasons for dividing use cases or joining them wholly or partially: A use case may become too complex to understand and manage, or the discovery of common functionality among multiple use cases may require that "reusable" use cases be created. The mechanisms of "**extend**" and "**include**" are then used to relate separated or recombined use cases back together.

A use case may be divided *vertically* by consolidating parallel steps within a use case into another use case, or *horizontally* by taking out a set of steps. Refactoring is a special case of horizontal division in which a set of steps common to multiple use cases are extracted and joined.

☑ **Activity diagram**

The activity diagram is a general-purpose diagram for visualizing and verifying a logical flow. For a use case with a complicated alternate flow, the activity diagram is a very helpful tool. Its simplicity facilitates communications, especially between development stakeholders.

☑ **Use case modeling as a framework for development & deployment**

The main mission of use case modeling is to model the system's behavior from a *conceptual* viewpoint. Its impact, however, goes far beyond that. Use cases provide a framework for discovering business objects, designing user interfaces, incremental development, user documentation and application help, test case definition, and training.

☑ **Use case supplements**

A use case should not go into a level of detail that would blunt the thrust of its narrative. However, the more we gather requirements and the closer we come to implementation, the more we need containers for organizing details. By creating supplemental documents, we can keep the relatively simple framework of use cases and, at the same time, satisfy the need for elaboration.

13. KEY CONCEPTS

For many of the concepts explored in this chapter, see the definitions in the previous chapter, Use Cases: The Basics. Some entries are repeated to take into account the context of *this* chapter.

Activity Diagram. A diagram that depicts the flow from activity to activity. It presents a visual, dynamic view of the system and its components.

Actor Generalization. Abstraction of actors with a shared role into one role. The resulting actor is called the *super-role* or *parent* actor, while the original actors are called *sub-roles* or *children*. The children *inherit* all responsibilities and privileges granted to the parent.

Alternate Flow & Exceptions. In the use case template, a field in which alternates and exceptions to the steps in the normal flow are arranged as distinct steps.

Audit Fields. In the use case template, fields that help us track the evolution of a use case: *Author, Revision, Date, Source*, etc.

Base Use Case. A fully formed, structured use case that serves as a *base* to develop other use cases and other analysis and design artifacts.

Business Actor. An entity outside the business who interacts with the business. A business actor does not appear as an actor in an information system use case, unless there is a *direct* interaction between the entity and the information system. (See also **System Actor**.)

Custom Fields. A custom field in the use case template specifies an attribute or requirement that is specific to one use case or a set of use cases within a system.

Dependency. When a use case depends on another use case for its functionality. In an **extend relationship**, the *extending* use case is dependent on the *extended* (**base**) one. In an **include relationship**, the *including* (base) use case is dependent on the *included* use case, which is an independent use case and needs the including one to function.

Exceptions. See **Alternate Flow & Exceptions**.

Extend Relationship. An extend relationship is one in which a use case is created to extend the functionality of a base use case. (See also **Include Relationship**.)

Field. In the use case template, represents a building block of the use case within the **template**. The fields are arranged in a predefined, orderly manner to allow easy communication and verification.

Horizontal Division. A technique to divide the use case if the flow is too complex or if the building blocks of the use case lack unity.

ID. A number that *uniquely* identifies a use case across the system. The number must not have a built-in meaning. Unlike the name of the use case, it cannot be changed.

Include Relationship. An include relationship is one in which one use case uses the functionality of another, independent, use case. (See also **Extend Relationship**.)

Initiator. An actor who starts the use case. Initiator is not necessarily the primary actor.

Name. A name that expresses the goal of the use case in an active voice. It must be unique within the system or subsystem but, unlike the ID, it can change.

Nonbehavioral Requirements. In the use case template, a field when nonbehavioral requirements for a specific use case are listed.

Normal Flow. In a use case template, a field in which the "best case" scenario is presented as ordered, discrete steps.

Open Issues. In a use case template, issues related to a use case that must be resolved before a use case can be considered complete. The field is removed after the issues are resolved.

Post-condition. Describes the **state** of the business or the information system *after* the use case has been completed.

Precondition. Defines the *required* **state** of the business or the information system *before* a use case is allowed to start.

Priority. A custom scheme that identifies the order in which use cases are elaborated, designed, and implemented. Must be consistent across the entire set of use cases.

Proxy. An actor who interacts with the information system on behalf of another entity.

Refactoring. Abstracts and reorganizes common behavior among use cases into new use cases.

Scope. The boundaries of the system or subsystem that the use case models.

State. One of the possible conditions of an object or a system as a result of one or more changes to its quantitative attributes.

Sub-Flows. In a use case template, a field in which details to normal steps are presented as discrete steps.

System Actor. An entity that interacts with the information system. (See also **Business Actor**.)

Template. A format to structure use cases by providing well-defined and ordered fields. Some fields in the template are required, while others are optional. We can add custom fields to the template if the development of a specific system demands it.

Trigger. An event that starts the use case. A use case may have more than one trigger.

Use Case Diagram. A meta-model that portrays associations among actors, use cases, and the system.

Use Case Generalization. Abstraction of a set of use cases when they achieve the same goal by different means. The generalized use case is called the *parent*; the original ones are the *children* who inherit the attributes of the parent.

Use Case Supplements. Documents, based on the framework of use cases, that organize details necessary for development but confusing within the flow of the use case.

Vertical Division. A method to divide a use case if it has too many parallel steps.

14. Review Questions

1. How do we discover business activities?
2. How is the name of a use case determined?
3. Why does a use case need a unique, numeric identifier?
4. Why should we assign priority to use cases?
5. Is the initiator of a use case the same as the primary actor? Explain.
6. What should we do if there is more than one primary actor for the use case?
7. Explain precondition and post-condition by examples.
8. Explain the difference between trigger and precondition.
9. Comment on the statement "normal flow is the best-case scenario."
10. When do we use sub-flows?
11. What we do if there are too many steps in a normal flow?
12. Provide an example for actor generalization. What is the significance of generalizing or specializing actors?
13. Provide an example for use case generalization. What is its significance?
14. What are the differences between "extend" and "include" use cases?
15. Could an "extend" use case have a primary actor? Explain.
16. Could an "extend" use case have a secondary actor? Explain.
17. Could an "include" use case have a primary actor? Explain.
18. Could an "include" use case have a secondary actor? Explain.
19. Could an "include" use case have an extend use case? Explain by providing an example.
20. Could an "extend" use case have an "include" use case? Explain.
21. Could an "include" use case have an "include" use case? Provide an example.

15. Exercises

The following exercises apply to each of the four narratives introduced in Chapter 4: *The* Sportz *Magazine*, *The Car Dealership*, *The Pizza Shop*, and *The Real Estate Agency*.

❶ After reading this chapter carefully, read the narrative again and see if you can discover additional use cases that you missed in Chapter 6.
❷ Create a use case template similar to Table 7.1.
❸ Generalize your actors if necessary.
❹ Identify "include" and "extend" use cases.

❺ Generalize your use cases if necessary.
❻ Create a use case diagram complete with "include" and "extend" use cases.
❼ Look at your diagram carefully. Is there a need to separate or join some of the use cases?
❽ Create activity diagrams for each subsystem.
❾ Write a list of information that you wish you had, but that is missing in the given scenario.

16. Research Projects & Teamwork

❶ Refer to the online registration system for Walden Medical School in Chapter 4 and the major use cases that you identified in Chapter 6. Select one of the use cases and, using Table 7.1 as the template, list the properties and their values for your selected use case; for example, name, ID, scope, etc. Make sure to involve all team members. Have a discussion to find meaningful steps for the normal flow, the sub-flows, and the alternate flows.

❷ Have a discussion session with your team members on the topic of actor generalization. Why is actor generalization necessary? How can you do it? Refer to the same online registration system and explore the possibility of actor generalization.

Have a discussion on use case generalization as you did for actor generalization and find potentials for generalizing use cases. Prepare a report on why (or why not) actor and use case generalization are good practices. Provide examples in the context of the online registration system and submit the report to the instructor.

❸ Refer to the automated research system (the "reference engine") in Chapter 4 and major use cases that you identified in Chapter 6. Draw a use case diagram for the system and look for possible "extend" and "include" diagrams.

Divide the team members into two groups. One group should draw the use case diagram without considering what you have learned in the previous chapters and the other group should draw a use case diagram for the same use cases by following step-by-step processes from Chapters 5 and 6. The first group analyzes the results and writes a report on the differences. The second group comments on the first group's report and writes its own comments. The final report summarizes these findings and is submitted to the instructor, who may ask to see all preceding work of both groups.

❹ Refer to the online shopping system in Chapter 4 and the major use cases that you identified in Chapter 6. Get all group members involved in answering the following exercises.

- Identify all actors for each use case, both primary and secondary. Generalize actors if necessary.
- Find all "extend" and "include" use cases.
- Generalize use cases if necessary
- Draw a use case diagram.

❺ Refer to your domain analysis for patient scheduling in Chapter 5 and get all group members involved to create a use case diagram. Make sure that you follow all the steps: considering generalization for both actors and use cases, identifying extend and include use cases for major use cases, and creating a complete use case template to start your efforts.

17. SUGGESTED READINGS

Since **Ivar Jacobson** introduced use case modeling, the concept has been expanded and refined. Nevertheless, one of the best introductions to use cases can be found in the related chapters of Jacobson's pre-UML book, *The Object Advantage: Business Process Reengineering With Object Technology*, coauthored with Maria Ericsson and Agneta Jacobson (Addison-Wesley, 1995). The style is straightforward and the examples are clear. The book also provides good introductions to BPR (business process reengineering), modeling, and object-oriented concepts.

One of the most comprehensive and practical books on use cases is *Advanced Use Case Modeling: Software Systems* by **Frank Armour** and Granville Miller (Addison-Wesley, 2001). It does not shy away from the complexities of software development in the real world; nor does it shortchange you on examples.

The emphasis of *Use Case: Requirements In Context* by **Daryl Kulak** and Eamonn Guiney (Addison-Wesley, 2000) is on requirements, as the title declares. With many example, the authors take you through many iterations that both gathering requirements and behavioral modeling demand.

Applying Use Cases, Second Edition: A Practical Guide by **Geri Schneider** and Jason P. Winters (Addison-Wesley, 2001) covers the same basic grounds as the previous book, but explores certain topics from a different perspective. For example, the chapter on "Estimating Work with Use Cases" contributes to project management by providing guidelines on how to translate use cases to a work plan. Another chapter, "Dividing Large Systems," discusses the relationship between use case modeling and the architecture of the system.

Chapter

8

Structural Modeling

1. OVERVIEW

Behavioral modeling is the starting point for modeling software, but any system must rely on a structure that supports that behavior. This chapter explores how to arrive at classes, the basic building blocks of an object-oriented information system, and their relationships. It also introduces the class diagram, the most widely used tool in modeling for object-oriented development.

- ▣ Inception
- ▣ Requirements Discovery
- ☐ Development
    - ☐ Analysis
        - ☑ Domain Analysis
        - ☑ Behavioral Modeling
        - ☐ **Structural Modeling** ⬅
        - ☐ Dynamic Modeling
    - ☐ Implementation

Chapter Topics

➤ Structural modeling within the context of a conceptual information system.

➤ Classes as building blocks of structural modeling and objects as units of information systems.

➤ Basic object-oriented concepts in the context of structural modeling.

➤ Discovering class candidates by parsing use cases.

➤ Elaborating and defining classes by specifying and expanding their responsibilities.

➤ Class relationships.

➤ Class diagrams.

Introduction

An information system is built from the *outside in*. It is not a system that exists in nature, but rather a product and, as a product, it does not exist until we build it. To build it, we must first know what is required of it. Then we must understand how those requirements are used in context. In other words, we must discover the workflow of the product. Therefore, the first conceptual model of an information system must be the *behavioral* model: use cases that describe how the system would satisfy functional requirements. We discussed the behavioral model in the last two chapters.

But no system, even one as dynamic as an information system, is pure function: It must have a structure that supports the system's behavior. Moreover, the structure of an information system cannot be monolithic, for monolithic structures are difficult to build, expensive to maintain, hard to understand, inflexible, and, consequently, susceptible to breakdowns.

A flexible and reliable structure, therefore, needs **building blocks** that satisfy the specific requirements of the structure, both in themselves and in their relationships with each other. One building block is one link in the structural chain: It must be reliable as a unit, and it must fit properly with other units to provide both strength and flexibility.

Objects are the elementary particles of an information system. At its most basic level, the structure of an information system is composed of objects. It is the objects and their relationships that give a structure its unique identity. Classes are both abstractions of objects and the blueprints from which they are built. Hence, the structural model is primarily the model of classes and how they relate to each other.

The first structural model of an information system must be *conceptual*: business concepts that are defined as classes and their connections. To this end, we first discuss those characteristics of classes and objects that define them as *units of structure*. Then we illustrate how to *discover* business classes by parsing the behavioral model—use cases, in other words—and how to *elaborate* class candidates into mature classes by specifying their **responsibilities**.

Finally, we introduce the **class diagram** to discuss the various relationships among classes. As we argued, interrelationships among building blocks of a structure are as important and as crucial as the building blocks themselves. The class diagram, though simple in its essentials, is the one tool that clearly and effectively models those relationships.

2. INTRODUCING STRUCTURAL MODELING

> Structural modeling represents a view of the building blocks of a system or an entity and their interrelationships within a given scope.

Structural modeling of an information system shares common traits with the structural modeling of any other entity—be it a building, a car, an aircraft, or a living organism.

❶ *View may be conceptual, logical, or physical:*
  - In planning for a building, we first express the *concepts*: an Art Deco, three-story building with 10 bedrooms, 5 bathrooms, etc.

Figure 8.1 Building the Conceptual Structure: From Use Cases to Structural Modeling

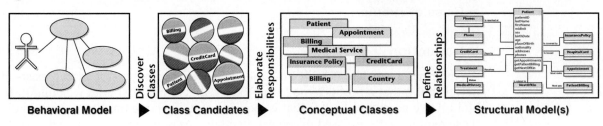

Behavioral Model ▶ **Discover Classes** ▶ **Class Candidates** ▶ **Elaborate Responsibilities** ▶ **Conceptual Classes** ▶ **Define Relationships** ▶ **Structural Model(s)**

☞ For a definition of ***domain***, see Chapter 5, Domain Analysis.

☞ When the building block is "coarse," we discuss the structure in terms of "***architecture***." See Chapter 16 on architecture in this book.

- Then we design the *logical* relationships: The library would be on the first floor, next to the drawing room which is accessible from the entry hall.
- Finally, we arrive at the *physical* specifications: the exact size, type, and features of the foundation; the location, the shape, and the diameter of water pipes; the wiring plan for electricity.

❷ *Scope can be any relevant or selected range:*

- For an animal, the model may represent the respiratory system, the skeleton, the digestive system, the vascular system, or a combination.
- For an information system, the scope of the model may be limited to one domain, may cover the entire enterprise, or may represent activities that are shared across several domains.

❸ *A building block may be fine or coarse:*

- A protein, molecule, gene, cell, tissue, and organ: these are all building blocks—or *units*—of an organism. Choosing one of them as the building block for a specific model depends on our *purpose*: anatomy studies organs, histology studies tissues, cytology studies cells, and so on. (See Figure 8.2.)
- In modeling an information system, the "building block" can be a class, a component, an architectural layer, or a subsystem.

A structural model can have any combination of **scope** (selected range), *texture* (fine-grained to coarse-grained), and **view** (conceptual to physical). Since different combinations of these three factors can result in a wide variety of models, a specific combination needs more than the term "structural modeling" to explain it. Therefore, **it is necessary to define expectations** when we set out to define structural modeling.

Structural modeling can have one of three aims:

❶ Understanding an existing structure.
❷ Changing an existing structure.
❸ Building an entirely new structure.

In the context of an information system, our aims are usually the last two. In understanding an *existing* structure, we do not have to solve all the mysteries and know everything, whereas in changing or building a structure, nothing can be left to imagination. Every building block and every relationship between the building blocks must be clearly specified and thoroughly understood.

> The structure of an information system must be able to accommodate both the behavior of the system and the dynamic interchange of the components required to support that behavior.

Figure 8.2 Defining the Building Block: Selecting the Right Viewpoint in Modeling the Structure

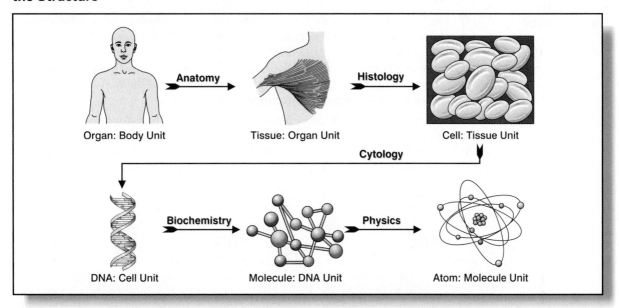

The definition of the "building block" for modeling depends on the nature of the structure, the viewpoint, and the purpose of analyzing the structure. In system development, choosing the right building block and the right viewpoint at the right time is critical.

3. CLASSES & STRUCTURAL MODELING

We outlined the basic concepts of the object-oriented approach to software development in the previous section of the book. Here we revisit classes by placing the concept of "class" within the context of structural modeling: how to define, shape, categorize, and relate classes into a structure that will support the behavior that was modeled by the use cases.

Classes as Object Templates

In the virtual world of software, a class is both an abstraction of an object and a template to create it.

In the real world, we classify *existing* objects by generalizing *selected* common traits into a "class": dog, cat, mammal, student, teacher, programmer, person, flower, tree, plant, and so on. Or we *create objects* that do not occur naturally but are nevertheless classified even *before* they are created: chairs, roads, cars, hats, computers, etc. (We even classify objects that are pure fantasies: dragons, unicorns, goblins, and the rest.)

In both cases, the process of *classification*—that is, definition of classes—starts with a *concept*: a general idea that is shaped into a distinct class through a mental and semantic process of **generalization**. (The exact nature of this process must be explained by cognitive sciences.) In other words, the concept always *precedes* classification, regardless of whether existing objects give rise *to* a class or the objects are created *from* a class.

☞ A **class** is:
  ❶ An abstraction of objects.
  ❷ A template for creating objects.
  ❸ A building block of modeling.

The relevance of the preceding analysis to the structural modeling of information systems is twofold:

❶ *The virtual world of an information system is composed of created objects.* For a software application to function, its components must be recreated *every time* we activate the application. The real world is made up of objects, not classes: The objects either exist naturally or continue to exist once they are created, regardless of whether we have classified them correctly or whether we have classified them at all. In a virtual world, by contrast, no class means no objects. (See Figure 8.3.)

❷ *Classes for creating a conceptual model originate from domain concepts.* It was no coincidence that we declared the definition of domain concepts as the primary task of domain analysis. We first developed these concepts into behavioral models and now we will transform them into structural models.

Class or Object?

It is not always easy to keep **class** and **object** separate. This confusion is not usually harmful. When we discuss a class, what we say often applies to objects that belong to that class as well, and *vice versa*. When we examine a floor plan, we might say "this balcony" instead of "this drawing of the balcony." Therefore, it is not necessary to become obsessive about separating the two. (In this book, we have often used the terms "class" and "object" interchangeably—instead of overusing "class and/or object" in phrases or sentences too close together.)

The confusion becomes harmful only if we do not distinguish between the two concepts when their differences are significant: Unlike objects, classes are never the actual components of a system, they do not hold values, they never act or interact, and they never change through interaction.

Classes as Building Blocks

Classes are the building blocks of structural modeling and the blueprints for objects; objects are the structural units of the actual information system.

Figure 8.3
Class as Cookie Cutter: Virtual Objects Come from Classes, Not Vice Versa

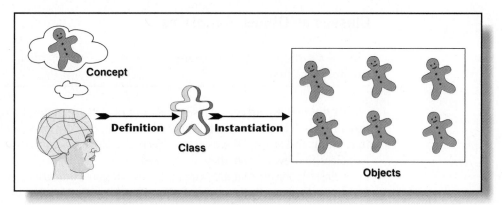

Classes are always shaped from the concepts of real or imaginary objects. However, whereas in the real world objects can exist without classification, in a virtual world objects are always created by the instantiation of classes. (The instantiated objects may look alike, but each would have its unique identity.)

☞ The structure of an information system and its models also consists of units *larger* than objects and classes: components, layers, and subsystems. (We are already familiar with subsystems, but the *macro-structure* of information systems will be explored more extensively in the chapters on *components* and *architecture*.)

A structure is made of units—or building blocks—that are arranged in a certain way and have certain relationships. Classes and objects are the *smallest* units of, respectively, the model of an information system and the actual system itself.

The *conceptual* modeling of the system *structure* is not concerned with the concrete layering or packaging of objects or components. Its primary concern is to discover, define, relate, and represent building blocks of the information system that are *independent* from design and the technology used to implement the design.

Objects as Black Boxes

> The internal structure of an object is known only to the object itself.

A black box is opaque: Its outside is visible but not what is inside it. An information system object is a *dynamic* black box; it interacts with outside entities to provide services but conceals its inner workings.

The same "black box" analogy holds true for classes as well. A main task of modeling is to make complexity more understandable. A model has to concentrate on what is essential for its mission and disregard the inessentials. It has to conceal those details that are irrelevant to its purpose within relatively simple symbols. (These symbols, if necessary, can be expanded and explored through other models.)

The objected-oriented approach to software development has a special affinity to modeling because, by definition, it is based on "enclosed" units. UML depicts classes and objects as boxes. (See Figure 8.4.) The box metaphor emphasizes two related concepts that are essential to object orientation: encapsulation and information hiding.

Encapsulation

> Encapsulation is enclosing data and processes within one single unit.

☞ All living creatures, from simple single-cell organisms to complex vertebrates, are the best examples of encapsulation. Units are what encapsulation produces. Numerous components and subsystems constitute a human being, and they can be studied or modeled rather independently of each other, but they cannot function—let alone make sense—unless they work as a unit.

The literal meaning of encapsulation is "enclosing something completely, as though in a capsule." In object-oriented terminology, encapsulation means that the data and processes that make up an object are placed *inside* a protective wall that separates them from *outside*. This separation ensures that the contents of the object function as *one unit*, under the control of the object and safe from unauthorized access: No entity outside the object can change anything within its protective walls without the object's permission and scrutiny.

Encapsulation results in two spaces:

- *Private.* Data and processes that are inside the object are labeled as "private."

- *Public.* Whatever the object *exposes*—that is, makes visible to the outside world—is "public." (See Figure 8.5.)

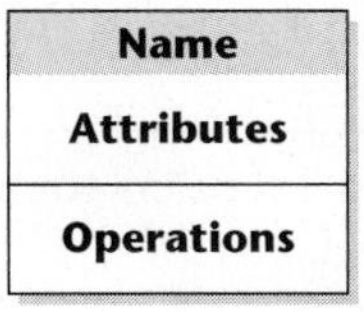

Name
Attributes
Operations

Figure 8.4
UML Shape (Symbol) for a Class

Figure 8.5   Encapsulation: Public Versus Private

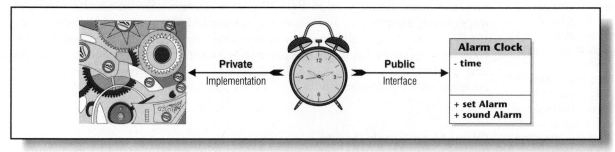

A clock's interface is simple, familiar, and elegant. How a clock performs its functions, however, may be anything but simple: There are a variety of mechanical clocks, electrical clocks, and even atomic clocks. But the "how" is private to the object; it is hidden (encapsulated) and does not become a distraction or a nuisance. (See the "Structuring the Interface" section for an explanation of the items in the right-hand box.)

Encapsulation also enables the object to enforce *business rules* with authority. If a **Customer** object does not allow the customer to purchase new merchandise unless the old purchases are paid for, no negligent or malicious code from any part of the system can manipulate the data inside the object or force the object to change its decision. If a business rule is implemented within a relevant class or classes (as templates for actual objects), then the rest of the system does not have to know about the rule and is not compelled to implement it anywhere else.

Information Hiding

> Information hiding conceals the inner entities and the workings of the object from outside entities.

How an object does something may be complex or simple, but as long the object meets its obligations, we need not be burdened with the details of the processes and data that it needs to achieve its goals. Information hiding is made possible by encapsulation that conceals irrelevant details from the public eye.

Another benefit of information hiding—and one that is no less important—is that the inner workings of an object may be changed or streamlined *without* any adverse effects on its use. How does a **Loan** object calculate premiums and interest? As long as it computes them correctly—given the correct parameters—we have no reason to be concerned about "how." And if it does its job *incorrectly*, or the rules for making a loan have changed, we do not need to be concerned about anything *but* the inner workings of the **Loan** object (or other objects on which the **Loan** object may depend). It resembles changing or fixing a tire that has gone flat: We do not have to disassemble the whole car.

☞ We can also define "interface" from a slightly different but equally valid angle: "The outside view of a class, object, or module, which emphasizes its abstraction while hiding its structure and the secrets of its behavior." [Booch 1994, 515.]

Interface

> The interface of an object is both the services that it offers to the outside world and how these services are structured and arranged.

Encapsulation and information hiding ensure that no entity can use or abuse the inner processes and data of an object. What, then, remains for us to work with? The answer is the object's interface: the services that it provides to the outside world—to other objects—and the structure and the arrangement of those services.

In other words, the interface of an object is defined by two factors: *what* it offers and *how* the offerings are presented to other entities. Therefore, we can state that the object and the outside world "agree" on both the **substance** and the **form** of the service that the object provides:

☞ Notice that the "how" refers to the arrangement and structuring of the interface, *not* the inner workings of the unit.

- An ATM *agrees* to conduct a transaction (substance) provided you slide your banking card through the correct slot (form) and enter the correct password.
- A battery *agrees* to provide an electrical current of known voltage (substance); it also *agrees* that the current flows from the pole marked with a negative sign to the pole with a plus sign (form).
- A movie theater *agrees* that if we buy a ticket for a specific movie, it will show us that movie—and not another movie—in full (substance), and *agrees* that the screening will start at a specific time and place (order and arrangement).
- A clock *agrees* to mean 10:30—and not any other time—when the hour hand is on the 10 and the minute hand is on the 6, even if "6" does not mean "30." (In this case, the substance and the form—the time and the location of hands—are intertwined.)

> An object's interface is a contract between the object and the entities that use it.

An agreement between two or more parties over the services that one or more parties must provide and the rules with which they must comply is called a **contract**. According to this definition, an object's interface is undoubtedly a contract since the object promises to perform services for an outside entity that behaves according to rules that the object expects. And since a contract is a **binding** agreement:

> The interface of an object, once formalized and made available for use, cannot be changed unless *all* parties to the contract agree to the change.

What does this statement mean *in practice*? In the real world, examples are numerous: *a standard*, formal or informal, *is a contract*, *even if it is not signed by all interested parties*. When you buy a TV set, you fully expect it to conform to the standard electrical current and the standard picture transmission of the market area in which it is sold. You might, mistakenly, buy a model that does not belong to your market area, but what you do *not* expect is that the manufacturer has decided to sell a TV set that does not follow *any* of the standards around the globe—for example, it needs 500 volts of electricity and a picture transmission of 900 horizontal lines. And what applies to television sets applies to thousands of other products and services.

In the development of information systems, many standards are local; that is, the standards are set by the development team(s) and have no effects beyond the confines of one information system or one enterprise. The limitation of scope, however, does not diminish the significance of standards (or the "contracts):

- Objects in an object-oriented structure must conform not only to the "spirit" of the contract, but also to its **letter**. Even changing the name of a service would violate the contract and rupture the structure. We might guess with a high degree of certainty that **Middle Initial** and **Mid Init** provide the same service. Objects, on the other hand, cannot *guess*: They are literal.

- The fact that many, if not most, standards are set by the development team and not by the market or an official agency makes a persuasive case for defining "contracts" that are clear, logical, and designed with foresight. When others besides the creators of the class need to understand, use, or change it, they cannot resort to the knowledge in the marketplace.

Structuring the Interface

> The interface of an object—its services—must itself be structured in a predictable manner.

We stated that the services of an object are provided through its interface. But how do we model, "read," or decipher this interface? The technological implementations of interfaces are different, but UML provides a simple notation to represent the structure of the class or, to be more exact, the structure of its interface: the **black box** that we discussed in the previous topic. It has three compartments that specify the class's interface: name, attributes, and operations.

To explore this structure, we turn to the simple but classic example of an alarm clock. (See Figure 8.5.) A clock's interface, even if stylized, is not confusing once we learn how to use it: ❶ We read the time, ❷ we set the time, ❸ we set the alarm, and when the time comes ❹ the clock sounds the alarm. The machinery behind the public interface—mechanical, electric, analog, or digital—is private to the clock and does not affect its use.

To turn the clock into a class that will produce *virtual* clock objects, we must abstract its *relevant* features into the three compartments of the class box:

❶ *Name.* **AlarmClock** is a perfectly good name for a class that abstracts alarm clocks. (We will discuss the name of *objects* later.) Name defines the *identity* of the class: Changing the name means that the old class *no longer exists* and a new class has been created.

There are rules and conventions that apply to naming classes:

- A class name must be a noun (**Patient**) or a noun phrase (**AlarmClock**). Unlike use cases, a class name must *not* express or imply action.
- A class name is usually singular: **Doctor**, not **Doctors**. The exception is the **collection** class (see the following "Composite & Collection Objects" section). Having a collection class (**Doctors**) implies that there is also a single version (**Doctor**).
- If the name is a phrase, then no spaces are allowed between words: **MedicalService**, not **Medical Service**.
- Definite or indefinite articles—**APatient**, **ThePatient**, **AnAlarmClock**— must be avoided. A class is an abstraction and an abstraction is *not* a specific thing.
- A class name is always capitalized. If the name is a noun phrase, then all words must be capitalized: **AlarmClock**, not **alarmClock** or **Alarmclock**.

❷ *Attributes.* A clock "knows" time, and this is the definition of attributes: what an object *knows*. A **Patient** object "knows" its name, its address, and its phone number; a **Dog** object "knows" its breed, its color, and its age; a **Car** object knows its model, its top speed, and its number of cylinders.

By "object" we do not mean "class" but an instance of the class. An abstract clock does not know time; an abstract patient has no Social Security Number; an abstract car has no top speed; you do not own **Dog** but *a* dog. In defining a class, attributes are placeholders: it is the objects that fill the placeholders—or *variables*—with values. In other words:

> Classes define the containers of data, while their contents are provided by objects.

In naming attributes we follow the same rules and conventions as in defining class names. However, there is one difference: attribute names begin with a *lowercase* letter. (The words following the first one, if there are any, are capitalized.) The lowercase start is a convention to distinguish attributes and operations from classes.

❸ *Operations.* We set the alarm on a clock and the clock sounds the alarm when the time comes. Operations define what an object *does* or what can be *done to* it: a car object is directed to move; a plane object is directed to fly; an order object is told to cancel an order.

Again, the term "object" is used intentionally: A class merely *defines* what an object is expected to do. It is the object that carries out the actual operation: A **Plane** class does not fly; a plane object does.

Rules for naming operations are the same as for naming attributes, except that instead of a noun or a noun phrase, you must use a verb or a verb phrase: **move** is correct; **moving** is not.

Operations may affect attributes: The **cancel** operation of an **Order** object that has yet to be shipped would change the object's status from "open" to "canceled."

Visibility

> The visibility of an object's attributes or operations defines their availability to other objects.

☞ Making an attribute private conforms to object-oriented guidelines: Data must be kept private *unless* there is very good reason to make it public. How, then, do we access attributes? We will discuss the answer in the next chapter.

We previously discussed the services that an object provides to the *outside* world. But UML and modeling tools allow us to define attributes and operations that are *not* public.

If we review Figure 8.5 (a clock's interface), we will notice that the single attribute is preceded by a minus sign while operations are preceded by a plus sign. These two symbols, plus two others, define what type of entity may use a service—or to be more exact, which object is allowed to *see* an attribute or an operation. (See Table 8.1.)

Table 8.1
Symbols that Define the Visibility of an Object's Services.

	Visibility of Attributes and Operations	
Symbol	**Visibility**	**Description**
+	**Public**	The attribute or operation is visible to all entities.
–	**Private**	The attribute or operation is private and cannot be (directly) accessed by outside entities.
#	**Protected**	The attribute or operation is available only to the object or its descendants. (See Chapter 15.)
~	**Package (Friend)**	Only other objects in the package (or component) can use the attribute.

Composite & Collection Objects

☞ Large-grain structural units, such as system components and subsystems, are by definition composite.

In object-oriented terminology, composite objects are the result of **composition**. (See "Aggregation & Composition" later in this chapter.)

[Taylor 1998, 28–31]

> A composite object is one that is composed of other objects. A collection object is a composite object that manages a set of objects instantiated from the *same* class.

Many objects, either in whole or in part, are made up of other objects:

- A company is made up of departments.
- An airplane is made up of wings, engines, landing gear, cockpit, etc. (See Figure 8.6.)
- A classroom is made up of a teacher and many students.

Moreover, an entity that is part of a composite object may itself be a composite object: A jet engine is an assembly of precisely aligned units that must cooperate fully. The same is true of the tail assembly, wings, etc. In other words, composite objects can be *nested* in a *hierarchy*.

The ability to combine objects into a composite object provides a capable, varied, and sophisticated structure—both in the real world and in a virtual one. None of the parts that make up an airplane can fly by themselves. In an

Figure 8.6 Composite and Collection Objects: When an Object Is Made Up of Other Objects

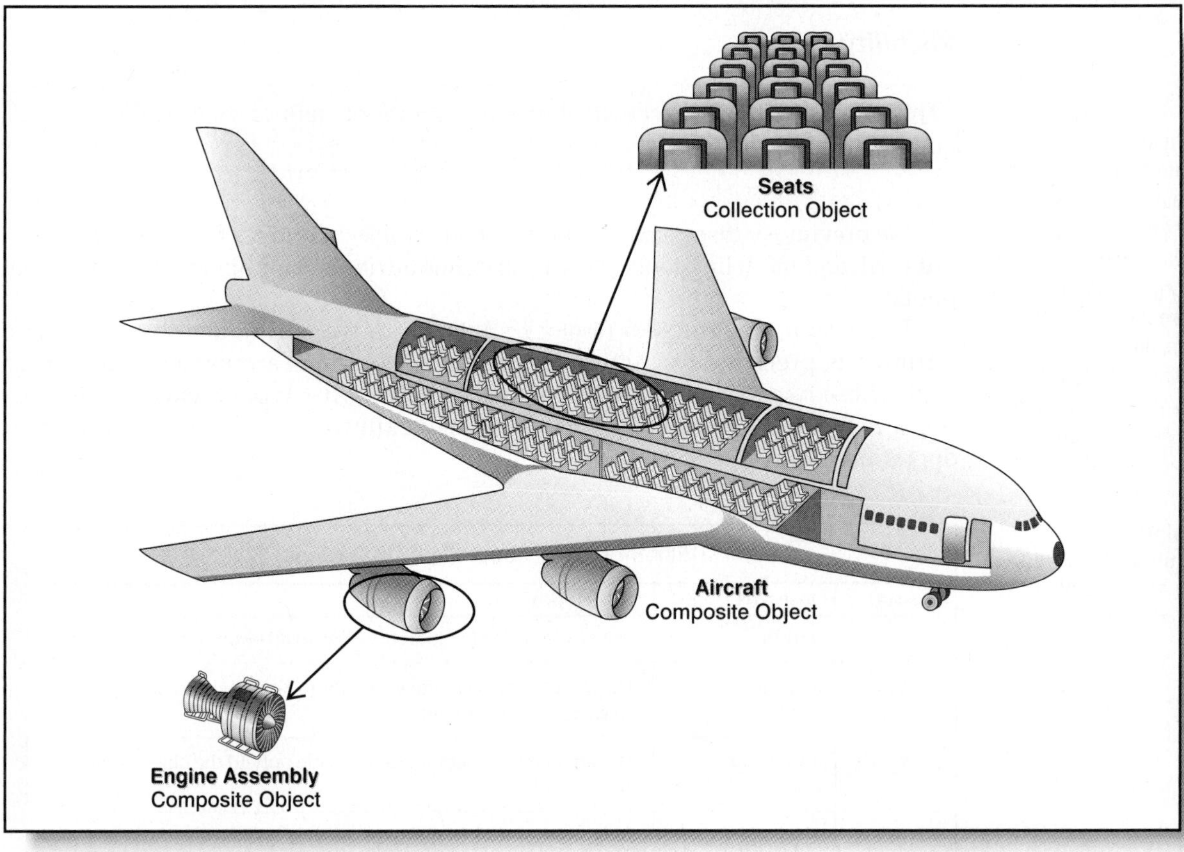

A jetliner is a good example for the nesting of composite objects and the need for recognizing collection objects.

☞ A collection class is exempt from the rule that class names must be singular, though it is not always necessary to have the plural form: We assume that a **Medical History** object is composed of one or more instances of **Medical Record**.

information system, objects with relatively simple interfaces can be combined to satisfy a very complex behavior.

A collection object is a special case of a composite object. Whereas, in a general sense, the building blocks of a composite object can be instances of many different classes, the constituent units of a collection object are all instances of the same class.

In assigning seats for a flight, show, or sporting event, it is not practical to treat every **Seat** object separately. (See Figure 8.6.) A **Seats** object, on the other hand, not only makes the task of navigation between the objects easier, but can also provide us with a snapshot of the whole rather than just parts.

4. FINDING CLASSES

To find use cases, we analyze the results of *domain analysis*. To find classes, we analyze *use cases*, gather more requirements and domain knowledge, and reinforce our findings by cross-checking the domain catalog.

From Use Cases to Classes

> To discover business objects, we must start by mining the flow of use cases.

State:
☞ If an action changes the value of at least one attribute, the "state" of the object is changed.

A more formal definition is: "A condition or situation during the life of an object during which it satisfies some condition, performs some activity, or waits for some event." [Booch 1999, 466.]

We will discuss "state" more extensively Chapter 9 under "Statechart Diagram."

☞ The classes that we discover through use cases are *business* classes. These classes are derived from the *concepts* with which

Let us restate what use cases do: A use case describes, in an ordered and logical manner, how an outside entity interacts with a system to achieve a goal. In the course of an interaction, the actor—the outside entity—sends *messages* to the system and, in return, receives messages. The messages are sometimes simple and sometimes not simple. Some messages carry values, called parameters, that tell the system or the actor how to interpret the message.

A use case proceeds towards a goal: It has a starting point and an ending point. Between these two points, the system keeps track of the interaction by examining the *state* of the objects affected by messages upon which it has acted. In other words, the system's "memory" is the sum total of the states of its constituent objects.

Use cases focus on the behavior of the system, not its structure. But what sustains the behavior of the system is a set of structural building blocks, each with its own characteristics and its own "memory."

> The messages exchanged between the actors and the system refer to objects that are affected by the interaction between the two.

Otherwise, the system would not know what to do and would not remember what it has done. Therefore, by *parsing* the messages that the steps in a use case scenario specify, we can start the discovery of classes.

Responsibilities

> An object's responsibilities consist of what it *does* and what it *knows*—in other words, its operations and its attributes.

the business is
concerned and form
the building blocks of
a conceptual model.
(Hence the
designation of
"conceptual.") To
design an information
system, however, we
need other class
types, which we will
discuss in the design
section of the book.

The services that a class defines and an object provides to the outside world are termed the "responsibilities" of the class or the object. Because the modeling of an object-oriented system represents its components by the services that they provide, defining the responsibilities of a class is defining the class itself.

We argued previously that if a system satisfies the behavior that use cases describe, then the system also satisfies the requirements. By definition, use cases are goal-oriented, and the sum of their goals defines the boundaries and the responsibilities of the *system* or the subsystem *as a whole*. Therefore, use case narratives are the most reliable sources for outlining the responsibilities of the components in **broad terms**.

A *preliminary* account of object responsibilities must be sketched "in broad terms" both by choice and by necessity. When the process of discovery starts, an overflow of details would be counterproductive by distracting from what is crucial. For example, in outlining the class **Patient**, we must focus on the premise that it is responsible for "knowing" all the information about the patient—personal, demographic, financial, and medical—that the hospital information system requires. If the premise is correct, then we can search for and identify the individual elements of the required information: name, date of birth, sex, health plan, etc. But if our assumption is wrong and we have invested too much in small-scale knowledge, then our investments would be wasted.

By necessity, use cases are summaries at some level. In a use case, we purposefully avoid overwhelming the scenario with too many details. In other words, use cases are necessary for starting the process of discovery, but they are not enough.

Finding Candidates & General Responsibilities

> Before we can define classes in detail, we must discover class candidates and outline their tentative responsibilities.

In scanning use cases, the first thing that we are meant to see is the behavior of the system. Beyond that, we do notice structural elements, but always in motion. As a

**Figure 8.7
Finding Class
Candidates:
Parsing
the Behavior
for Structure**

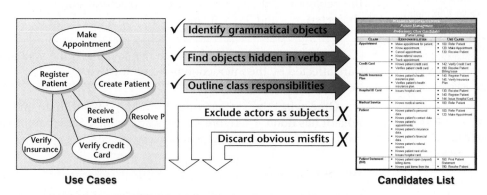

By parsing use cases, we discover candidates for analysis classes. We must then gather more knowledge to define and elaborate them.

result, the borders between the objects may appear blurred: Different attributes of one object may make it seem like multiple objects, while similar attributes of several objects may blend them together. Some objects may hide behind others. Consequently, the results of use case parsing must be considered as *preliminary* candidates, not as final class definitions.

The road to finding classes is not a clear-cut route with unambiguous signposts. Some points along the road have to be revisited after the first encounter. False steps and blind alleys await us. But is not a pointless or random journey. To arrive at the destination, there are things to do and things *not* to do; in other words, there are methods that enhance the chances of your success.

The following guidelines are not meant as ironclad rules. We always need to put on our detective hats and search for clues that we have missed at first glance.

❶ *Parse use cases for nouns as grammatical objects.* Grammatical objects—direct or indirect, simple or compound—are the best candidates for becoming classes. In the first pass through use cases, we should cast a wide net and mark anything that seems to qualify. (Actors are the exceptions, as we will explain later.)

As we go across use cases, we are bound to come across many duplicates. The more important a class is to the activities of the problem domain, the more likely that it will appear as a player in multiple use cases.

We will consolidate duplicate names later, but it might seem futile to keep tracking an object in step after step, and in use case after use case, subsequent to the first encounter. But the point of our search is not just to find class names, but also to discover how the object lives up to its **responsibilities**—what it has to *know* and what it has to *do*. By assembling pieces that we uncover about an object across steps and across use cases we can then outline a well-rounded class—not detailed yet, but full in its essentials.

Let us look at the normal flow of **Make Appointment**, the first use case for Walden's **Patient Management** (see Table 8.2). We have underlined grammatical objects, simple or compound, whenever they are encountered. (We have also underlined a noun—**Hospital**—that is not an object in the sentence, but appears promising. We will determine its value later.)

☞ It appears that we have used the terms "object" and "class" as synonyms here. Up to a point this assumption is true. But there is a subtle difference: When a "thing" participates in specific actions, we call it "object." When it is generalized, we label it as "class."

Table 8.2
Normal Flow of Walden's **Make Appointment** Use Cases. Grammatical objects have been underlined.

MAKE APPOINTMENT	
Normal Flow:	1. Appointment clerk verifies that the needed <u>medical service</u> is provided by the <u>hospital</u>.
	2. Appointment clerk records <u>patient</u>'s <u>personal and contact data</u>.
	3. Appointment clerk records <u>information</u> about the <u>referral source</u>.
	4. Appointment clerk consults <u>hospital's schedule</u> to find a <u>free slot</u> for the required <u>medical service</u>.
	5. Appointment clerk verifies that the <u>patient</u> is available for the <u>appointment</u>.
	→ Loop 1: **Repeat** steps 4–5 until <u>hospital's schedule</u> matches <u>patient</u>'s <u>availability</u>.
	6. Appointment clerk makes the <u>appointment</u>.
	→ Loop 2: **Repeat** steps 4–6 for each <u>appointment</u>.

Patient, **Medical Service**, and **Schedule** appear as solid classes, but is **Referral Source** an attribute of **Patient** or an independent entity? Is **Appointment** a class by itself, or some data that changes the state of **Schedule**? And what kind of an entity could **Free Slot** be?

We cannot answer these questions at this stage. We keep everything for now and separate the acceptable candidates from the unacceptable later. Nevertheless, be aware that not all nouns extracted in this way are eligible: Many are really attributes of a class and some do not fit in either category. Besides, differentiating a class and its attributes is not always easy. (We will discuss these complications in subsequent guidelines.) In the first attempt, however, we should stay clear of these concerns.

As you can see, we have *excluded* the appointment clerk, the sole actor in the normal flow of the use case. By arguing that only grammatical objects should be considered for becoming classes, the rationale for this exclusion should be clear. But, for some reason, the urge to include actors is considerable. So we restate the case: Actors must be excluded if they appear only as grammatical *subjects*; they are, by definition, entities *outside* the system, *not* part of the system's structure.

However, if the actor appears as a grammatical *object* within a message *to* the information system, then it becomes a class candidate (but only a candidate) because the reference hints that the system needs to record data about the actor. In other words, an entity can be an actor in one use case, but a class candidate in the same or another use case.

For example, in a **Prescribe Medication** use case, **Doctor** writes the prescription and is an actor. But the system needs to record the doctor's identification; therefore, **Doctor** *also* becomes a class. Or for the accounting department that pays the doctor's salary, **Doctor** is undoubtedly a class. (See Figure 8.8.)

Still, it is crucial to remember that actors and classes are two separate entities: Actors are outside the system and classes (or objects) are inside. An actor does not always have a class counterpart. For example, an information terminal at a railway station would provide anybody with arrival and departures times, but it is highly unlikely that it would record anything about them.

❷ *Parse use cases for hidden grammatical objects.* Use cases are written in natural language to be understandable to all development stakeholders. As a result,

Figure 8.8
Actor Versus Class: An Entity Can Be Both, But the Two Functions Are Not the Same

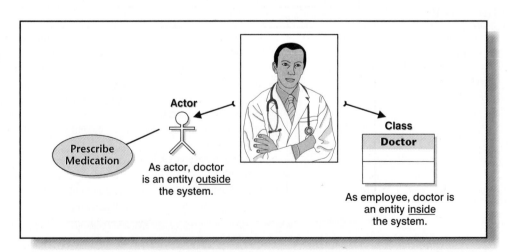

Prescribe Medication

Actor

As actor, doctor is an entity <u>outside</u> the system.

Class

Doctor

As employee, doctor is an entity <u>inside</u> the system.

the syntax is not always designed to make the task of finding classes easier. Look at the partial listing of a use case on buying books online:

Buy Books Online

Normal Flow: . . .

5. Customer adds a <u>book</u> from the search list to the <u>shopping cart</u>.

→ Loop 1: **Repeat** steps 3–5 until the customer proceeds to the checkout counter.

6. Customer orders the books in the shopping cart.

. . .

The word "book" is correctly identified as a candidate class. Another potential class, however, is hidden in the verb **orders**. We can restate step 6 as:

6. Customer places an order for the books in the shopping cart.

From a business point of view, an **order** is clearly a separate entity from a book or a set of books. In the same manner, the following partial use case hides a noun:

Prescribe Medication

Normal Flow: . . .

4. Doctor selects the <u>medication</u>.

5. Doctor prescribes the medication.

. . .

The hidden class is **Prescription** (or, actually, a prescription line item):

5. Doctor writes a <u>prescription</u> for the medication.

Verbs that hide nouns are usually verbs that have both *transitive* and *intransitive* forms. This duality allows the verb to conceal *direct* objects:

- He drives (his <u>car</u>) to work.
- I have already eaten (a <u>meal</u>).
- She hums (a <u>tune</u>) while working.
- The employees must punch out (their <u>timecards</u>) before leaving the office.

The second factor that may hide classes (or responsibilities of classes) are *assumptions* built into sentences. Natural language relies on the reader to make some assumptions in order to understand the correct meaning of a word, a phrase, or a sentence. In the normal flow of **Verify Credit Card**, the registration clerk exchanges messages with the system about **Credit Card**:

Verify Credit Card

Summary   Registration clerk verifies the patient's credit card for payments.

. . .   . . .

Normal Flow: 1. Registration clerk enters <u>credit card information</u> for verification.

2. Registration clerk transmits credit card information to the credit bureau of the bank.

3. Bank verifies the credit card.

☞ Close to "hidden objects" are sentences in passive voice: "Personal information about the patient is recorded (by the appointment clerk)." If you come across such sentences either ❶ do your best, or ❷ send it back. The flow of use cases *must* be written in an active voice: who does what, not what is done by who.

☞ How are we to decide the fate of **Free Slot** (see step 4 in Table 8.2)? There are two ways to visualize scheduling and appointments: one is like an actual appointment book—daily, weekly, monthly, etc.—with blank cells waiting to be filled; the other is a collection of appointments that, if we add them up, make up the schedule. The interface to scheduling applications usually appears like an appointment book, but behind the interface the second method is actually used. In any case, we must conclude that **Free Slot** is a synonym for either **Schedule** or **Appointment** and, therefore, must be excluded.

☞ The order in which we search for class candidates and their responsibilities will vary with resources, availability of use cases, and team or personal

The details in the normal flow are adequate for a use case, but they reveal nothing about the "credit card" (a possible class) or the "credit card information" or even to whom it belongs. The reason is that two sets of assumptions are at work here:

- *Logical Assumptions.* Even though the normal flow does not inform us explicitly that the credit card belongs to the patient, we assume that it does by other references in the use case (the **Summary** field, for example).
- *Cultural Assumptions.* What are the "responsibilities" of a **Credit Card** class? If we live in an economy where credit cards are pervasive, we assume that we know the answer: The class must "know" about a holder (the patient, as we concluded by making a logical assumption), a credit card type (Visa, Master Card, etc.), a number, an issuer, and an expiration date.

❸ *Eliminate obvious misfits.* Now and then, included in the natural language of use cases, are nouns or noun phrases that help the story along, but are obviously not candidates to become classes. For example, see step 1 in the normal flow of the **Make Appointment** use case (Table 8.2):

- Appointment clerk verifies that the needed <u>medical service</u> is provided by the <u>hospital.</u>

The noun "hospital" may tempt us to include it as a candidate. But if we change the phrase from passive (" . . . is provided by . . . ") to active, it becomes clear that only the "medical service" is the object:

- Appointment clerk verifies that the hospital provides the needed <u>medical service</u>.

Or step 2 of the same use case could have been written as follows:

- Appointment clerk enters patient's personal and contact data into the <u>computer</u>.

Though the statement is correct, the computer (which really stands for the information system) must not be included.

Use cases also include statements that are in no way related to the information system. In a **Checkout Groceries** use case, we may include steps for bagging the groceries to complete the overall picture, but if the information system does *not* track bagging, we should not concern ourselves with the class **Bag** and its properties.

❹ *Outline class responsibilities.* Finding class responsibilities is sometimes more complex and requires interpretation of the step (or steps) within the flow of the use case that we are parsing. However, for the preliminary list of classes, we need the responsibilities only in the most general terms, not as distinct attributes (or variables) and operations.

Responsibilities are suggested by the ***noun's relationships*** with other nouns and sometimes verbs (actions) within the statement:

- *Possessive relationship with other nouns or noun equivalents.*

1. Registration clerk enters or updates <u>patient's personal data</u>.

With this statement in the normal flow of **Register Patient**, "knowing" about patient's personal data becomes a responsibility of the **Patient** class.

preferences: We could first identify all class candidates across all use cases and then outline their responsibilities, or we could take whatever one use case has to offer and move to the next one. Chances are that whatever you plan will be disrupted by the events. One person or one team might not have completed use cases before you are asked to define classes. Or a use case is changed after you have parsed it. **Software development is iterative—by choice and by necessity**.

☞ The decision about the hospital card is a *preliminary* judgment. As we shall see, **Patient** will delegate most of its responsibilities, including the issuance of the hospital card, to "collaborating" classes.

- *Associative relationship with other nouns or noun equivalents.*

   1. Registration clerk asks the patient for health insurance card.
   2. Registration clerk sends data to the health insurance provider.
   3. Health insurance provider verifies that the insurance plan is valid.

We have to wait for the third sentence in the normal flow of **Verify Insurance Plan** to clarify that the "health insurance card" really means "health insurance plan." Since the plan belongs to the patient, knowing insurance data is a responsibility of the **Patient** class.

- *Associative relationship with actions.*

   3. Registration clerk issues <u>hospital card for the patient</u>.

Use cases does not speak with an object-oriented "dialect," but from this step in **Register Patient** we can conclude with a fair degree of confidence that since the hospital card is issued *for* the patient, **issueHospitalCard** should be an operation of the **Patient**class.

Earlier we said that, in parsing use cases, the borders between the objects may appear blurred. The argument was not meant as mere imagery. Notice the following statement from the normal flow of the **Make Appointment** use case (Table 8.2):

   3. Appointment clerk records information about the referral source.

Which object is responsible for "information about the referral source"? It is not quite clear. We have two candidates: **Patient** and **Appointment**. (The fact that that the **Referral Source** may qualify as a class by itself does not make any difference: Any object can be an attribute of another object.) Since the answer may be either, for the moment we assign the responsibility to both objects and resolve the issue later.

❺ *Consolidate the findings into a list of the candidates and their responsibilities.* Analyzing use cases provides us with a minimal collection of class candidates and their attributes. Nevertheless, use cases are the most important source for class discovery, because they outline the first and the outermost layer of the system's structure. No matter what lies in the innermost depths of the system, it is *this* structural layer that ❶ must satisfy the behavioral requirements and ❷ gives us clues as to what the rest of the structure should be or should do to support the outer layer.

Consequently, at this point we organize our findings before expanding classes into more solid and elaborate entities (Table 8.3). The presentation and the organization need not be very sophisticated: It is a working document and we will discard the list once we have elaborated classes and no longer need a "preliminary" list.

Entries in the candidates list share several features:

- *Names are preliminary.* We discussed the rules for naming classes, attributes, and operations. In the preliminary list, we come as close to the "correct" names as we can, but we do not go as far as removing spaces or changing capitalization. In addition, if we find synonyms for an entity, we include that synonym as well, since we have not yet verified that they are indeed the *same* entity. And if we do find that they are the same, then we must choose the name that the business prefers. Even though the "business" would not see the *inside* of the information system, software developers who work with the business do.

Table 8.3
Preliminary Class
Candidates for
Walden's **Patient
Management**, Partial
Listing.

Walden Medical Center *Patient Management* *Preliminary Class Candidates* (Partial Listing)		
CLASS	**RESPONSIBILITIES**	**USE CASES**
Appointment	• Makes appointment for patient. • Knows appointment. • Cancels appointment. • Knows referral source. • Tracks appointment.	• 100: Refer Patient • 120: Make Appointment • 130: Receive Patient
Credit Card	• Knows patient's credit card. • Verifies patient's credit card.	• 142: Verify Credit Card • 190: Resolve Patient Billing Issue
Health Insurance Plan	• Knows patient's health insurance plan. • Verifies patient's health insurance plan.	• 140: Register Patient • 145: Verify Insurance Plan
Hospital ID Card	• Issues hospital card.	• 130: Receive Patient • 140: Register Patient • 144: Issue Hospital Card
Medical Service	• Knows medical service.	• 100: Refer Patient . . .
Patient	• Knows patient's personal data. • Knows patient's contact data. • Knows patient's appointments. • Knows patient's insurance data. • Knows patient's financial data. • Knows patient's referral source. • Knows patient's next of kin. • Issues hospital card.	• 100: Refer Patient • 120: Make Appointment . . .
Patient Statement (Bill)	• Knows patient's open (unpaid) billing items. • Knows paid items from the last statement. • Prints billing statement.	• 160: Print Patient Statement • 190: Resolve Patient Billing Issue
Payment	• Knows the payment credited to patient's account.	• 190: Resolve Patient Billing Issue
Referral Source	• Knows the referral source.	• 120: Make Appointment
Hospital Schedule	• Knows appointments. • Knows openings for medical services.	• 120: Make Appointment

- *Names must be in singular form.* Names should *not* be plural. (There are exceptions, of course, such as **First Class Seats** for an airline reservation system.) Even if we arrive at collection classes later—as we will—at this point plurality leads to confusion, because our main concern here is to discover our most basic building blocks, not how they are put together.
- *Overlaps are tolerated.* Candidate classes such as **Payment**, **Cash Payment**, **Billing Activity**, **Adjusting Entry**, etc., are suspiciously close. They might be one class or might be the children of the same parent or parents. (We will discuss these terms later under the

"Generalization & Specialization" section.) But since we cannot be confident at this point, we leave them on the list as they are.

- *Responsibilities are not detailed on purpose.*   A use case, *by design*, hides details that do not help its flow. But even if it does not hide them, we disregard the details to find the *nature* of the responsibilities: A **Patient** object has to know a patient's personal data—whatever the details—and has to issue a hospital card—whatever information the card holds. We identify details when we define and expand classes.
- *Reference to sources (use cases) is highly recommended.*   It is not mandatory that we identify our source use cases, but remember that all development activities are iterative and we may need to consult our sources again, even if only for verification. The bigger and the more complex a project, the greater the need for *traceability*: What one person or one team discovers may have to be verified, changed, or expanded by another person or another team.

Elaborating Classes

> To fully define a class or an object is to define responsibilities in detail.

☞ For an explanation of domain catalog, domain dictionary, and domain experts, see Chapter 5, Domain Analysis.

Defining business classes from preliminary candidates is a process of elimination, expansion, and new discoveries.

The class candidates that result from parsing use cases are indispensable to creating a structure for the information system, even though they are not nearly enough for defining classes that satisfy structural requirements. But when we decide to proceed from use cases to outlining classes, we need those omitted details. Some of these details can be found in the domain catalog—the consolidation of domain dictionaries, business rules, interviews, and supporting documents—that resulted from *domain analysis*. It is, however, nearly impossible to gather relevant information in one pass. Therefore, throughout structural modeling, we must follow the leads that use cases provide *back* to the sources of domain knowledge. (We are still in the business territory, not the system space.)

And a class can change—many times perhaps—through defining its **relationships** with other classes. The more important an object is to the business, the more we find that it cannot dispense its responsibilities without *collaborating* with other objects.

Elaborating Patient

> Defining detail responsibilities must proceed from analyzing general responsibilities.

To illustrate how a class is defined through elaboration of its responsibilities and discovery of its relationships, we start with **Patient**, the undisputed central figure in the **Patient Management** subsystem. Even from the outline of responsibilities in the preliminary candidate's list, it is quite clear that class has an overwhelming number of obligations:

☞ By saying that **Patient** is "responsible" for so many pieces of information, we are

- Knows patient's personal data.
- Knows patient's contact data.
- Knows patient's appointments.

not implying that it
has to carry the whole
burden by itself. It is
very likely that
Patient would
end up as a
composite object.
(See "Composite &
Collection Objects"
earlier in this chapter.)

☞ We have added
one item to the list:
patient's medical
history. A patient's
medical history is the
collection of *medical
services* provided to
the patient. We have
yet to present a use
case that directly
explains how a medical
service is rendered.
(We will do so later in
the "Generalization &
Specialization" section)
But **Medical
Service** is
essential to
Appointment and
**Receive
Patient** use cases.

- Knows patient's insurance data.
- Knows patient's financial data.
- Knows patient's referral source.
- Knows patient's medical history.
- Knows patient's next of kin.
- Issues hospital card.

We undertake to clarify and elaborate each responsibility by reviewing use cases, consulting the domain catalog, conducting fresh research, and employing logical deduction.

❶ *Patient's Personal Data.*　Among all responsibilities, personal data is the most straightforward:

- Name: Last Name, First Name, Middle Initial.
- Sex.
- Date of Birth.
- Social Security Number.
- Place of Birth.
- Nationality.

The last two items, we discover, are not required by the hospital, but by government regulations. The introduction of the **nationality** attribute, however, raises an issue: Should the clerks enter the value of **nationality** as free form text or must they select it from a list? The hospital decides that the "list" solution is the better idea: the number of countries does not change constantly (which means minimal maintenance), it would prevent typographical errors and, most probably, we would need the list for other purposes, such as gathering statistics. (Satisfying this new requirement affects how the **nationality** attribute handles its responsibility. Since we have to explore some concepts first, we will explain the effect later in "The Conceptual Patient" section.)

We also come to the conclusion that although **dateOfBirth** is already an attribute, an **age** attribute would be helpful to both hospital clerks and medical staff. However, **age** does not have to be maintained: The object can calculate it from the date of birth. Therefore, we add another attribute to **Patient**:

- Age.

An attribute such as **age** is called a *derived* attribute. The object arrives at the value of a derived attribute internally—from what it already "knows," not from receiving a value from outside. As a result, if the "base" value or values change, the value of the derived attribute changes as well: As time goes by, date of birth stays the same, but the system date changes and, along with it, the value of **age**.

❷ *Patient's Contact Data.*　At first glance, this responsibility might seem as simple as the first one:

- Address: Building Number, Street, Unit Number, City, Postal Code (and perhaps Country).
- Telephone Number.

But it is not that simple. Many patients have at least two addresses: home and business. They may also have a cell phone and/or a pager. Sometimes the billing address may be different. And what about e-mail?

One patient may get by with just one address and one phone number; others cannot. A **Patient** object must handle all combinations—even, up to a point, new categories of addresses or phones that are yet to emerge: Just a few decades ago only police, government agencies, and the well-to-do had access to "mobile" phones. (They were mobile in the sense that vehicles carried and powered them. No shirt pocket was big enough or strong enough to transport them, even minus the power source.)

To satisfy current and upcoming demands, we might decide to give **Patient** a *set* of 10 addresses: one for office, one for home, one for billing, and seven unused addresses for any future use. Who would need more than 10 addresses?

☞ Numerous legacy applications have solved similar problems by designing "spare capacity" for future use into database tables. To be fair, sometimes the technology has "made them do it." But it is no longer justified.

Such a "solution" creates a few unpleasant problems of its own. First, we have no way of knowing whether a set of 10 addresses is too many or too few. If it is too many, we would waste resources—in processing power, in memory usage, and in storage. If it is too few, then we have to modify the object's interface to add new addresses. But remember that the interface of an object is a *contract*. As time goes by and the number of subscribers to the contract increases, changing the interface becomes more expensive and more disruptive.

Second, and equally important, is that adding 50 attributes (at least five variables per each address) to **Patient** defies a core reason for adopting an object-oriented approach: taming complexity by constructing a structure that at each level, at each viewpoint, is understandable and manageable. (There are other reasons for avoiding the "10 addresses" solution, reasons that relate to workflow and implementation. They will be discussed under the design section of the book.)

Fortunately, an object can discharge its responsibilities *without* carrying the whole burden by itself: It can *delegate* responsibilities to objects that *collaborate* with it.

[Jacobson 1992, 245]. *See also* [Booch 1999, 209].

"If the type [of an attribute] has a complex data structure, we often have to make a new class of the attribute type. . ."

We will come back to delegation and collaboration later. At this point, it is sufficient to say that if the complexity of one responsibility threatens the integrity and simplicity of one class, then we must delegate the responsibility to one other class or classes.

In the case of addresses for **Patient**, it is not difficult to conclude that we need two other classes:

☞ See "Composite & Collection Objects" earlier in this chapter. We will say more on the typical responsibilities of collection objects later.

- *Address:* a class that would produce as many instances as a **Patient** *object* may require, with no minimums or maximums.
- *Addresses:* a collection class that, when instantiated, would manage instances of **Address** for the **Patient** object.

By following the same reasoning for telephone numbers, we arrive at a simplified yet flexible structure for the **Patient**'s contact responsibilities:

- Addresses
- Phones

☞ The **number** attribute of a **Phone** object can hold a fax number, a pager number, or a voice phone number. Obviously, a **type** attribute is necessary to distinguish them. We can even argue that since a phone

❸ *Appointments.* Like addresses, a patient can have an open-ended number of appointments. Besides, even one appointment is not an "atomic" unit of data: at a minimum, it has date, time, place, and the type of medical service. Therefore, as the list of candidate classes has already shown, we need a separate **Appointment** class.

For addresses, we defined a collection class to manage individual addresses. For appointments, however, we take an alternate route that gives us the same results in *conceptual* terms, but without a collection object. This alternate method is to define an operation that returns appointments:

- getAppointments.

❹ *Patient's Insurance Data.* Insurance data (insurance policy) appears complex even at first glance: health insurance provider, plan type, plan number, deductible amounts, group number, and all other codes that providers are fond of displaying on insurance cards.

But, again, "first glance" can exaggerate. Insurance policies are not customized for individual patients, but "inherit" their rules and properties from "plans" that health insurance companies provide as a package to "groups." Therefore, the bulk of information should be managed by another object, **Health Plan**. Besides, insurance policy is not a collection: At any one time, only one policy is in effect for one patient. (When a medical service is rendered, the data on the active policy is recorded along with the service cost. As a result, a change in the insurance policy would not result in erroneous billing.)

So perhaps we should leave the responsibility of managing the insurance policy with the patient. There is no strong argument against this, but:

- The attributes that relate to the patient's insurance data form a *cluster*: a group of tightly knit elements that *only* together make sense. Such a group is always a good candidate for becoming a class by itself.
- As we previously mentioned, domain experts have told us that each patient has only one *active* policy at one time. But what if things change? In the chapter on domain analysis, we found out that Walden Medical Center is exploring the idea of offering "subscription plans"—very similar to insurance plans from health insurance provider companies—instead of, or in addition to, standard plans. If the hospital decides to realize such an idea, then we *must* create an independent class for insurance policy.

Delegating the responsibility to an **Insurance Policy** class involves some labor on our part, but it appears to be the right thing to do.

Why not start from domain objects?

We dedicated a whole chapter to *domain analysis* where, among other things, we discussed how to discover domain concepts, including *domain objects*. Then why not simply take domain objects and turn them into classes? Why waste considerable time and energy to rediscover the same objects? Now is the appropriate time and place to address these questions.

Remember the "M for Model" figure in the same chapter? The middle of the "M" is where concepts are shared by both the business and the information system: patient, appointment, medical service, medical record, etc. (See Figure 8.9.) The more we move to the right, the more the concepts are shaped for the system, even if they are basically business concepts. And this is the direction towards which we have been moving in the chapters on behavioral modeling and this chapter.

Let us illustrate the point with the object that we are in the process of defining into a class: **Patient**. The domain dictionary defined the patient as "any person who receives a medical service from medical staff." This definition, although short of particulars, is crucial to us: A patient is not anybody who is sick (the common definition), but a person to whom the hospital provides, or plans to provide, a medical service, whether that person turns up to be sick or healthy.

If we look for particulars beyond this general definition, we will find them scattered in a multitude of documents and departments throughout the hospital.

(Continued)

that a class must have a maximum of so many responsibilities and no more. But there is another rule: If we find that either the number of responsibilities for one class or the number of classes for one subsystem *seem too many*, then most probably they are. In the first case, we should delegate some responsibilities to other classes (as we are doing now). In the second case—too many classes—we must review the architecture of our system and collect related classes into new components or subsystems. (See Chapter 16.)

Which particulars are relevant to us in building an information system? The answer is those that are used in the information system; in other words, **those responsibilities that we can observe through use cases**.

Equally important is that the business does not see—and cannot see—the objects in terms of structural units for an information system. To make objects fit in the structure we must go through a process that we have been illustrating. Take the case of multiple addresses for **Patient**: Unless the enterprise is engaged in a business such as mail order, addresses would not be seen as independent entities. Regardless of how sharply we analyze the business, we cannot see all the ramifications of the modeling and the development process.

This raises another question: Is identifying objects through domain analysis a wasted effort? On the contrary; we must start there to get here. We cannot construct and/or understand use cases without having a reference point for objects on which they act.

Therefore, as far as **Patient** is concerned, its responsibility for "knowing" the patient's insurance data is reduced to exposing one other object:

- Insurance Policy.

Now, if we look at Walden's preliminary list of classes (Table 8.3), we will notice a candidate class named **Health Insurance Plan** that "knows patient's health insurance plan" (an attribute) and must be able to verify it (an operation). We now recognize that it is the same as **Insurance Policy**. We also recognize that the name on the list is *not* appropriate for the class, because **Health Insurance Plan** (or **HealthPlan** as we also called it) should refer to a class that is independent of **Patient**. (As we emphasized, the preliminary list should not be considered as final.)

❺ *Patient's Financial Data.* The term "financial data" presents the vaguest responsibility for the **Patient** class. What exactly do we mean by financial data? House mortgage? Bank account balances? Credit history? In developing an information system, this kind of vagueness and the resulting confusion is a regular occurrence. It is the task of the analyst to clarify the issues when they occur. (The preliminary list could have done a better job, but it did not. This happens frequently, too.)

In this case, fortunately, we do not need to search very far to find answers. By reviewing use cases cited as sources for the **Patient** class candidate, we find that the "patient financial data" consists of two distinct responsibilities: credit card

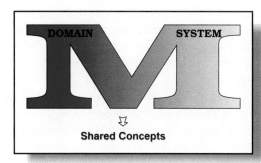

**Figure 8.9
"M" for Model:
Shared
Concepts**

Note: For a detailed description of this illustration, see Chapter 5, Domain Analysis.

**Figure 8.10
Delegation:
Assigning the
Actual Work to
Another Object**

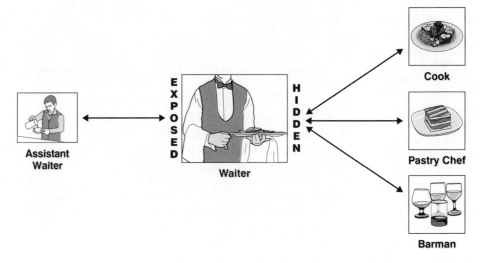

At a restaurant table, your orders for food, drink, and dessert are taken by the waiter, but the actual work is delegated to others. While the cook and the barman are "hidden," you can directly interact with the assistant waiter who also carries out some of the waiter's responsibilities.

information (if the patient wants to use it for payments) and billing activities (charges and payments).

Credit card information is very similar to the information on health insurance policy: one "cluster" of attributes (and a **verify** operation) and one credit card at one particular time. But for the same reasons that we discussed under insurance policy, we delegate the whole responsibility to a **CreditCard** class. The one major difference between the two classes is that whereas an **InsurancePolicy** directly belongs to the patient—even if the patient is not the *primary* policyholder—the credit card may belong to the guardian of the patient or even an unrelated person. The **CreditCard** object must find a solution to this issue, but the **Patient** object only needs to expose **creditCard** as an attribute. (The same credit card can cover multiple patients, siblings for example.)

"Billing activity" is similar to appointments: The number of billing activities for each patient is not fixed. Therefore we need a similar solution: a class for activities, **PatientBilling** perhaps, and an operation to retrieve the set.

The financial responsibilities of the **Patient** class, then, translate into one attribute and one operation:

- credit Card.
- getBillingActivity.

⑥ *Patient's Referral Source.* In discovering class candidates, we pointed out that by analyzing only the **Make Appointment** use case we cannot decide whether the responsibility for knowing the referral source falls on the shoulders of **Patient** or **Appointment**. Therefore, we ask the domain experts about the issue, and we conclude that:

- The referral source changes both with time and with the nature of the medical service that the hospital is expected to provide. A patient may be referred to the hospital by a general practitioner for a blood test and, almost at the same time, get an appointment for a biopsy as a result of a referral by a specialist.

☞ In calling the class **PatientBilling**, we have to be aware that the wishes of the accounting domain have yet to be taken into account. In the accounting profession's vocabulary, payments and charges are usually identified as *transactions*. Resolving these semantic issues to the satisfaction of the whole enterprise is a staple of the analyst's job.

- The referral source is not just a name, but an approved list. Only those on the list can refer the patient to the hospital. (This constraint should have been noted on the **Make Appointment** use case as a **Nonbehavioral Requirement**.) What is more, the list is not homogeneous: A referral source can be an outside doctor, an outside hospital, an outside emergency service, a paramedic who works for the hospital, or a doctor *inside* the hospital.

Based on this information, we conclude that the responsibility for knowing the patient's referral source should go to the **Appointment** class. And, at least at this point, we can feel some relief because it has become clear that managing the referral source involves much more than a simple note.

❼ *Patient's Medical History.* We have gained enough experience by now to lay out this responsibility rather quickly.

Medical history is really the accumulation of medical services provided by the hospital. (It is a near certainty that the hospital would want to access the records of medical services performed outside the hospital as well. But that is another matter to be reckoned with at a later time.) As such, we need a class that defines a single service for a patient. We cannot name it **MedicalService** because this term refers to services—X-ray, blood test, checkup, etc.—that must be defined as classes on their own, without any reference to a particular patient. Therefore, we choose **Treatment** because it has a tangible sound. And, this time, the collection object need not be a plural noun:

- Medical History.

❽ *Issue Hospital Card.* A hospital card is a piece of plastic, similar to a credit card, that identifies the patient to the hospital. (The hospital may issue a bracelet instead of, or in addition to, the card. The concept is the same in any case.) The magnetic strip behind the card holds minimal information about the patient, including the patient's ID to save the hospital staff from manual data entry (on equipment and computers that are provided with a card reader).

The hospital card does not seem too complicated: All the data that it needs is already available to the **Patient** object. Nevertheless, when we read **Receive Patient** and **Register Patient** carefully, we find that a replacement hospital card must be issued if the patient loses her or his card. This means that, as a security measure, the previous card must be cancelled before a new card is issued. This requirement, in turn, suggests that the card must have a unique identity, otherwise we cannot cancel it or validate it.

Upon further inquiry, we also find that the hospital card is time-limited, meaning that it becomes invalid after a certain date. (We find, furthermore, that the hospital has yet to decide on the criteria for the expiration date. If the hospital offers subscription services, then the subscribers must have access to the hospital for the entire duration of the contract. Other patients fall into many categories.)

Security considerations also add a twist: As far as we know, only one actor, **Registration Clerk**, through only one use case, **Register Patient**, is authorized to issue hospital cards.

Thus, we discover that a simple "issue hospital card" operation is not enough to cover all issues relating to the card. Unlike a printed report, a hospital card must be tracked. For the **Patient** class, therefore, we reduce the responsibility to one: **valid Card ID**. This one attribute, however, is very important. If the attribute holds a card ID, then the patient is registered. We leave other requirements to other classes that must manage the printing and tracking of hospital cards.

☞ Delegation might seem like a convenient delaying tactic. Like Scarlett O'Hara in *Gone With the Wind*, we can always say: "after all . . . tomorrow is another day." But at some point you have to attend to all the classes you have deputized. And each additional class translates into more resources and more maintenance. Only delegate when you are sure it is justified.

But how does the **Patient** object know about the card number? Does it delegate the responsibility to a **Patient Card** object? A benefit of **encapsulation** is that, at this moment, we do not have to know. This task falls on the design phase where we must weigh many considerations against each other and decide how to address the issue.

❾ *Patient's Next of Kin.* A patient's next of kin is optional for a normal adult and mandatory (as the guardian) if the patient is not an adult or legally requires a guardian. Moreover, one patient may have more than one guardian.

We know that, as a person, the next of kin's contact information can be as complicated as the patient's. But, unlike the patient, the next of kin is not woven into the fabric of the hospital's information system. Therefore, we need not go beyond a simple interface for the next of kin.

Still, the relationship between the patient and next of kin is one-to-many. As a result, we need a simple class, **NextOfKin**, and a method to access the whole set for a patient:

- getNextOfKins.

The Conceptual Patient

> Class definition through analysis results in conceptual classes.

Table 8.4 illustrates the results of defining **Patient** as a *conceptual* or *analysis* class. The term "conceptual" means that the responsibilities of the class have been defined as *concepts* and have yet to be shaped or adjusted for design or implementation. For example, none of the elementary attributes of **Patient** have a data type (alphanumeric, numeric, Boolean) or a specific size. In a conceptual model, we must suppress the temptation to specify anything that is dependent on a particular language, technology, or platform.

The Lessons

Not every business class is as exhausting to define as **Patient**. (Unfortunately, we cannot call it *exhaustive* as well because the collaborating classes are yet to be defined.) But what we encountered through the definition process applies to the definition of other classes as well.

❶ *Responsibilities of the class must first be defined only in general terms.* We must first understand the *purpose* of attributes and operations, not their details. Finding details out of order is counterproductive: We cannot decide whether the **postalCode** attribute belongs to the interface of the **Patient** class unless we understand its purpose and its significance within the context. As we discovered, the responsibility of **postalCode** belongs to the **Address** class, not **Patient**.

Premature attention to detail can also distort the verification and information gathering process by directing us towards wrong questions. If asked, a domain expert would assure us that **postalCode** does indeed "belong" to the patient. But a domain expert is not a system analyst and the answer, though technically correct, is misleading. The correct line of inquiry is to find the general meaning of "contact data" and its relationship to **Patient**.

❷ *No object is an island.* We found that **Patient** cannot live up to its responsibilities unless it delegates some of them to other objects. In the absolute majority of cases, one object needs other objects to fulfill its duties.

Patient: the Conceptual Class	
Attributes	
ATTRIBUTE	COLLABORATORS
patientID	
lastName	
firstName	
midInit	
sex	
birthDate	
age	
placeOfBirth	
nationality	• Country
addresses	• Address • Addresses
phones	• Phone • Phones
insurancePolicy	• InsurancePolicy
creditCard	• CreditCard
validCardID	• HospitalCard
medicalHistory	• Treatment • MedicalHistory
Operations	
OPERATION	COLLABORATORS
getAppointments	• Appointment
getPatientBilling	• PatientBilling
getNextOfKin	• NextOfKin

❸ *Definition of one class may lead to the discovery of other classes.* By trying to define **Patient**, we discovered some new classes (**Address**, for example) and rediscovered some that were already on the candidates list (such as **MedicalService**).

❹ *Definition of one class may lead to the redefinition of other classes.* We decided that **Appointment** rather than **Patient** is the right container for **Referral Source**. Had we defined **Appointment** earlier without a reference to the referral source, its definition would have to be changed now.

❺ *Classes may gain or lose responsibilities through definition.* We started with the assumption that **Patient** would be responsible for issuing the hospital card, but we found that the nature of the operation requires another class. Therefore, we stripped **Patient** of that responsibility, but made it responsible to know about a product of the new class, namely the **validCardID** attribute.

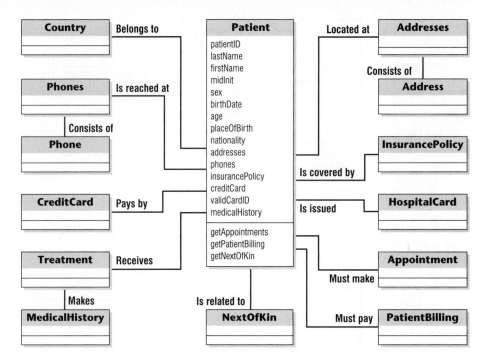

Figure 8.11 The Conceptual Patient: Analyze Responsibilities to Discover Collaborators

A collaborator is a class that carries out the responsibilities of another class.

Note: This illustration is an example of a class diagram. See the related topic in this chapter.

5. RELATIONSHIPS

A structure is more than the sum of its building blocks, or units. It is how the units *relate* to each other that makes a structure different from a storage container (at best) or a junkyard (at worst) where the objects do not interact with each other. Besides, even at the moment of its creation, a unit is often shaped by the expectations of relationships with other units (as we demonstrated in the previous topic).

Some types of relationships between classes are already familiar to you from previous discussions; we only need to formalize their definitions. Others were alluded to, but require a more extensive consideration. However, before exploring any of them, we must introduce a class diagram that visually represents those relationships.

Association

> An association is a structural relationship that defines the link between the objects of one class with the objects of another class.

We said that no object is an island: Objects must cooperate and combine their services to achieve a meaningful goal. Association describes how instances of one class cooperate with instances of another class:

- A **Patient** *is covered by* an **InsurancePolicy**.
- A **Patient** who *wants to receive* a **MedicalService** *must make* an **Appointment**.

- An **Employee** *works for* a **Department**.
- A **Student** *studies at* a **College**.

Association is *semantic*, meaning that it is expressed through language—a phrase (e.g., "*works for*") that describes the nature of the relationship between the *source* class (**Employee**, for example) and the *target* class (**Department**).

Association is also bidirectional. We can reverse the order of source and target and still have an association:

- An **InsurancePolicy** *covers* one **Patient**.

Class Diagram

A class diagram shows a set of classes and their interrelationships.

A class diagram is the most important visual tool in our modeling toolbox. All object-oriented development environments support it, and usually support it better than other modeling tools: Forward engineering (generation of code from class modeling) is commonly available and backward engineering (generation of class modeling from code) is not rare.

And yet it is a simple tool. You are already familiar with the icon for the class: a box with a name and (at least) two other compartments for attributes and operations. The rest are lines and arrows that indicate the relationships and labels that, tersely, explain those relationships.

We have already arrived at several classes through the process of elaborating one, **Patient**. It would be best, then, to employ them to introduce the class diagram. (See Figure 8.13.) However, before explaining the elements of the diagram, we must explain three related facts about class diagrams.

❶ *There are no "typical" class diagrams.* Even though the constituent elements of class diagrams are few, there are many ways to mix and match them (as we shall demonstrate). Making complicated things understandable is a main aim of a model. If a class diagram has too many classes, you must either hide responsibilities and show only the relationships or divide the classes into more than one diagram.

❷ *An entire system or subsystem cannot usually fit in one class diagram.* Unless your "system" is really small (or you are creating a component), a single diagram cannot represent the entire structure of a system. The main reason is the sheer size: Even a small system simply has too many classes to be grasped in one diagram. (Automated tools can produce an incredibly large diagram that would cover an entire wall of an analyst's office, but its usefulness would be mainly limited to impressing visitors.)

**Figure 8.12
A Simple Class
Diagram**

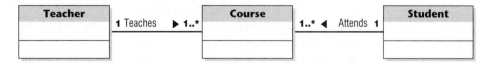

Class diagrams represent the relationships between classes. In this example, the diagram shows that one student may attend one or more courses, while the teacher may teach one course or more. (The elements of a class diagram are described later in the chapter.)

Figure 8.13 Patient and Its Associations: A Diagram Must Have a Point

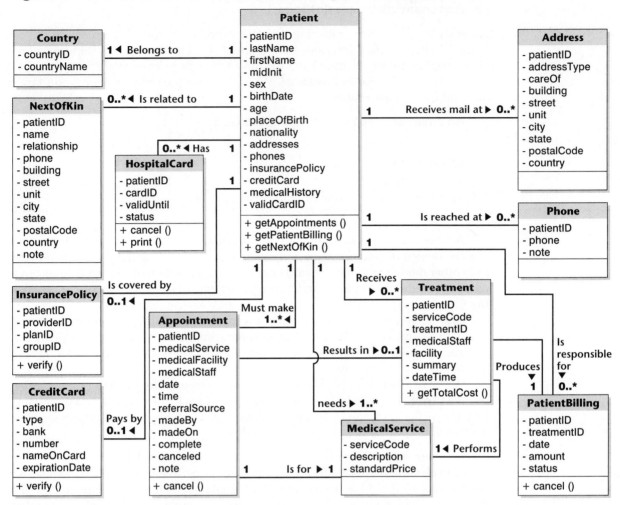

A model must convey a clear message. If an element confuses the message, it must not be included. For this diagram, we have ignored collections classes such as **MedicalHistory** since they make understanding the relationships more difficult. Responsibilities of other classes are for illustration and must be refined further.

❸ *A class diagram should have a viewpoint.* The main purpose of a class diagram is to show relationships. Unless we are merely interested in listing class responsibilities (a goal that is often justified), we must have a viewpoint. In Figure 8.13, our viewpoint is to show **Patient** and its relationships with its collaborators in a **cooperative** (or **associative**) context. Had we wanted to focus on any other class, or any other kind of relationships, the diagram would have been different—definitely in arrangement, most likely in the number and the identity of classes displayed. Figure 8.14 represents a different viewpoint that emphasizes a *compositional* context. Even if combining the two diagrams would not have made the picture too crowded, the two diagrams do not share the same purpose.

Elements of class diagrams, as we said, are few and mostly simple. Table 8.5 on page 280 describes those elements that are used in Figure 8.13. The rest we will explain as we discuss various relationships between classes.

Figure 8.14
**Patient and Its
Collection
Attributes:
Different
Message,
Different Model**

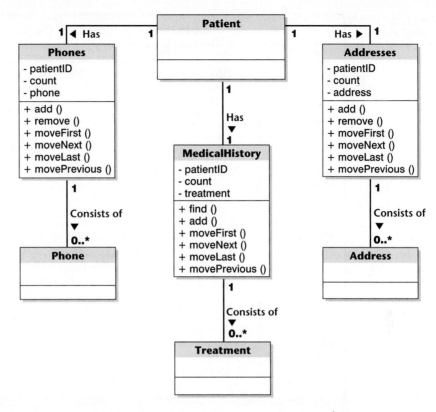

This class diagram models the relationships of the **Patient** class from a different viewpoint. The responsibilities that were already listed on the diagram in Figure 8.13 are hidden here. Operations listed for collections classes, such as **add** or **moveNext**, are usually defined during design (not analysis). They are shown here to acquaint you with the typical responsibilities of collection classes.

The **Relationship** (**Label**) is optional, and indeed if the viewpoint does not require it, it is not necessary. But if you are trying to compose a *cooperative* diagram such as "Patient & Its Associations" and cannot come up with halfway decent descriptions, then maybe a mistake has been made: Either a class does not belong to the diagram or it has been defined incorrectly.

Moreover, if you do have relationship labels and/or quantitative associations, it is better to have the direction symbols as well, as it makes the minimal wording of the label and the implication of the association clearer.

Multiplicity

> Multiplicity specifies how many instances of one class can associate with instances of another class.

The quantitative association between two classes can be limited to a specified set, can be one specific number, or can run the range from zero to infinity. The quantity in an association is specified *both* for the *source* (the grammatical subject of a relationship) and for the *target* (the grammatical object).

Multiplicity can be expressed as one number, as a set of numbers, or as a range of numbers. (See Table 8.6 for examples.) Negative numbers are not allowed, though zero can be used if multiplicity is a set of numbers or a range.

☞ Do not look for *this* definition of "multiplicity" in the dictionary. It is one of those terms that has been commandeered to express a concept with no established name. (At least it is shorter than "quantitative association" and impresses lay people more.)

Table 8.5
Basic Elements of the
Class Diagram.

Basic Elements of the Class Diagram

ELEMENT	SYMBOL	DESCRIPTION
Class	Class	The class, with or without attributes and operations, depending on the purpose and space.
Association		Shows that one class is associated with another class in some way. (There are other symbols specific to inheritance, aggregation, and composition that we will discuss later.)
Relationship (Semantic Association)	[Label]	A verb (transitive) or a verb (intransitive) plus a preposition that describes the relationship between the subject and the (grammatical) object classes. The label may also a specify a role (**Manager**, **Member**, etc.).
Direction	▶	Points from the subject of the relationship (source of the relationship) towards the (grammatical) object (the target). Many tools allow you to combine the direction symbol with the association line and use an *arrow* to represent both. Strictly speaking, in UML, a solid arrow means "uses," but the distinction is rather subtle and it might be easier to use an arrow.
Multiplicity (Quantitative Association)	[Number(s)] (See the following "Multiplicity" section.)	Describes the *quantitative* association between two classes.

- *One Number.* A single number indicates that only one quantitative association is allowed: the value of the number, no more and no less.
- *A Set of Numbers.* A set of numbers indicates that the quantitative association can vary, but can only be one of the numbers in the set.
- *A Range of Numbers.* A range in numbers is specified as **N1..N2**, where **N1** is the lower limit of the range and **N2** is its higher limit, separated by two dots. An asterisk (*) as **N2** indicates means "infinity", that is, there is no higher limit.

Table 8.6
Multiplicity
Examples.

Examples of Multiplicity

MULTIPLICITY	MEANING	EXAMPLE
1	Exactly one	A patient must have one, and only one, nationality.
0..1	Zero or one	A patient can have no insurance plan or can have one.
1..*	One or more	A patient must have at least one appointment to receive medical service, but can have as many as necessary.
0..*	Zero or more	A patient can have no billing activity or many.
20..40	A defined range	A part-time worker must work at least 20 hours a week, but no more than 40.
2, 4, 6, 8	A noncontinuous range	Tables are set for 2, 4, 6, or 8 people.

Aggregation & Composition

> Aggregation represents the relationship of a whole to a part. Composition is a form of aggregation in which the part is exclusively owned by the whole and its life cycle is dependent on the life cycle of the whole.

In the real world as well as in an information system, an object may be made up of other objects, either totally or partially. Earlier in this chapter we introduced composite objects to lay the groundwork for explaining how the responsibilities of an object, especially a complex object like **Patient**, can be divided up among parts (or components) that are less complex and more focused.

The object-oriented term for the whole-part relationship is "aggregation." In aggregation, one object acts as the "whole" while the second object plays the role of the "part." The whole object is called an **aggregate**, and in a class diagram is represented by a small diamond next to a line that connects it to the part.

If an aggregate relationship is very strong, it is called "composition." In composition, the part belongs to one, and only one, whole object. Moreover, the part can exist *only* as long as the whole exists. The "whole" in such a relationship is called a **composite**, and in a class diagram is represented by a filled diamond.

A (school) class is an example of normal or "weak" aggregation: one teacher and many students make **Philosophy101**, but both the students and the teacher are free to participate in other aggregations, that is, teach or study other courses. The windshield of a car, on the other hand, is the component of only one car. Therefore, the windshield has a composite relationship with the car: It cannot be shared with other cars.

Figure 8.15 represents examples of both "weak" aggregation and composition: Components of a TV set belong solely to the set, are not shared with other objects, and live and die with the set. Components of the sound system, on the other hand, can have independent lives: Speakers may be "switched over" to another system, and the system, as a whole, would remain a "sound system" even if the tape deck is removed. (Tape decks are actually disappearing fast.)

☞ An entertainment system can be much more complicated in reality. We can connect the sound output of the TV set to the tuner. A DVD player can play both DVDs and CDs and, therefore, can be aggregated into both a sound system and a "video system." We can increase the complexity by adding a game box with its console.

**Figure 8.15
Aggregation and Composition: How Parts Relate to the Whole**

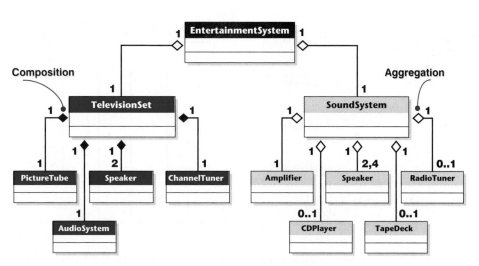

Note the aggregation does *not* replace associations, but simply expresses a different viewpoint. In another diagram, dedicated to associations, we could specify that **Amplifier** "enhances the signals of" **RadioTuner**, **CDPlayer**, **TapeDeck** (and even **TelevisionSet**).

Exercise
☞ Create a diagram of your ideal or actual entertainment system in terms of aggregation and composition. Reinterpret the system in an association diagram.

☞ In design and implementation, the difference between normal aggregation, called **loose coupling**, and composition, called **tight coupling**, becomes very important. (In implementation, the looser the coupling, the better.) But the conceptual aggregates are not necessarily converted one-to-one into concrete components. Therefore, in analysis, it is enough that the relationships among the classes be *conceptually* correct.

EntertainmentSystem is an aggregate of **TelevisionSet** and **SoundSystem**. As we discussed in the "Composite & Collection Objects" section, components of a composite (or aggregate) object can be aggregates themselves and so on. In other words, aggregation can be *hierarchical*.

Collection objects are a special kind of aggregation or composition. In collection objects, the parts are all instances of the same class. But like other aggregates, the parts themselves can be aggregates.

Even though we can identify a *single* aggregation or composition relationship between a whole and a part with relative confidence, calling the whole "composite" or "aggregate" is sometimes problematic. Figure 8.16 is a case in point. Instances of **Appointment**, **Treatment**, **Address**, etc., are exclusively owned by an instance of **Patient**. Remove **Patient** and they are removed as well. But **Country** has a simple aggregate relationship with **Patient** and will remain in existence even if a patient is removed. (We have chosen **Country** because it has a direct relationship with **Patient**. But there are other classes, such as **MedicalService**, that have the same aggregate relationship with "parts" of **Patient** as **Country** has with **Patient** itself.)

What, then, should we call **Patient**: aggregate or composite? The answer is that the label is *not* tremendously important, as long as individual relationships between class pairs are correct.

The aggregation relationship is *not* bidirectional: The whole and the part cannot exchange places. An **Engine** is a part of an **Airplane**, but an **Airplane** cannot be a part of an **Engine**.

Constraints

In structural modeling, constraints are rules that apply to associations.

In elaborating the **Patient** class, we concluded that a **HospitalCard** may become invalid either because it is lost or has expired. As a result, the hospital may issue more than one card to a patient, but at any one time *only* one card is valid. This

Figure 8.16
Patient as an Aggregation: Streamlining Complexity

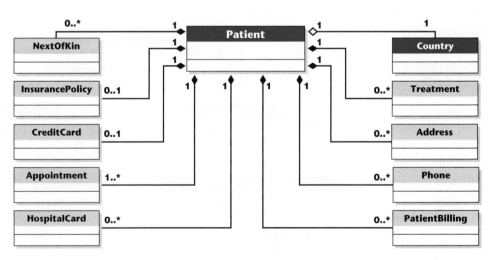

Notice that **Country** is a "loose" part of **Patient** because it exists even if no patient exists. Other parts, however, would not exist without a patient. It does not matter whether you call such a hybrid object an "aggregation" or "composition" as long as individual relationships are correctly identified. ("Compose" is a more popular term than "aggregate.")

Figure 8.17
Applying a Rule: Constraint in Structural Modeling

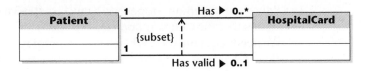

Patient may have many cards, but only a subset (one) can be valid at any one time.

is a *business rule* that we can model as a constraint to the association between **Patient** and **HospitalCard**.

☞ See Chapter 5, Domain Analysis, for a discussion on business rules.

Figure 8.17 illustrates the application of the business rule in a class diagram. The diagram shows *two* associations between **Patient** and **HospitalCard**. The association on the top is the general one that we saw before: A patient *has* zero or more hospital cards. The bottom association is a constraint on the first one: A patient *has* zero or one *valid* card. The relationship between the two associations is indicated by a dashed arrow that defines the direction of the relationship, and a label (between curly brackets) that expresses the nature of the constraint.

Generalization & Specialization

> Generalization is abstracting common elements shared by a set of classes into a *superclass*. Specialization is creating a *subclass* from an existing class by defining elements that are too specific for the parent class.

Generalization and specialization are opposite directions on the same road. In our everyday classifications—in our conversations, in our thinking, and in making decisions about the identity of objects that we encounter—we are engaged in repeated round-trips along this road. We continuously abstract categories into broader categories: **Dog** → **Canine** → **Mammal** → **Animal**. Or we deduce a more specific class from a more general one: **Plant** → **Tree** → **Oak**. (See Figure 8.18.)

We resort to generalization when we find common properties—attributes, operations, and constraints—among classes that, for some reason, we need to treat as one class. In other words, we need to further abstract the abstract. Through generalization, we arrive at a *superclass* (or "*parent*") that represents those common properties,

Figure 8.18
Generalization and Specialization: More Abstract vs. More Concrete

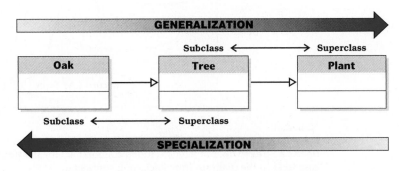

A class that is the result of generalization is called a superclass. A class that results from specialization is a subclass. In class diagram, generalization is indicated by a hollow-tip arrow from subclass to superclass.

and *only* those common properties: The class **Mammal** cannot have any attributes or operations that the **Cat** and **Dog** classes lack.

We need specialization when a class cannot represent the distinguishing characteristics of a subset of its members: The class **Mammal** does not "know" about the structure of the hands, feet, and brains of monkeys, gorillas, and humanoids that distinguishes them from other mammals; therefore, we need a **Primate** class who "knows" these attributes. Through specialization we arrive at a *subclass* (or "*child*") that has additional properties and/or more specialized attributes and operations, for example, a large domed cranium that protects the brain in primates. (In labeling the relationship between a subclass and a superclass, we can identify the subclass as "*a kind of*" superclass: "**Oak** is a kind of **Tree**.")

Walden's "Record Medical Service"

Generalization and specialization are often dictated by business needs.

In Walden's **Patient Management**, the most sensitive use case is **Track Medical Service**. It is also the most complicated. A hospital provides many types of medical services: medical procedures, X-rays, prescriptions, diagnoses, hospitalization, etc. And various kinds of people provide these services: doctors, nurses, lab technicians, and paramedics. But all these services have a property in common: They are *medical services*. The same is true for the people who provide them: They are the hospital's *medical staff*, distinct from managerial and clerical staff. As a result, we can generalize both the actors and the services. (See Figure 8.19.)

**Figure 8.19
Track Medical
Service: A
Source for Class
Generalization**

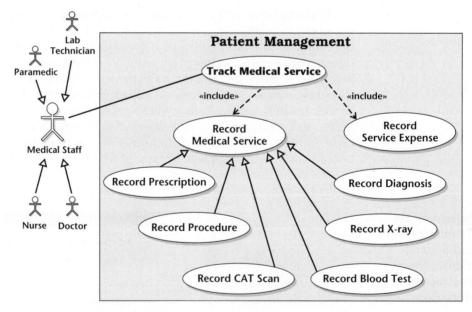

Note that:
❶ We have identified several—but not all—use cases that should be generalized into **Record Medical Service**, but have excluded a similar set for the **Record Service Expense** use case to keep the diagram from becoming confusing.
❷ Links between child actors such as **Doctor** and children use cases such as **Record Diagnosis** are not shown to focus on generalization. If a diagram becomes too crowded, you must resort to another diagram to display items that are left out from the first.

However, there is also a *business* imperative for generalization: At a high level, regardless of differences among services, the hospital must track the expenses and bill the patient and/or the health insurance provider. Similarly, the doctors need to access a *consistent* view of the patient's medical history.

We argued that parsing use cases is the best starting point for the discovery and the definition of classes. We must add that whenever we find use cases that are generalized (or can be generalized), the chances are that we will discover classes that need to be generalized as well.

Medical services are very different from each other and must be abstracted into classes that are, in some instances, very complex and unlike each other: a *prescription* may have many line items and each line item must be verified against a drug database and inventory; a *blood test* has a predefined format for recording the most common test results but must also accommodate special requirements; an *X-ray* produces a digital output that must be associated with a free-format text for diagnosis; medical operations and *procedures* have their own needs; etc.

Nevertheless, like "child" use cases in Figure 8.19, services that the hospital provides to patients have common properties:

- The *patient* who receives the treatment. (In Figure 8.13, we called a medical service that is *actually* provided to a patient a *treatment* to distinguish it from the class that describes medical services independent of the patient.)
- The *medical staff* who provides the service.
- The *facility* in which the service is provided.
- The *type* of the service.
- A *summary* of the results of the service.
- *Total cost* of the service. Some services have only one cost, while others may include multiple items. In all cases, we want to know the sum.
- *Date* and *time* of the service.

The hospital must keep track of the services for billing, medical, legal, and inventory purposes *regardless* of the intricacies of each particular service. To achieve this goal, all medical services must be *generalized* without losing their own distinct identity. (See Figure 8.20.) Through generalization, the system can choose to see an object of various treatment classes either as an instance of its own subclass—**Diagnosis**, **Prescription**, **XRay**, etc.—or as an instance of the superclass **Treatment**.

☞ We could have arrived at the same results through specialization; that is, had we begun with **Treatment** as a distinct class, we would have concluded that it needs subclasses to handle the complexity of various medical services. In any case, from now on, if we discover a new medical service that had escaped our attention before, we can retrofit it into the system with relative ease—provided we define it as a subclass of **Treatment**.

6. DELIVERABLES

- *Class Candidates & Their General Responsibilities.* Discovery of class candidates and their general responsibilities is a required first step for structural modeling. The results of this activity need not be very formal: they provide a framework for defining business ("entity") classes and their detailed properties (attributes, operations, and constrains). You may keep the results for traceability (and the inevitable iterations), but you need not pass them to later stages of development.

- *Business Classes.* Modeling tools are increasingly integrated within development environments. Therefore, it is likely that your IDE (Integrated Development Environment) would automatically translate your class models into code "skeletons" and save them in a repository. As a result, depending on the features of your

Figure 8.20
Generalization of Treatment Without Losing Specialization

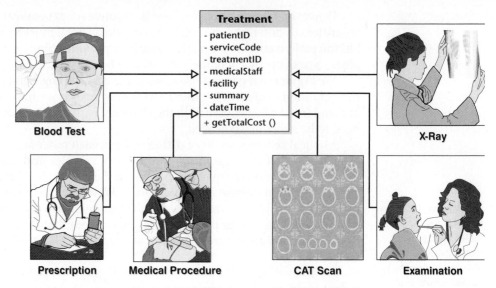

Treatment
- patientID
- serviceCode
- treatmentID
- medicalStaff
- facility
- summary
- dateTime

+ getTotalCost ()

Blood Test

X-Ray

Prescription   Medical Procedure   CAT Scan   Examination

getTotalCost relies on patient billing records to return the total cost of the medical service. (As a rule, in an information system, we do not store both the detail and the total that results from summing up the details.)

See Chapter 15, Components & Reuse, to see how the mechanism of inheritance relates to generalization and specialization.

development tool, you need not keep separate documentation unless it is required for traceability.

• *Class Diagrams.*   Unless the software under development is very simple, you need multiple class diagrams to clarify class relationships from different—but sometimes overlapping—viewpoints. Keep class diagrams simple: A diagram that overwhelms the eyes with too many classes and lines that cross each other is not a sign of mastery over complexity, but an evidence of defeat. Above all, a class diagram must have a *purpose*.

7. WRAP UP

Even the most dynamic system has a structure and this structure must be modeled before it is constructed. A structural model, however, is not meaningful in isolation: Ultimately, it must support the behavior of the system and the dynamic interaction among its building blocks to achieve that behavior.

☑ **Structural modeling within the context of a conceptual information system**

The structural modeling of an information system is, in essence, similar to the structural modeling of any other system: It must show the **building blocks** of the structure *and* their *interrelationships*. And, like others, its **view** may be conceptual, logical, or physical; its **scope** may be any relevant or selected range; and its building blocks may be simple or complex.

In conceptual modeling, however, we focus on concepts, such as a car has an engine that powers four wheels (concepts), not whether the engine is in the back or in the front (design), nor the exact radius of the axles (physical model).

☑ **Classes as building blocks of structural modeling and objects as units of information systems**

A structural model is distinguished from another structural model by ❶ the nature of its building blocks (or units) and ❷ how the units are connected. The structural model of information systems is composed of classes and their interrelationships. At runtime, when the information system is actually created, classes are "*instantiated*" into objects that function as the units of the information system. In other words, classes act both as units of modeling and as *templates* for units of the information system.

☑ **Basic object-oriented concepts in the context of structural modeling**

Classes and objects are black boxes: Their outside is visible while their inside is not. This characteristic is achieved through **encapsulation**, the enclosing of data and processes within one single unit. **Information hiding**, which follows encapsulation, ensures that the inner entities and the workings of the object are concealed (and safe) from outside entities.

Encapsulation results in two spaces: **public**, the outside, and **private**, the inside. What the object offers to the public is called its **interface**. The interface is both the *services* that an object provides and the *form* that these services take. Since, in an information system, the only reason for an object's existence is the services that it offers to other entities, the interface of the object is characterized as a "**contract**" or a binding agreement.

Under this "contract," an object assumes certain **responsibilities**. The responsibilities fall into two categories: what the object "knows," or **attributes**, and what the object "does," or **operations**. A class defines the responsibilities and its instances, the objects, carry them out.

Even though an object is a building block of an information system, it might be composed of other objects. Such objects are called **composite** objects. A **collection** object is a composite object that is made up of objects instantiated from the same class. Composite objects may belong to a *hierarchy*: A component of a composite object may itself be a composite object.

☑ **Discovering class candidates by parsing use cases**

For all practical purposes, a class *is* its responsibilities. And the best starting point for discovering responsibilities are the use cases. In very broad terms, use cases specify what a class must "know" and what a class must "do."

To discover class candidates, we ❶ identify nouns that serve as grammatical objects, ❷ search for grammatical objects hidden in verbs that have both transitive and intransitive forms, ❸ discard obvious misfits, ❹ outline the general responsibilities of the candidates by analyzing their relationships with other nouns and sometimes verbs within the flow of the use case, and ❺ consolidate our findings in a preliminary list of candidates and their responsibilities.

In this process, we *intentionally* avoid including details and, instead, outline the responsibilities *only*

in broad terms. (Even if use cases do offer details—which they usually should not and do not—we must disregard them for the moment.)

☑ **Elaborating and defining classes by specifying and expanding their responsibilities**

To create solid building blocks for the structure of an information system, discovery of class candidates and their general responsibilities is required but is not enough. We must also ❶ confirm that the tentative responsibilities *do* belong to the class and ❷ specify the exact nature of those responsibilities. In the process, we often discover new classes that must *collaborate* with the original class to fulfill some of its responsibilities.

To arrive at the precise meaning of class responsibilities, we must take actions that are iterative and intertwined; in other words, they are not necessarily sequential:

❶ *Reexamine use cases for details.* Use cases should not be inundated with detail, but if they do contain details, it is likely that the business stakeholders considered them important enough to be included. (And, in any case, grasp the business knowledge wherever you might find it.)

❷ *Make assumptions.* Regardless of the richness of detail that might result from gathering requirements, every enterprise relies on a set of assumptions that the business considers "intuitive" enough *not* to need definition: Everybody should know the components of an address, so it is not usually explained. Make your own assumptions to arrive at the specifics of a responsibility, but be aware: Every assumption must be verified with domain experts. It would be easier for them to make judgments if they grasp the full scope of a responsibility, but they must be the final arbitrators.

❸ *Review domain concepts.* The concepts that result from domain analysis, especially domain objects, functions, and business rules, have a great bearing on the definition of classes. Use cases rely on domain dictionaries to define the objects whose behavior they describe, and nonbehavioral requirements are usually excluded from use cases. Business rules, particularly **constraints**, must be taken into account in creating classes.

❹ *Return to domain sources.* Lack of detail is not necessarily a failure in gathering requirements. Knowledge gathering is incremental and must be so: Each set of details makes sense only at a certain stage of modeling and development. Prior to that stage, they would simply crowd out what is meaningful to the task at hand.

When the responsibilities are reasonably specified in detail, you might have to **delegate** some of them to other classes, new or existing. The more important a class is to the enterprise, the higher is the likelihood that it would be overwhelmed with too many responsibilities. Among the reasons for delegation:

❶ *A set of attributes are repeating.* If for *one* instance of the class a set of attributes repeats themselves, then it is impossible to keep the attributes within the class. "Medical History" and "Credit History" are typical examples: They must be delegated to a class, an instance of which would hold one, and *only* one, set of attributes. It might also be necessary to create a collection class to manage the repeating items on behalf of the original class. (Creation of collection classes is best left to design, unless the business recognizes the concept as legitimate or the modeling does not work without it.)

❷ *A set of attributes forms a distinct domain object.* For a hospital, an insurance policy is a distinct entity. Even if the attributes that relate to an insurance policy are few, it is preferable to make them into a class of their own.

❸ *A service is a candidate for reuse.* In conceptual modeling, we avoid design implementation features (as we should), but it is not difficult to conclude that a credit card has special processing needs that set it apart from simple attributes such as "middle name." In addition, the properties and requirements of a credit card make it a good candidate for reuse in other parts of the system. (Most decisions about reuse will be made in design and implementation, but if we see a strong candidate in analysis, we better pay attention.)

❹ *The number of attributes and/or operations is too high.* The decision in this case is very subjective, but a *business* object with five hundred responsibilities is certainly a mistake. In such cases, the responsibilities form *clusters* that can be turned into classes in their own right. If, for a research project, a hospital needs to record 20 physical measurements for each patient, a **PatientMeasurement** class is definitely in order.

Classes that we discover through analysis are **conceptual classes**. They mainly express business concepts and, as much as possible, they should be devoid of design and implementation features and constraints.

☑ **Class relationships**

To build a structural model we must identify its building blocks, but to complete the task we must also define how its constituent units relate to each other.

Association is a relationship that defines the connection between objects of one class with the objects of another class in *semantic*—that is, word-based—terms: a **Patient** *is covered by* an **InsurancePolicy**, a **Customer** *pays by* a **CreditCard**, an **Author** *is the writer of* a **Book**, and so on.

Multiplicity is the quantitative association between instances of one class with instances of another class: *1* patient can have only *1* nationality, *1* customer can purchase up to *100* books, *1* student must register for at least *6* credits per semester but cannot enroll in more than *18*, etc.

Constraints are rules that apply to associations: a *full-time* student must take *at least* 12 credits per semester, a patient can be issued many hospital cards but *only one card can be valid* at any given time.

Aggregation represents a "whole-part" relationship: A school class is an **aggregate** of many students and one teacher. **Composition** is a strong form of aggregation in which the parts exclusively belong to the **composite** object and do not live beyond its life cycle: The accounting department of a company disappears the moment that the company goes out of business. A **collection** object is a special kind of aggregate or composite in which all parts are instances of the same class.

Generalization is a relationship in which one class is the more abstract expression of the properties of a set of classes: A **Tree** class embodies properties common to **Oak**, **Birch**, and **Cedar** classes. Conversely, **specialization** is a relationship in which a class is the *less* abstract expression of another class: A **Rose** is a **Flower** but the **Flower** class does not express the specific features of a **Rose** that set it apart from other flowers. The result of generalization is a *superclass* (or a "*parent*"), while specialization arrives as *subclasses* (or "*children*").

☑ **Class diagrams**

Class diagrams are an indispensable tool for modeling class relationships. Elements of class diagrams are few and simple but can model a wide variety of actual relationships. No single class diagram can model all classes and all their relationships for even a small system. Therefore, to represent the structure of a system, we need to create a set of class diagrams, each with a recognizable focus and *purpose*.

8. KEY CONCEPTS

Abstraction. Selecting common properties among objects in order to generalize them into classes (classification).

Aggregate. A class that is the result of **aggregation**. An aggregate class is a "whole" that is made up of class "parts."

Aggregation. Represents the relationship of a whole to a part.

Association. A structural relationship that defines the link between objects of one class with the objects of another class.

Attribute. What the object "knows." Classes define the containers of data, while their contents are provided by objects.

Black Box. An entity, the outside of which is visible but whose internal structure and dynamism is concealed from the outside. A software object appears as a black box to other objects.

Building Block. The smallest unit of a structure, depending on the purpose of modeling. A building block in one model may consist of multiple units in another model, or it may become part of another unit in the third model. In the conceptual modeling of an information system, the smallest building block is a class. The smallest building block of an information system is an object.

Class. The result of classifying a set of objects with the same properties. In the virtual world of software, a class is both an abstraction of an object and a template to create it. In the conceptual modeling of an information system, class is the smallest building block.

Class Candidate. An entity that is discovered through analyzing use cases or domain concepts and that is likely to become a class.

Class Diagram. A diagram that displays a set of classes and the relationships among them.

Collection. A special kind of **aggregate** or **composite** object in which the parts are instances of the *same* class.

Composite. An object that results from **composition**. A composite object is a "whole" that has sole ownership of its "parts."

Composition. A form of **aggregation** in which the part (another object) is exclusively owned by the whole and its life cycle is dependent on the life cycle of the whole.

Conceptual Class. A class that results from analysis and that is used as a building block for conceptual modeling. A conceptual class has yet to acquire concrete attributes and operations that will be defined by design and implementation.

Constraint. In structural modeling, a rule that applies to an association between two classes.

Contract. The concept that an object's **interface** does not belong only to the object itself, but is a binding agreement between the object and entities that use it.

Delegation. When an object transfers a **responsibility** to another object. The second object may be part of the first object's interface (public) or can be hidden (private).

Encapsulation. Enclosing data and processes within one single unit. Encapsulation creates a wall between the inner workings of an object and its interface.

Generalization. Abstraction of common elements shared by a set of classes into a *superclass*. (See also **specialization**.)

Information Hiding. Conceals the inner entities and the workings of the object from outside entities. (See **Encapsulation**.)

Instance. The concrete realization of an abstraction. In software, an object is an instance of a class. The act of creating an instance is called *instantiation*.

Interface. The services that an object offers to the outside world, as well as how these services are structured and arranged. The interface is also a "contract" between the object and the entities that use it.

Multiplicity. Specifies how many instances of one class can associate with instances of another class. Multiplicity defines and constrains the quantitative association between instances of two classes.

Name. Uniquely identifies a class among other classes or, within one class, its attributes and operations. (In other words, different classes may have attributes and operations with the same name.) The name of a class must be capitalized, while the name of operations and attributes must begin with a lowercase letter.

Object. In software, the smallest unit of related behavior and data. An object is an "instance" of a class, that is, a concrete manifestation of its operations, attributes, constraints, and relationships.

Operation. What the object "does." In other words, an "operation" is a service that a class defines and an object carries out.

Private. Data and processes within an object that are not "exposed" to the outside world. That is, private data and processes are only available to the object itself.

Public. Data and processes that an object "exposes" to the outside world. That is, public data and processes are available to other objects as well as their owner.

Relationship. A connection between two classes or objects that is expressed through language. (That is, it is defined *semantically*, not through shapes or symbols.)

Responsibility. What an object does or what the object knows; in other words, an operation or an attribute.

Scope. Any relevant or selected range that applies to structural modeling. For an information system, the scope of the model may be limited to one domain, may cover the entire enterprise, or may represent activities that are shared across several domains.

Specialization.   Creating a *subclass* from an existing class by defining elements that are too specific for the parent class. (See also **generalization**.)

Structural Modeling.   A view of the building blocks of a system or an entity and their interrelationships within a given scope.

View.   In structural modeling, the view can be conceptual, logical, or physical. The conceptual view expresses the concepts or the "ideas" that the model represents. The logical view represents how the building blocks of the structure are logically related.

The physical view translates the logical view into specific properties of the building blocks and their relationships.

Visibility.   Defines the availability of an object's attributes and operations to other objects. A **private** attribute or operation that is marked as private is hidden to the outside world, while a **public** one is available to any entity on the outside. (Two other types of visibility, *protected* and *friend*, will be discussed later.)

9. Confusing Terms

Class & Object.   Class and object are often used interchangeably. Often, no harm results: Class is an abstraction of similar objects and an object is a concrete manifestation of a class. (Sentences would become very awkward if everywhere we repeat "class and/or objects" or "class and its instances.") In a majority of cases, what we say about classes also applies to objects, and vice versa. It is in those minority of cases that the distinction is crucial: Class is the concept; object is the realization of the concept. Class is the cookie cutter; object is the cookie. If we declare that the cookie cutter is round, we imply that the cookie will be round, too. But if we say that we want to eat a cookie, it is unlikely that we mean to eat the cookie cutter as well.

Structural & Static.   It is easy to confuse "structural" with "static." After all, this book discusses "behavioral" and "dynamic" modeling, so "static" modeling should not be a far-fetched conclusion. But whether "static" modeling is meaningful or not, structural modeling is not static: It models not only

the building blocks of an entity, but also the *relationships* among them. And in a system, closed or open, software or otherwise, relationships are never static.

Unit.   The term "unit" may *appear* confusing because it is flexible: "an entity defined as the elementary structural or functional constituent of a whole." In other words, the entity that plays the role of "unit" changes depending on what level of a hierarchy is defined as the "whole": a soldier is a unit in a company which is a unit in a battalion which is a unit in a division, and so on. When we say a "unit," we mean any entity that plays the role of the unit in a certain view. If we choose "battalion" instead of "unit," then we are declaring that what we are discussing does not apply to any unit, but only to a battalion. In an object-oriented approach, "unit" is often used to imply that a concept applies to components, layers, and subsystems as well as to classes and objects.

10. Review Questions

1. Explain briefly how you discover business classes and provide an example.
2. List and distinguish the three views of structural modeling in the context of an example.
3. How do you define structural modeling in an object-oriented approach?
4. How would you distinguish objects from classes? Provide an example.
    a. Comment on the statement: "A class is an abstraction of objects."
    b. Comment on the statement: "A class is a template for creating objects."
5. From where do classes originate?
6. To build an information system, which do you need to identify first, classes or objects?
7. Does structural modeling represent classes or objects?
8. How does encapsulation protect business rules from unauthorized access and manipulation?
9. How does an object's interface relate to services that the object provides?

10. Comment on the statement: "Classes provide the containers and objects provide the contents."
11. Why should operations be described by verbs?
12. What is "protected" visibility? Give an example.
13. Provide examples for composite and collection objects. How do they differ?
14. Responsibilities of an object define what they know and what they do. Provide an example for each.
15. How do you mine use cases to find classes?
16. What kind of responsibility (attribute or operation) are "personal data"? Explain.
17. Explain the difference between the **Address** and **Addresses** classes.
18. What is delegation? What is its significance in structural modeling?
19. What does a class diagram portray?
20. How does multiplicity relate to business rules? Give an example.
21. What is the difference between aggregation and composition? Give an example for each.

11. EXERCISES

The following exercises apply to each of the four narratives introduced in Chapter 4: *The* Sportz *Magazine, The Car Dealership, The Pizza Shop,* and *The Real Estate Agency.*

❶ Identify class candidates for the scenario. Be sure to refer to use cases from previous chapters.
❷ Identify responsibilities for each class that you have identified.
❸ Crate a table similar to Table 8.3 to summarize classes that you have identified, together with their responsibilities. Do not forget to report which use cases are your sources of information.
❹ Identify attributes for each class that you have identified.
❺ Identify operations and collaborators for each class that you have identified.
❻ Create a table similar to Table 8.4 for the scenario.
❼ Create a class diagram—complete with associations and multiplicity.
❽ Is there any relationship in this narrative that can be described by aggregation or composition? Explain.
❾ Are there classes that can be generalized? Explain.
❿ Are there classes that can be specialized? Explain.

12. RESEARCH PROJECTS & TEAMWORK

❶ Read the chapter and schedule a group discussion to debate the *differences* between **object** and **class**. Each team member should provide two examples.

❷ Select three of the best examples provided by the team members in project 1 and have all team members identify **attributes** and **operations** for each. Compare and critique each other's work. Prepare a report describing the process and the final results. Create a table with your classes, their attributes, and their operations.

❸ Refer to the online registration system for Walden Medical School in Chapter 4 and the major use cases that you identified in Chapter 6. Identify classes and objects.

❹ Have a discussion session with your team members on the topic of class generalization and specialization. When and why should we do either one? How should you do it?

Refer to the online registration system and explore the possibility of class **generalization**. Discuss class specialization the same way as you did for class generalization and find potentials for specialization of classes. Prepare a report complete with why (or why not) class generalization and specialization are important to the system development processes and submit it to the instructor.

❺ Refer to the automated research system (the "reference engine") in Chapter 4 and the major use cases that you identified in Chapter 6. Are there potential **aggregate** and **composite** classes for this application? Write a team report on aggregation and composition and validate your arguments in the context of this application.

❻ Refer to the online shopping system in Chapter 4 and the major use cases that you identified in Chapter 6. Involve all team members in the following:

- Identify class candidates for the system. Be sure to refer to use cases from the previous chapter.
- Identify responsibilities for each class that you have identified.

- Crate a table similar to Table 8.3 to summarize the classes you have identified, together with their responsibilities. Do not forget to report which use cases are your source of information.
- Identify attributes for each class that you have identified.
- Identify operations and collaborators for each class that you have identified.
- Create a class diagram complete with associations and multiplicity.

❼ Refer to your domain analysis for patient scheduling in Chapter 5 and, as a team, create a class diagram. Make sure that you follow all the steps; consider generalization and specialization, and identify relationships and multiplicity. Start by creating a class template.

13. SUGGESTED READINGS

A use case diagram is a *meta*-model; that is, it models use cases that are models themselves. The real work of UML starts with class diagrams. Classes and the relationships among classes, rendered as class diagrams, are the most important artifacts of structural modeling. Fortunately, in this respect, the references and books on system analysis and design and on UML are both many and strong. Even a large number of books on specific technologies, such as Java and .Net, devote many pages to UML concepts and diagrams.

In the general category, besides enormous resources on the Web, it is always useful to keep *the* original reference nearby: *The Unified Modeling Language User Guide* by the framers of UML, **Grady Booch**, James Rumbaugh, and Ivar Jacobson (Addison-Wesley, 1999). The book is *not* for reading cover to cover, but it is indispensable when you *do* need it for clarification or reference.

In the technology-specific category, we recommend two books. *Enterprise Java with UML: Second Edition* by **C. T. Arrington** and Syed H. Rayhan (Wiley Publishing, Inc., 2003), and *UML Applied: A .Net Perspective* by **Martin L. Shoemaker** (APress, 2004). Neither are devoted to structural modeling or class diagrams, but both do something very important: They place these abstract concepts in practical, hands-on contexts. Be advised, however, that the two books can only give you full benefit if you are familiar (or want to become familiar) with the technologies under discussion.

For the process from domain analysis and use case modeling to defining classes, the field is distinctively more limited. One book that we recommended in the last chapter, *Advanced Use Case Modeling: Software Systems* by **Frank Armour** and Granville Miller (Addison-Wesley, 2001), also does an excellent job in this regard.

The Object-Oriented Thought Process by **Matt Weisfeld** (SAMS, 2000) offers a jargon-free and relatively technology-independent treatment of the fundamental concepts of object orientation and structural modeling. This one *is* good for reading from cover to cover.

As its title implies, *Object Design: Roles, Responsibilities, and Collaboration* by **Rebecca Wirfs-Brock** and Alan McKeen (Addison-Wesley, 2003) is all about discovering and defining classes, the services that they provide, and their interrelationships. It does not leave many stones unturned.

Chapter

Dynamic Modeling

1. OVERVIEW

Modeling actions and interactions of a system's components to satisfy its behavioral requirements is the subject of this chapter. Virtual objects interact by exchanging messages that must follow strict rules and carry enough information to make a response possible. And since, oftentimes, entities that engage in an interaction change as a result of their participation, we will also discuss how to analyze and model changes that have significant consequences for the correct operation of the system.

- ☑ Inception
- ☑ Requirements Discovery
- ☐ Development
  - ☐ Analysis
    - ☑ Domain Analysis
    - ☑ Behavioral Modeling
    - ☑ Structural Modeling
    - ☐ **Dynamic Modeling** ⬅
  - ☐ Design
  - ☐ Implementation

Chapter Topics

- ➤ Dynamic modeling and its relationship with behavioral and structural modeling.
- ➤ How objects interact by exchanging messages.
- ➤ The role of parameters and return values in exchanging messages.
- ➤ Methods and their relationships with operations.
- ➤ Events and their significance in dynamic modeling.

- ➤ Sequence diagram.
- ➤ Collaboration diagram.
- ➤ Statechart diagram.
- ➤ Activity diagram.

Introduction

We take the challenge of system analysis from two opposite directions. First, we model the system as it should behave, with minimal attention to its structure. Then, by a close reading of the behavior—who does what to whom—we conceptualize what structure such a system must have.

But we are still left with a wide gap between the "skin" of the system and the building blocks behind it. We have more or less decided what those things—or objects—underneath the surface are, but how must they cooperate to achieve the behavior that we expect from the system? In what order? With what consequences? In short, we must open a third front: dynamic modeling.

Dynamic modeling adds a new perspective to analysis. We know what the system is required to do (behavior), and we know what elements it must have (structure); now, let us see and verify that the components of the structure can satisfy the behavior. To reach such an objective, we must understand what the specific features of dynamic modeling are.

Dynamic modeling features *objects*, not classes. Objects are created from class templates, but classes are abstractions and, as such, are unable to do anything. And, unlike classes, objects are not ever-present: Each object has a lifetime and may change during this lifetime.

Dynamic modeling is also about *interaction*. Unlike the real world in which objects interact in many different ways, residents of a virtual world can only interact through **messages**: requests and instructions that are passed between the system and the outside world, or among the system's components.

Interactions happen in *time*. Therefore, dynamic modeling must show not only who interacts with whom and how, but in what *order*. To satisfy the requirements and

Figure 9.1
Welding Structure to Behavior: Dynamic Modeling

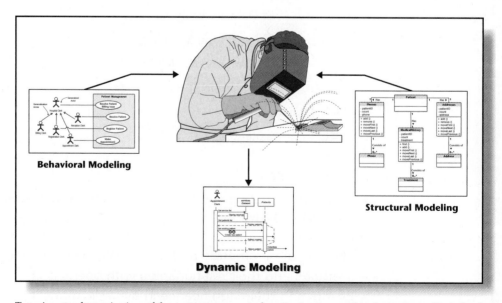

To arrive at a dynamic view of the system, we must place its structure within the context of its behavior.

the objectives of the system, actions—both individually and in groups—must obey rules of precedence. Objects are not free agents and cannot act randomly or at will.

Furthermore, any goal-oriented interaction requires a *logical flow*. A logical flow is more than merely the order of actions, but also their relationships: Can one action take place if another action has occurred? Can two actions happen at the same time? What are the consequences of a certain action?

To achieve a goal, objects must *collaborate*. Collaboration requires that objects must be *organized* in specific way, have specific capabilities, and accept specific responsibilities.

Finally, interaction often means *change*. And change, in turn, affects interaction: Actions that were not possible before a change now become possible, while others would no longer be allowed.

Objects, lifetime, interaction, messages, time, order, logical flow, collaboration, organization, and change—no model can represent all these features at the same time. But, as we shall see, dynamic modeling has various tools at its disposal, each fine-tuned for viewing the system from a specific angle.

2. INTRODUCING DYNAMIC MODELING

> Dynamic modeling represents the interaction of the building blocks of the information system with each other and with the outside world to satisfy the behavioral requirements of the system.

☞ Classes are abstractions and, as a result, cannot be expected to actually do anything. Class **Dog** specifies that a dog can bark, but it is **Fido**, an instance of the class, that actually barks.

Dynamic modeling represents *structure in motion*: It welds behavioral modeling to structural modeling to illustrate how a certain structure and its constituent components must work (or do work) to achieve the behavior that an entity must exhibit (or does exhibit) within a timeframe. (See Figure 9.2.)

Behavioral and structural modeling are concerned with *abstract units*: use cases and classes. Use cases describe how a system behaves with minimal attention to its structure, while classes describe the building blocks of the structure and their properties without revealing much about the flow of interactions and how the building blocks change. Dynamic modeling, on the other hand, is about *objects*—their interactions and how the objects change *through* interaction.

Dynamic modeling is greater than the sum of its parts. Moreover, the relationship among the components of dynamic modeling is not necessarily straightforward. Adding a timeline to a mixture of behavioral and structural models would not mechanically yield a dynamic model. As we shall see, dynamic modeling requires us to refine—and often revise—both the behavior and the structure of the system that we intend to build. Invariably, we discover that, in order to satisfy its behavior, the structure of the system needs components beyond those that are already discovered by analyzing business requirements.

Behavioral and structural modeling were discussed extensively in the preceding chapters. But let us illustrate the previous argument by a brief description of each component of dynamic modeling and point out why the relationship among them does *not* always follow a direct line.

- *Behavior.* Behavior is how an entity or a system interacts with the outside world or appears to the outside world. Behavior is dynamic, but not everything dynamic about an entity is behavior. In fact, by itself, a behavioral model cannot explain the

Figure 9.2 Dynamic Modeling: Structure in Motion

A horse has a structure: limbs, body, head, etc. A racehorse is also expected to satisfy a behavior: jump over hurdles. This set of pictures illustrates how the horse uses its structure to accomplish the behavioral requirement. (Eadweard Muybridge, *Daisy Jumping a Hurdle, Saddled,* 1887.)

☞ With **simulations** we can model a system in real time. Simulations, however, cannot be used as blueprints.

actual workings of an entity or a system. Two different vehicles can go from point A to point B with the same speed, but the engines might work very differently.

- *Structure.* Structure consists of the components of an entity and their *spatial* relationships. The structure of an entity must be able to support its behavior. But the similarity of the structure may not translate into the similarity of behavior: A penguin is structured like any other bird, but it cannot fly. On the other hand, similar behaviors can result from different structures: A hummingbird can hover just like a helicopter, but the structures are very different.

- *Timeframe.* Actions and interactions happen in time and, as a result, have *temporal* relationships. But even though a system might work in "real time," we must often model the system in two dimensions. (How to do this is the subject of this chapter.) Besides, the temporal relationship cannot always be presented as a simple sequence in which action A results in action B which results in action C, and so on. Events can happen simultaneously or result from an action that was taken outside the timeframe of the model: An ATM system must process numerous requests simultaneously, and an alarm clock sounds the alarm at a moment set a long time earlier.

In short, dynamic modeling requires us to make choices that may affect both the behavior and the structure of the system in their spatial *and* temporal relationships. What is not in doubt is that it will reveal the system from a new perspective.

3. OBJECT INTERACTION

In the real world, objects can interact in a variety of ways: physical contact, sight, sound, and smell—or a combination. In an object-oriented virtual system, however, the only possible way of interaction is through sending and receiving messages. A message may consist of a simple command, or it may carry additional information that qualifies the command. A message may also elicit a reply that is returned from the receiver of the message to its sender.

Messages

[Booch 1999, 463]

> Messages are instructions and information sent to objects in the expectation that the recipient objects will carry out certain actions.

We stated that an object has responsibilities. The responsibilities consist of what the object knows, or its attributes, and what the object does, or its operations. Furthermore, we argued that an object is a ***black box***. Its inner workings and its knowledge is hidden from the outside world, and the outside world—users of the system and other objects—may interact with the object only through its public **interface**.

How, then, is this interaction actually accomplished? For that matter, how do the users interact with the system? The answer is by exchanging messages.

To understand messages and their fine points, we will proceed in small steps. Let us start with a rather oversimplified example: a **Have Dinner** use case. (See Table 9.1 for a partial listing.) The use case is from the viewpoint of the customer as the primary

Table 9.1
Have Dinner Use Case, Partial Listing.
  We have simplified the case and overlooked certain complications. The most obvious omission is the number of guests: It would require us to add a *loop* around each "order" item.

Use Case:	Have Dinner
Scope:	Restaurant
Primary Actor:	Customer
Normal Flow:	1. Customer is seated at a table. 2. Customer asks the waiter for the menu. 3. Customer orders drink(s). 4. Customer orders appetizer(s). 5. Customer orders main course(s). 6. Customer orders dessert(s). 7. Customer asks for the bill. 8. Customer pays the bill and receives change (if any).
Alternate Flow/Exceptions:	1.a Customer asks the waiter for his or her name.

actor who interacts with the restaurant "system" to achieve a goal: have a full-course meal. (Notice that this is a real-world use case, not a virtual one.)

☞ See the previous chapter on discovering classes from use cases.

We analyze the use case to find classes. And we can easily find several: **Menu**, **Appetizer** (a superclass, because it generalizes many kinds of appetizers), **MainCourse** (another superclass), **Drink** (superclass again), **Dessert** (ditto), and **Bill**. Since the system is seen from the viewpoint of the customer, we also designate **Waiter** as a class: For the customer, a waiter is simply an "interface" to the restaurant. (Had the use case been described from the viewpoint of the restaurant—a **Serve Customer** use case, for example—the waiter would have been the primary actor.)

Figure 9.3 is a dynamic model. (It is not an official UML model, but it is a model nevertheless.) It illustrates how a unit of the system's behavior, the **Have Dinner** use case, is realized through time (the vertical axis) by the interaction between the actor and an object of the system (the horizontal bands).

Under the Operation column heading, we see the responsibilities of the **Waiter** class (or actually an instance of **Waiter**), but with details to which we paid little attention in defining use cases or discovering classes. These must be carefully specified now. (If you are wondering how the name attribute metamorphosed into the **getName** operation, we will cover this in the "Accessor Operations" section later in the chapter.)

Under the Message column, we observe how the actor actually demands the system (in this case represented by the **myWaiter** object) to carry out its responsibilities. To understand how a message ties to an operation, we must understand parameters.

Parameters

> Parameters, or arguments, specify the data that must be supplied to an object to carry out a specific operation.

☞ We will discuss **data types** in the design section. Data types are highly dependent on the language and on the platform, but fall into broad categories such as **Date**, **String**, **Number**, and **Object**. (Yes, a variable can hold an object, and objects can be sent and received like any other piece of data— exactly like the postal service that carries not only letters, but also parcels.)

When an object must carry out a responsibility, it often needs to know more about the operation than just its name. An instance of the **Waiter** class *must* serve the customer with drinks when ordered to, but it needs to know what kind of drink and how many of each. Therefore, the **orderDrink** operation must specify placeholders for the drink type and quantity of drinks:

```
orderDrink(drink, quantity)
```

These placeholders, usually enclosed within a pair of parentheses, are called parameters or arguments of the operation. Parameters specify what information the object needs (and in which order) to carry out an action.

Like classes and their operations, parameters are defined in abstract. They are *variables*; that is, they are *containers* that carry data of a certain type, but are *not* data themselves. (Remember that we defined class *attributes* the same way: containers for data, not data itself.)

When a system is actually in operation, however, abstract definitions must give way to concrete data. A customer who asks the **myWaiter** object to fulfill its **orderDessert** responsibility would not receive anything unless the name of a specific dessert and a specific quantity is supplied to the waiter along with the order. Therefore, the **message** from the customer that invokes an operation must fill the operation's placeholders with unambiguous information:

```
orderDessert(Ice Cream, 2)
```

Figure 9.3   Messages and Methods: How Objects Interact

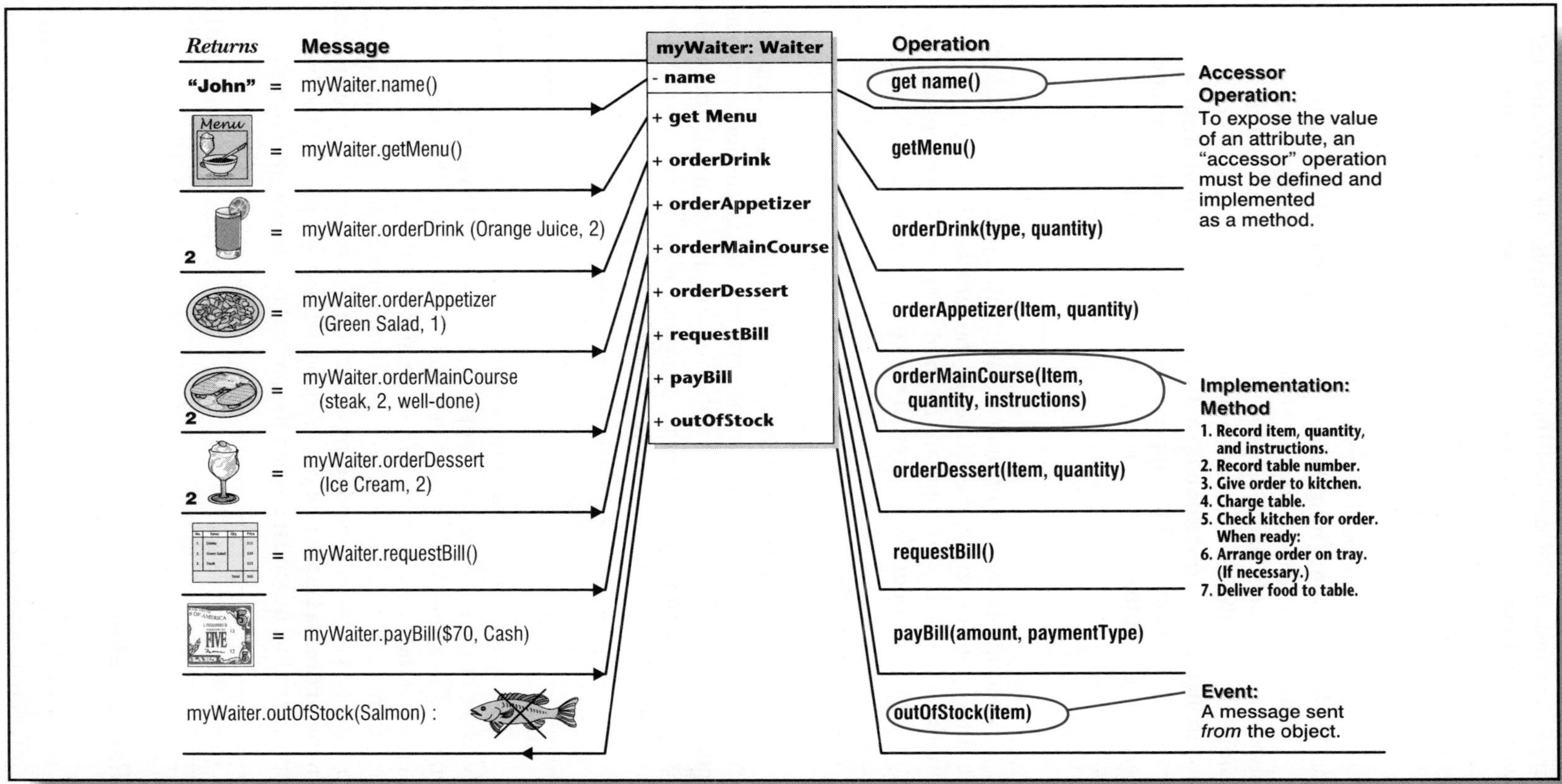

Returns	Message		Operation	Accessor Operation:
"**John**"	=	myWaiter.name()	get name()	To expose the value of an attribute, an "accessor" operation must be defined and implemented as a method.
[Menu image]	=	myWaiter.getMenu()	getMenu()	
[Drink image] 2	=	myWaiter.orderDrink (Orange Juice, 2)	orderDrink(type, quantity)	
[Salad image]	=	myWaiter.orderAppetizer (Green Salad, 1)	orderAppetizer(Item, quantity)	
[Steak image] 2	=	myWaiter.orderMainCourse (steak, 2, well-done)	orderMainCourse(Item, quantity, instructions)	Implementation: Method 1. Record item, quantity, and instructions. 2. Record table number. 3. Give order to kitchen. 4. Charge table. 5. Check kitchen for order. When ready: 6. Arrange order on tray. (If necessary.) 7. Deliver food to table.
[Ice cream image] 2	=	myWaiter.orderDessert (Ice Cream, 2)	orderDessert(Item, quantity)	
[Bill image]	=	myWaiter.requestBill()	requestBill()	
[Money image]	=	myWaiter.payBill($70, Cash)	payBill(amount, paymentType)	
[Fish image]		myWaiter.outOfStock(Salmon) :	outOfStock(item)	Event: A message sent *from* the object.

myWaiter: Waiter
- name
+ get Menu
+ orderDrink
+ orderAppetizer
+ orderMainCourse
+ orderDessert
+ requestBill
+ payBill
+ outOfStock

Messages are the means by which objects interact with each other and with the outside world. *What* an object does (or operations) is defined by the class; *how* the operations are carried out is decided by their implementation (or methods).

The message must abide by two constraints imposed by the operation: *type* of an argument and its ordinal ***position***. For example, the following message would not work (even though it might raise a few laughs in a comedy routine):

```
orderMainCourse(whisky, on the rocks, many)
```

"Whisky" is not on the menu as a main course and "many" is not an exact number. Besides, quantity must be the second argument, not the third.

Some operations, of course, do not need arguments. Since we assumed that the restaurant has only one kind of menu (or we assumed that the waiter knows that at dinnertimes only the dinner menu is offered to the customers, not the breakfast and lunch menus), the **getMenu** operation does not need an argument and the **getMenu** message does not need to supply a value. But we *do* display a pair of parentheses to leave no doubt that the lack of any argument is intentional:

```
getMenu()
```

A parameter can be *optional*, meaning that the sender of the message may leave it out. (In our example, the sender of the message is an actor, but it may as well be another object). If you compare the **orderAppetizer** message in Figure 9.3 with its counterpart operation, you will notice that the message has ignored the quantity:

```
orderAppetizer(Green Salad)
```

Take note, however, that the option to ignore the argument applies only to the message, *not* to the operation. In fact, an optional parameter needs a longer specification within an operation, not a shorter one. For example (depending on the language), the **orderAppetizer** operation must be specified with the following syntax for the quantity parameter to become optional:

```
orderAppetizer(appetizer, quantity=1)
```

This syntax means that if the sender of the message fails to specify a quantity, the receiver of the message must supply its own *default* value for the **quantity** parameter. The **appetizer** parameter, on the other hand, has no default value and the sender of the message must supply a valid value.

Conversely, the order of arguments in a message must exactly follow the order of parameters in the corresponding operation. For example, if the **quantity** parameter in the **orderMainCourse** operation is defined as optional, the message can forego a specific value, but must respect the ordinal position with a blank:

```
orderMainCourse(Steak, , well-done with french fries)
```

Return Value

Return value is the reply that a message may invoke from the receiving object after an operation is complete.

All operations in our example, except one, return something to the customer: **getMenu** returns the menu, **orderDrink** returns the drink(s), **requestBill** returns the bill, and so on. (See the entries in the Returns column.) Unlike parameters, return value is always a single item: An operation never returns more than one.

A *single* item, however, does not have to be a *simple* item: It can be a set, an array, an object, or another type of complex structure. (We will discuss complex data types in the section on design.) For example, the **orderDrink** operation can return one orange juice or many. In other words, the "single" item that it returns is a set of one or more orange juices. But if you need to have one orange juice and two apple juices, you must invoke the **orderDrink** operation twice, once for each type of drink.

An operation, of course, can return nothing. The **tip** operation of the **Waiter** class has no return value: The customer leaves a tip and might even leave before the waiter has a chance to express gratitude.

The Syntax

> The syntax of a message matches the operation's name and parameters, but a message and its corresponding operation are phrased differently.

The exact syntax for declaring operations and sending messages is language-dependent. Some elements, however, are common to most, if not all, object-oriented languages. We discussed the naming of **operations** in the previous chapter. Let us now look more closely at its syntax:

```
[Visibility] [Return Type] [Name](Param 1,  . . . , Param n)
```

Let us also provide an example before describing each element:

```
Public Currency payBill(amount, paymentType)
```

- *Visibility*, introduced in the last chapter, determines which entities outside the object have access to the operation. Visibility has four types: ❶ *public*, accessible to any entity; ❷ *private*, not accessible to any entity outside the object; ❸ *protected*, accessible only to the object itself and its descendants; and ❹ *friend* (or *package*), accessible only to objects within a component. In conceptual modeling (analysis), we are mainly concerned with public visibility.
- *Return type* defines what kind of a value is returned by the operation after its completion. In our example, the **payBill** operation returns the change, or a value of **currency** type. (A zero amount, meaning no change, is still a **currency** type value.) Return type is usually specified even if, as we said, it returns nothing. In the following example, the keyword **void** signifies that no value is returned:

```
Public void printSummaryReport(reportDate)
```

- *Name*, as we mention before, must be a verb or a verb phrase.
- **Parameters** are the information the object needs to carry out a certain operation. (Parameters are listed within a pair of parentheses and are separated by commas.) Whereas in conceptual modeling we usually rely on the name of the parameter to imply its data type, in logical modeling and implementation the data type of parameters *must* be specified explicitly. And, as we have mentioned, a

parameter *may* have a default value to be used in case the message fails to supply one. Fully specified, the previous example would appear with a data type (**Date**) and a default for its single parameter (**SystemDate**, or today's date):

```
Public void printSummaryReport(Date ReportDate = SystemDate)
```

The syntax for the message reflects the role of the sender, which is different from that of the receiver:

```
[Return Variable] = [Object Name].[Operation Name]
(Value 1, . . . ,Value n)
```

In the following example, the customer pays the bill and deposits the change in his or her wallet:

```
Wallet = myWaiter.payBill($70.00)
```

This message invokes the following operation of the **myWaiter** object (which now has a default value for the payment method):

```
Public Currency payBill(Currency Amount, PayMethod
paymentType = Cash)
```

In case the significance of the **Return Variable** element is not quite clear, let us look at Figure 9.4. As we have repeatedly mentioned, "data" never exists as an independent entity: It survives only within a container (or a variable). Even though it can be moved from one container to another, no container means no data.

When a message is sent to an object, the object has containers ready for the values transmitted by the message. And when the object returns a value to the sender, the sender must have a container ready. To sum:

> Any entity that expects a value must provide a container into which the value is deposited.

☞ Object-oriented languages provide a relief from "dot inflation" by allowing us to use **namespaces**. A namespace is a hierarchical naming scheme in which a name is evaluated within the space of the name above it. (See the "ID" topic under "Template Fields" in Chapter 7 for a more extensive discussion of namespaces.)

Of course, if the operation does not return a value, or the sender is not interested in the return value, the "return variable" can be disregarded. For example, the customer may leave the change on the table:

```
myWaiter.payBill($70)
```

The message must also identify the *recipient* object—very much like a letter that the postal service must deliver (and deliver back a receipt if there is a return value). Otherwise, the information system would fail to find the target. This task is accomplished by prefixing the name of the operation with the name of the object (the instance, to be more exact) and a dot.

This syntax is called the *dot notation*. If an object "owns" an object that owns another object—and so on—the number of dots will increase. For example, if our restaurant customer is a globe-trotter and is willing to travel across the world for a good dinner, the previous example could change to:

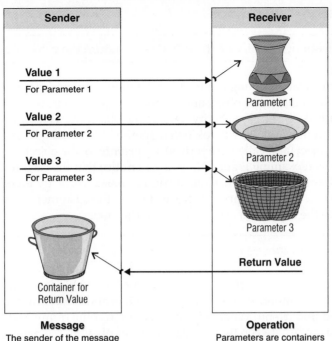

Figure 9.4
Variables Are Containers: No Container, No Data

A value is always stored in a container (or variable). Whenever an entity is to receive a value, it must have a container ready for it.

Sender

Value 1
For Parameter 1

Value 2
For Parameter 2

Value 3
For Parameter 3

Container for Return Value

Receiver

Parameter 1

Parameter 2

Parameter 3

Return Value

Message
The sender of the message must provide a container for the return value.

Operation
Parameters are containers (or variables) filled by the values from the message.

☞ Do not forget that we are referring to *object* names, not class names. Classes are not involved in dynamic modeling (or an actual information system as opposed to models of an information system).

```
US.NY.NewYork.SuperStakeHouse.myWaiter.payBill($70).
```

Methods

> A method is how an operation is implemented or actually carried out by the object responsible for the operation.

An operation identifies a goal or an action *in abstract*—as "what"—even when it receives concrete data through a message. *How* the action is carried out or the goal is reached is defined through a method. It is the method that implements the steps required to carry out a task. (See the Method column in Figure 9.3 for an example.)

Conceptual modeling does not need to delve deeply into how operations are implemented (though, as we shall see, sometimes it has to go a little deeper than the surface), but it is important to remember the distinction—for two reasons:

☞ As one would expect, the distinction between operation and method can easily become blurred. When sending a message to an object, are we calling (invoking) an operation or a method? As in the case of "class" and "object," this confusion is not usually harmful— except where keeping the distinction is crucial.

- The first reason may seem obvious but, nevertheless, needs emphasizing: Instances of two classes may have the same exact operation, but they can implement it differently even if the classes are related. For example, **Human** and **Horse** are both subclasses (descendants) of the **Mammal** class and have an operation called **Run**. But a horse would implement the **Run** operation very differently from a human. (This situation is called **polymorphism**, which we will discuss later in this book.)
- Instances of the same class may not carry out the same operation in the same way. A method does not follow a straight path from the invocation of the operation to the finish line of the action. A method may have to make decisions and branch out sideways depending not only on the values received through the message but also on the **state** of the object: A **run(fast)** message to a two-year old and a mature athlete would *not* be carried out the same way.

Accessor Operations

> Accessor operations are those that set or return the value of an attribute.

Information hiding is one of the defining characteristics of object-orientation: The inner workings of an object and its knowledge—that is, the data—are concealed from the outside world. If an entity outside the object wants to know something about the object, it must ask it by invoking an operation (or method). In other words, attributes of an object (also called properties) are *private* to the object.

If you examine Figure 9.3, you will notice that the class **Waiter** (represented by the object **myWaiter**) has one attribute, **name**, correctly identified (by the negative sign preceding it) as private. Nevertheless, the customer can send a legitimate message to the object and ask for the waiter's name:

```
myWaiter.name()
```

In response, the customer receives a return value from the object: "John."

Furthermore, if we examine the Operation column, we notice an operation named **get Menu**. Where did this operation come from? And why does the name—with a space between two words— not comply with the naming conventions that we previously described and emphasized?

The resulting confusion is justified, but rest assured that there is—literally—a method to this madness. Let us try to explain.

First, the examples in the previous chapter and this chapter must not lead us to believe that operations are necessarily all public and attributes (data) are unavoidably private. Our examples of operations have been public because we have been engaged in building a *conceptual* model, and during analysis we are not very interested in the inner workings of objects.

☞ By default, most modeling tools set the visibility of an attribute to "private" the moment that its name is entered. Some tools even prevent you from changing an attribute from private to public. The latter behavior, however, is a bad idea: Sometimes you *do* want to make an attribute public. Does it make sense to prevent a waiter from wearing a nametag (if the restaurant so desires)?

When we reach the point of implementation (or coding), we will find that many objects need numerous *private* operations and *private* data variables to satisfy just one public responsibility. (In our example in Figure 9.3, the waiter has to perform many functions before the main course reaches the customer. And the method that implements the operation does not even touch the complexity of the most important task—cooking dinner—that the waiter delegates to the kitchen—an aggregate object.)

But there is a very good reason why even data that is intended for *public* use is declared *private*. An operation must be implemented (i.e., coded) *intentionally* before it can do anything. In other words, if we fail to provide a *method* for the operation, invoking the operation will do nothing—neither good nor bad, just useless. On the other hand, an attribute is a *variable*, an *open* container that, unless it is protected, any entity with access to it can steal or change its contents. If this container is made public, the owning object would have no control over its contents.

As a result, a *convention* is used to guard against unauthorized or uncontrolled access to attributes: Define attributes as private, but for each attribute that is intended for public use, provide a single or a pair of **accessor operations**—*without*, however, listing them on the interface. (We will explain the "or.")

The syntax of an accessor operation is different from that of a normal operation. The name of an accessor operation has two parts: a **get** or a **set** keyword and, after a space, the name of the attribute (for instance, **get name** as in our example). The **get** operation returns the value of the attribute to the public, while its **set** counterpart changes the value. We then write **methods** to implement the **get** and **set** operations.

☞ Object-oriented languages and modeling tools (officially) recognize the difference between an accessor operation and a normal one. The exact treatment of the difference, however, is dependent on the language or the tool.

The outcome is that, by providing attributes with methods, we allow public access to private variables *and* protect those variables at the same time. Accessor methods, however, have other advantages as well.

- The object can analyze, change, edit, and format both incoming and outgoing values before they are stored in the attribute or released to the outside world. In our restaurant example, when the waiter's **name** method is invoked, the **myWaiter** returns "John," even though it is quite clear that it is not the waiter's full name: The method decided the first name is good enough for the interface of the object as a waiter. (Objects, as we mentioned in the previous chapter, may have multiple interfaces: The waiter might be an aspiring actor, with a stage name, in another interface.)
- Like normal operations, accessor operations can have parameters. For example, the **get length** property of an object might have a parameter through which you can decide the unit of the return value: inches, centimeters, or millimeters.
- We do not have to provide both **get** and **set** methods for an attribute. By dropping the **set** we make the property "read-only," which means no outside entity can change it: A waiter may give you his or her name, but would most certainly *not* allow you to change it. Or we can drop the **get** and make the property "write-only." Think of an object that asks for your password: You would not want the object to share your password with any other entity. (Hence our statement that an attribute can have a single *or* a pair of accessor operations.)

From the viewpoint of the clients (i.e., actors and outside objects), accessor operations appear different from normal operations, as the following example illustrates. (**placeBorn** is a variable to hold the return value.)

☞ Often, accessor operations are called **_properties_** by languages and modeling tools. It is much easier to use "get property" and "set property" instead of "get accessor operation" and "set accessor operation."

```
placeBorn = myPatient.placeOfBirth
myPatient.placeOfBirth = "USA"
```

The client does not have to use the **get** and **set** keywords (and does not even see them). Both operations appear as one and under one name—that of the attribute. To assign a value to an attribute, an equal sign is used instead of parentheses. (Parentheses are still used for arguments, if there are any. For example: **myBalance = myBankAccount.Balance(Euro)** if you want to know your bank account balance in euros instead of dollars.)

Events

> Events are actions by one object that interrupts the existing condition of one or more other objects.

Events have a crucial role in the operation of both modern information technology and the information systems that rely on them: Like the alarm of a clock, an event is what takes place when you press a key, click a button, or insert your card into an ATM. Or, when you request something from the Internet, your browser sends a request to the Web and redirects its attention to you, until an event tells it that the requested material has arrived.

Defining and understanding events, however, can be frustrating and confusing because the term applies to concepts that overlap but are slightly different.

[Booch 1999, 278–281]

Although the differences might be slight, they cannot be overlooked since each specific definition of "event" plays a distinct role. We will revisit events, but at this point a brief review is necessary as we will be working with one of the roles in this chapter. The following summary is not exhaustive but can serve as an introduction.

Call Events

Call events result from invocation of an operation.

As invocation, an event is the other side of the coin to the **message**: The sender, which may be an actor or an object, dispatches a message to an object who views the message as a *trigger* to carry out an operation. Let us clarify the point by elaborating, yet again, on our restaurant example.

Figure 9.3 represents a use case, **Have Dinner**, as a flow of messages and operations within time (oversimplified perhaps, but correct in essentials). The customer orders drinks first, then appetizers, then the main course until, finally, he or she asks for the bill and pays. From the **Waiter** object's point of view, however, the situation is not exactly the same. A waiter usually waits on more than one table and each table—even if customers obediently follow our sequence of events—may be in a different stage of having dinner: one is asking for the bill while two are requesting the menu and a fourth wants to order the main course. Between the *calls*—the more common word for "invocation"—the waiter object is "*idle*" and has no idea what the next call will be. Even though the waiter has "methods" to handle all messages from customers, when a message *does* arrive it is an "occurrence"—an event, in other words.

A call event is usually **synchronous**, which means that the message and the operation are in-sync or *in-phase*: Control is transferred from the sender of the message to the receiver and is not handed back to the **caller** (the sender) until the operation is finished. When you enter your password in an ATM, you cannot take any further action (and nobody else can use the ATM) until the machine returns and accepts or rejects your password.

Call events closely resemble a phone call (Figure 9.5): The caller must wait for the completion of response (and the subsequent conversation) before regaining the ability to engage in another task.

This is very interesting theoretically, but what is the practical benefit of understanding such a definition of event? By changing the viewpoint from the message sender to the receiver—who sees the message as an "occurrence"—you can make appropriate design decisions. A *synchronous* event ties up both the sender of the message and the receiver *until* the operation is complete. This type of event is the *simplest* form and usually the *fastest* method of communication between objects, but it has serious shortcomings in complex situations:

- The demand on the system and its components is high, but *resources are wasted* because some objects have to sit idle while others are overwhelmed: One waiter might be serving many customers, while others might be looking over empty tables or waiting on customers who are taking their time.
- Actions occur sequentially where they must take place, more or less, *simultaneously*: Orders for the main course do not arrive together and your companions are embarrassed to begin eating their dinners before yours is before you.
- Actions take place *outside the normal course of events*: You want to have your coffee *with* the main course but, regardless, it arrives early and gets cold before your meal arrives.
- Message senders and receivers are *not known to each other* (or, in a more technical term, do not have a "reference" to each other): You hail somebody who is

Figure 9.5
Events: Actions that Interrupt Existing Conditions

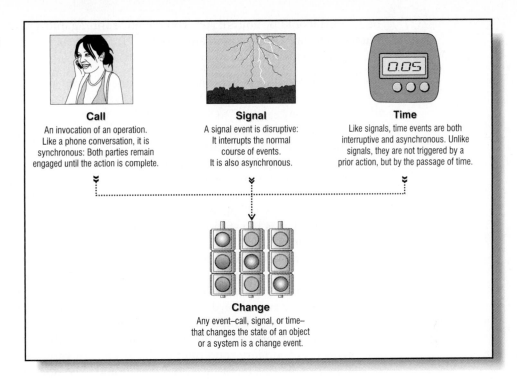

Call
An invocation of an operation. Like a phone conversation, it is synchronous: Both parties remain engaged until the action is complete.

Signal
A signal event is disruptive: It interrupts the normal course of events. It is also asynchronous.

Time
Like signals, time events are both interruptive and asynchronous. Unlike signals, they are not triggered by a prior action, but by the passage of time.

Change
Any event–call, signal, or time– that changes the state of an object or a system is a change event.

obviously a waiter and ask for a glass of water but he informs you that he is not *your* waiter, he is busy otherwise, and you have to wait for the waiter who is assigned to your table.

- *Errors* (exceptions) occur that must be handled immediately or an operation cannot go on: Your food is of the wrong kind, is undercooked, or is overcooked; you want to return it but the waiter is nowhere to be seen.

In such situations, you need another way of arranging communication between objects: asynchronous events.

Signal Events

> Signal events disrupt the normal flow of actions.

This kind of event is truly *interruptive*: You are in a train station because you commute to work. As you do every day, you are reading a book until your 5:45 PM train home enters the station. At 5:30 the public announcement system comes to life and informs everybody at the station that, for some reason, trains to your destination are not running. You are dismayed by this interruption but are not defeated because you have an emergency plan: first call home to say that you will be late and then leave the station and take a bus.

What you have just done is that you have handled an event as an *interruption*—an occurrence that *disrupts* a normal course of actions. This is not to say that all interruptive events have to be unwanted: You want the alarm clock to go off in the morning and interrupt your sleep (otherwise you would be late for work); you want the telephone to ring for an important call (otherwise you might lose the job that you had hoped would be yours); you would enjoy running into a person whom you have missed (and say "What a pleasant surprise!").

Signal events have the following traits in common:

- They are usually **asynchronous**; that is, they are *out-of-phase* with the recipient of the event: The action that triggers the event is outside the space and/or time frame of the "**catcher**" (a synonym for the "recipient"). The alarm is set long before it goes off. (What is more, the alarm may be set by somebody who is not among those whom the alarm awakens.)
- The object that *raises* the event (and sends the event message) also defines the parameters of the message and their order, while those who *receive* the event must comply with the sender's parameter sequence—the **reverse** of what happens with "call" events. When the news of the train cancellation is announced, it is the station that decides what to make public, when, and in what order.
- Signal events are usually **anonymous**; that is, they are not dispatched to a specific object, but are broadcasted to any object that qualifies (or "subscribes") to receive it and is in a position to catch it. The announcement about the train cancellation can be heard by everybody in the station but is "caught" only by passengers whose train schedule is affected (i.e., those who qualify for the event) *and* are present in the station (meaning that they can receive it).
- Signal events do *not*—and cannot—have a **return value**. This is a direct result of the fact that the message is anonymous and is *broadcasted*—unlike a call event that is targeted at a specific object. If your train is canceled, you may go to the ticket counter and get a refund, but you and other disappointed passengers cannot return anything in direct reply to the announcement, not even by shouting your displeasure. (However, in certain situations, you may be able to return something by manipulating the values of parameters contained in the event—just like any other message.)

How do objects interact through signal events? First have a look at the syntax. The class whose instances *send* the event message must also define it:

```
[Visibility] Event [Name](Parameter1 . . . ParameterN)
```

For example:

```
Public Event trainIsCanceled(trainIdentifier,
cancellationReason, suggestions)
```

☞ Like normal operations, you may have private, protected, or friend events. (Private events, however, are less common.) But in either case, conceptual modeling favors public visibility.

When a train is actually canceled, the object that *raises* the event replaces the parameters with actual values (or data), and "*throws*" (sends or broadcasts) the event message.

As we pointed out, from the viewpoint of the sender this type of event is *anonymous*; therefore, the sender does not prefix it with an object identifier. On the other hand, the receiver (the catcher) of the event must know the identity of the sender to evaluate its own course of action. To do this, the receiver must first *subscribe* to the sender, or *listen* to it, *intentionally*. (Both terms, "subscriber" and "listener," are widely used in the industry to identify the receiver of an interruptive event.) Then the receiver object must implement an **event-handler** method to take action *if* and *when* the event message is received. For example, in your "code" as a commuter object, you might have an event-handler such as the following:

```
myTrainStation_trainIsCanceled(trainIdentifier,
cancellationReason, suggestions)
If trainIdentifier is the same as myTrain
  1. Call home to report delay.
  2. Optional: get refund for the ticket.
  2. Take bus.
```

As you may have noticed, even though the event message provides the receiver with a value for the **suggestions** parameter, your event-handler ignores it, while the sender *must* supply the value. (The exact syntax of event messages and event-handlers, such as the underscore between the name of the object and the name of the event, are language-dependent.)

Time Events

Time events are triggered by the passage of time.

A time event signals the passage of time. As this description implies, a time event is really a signal event: It is asynchronous, meaning that whatever action has set the time in motion is not in sync (or in-phase) with the recipient (or the "catcher") of the event. It is also anonymous: It happens to everybody and everything.

But there is one important difference: A time event is not triggered by—and is not dependent on—any prior action. An alarm clock goes off because somebody has set it (and the setting can be changed or undone before the alarm sounds). But time moves on relentlessly. It cannot be stopped or restarted by any human agency. Its pace cannot be speeded up or slowed down for anybody: When your birthday arrives, you are a year older. Period.

Change Events

A change event is any kind of event that changes the state of one or more objects.

Change events are *significant* events. Of course, any occurrence that is significant is called an "event"—both in the real world and in object-oriented theory. The difference lies in the interpretation of "significant."

In dynamic modeling, a "significant" occurrence is one that changes the **state** of the system by changing the state of one or more of its objects. The state of an object is the *condition* of an object from a specific viewpoint. Your birthday is an "event" because it changes your state from the viewpoint of *age*: On your birthday, you are exactly one year older. (We will come back to "state" later in the "Statechart Diagrams" section.)

A **change event** is *not* a fourth *kind* of event after call, signal, and time events. In fact, a "significant" event can be any of these: Whether you receive money through you regular paycheck (call or invocation) or by winning the lottery (interruption), the state of your cash balance is changed.

☞ Event handlers clearly illustrate the difference between **operations** and **methods**: In an event-handler, the operation is defined by the sender of the message, while it is the receiver who must implement the method.

☞ A good description of event-handlers is: "**Expect the unexpected**!"

☞ In practice, a time event is handled the same way as a signal event. Thus you may consider the difference, as important as it is, as more academic than practical.

☞ As we mentioned, choosing the right event is more a problem for design than for analysis. However, one kind of dynamic modeling—**statechart diagrams**—requires an understanding of **change events** and, without a correct understanding of events in general, we risk a misunderstanding that would be difficult to unlearn later on. Having said this, remember *one important point*: Frequently, the term "event" is used in a very ordinary sense—an occurrence or something that happens.

UML offers four diagrams to model the dynamism of the system. The first, the **sequence diagram**, emphasizes the order of interactions in time. The second, the **collaboration diagram**, focuses on how the objects are organized and what set of messages they must exchange to satisfy a certain behavior. The third, the **statechart diagram**, traces the results of interactions on the state of objects belonging to a specific class. And the fourth, the **activity diagram** (introduced under behavioral modeling), concentrates on the logical flow of activities.

Dynamic diagrams have various levels of affinity with the structure of the system and its behavior. The collaboration diagram is closest to structural modeling, while the activity diagram represents actions in their most abstract form.

Sequence Diagram

> A sequence diagram represents the interaction between objects, or between actors and objects ordered in time.

☞ One reason for new additions is to illustrate collaboration among objects. But the primary reason is that any attempt at modeling is often a process of discovery as well. In this instance, we have already written a **Have Dinner** use case. If our use case is well-defined, creating a sequence diagram that merely repeats the behavioral model would gain us little. (A use case itself is an ordered sequence of interactions between actors and the system.) The main rationale for dynamic modeling is that by starting from behavioral and structural models we can fine-tune both. In this example, we discover that the waiter's behavior must be supported by objects deeper within the **system space**.

☞ See Chapter 5 for a full discussion on spaces and domains.

Figure 9.3 is really a sequence diagram, somehow simplified but, at the same time, a little embellished. Therefore, if we have been able to clarify concepts that the illustration presents—messages, methods, parameters, return values, timeline—you would have no difficulty in understanding sequence diagrams.

The Building Blocks

> A sequence diagram is composed of a timeline, objects that interact across this timeline, and the messages that they exchange.

To illustrate the basic building blocks of a sequence diagram, let us resort to the same use case that Figure 9.3 illustrates: **Have Dinner**. (Its familiarity and simplicity should prepare us to grasp more complicated concepts later on.)

In Figure 9.6, we meet the same entities as before: a **Customer** and a **Waiter**. But we have added instances of three other classes as well—**Kitchen**, **Bar**, and **Cashier**—to provide a view of interactions that take place *inside* the system.

The individual elements of the diagram are explained in Table 9.2. In the following text we concentrate on the concepts that underlie a sequence diagram.

• *Time & Space Axes.* Every sequence diagram has two axes. The vertical axis is the **timeline**, or a chronology of events. The horizontal axis identifies the *space* and the actions that take place within the space. Movement on the timeline axis is strictly one way. (You cannot go back in time.) On the space axis, however, the flow of action can go either way. (The arrows identifying the axes in the example are strictly for illustration. They are not explicitly used in sequence diagrams.)

The space may present only the *system* (or *solution*) space or both the system *and* the *problem* space. (If you have reason to model *only* the interaction among actors, then the space can be exclusively problem space.) One primary advantage of the sequence diagram is that it allows us to gradually and smoothly move from "problem domain" into "system domain" by discovering actions and objects that enable the system to support its behavior and properties.

Figure 9.6 Have Dinner Sequence Diagram

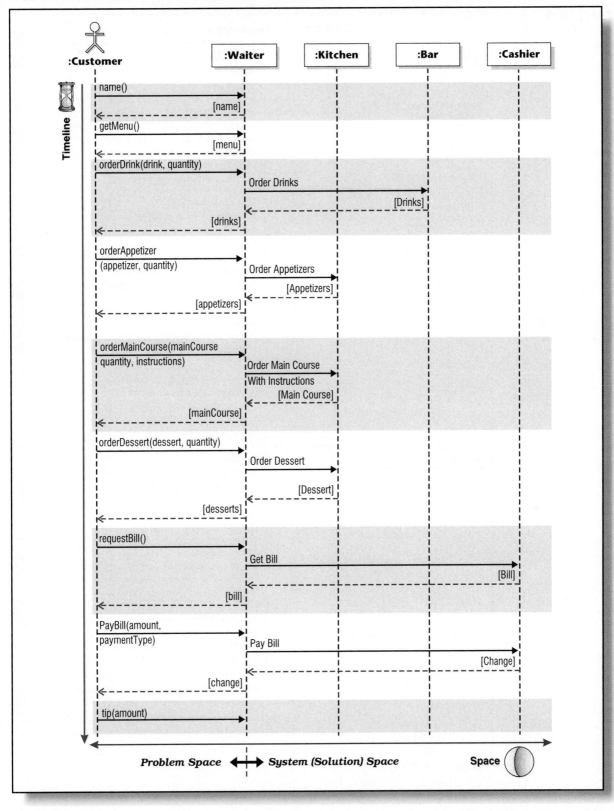

We have identified each interaction with a band of gray or white. Neither the bands nor the colors, however, are part of the sequence diagram.

The colon before the name of the entity identifies it as an object, or an instance of the class.

Table 9.2

Elements of a
Sequence Diagram.

Elements of a Sequence Diagram	
SYMBOL	DESCRIPTION
[Instance Name] **:Actor Name**	**Actor Instance.** The instance may be identified by placing a colon before the role name (for example, **:Customer**) or may be a fully qualified instance name (for example, **aCustomer:Customer**). If the diagram needs more than one instance of the *same* role, then all labels must be fully qualified (for example, **firstCustomer:Customer** and **secondCustomer:Customer**).
[Instance Name] **:Class Name**	**Class Instance.** Naming rules for an object are the same as for the actor instance. Entities inside the **system space** *must* be presented as objects, while entities outside (those in the **problem space**) *must* be shown as actors. The distinction does *not* result from whether an entity is real or virtual.
	Timeline. A dashed line that starts with the instance of an actor or an object and continues vertically to the bottom of the diagram. All events that relate to the instance start or end with this timeline or are placed on top of it. A timeline may **fork** and *merge* (with itself) if a conditional action is required. (See the entry in this table on "Message & Timeline Forking.")
Message ⟶	**Synchronous Message.** A synchronous message is represented by a label (see below) and a solid-head arrow that starts with the sender and ends with the receiver. (See "Call Events" in the "Events" section in this chapter for a description of synchronous events.)
Message(Argument 1, Argument 2, ... Argument n)	**Message Label.** As we saw in the "Messages" section, arguments in a message carry *actual* values—not variables—but in a sequence diagram they are usually presented with variable names, *unless* the value makes a difference in the *kind* of action taken by the message recipient. (See the entry in this table on "Message & Timeline Forking.") Labels need not be "official," especially if ❶ the final format of the operation is not known or ❷ the label must be easy to read: **Request menu** is as valid a label as **getMenu()**. Nor is the message label necessarily qualified by the instance name of the recipient as the arrows and timelines make the target clear.

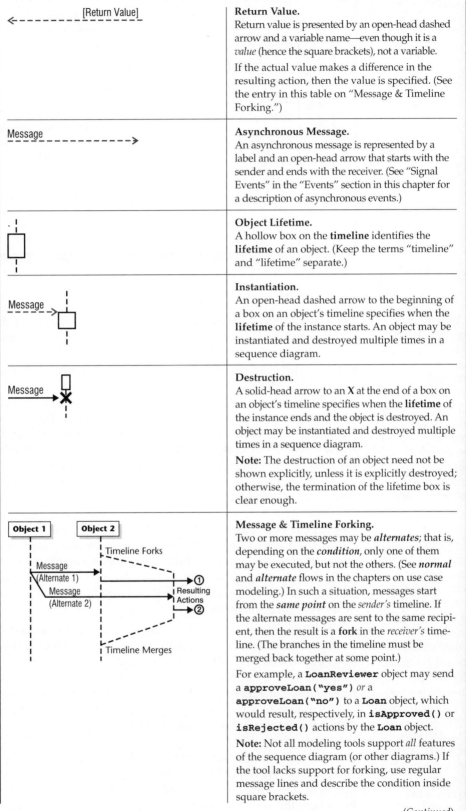 ← - - - - - [Return Value]	**Return Value.** Return value is presented by an open-head dashed arrow and a variable name—even though it is a *value* (hence the square brackets), not a variable. If the actual value makes a difference in the resulting action, then the value is specified. (See the entry in this table on "Message & Timeline Forking.")
Message - - - - - - - - - ->	**Asynchronous Message.** An asynchronous message is represented by a label and an open-head arrow that starts with the sender and ends with the receiver. (See "Signal Events" in the "Events" section in this chapter for a description of asynchronous events.)
	Object Lifetime. A hollow box on the **timeline** identifies the **lifetime** of an object. (Keep the terms "timeline" and "lifetime" separate.)
Message	**Instantiation.** An open-head dashed arrow to the beginning of a box on an object's timeline specifies when the **lifetime** of the instance starts. An object may be instantiated and destroyed multiple times in a sequence diagram.
Message	**Destruction.** A solid-head arrow to an **X** at the end of a box on an object's timeline specifies when the **lifetime** of the instance ends and the object is destroyed. An object may be instantiated and destroyed multiple times in a sequence diagram. **Note:** The destruction of an object need not be shown explicitly, unless it is explicitly destroyed; otherwise, the termination of the lifetime box is clear enough.
Object 1 **Object 2** Timeline Forks Message (Alternate 1) Message (Alternate 2) Resulting Actions Timeline Merges	**Message & Timeline Forking.** Two or more messages may be *alternates*; that is, depending on the *condition*, only one of them may be executed, but not the others. (See *normal* and *alternate* flows in the chapters on use case modeling.) In such a situation, messages start from the *same point* on the *sender's* timeline. If the alternate messages are sent to the same recipient, then the result is a **fork** in the *receiver's* timeline. (The branches in the timeline must be merged back together at some point.) For example, a **LoanReviewer** object may send a **approveLoan("yes")** *or* a **approveLoan("no")** to a **Loan** object, which would result, respectively, in **isApproved()** or **isRejected()** actions by the **Loan** object. **Note:** Not all modeling tools support *all* features of the sequence diagram (or other diagrams.) If the tool lacks support for forking, use regular message lines and describe the condition inside square brackets.

(Continued)

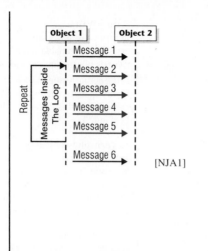

Message to Self & Looping.
Objects may send message to themselves. Although such a message may serve any purpose, it may be used for *looping*.

Looping is necessary if a set of messages are to be repeated until a certain condition is satisfied. (The syntax is usually `Repeat until [condition is true]` or `While [condition is true] repeat`.

(Even though it may appear that in looping the timeline is going backward, each repetition actually happens *after* the previous one.)

Note: A sequence diagram is not the best vehicle for representing loops. If the purpose of the model is more the depiction of a logical flow and less the presentation of interactions, then use an **activity diagram**.

☞ We emphasized before (see Chapter 7) that actors are not the same as classes within information system. But, as we suggested, they share many traits with classes: generalization, specialization, and—what is relevant here—instantiation.

☞ Sequence diagrams do not officially identify "bands" and, in fact, sometimes it is not possible to identify a "reasonably" complete transaction. (Though if you cannot find a complete transaction, you must clarify the reason to yourself. A *good* reason is often the level of detail, which usually happens when one is creating blueprints in the

• *Instances & Timelines.*   Within the axes, the sequence diagram is composed of *columns* and *rows*. Each column identifies an *instance* of an actor or a class. Hence the column headings are composed of a colon followed by the name of the class (or role) to which the instance belongs: `:Customer` instead of just `Customer`, or `:Waiter` instead of just `Waiter`. If more than one instance of the same class (or actor) participates in a sequence diagram, then you have to specify the object name as well—for example `primaryCare:Doctor` and `eyeSurgeon:Doctor`.

What sets an actor instance apart from an object instance is *not* whether one is real (a person, for example) and the other is virtual, but whether the entity is outside the *system space* or inside it. An entity in the *problem space* (i.e., outside the system space) is always an actor, even though it might be another component or subsystem. And if we are modeling an entire hospital as a system—as opposed to the information system *within* the hospital—then a `Patient` becomes an actor, but each `Registration Clerk` or `Doctor` turns into an object.

In a sequence diagram, instances of actors and classes move through time. For each instance, this movement through time is identified by a **timeline** (shown as a vertical dashed line that extends from the instance to the bottom of the diagram). Objects are born (instantiated), live (send and receive message), and die (are destroyed) on the timeline.

• *Interactions & Messages.*   As the model of a *space-time matrix*, a sequence diagram is also composed of horizontal rows and bands. Each *row* usually represents *one action* in time: a message, its direction (by an arrow), its sender, and its recipient. Each band is usually composed of a (reasonably) complete *interaction* (or *transaction*): one message (at least) and perhaps a return value (if any.)

Messages in a sequence diagram do not have to follow the formal syntax of **Message (Parameters)** that we previously described. Sometimes we are just discovering how the objects interact and *cannot* specify the operation; at other times the clarity and the audience of the model requires that the description of the model be informal. (We have illustrated both approaches in Figure 9.6. Where the interaction is between the customer and the waiter, we have followed the formal syntax; but where the waiter exchanges messages with objects inside the system space, we

implementation phase.) But any modeling tool is *your* tool: As long as you make it more understandable— not more difficult to understand—you should feel free to adjust the tool. (We did just this in the sequence diagram for **Have Dinner**.)

have used a phrasing that is looser and less formal.) As always with modeling, it is the ***purpose*** of the model that should decide which variation of the form you must use. If the purpose is to convey a general idea of the interaction, then strict adherence to a formal syntax might become counterproductive. If, on the other hand, the model is to serve as a blueprint for defining classes or implementation, then following strict rules is a necessity.

• *Scope.* The scope of a sequence diagram is completely dependent on the task at hand. No rule obligates you to limit the scope of your sequence diagram to a use case: The scope can be much smaller (even one complicated transaction), or much larger (a full system). But since a sheet of paper, or the screen of a computer monitor, would inevitably run out of space at some point, one has to make a compromise between the scope and the detail. (An infinite space for any diagram would not be helpful anyway.)

One common device for compromise is to roll up a set of messages into one message and later, if necessary, create a separate sequence diagram for that set. For example, verifying a credit card purchase usually comprises a set of messages and return values. (See Figure 9.7.) But if the verification detail is not required within the context of a certain sequence diagram, then the first four steps can be collapsed into one message: "Verify purchase." Such a reduction would save space on any sequence diagram.

Object Lifetime

> The lifetime of an object specifies when it is instantiated, how long it exists, and when it is destroyed.

Figure 9.7   Summarizing Transactions in Sequence Diagrams

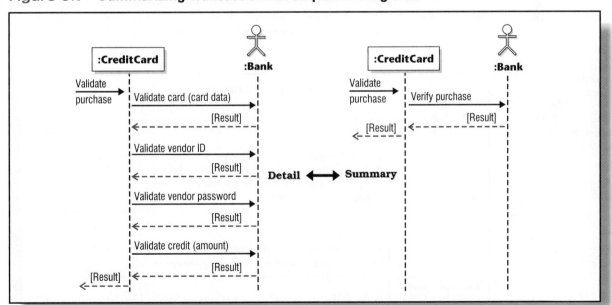

The "collapsed" section can be opened up with another sequence diagram.

In the sequence diagram for **Have Dinner** (Figure 9.6) we assumed that all objects exist from the beginning of the diagram to its end. In most scenarios, that is not the case: Objects have a lifetime that is a shorter than the timeline of the sequence diagram.

To explain lifetime and its significance, and to illustrate other building blocks of the sequence diagram, let us—at long last—return to the case history of Walden Hospital. Table 9.3 lists the normal and alternate flows of—by now—the familiar use case of **Make Appointment**.

Figure 9.8 shows the sequence diagram for the use case. We have added a new space to the diagram: the *public* space. The purpose is to show what drives the actions taken by the appointment clerk. **Appointment Clerk** is an actor to the information system, while **Patient** is an actor to the *hospital* system. (As we pointed out in discussing use case modeling, patients are *not* actors to the information system because they do not interact directly.)

Now let us compare the **Make Appointment** scenario as presented by the use case and as modeled by the sequence diagram. (Steps in the use case are identified by the round numbers on the sequence diagram.)

❶ *Appointment clerk verifies that the needed medical service is provided by the hospital.* Triggered by a call from the patient, the appointment clerk must verify that the medical service requested by the patient is offered by the hospital. (Most likely, the clerk already knows hospital services by heart, but we cannot count on the knowledge as the clerk might be new to the job.)

To verify the service, the clerk needs a list. What object can provide such a list?

As we have emphasized repeatedly, data always needs a *container*—a vehicle, if you will—and cannot float freely. All languages have one or more general-purpose *collection* objects to retrieve data from the database and pass it back and forth among objects who request the data. Such a vehicle is variously called a *result set*, a *dataset*, a *recordset*, a *data collection*, or simply a *list*, but whatever the name, the concept is the same.

In this case, the application creates an instance of the **Dataset** class to retrieve a list of medical services from the database. Since this object is general purpose, the instance's name is fully qualified: **services:Dataset**.

☞ The use case specifies **Referral Source** as the source of the trigger.

Referral Source is a generalization of multiple actors, *including* **Patient**. We have chosen to use this specialized actor for the sequence diagram.

Table 9.3
Normal & Alternate Flows of Walden Hospital's **Make Appointment** Use Case.

Make Appointment	
Partial Listing	
Normal Flow:	1. Appointment clerk verifies that the needed medical service is provided by the hospital. 2. Appointment clerk records patient's personal and contact data. 3. Appointment clerk records information about the referral source. 4. Appointment clerk consults hospital's schedule to find a free slot for the required medical service. 5. Appointment clerk verifies that the patient is available for the appointment. → Loop 1: **Repeat** steps 4–5 until hospital's schedule matches patient's availability. 6. Appointment clerk makes the appointment. → Loop 2: **Repeat** steps 4–6 for each appointment.
Alternate Flow/ Exceptions:	**2.a** Patient is not on file. Create new patient. (Extend: 141 – Create Patient.)

Figure 9.8 Make Appointment: Sequence Diagram

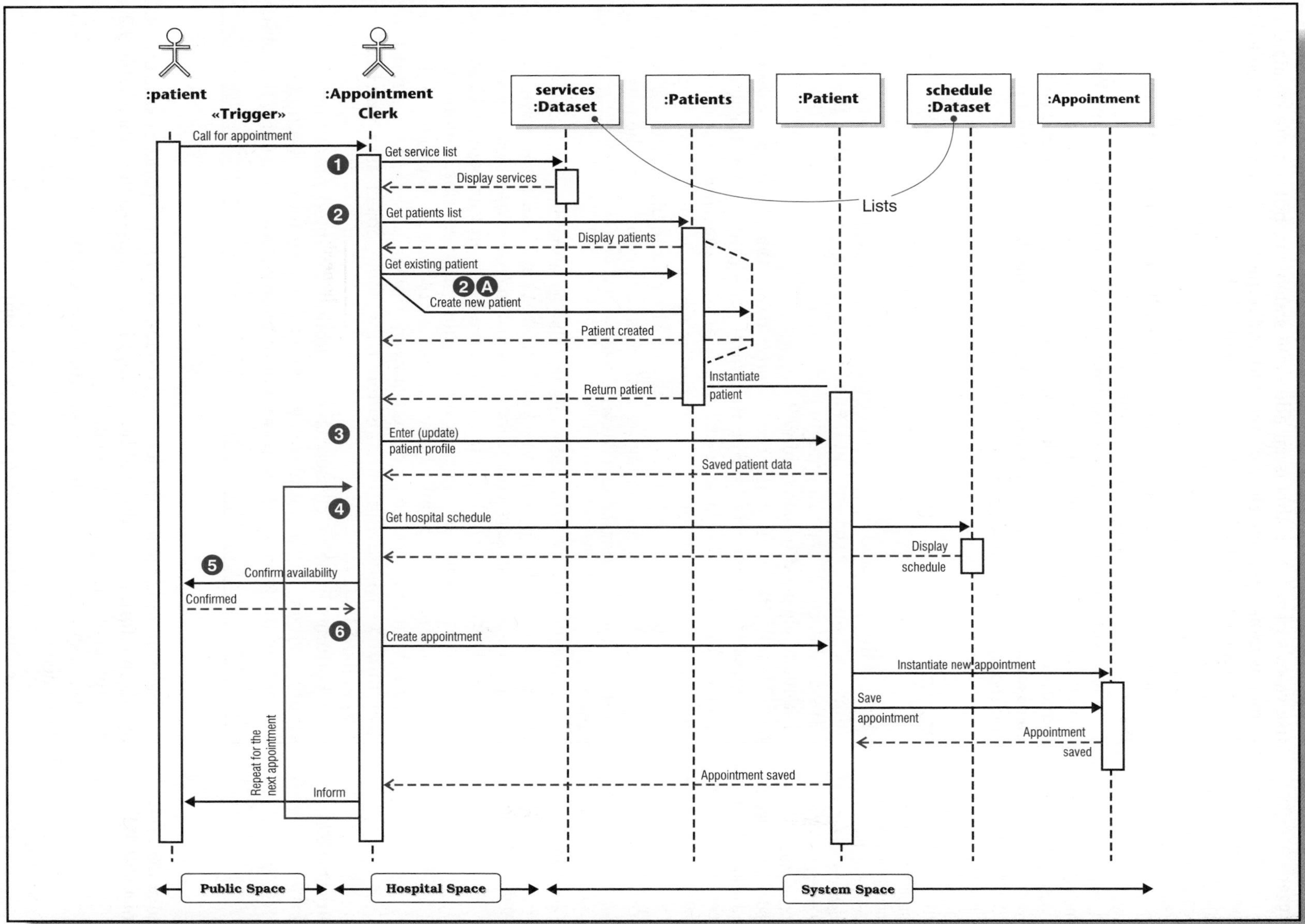

☞ The label **«Trigger»** above the first message from the patient to the appointment clerk is a called a **stereotype**. Stereotyping is the UML mechanism that allows us to extend UML elements by **typecasting** them. In this case, the stereotype specifies that the message is not just any message, but the trigger that starts the use case. The special characters around the stereotype names are called *guillemets*. (Since *guillemets* cannot be found on most keyboards, you may use a pair of angled brackets on each side of the stereotype name: **«Trigger»**, for example.)

☞ For more on collection objects, see the previous chapter.

[Arrington 2001, 88–89]

[Muller 1997, 114], [Strum 1999, 104]

❷ *Appointment clerk records patient's personal and contact data.* As far as the use case is concerned, this is an adequate statement, but a more detailed model demands more answers. How do we find and retrieve patient information to update it? And, come to think of it, how can we ensure that the patient exists on hospital files? If the patient is *not* on file, as the alternate step 2.a cautions, how do we create it?

First, the actor must request a *list* of patients by providing a search criteria, such as first and/or last name, partial or complete. It seems that another instance of the **Dataset** class would satisfy the requirement.

However, we need more than a collection of *data* about the patient: We require an object that manages individual instances of the **Patient** class. Therefore, the request of the appointment clerk creates an instance of a *customized* collection class, **Patients** (not to be mistaken with **Patient**, singular). This object provides a list and more, as we shall see next.

Patient & Patients

Both in this book and in the world outside its covers, you will come across classes that are paired: **Patient** and **Patients**, **Seat** and **Seats**, **Student** and **Students**, etc. This pairing might prove confusing, but is widely done and there is a relatively good reason behind it.

Usually, the class with the *singular* name (**Patient**, for example) is a *business* ("entity") class, while the *plural* class (**Patients**, for instance) is a *control* or *life cycle* class. (**Patient** is also a *collection* class that we introduced in the last chapter.) An "entity" object is usually *persistent*, meaning that its "state" is saved to the database. The plural "life cycle" object, on the other hand, is used for managing instances of the class with the singular name and is not *usually* persisted. (We will discuss class types in the design section of the text.)

Now, the names: Why not name the classes something quite distinct so that there would be less confusion—**PatientCollection** for example? Actually, there is no law that says you cannot. It is just that developers often prefer to type *less*, so **Patients** would be used more readily than **PatientCollection** or **ColPatient**. You can use your own naming conventions, as long as you can *consistently* show the affinity between the pair of classes. (If you think this is confusing, wait until you come across *case-sensitive* languages where a **Patient**—capitalized—would not be considered the same object as a **patient**—not capitalized.)

Fortunately, some classes have commonly accepted plural names that are more distinct than just a plural: **MedicalHistory** for a collection of medical records or treatments, **FirstClass** or **EconomyClass** for a collection of seats, and so on.

By examining the list, the actor can decide whether the patient exists or not. This results in a **fork** (or conditional branching) in the message flow. (See Table 9.2 for a description of forking and its symbol.)

What should be done if the patient does not exist? The alternate step 2.a specifies the remedy:

• Patient is not on file. Create new patient.

The actor notifies the **Patients** (plural) object that a new patient must be added to the file. (The message fork results in branching of the timeline for the **Patients** object.) In response, **:Patients** adds the new patient to the information system's database and notifies the actor of the result.

If the patient already exists, the actor simply asks for more information about the patient. This request seemingly does not elicit a response from the system but, in fact, it does: When a new patient is successfully created, it is incorporated in the **Patients** object, and when the timelines for this object merge back into a single flow, a requested instance of **Patient** (singular) is generated—regardless of whether it was a "new" patient previously or not.

The collection **Patients** object then returns the instance of **Patient** to the actor. Since the collection object is no longer needed, it is destroyed. (We will *not* enter into the mechanism by which objects are instantiated and destroyed. That remains for design.)

❸ *Appointment clerk records information about the referral source.* What happened to the original requirement of step 2—recording of patient's personal and contact data? The sequence diagram collapses steps 2 and 3 into one: "Enter or update patient profile." Since it is the **Patient** object's responsibility to save its own state, it carries out a method to do so and informs the actor of the results.

❹ *Appointment clerk consults hospital's schedule to find a free slot for the required medical service.* Here, again, the actor merely needs a list of free slots for a certain medical service. Therefore, a generic collection object, **Schedule:Datasetet**, is instantiated. (Unlike the **Patients** collection object in step 2, a customized collection object is not needed by this step.)

❺ *Appointment clerk verifies that the patient is available for the appointment.* The verification happens outside the scope of the *hospital* system, in what we have called the *public* space. Therefore, it puts no *direct* demands on the information system.

❻ *Appointment clerk makes the appointment.* In the previous chapter, we identified **Appointment** as a class that collaborates with **Patient**. Here we see how the collaboration works: The request for a new appointment is passed to the **Patient** object, which delegates the task to a new instance of **Appointment**.

In the use case, we also have two *loops* (actions that repeat until a certain condition is met), one within another. The diagram ignores one (regarding confirmation of the patient's availability). The second one, making multiple appointments for the same patient, is illustrated by a message that the actor sends to *itself*. (Entities in sequence diagrams can send messages to themselves—including, but not limited to, loops.)

Collaboration Diagram

> A collaboration diagram is a dynamic diagram that focuses on the organization of objects that must cooperate, by exchanging messages, to satisfy a certain behavior.

Sequence and collaboration diagrams are both *interactive* diagrams, meaning that they both depict interactions between actors or objects or among objects. But while sequence diagrams emphasize the *flow* of interaction through time, collaboration diagrams concentrate on the **organization** and the structure of objects that exchange messages.

☞ Sequence diagrams are not very good at modeling loops and conditional messages. If loops and conditional statements overwhelm the clarity of the diagram, it is better to collapse them into simple messages (as we illustrated in Figure 9.7) and compensate by providing additional sequence or **activity diagrams**. (Activity diagrams excel at modeling complicated logical flows.)

Nevertheless, both diagrams are very close and differ only on the point of emphasis. (In fact, good modeling tools can generate a collaboration diagram from a sequence diagram, and bring back any changes done to the collaboration diagram.)

In the previous chapter, we showed that by analyzing a class's responsibilities, we arrive at most of its collaborators. Structural modeling focuses on *associations*—qualitative as well as quantitative (multiplicity). At first glance, the collaboration diagram closely resembles the class diagram. But there are three important differences: ❶ as a dynamic model, the collaboration diagram represents the relationship among *objects*, not classes; ❷ the relationships in the collaboration diagram relate to the *exchange of messages* among objects, not their kinships; and ❸ the collaboration diagram is *goal-oriented* and, as a result, cannot show *all* collaborators to an object, save those that cooperate in achieving a certain behavior.

In the previous section, "Sequence Diagram," we discovered that by placing objects in a dynamic perspective, we need to invent new classes (**Patients**, for instance) so that the required behavior of the system can be satisfied. The same results should be expected from collaboration diagrams.

The main benefit of the collaboration diagram is that by removing all distractions, it presents a clear picture of what an object expects from another. Therefore, a *set* of collaboration diagrams for the behavior of the system and its components would contribute greatly to the refinement of class responsibilities.

From Sequence to Collaboration Diagram

> The best way to arrive at a collaboration diagram is to start from a sequence diagram.

Collaboration diagrams, as we said, disregard the timeline of a behavior and, instead, focus on messages and the organization of the objects as a *task force*. We must slightly qualify this assertion: To be useful to design, a collaboration diagram must show the *ordinal* position of messages that are necessary to achieve the task. That is, even though messages are not arranged *chronologically*, we must be able to verify their relative position, because objects must be in a certain **state** before they can fulfill a responsibility. (See the following "Statechart Diagram" section.)

But *because* the messages are not visually in chronological order, identifying the sequence becomes rather difficult, unless the collaboration diagram is about a very simple task with very few objects (in which case, perhaps we would not need a diagram at all). Therefore, it is more advantageous if we start from a sequence diagram and arrive at its collaboration diagram.

Figure 9.9 is the collaboration diagram for Walden's **Make Appointment** use case, the same one that we used to illustrate a sequence diagram. (We have dropped the interaction of the appointment clerk with the patient as it does not add anything to the diagram. Furthermore, since a collaboration diagram is not about the flow of events, conditional branching *cannot* be included.)

The collaboration diagram has no building blocks that you might not recognize:

- An instance of an *actor* (role) is identified by the actor symbol and the name of the instance in the **[instanceName]:Actor** format.

Figure 9.9 Make Appointment: Collaboration Diagram

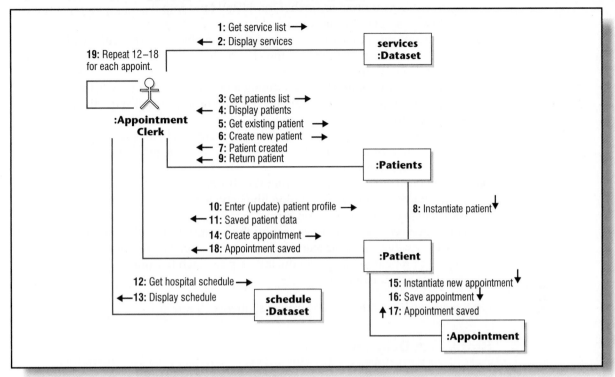

A collaboration diagram organizes messages passed between objects, minus the time and space matrix of the sequence diagram. Its advantage is that responsibilities are clearly defined.

- An *object* is identified by a rectangle labeled by the name of the object in the **[instanceName]:Class** format.
- Collaboration between entities is indicated by **a *simple line*** between two instances. (The line does not indicate a direction.)
- **Messages** that pass between two entities are grouped somewhere next to the association line between the two. Each message starts with a *number* that agrees with the *chronological order* in which events occur. As a result, ❶ each message has a unique number, and ❷ messages in one group are not necessarily numbered consecutively. (But *within* a group, the lowest number must be listed *first*, and the highest number *last*.)
- The direction of the message (or the return result) is indicated by a small arrow next to the message.
- As in the sequence diagram, an object can send *messages to itself*, in which case a direction arrow is not necessary.

Guidelines for Building a Collaboration Diagram

If you do *not* start from a sequence diagram, then you should follow a set of guidelines to build a collaboration diagram:

❶ Identify and list all objects (or actors) that must cooperate to satisfy a *specific* behavioral goal. If you cannot describe the *goal*, you cannot create a satisfactory collaboration diagram. In our example, the goal of the diagram is the same as the use case and, therefore, rather easy to identify because the work is already done. But as you proceed further into detail (and into design), you must model what happens at lower levels.

❷ List the messages that are exchanged between objects in *chronological order*— regardless of the significance of the objects that exchange them—and consecutively number them.

❸ Identify the *central entity*. In modeling a use case, the primary actor is the most likely central figure. When there is no actor, the object that starts the interaction is a good candidate.

❹ Place the central entity on the diagram and, around it, arrange objects with which it *directly interacts*. (Remember to draw a line between the central entity and each such object.)

❺ One by one *transfer messages* from the chronological list of events to an appropriate place next to the association line between each pair of objects. Identify each message with a direction arrow.

❻ For each object in the first tier around the central figure, place objects with which they *directly* collaborate (if they are not already present). Repeat the last step. And repeat *this* step and the last step for each tier until *all* messages on the event list are transferred.

On the whole, it is better to start from a sequence diagram.

Statechart Diagram

> A statechart diagram represents milestones in the lifetime of an object when its state changes.

Like living objects in the real world, a virtual object is born and changes during its lifetime. Like living objects, it might also cease to exist. A statechart diagram models the stages in the life of an object when its state is changed by a **change event**. (See the "Events" section in this chapter.) But what exactly is a "state"?

☞ **State**. "A condition or situation during the life of an object during which it satisfies some condition, performs some activity, or waits for some event." [Booch 1999, 466]

> A state is an object's *condition* at a certain stage and from a certain viewpoint. It is a snapshot of the object at a (usually important) point in time.

A few examples are necessary to explain this definition:

- Your cousin receives her B.A. with honors. Her state has now changed (from **high-school graduate** to **college graduate**).
- Your grandfather celebrates his 80th birthday. He is no longer 79, so his state has changed (from **septuagenarian** to **octogenarian**).
- A patient has been given an appointment at the hospital. His state has changed from **has no appointment** to **waiting for appointment**.
- You have ordered a set of books online and the bookseller ships them. The state of your books has changed from **ordered** to **shipped**.
- A waiter is **idle**. When a customer orders, the waiter's state changes from **idle** to **active**.

☞ States can be repetitive or simultaneous. A waiter may be in the **Idle** state at one point, become **Active** next, and return to **Idle** again. A patient may have been **Treated** a few times before, but can have a state of **Waiting Treatment** at this time. The state of a waiter object can be both **Active** and **Fulltime** depending on your interest or viewpoint.

Although any change in the "condition" of an object results in a state change, *no* statechart diagram attempts to model *every* change in the state of an object. For example, a credit card holder may charge many purchases to the card and the state of the account changes with every purchase, but the statechart may find that only **paid-in-full** or **over-the-limit** states are worthy of attention. In the same manner, every day that your cousin has spent at college has changed her "state" by teaching her something new, but only her graduation is celebrated as a "state change."

To sum, a statechart diagram depicts only those states that are deemed as *milestones* from a specific *viewpoint*—either for reasons of the problem domain (business reasons) or because the solution domain (the information system) considers them significant.

Anatomy of a Statechart Diagram

> A statechart diagram is composed of the states of an object and the flow of events that change its state.

A statechart diagram has very simple components. In fact, symbols used by this diagram are merely a subset of those used by the **activity diagram** (which we introduced in Chapter 7).

Figure 9.10 is a statechart diagram that represents milestones in the lifetime of an instance of the **Treatment** class (from an accounting viewpoint, mostly). The object is born when the patient calls the hospital and the appointment clerk instructs the **Patient** object to create an appointment. (See the "Sequence Diagram" and "Collaboration Diagram" sections earlier in this chapter for the interactive modeling of this event.) If the appointment is saved, then the **Treatment** object enters the state of **Scheduled**.

Each state is triggered by an **event**, shown as a label over an arrow that signifies the *transition* from one state to another. (For the initial state, we have also identified

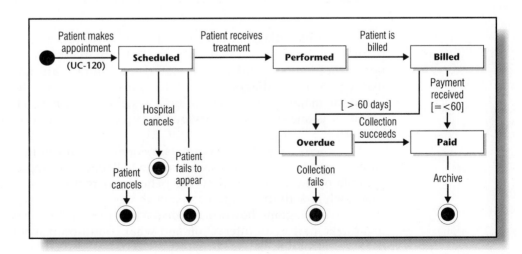

Figure 9.10 Treatment: Statechart Diagram for an Object

☞ The termination is usually indicated by some kind of a **status** attribute with values such as "active," "not active," "canceled," etc. But variations are many and a class may not have a **status** attribute at all; instead, its state might be *inferred* from the "***sum total***" of all or some of its attributes (as we previously stated).

the use case, **UC-120: Make Appointment**, during which the event occurs. We will explain why later.)

Three events may end the lifetime of the **Treatment** object before it is actually performed:

- The patient cancels the appointment.
- The hospital cancels the appointment.
- At the scheduled time, the patient fails to appear.

The symbol for the lifetime termination (a hollow circle around a solid circle) signifies that the object's state will no longer change—for any reason.

If the patient appears and receives the treatment, then the object is flagged as **Performed**. Next, the hospital bills the patient for the treatment and the **Billed** state is entered. If the payment is received on time (within 60 days), the state of the **Treatment** object is changed to **Paid** and the object is removed from "open" receivables and placed in archive.

However, if the payment is *not* received within 60 days, the object enters the **Overdue** state. If the hospital is successful in collecting the payment then, again, the state is changed to **Paid**. If, however, the hospital gives up hope of ever receiving the payment, the object is deactivated without entering the **Paid** state.

Like activity diagrams, statechart diagrams indicate *conditions* by placing them within square brackets over the transition arrow. However, the term "condition" is not quite adequate by itself, since a transition is *always* triggered by an **event**—something that occurs: an action, not a situation. In our example, the passage of 60 days, a **time event** (see the earlier "Events" section), triggers the transition. In other words, a transition indicates conditions that happen (a change in conditions), not conditions that simply exist.

Table 9.4 lists the components of a statechart diagram.

The Value of a Statechart Diagram

A statechart diagram is the only dynamic model that can illustrate the milestones in the lifetime of *one* class of objects in its entirety.

A statechart diagram is usually treated with less reverence than its more popular siblings—class, sequence, and activity diagrams. Undoubtedly, situations where you would need a statechart diagram are far fewer than those that require a class diagram. (Class diagrams are *always* needed.) Objects belonging to the majority of classes within a system do not need statechart diagrams. **Country** is one of the most obvious examples whose objects are either there, or are not.

But when a statechart diagram is *really* needed, it can make a distinct difference. Interactive diagrams (sequence and collaboration) represent how the components of the system satisfy the behavioral requirements in *units*, large or small, while activity diagrams depict the logical flow in or out of the system. A statechart diagram, however, models what *condition* an object must have *before* it can take part in an interaction and what condition it would have *afterwards*.

Table 9.4
Elements of a
Statechart Diagram.

	Elements of a Statechart Diagram
SYMBOL	**DESCRIPTION**
●	**Initial State (Starting Point).** A solid circle identifies the point in time that an object is born. A statechart diagram always starts with an initial state. A statechart diagram has *one*, and only *one*, starting point.
[State]	**State.** A rectangle with a name for the state in the middle. The name must be a condition. It is not always easy to find a good state name. For example, a *new* patient is created when an appointment is made. But what is a good name to describe the state of the patient at this point—"waiting treatment," "waiting appointment," "scheduled," "appointed"? Do not skip a state because the name might prove awkward.
Event [Condition] → (Use Case ID)	**Transition & Event.** An arrow between two states indicates transition from one state to another. The transition symbol is always accompanied by a description of the event that triggers it. For example: "Treatment is performed." If the event is based on a *condition*, then the condition is enclosed within square brackets. For example "[60 days]" may mean than a transition would occur on the 61st day. (The condition is also called *guard* and must be "Boolean"—that is, it must be either **True** or **False**.) You may also identify the event with the ID of the use case where the event occurs, *if* the use case is available and the event is a step in the flow of a use case. Events can be described informally or formally. For example: **Patient makes appointment**, or **makeAppointment (patientID, serviceID, date, time)**.
◉	**Final State (Termination Point).** A circle around a solid circle (target symbol or a bull's eye) means that the object has reached *a* final state and can no longer change. (An object can have more than one final state: **Canceled**, **Paid**, **Not Collectible**, etc.). A statechart diagram may have more than one termination point, but it *usually* has at least one. (A certain object may never retire.)

As such, it takes the entire lifetime of an object into account and is not limited to units of that lifetime.

A few examples will better clarify this explanation:

- A patient must not be billed *before* the treatment enters the state of **performed**.
- An order cannot be shipped unless it has a state of **placed**.
- A person may not vote until he or she is **eligible** (18 or over).
- A document must not be saved unless it is **edited**.
- A credit card purchase must not be processed unless the card is **validated**.

These are rather simple examples (as examples should be) but, when building a system of even medium complexity, it is easy to lose track of when a specific object is ready (or eligible) to take part in an interactions. (To turn the popular metaphor around, we might lose sight of the trees because we are looking at the forest.)

For example, when a patient arrives at the hospital to receive a medical treatment, it is easy to remember that the patient must have an appointment, but it is also easy to forget that the patient must be properly **Registered**. (See the use case **Receive Patient** in Chapter 7.)

Therefore, a statechart diagram is an effective verification tool. As a result, it would be helpful if events are referenced by the use case during which they occur.

Activity Diagram

> An activity diagram provides the most lucid tool for modeling the *logical* flow of activities that takes place between the system and the outside world or within the system among its components.

We introduced the activity diagram before (in Chapter 7) and illustrated the concept with a diagram for the **Make Appointment** use case. Here we add a little more sophistication to our understanding of this important (and very popular) modeling tool.

Now that we are familiar with **sequence diagrams**, let us state that the activity diagram is another view of the same activities that the sequence diagram illustrates. But whereas the sequence diagram focuses on the exchange of messages between objects and object lifetimes, the activity diagram is concerned with the *logical flow of activities* in an almost pure form. And whereas the sequence diagram is basically a *sequential* presentation of actions (hence its name), the activity diagram can efficiently portray parallel activities.

Two more tools within the toolbox of the activity diagram give it a wider range of representation: swimlane and synchronization bar.

Swimlane is a vertical partition on the activity diagram that organizes responsibilities for actions. Figure 9.11 represents one set of activities within **Make Appointment**: entering (or editing or updating) patient information before the actual appointment is made. The diagram has three swimlanes for each entity responsible for a subset of actions: the appointment clerk, the **Patients** collection object, and an instance of **Patient**.

Swimlanes are not limited to objects. In an activity diagram for workflow (also called the *workflow* diagram), swimlanes can represent divisions within an enterprise: inventory, shipping, sales, account, etc.

A synchronization bar is where parallel actions **fork** or *merge* back. For example, in a **Ship Order** activities diagram (Figure 9.12), the inventory department may be packing order items into a box, while the shipping department is preparing the mailing label. Both flows then merge in the shipping department, where the mailing label is attached to the box and shipped out. Synchronization bars must be paired: Each **fork** must be matched with a *merge*. (Bars can be nested to as many levels as necessary, as long as they are paired within their own level.)

Figure 9.11
**Enter Patient
Data: Activity
Diagram**

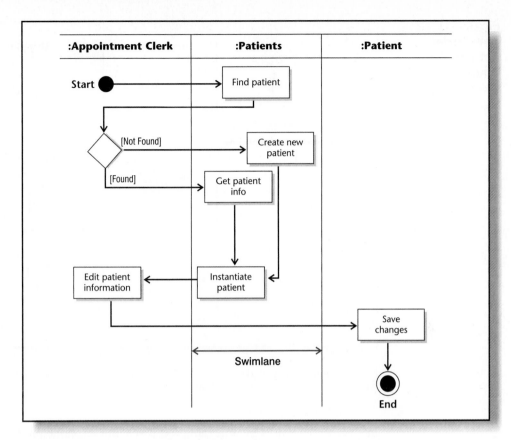

Entering patient data is a part of the **Make Appointment** use case. Compare this diagram with the same set of activities on the sequence diagram earlier in this chapter.

5. DELIVERABLES

Use cases must cover the entire behavior of the system and each class must appear in at least one class diagram. Dynamic modeling, however, should be used on an "as needed" basis. Though most systems need a great number of dynamic diagrams, you should not be tempted to provide one diagram for every entity in the system.

• *Sequence Diagram.* Sequence diagrams may be used at any stage of development to help you visualize the sequence of events, messages, and object responsibilities. Since a sequence diagram's level of detail or scope is not predetermined, you may choose a level or scope that suits your needs or the complexity of the scenario that the diagram represents.

In analysis, by modeling use cases or sections of them, you can use sequence diagrams to ❶ find new classes that were missed in structural modeling and ❷ clarify the messages that must pass between objects and, consequently, refine class responsibilities. In addition, as we shall see, sequence diagrams are the best method for crossing from analysis to *design* by going deeper into messages and responsibilities.

• *Collaboration Diagrams.* The primary purpose of collaboration diagrams is the verification of object responsibilities. We start the definition of class responsibilities

**Figure 9.12
Ship Order:
Activity
Diagram for
Workflow
Modeling**

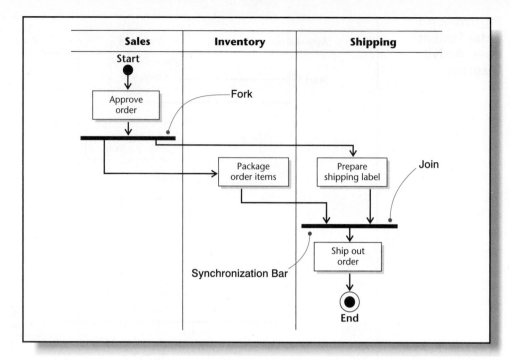

Each fork must be matched by a join. Both are represented by a synch bar. (The exception might be when a fork results in the termination of the activity.)

in structural analysis by analyzing use cases. But dynamic modeling either reassigns responsibilities or expands them. Therefore, by turning sequence diagrams into collaboration diagrams you can ensure that class definitions are mature enough to support their *conceptual* responsibilities.

• *Statechart Diagrams.*   You need statechart diagrams *only* for those objects whose states affect specific behaviors of the system. Changes to instances of most classes, and most changes to instances of all classes, do not warrant statechart diagrams. But, for certain crucial classes, a statechart diagram can make all the difference to the success or the failure of the system as a dynamic entity, especially if a system is complex and instances of the same *business* ("entity") class appear in many scenarios.

• *Activity Diagrams.*   Activity diagrams are the most popular form of dynamic modeling, and for a good reason: They are the best in representing the complexities of logical flow. By adding "swimlanes" to activity diagrams, you can compensate for the shortcomings of sequence diagrams where the logic of the interaction is complicated beyond a certain point.

6. WRAP UP

☑ **Dynamic modeling and its relationship with behavioral and structural modeling**

Dynamic modeling represents how the structure of a system and its components act and interact to satisfy its behavioral requirements. Whereas behavioral and structural models represent *abstract* units, dynamic modeling is concerned with *actual objects* (and components).

Dynamic modeling is not a straightforward combination of structure and behavior. It demands new decisions and often leads back to refinements in both behavioral and structural models.

☑ **How objects interact by exchanging messages**

In a virtual system, a message is equivalent to an action in the real world. And interaction in a virtual world consists of exchanging messages.

Messages are instruments of communication that carry instructions and information necessary to carry out those instructions, in the expectation that that the recipients will carry out the intended action.

However, an object will not perform any task unless the task is its **responsibility**. In other words, if the message sent from one object to another does not correspond to an **operation** included in the **interface** of the recipient, the second object will take no action.

☑ **The role of parameters and return values in exchanging messages**

Parameters (or **arguments**) are the *types* of data that an object requires to perform a certain task. While the object that is responsible for an operation defines the types (and provides the containers or *variables*) for the data that it needs to carry out the operation, the sender of the message—the object that requests the action—must provide the *values*.

The values that the message carries to its recipient must agree in both type and in order with those that are defined and expected by the operation. (The recipient might supply a *default* value for a parameter, but the order must be preserved by indicating where a value is *not* supplied because a default value exists.)

After the recipient object has carried out an operation, it might send a *return result* to the sender of the message. In this case, it is the recipient of the original message that must provide a container.

☑ **Methods and their relationships with operations**

An operation defines *what* the objects instantiated from a class must do, but not *how* they are expected to do it. It is the method that implements the actual steps required to carry out a task.

Conceptual modeling usually ignores *how* operations are implemented, but the distinction between operations and methods must be understood long before we actually attend to the latter.

First, instances of two classes may have the same exact operation, but they can implement it very differently even if the classes are related.

Second, instances of the *same* class may not carry out the *same* operation in the *same* way *if*

their **states** are different. (And this is very important to dynamic modeling, conceptual or otherwise.)

Finally, attributes of objects, usually private, are exposed to the outside world through **accessor operations**. These types of operations conform to a syntax different from normal operations and are not usually declared on the interface of a class. The task of methods that implement such operations is to guard private data from unauthorized access or actions and retain the control of the variable in the hands of the object.

☑ **Events and their significance in dynamic modeling**

Events are occurrences that interrupt the existing condition of one or more objects. Events are basically of three types.

The first type are **call events**, those that *invoke* an operation. When an object sends a message to another object, the recipient of the message views the arrival of the message as an event to which it must respond. As such, "call" events are the other side of the coin to messages. Moreover, such events are usually both *targeted* (directed to a *specific* object) and **synchronous** (the event and the response to it work within the *same phase* or timeframe).

The second type are **signal events**. They are **anonymous**, meaning that they are not directed to a specific object, but will be received by any object that "catches" them. ("Call" events may be compared to receiving a personal telephone call, while "signal" events are like buying newspapers or tuning to a radio station to learn about "events.") Furthermore, signal events are usually **asynchronous**, meaning that the action that results in the event may not occur in the same "phase" or timeframe in which the event occurs.

Time events are like signal events: disruptive, asynchronous, and anonymous. The important difference is that they are triggered by the passage of time, not by any prior action.

From the viewpoint of object-orientation, all these types could be *significant* (or **change**) events if they change the state of an object (or a system).

☑ **Sequence diagram**

A sequence diagram represents the interaction between objects, or between actors and objects ordered in time. A sequence diagram is composed of a timeline, objects that interact across this timeline, and the messages that they exchange.

A sequence diagram is basically a *space-time matrix* for interactions. Two axes contain the diagram. The vertical axis is a **timeline**, or a chronology of events. The horizontal axis identifies the *space* and the actions that take place within the space. Movement on the timeline axis is one way, but bidirectional on the space axis.

Each column in the sequence diagram identifies an *instance* of an actor or a class. Each "row" is a message sent or received by the entities in the column.

The scope of a sequence diagram (and other dynamic models as well) is a matter of choice and judgment. You may use it to model a use case, part of a use case, or interaction among components or between subsystems.

☑ **Collaboration diagram**

A collaboration diagram focuses on the organization of objects that must cooperate, by exchanging messages, to satisfy a certain behavior. A collaboration diagram is *goal-oriented* and, as a result, must show only those objects that cooperate in achieving a certain behavior.

The main value of a collaboration diagram is that it presents a clear picture of what an object expects from another. Therefore, a *set* of collaboration diagrams for the behavior of the system and its components would contribute greatly to the refinement of class responsibilities.

☑ **Statechart diagram**

Like a living object in the real world, a virtual object is born and changes during its lifetime. Like a living object, it might also cease to exist.

A statechart diagram models the milestones in the life of an object when its state is changed by a significant event.

A statechart diagram is the only dynamic model that illustrates the milestones in the lifetime of *one* class of objects in its entirety.

☑ **Activity diagram**

An activity diagram provides an effective tool for modeling the logical flow of actions. An activity diagram is another view of the same scenario that the sequence diagram illustrates, but while a sequence diagram focuses on the exchange of messages between objects and object lifetimes, an activity diagram is concerned with the *logical flow* of activities. And whereas a sequence diagram is basically a *sequential* presentation of actions, an activity diagram can efficiently portray parallel activities.

We introduced the activity diagram under use case modeling, but it has two very useful tools that we left for later: **swimlane**, a vertical partition on the activity diagram that organizes responsibilities for actions, and the **synchronization bar**, where parallel actions (or forks) merge back.

With these tools, an activity diagram can be employed as a *workflow* diagram to model actions across an enterprise.

7. KEY CONCEPTS

Accessor Operation. An operation that sets or returns the value of an attribute. **Methods** that implement accessor operations are called **accessor methods**.

Activity Diagram. A diagram that models the *logical* flow of activities that takes place between the system and the outside world or within the system among its components.

Alternate Messages. Two or more messages, only one of which may be executed. In a **sequence diagram**, alternate messages start on the same point of the object's **timeline** and, often, result in a **fork** in the **timeline** of the receiving object.

Anonymous Message. A message that is broadcast and is not *targeted* towards a specific object. An anonymous message is usually an "event" message; that is, a message that is broadcasted as a **signal** or **time event**.

Arguments. See **Parameters**.

Asynchronous. An interaction in which the action and the response to it are not in the same timeframe (or are *out-of-phase*). An asynchronous **event** is one in which the action that triggers the event and the event itself are not within a common timeframe. The object that is the source of action immediately regains control.

Call Event. An **event** that is triggered when an operation is invoked. A call event is usually **synchronous** and *targeted*.

Catcher. An object that chooses to receive an **asynchronous** event. Also called **listener** or **subscriber**.

Change Event. An **event** that changes the **state** of an object. Any **call**, **signal** or **time event** can qualify as a change event.

Collaboration Diagram. An *interaction* diagram that focuses on the organization of objects that must cooperate, by exchanging messages, to satisfy a certain behavior.

Dynamic Modeling.   Represents the interaction of the building blocks of the information system with each other and with the outside world to satisfy the behavioral requirements of the system. It models the structure of the system as it moves through space and time.

Error-Handler.   See **Event-Handler.**

Event.   An action by one object that interrupts the existing condition of one or more other objects. Event types are **call**, **signal**, and **time**. Any event that changes the state of an object is called a **change** event.

Event-Handler.   A method that implements the response of an object to an event raised by another object. If the event is an exception (an error) then the method is called an **error-handler.**

Fork.   When a single flow of action splits into *parallel* timelines (**sequence diagram**) or parallel set of activities (**activity diagram**). Each fork must be balanced by a *merge*, where parallel timelines or activities are joined back into a single flow.

Interface.   The services that an object offers to the outside world, as well as how these services are structured and arranged.

Lifetime.   In a sequence diagram, an empty rectangle that specifies when an object is instantiated, how long it lives, and when it is destroyed.

Listener.   An object that chooses to receive an **asynchronous** event. Also called **catcher** or **subscriber.**

Message.   Instruction and information sent to an object in the expectation that the recipient will carry out a certain action. A message is the invocation, by the sender, of an operation for which the recipient is responsible. The data included in the message are defined—both in type and in order—by the **parameters** specified in the invoked operation. After the operation is complete, the *recipient* of the message may *return* a *result* to the sender.

Method.   How an operation is implemented or actually carried out by the object when it receives a message. In **call events**, both the operation and the method exist within one object. In **signal** and **time** *events*, the message sender specifies the event and the *recipient* implements it.

Operation.   What the object does, identified by a name and one or more **parameters**. An operation may also send back a **return value** to the object from which it receives the message.

Parameters.   Specify the data that must be supplied to an object to carry out a specific **operation**. (Parameters are also called **arguments**.) The type and the ordinal position of each value that must be received for each parameter is decided by the operation defined in the **interface** of the class to which the object belongs.

Responsibility.   Any action that an object must take in response to a correct message. Responsibilities of an object are defined in the **interface** of the class to which it belongs.

Return Value.   The response that a message may invoke from the receiving object after an operation is complete. Each operation may have only one return value. The return value, however, may be complex or might even be an object or a set of objects.

Sequence Diagram.   An *interaction* diagram that represents the interaction between objects, or between actors and objects ordered in time. A sequence diagram is composed of a **timeline**, objects that interact across this timeline, and the messages that they exchange.

Signal Event.   An **event** that disrupts the normal flow of actions. A signal event is **synchronous** and **anonymous.**

State.   The condition of an object at a certain stage from a specific viewpoint. A state is a snapshot of the object at a (usually important) point in time. An object may arrive at a certain state repeatedly, or it might have multiple states simultaneously (depending on the viewpoint).

Statechart Diagram.   A diagram that is composed of the **states** of an object and the flow of **events** that change its state. A statechart diagram is the only dynamic model that can illustrate the milestones in the lifetime of *one* class of objects in its entirety.

Subscriber.   An object that chooses to receive an **asynchronous** event. Also called **listener** or **catcher.**

Swimlane.   A vertical partition on the **activity diagram** that organizes responsibilities for actions depicted by the diagram.

Synchronization Bar.   A horizontal line on the **activity diagram** where parallel actions **fork** or *merge*.

Synchronous.   An interaction in which both the action and the response to it occur in the same timeframe (or are *in-phase*). A synchronous **event** is one whose triggering action occurs immediately before the event is "fired" and neither side of the interaction can gain control until the operation is complete—that is to say, "the event runs its course."

Targeted Message.   A message that is targeted towards a specific object. (See also **Anonymous Message.**)

Time Event.   An event that is triggered by the passage time. Like **signal** events, time events are **asynchronous** and **anonymous**; unlike signal events, they do not result from a prior action in the ordinary sense of the word.

Timeline.   An axis in the sequence diagram that signifies the chronology of events.

8. CONFUSING CONCEPTS

Creation & Instantiation. Even though these two terms are often used interchangeably, sometimes we should (at least) try to keep them separate. When a patient does not exist on the hospital's file—in other words, when a patient is new to the *hospital*—it is *created*. When the *information system* needs to exchange messages with the `Patient` object, it is *instantiated*, regardless of whether the hospital considers the patient "new" or "existing."

In a play, an actor "instantiates" a role when he or she appears on the stage, and "destroys" the role when he or she leaves the stage. But neither the actor nor the role are created onstage or die offstage.

Nevertheless, it is hopeless to expect that anybody can follow the distinction strictly and faithfully. We may create both patients (for the hospital) and `Patient` objects (for exchanging messages within the information system). Our only real option is to interpret the word based on its context.

Events. Even in books on information systems (such as this one), usage of the term "event" runs from loose and general to very specific. Any action, any occurrence, can legitimately be called an event. Any action that changes the **state** of an object is a **change** event. Sending a message to an object is an event because, at the very least, it turns the state of the object from `Idle` (doing nothing before receiving the message) into `Active` (after receiving it). The most specialized type of events are signal and time events that need **event-handlers**. As usual with confusing terms, you often have to rely on the context to grasp the implication.

Events & Messages. Events are always related to messages. (As we emphasized, messages are the *only* mechanism by which objects in a virtual world interact.) The possible confusion lies in the *direction* of the message: **call** events result from receiving messages, while **signal** and **time** events send them. You send a message to a waiter to provide you with a menu, while the clerk at the train station sends *you* (and most likely others like you) a message when your train is delayed or canceled. As a result, sometimes we say that a message raises an event while, at other times, we may refer to an "event message."

Lifetime. The term may be used in two different ways. If you have "instantiated" the application (you are running the program, in other words), "lifetime" refers to the lifespan of an object while the system is running. (**Sequence diagrams** represent this definition.) But the term might go beyond this definition: A bank account starts life when it is opened and ceases to exist when it is closed—regardless of whether the bank's information system is running or not. In other words, the *persistent*—or, more or less, business—meaning of "lifetime" is not the same as its *transitory* (role-playing) sense when the application is running.

State. Any change to the "condition" of an object changes its state. If you change the address of a `Patient`, its state (in programmer's vocabulary) changes from `Clean` to `Dirty` and must be saved to the database. But usually it has a narrower meaning and refers to a "significant" change or a *milestone* from a specific *viewpoint*. Therefore, depending on the viewpoint, an object may have *multiple* states at the same time: a car may be simultaneously `Empty` or `Full`, `Stationary` or `Moving`, `New` or `Old` or `Refurbished`. For each viewpoint, you need a different **statechart** diagram. (Moreover, some states, such as `New`, cannot be regained, while others, `Empty` for example, can be repeated for the same object.)

9. REVIEW QUESTIONS

1. Describe the relationship between dynamic modeling, behavioral modeling, and structural modeling.
2. Comment on this statement: "Dynamic modeling is about interaction."
3. How does a sequence diagram differ from use case modeling?
4. Explain how objects interact by exchanging messages.
5. Explain the role of parameters and return values in exchanging messages.
6. Describe "events." Provide an example.
7. Describe the different types of events and compare them.
8. What are the building blocks of a sequence diagram?
9. What are the building blocks of a collaboration diagram?

10. Explain the lifetime of an object. Provide an example.
11. How do actors and objects fit in a sequence diagram?
12. Why is dynamic modeling based on objects, but not classes?
13. Explain the following pairs in relation to each other:
    a. Method and operation
    b. Event and state.
    c. Interaction and message.
14. Explain events and their importance in dynamic modeling.
15. What are the main differences between sequence and collaboration diagrams? When would you use each?
16. Explain the significance of "collection class" and provide two examples.
17. Refer to Figure 9.8, the sequence diagram for the **Make Appointment** use case. Three spaces are identified in this diagram. Explain the significance of each.
18. Discuss how a collaboration diagram represents the organization of objects that must cooperate to reach an objective.
19. What are the components of a statechart diagram?
20. What is the significance of a statechart diagram?

10. Exercises

The following exercises apply to each of the four narratives introduced in Chapter 4: *The* Sportz *Magazine, The Car Dealership, The Pizza Shop,* and *The Real Estate Agency.*

❶ Create **sequence diagrams** for significant use cases in the following subsystems:

- Subscription, advertising, and editorial in the *Sportz Magazine* scenario.
- Sales in the *Car Dealership* scenario.
- Matching buyers and sellers, gathering data about buyers and sellers, and advising buyers and sellers in the *Real Estate Agency* scenario.

Note that it is unlikely that a single use case and, as a result, a single sequence diagram can cover the whole subsystem. Therefore, be selective: Not every use case (or combination of use case) needs a sequence diagram.

❷ Convert the sequence diagrams to **collaboration diagrams**.

❸ For each system or subsystem reference, select an object that can have a meaningful **statechart diagram**. ("Meaningful" means that changes to the state of the object have a noticeable impact on the system.)

11. Research Projects & Teamwork

❶ After reading the chapter, schedule a *group discussion* to outline the significance of **dynamic modeling** to system development. One team member should search the Web to find discussion panels on the subject. The second should look at system development magazines, and the third (someone who might have contacts in an organization engaged in software development) should obtain firsthand information on dynamic modeling.

Write a short report to summarize your findings. The emphasis should be on the relationship between dynamic modeling and behavioral modeling and how dynamic modeling ensures the correct operation of the system.

❷ Refer to the online registration system for Walden Medical College in Chapter 4. Each team member should review the system's major use cases and classes (identified previously) to determine whether *sequence* and/or *collaboration* modeling is appropriate for each use case. Write a short report explaining your decision. Create a table with two columns: the first column for use cases, the second for the selected dynamic modeling.

Repeat the same process for the online shopping system (Chapter 4), the automated research application (the "reference engine," Chapter 4), and for the patient scheduling system (Chapter 5).

Based on your decision, create **sequence** or **collaboration** diagrams for the selected use cases.

❸ Create **sequence**, **collaboration**, and **activity** diagrams for the selected use cases in the previous scenarios.

❹ Choose a task that you carry out regularly and understand well (for example, getting ready to go to work). Draw an **activity diagram** to summarize steps in the task.

❺ Plan a discussion session with your team members on the topic of the **statechart diagram**, its properties, when to use it, and for what purposes.

❻ For each of the following scenarios, identify an object, the state of which affects the behavior of the system, and create a **statechart diagram** for it: the online shopping system (Chapter 4), the automated research application (the "reference engine," Chapter 4), and the patient scheduling system (Chapter 5).

12. Suggested Readings

Structural modeling, dynamic modeling, and related UML diagrams and tools are usually discussed together, within the same book. Therefore, for *analysis*, you can refer back to the same sources that we recommended in Chapter 7 for behavioral modeling and in Chapter 8 for structural modeling. In design, which starts with the next chapter, we will explore the same concepts from a new perspective and suggest other titles.

Chapter

10

The Design Challenge

1. OVERVIEW

Design is the concrete modeling of the solution. This chapter provides the foundations on which the later discussions on design are built. It also explains why design is fundamentally different from analysis and how we should move from conceptual modeling to concrete modeling.

- ▇☑ Inception
- ▇☑ Requirements Discovery
- ▇☐ Development
    - ▇☑ Analysis
    - ▇☐ Design
        - ☐ **The Design Challenge** ⬅
    - ▇☐ Application Design
        - ☐ Patterns
        - ☐ Components & Reuse
        - ☐ Architecture
- ☐ Implementation

Chapter Topics

- ➤ Design and its place in the development process.
- ➤ Moving from analysis to design.
- ➤ Logical design vs. physical design.
- ➤ The significance of domain analysis to design.
- ➤ Design objects.
- ➤ Stereotyping and other UML extension mechanisms.
- ➤ Packaging, a UML mechanism for managing the complexity of models.

Introduction

Development is preceded by the articulation of a goal—a product or a service—that solves a problem, exploits an opportunity, or satisfies a desire. To arrive at the goal, the development venture must start with *analysis:*

❶ *Requirements Discovery:*   define the scope, or the boundaries, of *what* the product must do.
❷ *Domain Analysis:*   define the meaning of what the product is expected to do, clarify the *concepts* that relate to the product, and discover the *context* in which the product will operate.
❸ *Behavioral Modeling:*   define the behavior of the *conceptual* product in units of behavior, or *use cases,* in which one user type (or actor), alone or in cooperation with others, interacts with the system to achieve a meaningful goal.
❹ *Structural Modeling:*   discover and define the building blocks that are necessary to support the product's behavior.
❺ *Dynamic Modeling:*   define what interactions between the building blocks of the product are required to satisfy the behavior, and refine the building blocks when necessary.

In short, analysis results in a ***conceptual model*** that defines the "***what***" and the "***where***" of the product or the service. But to build an actual product, *what* it must do and *where* it will be used are not enough. We must also decide ***how*** the product will achieve the goal. Bringing everything together and creating a workable solution is the task of **design,** which adds the "how" to the "what" and the "where" of analysis.

The mission of design is defined by analysis, but design is a more daunting challenge.

* *Design must create something new.*   Design is needed when a required solution does *not* exist or is not completely satisfactory, whereas analysis identifies (or tries to identify) an *existing* problem within an *existing* context. Creating something new is never easy or straightforward.
* *Design must make compromises.*   One problem can have many solutions and each solution imposes its own compromises. Even if we find the "best solution," it would most likely be more expensive than other solutions. Many miracle drugs really do perform miracles, but with side effects. A notebook computer can be hardened to withstand shocks, but it might become too heavy to carry around (which is the primary purpose of buying a notebook in the first place).
* *Design must work in context.*   Depending on the product and its context, analysis may be simple or complex. Sometimes a simple product must operate in a complex (or at least unusual) environment: A wrench is not an exceptionally complex product and is supposed to do the same thing everywhere, but to use it in outer space it must be redesigned so that the lack of gravity would not cause the astronaut to turn instead of the screw. Sometimes a complex product must operate in an unsophisticated context: tanks in deserts, cars by inexperienced drivers, game consoles by children, and PCs in our dens and dorms. **Analysis *must* see the solution in abstract; design *cannot* afford to do so.**

Since design is primarily concerned with the solution, not the problem, it works with concepts that, to varying degrees, are different from those of analysis. In this chapter,

Figure 10.1
**Design: The
Path from the
Concept to
the Product**

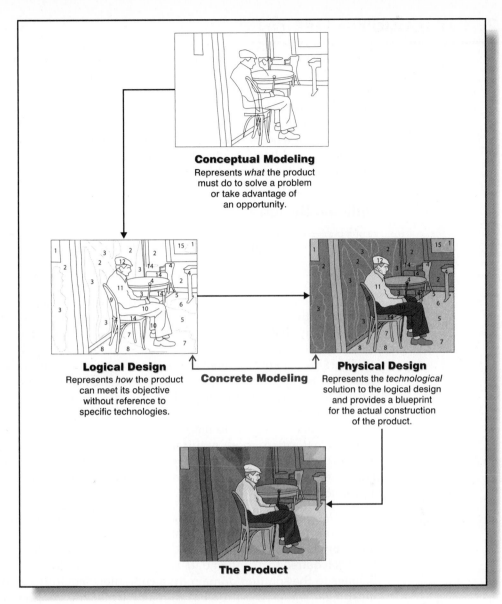

Design extends modeling from conceptual to concrete. The two activities within design can be compared to children's paint-by-numbers books: Logical modeling maps the concept of the product into identifiable building blocks without concern for specific technologies, whereas physical modeling translates the logical artifacts into engineering blueprints.

we lay the groundwork for exploring design concepts and expand on ideas that can apply both to analysis and design but are more relevant to the latter.

Design cannot be learned as a set of recipes, but the creativity that it needs can be nurtured and sharpened by following methodologies that have worked in the past, by personal experience, and last, but not least, by studying *failures,* not only in one's field but also in product and services that might seem far removed from software development.

The simple term "design" covers a set of concepts expressed through the same term, even within the confines of software development. We talk about "good design" to convey our approval, but we might mean many different things: pleasing aesthetics, ease-of-learning, ease-of-use, elegance of engineering, reliability, consistency, etc.

Like other complex concepts, design cannot be understood by a single definition or a single viewpoint. The idea must be explained and illustrated many times to become reasonably intelligible. Furthermore, like other relatively complex concepts, agreement on its meaning is hard to come by.

Defining Design

> Design is a model-driven activity that aims to arrive at the specifications of the solution.

A finished product has two set of features: One set satisfies the objectives of the product (or the *requirements*) while the second set (or the ***solution features***) includes those features that are necessary to make the first set possible *and* workable within the intended context.

Tracking patient treatment is a requirement; a treatment-tracking application is a solution. Listening to music programs is a requirement; a radio and a computer connected to the Internet are alternate solutions. Traveling is a requirement; trains, planes, and automobiles are competing or complementary solutions.

The task of design is to map requirements into models and specifications of a product that satisfy those requirements. Requirements, however, are conceptual and relatively abstract, while products and services are concrete. As a result, requirements, though necessary, are not sufficient for designing a product. To build a product:

- *Design must discover or create the components of the solution.* Invariably, a solution has features that are not related to the problem. In an information system, objects such as `Patient` and `Invoice` belong to the problem domain, but what is required to maintain data about the patient or to create and send an invoice belongs to the solution domain. In a computer, "computing" (with its myriad of meanings) serves the problem domain, while the cooling fan and the cables between the computer and its peripheral equipment are features of the solution. What is more, design must integrate both the problem features and the solution features into *one* product.

- *Design must select between alternate solutions.* Frequently, more than one solution can satisfy the same problem. Even if the components at hand are restricted in number, the design can combine them differently: witness the countless architectural styles in buildings that are constructed from the same material, or the variety of applications built on the same computer platforms that address the same requirements such as browsing the Web or editing a picture.

Each solution, however, exacts a price and demands a compromise. A picture phone is convenient to carry but too small to view details. A powerful database management system is expensive and requires dedicated servers and an expert maintenance crew, while a less expensive and easy-to-maintain DBMS does not offer many desirable features.

• *Design must start from an architectural view of the solution.* Analysis does not have to round up its artifacts into an integrated whole. It states, in effect: "Here are the problems. Solve them!" Design, however, must offer the solutions as *identifiable* and *integrated* wholes, the components of which must work together: an information system, a car, a book, a computer, a railroad system, an application. To achieve this goal, design must decide on the architecture—the highest view of a product or service that defines not only what components are required but how they are grouped, how these groups are arranged, and how they interact.

☞ See Chapter 4 for a description of common **nonfunctional requirements.**

• *Design must take into account nonfunctional requirements and the target environment.* Nonfunctional requirements are overwhelmingly related to the solution, not to the problem. Analysis may gather and catalog them faithfully but, in modeling, it treats them mostly as secondary observations. Design, however, must address nonfunctional requirements. Requirements discovery, however, might miss the issues that are not directly related to the problem at hand. For example, a screen for searching and selecting video titles may seem to satisfy business requirements until we notice that the search must be done by the customers in a video shop, which then raises other related issues such as the size of fonts and icons, the desirability of a touch-screen monitor instead of a keyboard and a mouse, and so on. (Testing of products in their target environment—if possible—is necessary but a great amount can be achieved, for a much cheaper price, by analyzing the context *before* the product is developed.)

☞ See Chapter 6 for a discussion of analyzing the **context.**

• *Final design artifacts must be sufficiently specific and exact to serve as blueprints for building the product.* Some analysis artifacts, such as use cases, must intentionally avoid too much detail to keep the "big picture" visible and clear. Others, such as class and sequence diagrams, are detailed (and also serve as tools for discovering details) but must stay on the business message—that is, they must focus on the problem domain and not the solution space. The *final* artifacts of design, however, must be detailed enough for the actual building of the product. Notice that the operative word here is "final," for design must actually start from an overall view. (See the "Design Concepts" section later in this chapter.) Also, as we shall soon see, **concrete modeling** (as design is also called) consists of two overlapping activities: *logical* design that avoids specific technologies and *physical* design that maps the logical design into specific technology or technologies.

Design & Methodology

> Object-oriented design is the definition and refinement of objects of which the solution is composed, their relationships, and their interactions with each other and the outside world.

Creating an artifact requires forethought: envisioning what to build and planning how to build it. The combination of experience, theory, methods, and techniques that we follow to build something constitutes a methodology—regardless of whether it is effective or not, is consistent or not, is elegant or not, or has a name or is nameless. But just as a problem may have more than one solution, development itself can follow more than one methodology. Simply using an object-oriented technology does not mean that our methodology is (or should be) object-oriented as well. Furthermore, all object-oriented methodologies are not the same.

Our approach to object-oriented design in this book is **component-based** and **architectural,** both for the product and the development process that aims to arrive at the product. "Architectural" does not mean that designing software is exactly like constructing a building. No two product types can be designed the same way. What we mean by the term is that, first, design models start from a very high-level view and are refined iteratively and, second, the final product is viewed as a system composed of identifiable components, their behaviors, their interrelationships, and their own identifiable subcomponents. (We will explore this concept further in Chapter 16.)

No methodology can become successful by simply issuing a mission statement. The quality of a methodology is reflected in how it meets the individual challenges that arise in the course of designing the product. There are, nevertheless, general guidelines that should be taken to heart, including the following.

- *Design is iterative.* The fact that we champion starting design from a high-level view should not suggest that design is a one-way trip from top to bottom. On the contrary, design is both iterative and incremental. We often return to the starting point to refine our artifacts and, by following an object-oriented approach that views the product as a set of components, we do not necessarily have to wait for the final specification of each and every component before implementation can start.

- *Design discovers from the outside but refines from the inside.* Object-oriented design discovers objects from *outside* by behavioral modeling but refines them by studying the inside of the system or the component by structural and dynamic modeling.

- *Design cannot follow a cookbook approach.* We can learn much from the examples presented in various books on design, but design cannot be achieved by following a recipe. (If somebody has a recipe that exactly matches your design needs, use it by all means—but in that case you are not the one who is doing the design.)

- *Design must avoid functional decomposition.* As we discussed in the chapter on methodology, functional decomposition is a methodology by which a big problem is broken into smaller problems until we arrive at functions that solve the smallest piece of the problem. We will not repeat our arguments about functional decomposition, but be aware that the temptation is always there. Object-oriented concrete modeling is about discovering and defining objects and components, not about functions.

- *Design must avoid preempting implementation tasks.* To varying degrees, a designer must get involved in implementation, in the same manner that an analyst must remain as a moderator and communicator between business and design. (An analyst who is a stranger to design and a designer who is a stranger to implementation have serious shortcomings to overcome. How can a designer suggest and model technologies about which he or she knows nothing?) Design, however, must know its own scope and boundaries. During coding, programmers can use models such as activity diagrams to solve their own problems. They might even judge that a class structure needs modifications to be workable. More often than not, such modifications may require the involvement of the designer. But such decisions cannot and should not be made beforehand.

From Analysis to Design

Analysis artifacts are the foundations of design artifacts.

Though we have often used the terms "phase" and "stage," they are really terms of convenience and do not give the exact meaning of what is expressed by them. In the object-oriented development methodology, analysis, design, and implementation are *activities* rather than clearly delineated phases (such as stages in a rocket or stories in a building). What makes the use of "phase" excusable is that these activities, more or less, follow each other. But they also overlap. In fact, at the start of each "stage" of development, the activities are very similar both in type and in the artifacts that they produce. The distinguishing features of each activity emerge only as the development process goes forward. Requirements discovery turns into domain analysis which, in turn, feeds behavioral modeling, and so on.

To illustrate the point we turn to Figure 10.2, which has a slightly different emphasis from our previous references to the same model. Analysis starts with business concepts and builds a conceptual model of the system (the product). Design receives analysis artifacts—behavioral, structural, and dynamic models—and launches the development into the system space or the solution domain.

The figure emphasizes two points: ❶ The problem space and the solution space overlap, indicating that a set of concepts are *shared* between the problem and the solution; and ❷ the conceptual models are turned into concrete models *incrementally,* not in one leap.

In design, we use basically the same modeling tools as in analysis: class diagrams, sequence diagrams, etc. Two exceptions, however, exist:

- **There are no *design* use cases.** Use cases capture business requirements and model the behavior that the system must have to satisfy those requirements. In other words, even though they provide a conceptual model of the system, their viewpoint is from the vantage point of the problem space, not the solution space

Figure 10.2 "M" for Model: From *What* and *Where* to *How*

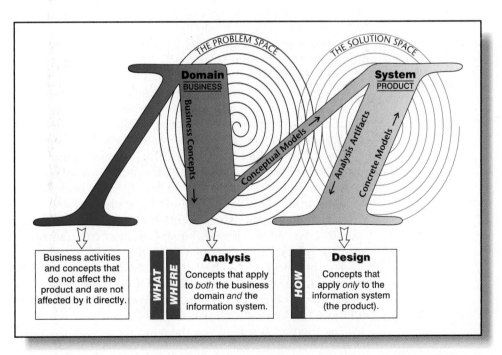

"M" again! Design uses the artifacts of analysis to produce a model of the solution. While the problem and solution spaces always overlap, analysis belongs more to the problem space and design more to the solution space.

(concepts that apply *only* to the product). This, of course, does not mean that there is no need to correct or amend use case modeling during design. Object-oriented analysis and design is an iterative process and *expects* such modifications. (The object-oriented approach actually encourages us to refrain from capturing every detail at once.) This does not mean that when we start design, we have all the relevant facts. To capture details required for design we must resort to tools that are available and appropriate for design. (We shall explore these tools in the following chapters.)

- The modeling tool that is primarily meant for design is the ***component diagram.*** A component diagram is a type of structural diagram that shows a set of components and their relationships. (To understand components in object-oriented and UML contexts see Chapter 15.)

Concrete Modeling: Logical & Physical

> Logical modeling represents the solution without reference to a specific technology; physical modeling maps the logical modeling to specific technologies.

We stated that design is the path between the concept of the product and the product itself. The design itself, however, must follow a path, as the two middle panes of Figure 10.1 illustrate in the form of "paint-by-number" kits or booklets offered by most toy stores: logical design and physical design.

Logical design transforms the conceptual model into a representation that shows how the components of the solution are logically related and interact. If you are constructing a house, the conceptual model identifies the scope of the building: the location, the area under construction, number of bedrooms, number of floors, number of bathrooms, etc. Logical modeling would then identify the exact location of rooms, halls, and staircases; the walls between them; the path of electrical wiring; the plumbing routes; and so on.

In modeling an information system or an application, your logical model would identify the logical architecture, the flow of the application, the exact messages that must pass between the user interface and the application to satisfy behavioral requirements, objects that must control the flow and pass on these messages to other objects, and blueprints for persistence (or database design).

Physical modeling carries modeling to actual choices that you must make to construct the product. For constructing a home, you must choose the make of the bricks, the type of the pipes, the wood paneling, the steel beams, and other items that satisfy the requirements of logical design. For an information system or an application, physical modeling includes the choice of the physical architecture (the network, the operating system, the physical distribution of components), the development platform, the programming language, visual controls, and the database.

The physical model should be almost indistinguishable from a reverse-engineered model of the product if it existed (except, perhaps, for building instructions or engineering specifications, such as the numbers in the third frame of Figure 10.1).

The relationship between the concept of a product and logical and physical design is not one-to-one:

- **A conceptual product might not have any logical solutions.** For a long time, science fiction writers have written stories—some very good—about travel aboard faster-than-light spaceships. Unless we find a loophole in the theory of relativity, no design for such ships will be forthcoming.

- If the product (or service) *can* have a solution, it might have *more than one logical design.* Our example about shellfish distribution (see Chapter 5) is but one of many examples that can express this concept.
- The same logical design can translate into *many physical designs* (or sometimes none). Again, transportation by automobile and the multitude of car designs provide a good example.

☞ In this book, except for certain examples, we will focus on logical design. As we shall explain, as long as the "technological paradigm" is the same, logical modeling applies to many technologies.

Sometimes physical constraints may define logical design. If a building exists, your choices for changing the building are limited to what the existing foundation or structure allows. The same is true if an enterprise asks you to produce an application that runs on its existing network, operating system, and/or database management system. Some existing frameworks, of course, are more flexible than others. Therefore, existing physical constraints may or may not allow a satisfactory logical design.

Last, but not least, **there is no exact threshold where logical design is transformed into physical design.** Physical design is achieved by successive refinements of logical design and the gradual inclusion of physical elements and constraints. Even from a purely physical viewpoint, this approach is prudent, because one physical choice often affects another one. For instance, if the floors of a multistory building are to be built from marble or stone, the columns supporting the floors must be designed to support the weight.

The Design Paradigms

> A design usually works only within one technological paradigm.

☞ The term "**paradigm**" has many meanings (and is frequently used carelessly). What we mean by the term *here* is an intersection of the following definitions: ❶ a broad theoretical or technological framework, ❷ a general agreement on how the world (or an aspect of it) works, and ❸ a fundamental model or pattern.

The distinction made between logical and physical modeling must *not* lead you to believe that logical design has no relationship whatsoever to technology. This is a dangerous error since it can lead to partial or total design failure.

Logical design must take into account the existing technological paradigms while steering clear from specific technologies within those paradigms.

For example, modeling elevator shafts and electrical conduits is meaningless (and would not be done) unless electricity and elevators are part of the technological landscape. In information systems, the logical persistence modeling for a relational database would be different from a design for an object-oriented database, and the technological paradigms within which Web and client/server applications work have noticeable differences.

Considering the dependency of design—both logical and physical—on technology, can a design survive rapid technological changes and "paradigm shifts"? The answer is both no and yes. No, because at a certain point a design cannot absorb technologies that emerge: A candle design is not able to adapt electricity to its own use, no matter how clever the design. Yes, if the design is flexible and captures the essence of the paradigm for which it is created. A good logical design for relational databases can easily be transferred to various implementations of the technology.

Another approach to making design adaptable to change is *loose coupling*—an architectural concept (discussed in Chapter 16). In a loosely coupled design, the system is constructed from **components** and *layers* that are, as far as possible, independent from each other. With loose coupling—within limits, of course—parts of the product (or service) can be repaired or upgraded with a minimum amount of cost and/or disruption.

If the technological paradigm is the envelope that surrounds design, is there any chance for design to push the envelope? In other words, is *revolutionary design* really possible? The answer is a resounding "yes," except that all revolutions are not the same thing.

☞ Tim Berners-Lee is credited with creating the first Web applications. His contribution, however, built upon the work of others such as Doug Engelbart and Ted Nelson who contributed to the concept and the implementation of hypertext, the foundation of HTTP (Hypertext Transfer Protocol).

- Often a revolutionary design is the creative use of an *existing* technological paradigm. As we stated in Chapter 1, technology is not one thing, but a set of interrelated components: know-how, methods, methodology, and material. *Refining one component of technology may result in a revolutionary design that makes the best use of other components.* We have already mentioned Henry Ford's refinement of the assembly line that changed the landscape of manufacturing. Closer to our subject matter is the World Wide Web, which took advantage of an existing technology, the Internet, but started a revolution that is still ongoing.
- If motivations are strong and resources available, a design can bring about technological innovations that satisfy its demands. The U.S. space program that resulted in manned missions to the Moon is such an example. Such technological leaps, however, are not cheap and require vast resources that are usually justifiable only in times of war (or cold war). Market forces also play such roles, but their pace is much slower and less focused.
- Some technologies that are overlooked or viewed from one perspective often find other uses later, and some of these uses can be revolutionary. Laser (**l**ight **a**mplification by **s**timulated **e**mission of **r**adiation) was put forward by Bell Lab scientists in the 1950s and gave rise to a wave of "ray gun" speculations. No one could foresee that it would become revolutionary in so many other areas: surgery, entertainment, supermarket checkouts, etc. The compass was considered a curiosity until European navigators tapped into its potential and started the "great age of discovery" in the 14th and 15th centuries. *Good design can make a technology revolutionary.*
- Technological revolutions do not happen in a vacuum, but result from decades, centuries, or even millennia of incremental development, both theoretical and technical. **Demands of design and technological innovations often drive each other forward.**

The Significance of Domain Analysis

Without a sound domain analysis, even an ingenious design is likely to fail.

We devoted one chapter to domain analysis. Most probably some ideas that we discussed in that chapter seem very reasonable: discover the meaning and the scope of the concepts that we are expected to transform into a solution—a product, a service, an application, or an information system. Other ideas might have seemed irrelevant (or even annoying): an illustration and a discussion about a rope, a knot, and a pair of hands. Therefore, it is equally probable that some of us would ignore *the second mission of domain analysis*: discover the context in which the product or the service must work.

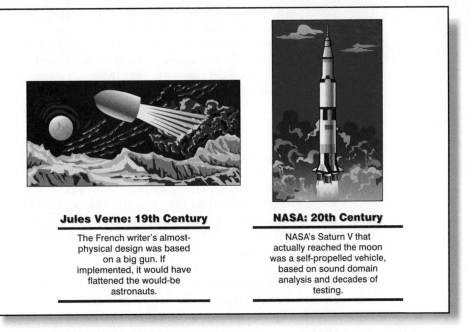

Jules Verne: 19th Century

The French writer's almost-physical design was based on a big gun. If implemented, it would have flattened the would-be astronauts.

NASA: 20th Century

NASA's Saturn V that actually reached the moon was a self-propelled vehicle, based on sound domain analysis and decades of testing.

Jules Verne's moon gun (in the famous science fiction novel *From the Earth to the Moon*) was to be poured into a well 274 meters deep, the first 61 meters of which were to be filled with 122 tons of guncotton. When fired, the gun was supposed to create a velocity of 12,000 yards per second. (His technical specifications are not limited to the above.) Even if everything else worked and the space-craft survived the launch, one piece of domain analysis was missing: No human can take this velocity and remain whole; not in the 19th century, not before, and not after. (Notice the difference between velocity and speed.)

This second mission is not less important than the first. In fact, a good design may fail to work due to factors that are not *directly* related to the product itself. The following instance from aircraft design is a succinct example.

[Graham 2001, 378–379]

A requirement was stated that [a plane's] reverse thrusters should not cut in until the aircraft was in contact with the runway. The designers reasoned that one could only be sure that the plane has touched down when its wheels began to spin forwards, which would be the case when in contact with a runway or similar [surface]. Therefore they arranged the system such that the thrusters would fire automatically when the wheels so span. This worked very well . . . until the first time the plane had to land on a runway covered with water . . . ! The plane overshot the runway. So, **even if the system can be proved to meet its specifications**—and there is no principled reason why this could not have been done in our aircraft example—**then there is still no guarantee that the specification meets the true requirement.** [Emphasis added.]

3. DESIGN CONCEPTS

Design poses problems that are different from those presented by analysis. In design we may use, more or less, the same modeling notations and the same diagrams as in analysis, but design models convey different concepts. In their essence, design concepts are expressions of one goal: *how* to create a product that satisfies *what* the conceptual model of analysis specifies.

In object-oriented system development, of course, analysis and design are not phases that are separated by a marked border line, but activities that overlap. They operate on concepts that intersect each other, even though they may point to different directions. Our approach to learning design, however, has to be different from the one that we adopted for understanding analysis. (See Figure 10.4.)

In analysis, we start by trying to understand *existing* problems within an *existing* context. And we learn analysis by going in the same direction: requirements discovery, domain analysis, behavioral modeling, and so on. In design, by contrast, we aim to build something that does *not* exist and, once it comes into existence, would most likely change the context into which it is introduced. A building, at the very least, changes the landscape around it; automobiles have changed the landscape everywhere with gas stations, service stations, car washes, expressways, toll-booths, and (regretfully) junkyards.

If you want to build a town hall, you set up a design competition: Would the design embody the ideals of the town, how would it look within its setting, what are the services that the city must provide for the hall once it is built, what are the undesirable consequences, and how much would it cost? After declaring a winning design, you then ask for well-formed architectural models and, most likely, the lowest-priced offer to build the desired building. The contractor then has to come up with engineering blueprints, organize a project, buy material, and start the actual building.

You do not, though, become an architect or a civil engineer by designing or constructing buildings, roads, and bridges. You become one by first studying all the tangible and intangible elements that must be put together properly to result in a building, a road, or a bridge: the building blocks of architectural and engineering artifacts, materials science, building codes and regulations, solutions that have worked (or have not worked) in the past, structural modeling from fine-grained components to large-grained ones, layering, etc.

In a sense, we undertake both analysis and design from the same starting point: the "big picture." The difference, as we said, is that in analysis the big picture exists while in design the big picture is the goal. Hence the different routes in learning each.

Figure 10.4 illustrates the most important design concepts that we will discuss:

- *Design Objects.*   A design object is an object that is not part of the problem domain but which is necessary for building the solution. We introduce design objects in this chapter and discuss them, extensively, in the next three chapters on application design.
- *Patterns.*   A pattern is the core of a solution to a recurring problem—a solution that has worked in the past. Patterns will be explored in Chapter 14.
- *Components & Reuse.*   A component is a reusable and replaceable software unit that provides services independent of particular applications. Reuse consists of technologies and concepts that allow software units to be used by more than one application or information system. Both concepts are the subject of Chapter 15.
- *Architecture & Layers.*   Architecture is the arrangement of the parts and their interrelationships within the structure of the product. A layer is a collection of components that provide similar services and/or are highly dependent on each other for performing their services. Chapter 16 is dedicated to both concepts.

Figure 10.4   Design Concepts

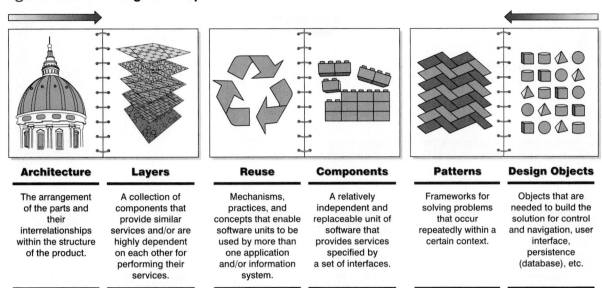

Architecture	Layers	Reuse	Components	Patterns	Design Objects
The arrangement of the parts and their interrelationships within the structure of the product.	A collection of components that provide similar services and/or are highly dependent on each other for performing their services.	Mechanisms, practices, and concepts that enable software units to be used by more than one application and/or information system.	A relatively independent and replaceable unit of software that provides services specified by a set of interfaces.	Frameworks for solving problems that occur repeatedly within a certain context.	Objects that are needed to build the solution for control and navigation, user interface, persistence (database), etc.

Actual design must start from the "big picture," but we must first understand the building blocks and the methodology.

Design Objects

> Design objects are those objects that are needed to build the solution.

☞ Until now, we have called analysis classes variously as "business" or "domain" classes. The official UML term for such classes is **entity** and, from now on, we are going to refer to them as "entity classes."

Analysis discovers objects that have, more or less, counterparts in the problem domain—patient, appointment, medical history, address, invoice, payment, doctor, etc.—regardless of whether the domain expert describes them exactly as the system analyst does. These objects usually have a "real life" outside the information system and, as a result, are "persisted," that is, their state (the values of their attributes) is saved in a database of some sort.

As Figure 10.2 illustrates, design classifies concepts that are concerned with the *solution*. The mission of an application is to serve the business by extending the reach of business activity or automating an existing workflow but, strictly speaking, the task of design classes is to serve the application, not the business. Therefore, in most cases, design classes need not be persisted in a database and disappear when the application is terminated. In other words, the majority of design objects have no state that needs persistence (except to satisfy application-specific requirements such as saving **User Preferences** or **Options** that many mass market productivity tools offer).

☞ The transition between the problem space and the solution space is never a clear-cut line but happens gradually and incrementally. Therefore, sometimes we have to redesign entity classes to work for our design, and some design classes are concerned with managing entity classes.

Figure 10.5 presents a general view of (common) design classes. The goal of analysis is discovering entity classes that, in spite of their diversity, are essentially of the same type as far as modeling is concerned. Design, however, requires many more *types* of classes—the same way that a toaster needs heating elements, screws, a casing, insulation, latches, springs, and other parts to satisfy a simple requirement: toast a piece of bread that in older times was done by holding the bread over a fire.

Design classes reflect the needs of the application: how it flows, how it interacts with the outside world, and how it manages it own needs. They fall into three general categories.

Figure 10.5   Common Design Classes: Making the Solution Work

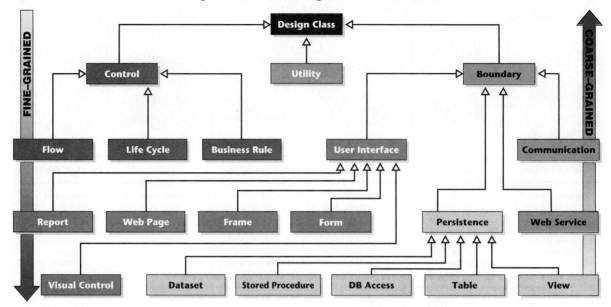

The categories in this illustration present a *general* view, not a *definitive* view. In design, you may need different objects or classify them differently.

[Jacobson 1999, 185]

❶ *Control.*   Classes that control the *flow* of the application, direct the sequencing of events, manage the interaction of other objects, and are "often used to encapsulate control related to a specific *use case.* Control classes are also used to represent complex derivations and calculations, such as business logic, that cannot be related to any specific, long-lived information stored by the system (i.e., a specific entity class)."

Control classes are not *directly* involved with the interaction between the actors (including non-human actors) and the system, nor are they responsible for persistence, but delegate these tasks to **boundary classes.**

❷ *Boundary.*   Classes that control the interaction between the system and *all* entities outside the system such as actors (user interface), persistence (databases, files, etc.), and Web services.

❸ *Utility.*   Classes that encapsulate a functionality that fall in neither control nor boundary classes. They are also called "helper" or "service" classes.

Depending on the dictates of the design, these categories can be further subcategorized. As we indicated before, two designers can produce completely different designs for the *same* product using the *same* technology and following the *same* methodology. As a result, except for the first tier of class types, there is **no standard way** to delineate design classes. What appears on Figure 10.5 would probably not match any other designer's or writer's concept of design subclasses.

Furthermore, since no standard exists, the same exact concept may appear under a different designation. In addition, the *context* may be different: In client/server applications, a **Form** is what the main unit of the (visual) user interface is called, whereas one Web page may contain *many* "forms" or input areas.

As we shall see in the next three chapters, the discovery and the definition of design classes starts with analysis artifacts:

- *Behavioral* models—that is, use cases—tell us what the user interface must do to satisfy the requirements. In design, this means not only the "what" of requirements, but also the "how" of navigation and workflow.
- *Structural* models identify entity classes that must be managed and persisted by design. Design requirements often force us to streamline the structural arrangement of the system (without, however, compromising the integrity of entity classes within the structure).
- *Dynamic* models, such as sequence and activity diagrams, are often the main stepping stones for discovering the user interface and control classes.

In different phases of modeling for design, you would need different kinds of *granularity.* That is, at first you would use *coarse-grain* class types such as **Control** and **Boundary** to create high-level but less detailed models. (We shall do so in the next chapter.) Then, as the need arises, you will use more *fine-grained* types like **Form** and even **Visual Control** and add details.

Note that actual design artifacts seldom follow clear-cut theoretical lines. When defining design classes, countless factors come into play—not the least of which are the nature of the application, the preferences of the designer, and the vision of the architect. For example, one designer might decide to assign the responsibility of communication with the database to individual entity classes and dispense with **DB Access** type classes. Another might choose to give this responsibility to classes that coordinate a set of transactions *across* various classes. A third might adhere to our concept of separating the mechanics of persistence from the business logic embodied in entity classes. In fact, you may be forced to employ all such solutions within a single application. (We will clarify this example in Chapter 13.)

All told, what makes one product better than its competitor is the quality and the ingenuity of the solution, not the nature of the problem.

UML Extension Mechanisms

UML offers a set of mechanisms that allow modeling to be refined, extended, and adapted to specific needs.

☞ The framers of UML are, of course, not anonymous. Many writers have made impressive contributions to object-oriented modeling and have expanded the horizons of UML, but the originators of UML are Grady Booch, Ivar Jacobson, and James Rumbaugh. (See *Chapter 2.*)

The framers of UML had the foresight to know that no modeling language can foresee or incorporate all the symbols that would satisfy future modeling requirements. (Such an assumption would have been similar to the famous story about the 19th century patent official who declared that since everything worth inventing had been already invented, there was no need for issuing further patents.)

UML is periodically updated and expanded officially, but its inherent simplicity is its main strength, not a weakness (as some would have you believe). The basic concepts of UML—actor, class, package, etc.—are each represented by one symbol and, furthermore, there are very few such symbols in total.

Compared to design, the modeling needs of analysis are modest. Therefore, in chapters on analysis, the extension mechanisms of UML were mentioned only in passing. Design, however, must produce a *builder's view* of the system and, as a result, has more rigorous and demanding modeling requirements than analysis. UML provides for such requirements by providing a set of mechanisms: stereotyping, notes, adornments, tagged values, and constraints. These mechanisms enable us to clarify modeling elements and add new properties to UML building blocks. (The compliance of modeling tools with these mechanisms, unfortunately, is uneven.)

The first thing that you must consider *before* using UML extension mechanisms is not to use them. Extending UML must be the last resort—*after* you have made certain that standard UML notation cannot satisfy your modeling needs.

Stereotyping

> Stereotyping is the specialization of standard UML notations.

[Booch 1999, 466]

Stereotyping extends the vocabulary of UML by allowing you to "create new kinds of building blocks that are derived from existing ones but are specific to your" needs.

UML stereotyping is typically simple but powerful: If any building block of UML is not **specialized** enough to express your specific needs, you may specialize it yourself by specifying a tag and/or assigning an icon. Besides, if need be, such an icon can be used *instead* of the original UML symbol.

The lack of "standards" for the design classes that we have mentioned is actually intentional—and very wise since, otherwise, UML would become a repressor instead of an enabler. But with freedom comes a responsibility: Stereotyping is not for entertainment. Modeling is first and foremost for communication and if a model loses its simplicity, its message is lost as well. While it is true that you may not find official or standard symbols for your needs, if you come across *de facto* standards—that is, a designation or an icon that somebody else has put forward and which has become popular—try using it first.

In previous chapters we mentioned stereotyping briefly, but in design it is seriously needed. Not only are design models more crowded than analysis models, but there is also a greater variety of element *types*. Figure 10.6 illustrates the same design classes that we discussed in the previous section, but in this rendition they are "stereotyped" by icons. (As we shall see later, we can stereotype a class simply by assigning a tag instead of, or in addition to, an icon: «**Control**», for example, to specialize a class as responsible for controlling the flow of the application.)

Table 10.1 explains the stereotypes that appear in Figure 10.6 (plus one for *entity* classes that mostly result from analysis). It is worthwhile to emphasize that another source may view the same concepts differently or produce new ones. The first three stereotypes—**Entity**, **Control**, and **Boundary**—come from standard UML notation. We have adopted some of the others (such as **Table** and **View**) from other writers.

Figure 10.7 illustrates the various ways in which stereotypes may be used.

❶ A class diagram from Walden's **Patient Management** subsystem that includes two design classes (**Appointment UI** and **Appointment Agent**) and one class from analysis (**Patients**, plural) that we have redefined as a design class. **Patient** and **Appointment** are entity classes and are not explicitly stereotyped here. (We can, of course, do so.) All classes are presented as the standard UML "box" icons with compartments for the attributes and operations. The stereotypes are identified by a simple tag above the class name: «**UI**», «**Flow**», and «**Life Cycle**». (The typographical symbols around stereotype labels are called *guillemets*; since they cannot be found on regular keyboards and you must create them by entering key combinations, you may use angled brackets—« and »— instead.) As in the previous class diagrams with which you are familiar, specifying operations and/or attributes is optional and depends on your needs.

☞ **Appointment UI** is especially coarse-grained because we can be sure that it involves more than one form and many visual controls. But using such coarse-grained classes in the early stages of design ensures that the model stays focused on its message and does not lose its way in details that are irrelevant to its purpose.

Figure 10.6 Design Classes with Stereotypes: Specialization of UML Notation

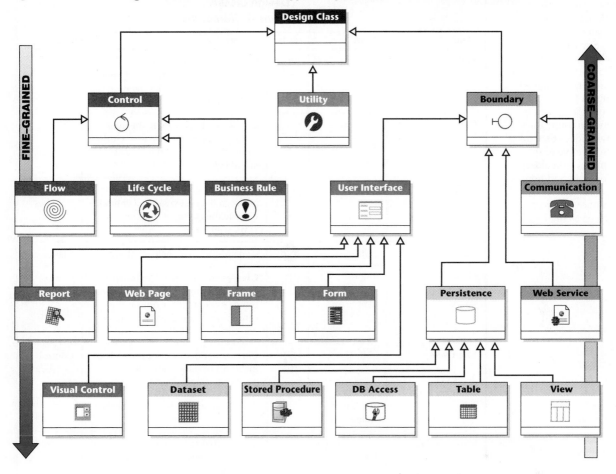

➋ The same class diagram as in the first example, except that the attribute and operation compartments have given way to an *icon* that identifies the stereotype. (We have also included the icon for entity classes.)

➌ A simplified collaboration diagram in which the standard UML icon for class has been replaced by an icon specific to each stereotype. Stereotype tags have been discarded because the assumption is that the icons are either familiar or self-explanatory. (Hence a warning on using stereotype icons: If the icons that you want to use are not standard, familiar, or self-explanatory, you must do your best to make the consumers of your models familiar with them—perhaps by an index similar to Table 10.1.) This modeling technique lacks detail but can convey a complex view very fast and very effectively.

Even though in the first example of Figure 10.7 we did not identify entity classes with any specific stereotype, you may do so if the need arises. For example, in Walden Hospital's information system, we might want to distinguish all patient-related classes—such as **Medical History**, **Addresses**, **Appointment**, etc.—from other classes. To accomplish this, we can stereotype them as «**Patient-Related**» and assign an icon to this stereotype.

Stereotyping is by no means limited to classes. We may stereotype any and all modeling elements within UML, including actors, relationships, use cases, etc.

Table 10.1

Design Classes:
Definitions &
Stereotypes

Such a list of design
classes can neither be
comprehensive nor
universally agreed
upon. Building a
solution generally
means coming up
with ideas that are
innovative or that
improve on older
ideas. In addition,
certain concepts
cannot be forced on a
given technology.

Design Classes
Definitions & Stereotypes

STEREOTYPE	LABEL	ICON	DESCRIPTION	PARENT
Entity	«Entity»		Classes that usually have a counterpart in the problem domain and that are persisted. (The icon is a UML *standard*.)	Class
Control	«Control»		Classes that coordinate the interaction among other classes within the system. (The icon is a UML *standard*.)	Class
Boundary	«Boundary»		Classes that control the interaction between the system and *all* entities outside the system. (The icon is a UML *standard*.)	Class
Utility	«Utility»		General-purpose "helper" classes.	Class
Flow	«Flow»		Classes that control the flow of the application and the sequencing of events. Their operations often match the events within a use case.	Control
Life Cycle	«Life Cycle»		Classes that manage the life cycle of instances of a specific class.	Control
Business Rule	«BR» or «Business Rule»		Classes that enforce business rules that go beyond individual classes.	Control
User Interface	«UI» or «User Interface»		Classes that manage interaction with the users. They may be visual or nonvisual.	Boundary
Persistence	«Persistence»		Classes that manage the interaction between the application and the database.	Boundary
Communication	«Comm»		Classes that manage the communication between the application and automated sources such as remote sites and the operating system.	Boundary
Web Service	«Web Service»		Classes that offer packaged functions using Web technology.	Boundary
Report	«Report»		Classes that provide information about a specific topic in a structured format.	Boundary: UI
Web Page	«Web Page»		A page sent by a Web server and received by a browser.	Boundary: UI
Form	«Form»		In client/server applications, the main unit of interaction between the user and the application. On a Web page, an area that allows the user to maintain data.	Boundary: UI

Frame	«Frame»		In client/server applications, part of the form that manages its own set of visual controls. On a Web browser, an area that is populated with a page independent from other frames.	Boundary: UI
Visual Control	«VC» or «Visual Control»		A constituent element of a form or a Web page. Text boxes and dropdowns are examples of visual controls.	Boundary: UI
DB Access	«DBA» or «DB Access»		Classes that manage the communication between the database and the application.	Boundary: Persistence
Dataset	«Dataset»		A vehicle for transporting data within the application. Also variously called **Recordset**, **Resultset** or simply (though not quite accurately) **List**. Datasets are usually standard components of development platforms.	Boundary: Persistence
Table	«Table»		❶ The basic structural unit of relational databases in row-column format. ❷ Any data structure in row-column format.	Boundary: Persistence
View	«View»		A *virtual* (or logical) table created by the relational database management system from joining columns from various tables.	Boundary: Persistence
Stored Procedure	«SP» or «Stored Proc»		A procedure stored within a database that, according to predefined rules, processes data for reading and/or writing. In many cases, stored procedures embody business rules, independent of any application.	Boundary: Persistence

(The labels **«Include»** and **«extend»** that were introduced in Chapter 7 are actually stereotypes of relationships.) Figure 10.8 illustrates the application of stereotyping to some of the use cases that we introduced in Chapter 7. (There, we also used the solid triangle to stereotype the **Make Appointment by Referral Source**.)

We must make one very important point about Figure 10.8: To illustrate stereotyped relationships—that is, between a stereotyped class and its "parent"—we use a blank-headed arrow that is the UML symbol for generalization. We must, however, distinguish between generalization as it applies to the elements of the information system and the elements of UML.

> Specialization and generalization by stereotyping applies to modeling elements, not to what those elements represent.

Stereotyping does not imply inheritance. For example, the design class **Form** is a sibling of **Report** and a child of **User Interface** that, in turn, is a specialized type

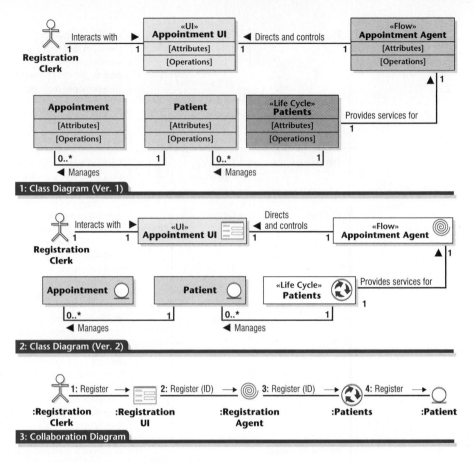

Figure 10.7
Modeling with Stereotypes: The Alternatives

Class diagrams usually do not include actors but, as we mentioned in Chapter 8, Structural Modeling, a class diagram must have a purpose and since the purpose of diagrams in this illustration is to introduce the function of design elements, the class diagrams include the actor to clarify the role of user interface and control classes. (In the next three chapters, we will discuss these objects in detail.)

of **Boundary**. These relationships do not mean that any **Form** class inherits any attributes and/or operations from a certain **Boundary** class or shares any with a **Report** class. In fact, the relationship between a superclass and a subclass in stereotyping can itself be stereotyped (with a «**Stereotype**» tag) to distinguish it from "normal" generalization. (However, this is rarely necessary since, first, you would seldom need such diagrams in a real development project and, second, it is mostly superfluous—except as a training wheel.)

☞ Again, do not use stereotypes (especially stereotype icons) indiscriminately. It is true that stereotypes extend the UML notation (and it is a good thing), but you may end up extending it beyond recognition (which is *not* a good thing).

[Booch 1999, 78]

Notes

Notes "specify things like requirements, observations, reviews, and explanations."

In any field, and within any modeling notation, modeling elements are—by necessity—rather simple and minimal because the value of modeling depends on the use of a limited set of symbols that can be more or less readily understood. This simplicity, however, cannot be enough in many situations where the basic

Figure 10.8
**Stereotyping
Use Cases and
Actors: All UML
Elements Can
Be Stereotyped**

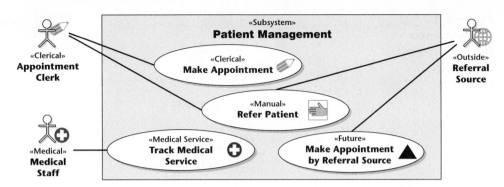

Most modeling tools allow stereotyping by tag while support for icons is more limited.

modeling symbols fail to provide the full significance of an entity. Using notes is one mechanism to remedy this shortcoming.

Notes may consist of any number of textual or graphical elements. Depending on the modeling tool, you may even embed a URL within a note that directly takes you to a lengthy document or a Web page.

☞ Notes do *not* change the meaning of the models to which they are attached, but simply clarify them.

The UML icon for presenting notes is a rectangle with a dog-eared corner, containing textual and graphical elements.

Do not obscure a model with too many notes or long notes. If long comments are needed, use the note to direct attention to a detailed document.

Adornments

[Booch 1999, 79]

> Adornments "are textual or graphical items that are added to an element's basic notation" to show a detail or details about the element's specifications.

In a class diagram, the association between classes is represented by a simple line but, as we saw in Chapter 8, this simple connection can take on extra significance by specifying the role of the association, its direction, and the quantitative relationship

Figure 10.9
Notes: Specify, Explain, Review, and Link

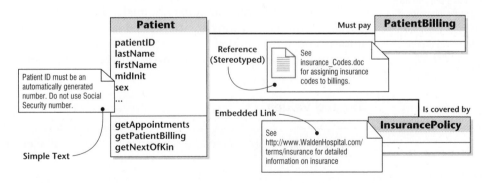

By adding notes, you can explain or ask questions. Indiscriminate use of notes, however, can obscure the model.

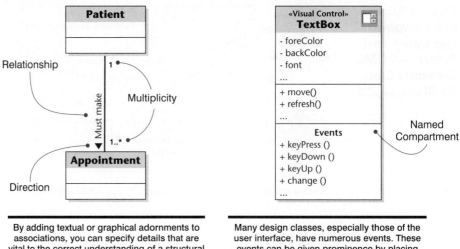

Figure 10.10
Adornments:
Add Details to
the Basic
Notation

By adding textual or graphical adornments to associations, you can specify details that are vital to the correct understanding of a structural or dynamic model.

Many design classes, especially those of the user interface, have numerous events. These events can be given prominence by placing them in a compartment of their own.

By using adornments, you may show details about an element's specifications or its association with another element.

[Booch 1999, 79]

☞ "Unless it's obvious by its content, it's good practice to name any extra compartment explicitly so that there is no confusion about its meaning. It is also good practice to use extra compartments sparingly, because if overused, they make diagrams cluttered."
[Booch 1999, 80]

(or "multiplicity") between the two classes at each end of the line. For example, the association between **Patient** and **Appointment** is specified as one in which a patient **Must Make** one or more (**1 to 1..***) appointments. In UML terminology, such extensions are called **adornments.**

Adornments are usually "rendered by placing text near the element of interest or by adding a graphic symbol to the basic notation." (This is how the association between classes and multiplicity is presented.) Sometimes, however, we may need "to adorn an element with more detail than can be accommodated by simple text or graphic." In classes—more so in design but also in analysis—we can add an extra compartment to provide the desired information. For example, we may want to distinguish *events* from other operations (or *exceptions* from other events) by assigning them to a separate compartment. Such compartments may be anonymous (without name) or named (identified by a label).

The term "adornment" must not mislead you into believing that they are simple decorations and may be dispensed with. For example, we may (perhaps) understand individual classes without the specification of multiplicity, but our perception of the system's structure would become severely defective.

Tagged Values

Tagged values allow us to add new properties to UML elements.

[Booch 1999, 81]

Each UML element has "its own set of properties: classes have names, attributes, and operations; associations have names and two or more ends (each with its own

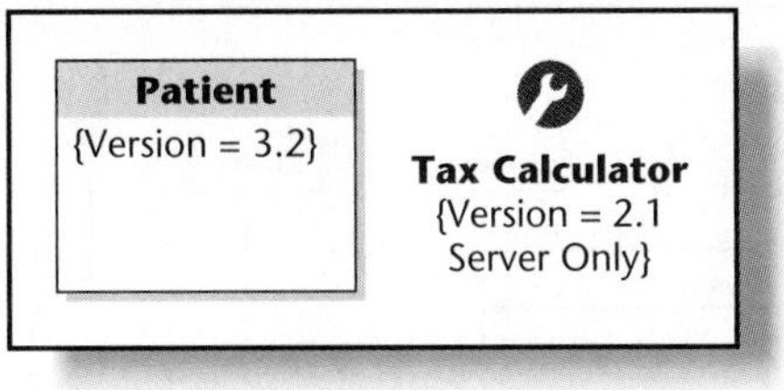

Figure 10.11
Tagged Values:
New Properties
for UML
Elements

We may use tagged values to assign new properties to modeling elements. Note that the new properties do not apply to what those elements represent.

properties); and so on. With stereotypes, you can add new things to the UML; with tagged values, you can add new properties."

Tagged values are often used to add properties relevant to code generation and/or configuration, *not* to instances of what the UML symbol signifies. For example, if we add the tag **{Version = 2.3}** to a **Patient** class icon, it does *not* mean that instances of **Patient** (i.e., **Patient** objects) have a new property like **firstName** or **lastName**, but simply that *this* concept of **Patient** is in its second major revision and its third minor one. Therefore, tagged values must be considered as *metadata* (and tags as *meta-properties*).

We can assign tags to existing UML elements as well as to stereotypes, in which case all "children" of the stereotype receive that tag as well. If, for instance, we create a stereotype called «**Tax Calculation**» and assign it a tag such as **{Server Only}**, then we have, in effect, declared that any class that uses this stereotype *must* be installed on the server, not on the client workstations (so that they may updated without needing to update individual workstations).

A tagged value is commonly rendered as a string enclosed by curly brackets and placed below the name of the element that receives the new property. The string starts with the name of the tag, includes a symbol (such as =) that defines the relationship between the tag and its value, and ends with the value of the tag. If the value is unambiguous, you may omit the tag name: **{Server Only}** instead of **{Location = Server Only}**.

Constraints

A constraint specifies a condition that must be true for a relationship to be correct.

UML models often depict relationships that must be qualified with a constraint to be understood correctly. For example, as we explained in Chapter 8, a patient may be issued many hospital cards but, at any one time, only one card is valid. In other words, the valid card is a *subset* of all cards. In the same manner, a department may have many employees, but only one employee can be the manager. Or, for an online purchase, the connection for entering payment information must be secure. (See Figure 10.12.)

A constraint is shown as a string enclosed within curly brackets, placed near the element that it qualifies. This is similar to tagged values, except that constraints apply to relationships within the information system, while tagged values qualify UML elements. Removing tagged values does not change the meaning of the model, while removing constraints does.

Figure 10.12
**Constraints:
Qualifying the
Relationships**

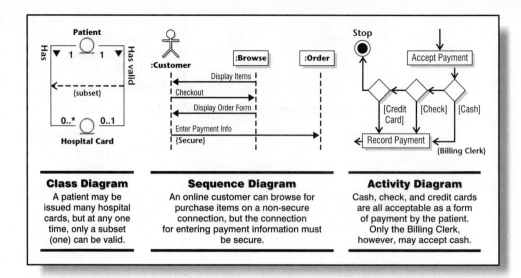

Class Diagram
A patient may be
issued many hospital
cards, but at any one
time, only a subset
(one) can be valid.

Sequence Diagram
An online customer can browse for
purchase items on a non-secure
connection, but the connection
for entering payment information must
be secure.

Activity Diagram
Cash, check, and credit cards
are all acceptable as a form
of payment by the patient.
Only the Billing Clerk,
however, may accept cash.

4. PACKAGING

The UML models in the analysis section of this book illustrated only a tiny fraction of the models that are needed to represent the **Patient Management** domain, let alone the whole enterprise-wide system for Walden Medical Center. Even then, we separated use cases and classes into diagrams with relatively few elements to avoid overloading the model.

Design increases the need for models exponentially since ❶ design artifacts, especially in physical modeling, must be comprehensive and precise enough not only for understanding the concepts but also for building a product; and ❷ a vast amount of detail is discovered during design. We can accommodate design needs by producing huge models, but a model that is difficult to decipher is not a good model.

A larger page to print a larger diagram would help but would not resolve the issue. It is the number of elements within the diagram that is the culprit. When we consult an unfamiliar map, we cannot readily memorize the absolute majority of elements that the map represents. After the first scan, we may remember a few names, the shape of a road, and perhaps the bend of a river. Our short-term memory is not able to retain too much information and relate them together:

[Evitts 2000, 19]

This is where Seven Plus or Minus Two [pattern] comes in. Pattern recognition is itself dependent on the capabilities of human short-term memory. Individual elements in a potential cognitive pattern can be related and organized only if they are in short-term memory, and short-term memory can manage only a limited number of items. It turns out that this number, which varies only slightly—depending on the circumstances—is . . . Seven Plus or Minus Two (7±2).

The effectiveness of any diagram—not just UML diagrams—decreases as the number of elements passes the 7±2 threshold. Since an important reason of modeling is to *manage complexity,* we cannot allow models themselves to become too complex.

The most common approach to resolving this issue is called *chunking:* breaking down a large model into pieces that can be grasped more easily. In other words, we should build models that adhere, more or less, to the 7±2 rule and then organize *logically related* items into meaningful groups. In UML, the chunks that organize models are called packages.

What Is a Package?

[Booch 1999, 169–181]

> A **package** is a general-purpose mechanism in modeling tools for grouping related items within a hierarchical structure.

We introduced Walden's **Patient Management** first as a *domain* in which related business activities take place and a set of business concepts are shared. We then argued that domains provide a conceptual framework for organizing the information system into *subsystems* that correspond to the business workflow.

A subsystem is an **architectural** unit and the term "architecture" applies to both the actual arrangement of building blocks within a system and the various views (or models) of such an arrangement. We can also define a subsystem as a **package** of behavior and operations, and the models that represent the subsystem as a "package" of views.

Up to now we have used packages transparently, as models on a *flat* surface. However, to resolve the issue of model *overloading,* we should explore the three-dimensional facilities of modeling tools.

Figure 10.13 illustrates one (rather simplified) way of packaging models for Walden's **Patient Management** system. To suggest that models of a large system can proliferate into an enormous volume of analysis and design artifacts, we have included all subsystems that make up the system as the top-level package.

The **Patient Management** package, in turn, consists of three other packages—behavioral, structural, and dynamic models—each of which owns a set of models. We could have organized **Patient Management** differently, grouping its models into functional packages such as **Appointment**, **Registration**, **Medical Services**, etc. (See Figure 10.14. This latter approach is especially useful if the number of models is high.)

A package can contain any number of items: use cases, use case diagrams, class diagrams, components, other packages, etc.

There are no limits on nesting packages within each other—except those required by good judgment and dictated by the capabilities of modeling tools.

Packaging Namespace

> A namespace is a *hierarchical* scheme of naming in which each name is unique within the sphere of the one above it.

Figure 10.13
Packaging Walden's IS: Nesting Models within a Hierarchical Structure

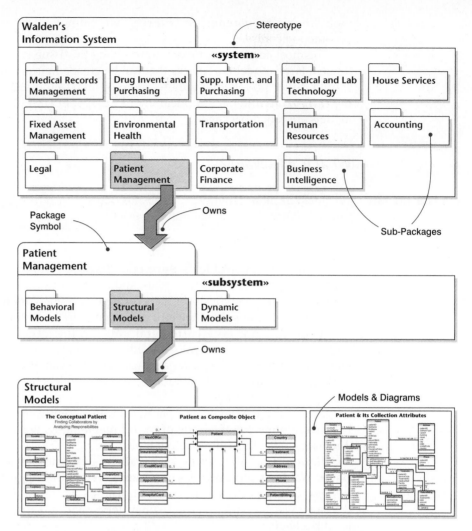

Packaging allows models to be nested in a hierarchical structure. One model or package can belong to one, and only one, package, although packages can "import" elements from other packages.

Packaging hierarchy enforces a *namespace*, meaning that at every level the name of an item must be **unique** within the boundaries of the package that owns it. For example, if we follow the packaging scheme illustrated in Figure 10.14, the **full name** of the **Register Patient** use case becomes **Walden Information System::Patient Management::Behavioral Models::Register Patient**. (Some modeling tools do not allow spaces in names; most do not accept special characters.) Unlike the names of use cases, the names of packages are *not* active; that is, they do not signify an action but an area of activity.

The full name is formally called the *path*, following the tradition of a hierarchical file system (such as those in Windows or Unix). In such a system, *folders* contain *subfolders*, and subfolders may own other subfolders, and so on. **Register Patient** is called the *simple name*. The double colon in the full name indicates that the left-hand entity contains (or owns) the right-hand one.

Figure 10.14
**Patient
Management
Package:
Visibility and
Importing**

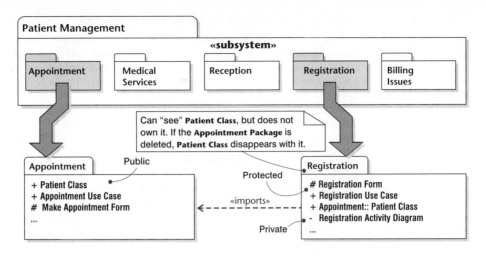

As in the case for classes, the elements within a package can be public, private, or protected.

Visibility & Importing

> Visibility of an element inside a package decides what other packages can access that element.

The UML packaging concept is hierarchical: Packages may **branch** into other packages until they end in **leaves,** the actual artifacts such as classes, use cases, or diagrams. But if a system or subsystem is complex enough to require packaging, then the chances are high that a good number of analysis or design artifacts cannot be assigned exclusively to one branch or one package alone. This situation is especially true of individual classes that are the building blocks of modeling. For example, in Walden's information system, the class **Patient** and its associate classes are needed not only by *all* areas with **Patient Management** but also by a number of other subsystems.

The mechanism employed by UML to address this issue is *importing.* This mechanism, in turn, relies on the *visibility* of package elements. Like the attributes and the operations of a class, the elements owned by a package can be assigned a specific visibility:

- *Public.* Identified with a plus sign, public elements are visible to all other packages. In most modeling tools, elements are public by default.
- *Private.* A minus sign next to an element specifies that the element may be seen only by members of the same package.
- *Protected.* Like classes, packages can be *generalized.* For example, you may define a package called **Search** that contains a certain set of classes common to search activities within the system. You may then define other packages such as **Patient Search** or **Medical Service Search** that inherit the artifacts within the **Search** packages. These *child* packages can see both public and protected elements within **Search**, while other packages have access only to public items. (As in classes, child classes can override what they inherit. See Chapter 15.) Protected element are identified by a pound (#) sign.

A package may import the public elements owned by another package. For example, in Figure 10.4 the **Registration** package imports the **Patient** class from the **Appointment** packages. (Most likely, the other packages within **Patient Management** will have to do the same.) On the *importing* package, the imported item appears like other elements, with two distinguishing features:

- The name of the imported element is not "simple," but carries the name of the *exporting* package as well. In our example (see Figure 10.14), the name of the **Patient** class in the **Registration** package consists of two parts: **Appointment::Patient**. The first part of the name, **Appointment**, refers to the package that exported the item.
- If the owner package (**Appointment**, for example) is removed from the system, the element disappears from *all* importing packages (e.g., **Registration**) as well. Importation does not bestow any protection to the imported element.

The importing package can mark the visibility of the imported items without restrictions. For example, the visibility of **Patient** within **Registration** can be public, private, or protected. If the imported element is public, then other packages may, in turn, import the item from the importing package. Since the inside of a package is *encapsulated* and only its *interface* is accessible to other packages, whether an item actually belongs to the package or is merely imported becomes irrelevant.

[Booch 1999, 177]

In fact, a package can be just a *façade*; that is, it can own nothing of its own and simply represent a view on the elements owned by other packages. This is a powerful feature (if the modeling tool supports it), since it eases the task of creating new packages as the need arises. It is also an argument in favor of packaging analysis and design artifacts along types (as in Figure 10.13) because you do not have to decide, beforehand, how the artifacts are presented from various viewpoints.

The public parts of a package are also called its *exports*, even though the package does not actively engage in exporting but rather cooperates with importing packages.

When to Use Packaging

> Whether or how to use packaging depends on the complexity of the system, the context of the problem, judgment, and experience.

One thing that we *must* avoid is to package because it seems sophisticated or proves that we are masters of UML. *Do not take lightly the effort needed to create and maintain packages.* Packaging without a clear vision and good planning will create more problems than it can resolve:

❶ Once we group our artifacts into packages, CASE tools do not allow us to easily or cheaply change our minds (though the mechanism of importing may ease the problem).

❷ The earlier in the development process, the less we can be sure how things relate to each other. In other words, the earlier it is, the more misunderstandings we will have, which returns us to number ❶.

However, there are factors that may weigh in favor of using multi-level packaging:

[Bittner 2002, 165–166]

- *Identifying Functional Areas.* Even without complexity, we may want to distinguish between areas of activity. (As it happens, when we do have separate areas of activity, complexity usually follows.) If, however, our problem domain is small and well-defined, we should stay with single-level packages.
- *Complexity.* We must use every device at our disposal to make complexity comprehensible. Packaging is one such device—even though it has its own side effects, such as making the management of analysis and design artifacts more complicated.
- *Team Work.* If a project is large enough that it requires us to partition our models for use by different development teams, then packaging is an answer (though not the only answer and not enough by itself). If this is the primary factor, then extra effort must be made so that each bundle of packages is as comprehensive and self-contained as possible.
- *Confidentiality.* If the client wants to keep certain areas of the system confidential, then packaging becomes a useful mechanism, since package elements can be marked as "public" or "private."

5. Wrap Up

☑ **Design & its place in the development process**

Design is the path between the concept of a product and the building of the product itself. While analysis studies the product from the viewpoint of the problem domain—what it can do to solve a problem, satisfy a desire, or take advantage of an opportunity—design does the same thing from the view of the solution: what the product must *be* to satisfy requirements. In short, design is about "*how*," whereas analysis is about "*what*" and "*where*."

Design is a model-driven activity that must, eventually, produce engineering blueprints for actually building the product. Our approach to design is *object-oriented, component-based,* and *architectural.* This approach views the product as a *system* composed of objects, both coarse-grained and fine-grained, and holds that the design process must start from an overall view that is refined through round-trips and iterations, not through successive decomposition of the features.

Like object-oriented analysis, design starts its voyage of discovery by going from outside in, and refines its views from inside out if new objects are discovered or required.

☑ **Moving from analysis to design**

Analysis and design are not phases divided by clearly defined lines. They are activities that overlap, and the transition between the two occurs only incrementally. Design objects—objects that serve the product—are discovered by starting from analysis artifacts.

Essentially, design uses the same modeling tools as analysis, but turns its focus from the problem space to the solution space. There are two exceptions: use cases that are used by design but not created for it, and component diagrams that are primarily for use by design.

☑ **Logical design vs. physical design**

Since design is about modeling the product, it is also called **concrete modeling.** Concrete modeling is composed of two activities: **logical modeling** that represents the solution but avoids references to specific technologies, and **physical modeling** that maps logical models into specific technology or technologies. The detailed physical models are comparable to *engineering blueprints* in construction or manufacturing.

We must not conclude that since logical design avoids *specific* technologies it is technology-agnostic. Logical design must take into account a technological **paradigm** while disregarding technologies as products.

A problem may have no solution and, therefore, lack a meaningful logical design. But if there is a solution (or more than one solution), it is likely than one logical design can be mapped into multiple physical designs.

☑ **The significance of domain analysis to design**

Simple requirements gathering might overlook factors that are not directly related to the problems that the product must solve. A sound and extensive domain analysis is critical to the success of design, since a product might satisfy all stated features but fail in the context in which it must operate.

☑ **Design objects**

Analysis discovers objects that belong to the problem space. Design must define objects that are necessary for the product to operate. While analysis objects, called *"entity"* objects in object-oriented terminology, must be persisted because the business must know their states across a period of time, design objects are usually (but not always) stateless: They vanish if the system is shut down or the application is closed.

One characteristic of design objects is their variety. In essentials, design classes fall into three major categories but, depending on the available or selected technology, the requirements of the application, and the designer's decisions or preferences, they might be further refined into subclasses:

- **Control.** These classes control the flow of the application, direct the sequencing of events, manage the interaction of other objects, and frequently enforce such business rules that go beyond the domain of a specific class but relate to a specific use case or go across use cases. Control classes are not directly involved in the interaction between the application and the outside world, but delegate these tasks to "boundary" classes.
- **Boundary.** Boundary classes control the interaction between the system or application and entities outside the system such as human actors (user interface), communications, and persistence (databases, files, etc.).
- **Utility.** These "helper" classes offer services (such as calculations) that are usually independent of the application's flow and do not go beyond its boundaries.

As we said, these superclasses might be refined into subclasses such as `Life Cycle` classes that manage entity classes, `Web Page` and `Form` classes that manage the interaction with the users, and `Dataset` classes that function as data carriers. (There are, however, no standards for doing so. Therefore, you must follow your own judgment or examples that have become *de facto* standards.)

☑ **Stereotyping & other UML extension mechanisms**

UML modeling notations are few and simple. To allow creating richer models both in content and in form, UML provides a set of extension mechanisms:

- **Stereotyping:** extends the vocabulary of UML by creating *specialized* building blocks for modeling. For example, you can specialize the UML class symbol by labeling it as «`Control`» and adding an identifying icon. You may then use the label to identify all control classes or use the icon as a substitute for the standard box. *Every* UML notation can be stereotyped.
- **Notes:** specify comments that express requirements, observations, reviews, and explanations. Notes should be used sparingly and, if long comments or documentation is necessary, they can serve as references to other documents or hold embedded links.
- **Adornments:** are textual and graphical items that show details about modeling elements. Contrary to the low expectations that the term inspires, adornments are often essential to understanding the model, for they include things like multiplicity (quantitative relationship between instances of classes), the nature of class associations, and the direction of the association.
- **Tagged Values:** allow us to add new properties to modeling elements, such as version number. Note that these tagged values are *metadata* about the *modeling* elements and *not* what they symbolize (such as an entity class).
- **Constraints:** specify a condition that must be true for a relationship between modeling elements to be correct. For example, one department may have many employees but only *one* manager (a subset, a type of constraint).

☑ **Packaging, a UML mechanism for managing the complexity of models**

Design increases the complexity of models exponentially. The most common approach to resolving this issue is called *chunking:* breaking down a large model into pieces that can be grasped more easily. The mechanism provided by UML for this purpose is packaging. A **package** is a general-purpose mechanism in modeling tools for grouping related items within a *hierarchical* structure.

A package can contain any number of items: use cases, use case diagrams, class diagrams, components, other packages, etc. Depending on the circumstances and choice, packages can be organized functionally or based on some other criteria such as the type of model.

A package and the elements within the package can belong to one, and only one, package—even though packages can *expose* their elements to other packages that may then *import*

such *public* elements. Nevertheless, the life of a package element is dependent on the life of its owner: If the owner is removed, all its owned elements disappear as well.

Packaging should not be done early and should not be done often. Only when you have a clear picture of how you want to organize your models should you attempt packaging, for "repackaging" is not easy.

6. KEY CONCEPTS

Adornments. Textual or graphical items that are added to an element's basic notation to show a detail or details about the element's specifications. Even though the term might suggest the idea of luxuries that we can dispense with, adornments often are essential to understanding the significance of a modeling element.

Architecture. The arrangements of a system's components and the relationship of these components to each other and to the whole.

Boundary Classes. Classes that control the interaction between the system and *all* entities outside the system such as actors (user interface), persistence (databases, files, etc.), and Web services.

Component. A reusable, replaceable, and sometimes recombinable unit that provides services independent of a particular product or application.

Concrete Modeling. Modeling of the solution through design. It consists of two related and overlapping activities: **logical modeling** and **physical modeling.**

Constraint. A UML extension mechanism. A constraint specifies a condition that must be true for a modeling relationship to be understood correctly.

Control Classes. Classes that control the flow of the application, direct the sequencing of events, manage the interaction of other objects, and often enforce business rules that cross class boundaries. Control classes are not *directly* involved with the interaction between the actors (including non-human actors) and the system, nor are they responsible for *persistence,* but delegate these tasks to **boundary classes.**

Design. A model-driven activity that aims to arrive at the specifications of the solution. The modeling done during design is often called **concrete modeling.** Our design methodology is object-oriented, component-based, and architectural.

Design Objects. Objects that are needed to build the solution and are defined by design. Design objects are

instances of classes that fall into three broad categories: **control, boundary,** and **utility.** Unlike **entity classes,** design classes usually do not need *persistence.*

Domain Analysis & Design. Domain analysis defines the *context* within which the product must work. Therefore, it is critical to the success of design. Seen from the opposite angle, without sound domain analysis, even an ingenious design is likely to fail.

Entity Class. A class that often has a counterpart in business (problem domain). The majority of entity classes result from analysis (even though some are refined or broken into more than one class during design). Entity classes are usually *persisted* (i.e., their state is saved).

Extension Mechanisms of UML. A set of mechanisms that allow modeling to be refined, extended, and adapted to specific needs. They include **stereotyping, notes, adornments, tagged values,** and **constraints.**

Logical Modeling. Models the solution without reference to a specific technology. Even though logical modeling avoids specific technologies, it must take into account the technological **paradigm** (or framework).

Notes. A UML extension mechanism that adds comments about things like requirements, observations, reviews, and explanations. A note can work as a container for a hypertext link.

Packaging. A general-purpose mechanism in modeling tools for grouping related items within a hierarchical structure.

Paradigm. ❶ A broad theoretical or technological framework, ❷ a general agreement on how the world (or an aspect of it) works, and ❸ a fundamental model or pattern. Logical design is based on a technological paradigm, but not on specific technologies *within* that paradigm. (Our usage of the term is an intersection of all three definitions.)

Pattern. The core of the solution to a problem that occurs repeatedly in an environment. Design patterns are the most well-known and explored type of patterns.

Physical Modeling. Maps the logical models to specific technologies. Often, one logical design can be mapped to multiple physical designs.

Reuse. The concept that, with proper planning and design, any product, experience, and expertise that is required in the development process can be reused.

Stereotyping. Extends the vocabulary of UML by allowing the creation of *specialized* building blocks with customized labels and/or icons. Such icons may be used instead of standard UML symbols.

Any UML notation, including classes, actors, use cases, and associations, can be stereotyped. (Specialization and generalization by stereotyping applies to modeling elements, not to what those elements signify.)

Tagged Values. A UML extension mechanism that allows adding new properties to UML elements. Note that this kind of "metadata" applies to the modeling element itself, not to what the element signifies.

Utility Classes. Classes that encapsulate such functionality (like calculations) that they fall in neither **control** nor **boundary classes.** Also called "helper" or "service" classes.

7. REVIEW QUESTIONS

1. Briefly describe how development moves from conceptual modeling to logical and physical designs. Provide one example for a non-IS product and one for an IS product.
2. Compare the objectives of a product to its features.
3. Identify objectives and solution features for the following products:
   a. An ATM.
   b. An accounting information system.
   c. A carwash.
   d. A car.
4. Briefly describe the role of technology in conceptual, logical, and physical modeling.
5. What is the role of domain analysis in designing a product?
6. Briefly describe design classes: utility, control, and boundary. How do they differ from "entity" classes?
7. How can we use packaging to structure modeling artifacts?
8. Explain the three types of visibility for package elements: public, private, and protected.
9. When should we use packaging? Discuss its pros and cons.
10. Describe the significance of constraints and how they relate to business rules.

☞ This chapter sets the framework for the work on design. *Exercises* and *Research Projects & Teamwork* will resume with the next chapter.

8. SUGGESTED READINGS

The following chapters discuss the individual design concepts that we introduced in this chapter. In each chapter, we will suggest a set of selected titles that we believe will expand your knowledge of the subject at hand. Software design, however, is a type of industrial design and all industrial designs share common features and patterns: usability, cost-effectiveness, reliability, and so on. Furthermore, design is always a compromise between competing forces and, consequently, there is no perfect design.

Since the concepts of design in general are older and better-established than those for software design in particular, reading good books on industrial design can provide valuable knowledge about designing software. *Small Things Considered: Why There Is No Perfect Design* by **Henry Petroski** (Vintage Books, 2003) breezes through various design problems and skillfully discusses the relationship of design to its broader context, including prevailing perceptions that make a design "good" in a certain timeframe and "bad" at another juncture.

Perfect design may not be possible, but design *failures* are easy to come by. However, studying failures provides a superb path towards good design. (Depending on the failure, the lessons might be amusing or heart-breaking.) *Why Things Bite Back* by **Edward Tenner** (Vintage Books, 1996) discusses "technology and the revenge of unintended consequence." Its conclusion on the effects of computers on productivity may be dismaying to some of us but, at the very least, it can persuade both designers and consumers to become more realistic and more vigilant about technology.

Another book by **Henry Petroski,** *To Engineer Is Human: The Role of Failure in Successful Design* (St. Martin Press, 1985), argues that "the concept of failure . . . is central to understanding engineering, for engineering design has as its first and foremost objective the obviation of failure. Thus the colossal disasters that do occur are ultimately failures of design, but the lessons learned from those disasters can do more to advance engineering knowledge than all the successful machines and structures in the world." (Page xii. The book has been very popular and has gone through many editions.)

Two books by **Donald A. Norman,** *The Design of Everyday Things* (Basic Books, 2002) and *Emotional Design: Why We Love (or Hate) Everyday Things* (Basic Books, 2004), go beyond engineering and discuss both rational and irrational factors that contribute to design and its reception by its intended users.

Chapter 11

Application Design I
Flow & Control

1. OVERVIEW

The flow of an application is decided by entities that are known as control objects. This chapter explores the concepts that lie behind these objects and illustrates the concepts by applying them to the scenario of Walden Hospital.

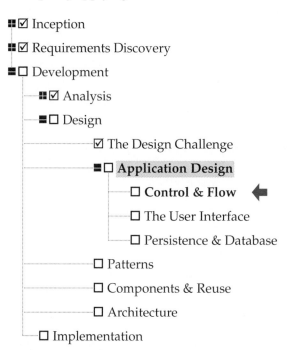

Chapter Topics

➤ Control classes and their role in the flow of applications.
➤ Building on analysis models.

- ➤ Characteristics of flow objects.
- ➤ Applying structural modeling to design.
- ➤ Life cycle objects.
- ➤ Dataset, a utility object.
- ➤ Application control and security.
- ➤ Design requirements for defining methods and messages.
- ➤ Construction and destruction of objects.
- ➤ The control flow of Web applications.

Introduction

Conceptual modeling presents an *idea* of the solution in which only the most basic functions of the solution are conceived. Concrete modeling, however, is literally about the *"nuts and bolts"* of the solution. The idea of a plane is to fly passengers and cargo across vast distances, but a Boeing 747 (model 400) has about *six million* parts, half of which are "fasteners." In other words, a Boeing 747 needs around three million nuts, bolts, and their equivalents to make the idea of a plane fly.

Sometimes, at first glance, it is difficult to understand the relevance and the significance of a component that serves the concrete solution, unless the solution is so widespread that we accept it as a fact of life—as "how things are"—not as an artifact. A simple, random example is the rearview mirror in a car. It has no relationship to the functionality of the car and was not invented along with the automobile. As the number of the cars on the roads grew, however, experience taught that driving without this device could be dangerous.

Applications are solutions to information needs. An information system without applications is similar to a network of roads, highways, gas stations, and parking areas minus the cars. Without applications, an information system becomes a mere collection of computers, communication devices, and databases.

The task of an application is to permit users of an information system to maintain and make sense of a set of entity objects: paragraphs and documents in a word processor; pictures in an image editor; medical history, treatments, and financial transactions in a hospital information system; stocks and bonds in a portfolio management system, and so on.

Like any other solution, an application has components that may appear unrelated to the "idea" or the conceptual model. What is more, except for the visual user interface, software components are not visible and, unlike the wheels of a car, it takes a leap of imagination to picture them in action. Nevertheless, the *overwhelming* majority of components in a software application are parts that have no counterparts in the problem domain. Design is the definition of these building blocks, their interactions, and their relationships to entity classes, regardless of whether they are easy to understand or difficult to comprehend, seem strange or familiar, or appear related to the conceptual solution or not.

> Any task that an application performs and every piece of data that it displays, accepts, saves, or retrieves is handled by an object or the collaboration of a set of objects. For each and every individual action, interaction, keystroke, attribute, picture, sound, warning, menu, button, etc., you must ask yourself: What object provides the service and how?

Figure 11.1
**Application
and Its Major
Components**

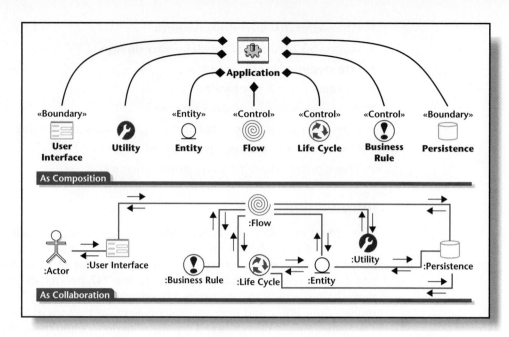

An application can be seen as both a structure composed of various objects and as the dynamic interaction or collaboration among its components.

An application can be seen both as a composition of objects and as the collaboration among those objects to fulfill the requirements of the application. As Figure 11.1 shows, an application is composed of many types (or "stereotypes") of classes, of which domain or "entity" classes are just one type. Furthermore, as the second section of the same illustration indicates, classes stereotyped as **<<Control>>** have a pivotal role in the application.

How an application flows and how the interaction among its components is controlled is the main subject of this chapter. In addition, we will also explore the concrete design of **methods**. Objects must expose methods to provide services requested by messages, and messages are the real nuts, bolts, and transmission mechanism of software applications. A brief discussion of the *Web control model* and its impact on design concludes this chapter.

2. INTRODUCING FLOW & CONTROL

[Jacobson 1999, 185]

> Control objects control the flow of the application, direct the sequencing of events, manage the interaction among other objects, and are "often used to encapsulate control related to a specific *use case*."

An application is a dynamic entity: What it *does* decides the value of what it *is*. Therefore, the flow of the application and how it controls and drives its components must be placed very high on a designer's agenda.

Examples and case studies are the best way to learn about flow and control, as they are for design. A concise definition, however, will help to pave the way:

Control objects provide workflow and session services to other objects. The control object bundles the complex series of requests to the entity objects into a common workflow that is easily accessed by the boundary objects. A high-level message from a boundary object to the control object is converted into a series of messages from the control object to the entity objects. This allows the boundary object to concentrate on its responsibilities while the domain object stays simple.

3. PLOTTING THE FLOW

> To plot the flow of an application we must rejoin use cases with the artifacts of analysis.

☞ An **entity class** "is used to model information that is long-lived and often persistent. Entity classes model information and associated behavior of some . . . concept such as an individual, a real-life object, or a real-life event." [Jacobson, 1999, 184]

Design is not a break with analysis, but an evolution from a conceptual solution to a concrete one. The individual building blocks of design also follow this evolutionary path. In analysis, a close examination of use cases (behavioral modeling) led us ❶ to the discovery of entity classes and their relationships (structural modeling) and ❷ to the relationship between the structure and the behavior of the system (dynamic modeling).

To plot the flow of an application, we must *revisit the use cases* and reexamine them from the viewpoint of design. In doing so, we follow a slightly different sequence of steps from what we followed in analysis.

Analysis and design are both iterative and different models refine each other. In analysis, however, the emphasis is on the *problem space*. In other words, the process of defining entity classes is primarily a process of *discovering objects* in the problem space and abstracting them into information system classes. Therefore, to a large degree, the basics of structural modeling can precede dynamic modeling. In design, by contrast, we must discover the concrete *needs of the solution*. Then we examine our conclusions to *invent classes* that we believe can best answer those needs.

In analysis, classes such as **Patient**, **Invoice**, and **Insurance Policy** point toward concepts or actual objects in the problem space, whereas objects specific to the solution either do not correspond to anything in the problem space or are only *superficially* similar. For example, operating systems allow you to perform actions through "menus," organize your "files" into "folders," or remove them by dropping them into "trash cans," but these terms merely serve as user-friendly metaphors and in no way signify *how* the operating system actually accomplishes its tasks.

To sketch the flow of an application and the objects that it requires, we return to the **Make Appointment** use case.

☞ The **Make Appointment** use case was presented in Chapter 7. The analysis sequence diagram for the use case (and a general discussion of sequence diagrams and their components) appeared in Chapter 9.

Moving to Design: Magnifying the Use Case Flow

> Design modeling starts with identifying the generic components of the solution. It continues by fine-tuning the structure of the application until it arrives at detailed objects and detailed messages exchanged between these objects.

If you review the analysis version of the sequence diagram for the **Make Appointment** use case, you will notice that its participating objects were limited to instances of classes that could be readily understood by people engaged in running the hospital: **Patient** and **Appointment Clerk** as actors, **Patient** as object, **Patients** as a collection of patients, **Appointment**, a list of hospital **Services**, and another list for the **Schedule** of those services. (We labeled the class whose instances carry the lists as **Dataset**, but the concept of a "list" or a "schedule" is easy enough to understand, regardless of whether the medium is paper or virtual.)

Figure 11.2 shows the first "transaction" of the same sequence diagram, revised and expanded for design. The design version adds instances for three new classes: ❶ **Appointment UI**, responsible for interaction with the user; ❷ **Appointment Agent**, which controls the flow of interaction among objects; and ❸ **Persistence**, which saves and retrieves data or the "state" of objects. (In this chapter, we treat both **Appointment UI** and **Persistence** as single "black box" objects. Neither, however, is so simple. We will discuss user interface and persistence in the next two chapters.)

☞ For a discussion of stereotypes see Chapter 10.

As shown in Figure 11.3, the design version also renames **Patients** as **Patient Mgr** and tags it as a **<<Life Cycle>>** stereotype, indicating that instances of this class are responsible for managing other objects (which, in this case, are instances of the class **Patient**).

By introducing the three design classes, both diagrams in Figure 11.2 and Figure 11.3 (let alone the full version) seem much more crowded, even through the workflow is the same and the objects exchange no new messages. As we discussed in the previous

Figure 11.2
Make Appointment: The Design Sequence I

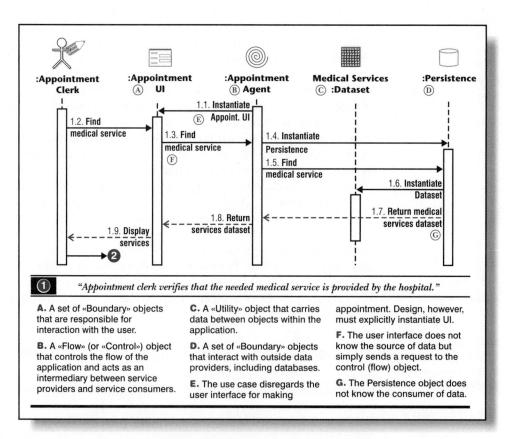

① *"Appointment clerk verifies that the needed medical service is provided by the hospital."*

A. A set of «Boundary» objects that are responsible for interaction with the user.

B. A «Flow» (or «Control») object that controls the flow of the application and acts as an intermediary between service providers and service consumers.

C. A «Utility» object that carries data between objects within the application.

D. A set of «Boundary» objects that interact with outside data providers, including databases.

E. The use case disregards the user interface for making

appointment. Design, however, must explicitly instantiate UI.

F. The user interface does not know the source of data but simply sends a request to the control (flow) object.

G. The Persistence object does not know the consumer of data.

This diagram corresponds to the first step in the normal flow of the use case.

Figure 11.3 Make Appointment: The Design Sequence II

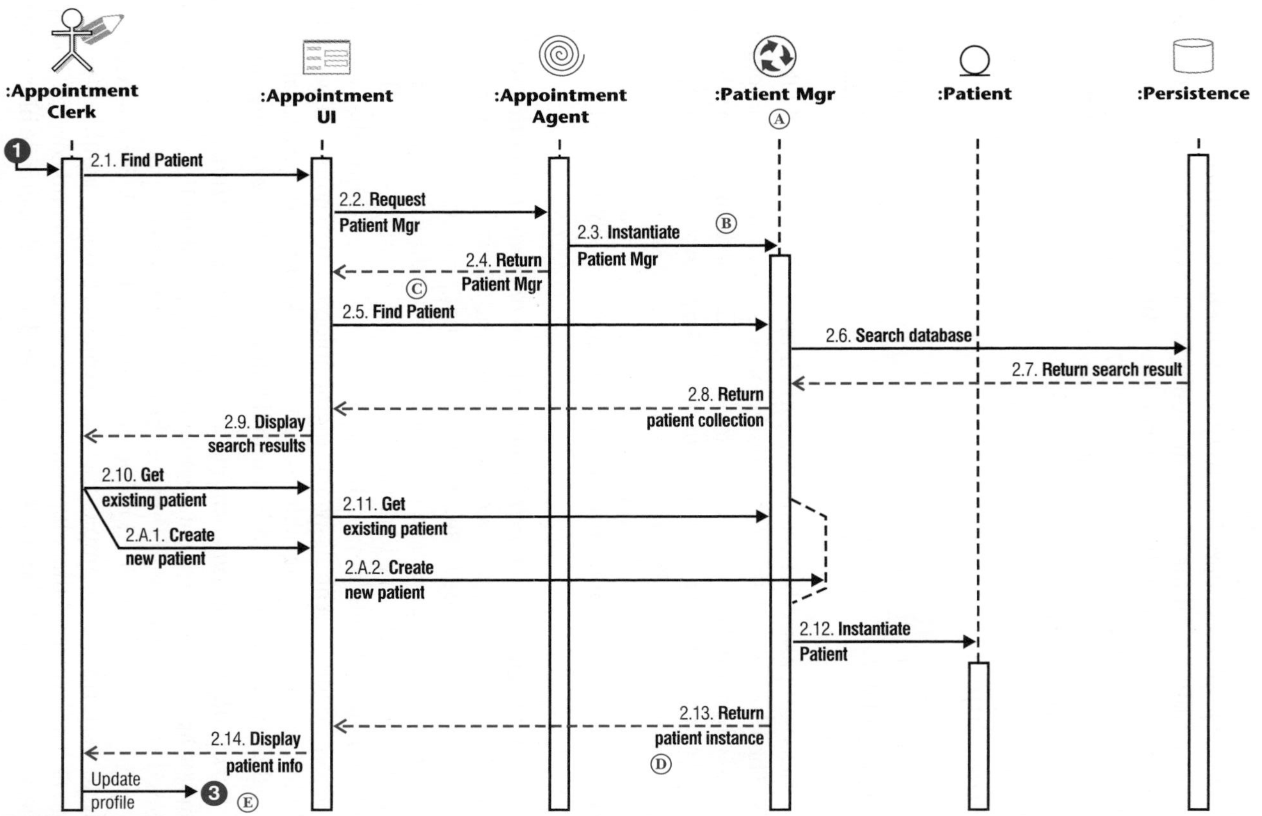

"Appointment clerk records patient's personal and contact data."

A. A«Life Cycle» («Control») object that is responsible for managing a set of Patient («Entity») objects.

B. By "constructing" the Patient Mgr instance, the flow object can give it the address of the Persistence object which it would

need later to retrieve data.

C. The flow objects do not intercept every message in the application. After Appointment UI receives an instance of Patient Mgr, the two objects can communicate directly.

D. Regardless of whether the patient is existing or new, Patient Mgr returns an instance of Patient to the user interface. Once the UI has received an instance of Patient, both objects can communicate directly.

E. Whereas in the use case the appointment clerk updates the patient profile in two steps to emphasize the importance of the referral source, the design model consolidates both actions in step three. The workflow, however, is essentially unchanged.

This section in the diagram covers only part of step 2 in the use case. (See Appendix A for subsequent steps of the use case.)

☞ Analysis models are not merely incomplete versions of design models and are *not* replaced by them. Analysis artifacts do provide the foundations for design, but their other vital task is the illustration and the verification of business concepts and requirements.

☞ See Chapter 8 for a discussion on interfaces. We will return to interfaces in Chapter 15.

☞ As the name implies, a placeholder object represents another object or a set of objects whose exact specifications are to be worked in subsequent iterations. In object-oriented terms, a placeholder object represents an *interface* (discussed earlier). An interface specifies the services that an object or a component offers to the outside world, but hides how these services are performed.

chapter, design adds many more elements to analysis artifacts. (In modeling, at some point, the law of diminishing returns takes effect: As you increase the number of elements within a model, the model's efficiency and focus decreases.)

The diagram, however, serves an important purpose: It introduces *design objects* into the diagram, pointing the model towards the creation of the *concrete* solution. Of course, some of the objects introduced in Figure 11.2 are not fully formed and refined, but are simply *placeholders.*

We may use placeholders in any type of model to reduce overcrowding, but they are especially useful for design modeling with its myriad of additional objects and components. Of the three objects introduced in Figure 11.2 only one, **Appointment Agent**, is likely to remain a single object because it performs a relatively straightforward task. The other two, **Appointment UI** and **Persistence**, will each be transformed into a set of objects.

The Flow Object

> Flow objects enforce the workflow and the sequence of events as envisioned by behavioral and dynamic models.

The messages passed between objects in Figure 11.2 are essentially the same as in analysis. The difference is that three design objects now intercept and either execute them or pass them on. For example, the message "Get medical service schedule," initiated by **Appointment Clerk**, is transmitted by **Appointment UI** to **Appointment Agent**, which passes it to **Persistence**. In the analysis version, the appointment clerk sent the message directly to the data-carrier object, **schedule:Dataset**. Why can't we use the same simple structure for design? Why do we need intermediaries? The answer is twofold:

❶ *The challenge of complexity can be met only through a policy of divide and conquer.* An object must have a clear, specific, and *specialized* mission. For the actor to interact with the **Medical Services** object that provides the list, the latter must be equipped with an appropriate user interface and, additionally, it must also incorporate all the logic necessary to retrieve data from the database. By following such a path, we will end up with a monolithic "object-less" application that was the norm before object-oriented technology and methodology. The results will be predictable: overwhelming and unmanageable complexity, lack of reuse, structural weaknesses (so far as there is a structure), and an uphill battle to maintain or change applications.

❷ *Entity objects are independent of specific applications.* Objects such as **Patient** or **Appointment** have no notion of an application flow. They perform services based on their own built-in rules, but they are not equipped to know how an outside entity should be guided to the point where it can ask for a service that they are able to perform. For example, the **Appointment** object would refuse a "Save" message unless it decides that all required data are present and correct. The appointment clerk, on the other hand, must follow several steps that enable him or her to create an appointment—requirements that are outside the knowledge and/or the abilities of the **Appointment** object.

To sum:

[Arrington 2003, 90]

The easiest way to understand the necessity of control objects is to imagine the system and its components *without* them.

In addition to command and control, the **Appointment Agent** object provides other objects with services that they cannot find for themselves. The services that the flow object provides are usually not its own, but are delegated to other entity and design objects.

By analyzing the sequence diagram, we can create a preliminary definition of the **Appointment Agent** class, as shown in Figure 11.4. We still have to cover a considerable territory before we can arrive at a physical "blueprint" for any of the design objects that we have introduced. This class diagram, however, illustrates how we can define design classes by studying the needs that we discover when we reintegrate the flow of use cases with classes from analysis.

The Life Cycle Object

> A life cycle object creates, organizes, tracks, and destroys other objects, often instances of an entity class.

Exchanging messages is how an object-oriented application works. When we send a message through the postal system, we must know the identity and the address of the recipient. What is true for the real world is true for an object-oriented application as well. The difference is that the postal system is not responsible for managing the lives of those to whom it delivers the mail, while an application must create, change, track, and sometimes destroy hundreds or thousands of objects.

Life cycle classes are responsible for managing a set of other objects, especially when a large number of entity classes are involved. The need for them arises from a central maxim of object orientation that we mentioned before: *divide and conquer.* Although the term "life cycle object" may not be in common usage, the application of the concept is very common in the real world: A general does not manage the affairs of every soldier under his command, but delegates the task to the commanders of smaller units who, in turn, delegate it to the leaders of progressively smaller units until it reaches the level of squad leaders.

Another real-world counterpart to this concept is *inventory,* a distinct business domain with its own organization, rules, procedures, and people by which the resources of a business are tracked and managed. (Depending on the resource type, the designation of "inventory" may change to *asset management* or *human resources.*) Other business domains do not have to track the on-hand quantity of each merchandise or the specific warehouses in which they are stored. The purchasing department has merchandise shipped to inventory and the sales department asks inventory to ship out the merchandise. The inventory domain is responsible for adding, removing, and tracking the individual items.

Life cycle objects help both the management of complexity and *reuse.* During even a short period of time, a large hospital must provide treatment to a vast number of patients. Many applications within Walden's information system would want to interact with a set of **Patient** objects that conform to a certain criteria—for billing, treatment, research, etc. Without a specialized class such as **Patient Mgr**, each application must know how to search and retrieve patients, must instantiate them, and must track them one by one. (We explain the possible complexities of instantiation later in this chapter in the "Construction & Destruction of Objects" section.)

Life cycle classes have similar missions; therefore, they have similar attributes and operations as well. (See Figure 11.5.) Although the specifics will vary according

☞ The **naming of control classes** and objects follows the same rules that we presented in the chapters on structural and dynamic modeling. The only additional guideline that we can offer is that the name of control classes should reflect what they **do**—**AppMgr**, for instance—unlike entity classes whose names express what they **are**—for example, **Patient** or **Appointment**. Nouns that result from adding the "-er" suffix to verbs, like "verifier," and combinations using "manager," "agent," or "admin" are more or less the obvious choices.

☞ **Inventory** must not be mistaken for **storage**, which is a *function* of inventory, not the inventory itself. In an information system, the database provides the storage for *data,* while object managers handle *objects.*

Figure 11.4 Make Appointment: The Control Structure

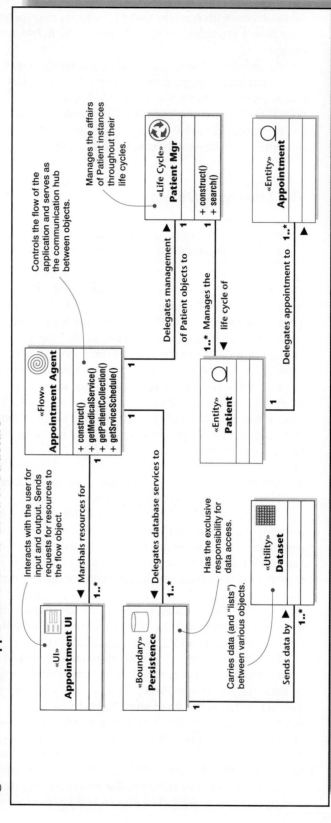

The operations defined for the control classes (**Appointment Agent** and **Patient Mgr**) are preliminary. They have to be refined in a later iteration of design. For a description of the **construct** method, see the "Construction and Destruction of Objects" section in this chapter.

Figure 11.5
**The Life Cycle
Object:
Controlling
the Chaos
of Multitude**

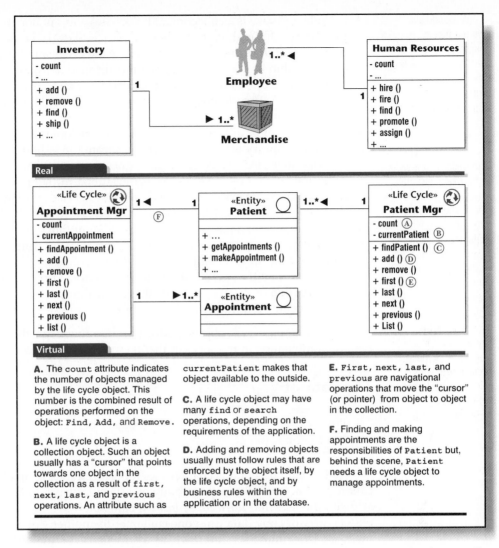

Life cycle classes are collection classes, and since they perform similar functions they have similar attributes and operations, even if the labels are different.

to requirements and designer preferences, the following features are common among life cycle classes:

☞ See Chapter 8
for a discussion
of collection objects.

- Life cycle classes are *collections.* As a result, they are responsible for managing multiple objects, from a few to thousands. This number is exposed to the outside world through one or more methods. For example, the **count** attribute of the **Appointment Mgr** class in Figure 11.5 identifies the number of appointments for a particular patient. We may also want to distinguish between the number of past and future appointments, in which case we may add two more attributes: **pastCount** and **openCount**.
- To move among objects within the collection, life cycle classes provide a set of *navigational* operations including, but not limited to, **first** for the object on top, **last** for the object at the bottom, **next** for the object after the current one, and **previous** for the preceding one. The life cycle object keeps track of these movements by keeping a "*cursor*" that points towards the selected object.

☞ We should also point out that even though the concept of "life cycle" classes is widely used, the designation is not. "Entity, boundary, and control classes have a long history as analysis classes. Life cycle classes, at least by this name, lack this pedigree . . . [but] almost all designers introduce something similar late in analysis or very early in design. Most designers use names from the intended implementation technology or from their design experience. Some common examples include *home, factory,* and *container.*" [Arrington 2003, 92]

- A lending library is a collection of books that you can borrow to read outside the library. Although you may borrow each and every book, you may not borrow all at the same time. Likewise, the life cycle object (usually) offers the objects within its care only one at a time, through a **current** attribute or a **getCurrent** operation, like the **currentPatient** attribute of **Patient Mgr** in Figure 11.5. The identity of the object available for "borrowing" is decided by the navigational operations previously described.
- You may never be able to find the book you are looking for if your only search option in a library is to scan bookshelves from top to bottom. Fortunately, libraries offer card or electronic catalogues that allow you to search their collection by various criteria such as the author, the subject, etc. Depending on specific needs, life cycle objects may provide services for *listing* or *filtering* their contents, like the **list** operation of **Patient Mgr** in Figure 11.5.
- Appointments for a patient may be limited in number, but a stock trading application may have to work with millions of trades during even a short period of time. Consequently, instantiating all objects that belong to even one class may be neither practical nor desirable. Most life cycle classes offer one or more **search** or **find** operations that allow the application to narrow the field and select only a limited number of objects for instantiation.

Again, although life cycle objects perform similar functions, the naming, the number, and the combination of the services that they offer are not necessarily the same.

The Dataset

> A dataset is a general-purpose utility object that carries data between objects within an application.

At the beginning of this chapter we emphasized that, in an object-oriented application, *every* action is the responsibility of a specific object. In earlier chapters we also stressed the fact that *data must have a container.* Messages exchanged between objects carry or copy data from one container to another. For example, the following message from the user interface to an instance of the **Patient** object called **myPatient** copies the value 11/10/1980 from a variable in the UI to a variable (attribute) in the latter object:

```
myPatient.birthdate(11/10/1980)
```

This works perfectly well for transferring a limited and predictable amount of data. However, to carry bulk data among objects another solution is required. You may be able to carry your daily grocery shopping by hand, but to distribute merchandise to even a small town you need more powerful vehicles.

Collection objects such as the "life cycle" are good tools to manage objects, but they themselves need some sort of object to carry the required data from and to the database. Besides, life cycle objects are resource-intensive, are overkill when all you need is just a list of values, and are closely coupled to the specific objects that they are to manage.

To address the need for general-purpose data-carrier objects, all current development platforms and languages offer a collection class that is variously called **Dataset**, **Resultset**, **Recordset**, **List**, or something similar. If we use inventory

☞ How various technologies implement the dataset concept is sometimes much more complex. For example, an item in the column may in turn point to another tabular construct, making the dataset *multi-dimensional* instead of simply *two-dimensional.* In all cases, however, the basic idea and functionality are the same.

☞ See Chapter 8 for a discussion on aggregation and composition.

☞ Datasets and their constituent objects are not designed by developers but are put together at runtime from *prefabricated* components. In other words, you have no part in deciding what services row, column, and "primitive" objects offer, but you can decide the combination that satisfies your requirements.

as a metaphor for life cycle objects, then cargo carriers—trains, boats, and trucks—would be appropriate similes for datasets: They carry large amounts of data between data providers and data consumers. (In fact, an efficient design would have **Patient Mgr** receive its data in a dataset rather than through requesting it piecemeal by sending numerous messages to the **Persistence** object.)

Dataset is a collection in which objects are aggregated in **tabular** format: *rows and columns,* similar to how spreadsheets accept and display data. (See Figure 11.6.) Each row represents a collection of attributes for a single item. Each column, on the other hand, represents one attribute that is shared by all items within the dataset. (Sharing the same *attribute,* however, does not mean sharing the same *value* for the attribute: All patients have a first name, but not all first names are the same.)

Each *cell* within the dataset is a "primitive" object that exposes a single piece of data of a certain type. This data type is the same for all members of the column. Depending on the specific platform, the number and the names of data types are different. The most important attribute of these "primitive" objects is the **value**, or similarly named, attribute that holds only one piece of data. This attribute is explained by *metadata* attributes at the column level. For example, if the data type is **number**, the column may have attributes about the data's precision and the number of decimal points.

A dataset shares with other collection classes operations such as **first**, **next**, etc., and attributes such as **count**—adjusted for its tabular, two-dimensional structure. But whereas a life cycle object can be described as a simple *aggregation,* a dataset is both an aggregation of "primitive" objects and a *composition* (or a *strong* aggregation) of rows and columns that cannot retain their identity outside the dataset.

Datasets are extensively used by persistence objects to transmit query results from the database to other objects within the application. (Hence the alternate designation of **Resultset**.) Consequently, there is a strong tendency towards identifying the dataset as a boundary class. Datasets, however, may be created and used exclusively within the application, without coming into contact with the outside world.

The Application Control

> The control of an application is the composite of ❶ flow objects for individual use cases and ❷ objects that direct the application-level flow, including security-enforcement objects.

The difference between the flow of the application and the flow of its individual use cases is a difference in scope, not in quality. Both flows must enforce a predetermined sequence of actions, including conditional steps (which in use cases are known as the alternate flow). In fact, a large-sized application is usually made of multiple "mini-apps," each with its own flow objects, and, as we mentioned before, a complex use case may delegate its flow to several objects.

Two features, however, distinguish the application flow from the flow of use cases:

- The application flow must fulfill *nonfunctional requirements* that go beyond individual use cases, notably *security.* Use case flow objects should not be concerned about the specifics of security or how the security settings are decided, but only with what a certain user can or cannot do, and what the user can and cannot see.
- As a rule, *the application flow does not directly interact with entity objects.* Entity objects must be managed through use case control objects that embody the

Figure 11.6 Dataset: The Data Delivery Vehicle

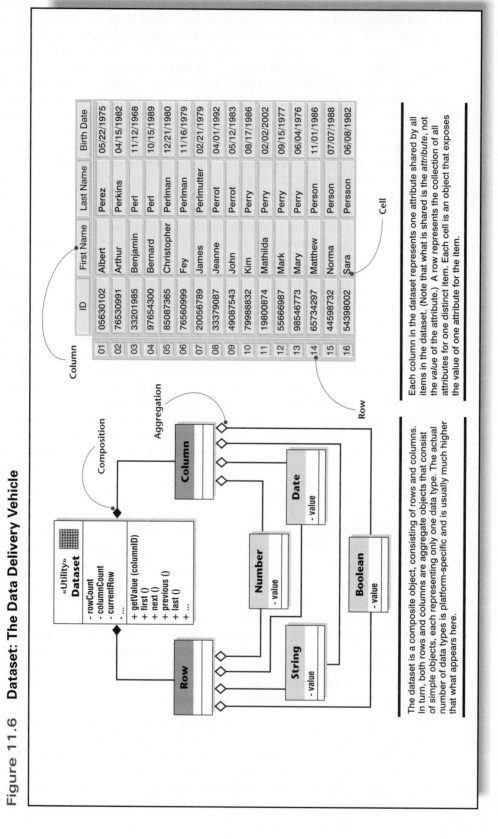

The dataset is a composite object, consisting of rows and columns. In turn, both rows and columns are aggregate objects that consist of simple objects, each representing only one data type. The actual number of data types is platform-specific and is usually much higher than what appears here.

Each column in the dataset represents one attribute shared by all items in the dataset. (Note that what is shared is the *attribute*, not the *value* of the attribute.) A row represents the collection of all attributes for one distinct item. Each cell is an object that exposes the value of one attribute for the item.

Each cell is an object that represents one primitive data type.

workflow. In general, the interaction of the application flow should be limited to other control objects, including security and flow objects that perform application-specific services such as those that display menus and return user selection.

Figure 11.7 is a simple example that illustrates how applying security affects the opening menu of Walden's **Patient Management** application. The example assumes that **Clerical Supervisor** is a super-role, a generalization of all primary actors for use cases that constitute **Patient Relations** (a component of **Patient Management**, which, in turn, is a subsystem of Walden's information system). The first user is a **Clerical Supervisor** and, as a result, has access to all options on the menu.

The second user is a member of both the **Appointment Clerk** and **Reception Clerk** roles, but is not a member of other roles that are allowed access to the patient's financial data. Therefore, the second user can make appointments and receive patients, but cannot register patients, arrange admissions (hospitalization), or resolve billing issues.

The simplicity of the outside view, however, is deceptive. The application must do a considerable amount of work, involving several objects, to arrive at a menu that conforms to the user's security settings. The sequence diagram in Figure 11.8 (somehow

Figure 11.7 Designing Application Security: The View from Outside

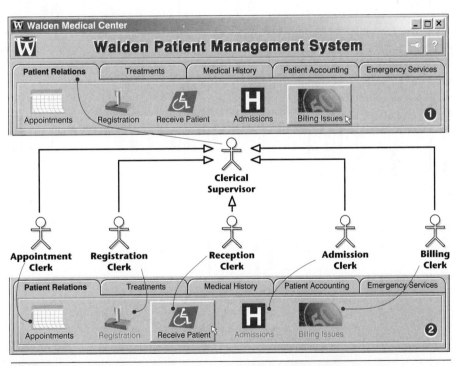

1. The first user is a Clerical Supervisor, a generalized actor. As a result, this user receives all the privileges enjoyed by the specialized actors.

2. The second user receives the privileges of two roles, the appointment clerk and the reception clerk, but cannot access options that are not open to these two actors.

Security is but one of many nonfunctional requirements to which design must attend. (An alternate to disabling buttons is to make them invisible, or present a completely different menu to the users depending on their security privileges.)

Figure 11.8   Designing Application Security: The View from Inside

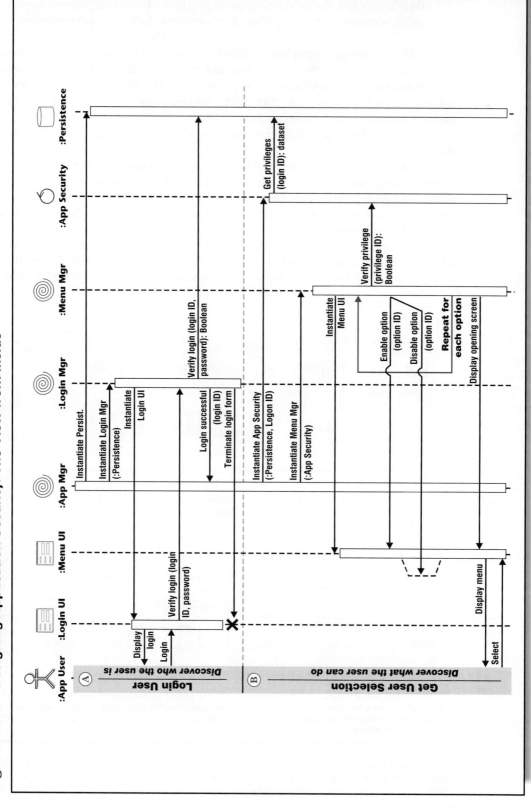

The items within parentheses identify arguments that are passed from the sender of the message to its receiver. The item after the parentheses is a return value. (See the "Defining Concrete Classes" section in this chapter.)

☞ In this chapter and most others in design, we have allowed spaces in the names of classes, objects, and actors to make them more readable. An actual modeling or development platform usually does not allow spaces, as we emphasized when introducing these entities in the chapters on analysis.

summarized, as usual) illustrates the interaction between various control and boundary objects *before* the user can see a screen similar to the one in Figure 11.7. To know *what* the user can do, the application must first know *who* the user is. This is the task of objects that must satisfy the design of a **Log In User** use case: **Login Mgr**, **Login UI**, and **Persistence**. The **App Mgr** flow object, responsible for controlling the overall flow of the application, supplies the address of the **Persistence** object to the **Login Mgr** object at the moment of the latter's instantiation, so that the two objects can exchange messages directly. (See the "Construction & Destruction of Objects" section later in this chapter for a discussion on arguments used in instantiation.)

Having established the identity of the user, the application must then establish the *privileges* that the user may exercise. To this purpose, **App Mgr** creates an instance of **App Security**, whose task is to retrieve and provide security settings for the user. Since the security settings are needed throughout the lifetime of the application, **App Mgr** does not destroy the instance of **App Security** until the user exits the application. Instead, its "address" is passed to all components that must use its services.

The first control object that needs to know about the user privileges is the flow manager for a **Get User Selection** use case, **Menu Mgr**. After instantiating the user interface object but *before* anything is shown to the user, **Menu Mgr** goes through a loop in which it asks **App Security** whether the user enjoys a specific privilege or not. If the answer is affirmative, then **Menu Mgr** orders **Menu UI** to enable the corresponding button and/or menu option. Otherwise, the button or the menu option is disabled or hidden.

Menu Mgr does not know how or what the user interface displays to the user—buttons, dropdown menus, both, or something else—or whether the options are enabled or disabled by default; therefore, it sends a message to the UI regardless of whether the result of the query to **App Security** is positive or negative.

When the user interface component is fully informed about the tasks that the user may or may not perform within its domain, **Menu Mgr** sends it a message to display itself.

4. DEFINING CONCRETE CLASSES

If a friend asks you to "buy me a book," you would want to know a few things before you actually try to fulfill the request: Is it a specific title? Any book by a particular author? A book that belongs to a particular genre, period, or subject? In what price range? Such questions are, in fact, similar to what the Web site of an online bookseller would ask you before you place an order.

Up to now, however, we have largely followed the incomplete guidance of messages such as "buy me a book" and ignored their finer points: In Figure 11.3 the **Appointment UI** effectively tells the **Patient Mgr** "find me patients," but does not communicate the criteria for doing so.

This omission has been intentional: The primary task of both object-oriented analysis and object-oriented design is to identify objects that are needed for building the information system. Refining them is equally important but must necessarily happen one step behind the identification of objects and the services that they must provide.

That time has now arrived. We must set out to provide *concrete* classes with enough precision so that they will be ready for construction, namely for implementation and coding. By "concrete" we do not mean only design classes but any class, including "entity" classes that correspond to "domain" or "business" objects. How is this done?

As you may have noticed, the sequence diagram has been the primary modeling tool in this chapter. We arrived at the class diagram in Figure 11.4 only after analyzing the design sequence diagram for **Make Appointment**. The reason is that the sequence diagram tracks the interaction between objects both in time and in space, and any gap in this time-space matrix is more noticeable than in other types of modeling. The sequence diagram, therefore, is the most precise tool for discovering messages.

Methods Revisited

> Methods are implementations of an object's public services. To ask an object to perform a service, another object must send it a message that corresponds in both substance and form to the method that provides the service.

We have discussed messages extensively before, in the chapter on dynamic modeling. We need, however, to repeat the basic facts about messages before we turn to the issue of designing methods.

- *Attributes & Operations.* An object is defined by what it *knows* and what it *does.* Things that an object knows are called "attributes." Things that it does are called "operations." Both attributes and operations are enclosed, or *encapsulated,* within *one* package.
- *Public Versus Private.* Encapsulation creates a *black box* that hides how the object works inside. What is inside the box is private; what the object exposes to the outside world is public.
- *Services & Interface.* What the object offers to outside entities are called its services. The collection of an object's services are called its *interface.* An object's interface is also known as its *signature* because by making its services public, the object is signing a *contract* that requires it to provide those services to entities that ask for them.
- *Methods & Messages.* Whatever the object knows or is able to do is private. Therefore, the object implements its services as methods. To access a specific service, an outside entity must send a message to a specific method.
- *Parameters & Arguments.* Often, to perform a service, the object must receive more data from the message than merely the name of the method. This additional data or instructions are known as "parameters" or "arguments."
- *Variables.* Data are values, not things or objects. Therefore, to send, receive, or store data we need *containers.* Such a container is called a "variable" because its value, or data, can change. Attributes are variables; so are a method's parameters or arguments. We must never ignore or forget the difference between the container and the contained, between the variable and the data.
- *Return Value.* Frequently, objects return a value after executing methods. This value can be a simple piece of data, it can be complex, or it can be the "address" of another object. Regardless of what is returned, the sender of the message must provide a container—a variable—to accept the returned value because, as we said, data cannot exist unless it has a container.
- *Method Signature.* A method's name, its parameters, the type and the relative position of each parameter, and the type of its return value are known collectively as the method's "signature."

☞ Logging into an application is a very familiar scenario and that is the reason we are using it as a sample. But do not, ever, imagine that all logins are created the same way. If you are logging into your bank online, the login must be encrypted and secure. Furthermore, many applications require extra parameters, such as "Remember Me" on many Web sites.

On the other hand, large enterprises are increasingly incorporating user authorization into their IT infrastructures, so the responsibility is taken off the shoulders of individual applications *behind* the "firewall" (meaning applications that do not interact with entities outside the security fence).

- *Data Types.* Variables are specialized. Like real-world containers, they can accept only what they are designed for. You may not put a text value into a container that is designed for date. Fortunately, the variety of containers provided by development platforms and languages is enough for most needs. For the rest, you may design your own containers from the parts or the components provided by the development platform.

Deriving Methods from Messages

> Arriving at blueprints for methods is a progressive refinement of messages into detailed logical and physical models.

The responsibilities of "entity" classes such as **Patient**, **Customer**, or **Appointment** are essentially what the business domain requires. The problem domain, however, is not explicitly concerned about design classes as long as the solution does what it is required to do. As a result, the shape of design classes emerges slowly from going back and forth among objects as they interact.

This does not mean that entity classes can remain as we found them in analysis. But whereas entity classes must be adjusted and detailed for design, design classes are built from the ground up.

As long as we are at the discovery stage, we can—indeed we should—avoid designating methods with names that are too terse for easy understanding. We should also avoid the temptation to specify every argument and every parameter type right at the beginning. In the process of discovery, a little always goes a long way.

So when and how do we start to solidify our finding into *detailed* design? When we are reasonably convinced that we have captured the basic messages that satisfy the behavior of the application, and by placing those messages under a critical lens.

Figure 11.9 illustrates how a simple message is mapped into the logical design for a method. In an earlier iteration for the design of the **Login User** use case

Figure 11.9   The Method and the Message

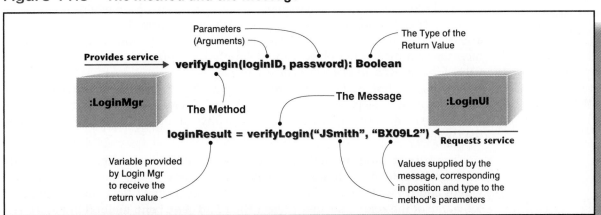

A variable of the Boolean data type can hold only one of the two values: **true/false, yes/no,** etc.

(see Figure 11.8), the label **verifyLogin** would have sufficed: Its intention is clear and it is concise enough. Eventually, however, we must establish what exactly we mean by "verify login":

- *The Names.* In analysis and early in design, names and labels are free-format: Their purpose is clarity, not precision. Like architectural plans, however, physical design demands precision and late logical design must start this process.

Therefore, the names must be changed to comply with general rules first, and with the requirements of the physical platform second. It is no longer **Find Patients** but **findPatients**, and no longer **Verify User Login** but **verifyLogin**. This process makes labels more difficult to understand, but so are detailed engineering blueprints for building a house.

The names and labels must be *unique* within a *namespace.* For methods, the namespace is the class. As a result, there can be only one **LoginMgr.verifyLogin** method. (There is an exception to this which is explained later in the "Overloading Methods" section.)

- *The Parameters.* For detailed design, parameters must be clearly specified. Methods cannot rely on guesswork. The **verifyLogin** method needs both **loginID** and **password** to be able to ascertain that the user, in fact, has access to the application. In addition, we must eventually define the **data type** for each parameter. For example, the following indicates that both parameters of **verifyLogin** are of data type **string**:

```
verifyLogin(loginID:String, password:String): Boolean
```

- *The Return Value.* Each method may have *one* value that is returned by the provider of the service to the sender of the message. The object that requests the service must provide a variable to receive the returned value. This variable is not usually public, but private to the *sender* of the message. For example, in Figure 11.9, the private variable **loginResult** in object **LoginUI** receives the answer of **LoginMgr** to the message **verifyLogin**.

The return value is not limited to simple data types. Depending on the language, the return value can be a complex structure or even objects (or rather the address of the objects). In Figure 11.3, **AppointmentAgent** returns to the **AppointmentUI** object an instance of **PatientMgr**, which in turn exposes **Patient** objects on request.

- *The Syntax.* As we have stated, concrete modeling for methods requires not only the specification of substance, but also of form. If we specify that the **loginID** parameter in the **verifyLogin** precedes the **password** argument, then a message sent by another object cannot supply the value for **password** before the value for **loginID** and expect a correct answer.

For logical design, the syntax shown in Figure 11.9 is sufficient: the name of the method, followed by parameters within a pair of parentheses, followed by the return type of the method (if any). The syntax of the physical design, of course, depends on the language.

The **verifyLogin** method is really simple, but some methods are only *seemingly* simple. An online movie vendor must allow its customers to search for videos and DVDs by a variety of criteria: the title, partial title, name of the director, name of the actors, the genre, etc. (The **Find Patient** method in Figure 11.3 would have a comparable variety of criteria.) Additionally, some parameters may

☞ In everyday life and language, "nothing" is conspicuous only by its absence. For most object-oriented languages, however, absence is not an option. You must specify the "nothing" return value by a keyword. (The keyword is usually **void**.)

constrain others. For example, the customer may want to search for comedies in which a certain actor appears.

Obviously, one **search** method cannot satisfy such demands. We might be tempted to provide **DVDSearchMgr**, a life cycle class similar to **PatientMgr**, with a set of alternate operations such as the following:

```
+ searchByTitle(movieTitle)
+ searchByDirector(directorName)
+ searchByGenre(movieGenre)
+ searchByActor(actorName)
```

Such an approach would work for certain situations, but even if we add secondary parameters to each operation, we cannot implement all the variations that the business flow requires.

One solution to this issue is provided by Figure 11.10. In this example, each search criterion is implemented as an attribute, while the **search** operation remains simple. The actual search is still complex, but how to use the search service is streamlined and easy to understand: The **DVDSearchUI** assigns values entered by the user to the attributes of **DVDSearchMgr** and then sends a message to its **search** method.

Note that you should not confuse operations with methods. For **DVDSearchMgr** we need to design at least 33 methods: one for the **search** operation and *two* for each attribute. The following section explains why.

Exposing Attributes

> The attributes of an object should be exposed to the public only through accessor methods.

If you review class diagrams in this book or design a class in a modeling tool, you will notice that attributes default to *private* (with a minus sign) while operations

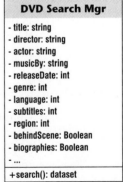

Figure 11.10 Complex Search: When One Method Does Not Suffice

Remember that designing methods applies not only to operations, but also to attributes. (See the "Exposing Attributes" section in this chapter.) The search criteria in this illustration is modestly complex, but it does not present all possible items or variations. To see a full variety, visit the Web sites of online retailers such as Amazon.com.

are designated as *public* (with a plus sign). There is nothing to prevent you from doing the reverse—making an attribute public and an operation private. Indeed, most objects have many private variables and methods that are never exposed and, under certain circumstances, they might allow the public unrestricted access to a variable.

In object-oriented modeling, however, we do not try to intrude into the inner workings of objects. Then why show private attributes at all? If you are confused, you have every right to be. But the question has a simple answer, even though it is not very straightforward: The attributes that appear on a class diagram are private and *controlled,* but the object must somehow make them accessible to the outside world. When you create a new **Patient** instance, the object must somehow allow the values of the **firstName** and **lastName** attributes to be set by an outside entity, and an outside entity must somehow be able to read their values.

To make this access possible, you should build **accessor methods** for an attribute. An accessor method has a language-dependent syntax that allows an outside entity to *set* or to *get* the value of an attribute, meaning that full access to an attribute needs *two* methods. The following example is the Java format for setting or getting the value of the **firstName** attribute:

```
public String getFirstName()
public void setFirstName(String _firstName)
```

In most languages, the two methods appear to the outside world as one, hiding the distinction between the two methods. For example, **AppointmentUI** in Figure 11.3 can set and get the value of **firstName** through the same syntax:

```
newPatient.firstName = "Benjamin"
first_name = selectedPatient.firstName
```

If necessary, the object may omit the **set** method, making the attribute *read-only.* For example, the **age** attribute cannot be set by an outside entity since it is derived, or calculated, from the birth date. Omitting the **get** method makes the attribute *write-only,* meaning that an outside entity can set the value but cannot read it. Such a requirement is not common but, nevertheless, it is possible.

The two accessor methods can have different *visibilities.* (See Chapter 8 for a discussion of visibility.) For instance, the **Patient** object may have a unique identifier that is generated by the database. (For an explanation of "auto-numbers" see Chapter 13.) Outside entities should be able to read this identifier, but only a privileged group of objects (called **package** or **friend** objects) should be allowed to set it. (Think of such a method as being "confidential.") As a result, the **get** method remains public whereas the visibility of the **set** method is changed to **package** (specified by a *tilde* sign):

```
+ getPatientID(): String
~ setPatientID(_patientID:String): void
```

To summarize: Specification of *private* attributes on class diagrams means that we have to create accessor methods for those attributes.

Construction & Destruction of Objects

> Objects must be instantiated explicitly. Constructor methods provide the object with the minimum data that they require to start their existence.

The first object of an application is instantiated by the operating system. Thereafter, each object *must* be created by another object: ***objects do not instantiate themselves.*** They are born, have a lifetime, and are eventually disposed of, exactly as sequence diagrams show.

Earlier in this book, we defined the class as a template or a "cookie cutter." Objects are instantiated, or "cut," with a statement similar to the following that creates an instance of **Patient** called **myPatient**:

```
myPatient = new Patient();
```

We cite this example not to discuss programming languages, but because there is a hidden method within this statement. Note the pair of parentheses after the name of the class. The syntax resembles the syntax of a message that invokes a method and, in fact, it *does* indicate an ***implicit*** call to a special type of method called a **constructor method**. Unlike normal methods, constructors have the *same name as the class* that they belong to and can *never* be invoked after the class is instantiated. Like other methods, however, constructors can have parameters.

In Figure 11.8, the instantiation of **LoginMgr** by the **AppMgr** object includes a reference to the **Persistence** object, because **LoginMgr** requires this information to verify the login data against the database.

Destruction of objects usually does not require explicit actions: When all other objects stop referring to (or "forget about") an object, it is automatically destroyed by the runtime environment. This activity is commonly called *"garbage collection."*

Sometimes, however, you need to destroy objects explicitly. In Figure 11.8, the application must remove login from the screen after the login has been verified. Therefore, it is explicitly destroyed by **LoginMgr**. (This is merely an example: As a rule you do not need to show the destruction of an object on a sequence diagram, since the *lifetime* box on the object's *timeline* is usually sufficient.)

Overloading Methods

> Overloading is defining the same method in several versions, using the same name but different parameters.

As we stated earlier, what identifies a method to the outside world is its *signature,* the combination of its name, its return type, the number of parameters, the type of each parameter, and the arrangement of arguments.

Sometimes several methods represent functions that are very similar. For example, the **Patient** object may expose the following two methods for applying payments:

```
applyPaymentByName(lastName:string, firstName:string,
  Amount:currency):Boolean
applyPaymentByID(ID:number, Amount:currency):Boolean
```

To simplify the interface, many object-oriented languages allow you to combine such methods into one:

```
applyPayment(lastName:string, firstName:string,
  Amount:currency):Boolean
applyPayment(ID:number, Amount:currency):Boolean
```

When another object sends a message to the **applyPayment** method of the **Patient** object, the latter automatically executes the correct method by analyzing the "signature" of each and comparing it to the components of the message.

All methods, including constructors, can be overloaded. Overloading, however, is not as simple as it might appear: Overloaded methods must have the same name, but their "signatures" must be different. In other words, they must be different in at least one of the three following aspects:

- The number of arguments.
- The data types of the arguments.
- The order of the arguments in a manner that changes the signature of the method.

For example, if all versions of an overloaded method have three arguments, of which the first is a **string**, the second is a **number**, and the third is a **Boolean**, there is no way to tell them apart and overloading would not work.

5. THE WEB CONTROL MODEL

Web connections are "stateless." The application, therefore, must recreate the state every single time that it receives a message from the Web.

The meaning of the term "state" is not easy to retain. The primary reason is that it is a far-reaching concept. A 7-year-old boy and a 70-year old man are in different stages of life and, therefore, have different states. If, however, they are both waiting for their lunches, we can say that they are in the same state (i.e., "hungry"). In other words, the term "state," or "condition," can apply to the sum of a wide range of attributes, to the collection of a few attributes, or to just one attribute. In addition, "state" can be repeating or it can be irreversible: The 70-year-old man cannot revert back to being 7 years old, but waiting for lunch may happen every day.

Figure 11.11 The Web Flow: State Is Recreated with Every Message

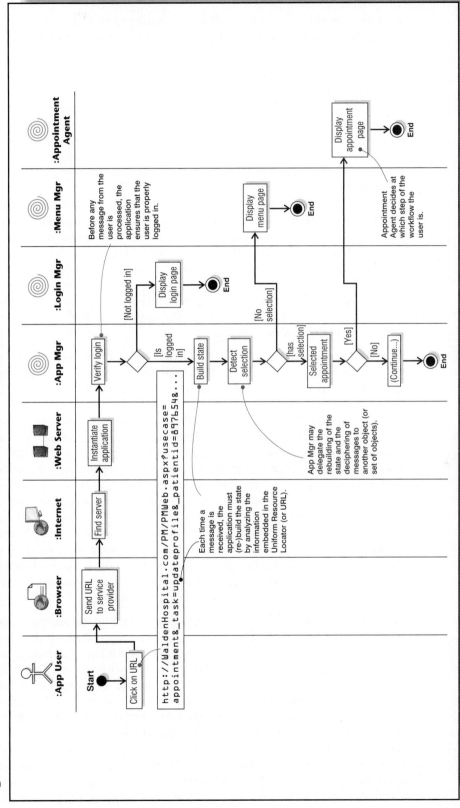

Designers use various techniques to save and recreate the state of a Web application. In this example, the application uses both a cookie (for login verification) and the URL (or link) for rebuilding the state.

☞ See the "Statechart Diagram" section in Chapter 9 for a discussion of state.

By now we should be familiar with the state of objects. As we said before:

A state is an object's *condition* at a certain stage and from a certain viewpoint. It is a snapshot of the object at a (usually important) point in time.

Likewise, the state of an application is a snapshot of the application in time. By keeping state, an application "knows" what the user has been doing, where in the workflow the user is now, and what actions are allowed or possible from this point on. When you edit a document in a word processor, the application keeps track of what you have been doing and allows you to "undo" a certain number of actions. In a client/server application for Walden Hospital, the control object would remember the ID of an existing patient that you have selected from a list and returns the patient profile so that you may edit it.

What makes the Web platform different? The answer, in few words, is *lack of state.*

The Internet was designed as a fault-tolerant network for packets of information to find their targets even if parts of the network have ceased to function. This architecture fits well with the World Wide Web where the user can "surf the Net" at will and the only responsibility of a Web site is to return the page that the user has requested, after which the user can forget about the site and the site can forget about the user. An application, however, embodies a workflow that progresses through distinct steps to achieve a goal *incrementally.* The application must remember who you are and where in the process you are.

[Conallen 2003, 22–23]

The distinction between Web sites and Web applications is subtle and relies on the ability of a user to affect the state of the business logic on the server. Certainly, if no business logic exists on a server, the system should not be termed a Web application . . .

One common challenge of Web applications is managing client state on the server. Owing to the connectionless nature of [Web] client and server communications, a server doesn't have an easy way to keep track of each client request and to associate it with the previous request, since each and every Web page request establishes and breaks a completely new set of connections.

Managing state is important for many applications; a single use case scenario often involves navigation through a number of Web pages. Without a state management mechanism, you would have to continually supply previous information entered for each new Web page. Even for the most simple applications, this can get tedious. Imagine having to reenter the contents of your shopping cart every time you visit it or to enter your user name and password for each and every screen you visit while checking you your Web-based e-mail.

The mechanisms by which Web developers keep state is not the subject of this book. Suffice it to say that the application recreates the state each time it receives a message from the client by analyzing a "*marker*" that it has transmitted to the client in the previous exchange. The most common form of such a marker is a small text file called a *cookie* that encodes the necessary data for building the state. Another method is to encode the "state data" inside the **URL** (Uniform Resource Locator), also known as a *link,* that is clicked by the user to send a message to the Web server. It is not unusual for a designer to combine several methods.

The activity diagram in Figure 11.9 provides an example of how the repeated need for recreating the state affects the flow of a Web application. Each time a message is received, the main control object of application, **AppMgr**, decodes the "marker," determines the state, decides which object is responsible for the user request, instantiates the object, and sends it the decoded message. Part of the coded marker indicates the login status: If the user has not logged into the application or if the login has "timed out" (expired), the control object forces the user to log in. This last point is an important *security requirement:* A Web application never knows whether the message it receives from the user is legitimate or whether it has been created fraudulently. (Even a legitimate user can cheat by saving a page from a previous session.)

A *warning,* however, is in order: In designing a Web application, you should *not* include such a scenario in every model because the models will become hopelessly cluttered. Following the tenets of object orientation, the control objects should delegate the decoding and the encoding of Web messages to specialized objects and let other objects free to pursue their own tasks. The best approach is one that can minimize the effects of specific platforms on the design of objects and/or use cases. A sequence diagram that follows every message through the twisted pathways of Web communication and back is worse than useless.

6. DELIVERABLES

We argued in the previous chapter that design must start with the overall view of the information system, or its **architecture.** Design has smaller and faster iterations than analysis: Concrete modeling does not follow a straight line from top to bottom or from outside in, or *vice versa.* Each aspect of concrete modeling—behavioral, structural, or dynamic—*incrementally* enhances, corrects, and leads to a more precise version of another aspect.

By modeling the flow of the application, we provide the **framework** that supports the *façade* of the system that interacts with the outside world. In this endeavor, we can use all the modeling tools at our disposal as required:

- *sequence diagram* to discover both control objects and the messages that they pass to each other and to entity or boundary objects,
- *collaboration diagram* to consolidate the messages and, consequently, the responsibilities of classes,
- *activity diagram* to sort out confusing flow logic and, last but not least,
- detailed *class diagrams* that must function as engineering blueprints.

Often, however, we must travel to the boundaries of the system and return inside to refine our discoveries. As we saw in Figure 11.8, sometimes we must know the demands of the user interface (or persistence) to design a control object correctly.

The deliverables of design are not produced at the end of clear-cut stages, but result from activities that, as a rule, take place in *clusters.*

7. WRAP UP

☑ **Control classes and their role in the flow of applications**

A software application is a dynamic entity. Consequently, its usability depends on how well it flows and how successfully it can control and direct its building blocks towards goals that the application must help its users to achieve.

Objects that control the flow of the application, direct the sequencing of events, manage the interaction among objects, and encapsulate the behavior specified by use cases are called *control* objects.

A seemingly simple message from the user interface, such as "update the patient profile," usually translates into a set of messages that the control objects direct towards entity and other design objects such as those responsible for persisting the data in a database.

The central concept behind control objects is a rule that flows from object-oriented design: *divide and conquer.* By distributing the responsibilities of the solution among control and flow objects, the user interface, persistence, and entity objects can remain focused on their own responsibilities.

☑ **Building on analysis models**

Design focuses on the product that solves the problem, but it is not a sudden break with analysis. On the contrary, design is an evolution from a conceptual solution to a concrete one. The same evolutionary path is also followed by individual building blocks of design. Concrete modeling revisits *use cases* from the viewpoint of design and develops its artifacts by expanding structural and dynamic models of analysis.

Analysis and design are two sides of the same coin. Nevertheless, they look at opposite directions to define their structural entities. In analysis, the process of defining entity classes is primarily a process of *discovery*: what objects in the *problem space* must be abstracted into the entity classes of the information systems. Design, by contrast, arrives at concrete classes by *invention*: what entities *would* answer the needs of the *solution space.*

☑ **Characteristics of flow objects**

Flow objects enforce the workflow and the sequencing of events as specified by behavioral modeling, as described by use cases, and by dynamic models. To enforce the workflow, flow objects must intercept most messages exchanged between objects to ensure that the interaction between them follows the correct sequence or scenario.

One important result of this intervention is that other objects can retain their clear, specific, and *specialized* missions:

- The user interface can focus on presenting data *to* the user and accepting data *from* the user. It does not have to retrieve data from the database or save it.
- Persistence objects, those objects that manage the interaction with external data sources, can hide the complexities of data management from other components of the applications. Furthermore, they are not charged with controlling how the data is consumed or by whom.
- Entity objects can remain as independent from specific applications as possible.

Thus, besides command and control, *flow objects provide other objects with services that they cannot find for themselves.* The services that the flow object provides are usually not its own, but are delegated to other entity and design objects.

Without flow objects, boundary and entity objects would have to assume responsibilities that would reduce their flexibility and increase their complexity.

☑ **Applying structural modeling to design**

The ultimate mission of concrete modeling is to produce blueprints for building the information system and its components. This task involves both the refinement of entity classes that originate from the problem domain and the definition of design classes that serve the solution.

Design classes are not abstractions of objects that have counterparts in the problem domain. Therefore, to define their responsibilities, we must parse dynamic models, such as sequence diagrams, that identify services that the solution requires. In other words, we can define design classes by studying the *needs* that we discover when we reintegrate the flow of use cases with classes from analysis.

☑ **Life cycle objects**

Life cycle classes are responsible for managing a set of other objects, especially when a large number of entity classes are involved. They create, organize, track, and destroy other objects, often instances of entity classes.

Life cycle objects help both the management of complexity and *reuse.* Life cycle classes have similar missions; therefore, they have similar attributes and operations as well: They are *collections,* responsible for managing multiple objects, from a few to thousands; they provide a set of *navigational* operations such as **first**, **next**, **previous**, and **last** that allow outside entities to browse among objects within the collection; they *expose* individual objects upon request; they provide *lists* of objects in their care; they often provide operations such as **search** or **find** to *select* subsets that satisfy specific criteria.

☑ **Dataset, a utility object**

Besides control and flow, the internal workings of an application require a wide range of *utility objects.* One such object is **dataset**, which, depending on technology, is also called **resultset**, **recordset**, or simply **list**.

Data are values and as values they must have containers. Messages exchanged between objects carry data in containers called "variables," the same type of containers that objects use privately to hold the values for their attributes. This mechanism, however, would be unwieldy and inefficient for carrying large amounts of data among objects.

Dataset is a general-purpose utility object that carries data between objects within an application. It is a collection object in which the objects are organized as *rows* and *columns,* similar to spreadsheets. Each *cell* within this *tabular* format is a "primitive" object that exposes a single piece of data of a certain type. This data type is the same for all members of the column. The exact variety of **data types** depends on the technology and language, but they fall in general categories of **string** (text), number, Boolean, or object (or rather, the *address* of an object).

☑ **Application control & security**

The control of an application is composed of control objects for individual use cases, plus objects that control application-level flow, including security enforcement objects.

The difference between the flow of an application and the flow of its individual use cases is a difference in scope, not in quality. Both flows must enforce a predetermined sequence of actions, including conditional steps (or the "alternate flow"). Typically, a large application is usually made of multiple "mini-apps," each with its own flow objects.

Security and user privileges are usually decided when the user logs into the application and are communicated to individual control objects as the need arises.

The application flow does not directly interact with entity objects. In general, the interaction of the application flow should be limited to other control objects, including security and flow objects that perform application-specific services such as those that display menus and return user selection.

☑ **Design requirements for defining methods & messages**

Messages are how objects interact within an object-oriented context. To define a concrete class, we must provide it with exact and detailed methods so that its instances can respond to exact and unambiguous messages from other objects and provide them with its services.

Methods are implementations of an object's public services. To ask an object to perform a service, another object must send it a message that corresponds *both in substance and in form* to the method that provides the service.

To arrive at blueprints for building methods, we must progressively refine messages into detailed logical and physical models. For concrete modeling, **parameters** within a method must be clearly specified: Methods cannot rely on guesswork. We must also define the **data type** for each parameter. Furthermore, concrete modeling of methods requires not only the specification of *substance*, but also of the *form.*

Methods implement not only operations, but also provide access to *attributes.* Such methods are called **accessor methods** and are usually defined in pairs, one for reading the value of the attribute and the other for setting it. By removing one, we can make an attribute *read-only* or *write-only.*

A method's name, its parameters, the type and the relative position of each parameter, and the type of its return value are known collectively as the method's *signature. Overloading* is a mechanism by which you may define several methods with the *same name but with different signatures.*

☑ **Construction and destruction of objects**

Objects do not create themselves: Each object must be instantiated by another object. In most object-oriented languages, an object may implement **constructor methods** that allow the entity that instantiates the object to provide it with information that it needs from inception to provide any service. Constructors are like other methods and can even be "overloaded," but they have the *same* name as the class and cannot be accessed after the object has been instantiated.

Destruction of objects often does not require explicit actions: When other objects no longer refer to an object, it is automatically destroyed by the runtime environment. Sometimes, however, you need to destroy objects explicitly.

☑ **The control flow of Web applications**

The state of an application is a snapshot of the application in time. By keeping state, an application "knows" what the user has been doing, where in the workflow the user is now, and what actions are allowed or possible from this point on.

The Web, however, is a "**stateless**" environment: A Web server does not keep track of the identity or the actions of the users after responding to individual messages. A Web application, therefore, must recreate the state every single time that it receives a message from the Web.

The mechanisms by which Web developers keep the state of an application are varied. In essence, the Web application recreates the state each time it receives a message from the client by analyzing a *"marker"* that it has transmitted to the client in the previous exchange. The most common form of such a marker is a small text file called a *cookie* that encodes the necessary data for building the state. Another method is to encode the "state data" inside the *URL* (Uniform Resource Locator), also known as a *link*, that is clicked by the user to send a message to the Web server.

8. KEY CONCEPTS

Accessor Methods.   Methods that make an object's attributes accessible to the outside world. They are usually done in pairs, one for reading the value of the attribute and one for setting it. By removing one, the attribute can be made into "read-only" or "write-only."

Application.   A dynamic composite of control, entity, boundary, and utility objects that provides specific solutions for information needs. The task of an application is to permit users of an information system to maintain and make sense of a set of *entity* objects.

Arguments.   See **Parameters.**

Constructor Method.   A **method** with the same name as the class that is executed when an object is instantiated. It is often used to supply the object with information that it needs from the start to perform its services. It cannot be called again after the object has been instantiated. (See **Method Overloading**.)

Control, Application.   The composite of ❶ flow objects for individual use cases and ❷ objects that direct the application-level flow, including security-enforcement objects.

Control Class.   A class whose instances control the flow of the application, direct the sequencing of events, manage the interaction among other objects, and often encapsulate control related to a specific use case.

Dataset.   A general-purpose utility object that carries data between objects within an application. A dataset is a collection object that organizes objects in a tabular format, as rows and columns. Each cell within the dataset is a "primitive" object that exposes a single piece of data of a certain type.

Data Type.   Identifies the type of data, depending on the platform and language. Usually number, string (text), Boolean (true/false), data, or (the address of an) object.

Entity Classes.   Classes that result from the analysis of objects within the problem domain. Entity classes usually have counterparts in the problem domain.

Flow Class.   A type of **control class** whose instances enforce the workflow and the sequence of events as envisioned by use case and dynamic modeling. Furthermore, flow objects act as intermediaries between entity and other design objects and provide them with services that they cannot perform by themselves.

Life Cycle Object.   An object responsible for managing a set of other objects, especially when a large number of entity classes are involved. A life cycle object creates, organizes, tracks, and destroys other objects, often instances of entity classes.

Method.   Implementation of a public service provided by an object. To ask an object to perform a service, another object must send it a message that corresponds in both substance and form to the method that provides the service. Concrete modeling must provide engineering blueprints for the construction of methods.

Method Overloading.   When more than one method has the same name but different signatures. See also **Method Signature**.

Method Signature.   A unique combination of a method's name, its parameters, the type and the relative position of each parameter, as well as the type of its return value. See also **Method Overloading.**

Parameter.   A piece of data or instruction that must be supplied to an object to carry out a specific **method**. (Parameters are also called **arguments**.) The type and the ordinal position of each value that must be received for each parameter is decided by the operation defined in the *interface* of the class to which the object belongs.

Return Value.   The response that a message may invoke from the receiving object after the execution of a method is complete. Each method can have only one return value.

State, Application.   A snapshot of the condition of an application in time. By keeping state, an application "knows" what the user has been doing, where in the workflow the user is now, and what actions are allowed or possible from this point on.

State, Object.   An object's *condition* at a certain stage and from a certain viewpoint. It is a snapshot of the object at a (usually important) point in time.

Stateless. An object, a component, or an application that does not or cannot keep **state**. The *Web* is a stateless environment; therefore, Web applications must devise mechanisms to keep state.

Variable. A container to hold data or values.

Web Application. An application that runs on the World Wide Web. It must provide the user with the ability to affect the state of the business logic on the server.

9. REVIEW QUESTIONS

1. Explain the statement that "applications are solutions to information needs." Provide examples to make your point.
2. How do sequence diagrams for design differ from those for analysis? In which one do boundary objects appear? Why?
3. Explain the role of interface in encapsulation. Provide examples.
4. Describe the concept of the life cycle object, how it relates to collection objects, and give an example of a life cycle class with appropriate attributes.
5. How does the application flow handle nonfunctional requirements? Give an example.
6. Describe the difference between concrete and abstract classes and give an example for each.
7. Explain, through an example, how methods can be derived from messages.
8. Explain parameters and return values in the framework of messages. Provide examples.
9. How do we apply structural modeling to design?
10. How do we use the requirement of design to define messages and methods?

10. EXERCISES

The following exercises apply to each of the four narratives introduced in Chapter 4: *The* Sportz *Magazine, The Car Dealership, The Pizza Shop,* and *The Real Estate Agency.*

❶ Select "base" use cases from the scenarios above. Identify *design objects*—control and flow, user interface (UI), life cycle, etc.—for each use case. Create **structural diagrams** that show the relationships between design objects.

❷ Select a use case and represent it in a *sequence diagram* that includes the design objects identified in the previous exercise.

❸ Create a *design collaboration diagram* for *another* use case that you worked on in the first exercise.

❹ Create design *activity diagrams* for a selected set of use cases.

11. RESEARCH PROJECTS & TEAMWORK

In analysis, you interpret the world. In design, you create a virtual one. In this creation, your hands are not completely free: requirements, business rules, and "entity" classes constrain whatever decisions you make—to say nothing of the technology. Within these constraints, however, you can choose alternate solutions for the exact same design challenges. Therefore, do not look for one ultimate design. One design can be as good as another—and very different.

❶ Refer to the online registration system for Walden Medical College (Chapter 4). Each team member should identify design objects for the system. Consolidate the team's work and create a *design class diagram* for the system.

❷ Do the same for the online shopping system (Chapter 4), but also create a *design sequence diagram* for one of the use cases.

❸ Identify *control and flow* objects for use cases that relate to the registration system for Walden Medical College (Chapter 4), the online shopping system (Chapter 4), and the patient scheduling system (Chapter 5). Look at Figure 11.4 and try to create similar diagrams.

☞ The Web, as we said, is "stateless." As a result, certain activities take place repeatedly whenever a message is received from the actor. Since this can produce a very confusing diagram, feel free to ignore Web-specific features—unless you want to try your hand in creating something like Figure 11.8.

❹ Discuss, as a team, what the *security* features of an online shopping system should be. Create diagrams, like those in this chapter, that show the application of security from *inside* and/or *outside*.

❺ Individually, try to come up with **life cycle objects** in any of the scenarios in assignment 3. Compare notes in a discussion session. Create structural and/or sequence diagrams that represent these life cycle objects (if any).

12. SUGGESTED READINGS

The literature on application design is vast. Most, however, is tightly focused on specific technologies, not on general concepts. (To be fair, it is not easy to express or understand many design concepts without reference to technology. Besides, the market is less kind to general-purpose books in this field.) Furthermore, the subject of control and flow is seldom given the prominence and the visibility that it deserves.

Enterprise Java with UML by **C.T. Arrington** and Sayed H. Rayhan (New York: Wiley, 2003) explores application design extensively and in depth. Although the book presents its examples in the framework of Java, its narrative and UML models are clear and comprehensive.

Building Web Applications with UML by **Jim Conallen** (Boston: Addison-Wesley, 2003) provides a much-needed guide to the "big picture" in developing applications for the Web. Compared to client/server applications, Web applications are more difficult to design and understand, which makes this book especially helpful. Again, the examples are in Java, but a considerable part can be understood by people with little or no programming knowledge.

Be aware that neither book can be considered "light" reading. You can skip parts that are bound to technology and still learn a lot, but they still demand a good deal of attention and focus.

12

Application Design II
The User Interface

1. OVERVIEW

The user interface is where the interaction between the user and the application takes place. The components of the user interface, its language, and the requirements for its design are discussed in this chapter.

- ☑ Inception
- ☑ Requirements Discovery
- ☐ Development
    - ☑ Analysis
    - ☐ Design
        - ☑ The Design Challenge
        - ☐ **Application Design**
            - ☑ Control & Flow
            - ☐ **The User Interface** ⬅
            - ☐ Persistence & Database
        - ☐ Patterns
        - ☐ Components & Reuse
        - ☐ Architecture
    - ☐ Implementation

Chapter Topics

➤ The user interface layer and its responsibilities.

➤ The language of graphical user interface (GUI).

- Visual metaphors and their roles in the design of user interface.
- The significance of patterns, consistency and aesthetics in UI design.
- Mapping messages, parameters and attributes to the user interface.
- Modeling for UI: navigation diagram, storyboarding, simulation and prototyping.

Introduction

An information system and all its components are useless unless human beings can interact with them. In the vast and growing literature on system analysis and design, user interface usually occupies a humble niche, but such a modest treatment should not be seen as a reflection on its significance. Most everybody knows that the user interface can make or break the application and, consequently, the entire information system. The difficulty in writing about the user interface lies in the fact that UI lends itself *less* to guidelines and rules than any other building block of the information system.

The user interface is primarily *an interpreter* that makes the interaction between two different worlds—human and machine—possible. In this process, the danger always exists that, as they say, something is lost in translation: A virtual information system works on different principles and has a different structure than the workings and the environment in which humans live.

To call the user interface an "interpreter" is not taking poetic license but is a literal description. In communicating with modern computers, you do not use a digital or binary language, but enter human-readable text, click buttons, select from menus, and manipulate scrollbars. In short, the graphical user interface translates the binary language of the computer into the **metaphors** of the real world.

Since the two sides of this communication—the *problem domain* and the *solution domain*—do not speak the same language, the UI designer becomes responsible for the translation. As with any kind of translation, the designer may refer to dictionaries and grammar books, but cannot rely on them for success. Rather, the translator must have a good grounding in both languages, be aware of common usage, know the target audience, take precedents into account, learn from others, and possess an aesthetic sense.

This, no doubt, is a tall order. Aptitude cannot be taught but it can be nurtured and sharpened. The rather short history of the graphical user interface provides a treasure trove of patterns and precedents, both positive and negative (and occasionally annoying

Figure 12.1
User Interface: The Boundary Between the Real and the Virtual

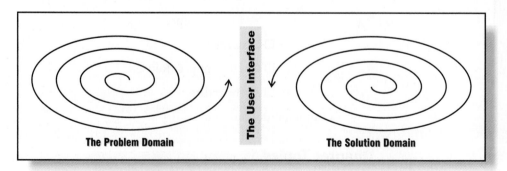

The Problem Domain   The User Interface   The Solution Domain

User interface is where the problem domain and the solution domain meet and interact.

or funny). In addition, the design tools, whether for modeling or for development, are constantly improving.

The user interface serves two masters: the application and the user. To design a good user interface, we must understand both masters adequately. In previous chapters we discussed *messages* that constitute the language of an object-oriented information system. In this chapter, we first explore the language of the user interface as presented to users. We then discuss how, and with what tools, the two languages can be mapped together.

2. INTRODUCING THE USER INTERFACE

> The user interface is the area of interaction between an application and its *human* users.

This definition sounds more or less obvious. You can find many other descriptions that define the user interface equally well, each from a slightly different point of view. It is, however, precisely the differences among viewpoints that turn designing the user interface into a challenge. These differences are, paradoxically, both necessary and problematic.

When the users and domain experts explain their business or their requirements, system analysts, designers, and developers take it for granted that the "problem domain" is really outside their domain, even though they must do their best to understand it. And when designers and developers talk about the requirements of the "solution domain," such as database, control objects, inheritance, etc., users generally see no need to understand any of it and consider it outside *their* domain.

The user interface is where two worlds collide, where the problem domain meets the solution domain. The two, however, come from opposite directions. The users, in general, view the user interface as the whole application and the application as the whole information system. System designers, on the other hand, see the user interface as one of many possible expressions of the same application and an application as merely how the resources of an information system are applied to a set of tasks.

This, as we said, is both necessary and problematic: users should be concerned about doing their own jobs; and analysts, designers, and developers who start building an application from the user interface will produce, at best, a mediocre product. How, then, is this challenge to be answered?

To create a well-designed interface, the designer must move on two tracks:

❶ Revisit the starting point of the development process, or behavioral modeling. Use cases provide the general outlines of how the users view the system and what they expect from it. In the succinct words of one author, "a user interface is well designed when the program model conforms to the user model."

[Spolsky 2001, 8]

❶ Ask the users. The application can have superb flow and database design but fail miserably because the designers take it upon themselves to decide how the users *should* work. Sometimes the users may seem *too* helpful by telling the designer to put a dropdown here and a check box there. This means that, besides everything else, the designer must be endowed with the virtues of patience and persuasiveness. The user interface is *not* a "necessary evil" but an element without which an information system is meaningless.

The Responsibilities of the User Interface

> The user interface is responsible for ❶ accepting and editing user input, ❷ producing human-intelligible output, and ❸ guiding users to accomplish tasks.

The interface is the boundary between the *inside* of an entity and the world *outside* it. It applies to any object-oriented entity: objects, components, subsystems, systems, and applications. *Encapsulated* entities communicate by sending *messages* to each other's interface.

The user interface is an interface like any other, but with two added responsibilities that distinguish it from the rest:

☞ See Chapter 2 and Chapter 8 for a detailed discussion of *interface, messages,* and *encapsulation.*

- *The user interface is responsible for translating real-world messages into virtual ones and virtual messages into real ones.* Messages exchanged between virtual objects are meaningless to humans. Similarly, human-understandable messages are meaningless to virtual objects. The *primary* task of the user interface is to make the virtual world and the real world intelligible to each other. To accomplish this task, the user interface must rely on digital-to-analog and analog-to-digital hardware that is managed by the operating system and its components.

Depending on whether we define the user interface broadly or narrowly, it can include or exclude hardware such as the keyboard, mouse, display, etc. In application design, however, we generally confine ourselves to the narrow interpretation of the user interface as a *layer* of virtual objects.

The messages that are received by the user interface layer and transmitted to the application are classified as **input.** Those that travel in the opposite direction, from the application to the user, are called **output.** Input and output, or *I/O,* usually happen as a pair: The user presses a key and a letter appears on the screen, or the user clicks on a link and a Web page is displayed.

- *The user interface must guide the users through the steps necessary to accomplish tasks.* In the previous chapter, we discussed application design in the context of its *flow:* what objects control the movement of the application and how they do it. Within the confines of a platform such as the client/server or the Web, however, the application flow is more or less independent of the user interface. (This is why it was discussed *before* the user interface.) Modeling the application flow identifies *what* in terms of messages, data, objects, and sequencing of messages is needed for the application to carry out its responsibilities. It does not identify *how* the user experiences or participates in the flow.

The manner in which the *user interface* guides the users through the flow of the application is called **navigation.** In other words, *navigation is the flow of application as experienced by the users.*

Navigation is a critical aspect of the user interface that is, nevertheless, organically integrated with its other aspects, such as its *layout.* The layout is how various elements of the user interface are arranged for input and/or output. For most tasks, it is neither possible nor desirable to present every I/O element all at once. Therefore, visual elements must be divided into discrete groups. Moving efficiently and effortlessly among these groupings requires a good navigation design.

The Evolution of the User Interface

> Mass-market software is the driving force behind the evolution of the graphical user interface.

The "user interfaces" of early computers look so alien today that even describing them takes a good amount of effort on the part of the storyteller and a leap of imagination by the listener: no keyboard, no mouse, no monitor, but a set of mechanical switches that were set to on or off positions to program the computer by entering binary 1s and 0s. Punched cards, which we described in a previous chapter, were invented before digital computers but were adopted later, after the introduction of card readers that could translate them into digital signals.

The *command-line* interface, in which the user types instructions to the computer in a special language, arrived with the adoption of the teletype printer (TTY), a device consisting of a keyboard and a printer. Later, the printer was replaced with a monitor (actually a television set at first). For computer professionals—and only professionals worked with computers—this was a giant leap forward, because it allowed *real-time* interaction with the system.

The invention of printed circuit boards and microchips made computers affordable to small businesses and then to individuals who were not computer professionals. To sell products to these nonprofessionals, software makers had to find a better way than the command line. (The software industry itself is largely a product of affordable computers.) The first products to offer a more user-friendly interface were word processors. By presenting character-based menus, these programs relieved the users from having to memorize cryptic commands.

Around the same time, in the late 1970s, computer scientists at Xerox's Palo Alto Research Center (PARC) were developing a radically new approach for managing the human–computer interaction Later named *graphical user interface,* or GUI for short, this approach enabled users to interact with the computer through real-world **metaphors:** desktop, menus, icons, command buttons, and so on. In the 1980s, GUI was first adopted by Apple (Macintosh) and then by Microsoft (Windows).

Today, the command-line interface is still used for a limited number of purposes but, for most people, "user interface" and GUI are one and the same. Without GUI, user interface design would not be a subject of study or discussion, for "designing" a command-line interface is not a great challenge.

User Interface Objects

> The user interface is a layer of boundary objects that manage interaction with the user.

A user interface is composed of objects that form a *layer.* A layer is a collection of components that provide similar services and/or are highly dependent on each other for performing their services. The emphasis on the concept of layer is warranted for two reasons:

- No user interface object should be treated as an island, but as an element within a dynamic context. The efficiency and the usability of the user interface are decided not only by the suitability of its individual components, but also by the flow of the whole.

- The *specialized* function of the user interface is to serve as the interaction point between users and the application. Any other task that is not related to this function—business logic, database access, security, and so on—must be kept out of this layer.

UI objects that are visible to users are called **visual controls.** Not all objects that participate in the user interface are visual. Those that *are* visual, however, have two faces: one towards the user in the real world and another towards the application in the virtual world. What the user sees on the screen is only one aspect of the user interface. UI design must be aware of both aspects.

3. THE LANGUAGE OF THE USER INTERFACE

The user interface is the means by which the application communicates with people. Any kind of communication is based on a language and any language consists of *symbols* and *syntax* or the rules for organizing symbols. The sender and the receiver of a message must agree on both the meaning of symbols and how they are organized. Lack of such a mutual understanding results in *mis*communication. This point is valid regardless of whether the language is visual, vocal, verbal, or a combination.

Furthermore, symbols and syntax are *not* equal partners: Syntax can—and often does—change the meaning of the symbol. In the English language, it is the organization of the sentence or the phrase that decides whether the word "sleep" is a noun or a verb, whether "good" is an adjective or a noun, or whether "what" is a pronoun, an adjective, an adverb, or a conjunction. To sum, usage can decide the *role* of the symbol.

We will see how the same building blocks of the visual interface can play different roles after the following section.

The Metaphors

The vocabulary of the user interface is dominated by metaphors.

The language of the user interface is predominately visual and metaphors constitute the majority of the symbols in its vocabulary. A metaphor is simply a symbol or an expression that represents something beyond its literal or immediate meaning: A skull-and-crossbones sign does not actually point to any skulls or bones but implies "danger!"; the trashcan icon on a computer screen does not point to a real garbage can but indicates where to dispose of files.

The metaphors of the graphical user interface constitute an ever-growing set: buttons, menus, text boxes, scrollbars, dropdowns, sliders, gauges, icons, tree views, etc. Some metaphors are easy to understand while some need textual explanations or "bubble" help. The most successful "after-market" vendors for software development tools are those that offer better, more attractive, or newer metaphors.

Prior to the graphical user interface, interaction with computers did not involve metaphors, but consisted of punched cards and typed-in commands. At the same time, an easy-to-use computer was an oxymoron: Persons who fed the punched cards or cryptic commands to the computers where trained technicians, not "users" as the term is understood today. Neither were aesthetics or usability important issues in the development of information systems. Metaphors have made computers easy to use, but have added a layer of complexity to the design of software.

In the real world, metaphors use symbols of real things to enhance the impact of messages by brevity or by imaginative association. Software applications belong to a *virtual world* but they must rely on *real-world metaphors* for the very essence of their messages. Symbols and labels on elevator buttons refer to what the buttons do, but the buttons themselves are not symbols or metaphors. On a computer screen, on the other hand, the button itself is also a metaphor.

The Roles

> Each metaphor in the vocabulary of the user interface can signify multiple roles.

What we have described presents both opportunities and risks. In the real world, a bare minimum of relationship exists between form and functionality: There is a limited number of widgets that can turn a faucet on or off. On a computer screen, *any* shape can symbolize *any* action because form is not dictated by function: You may open a document by clicking a button, double-clicking an icon, selecting a menu item, typing its name, and so on.

The building blocks of the user interface come in a vast variety of shapes and forms. Designers are constantly experimenting with new visual controls. A few succeed and the rest are consigned to oblivion, but the effort goes on for two reasons: market demand for better or newer metaphors and, as a result, market competition.

Any catalog of visual controls will look outdated in a very short time. The roles, however, are more stable and result from the requirements of human–computer interaction. We must emphasize that most visual controls can, and do, play multiple roles. (See Figure 12.2.)

The Containers

> Containers organize and present visual controls.

Containers, such as forms and Web pages, are the major *units* of the visual interface. They organize and present visual controls for a *specific* purpose: The main form of a word-processing application offers buttons, menus, toolbars, and other things that are required to edit documents; a spreadsheet application contains what is necessary for maintaining columnar data; and a form such as the one in Figure 12.2 shows controls that serve its stated task, finding and managing patients.

Containers can house other containers, such as frames, that further refine the organization of visual controls. In other words, containers may have a hierarchical relationship with each other.

The Displayers

> Displayers provide textual or pictorial information.

Every visual control, by definition, displays something. Most user interfaces, however, must employ dedicated controls for displaying textual or pictorial

Figure 12.2 The Language of the User Interface: A Vocabulary of Metaphors

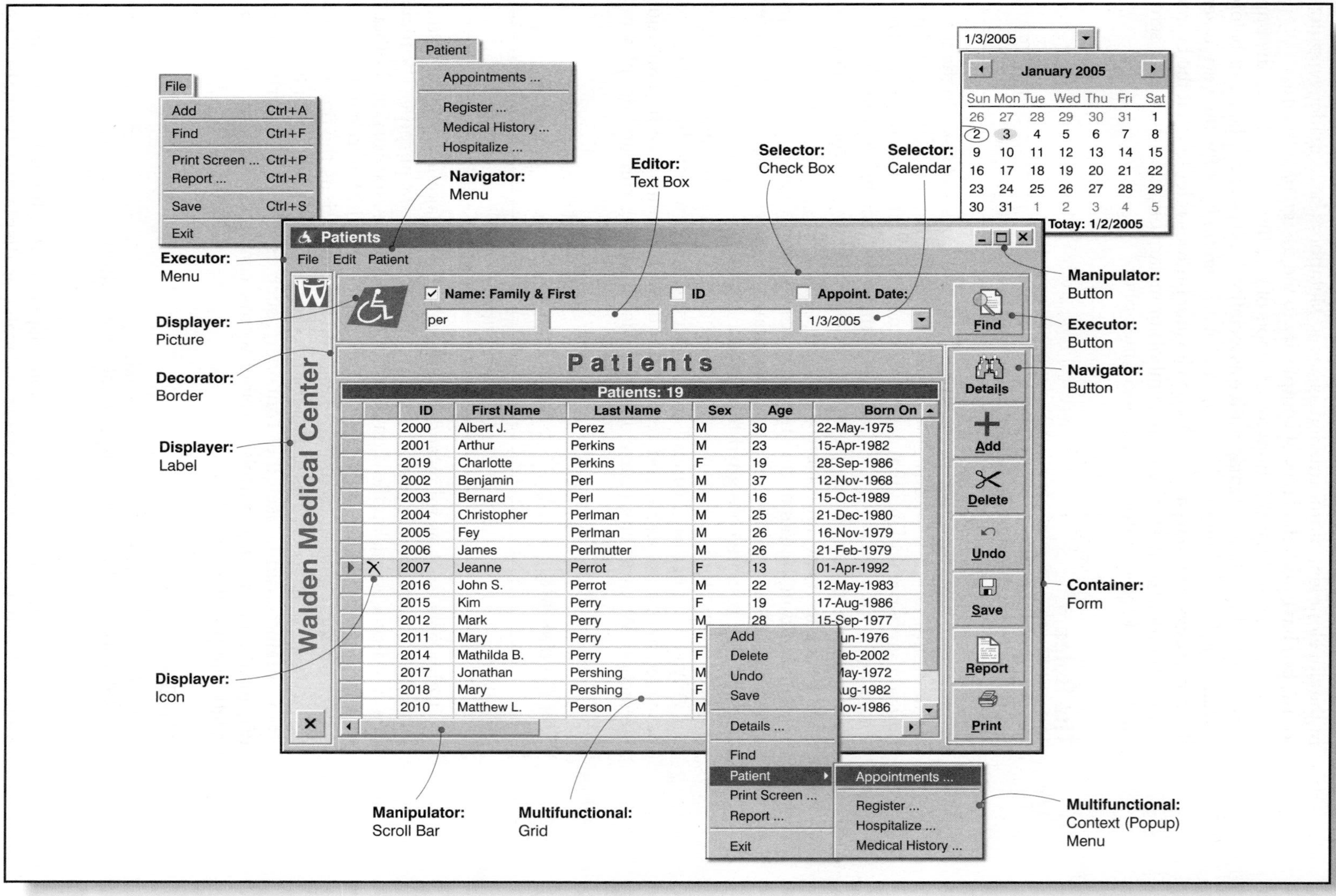

Visual controls are metaphors of real-world objects. Each metaphor can play multiple roles, sometimes at the same time.

information to clarify their purpose. Without the **Patients** label, the function of the form in Figure 12.2 would not be readily understandable. In the same illustration, an **X** icon on a grid row provides a visual feedback for an action performed by the user: mark the patient for deletion.

The picture of the wheelchair patient on the form is also a displayer that indicates the function of the form, but its role is more subtle than the label. Without the **Patients** label, users who are newcomers to the application might guess the form's function from the picture, but they cannot be certain. As they become more experienced, however, the picture would become shorthand for the label. In Walden's patient management application, many forms and menus are likely to refer to the patient search screen and the experienced user would have an easier time differentiating among icons than among textual labels.

The behavior of displayers can be *dynamic* or *non-dynamic.* A label such as the one in our illustration usually shows the same thing throughout its lifetime. A progress bar, on the other hand, is used to display the changes in the status of something: number of files copied, number of e-mail messages downloaded, the percentage of a task accomplished, and so on. *Cursors* are the ever-present displayers that indicate where an action by the user is taking place or will take place.

Although the behavior of a control may be non-dynamic, the control itself cannot be called "static," as the application may decide to change the message on a label or the picture in a picture box. Some controls, however, are designed only for dynamic use: A gauge or a progress bar is a waste of space if it is not used to display a kind of change.

The appropriate use of displayers is more art than science: Both too little and too much can confuse the user. What is more, their use is not always dictated by the *functional* requirements of the user interface but depends on the judgment of the designer and/or the taste of the client, which may or may not serve the user. The best available guideline for using displayers (and decorators, described later), is this: Use the minimum necessary but not more—valuable advice but of little practical value.

The Editors

Editors accept textual or graphical input from the user.

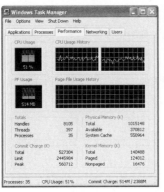

Figure 12.3
The Displayer

In Windows Task Manager, which monitors the resources of the workstation, the graphs are obviously dynamic, but some of the labels are continuously changed as well.

The most familiar embodiment of the editor role is the omnipresent text box. In the majority of cases where user input is required, a text box is used to accept and evaluate the input. In most cases where a text box is used, it is much more than a passive or inert receptacle for the input. It is, on the contrary, an *editor:* The text box interprets and formats the text. When you enter your password, what the text box displays is not what you typed, and where the entry must be numerical, nonnumerical entries (except, perhaps, the decimal point) are discarded.

The main window of a word-processing application is a large and very sophisticated editor. The editors, however, are not limited to textual receptacles. Painting and drawing applications offer graphical editors that interpret the input—by mouse, drawing pen, touch-sensitive screen, or even keyboard—as graphical shapes. (See Figure 12.4.)

Whether textual or graphical, the behavior of an editor is decided by the context. To be more exact, it is the application that decides how the editor must behave based on settings, prior user selections, and user actions. In a drawing application, mouse movements would not produce the same results every time: If you have selected the circle tool, holding the left mouse button and dragging the mouse would produce a circle; but if you have selected the rectangle tool, the same action would result in a rectangle. In a word processor, the font and the formatting of the text that you type result from the paragraph style or the keyboard actions that you perform to make a word or a phrase bold or italic.

☞ The previous examples can also serve as reminders of **polymorphism,** which was discussed in Chapter 2. As we said, polymorphism is the ability of objects belonging to different classes to perform the same operation differently. In a drawing program, when the application passes user mouse movements to a "square" object, the messages are translated to a square, while the "circle" object would convert the same messages to a circle.

The Selectors

Selectors allow the user to choose between two or more options or values.

Editors are more or less free-format while selectors accept user input as a selection of predefined values. The choices may be limited, like *yes* or *no,* or may cover a vast range, such as dates. They might also be **dynamic** or **static**. In Figure 12.2, the options for finding patients are limited to three: by name, by ID, or by the appointment date. (A real system must provide many more search options.) Once the search is done, however, the number of patients from which you may select is not predefined. In our example, the search returned 19 names. It might have returned less, more, or none at all.

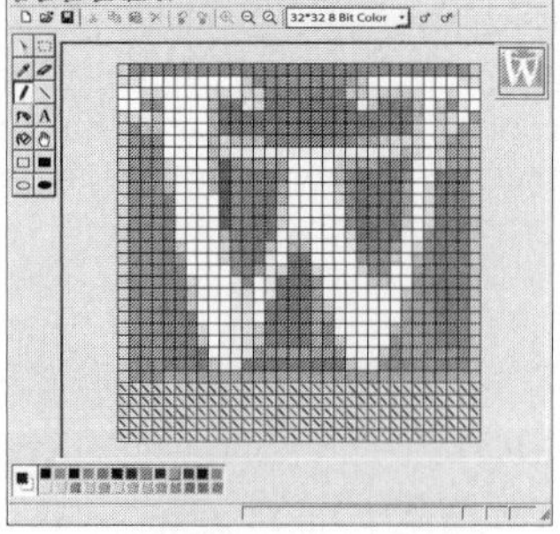

Figure 12.4
The Editor

Editors accept and evaluate user input. This example, from Windows Paint, illustrates an editor that allows users to draw icons.

Figure 12.5
The Selector

Selectors allow the user to choose among predefined options. They encompass a very wide variety, from simple check boxes and dropdowns to maps. This example, from Creative Mixer (by Creative Mixer, Ltd.), offers sliders to control the sound level and the balance of various devices connected to the sound card. Slider is a real-world metaphor that fits well with a sound device. The boxes over the vertical sliders are also selectors, but are of a binary type: By clicking on them, the user can turn the input/output for a particular device on or off.

Source: Creative Labs, Inc., http://us.creative.com.

Controls that play the role of selectors constitute a vast variety: dropdowns, lists, option buttons, push buttons, calendars, menus, and more. Choosing the selectors depends on the *quantity* of options and their interrelationships. Option buttons are used when the choices are mutually exclusive. For example, you may not select *male* and *female* together. Check buttons allow you to select more than one option at the same time. When the values are dynamic or their number exceeds what can be accommodated within the form's limited area, dropdowns are used.

In certain environments, such as train stations, airports, factory floors, and video shops where keyboards or mice are not practical, selectors are the only available option for receiving user input. The interface may even offer the user a virtual keyboard on the touch-sensitive screen for entering free-form text.

Some controls combine the editor and the selector roles in one. Dropdowns often allow the user to type in characters while the control displays options that correspond, in part or in whole, to the typed characters. Sometimes you may add values that are not already present. Instead of scrolling up and down a long list, a directory listing may allow the user to type a character and then immediately go to entries that start with that letter.

The Executors

> Executors allow the user to request the execution of specific commands from the application.

Executors take action. In Figure 12.2, after you have specified the search criteria, you click on the **Find** button to order the application to conduct the search. Buttons and menu entries are the primary controls that can play the executor role, but since in the virtual world of the user interface the form is not constrained by the function, UI designers have used almost every available control as executors. On many Web applications, some from prestigious online vendors, setting the value of a check box may trigger an action. The designers might believe that by using such methods they have saved the user an extra click of the mouse, but what they have really done is to confuse the user because they have acted against *precedence* and expectations. (See "The Grammar of the User Interface" section later in this chapter.)

Figure 12.6
The Executor

The icons on these buttons from the Microsoft Word toolbox represent execute commands: create new document, open document, save changes, email document, print, and print preview.

Designers must be very careful in choosing metaphors that play the executor role. The result of bad choices may range from simply annoying to extremely destructive. If our sample form in Figure 12.2 conducted a search the moment that you clicked on a check box, you would be irritated because the application gave you no chance to ponder your choices and change your mind. In a banking application, such a misuse may create serious problems by sending money to where it should not go. Selecting inappropriate "executor" metaphors for applications used by the military and nuclear power plants can have catastrophic results.

The Navigators

Navigators allow the user to move among containers.

Rare are applications whose functionality can be contained within one form or one Web page. Even a word processor that offers most of its services in one window has to provide the user with numerous forms to customize the settings, open and/or save documents, choose options, or define styles. To enable the users to plot a course among the functional units of the user interface, the application must provide them with navigators.

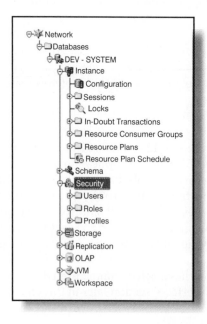

Figure 12.7
The Navigator

The tree view control organizes navigational choices in a hierarchical structure. It is especially useful when the choices are too numerous to be accommodated by other navigators such as menus or buttons. (This example is from Oracle's Enterprise Manager Console.)

☞ Beware of incompatible terminology. On the Web platform, "page" is the main container unit, whereas in desktop platforms, such as Windows, the major user interface units are called "forms." Thus, on the Web, one page may contain multiple "forms" or sections of the document that accept user input. In Windows, however, a form may be "paged," meaning that it may consist of multiple "pages," or groupings of controls, that overlay each other on the same form.

Navigators are specialized subclasses of executors that sometimes resemble selectors. What makes navigators different from selectors is that the choices offered by navigators relate to the dynamic behavior of the application, not to data. They are subclasses of executors because navigation often results not only in a change of containers, but also in some action. In Figure 12.2, clicking on the **Details** button would trigger two actions: retrieve the full patient profile *and* display the information on a different form.

Menus were one of the earliest controls used to offer navigational choices. Menus and buttons are still the most popular and well-suited navigators. Tree views come next, for situations where the choices are too many for a clean and clear presentation by buttons and menus. In spite of the similarity between navigators and selectors, some selectors such as dropdowns and check boxes should not be used as navigators: As we indicated, selectors primarily relate to *state* and data whereas navigators focus on *behavior.* A control that serves one role well may not suit the other.

Controls such as tabbed pages function both as containers and *local* navigators. On a tabbed page, controls are organized as "pages" that are displayed when the user clicks on a tab.

Object Signifiers

> Object signifiers represent objects, their properties, and/or their methods.

Containers and other visual controls are objects. Unlike other virtual objects, you can *see* what they are and what they can do. In fact, they exist to make invisible objects visible and accessible. Without a word processor or a printout, a document is just a collection of digital bits and bytes on the hard drive, and only through user interfaces such as the one in Figure 12.2 can users interact with `Patient` and other entity objects.

Visual objects, however, do not necessarily correspond with *entity* objects. Use cases model the behavior that the *system* must provide to satisfy requirements, and this behavior is much more complex than the behavior of its individual building blocks. For example, as we previously described, the appointment clerk must follow a precise set of steps and work with more than one entity object before he or she can order the `Patient` object to create an appointment.

Sometimes, though, both the workflow and the complexity are better served if we create the *illusion* that the user can interact directly with entity objects. Since the graphical user interface won over the marketplace, every computer user has become familiar with object signifiers: *icons* for folders, files, trash cans, documents, pictures, etc. Indeed, it has become almost second nature for computer users to click on an icon to launch an application.

Icons, as object signifiers, are very effective because they can pack a large number of options within a very small but distinctive image, sometimes clarified by a short label. Each object signifier has a default action, usually triggered by a double-click or by pressing the **Enter** key, and a set of operations, displayed when the user presses and holds down the right mouse button. (This is usually called the **context menu.**)

Without the compactness of icons, the user would have to type in cryptic commands or wade through a varying number of menus to accomplish something. Icons also allow the user more freedom in defining the workflow. From a shortcut icon for

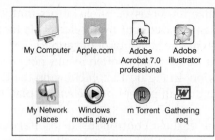

Figure 12.8
The Object Signifier

Object signifiers point towards anything that can be represented as a distinct entity: a document, a Web site, an application, a computer, etc. In this example from a Windows desktop, a chapter of this book is shown as an icon in the lower right-hand corner. The context menu would present us with all the actions that are possible with this object: open for editing, copy, email, etc. The Apple icon on the row above would have different actions. By clicking on this icon, we can directly go to the company's Web site, without having to open the browser first and selecting a site afterwards.

a document on your desktop, you can directly choose actions that relate to the document: edit, copy, move, e-mail, etc.

We used the term "illusion" in describing object signifiers. This characterization is accurate in two ways. First, an object signifier is *not* directly wired to any entity object, but to the operating system or applications that interpret the user action and apply it to the object. Second, ease of use is not the same as ease of implementation. If you double-click an icon for a snapshot of your family on vacation, the operating system must decide which of many applications can handle the object, launch the application, and point it towards the object. In turn, the application must be equipped to accept the message supplied by the operating system and process it correctly.

☞ Not all icons are object signifiers. Like most other visual controls, an icon can play several roles. Often icons are used as simple displayers, on buttons or next to branches on a tree view control. (See Figure 12.7.) An icon for opening documents is an executor: It executes an action but does not point to a specific object.

Though icons are the most familiar controls for object signifiers, other controls may perform the same role as well. In many applications where a list is displayed, double-clicking on a row would perform some action related to the entry on that row. In our example in Figure 12.2, double-clicking on a row would launch the **Details** form. The context or "popup" menu in the same illustration is displayed as a result of right-clicking on a row: if you select the **Medical History** entry on the context menu, the application will display the medical history for the specific patient on which you right-clicked.

As we stated, the actions that object signifiers perform or offer depend entirely on how they are "wired" or programmed. In addition, the platform may constrain the manner of interaction between the user and the object signifier. For example, in standard Web interface, double-click is not used. Instead, the object signifier is presented as a URL (Uniform Resource Locator) that is activated by a single click. Or where the mouse has only one button, "right-clicking" is irrelevant.

The Manipulators

The manipulators allow the user to control the appearance of the visual interface.

The computer screen is a limited space and the forms displayed by applications are constrained by this fact. Even if there were no limitations on the screen

The term "scrollbar" is a witness to the power of, and the need for, real-world metaphors in defining the user interface, even though scrolls started to lose ground to the modern book form (called "codex") from around two thousand years ago. Ancient scroll "bars" functioned very much like their modern, virtual, namesakes: They were attached to both ends of a scroll so that the "user" could control a "window" of the written surface by unrolling one end of the scroll while rolling it at the other end.

size, the human eye can handle only a limited number of elements at the same time. Therefore, managing the size and the layout of elements within a form, and managing the size and the arrangement of forms themselves, is a crucial UI design issue.

The primary controls that perform the manipulator role are the forms themselves. Most forms allow the user to resize, move, maximize, and minimize them. In performing these actions, forms also trigger *events* that the programmers can use to resize and/or arrange controls *within* the form. If done well, most users will not even notice the flurry of activity that follows a simple resizing of their word processor window: some controls are resized while others are moved around or are stacked differently. Such events might seem "natural," but there is nothing natural or automatic about them: Every movement or change of size is foreseen, and provided for, by the designers and/or programmers. However, *failure* to provide for these events will be immediately noticed by the users who will rightly judge the application as poorly designed.

Some containers are designed solely for playing the role of manipulators. "Splitters," as the name implies, split the form into vertical or horizontal panels. When the user drags the splitter by moving the mouse, the visual controls within its confines are moved and or resized. (See Figure 12.9.)

Scrollbars are the most widely used manipulators after forms. By dragging or clicking on scrollbars the user can move a "window" over large amounts of information that *must* be on one form but *cannot* fit on one form. Without scrollbars, editing even a moderate-sized document in a word processor would become similar to using an old-fashioned typewriter.

The Pointers

> Pointers are moving or movable symbols that indicate the position and the type of user actions.

Like icons, pointers are usually very small, but they play a significant role in the usability of the user interface. They tell you where and what you can do with *other* visual controls. When you move the normal pointer (usually an angled arrow) over

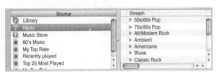

Figure 12.9
The Manipulator

In Apple's iTunes music management program, clicking on an item in the left pane displays the details on the right pane. A splitter allows the user to change the relative size of each pane (above and below). The combination of the splitter and scrollbars enables the user to decide what should be displayed in a limited space.

Chapter 12   Application Design II   **413**

Figure 12.10
The Pointer

Pointers must be "strong" metaphors: They must be familiar enough to be recognized almost immediately, but must not require too much detail.

the edge of a container such as a form, it may change to a two-headed arrow to indicate that by dragging the edge of the container you may resize the form. If the pointer does not change shape, you conclude that this specific container cannot be resized. Without pointers, the user cannot predict the results of pressing a key or clicking a mouse button.

The pointers walk a very fine line: They must be helpful but unobtrusive, familiar but distinctive, functional but pleasing. As a result, the pointers are the most "minimalist" metaphors of the user interface: various types of arrows, hourglass, pointing hands, I-beams, cross-beams, question marks, and other very simple signs. Designers tirelessly try to contribute to the rather limited vocabulary of pointers by introducing new metaphors: animated pointers of sniffing dogs, running horses, blazing fires, etc. Many are distinctive, some are pleasing, but most fall far short of the first required attribute for a pointer: helpful but *not* obtrusive.

Many applications use two pointers. The first shows where the immediate action would take place, while the second allows the users to select another area. For example, in a word processor, an I-beam (often called a "*cursor*") specifies where the next character that you type will appear, while the second one allows you to move the I-beam to another location in the text stream, or perform actions that do not change the location of the I-beam, such as resizing the window, selecting a paragraph style, or printing the document.

The Decorators

Decorators enhance the appearance and the aesthetics of the user interface.

Lines, frames, and borders that separate or emphasize visual controls are the most evident category of decorators. Members of the most widely used category, however, hide in plain sight: fonts and colors. The selection and the placement of typefaces and colors has a deciding impact on the appearance, usability, and the aesthetic effect of the user interface: A bold font overshadows a regular font and a red color draws attention away from more subdued colors.

Some displayers, like the icon of the wheelchair patient in Figure 12.2, walk a fine line between decoration and information: The figure is not absolutely necessary,

Figure 12.11
The Decorator

Walden Medical Center's Web site uses fonts, colors, lines, boxes, and semi-decorative images to distinguish certain items from the rest of its main page.

but, in addition to serving as a visual identifier, it helps to distinguish forms and buttons from each other and reduces the dullness of the user interface.

Decorators can hurt the design as much as they can help it: They must be used to enhance the user experience, but must not overwhelm it. (See "The Aesthetics" section later in this chapter.)

The Multifunctional Controls

> One instance of a multifunctional control can play multiple roles.

Each visual control usually can play more than one role. As Figure 12.2 shows, buttons and menus may be used as executors, navigators, or manipulators. Some controls, however, can play multiple roles within the *same* instance.

Grids are the most prominent members of the multifunctional controls. They are used to maintain varying amounts of relational or hierarchical data in the tabular format of rows and columns. These data usually represent or interpret attributes that belong to a set of objects (like patients, as in our example) and, often, these attributes require a wide variety of tools for display and maintenance: calendars to select dates, dropdowns to select from lists, navigator buttons to display forms with complicated search criteria, editors to evaluate user input, icons to display visual identifiers, etc.

During the lifetime of the graphical user interface, grids have evolved from simple display tables to highly sophisticated controls that allow the cells within their tabular format to play many of the roles previously described: selector, navigator, editor, etc. In addition, some grids allow the programmer to attach other controls to their cells, thus expanding the range of their own functionality.

In our example, the leftmost column of the grid is graphical instead of textual: An icon shows that one patient record has been marked for deletion. This graphical notation is likely to be more effective than a textual marker in drawing the attention of the user.

Input/Output Devices

> I/O devices are hardware that allow real-world users to interact with the virtual world of the information system.

Input/output devices such as a keyboard, a monitor, and a mouse are, of course, not metaphors but very tangible objects that make the human–computer interaction possible by turning analog signals into digital signals and vice versa. They are also usually part of the *general* technological framework, meaning that they are often taken for granted regardless of the specific platform or the specific technology for which the user interface is designed.

Application designers do not design the I/O devices, but they do design *for* them. Before the advent of the mouse or its predecessors such as the optical pen, keys and keyboard combinations were the only means available to users to issue commands to the computer. Before that, punched cards performed the same function—better, by an order of magnitude, than flipping on/off switches with which the users of the first computers had to contend.

By necessity, designs for different technological frameworks are different from each other. Without mouse or graphical displays, the user interface would not need, and could not use, most of the visual metaphors described in this chapter. This, however, does not mean that user interface designers can safely ignore the I/O issue and wrongly assume that one design fits the entire technological framework. In fact, the more advanced the technological framework becomes, the more work is required from designers to accommodate choices that the technology offers.

The keyboard-mouse-monitor combination may be the most common I/O device combination in the current technological framework, but it is not the only one. Games and simulations cover a considerable part of the software landscape and often require specialized "consoles." Notebooks are equipped with touch-sensitive pads or mouse imitations that are never as easy to use as the desktop mouse. Terminals in public-access areas such as railroad stations lack both a keyboard and a mouse and are be operated by using touch-sensitive screens. The same is true of restaurant systems where waiters must enter orders fast.

Ergonomics, design factors that are intended to maximize productivity and minimize work fatigue, do not stop at hardware, but must be carried over to the user interface as well. Even when designing for the most mundane applications, the designer must not forget that not all hardware combinations are the same, not all environments in which the users operate are the same, and, last but not least, not all users are the same: Some users prefer to learn and use keyboard short-cuts to issue commands while others are either newcomers to the application or prefer to click on some control.

The Vocals

Vocals are sounds or speech that reinforce the visual interface.

Sound support in computers has indeed come a long way. Not only have computers become entertainment centers in their own rights, entertainment equipment from stereo systems to DVD players to television systems are really computers at heart.

With certain exceptions, however, the user interface of applications remains predominately visual: With all the advances in voice recognition and voice rendition of digitized text, the science-fiction vision of total interaction with computers through normal conversation is still some time away. The reasons are only partly technical: Automated telephone systems, supposed to guide the user through a maze of options, have not been very endearing to the users whom they are supposed to help. On the other hand, the mostly visual Web interface has been enormously successful, even though its native controls are far fewer and poorer than the rich environments provided by Mac or Windows platforms.

Nevertheless, for better or for worse, sound has been used to enhance the effect of the user interface. The most familiar examples are the beeps and alarm bells that accompany alerts and error messages. Mouse clicks in certain applications are translated back into audible clicks—as annoying as they are to most users.

The usability of vocals in the user interface will no doubt grow as designers learn how to use them and, more importantly, *when* to use them. At least one vocal, "you've got mail" was treated affectionately in a movie, a romantic comedy. But, for some reason, people are more forgiving of a bad visual interface and less tolerant of any sound effect that does not please them. Therefore, designers must take extra care in using vocals in the user interface.

The Grammar of the User Interface

> The grammar of the user interface is based on usage and the requirements of the application.

The composition of any language changes over time: words and metaphors are invented, rediscovered, and discarded; accepted usage becomes old-fashioned; and newly coined expressions become fashionable over the protests of language purists. The language of the user interface is no exception. It is, however, characterized by an exceptionally fast pace of mutations and experimentations: It is, truly, a work in progress.

Modern languages began to stabilize when a successful technology, printing, converged with successful and trendsetting "content": the King James Bible and Elizabethan drama in England, and Renaissance literature in Italy. For the user interface of information systems, this convergence might be the unstoppable success and evolution of the Web, even though, at this moment, the Web is a relatively control-poor environment and, as far as the stability of the visual language is concerned, is far from stable.

Since there are no authoritative or time-honored guidelines for using the language of the user interface, what is a designer to do? Fortunately, there is a vast body of *precedents* that designers can use as a starting point. These precedents provide not only positive guidelines—what to do—but also negative ones—what *not* to do. In other words, existing applications provide designers with a *usage* guide in the form of patterns and anti-patterns.

Patterns

> The design of the user interface often consists of solving similar problems repeatedly.

☞ We will discuss patterns in detail in Chapter 14.

Existing applications supply a rich source for discovering **patterns** in user interface design. A pattern is the *core* of the solution to a problem that occurs repeatedly in an environment. Unlike rules, patterns must be adapted to the problem at hand and cannot be followed uncritically.

Recurring Problem	Solution	Role
How to display a large amount of information that cannot fit within one window.	Scrollbar	Manipulator
How to allow the user to select from a long list of hierarchical data and options without losing focus of the relationships between them.	Tree View	Navigator & Selector
How to identify actions that relate to *one* object—dynamically and without wasting space.	Context Menu	Multifunctional Control
How to allow the user to select only *one* option from a set of options.	Option Box	Selector
How to present clear and easy-to-understand choices of action to the user.	Button	Executor
How to distinguish a set of related items on a form from other items.	Frame	Decorator

Each of the metaphors and roles that we described can be seen as a core solution within a recurring problem:

These are, of course, "mini-patterns"—problems that can be solved by using single words and phrases from within the language. The challenge arises when a more complex communication between the computer and the user must take place: when the user must navigate from form to form and, along the way, work with many visual controls to accomplish a *meaningful* goal. To meet such challenges we must turn, yet again, to **use cases.** The paramount task of the designer is to employ the vocabulary of the user interface to realize the behavioral requirements of the system.

Use cases are the *user model* of the system, and the closer the user interface comes to this model, the better it is. Since visual controls are metaphors, the designer *must* rely on what the user already knows or is reasonably expected to know. To put it slightly differently, the designer must use precedents creatively but with **consistency.**

Consistency

> Consistency in the user interface is achieved when the user can predict what kinds of actions produce what kinds of results.

In designing the user interface, another meaning of the term "pattern" applies as well: a consistent and characteristic form.

[Cooper, 1995, 43]

> If our conscious mind had to grapple with every detail of what our eyes saw, we would be overwhelmed with meaningless detail. The ability of our unconscious mind to group things into patterns based on visual cues is what allows us to process information so quickly and efficiently. Understanding and applying this model of how the human mind processes information is one of the key elements of visual interface design. The philosophy is to present the program's components on the screen as recognizable visual patterns with accompanying text as a descriptive supplement. The user can choose, on a purely pattern-matching, unconscious level, which objects to consider consciously.

Consistency and predictability of expectations are essential both to the vocabulary and the syntax of the user interface. Users cannot learn everything from scratch every time they work with a new application. If the users expect the key combination **Ctrl-C** to copy something or the **F1** key to display help, the designers must not go against their expectations, even if they believe that they are far more qualified than Microsoft or Apple to create the world.

Still, the urge to be creative may win over prudence and common sense. There is nothing special or sacred about the location of the "file" menu or other official or de facto standards such as the 110-volt electrical current used in North America or the 220-volt electrical current used in Europe, but a designer must have a much better reason than creativity to go against standards. (You can easily imagine the fate of an electronics manufacturer whose merchandise can work only with a 90-volt current.)

The following quotation briefly describes the situation when de facto standards for the user interface did not exist:

[Spolsky 2001, 44]

> It is hard to underestimate just how much consistency helps people to learn and use a wide variety of programs. Before GUIs, every program reinvented the very fundamentals of the user interface. Even a simple operation like "exit," which every program had to have, was completely inconsistent. In those days,

people made a point of memorizing, at the very least, the exit command of common programs so they could exit and run a program they understood . . .

Consistency is a fundamental principle of good UI design, but it's really just a corollary of the axiom "make the program model match the user model," because the user model is likely to reflect the way that users see *other* programs behaving.

The Aesthetics

> The aesthetics of the user interface must be a *functional* aesthetic.

Applying the term "aesthetics" to interface design is quite appropriate but may lead to extremely bad decisions by the designer. First and foremost, the user interface is *not* art. Applications are functional products, not artwork, and the reason for the existence of a product is primarily *what* it does and *how* it does it.

The issues faced by user interface designers are more similar to those that industrial and graphic designers must solve than to challenges that painters and sculptors must confront. In industrial design, function comes first, beauty second. If aesthetics harms the functionality, then the aesthetics must be revised—a rule that should *not* apply to any work of art.

Nevertheless, aesthetics itself must not be discarded. Finding the most pleasing or informative picture for a button would not be in vain, nor would agonizing over choosing a dropdown versus a set of option boxes and where to place the controls.

The most praiseworthy aesthetic decisions are those that enhance the functionality of the user interface. One of the most basic aesthetic challenges is the management of forms with too many elements. One easy answer is to break one form into two or more forms. The easy answer may work in certain circumstances, but not in others: imagine a word processor where you have to go back and forth between forms to italicize a word, center a paragraph, choose a font, etc.

In certain contexts, the use of decorators such as lines and frames would add both to the aesthetic value of the user interface and to its functionality. How to use decorators, though, depends on the problem at hand and the aesthetic sense of the designer: use too little and the result would resemble the excruciating uniformity of tax or registration forms; use too much and the user interface would look like advertising pages or grocery store brochures where every element on the page is fighting with other elements for your attention—and none succeeds.

4. Shaping Messages into the User Interface

> The user interface is the concrete realization of messages passed between the actors and the system.

As we have stated in various forms, analysis and design are a spiral iteration of what we discover through behavioral modeling. It is **iterative** because at every development milestone we revisit use cases to expand and reinterpret what we have discovered since the previous visit; it is **spiral** because we do not exactly return to the previous point in time or place, but view the models from a higher level that is, at the same time, more advanced and more detailed.

In discovering and defining the application *flow,* we arrive at objects, messages, and methods that the application needs to satisfy the functional requirements of behavioral modeling. Methods, as we explained, implement the messages that objects exchange to ask for services or to provide them.

☞ See Chapter 11 for a summary of messages, methods, parameters, and return values.

We first come upon messages in conceptual modeling where dynamic diagrams depict the interaction between *entity* objects. The logical design refines these messages into methods and maps them to *design* objects, including objects that are specific to the solution. Finally, physical modeling specifies the particulars of the methods: the type and the order of parameters that are carried by the message to the service-provider object and the return value that the service-consumer object receives from the service provider.

If the job of concrete modeling is done well, then the user interface is close to realization because the ***essential purpose of the user interface is to enable the user and the system to exchange messages.*** That is to say, the user is simply one object among other objects that exchange messages with each other to perform tasks. If the user can send correct parameters within the body of correct messages and understand the return values, then we have the correct user interface.

Mapping Parameters & Attributes

UI design must map messages, their parameters, and their return values into UI metaphors.

To illustrate *how* defining methods shapes the user interface, we have selected one of the simplest, most familiar examples: login to the application. In Walden's **Patient Management** application, most everything is more complicated than this example (Figure 12.2, for instance), but here its simplicity serves our purpose well.

Login App User (Table 12.1) is the kind of use case that is frequently *not* written since it appears almost obvious. (It is not, though, *always* so simple.) In the previous chapter, we presented it as a part of the discussion on application flow and security, and modeled it in a sequence diagram with another use case, **Get User Selection**. By nature, however, a sequence diagram is not very agreeable towards *conditional* interactions, and therefore cannot represent the alternate flow and exceptions effectively. (As "The Web Flow," Figure 11.2, illustrates, an activity diagram is much more suited to conditional flow.)

☞ See the diagram "Designing Application Security: The View from Inside" in Chapter 11.

As the normal flow of the use case indicates, the message that the user interface must relay from the user to the control object (**Login Mgr**) is very simple:

```
verifyLogin(loginID, password): Boolean
```

The user must enter an ID and a password to enter the application. If the login is successful, the **Login UI** object will receive a **true** (Boolean) return value from **Login Mgr**. To satisfy the requirements, **Login UI** must provide the user with the following *minimal* visual controls:

- A **container** (form) to accommodate all other controls and define the visual boundaries of the interaction.
- Two **editors** (text boxes) for accepting and evaluating the user ID and password. The text box for password input must be encrypted so that its contents will be hidden from the view of persons other than the user.

Table 12.1
Patient
Management's **Login
App User** Use Case.
In the previous chap-
ter, we presented the
sequence diagram for
this use case in the
context of defining
the application flow
and security.

Walden Patient Management	
Use Case:	Login App User
ID:	10
Scope:	Patient Management System
Priority:	High
Summary:	Logs the user into the Walden's Patient Management application.
Primary Actor:	App User
Supporting Actors:	
Stakeholders:	• Hospital: The application user has access to the hospital's information system.
Generalization:	
Include:	
Extend:	
Precondition:	
Trigger:	App user starts the application.
Normal Flow:	1. App user submits his or her user ID and password for using the application. 2. The application verifies the login and displays the opening menu.
Sub-Flows:	
Alternate Flow/Exceptions:	1.a App user fails to enter the user ID and/or the password. A warning is issued. 2.b System fails to recognize the user ID and/or the password. A warning is issued. 3.c After three logon failures, the app user is notified of the failure and the login is terminated.
Post-Condition:	App user is logged in to the application and may use services determined by his or her privileges.

- Two **executors** (buttons) to allow the user to submit or cancel the operation.
- **Displayers** (labels and icons) to identify the use case (**Logon**), the system (**Patient Management**), and the owner (**Walden Medical Center**).

The result is illustrated in Figure 12.12. Neither the use case, which originates from analysis, nor the design sequence diagram, which identifies design objects and messages, dictates the exact choices made by the interface designer. The designer must satisfy the requirements of analysis and flow design, but it is the interface design that decides *how*.

To be sure, as we have explained, analysis may also define *non*functional requirements, such as the workplace environment and performance, that *must* be taken into account by design. Beyond that, however, analysis must avoid intruding in design issues. The basic task of analysis, as the term itself implies, is to separate a whole into its constituent parts, while design must create a *concrete* model of the whole. The issues faced by design cannot be clearly or reliably seen by analysis, and specifying inappropriate design guidelines in analysis can only hurt development, not help it.

Figure 12.12 The Logon Flow: The User Interface as the Realization of Use Cases

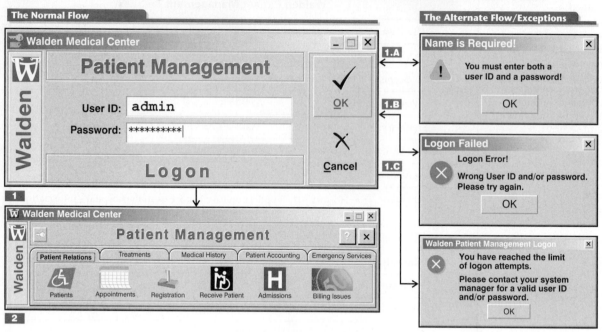

The user interface joins the methods defined during the discovery of the application flow with the workflow as described by use cases. (See Table 12.1, the **Login App User** use case.)

In Figure 12.2, the mapping is more complicated than in the example for **Login App User**. In the process of analysis and design, we discover that finding patients is repeated across many use cases. Following the guidelines for refactoring (see the "Refactoring" section in Chapter 7), we decide to make **Find Patient** into an independent use case. (We will talk more about the relationship between such an independent use case and other use cases in the "Constraints in UI Design" section.)

Elevating **Find Patient** from a single step into a fully independent use case, however, has consequences: The use case becomes more complex because it has to satisfy a larger number of requirements. The appointment and registration clerks need one set of criteria for finding patients, accounting needs another set, and the medical staff needs yet a third. The resulting complexity cannot be solved by the simple mapping between methods and interface elements that we presented for **Login App User**. Imagine mapping the interface to all the messages that the database management system must process to retrieve a patient list:

```
. . .
findPatient(lastName)
findPatient(lastName, firstName)
findPatient(appointmentDate)
findPatient(appointmentDate, lastName)
findPatient(appointmentDate, lastName, firstName)
findPatient(patientID)
findPatient(birthDate)
findPatient(lastName, birthDate)
. . .
```

And many more. Assigning one button or one menu item to each message would not only overwhelm the user, but would not leave much room on the form for anything else. The situation is similar to the online DVD search that we presented previously. (See the "Deriving Methods from Messages" section in Chapter 11.) One indisputable advantage of object orientation is that complexity can be encapsulated in those objects—and *only* those objects—that must deal with it.

As the sequence diagram in Figure 12.13 illustrates, to find the patients the user interface must communicate only with **Patient Mgr**, a control/life cycle object. (To keep the sequence diagram simple, we have ignored the **Find Mgr** object that is responsible for instantiating and managing all other objects.) How the **Patient Mgr** communicates with **Persistence**, which is responsible for managing the communication with the database, does not concern the **Find Patient UI** object.

Instead of exposing one method for each message that it must send to the **Persistence** object, **Patient Mgr** exposes search parameters as *accessor methods* to a set of attributes. The user interface must only map the appropriate attributes that, as accessor methods, have only *one* parameter to "set" and *one* return value to "get." The principle, after all, is the same as we explored for **Login App User** except that the **search** method relies on the *state* of **Patient Mgr** to select the messages that must be sent to the persistence object.

Figure 12.13
Mapping Attributes to the User Interface

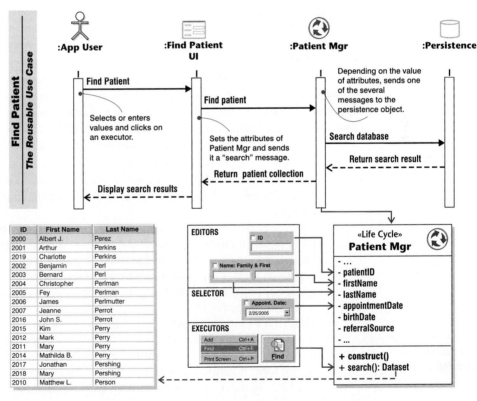

Attributes and operations are both implemented as methods and, as a result, are mapped the same way, except that each message to an accessor method carries a single value. (Accessor methods are how private attributes are exposed to the outside world.)

Constraints in UI Design

> Factors such as availability of visual controls, demands of workflow, and preferences of clients can have profound effects on the design of the user interface.

In every iteration of development, we have to ❶ revise certain aspects of the previous work and ❷ address the issues that are specific to the current activity. In the design of the user interface, there are constraints that apply only to the *user interface*:

- *Availability of Visual Controls.*   Unless you are developing visual controls, you may use only the visual tools that are available, regardless of whether the tools come with the development environment or you can buy them from third parties. A tree view is an excellent tool for packing a large amount of hierarchical choices but, both as a navigator and as a selector, menu precedes it. Therefore, at some point in time, you would not have been able to use a tree view even though you may have needed it badly.

The Web, as we mentioned, is a relatively control-poor environment, meaning that—compared to desktop operating systems—the *native* controls of HTML, the language of the Web, are very few: two types of text boxes, dropdowns, displayers for text and images, check boxes, tables, frames, buttons, and hypertext links. On the other hand, this scarcity of controls has not prevented Web developers from coming up with ingenious solutions. For example, the dropdown or popup menus that you can find on many Web pages are actually illusions: HTML lacks a menu control; the effect that you see as a menu is actually achieved by moving around text areas and changing the visibility of such areas in response to the location of the mouse.

- *Demands of the Workflow.*   It is usually possible to map the *same* set of messages to different UI styles and arrangements. For example, as we mentioned, if we analyze the use cases for Walden's **Patient Management** system, we will discover that many of them need to find a particular patient before they can take other steps. There are a few ways to satisfy this requirement; among them:

❶ Provide the appropriate form in each use case with its own search engine and display area. This approach is the least desirable since it leads to duplication of code and, most probably, to incompatible interfaces for the same function.

❷ "Refactor" the search part of each use case into one **Find Patient** use case that can be "included" in other use cases. It would display a dedicated form for patient search and return the selected patient to the calling form. This approach unifies the search function and its interface, but would be annoying for appointment, reception, or information clerks that must continuously search for patients.

☞ See Chapter 7 for a detailed discussion of *including* and *included* use cases.

❸ Make the **Find Patient** not an "included" use case but an "including" one. Provide a form that allows users to find a patient *and* access major use cases at the same time. The shortcomings of this solution are that the space on the form is limited, not all users would want (or are allowed) to see all available options, and, as the system expands, the form (and its supporting objects) must be constantly renovated.

❹ Combine options 2 and 3 so that the form (or the use case) can be both "including" *and* "included." To put it differently, the form must be polymorphous: It should work independently and, at the same time, be able to return the selected patient to the "including" object. (Though you will not be able to infer this from a picture, our example in Figure 12.2 follows this approach.)

No matter what solution you choose, there are simply no perfect solutions. It may seem that the fourth approach comes as close to perfection as possible, but such a conclusion is simply not true: Our example is more complex, suffers slightly from overcrowding, and is more difficult to maintain. Last, but not least, it would consume more development resources than the second approach and, as a result, would cost more. However, as far as we know, it satisfies the demands of the hospital workflow better than other solutions. Therefore, we have chosen it as the *compromise* solution for the specific *context* of the hospital. In a different context and with different resources, the designer must find a different solution.

• *Client's Preferences.* We previously mentioned aesthetics but, more often than not, the term is really a cover for "taste," specifically for the taste of whoever pays the development expenses. Work in the field and you will be surprised at how much energy and time your clients are ready to spend over points that might seem utterly trivial: the background color of a panel, the size of a text box, the fonts, etc. (For packaged software, focus groups and marketing departments play the same role.) Argue for your case as forcefully and as persuasively as you can, but remember: In the final analysis, the application belongs to whoever pays for it. As we stated in introducing this chapter, no matter how complex or intricate the inside of an information system is, for users the UI *is* the system.

To define the physical methods is to come very close to defining the user interface, but crossing the remaining gap is affected by many factors.

5. MODELING THE USER INTERFACE

> The user interface requires models that are intelligible to owners and users as well as to analysts, designers, and developers.

Throughout this book, we have emphasized the essential role of modeling in collaborative development. Designing a user interface is no exception. As classes and objects, the visual building blocks of the application are no different from entity or control classes and objects, and they can be modeled with the same UML tools: class, sequence, activity, statechart, and other diagrams. When it comes to features that are *specific* to the UI design, however, there is no general agreement as to how they should be modeled.

What are these UI-specific features? In general, they fall into two categories:

- **Layout:** how to present and organize visual controls on containers.
- **Navigation:** how to organize the sequence of containers that the user must traverse to accomplish a task.

None of the UI's distinctive features can be effectively modeled with a single tool or a single diagram. The primary reason is that whereas modeling entity or control classes must be meaningful to a limited set of people who are more or less specialists, the user interface concerns everybody with a stake in the application—the users of the information system as well as its builders.

UML diagrams are *engineering* diagrams and they can model, with engineering precision, the structure and the behavior of the system. Like other engineering blueprints, however, they cannot effectively communicate the "look and feel" of the final product.

Modeling the user interface involves both structure and motion. Therefore, it should come as no surprise that UI designers use the same techniques that are employed to develop the most typical product in each category: architecture and movies. In architecture, the designers resort to any available tool that can satisfy the expectations of their clients—from scaled-down physical models to sometimes fanciful drawings to computer **simulations.** To make movies, directors often resort to **storyboarding** to communicate their vision to producers, set designers, photographers, and actors.

In the course of this chapter and the last, we used both sequence and activity diagrams to arrive at the messages that the user interface must satisfy. Before discussing techniques that are specific to the user interface, we return to the class diagram.

Class Diagrams

> Class diagrams identify the units of the user interface and the services that the units must perform.

Among all UML diagrams, the class diagram is the most indispensable. We use sequence, statechart, and activity diagrams to discover and/or refine classes, but class diagrams are the definitive blueprints from which developers must build the final product. And, in case it might appear otherwise, behind the user interface are virtual objects that, in every aspect, are similar to entity and control objects.

A class diagram shows a set of classes and their associations. The associations can be presented from multiple viewpoints and every viewpoint can be used to model the user interface:

- *Relationship,* or the nature of the connection between classes. For example, the **Find Patients** form displays the **Patient Profile** form to display detailed information about a patient. (See Figure 12.14.) In fact, to a modest degree, class diagrams can be used to model navigation.
- *Multiplicity,* or how many instances of one class can associate with instances of another class. As Figure 12.14 shows, the **Find Patients** UI needs multiple instances of the **Dialog Box** class to display messages and exceptions. In addition, since **Find Patients** might display multiple patients, its relationship with forms such as **Patient Profile** and **Appointments** is one-to-many. (The "many," however, is not limitless: The resources of a workstation are limited and developers usually limit the number of forms that can be displayed at the same time.)
- *Aggregation* and *composition,* which represent the relationship of whole to its parts. Even the simplest form, such as a dialog box that displays error messages, is composed of multiple objects: a displayer, an icon perhaps, and a button to close the form.

**Figure 12.14
The UI Class
Diagram:
Modeling the
Structure of the
User Interface**

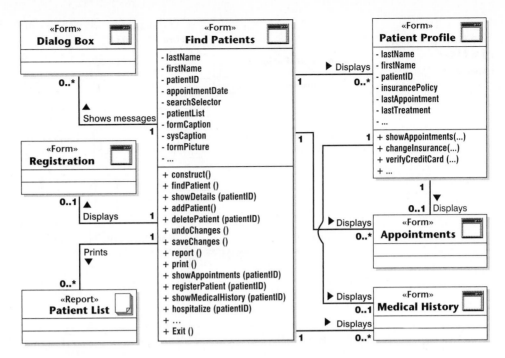

Although modeling association and multiplicity is the most common use of class diagram for UI, any type of class diagram can be helpful in designing the user interface.

- *Generalization,* or the abstraction of common elements shared by a set of classes into a superclass, and *specialization,* or the creation of a *subclass* from an existing class by defining elements that are too specific for the parent class. Modern development tools allow developers to *inherit* general-purpose components and specialize them, or create *templates* that can be reused to provide common functionality and harmonious appearance across the application.

The class diagram in Figure 12.15 displays an abbreviated view of **Find Patients UI** as a composite object. This diagram is *for illustration only:* Composition diagrams for the user interface are often unnecessary because, first, storyboarding and simulation (discussed later in this chapter) perform the same task more efficiently and, second, visual controls are normally used as ready-made components and developers do not create them for each UI unit. It helps, however, to emphasize the following points:

- Visual controls—textboxes, dropdowns, grids, and menus that you see on a form or a Web page—are *instances of classes* that, like all other classes, have attributes and operations. They send messages to other objects to request services and, in turn, respond to messages requesting *their* services. What distinguishes them from others is that some of their attributes are visual and some of the messages that they receive originate from *real* users. (We use the term "originate" because it is the operating system, not the visual control itself, that converts the analog signals of the keyboard and the mouse into digital messages.)

Figure 12.15
**The Composition
of a User
Interface**

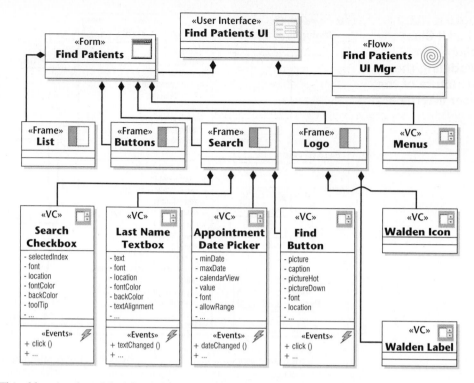

This abbreviated model of the **Find Patients** UI barely conveys the amount of detailed work that one unit of user interface requires. Fortunately, this diagram is for illustration only and you do not have to model the user interface this way since the UI is visible.

☞ See Chapter 9 for a discussion of *events.*

- Interruptive *events,* such as **click** for a button and **textChanged** for a text box, play a much larger part in visual controls than in entity classes. User actions through mouse, keyboard, or other input devices do not follow a well-ordered or predictable sequence; rather, as far as the application is concerned, they "happen." Furthermore, as independent components, visual controls have a limited awareness of the context in which they operate: When the user clicks a button, the button cannot judge the purpose of the user; it only broadcasts a **click** event that is interpreted and implemented by its container. While one instance of the **Button** class may result in a search, another instance of the same class may close the form, and the third may stop the assembly line of a factory.

☞ The **Find Patient UI Mgr** is mostly conceptual, not concrete: Often the containers such as forms play the part of the control object as well, even though they may delegate some of their functionality to other specialized objects.

- Creating a user interface that is aesthetically acceptable embodies the desired workflow, satisfies the required performance, and guards the application from the unforeseen behavior of the user and the user from the inevitable shortcomings of the application is a painstaking task. The "wiring" of the user interface must be done with an obsessive attention to detail.
- The user interface can be compared to an iceberg: What you see is only a small fraction of what is below. As the class **Find Patients UI Mgr** in Figure 12.15 indicates, user interface is only partly visual. The bulk of the work is done by UI-specific *control* objects that decide how the user interface must behave and *event-handlers* or methods that translate user input into appropriate actions.

Navigation

> Navigation specifies the sequence of user actions across multiple containers to achieve a goal.

Navigation has two related meanings: plotting a course and following the course; that is, navigation is both the theory of navigating and its practice which, in turn, expands the theoretical knowledge. In designing the user interface, the theory is represented by modeling and the practice by the user experience. (See the following "Storyboarding" and "Simulation & Prototyping" sections.)

☞ See Chapter 9 for a discussion of the *statechart* diagram.

As we illustrated, a class diagram can serve as a navigation model in a limited manner. A class diagram, however, is not dynamic and its purpose is to show the responsibilities of classes, their relationships, and their composition. A UML modeling tool that can be more successfully adapted to navigation is the *statechart* diagram.

We described the statechart diagram as a tool to model the major states of an object and the flow of events that change its "state" (or overall *condition*). In adapting this diagram for navigation, we keep the events but assign the rectangles to containers such as forms or Web pages. In other words, the events in such a **navigation diagram** identify what must happen for a form or a page to be displayed.

Figure 12.16 shows a statechart diagram that models the navigation for ordering books from Amazon.com, the well-known online merchant. The model is abbreviated and the company changes its navigation model over time. In general outlines, however, it illustrates how the Web site guides the customer through tasks that must be accomplished before a book order is actually placed and processed.

☞ Also notice that, unlike most client/server applications, the login does not occur at the start of the application, but only when the customer has to view, enter, or update confidential information over a secure connection. Otherwise, everybody is free to browse the site and remain anonymous. (This approach is often called "lazy login.")

The *events* in Figure 12.16 are similar to those in the example that was used to introduce the statechart diagram in Chapter 9: user selects a merchandise category, user searches for a book, user adds the book to the shopping cart, etc. The boxes, however, are labeled not as abstract states such as "billed," "paid," or "overdue" but with a short description of a *concrete* page (or form): **Search Results** *after* the user has instructed the application to conduct a search, **Shopping Cart** *after* the user has selected a book *and* wants to view and/or change the selections, **Place Order** *after* the user has confirmed and/or updated shipping and credit information, and so on.

The navigation diagram in Figure 12.16 also contains an element that our example in Chapter 9 did not need: the **synchronization bar.** We introduced the synchronization bar in the context of an activity diagram, when activities *fork* (travel in separate but parallel routes) or *merge* (join back into one stream). Here, the synchronization bar plays the same role: The user may choose to navigate the application through alternate routes, but the alternate routes can merge at some point.

☞ See Chapter 10 for a discussion of UML's *extension mechanisms.*

In the navigation diagram, you can use all the *extension mechanisms* of UML. For example, the option for proceeding to checkout should not be available unless the user has added at least one item to the shopping cart. The diagram expresses this condition with the UML notation for **constraints.**

Storyboarding

> Storyboarding is the use of a sequence of static pictures or drawings to narrate a story.

Figure 12.16   **Modeling the Navigation: Adapting the Statechart Diagram**

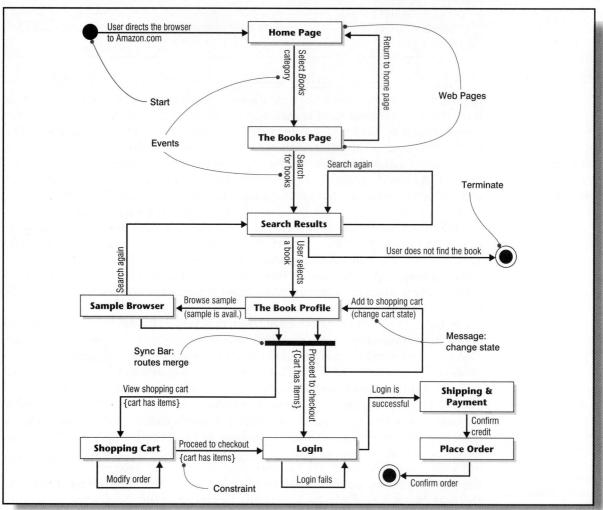

In such a navigation diagram, events lead to the display of UI units such as forms or Web pages.

Storyboarding evolved from *comic strips,* which in turn originated from the multi-frame cartoons of the 19th century mass-circulation newspapers and periodicals. The most famous pioneer of applying storyboarding to modeling is Walt Disney, who used it to produce his 1937 full-length animated feature film *Snow White and the Seven Dwarfs.* By taking advantage of this technique, Disney succeeded in employing multiple teams of animators to create an unprecedented 83 minutes of color animation for a single storyline. Since then, storyboarding has been a staple of movie-making and advertising.

Increasingly, the costs of producing software are rivaling those of big-budget movies, if not exceeding them. Storyboarding presents a low-cost technique for ensuring that the finished product meets user expectations.

The basics of storyboarding are straightforward: a set of frames, connected by navigation lines, tells a story or scenes from a story. The frames can be simple or elaborate, and the same frame can be used to narrate the same story from a different viewpoint or under different conditions.

In designing the user interface, the "story" is the application and the storyboards usually represent the narrative of use cases. Storyboarding, however, does not have to start with design. On the contrary, the storyboarding technique can be used *throughout* the development to communicate with the full spectrum of people who are involved in the process:

- *Conceptual* storyboards can be used to elicit response from domain experts, to gather requirements, and to verify the narrative of use cases. Such storyboards must not be so elaborate as to be mistaken for the ultimate user interface design, must avoid implementation and technological detail, and must contain only the highlights of the "story." Pencil and paper should prove sufficient for creating conceptual storyboards.
- The flow of the application and the contents of forms and Web pages can be presented by *logical* storyboards that are more elaborate than the conceptual ones but stop short of serving as engineering blueprints. These models should specify the relationship among user interface units and, optionally, *what* they contain but not *how* the content is presented.
- Modeling the layout of forms and pages in a format that comes as close to the finished product as possible, you may resort to *physical* storyboarding by rendering the exact location and the type of visual controls. Again, pencil and paper should suffice even for such exact storyboards, but modern development environments make the task of placing visual controls on the containers so easy that there are hardly any reasons *not* to use them.

☞ For the **Register Patient** use case, see Chapter 7.

Figure 12.17 illustrates the `Register Patient` use case as narrated by three bands of storyboards. The *Conceptual* band renders the flow of the use case in its most basic form. In the *Logical* band, we have identified the attributes and operations that are required for registration, but not *how* they are presented to the actor. The third band, *Physical*, maps the "story" of the use case to specific visual controls such as dropdowns, text boxes, and buttons. Two things about Figure 12.17 however, must be pointed out:

❶ The flow of the story in the *Physical* band is somehow different from the flow in the *Logical* band: The application does not force the user to perform tasks such as providing patient profile detail and insurance verification sequentially. Such a "course correction" is often necessary since the clearest narrative in the conceptual or logical sense is not always the best way to construct the physical user interface.

❷ The *Physical* band may appear as complete, but it is not: The frames, created by using a development environment, show the bare minimum of controls necessary, but do not include usability features such as **Cancel, Print,** or **Close** buttons. (The aesthetics leaves something to be desired, as well.) These omissions are intentional since the purpose of storyboarding is modeling the essentials in the clearest fashion possible.

How does storyboarding relate to UML? Storyboarding lacks formal notation; that is, no standards exist about what a frame in a storyboard must contain or how the frames must relate to each other. This absence of formal notation can lead to miscommunication and overwrought storyboards. On the other hand, storyboarding's flexibility and its ability to break down complex scenarios into simple frames makes it an appropriate tool for modeling the user interface.

The flexibility of storyboarding is such that it can adapt itself to many modeling notations, *including* UML. In fact, Figure 12.16 can be viewed as a logical storyboard that contains UML elements. In creating storyboards, you may use all the

Figure 12.17 Storyboarding: A Flexible Technique for Modeling

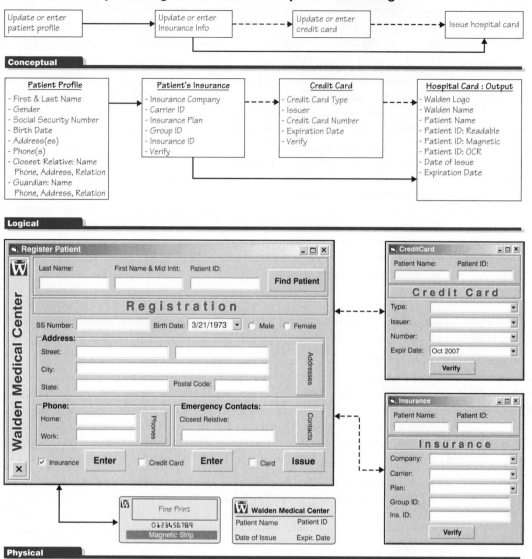

Storyboarding can be used throughout development, but it is especially useful for creating mock-ups of the user interface. Note that the even though the frames in the "Physical" band may appear as snapshots from a real application, they are merely mock-ups created by using a development environment.

extension mechanisms of UML, including stereotypes, ornaments, and constraints. You must not, however, forget the most important advantage of storyboarding: its simplicity.

Simulation & Prototyping

Prototyping is the creation of a working model for testing and verification of requirements.

Regardless of the methodology that we may use to develop a new product, the product itself always presents unexpected challenges. This observation holds true whether the product is a new car, a new medicine, or a new software application. The causes are many: faulty requirements or faulty requirements gathering, insufficient attention to the *context* in which the product must operate (i.e., inadequate domain analysis), poor design, and, last but not least, factors that no one foresaw or *could* foresee (meaning that sometimes nobody can be blamed).

Two closely related techniques are used to reduce the risk of unexpected factors:

- With **prototyping,** a model is created to test and verify the product before full-scale production starts.
- With **simulation,** a virtual or a real model of the product is subjected to an environment that tries to mimic the target context of the product.

In manufacturing, prototyping is a routine part of development and simulation is a close second. In software development, both methods have been used but success has not always been forthcoming. One reason is the crucial difference between the production of real products and virtual products such as software, movies, and music. The prototype of a car, for example, is expected to work fully in accordance with the requirements. But even if the prototype passes all tests and satisfies all requirements, the challenge of *reproduction* remains: how to retool the factory to mass produce the car, how to ensure a reliable supply of raw material and spare parts, how to keep manufacturing costs down, etc. On the other hand, a software application that satisfies all requirements is essentially the end of the (production) line because the reproduction costs are comparatively low.

The Definitions

What exactly is a software "prototype"? The answer, it seems, depends on whom you ask:

❶ A prototype is a *light version* of the application that implements only the most essential features of the final product. (This kind of prototype is also called a *"pilot."*) Once these essential features have been tested, verified, and corrected, the application can be completed with a high degree of certainty because only the "nonessentials" remain to be worked out and they cannot, logically, pose a great risk.

❷ A prototype presents a rather *complete user interface* which is then completed from outside in by adding whatever is necessary, including entity classes and persistence (or database). This approach is sometimes labeled—not very accurately—as RAD, or rapid application development.

❸ A prototype represents the *solid skeleton* of the application with a *minimal user interface.* This approach considers the user interface as rather incidental to the real functioning of the information system or the application.

❹ A prototype is a *throwaway construct* that serves as a *proof of concept.* Depending on the concept that needs proving, the prototype can offer an extensive user interface or not. In any case, the prototype is discarded once it accomplishes its purpose: whether an idea works and whether it conforms to client requirements and expectations.

⑤ Prototyping represents an *iterative process* in which not the whole application but *relatively independent units* of it are prototyped and tested. As new units, or subsystems, are developed, the old units are refurbished and retrofitted to fit within the evolving structure. Since each unit is iteratively tested and verified within the context of other units and the whole application, disruptive misunderstandings are avoided and the finished product would come as close to user expectations as possible.

Obviously, these interpretations of "prototyping" are largely incompatible even though they use the same term. Furthermore, we cannot reduce the risks of each approach and enhance their advantages by combining them: We either prototype the whole application or we don't, we either present a sophisticated user interface or we don't, we either construct a solid skeleton or we don't. Nevertheless, promises of prototyping as a magical solution are a recurring fact of the marketplace and are readily welcomed by clients who are desperate for a quick fix to their software development problems.

This is not to say that prototyping never works or can never work. Different situations require different approaches that may be incompatible with each other and may not work under different circumstances. Besides, as the proponents of one approach or another would not hesitate to remind us, in quite a number of cases prototypes have led to software products that work. The problem is the definition of the term "works." Cost-effectiveness—nowadays characterized by the more fashionable term of ROI, or "return on investment"—is one consideration, but there are others. An application may satisfy most immediate user requirements but fall short of one crucial goal: *changeability.*

Seldom can an application function for any considerable amount of time and not become a candidate for change. Change is necessitated by many factors, individually or in combination: incomplete or erroneous requirements, competition in the marketplace, the need to add new features, and so on. But the need to change is inevitable and when the need arrives, applications that are not constructed with foresight reveal their true costs. Frequently, such applications started life as prototypes of the user interface to which everything else was then appended—an approach that strongly resembles building a house by constructing the façade first and the foundation last.

Object-Oriented Prototyping

Is an *object-oriented approach* to prototyping possible? The answer, previously suggested by the definitions in 4 and 5, is affirmative but needs a reexamination of the concept. Indeed, we must return to the idea of prototyping in manufacturing and correct a misinterpretation: the illusion that the production of a car or an airplane, for example, *starts* with prototyping.

In manufacturing, the prototyping of a complex product takes place close to the middle of the production process: before reproduction but *after* development, that is, after conception of the idea, a feasibility study, requirements discovery, analysis, design, and, of course, modeling. A Boeing passenger plane or even a modest home entertainment system is *not* immediately prototyped once the idea is born, but goes through a development process that is very similar to what we have tried to explain in this book.

Far more crucial, however, is another aspect of manufacturing: *complexity* is harnessed by the use of *components.* A prototype is not a monolithic artifact, but a composite object whose components have been more or less independently

☞ For a more detailed discussion of components, see Chapter 15.

developed and tested, most likely through prototyping. In turn, each component itself may be composed of other components that are developed, prototyped, and tested separately. In short, manufacturing follows a *component-based* approach, a logical evolution of the object-oriented methodology.

Applying this methodology to software prototyping means the following:

- A prototype must be constructed from components. As a rule, arriving at the components *from* the prototype is the wrong approach. (The exception is when, despite our best efforts, we find missing components by testing the prototype.)
- Components must be envisioned and developed as independent units that can be tested *outside* the product, even though testing them *within* the product is indispensable and might discover shortcomings that result in modifications to the component.
- The issue of retaining versus discarding prototype code becomes irrelevant. Rather, it becomes a question of *reuse.* Prototypes of components consist of two entities: an object or a set of objects that will be reused in the final product or in a more complex component, and a *test harness* that is built around the component both as a "*proof of concept*" and as a test environment. Neither entity is necessarily a throwaway: the first for obvious reasons, the second because chances are high that it would be needed again to test changes or enhancements.
- Analysis and design do not follow the prototyping of the full product or its components, but precede it. (Note that all activities in an object-oriented methodology are *iterative* and, therefore, "precede" does not mean "finished"; rather, it means "as much as can be done at a certain time.")
- The question of prototyping the user interface versus prototyping the structure or some other aspect of the application becomes moot because our approach is *component-based* and a component can be anything as long as it keeps a clear identity and a distinct mission.
- If the client and/or the circumstances demand a general view *before* a considerable amount of time and money is spent, consider **simulation.** As we have stated before, simulation is a kind of modeling that is successfully used by the military for training soldiers and pilots, by NASA for space programs, by the manufacturers of many commercial products, and by building architects. Considering that most simulation tools are software, it is strange that it is so underutilized in software development.

The previous guidelines are backed by centuries of industrial development. In the field, however, you will find a very strong resistance to adopting them. This resistance comes not only from the clients but from the developers as well. In this regard, manufacturing has a clear edge over software development: Both its market and its practitioners accept the logic of experience.

6. DELIVERABLES

In theory, the design of the user interface can start only when we have a good grasp of the requirements and the application flow. In practice, however, this is not usually the case. As we said, for most users, the user interface and the information system are one and the same. Until you show them "something," they would not believe that anything has been done.

What is more, most of us—and this includes analysts and developers, as well as users—cannot fully connect with abstract models and need something concrete to awaken our critical faculties. As a result, only when some kind of user interface is offered do we discover serious omissions or misunderstandings in the specifications of requirements. In other words, what is intuitive and what is correct sometimes work against each other: A *finished* product may become a tool to elicit requirements about what it should be!

The best tool for escaping this paradox is **storyboarding:** It is cheap and it is effective. As we mentioned, you can use storyboarding in *any* development activity, from analysis to concrete modeling, both logical and physical. You will find that a few simple storyboards can perform miracles, from gathering requirements to formulating the workflow.

If the user interface flow is complex or confusing, then you can use **navigation diagrams.** As implementation blueprints, *class diagrams* are the most exact tools but, generally, you do not need to go deeper than the `<<Form>>` stereotype to create aggregation and composition diagrams identifying every visual component on forms or on Web pages. (Our example in this chapter was for illustration only.) Finally, if certain segments of the flow must be further clarified, *activity* or *sequence* diagrams are at your disposal.

7. WRAP UP

☑ **The user interface layer & its responsibilities**

The user interface is where the interaction between the application and its human users takes place. It is the *boundary* between the problem domain and the solution domain. The user interface is an interface like any other, but with two distinct responsibilities:

- The user interface is responsible for translating real-world messages into virtual ones and virtual messages into real ones.
- The user interface must guide the users through the steps necessary to accomplish meaningful tasks.

The user interface is a layer of "boundary" objects that manage interaction with the user. The efficiency and the usability of the user interface, however, are decided not only by the suitability of its individual components, but by the flow of the whole. Furthermore, any task that is not related to the interaction between the application and the user—business logic, database access, security, and so on—must be kept out of this layer.

UI objects that are visible to users are called **visual controls.** Not all objects that participate in the user interface are visual.

☑ **The language of graphical user interface (GUI)**

Any kind of communication, including that between the user and the application, is based on a language and language consists of *symbols* and *syntax,* or the rules for organizing symbols. The sender and the receiver of a message must agree on both the meaning of symbols and how they are organized.

The language of the user interface is predominately visual and **metaphors** constitute the majority of the symbols in its vocabulary. A metaphor is simply a symbol or an expression that represents something beyond its literal or immediate meaning.

☑ **Visual metaphors & their roles in the design of user interface**

Software applications belong to a *virtual world* but they must rely on *real-world* **metaphors** to communicate with real-world users. The metaphors of the graphical user interface constitute an ever-growing set: buttons, menus, text boxes, scrollbars, dropdowns, sliders, gauges, icons, tree views, etc. Some metaphors are easy to understand while some need textual explanations.

Each metaphor in the vocabulary of the user interface can signify multiple roles. The most common roles are:

- **Containers,** such as forms, Web pages, and frames, organize and present visual controls. They constitute the major *units* of visual interface.
- **Displayers,** such as labels, graphs, or pictures, provide textual or pictorial information. The behavior of displayers can be dynamic or non-dynamic.
- **Editors,** such as text boxes, accept textual or graphical input from the user. Whether textual or graphical, the behavior of an editor is decided by the context.
- **Selectors,** such as dropdowns, option buttons, check boxes, and tree views, allow the user to choose between two or more options or values.
- **Executors** allow the user to request the execution of specific commands from the application. Buttons and menus are the most familiar examples of this category.
- **Navigators** allow the user to move among containers. Buttons, menu items, tree views, and hyperlinks are widely used as navigators.
- **Object signifiers** represent objects, their properties, and/or their methods. Icons are well-known as object signifiers, but not all icons are object signifiers, nor are all object signifiers icons. Each object signifier has a default action, and can perform a set of operations that are presented as a "context menu."
- **Manipulators** allow the user to control the appearance of the visual interface. The primary controls that perform the manipulator role are the forms or Web pages. After the forms, however, scrollbars are the most widely used manipulators.
- **Pointers,** such as cursors, are moving or movable symbols that indicate the position and the type of user actions.
- **Decorators,** such as lines, colors, fonts, and pictures, do not contribute directly to the functionality of the user interface, but enhance its appearance, clarity, and aesthetic value.
- **Multifunctional controls,** such as grids or menus, can play multiple roles in the same instance.
- **Vocals** are sounds or speech that reinforce the visual interface.
- **Input/output devices** are hardware that allow real-world users to interact with the virtual world of the information system. Application designers do not design the I/O devices, but they do design *for* them.

☑ **The significance of patterns, consistency & aesthetics in UI design**

The design of the user interface often consists of solving similar problems. A **pattern** is the *core* of the solution to a problem that occurs repeatedly in an environment. Unlike rules, patterns must be adapted to the problem at hand and cannot be followed uncritically.

The user interface is composed of visual controls that are metaphors. Therefore, the UI designer must rely on what the user already knows or is reasonably expected to know. **Consistency** in the user interface is achieved when the user can predict what kinds of actions produce what kinds of results. Consistency and predictability of expectations are essential both to the vocabulary and the syntax of the user interface. Users cannot learn everything from scratch every time they work with a new application.

The *aesthetics* of the user interface must be *functional*. The issues faced by user interface designers are more similar to those that industrial and graphic designers must solve than to challenges that artists and fashion designers must confront. In industrial design, function comes first, beauty second.

☑ **Mapping messages, parameters & attributes to the user interface**

The user interface is the concrete realization of messages passed between the actors and the system. UI design must map messages, their parameters, and their return values into UI metaphors. Therefore, the discovery and the modeling of the application *flow,* discussed in the previous chapter, is essential to the correct design of the user interface. We should be aware, however, that the *same* flow and the *same* set of messages can translate into *different* user interfaces, depending on the designer or client preferences, the platform, the development tools, and so on.

☑ **Modeling for UI: navigation diagram, storyboarding, simulation & prototyping**

The user interface requires models that are intelligible to owners and users as well as to analysts, designers, and developers. As classes and objects, the visual building blocks of the application are no different from entity or control classes and objects, and they can be modeled with the same UML tools: class, sequence, activity, statechart, and other diagrams. Features that are specific to UI design are *layout* and **navigation**.

None of the UI's distinctive features can be effectively modeled with a single tool or a single diagram.

Navigation specifies the sequence of user actions across multiple containers to achieve a goal. A **navigation diagram** is an adaptation of a statechart diagram that shows what forms or Web pages are displayed in response to application events. We may use all the extension mechanisms of UML to make this diagram more suitable for presenting the flow of the user interface.

Storyboarding is the use of a sequence of static pictures or drawings to narrate a story. The basics of storyboarding are straightforward: A set of frames, connected by navigation lines, tells a story or scenes from a story. The frames can be simple or elaborate, and the same frame can be used to narrate the same story from a different viewpoint or under different conditions. Storyboarding is a cost-effective and flexible modeling technique that can be used not only in design, but throughout the development process.

Prototyping is the creation of a working model for testing and verification of requirements. There are conflicting definitions of prototyping and conflicting opinions on how useful it is. In an object-oriented and component-based approach, prototyping represents an iterative process in which not the whole application but relatively independent units of it are prototyped and tested. As new units, or subsystems, are developed, the old units are refurbished and retrofitted to fit within the evolving structure.

8. KEY CONCEPTS

Consistency. In UI design, consistency is achieved when the user can predict what kinds of actions produce what kinds of results.

Containers. Organize and present visual controls. Containers, such as forms and Web pages, are the major units of visual interface. They are usually constructed with a *specific* purpose.

Context Menus. Menus that offer options based on a *specific* context. Also called "*popup*" menus, they are usually associated with **object signifiers** where they identify actions that are allowed for a particular object.

Decorators. Pictures, shapes, and lines that enhance the appearance and the aesthetics of the user interface.

Displayers. Visual controls such as pictures, labels, or gauges that provide textual or pictorial information. The behavior of displayers can be dynamic or non-dynamic.

Editors. Visual controls that accept textual or graphical input from the user.

Executors. Allow the user to request the execution of specific commands from the application.

Input/Output Devices. Hardware such as a mouse, keyboard, and card reader that allow real-world users to interact with the virtual world of the information system.

Manipulators. Controls that allow the user to control the appearance of the user interface.

Metaphor. A symbol or an expression that represents something beyond its literal or immediate meaning. The vocabulary of the user interface is dominated by metaphors such as buttons, menus, and scrollbars.

Each metaphor in the user interface can signify multiple *roles*. For example, the *button* metaphor can execute commands or navigate the user across **containers.**

Multifunctional Controls. Visual controls, such as grids or menus, that can play multiple roles at the same time.

Navigation. The course and the sequence of user actions across multiple containers, such as forms and Web pages, to perform a task.

Navigation Diagram. An adaptation of a *statechart diagram* to model the **navigation** of the user interface.

Navigators. Visual controls that allow the user to move across units of application such as forms, tabs, or Web pages.

Object Signifiers. Represent virtual objects, their properties, and/or their methods. Icons are the best-known metaphors for object signifiers, but almost any visual control can represent objects.

Pattern. The core of the solution to a problem that occurs repeatedly in an environment. In the design of user interface, patterns provide the richest source for obtaining guidelines.

Pointers. Movable or moving symbols that indicate the position and the type of user actions. A *cursor* is a (usually blinking) pointer that identifies the location where a character typed from the keyboard will be inserted.

Prototyping. The creation of a working model for testing and verification of requirements. Object-oriented methodology favors a component-based approach to prototyping. As a concept, prototyping is closely related to **simulation.**

Selectors. Visual controls that allow the user to choose between two or more options or values. While **editors** are often free-format, selectors usually accept user input as a selection of predefined values.

Simulation. Placing a virtual or real model of the product in an environment that mimics the target context as closely as possible.

Storyboarding. The use of a sequence of static pictures or drawings that narrate a story. In designing the user interface, the narrative usually describes a use case or a set of use cases.

Synchronization Bar. A bar used in activity and navigation diagrams to show forking and merging of activities or events.

User Interface. The point of interaction between the problem domain and the solution domain, between the virtual world of the software and the real world of the user. The user interface is the concrete realization of messages passed between actors and the system.

Visual Control. An object within the UI layer that is visible to the user.

Vocals. Sounds or speech that reinforce the visual interface. In some cases, such as automated telephone systems, speech is the primary UI element.

9. REVIEW QUESTIONS

1. Explain why the "user interface is primarily an interpreter." Can you provide examples?
2. What is the role of navigation in user interface?
3. What are the characteristics and advantages of the graphical user interface (GUI)?
4. Explain the role of polymorphism in the user interface.
5. In interface design, what role do patterns play (or what role should they play)? Provide an example for patterns when you use an ATM to withdraw cash.
6. What is consistency in user interface design? What problems might lack of consistency cause?
7. Comment on the statement that the "essential purpose of the user interface is to enable the user and the system to exchange messages." Provide two examples.
8. What are some constraints in user interface design?
9. Relate multiplicity, aggregation, and generalization to designing user interface classes. Provide examples.
10. Draw a storyboard for registering students online.

10. EXERCISES

The following exercises apply to each of the four narratives introduced in Chapter 4: *The* Sportz *Magazine, The Car Dealership, The Pizza Shop,* and *The Real Estate Agency.*

❶ Create **storyboards** for the major use cases in the above scenarios.

❷ Create *activity diagrams* for the storyboards above.

❸ Create a **navigation diagram** for the billing use case in the *Car Dealership* scenario.

❹ Select one of the storyboards you have created and turn it into a *sequence diagram.*

❺ Create a structural diagram for the user interface of one of the storyboards. (Usually, as we said, you do not have to do this in the real world—unless you are designing a "visual control." It is a good exercise, however, and—who knows?—your assignment might actually involve designing visual elements.)

11. RESEARCH PROJECTS & TEAMWORK

❶ Choose a **user interface** with which the team is familiar—Amazon, for example, or Microsoft Word. Individually, identify features that you consider "friendly" or "unfriendly." In a team session, discuss your findings and document various "pro" and "con" views.

❷ Refer to the online registration system for Walden Medical College (Chapter 4). Have each team member identify *UI boundary objects* for the selected use cases. Consolidate the team's work and create a UI class diagram for the system.

❸ Do the same as above for the online shopping system (Chapter 4). Ask the team members to "discover" design objects for a set of use cases. Consolidate the team's work and create a *statechart diagram* that shows the states of an `Order` object.

❹ Select a "busy" use case from one of the scenarios above. Have each team member create a **storyboard** for it: logical or physical. Compare them in a team session and give them to the instructor.

❺ We said that the "visual controls" (visible elements) in the user interface are **metaphors.** Agree on a Web site or an application and *individually* categorize the metaphors used. Compare your conclusions in a team session.

12. SUGGESTED READINGS

Most "how-to" and technology-specific books devote varying amounts of space to the user interface, but the literature on UI *concepts* is sparse. One popular book is *About Face 2.0: The Essentials of User Interface Design* by **Alan Cooper** and Robert M. Reimann (Wiley, 2003). The book leans towards the Windows operating system to present and illustrate its arguments, but referring to specific technologies is inescapable in any design book and in no way compromises its value.

A very short and readable book is *User Interface Design for Programmers* by **Joel Spolsky** (APress, 2001). Do not allow the title to mislead you: The book is *not* about programming, but about design. The author is forthright in expressing his viewpoints, which makes the book all the more enjoyable.

Studying design failures is always a prerequisite for good design. *GUI Bloopers: Don'ts and Do's for Software Developers and Web Designers* by **Jeff Johnson** (Morgan Kaufmann Publishers, 2000) explores the *worst* practices of UI design in commercial software and on Web sites. It is both instructive and entertaining.

Chapter 13

Application Design III
Database & Persistence

1. OVERVIEW

The database is a major component of the information system. This chapter examines the concepts of data management and database management systems, database design, and the mapping of objects to the database. It concludes by discussing the persistence layer, a set of design objects that are responsible for communication between the application and the database.

- ☑ Inception
- ☑ Requirements Discovery
- ☐ Development
    - ☑ Analysis
    - ☐ Design
        - ☑ The Design Challenge
        - ☐ **Application Design**
            - ☑ Control & Flow
            - ☑ The User Interface
            - ☐ **Persistence & Database** ⬅
        - ☐ Patterns
        - ☐ Components & Reuse
        - ☐ Architecture
    - ☐ Implementation

Chapter Topics

➤ Data and data management.

➤ Database management systems.

➤ The relational model and its major components.

➤ Database mechanisms that safeguard data integrity.

➤ SQL, the database management language.

➤ Encapsulating data management: views, stored procedures and triggers.

➤ The concept and the rules of data normalization.

➤ Intersection tables and the issues they address.

➤ Lookup tables.

➤ The entity-relationship diagram (ERD).

➤ Mapping to relational databases.

➤ Persistence layer and serialization.

Introduction

The most visible, prominent, and recognizable face of an information system is the user interface of its applications. The primary reason for having an information system, however, is to process data into information, and data must be stored, organized, protected, maintained, and retrieved. Applications are the providers and the consumers of data, but not its guardians. This task falls on the database management system, a distinct domain with its own specific concepts, requirements, and rules, which are different from applications.

On the other hand, it is the applications that must provide data and, ultimately, put it to use. As a result, applications must manage a second *boundary*, this time not between the outside world and the information system, but between two components of the system itself: the *object space*, where things are done, and the *data space*, the inventory or the storehouse of the system.

The design of the user interface and the application flow can be narrowly focused and selective. The design of the database, however, must satisfy the requirements of the *entire* information system and, possibly, even its future requirements. In addition, database design requires an expertise that is very different from application design. As a result, we must first arrive at an understanding of some abstract concepts about data and data management before we can

Figure 13.1
Data Management: The Joint Responsibility of Applications and the Database Management System

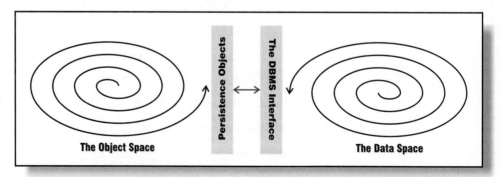

Persistence objects are specialized for communicating with the database, the same way that user-interface objects communicate with the users.

design object-oriented applications that will work well with the database and databases that will provide efficient service to applications.

2. DATA & DATA MANAGEMENT

The tools for building a modern information system, including database management and object-oriented languages, originate from *theoretical models*. Doubtless, the tools have benefited greatly from incremental development and fine tuning, but they were brought about by the implementation of innovative concepts. Therefore, understanding these concepts is crucial to using the tools: We must understand the concept of objects before using an object-oriented technology, and we must comprehend the meaning of data and data management before we can design a database.

Data management, in general, has moved more slowly than other fields of computerized information systems. The reasons are not difficult to understand: It is far less disruptive to adopt a faster CPU or even a new programming language than to adopt a data-management system. The other side of the coin is that when data management systems do change, the necessary adjustments in concepts are often more revolutionary than incremental. How you view data is not merely a theoretical question but deeply affects how you manage it practically.

Data

> Data are values of variables. In an object-oriented approach, variables belong either to objects or to the messages that the objects exchange with each other and with the outside world.

Interpretations of what we nowadays call "data" have always had a *practical* side. This is to be expected since we aim to *use* data to arrive at information, conclusions, meaning, and, hopefully, knowledge. Within this practical constraint, however, the room for producing variations on the same theme is vast. The original meaning of data is "something given," as in the numbers *given* to school children for an arithmetic exercise, but it has adopted an overabundance of definitions: facts, assumptions, representations of facts and concepts, binary representations of the same, evidence of any kind, and so on.

These definitions are general, but none are comprehensive, or could be so, because we see data from a *biased* viewpoint: how we want to use it and how we can capture, store, communicate, or process it. In other words, we tend to formulate a definition that fits both our purpose and our methodology.

Attributes of Data

> Data are highly abstract values, but they can be classified in relation to each other and to their contexts.

☞ "Quantifiable" data are not limited to numbers in natural language. Computers treat many kinds of symbols, including the characters, as quantities. As a result, "ford" and "fort" are considered different *quantities*.

Data does not exist in a vacuum. It exists in relation to other data and to its context (see the following section). These relationships provide data with attributes that affect how we manage them:

- Data can be **quantitative**, such as a number, or **qualitative**, such as an adjective. *Automated* information systems, however, can only process data that is quantified. For example, a questionnaire might ask respondents to evaluate their job satisfaction by checking a box labeled *Poor*, *Fair*, *Good*, or *Excellent*—all qualitative adjectives—but the program that inputs the responses into the information system must give each one a quantitative weight such as 1, 2, 3, etc. The digitized version of a work by Michelangelo can be stored in a database, but it must be given quantitative attributes such as the artist's name and the work's title, or else it can never be retrieved.

☞ "Continuous" does not mean "infinite." Continuous data, such as temperature, usually has a knowable *range*.

- Data can be **discrete** or **continuous**. Discrete data form a *finite* set of values that are distinct from each other: number of pages in a book or number of soldiers within a platoon. Continuous data, on the other hand, are not distinguished from each other by a distinct marker but change into each other gradually: the rise and the fall of temperature during the day or the weight of a child as he or she grows into adulthood.

  Digital information systems cannot handle continuous or **analog** data, but must rely on **sampling**—the selection of values that we decide are relevant within an arbitrary unit of time or space. For example, digital music—CD, MP3, etc.—is not a continuous replay of the original music (like analog vinyl records), but a reproduction of discrete zeros and ones that are sampled from the recording session. (The higher the rate of sampling, the higher the fidelity of the music.)

☞ In general, it is also wise *not* to build meaning into identifiers because it usually backfires as the context changes. Some years ago, the United States had to abandon an area code numbering scheme (for the phone system) in which the middle digit of an area code was always a 1 or a 0. With the rush of demand for cell phones, however, the scheme ran out of numbers. As a result, phone exchanges across the country had to be reprogrammed.

One root of such practices goes back to the time when computer networks did not exist or were not as pervasive as today and, therefore, cross-indexing data was time-consuming and difficult. As a result, people tried to make an identifier do double or triple duty as a provider of data. (The other root is laziness, pure and simple.)

- Data can be **categorical** or **non-categorical**. Non-categorical data, such as the examples in the previous item, represent quantities that are not made meaningful by other quantities. Categorical data, on the other hand, have significance only within the context of a *set*: 10 degrees Fahrenheit is a quantitative item of data, while "cold" (or a number representing coldness) makes sense only if some other data represents "hot," "freezing," or "warm."

  Categorical data can be **ordinal** or **nominal**. Ordinal data belong to an ordered *set*: school grades or the Richter scale for measuring earthquakes. Nominal data, by contrast, do not follow an obvious order: male/female, eye color, or nationality.

  Identifiers form the most widely used group of categorical data. The only function of an identifier, such as a Social Security Number, is to be *unique* within a set. Sometimes an element within an identifier has a built-in meaning, like the area code in telephone numbers. Usually, however, identifiers are strictly serial: a number is used in sequence as the previous number is assigned to an entity.

- Data can be **structured** or **unstructured**. By completing a tax form or a job application, you are *structuring* the data about yourself. A tax auditor (or an application that processes tax forms) knows exactly where to look to find the value of a certain attribute such as "gross income" or "charitable donations." A newspaper article or an essay has no such structure and, mere decades ago, would have been judged to be outside the realm of automated information systems. However, as any student today knows (and undoubtedly approves of), this is no longer the case: Web and desktop search engines are in a heated competition to mine an ever-increasing mass of unstructured data.

The Context of Data

> Data is meaningful only within the context of a variable, and a variable is meaningful only within the context of an object.

Data, by itself, has no significance. A data item finds significance when it is associated with a **variable**, so called because it varies depending on its data: 18 is a data item that has no meaning unless it is associated with `Age`, a variable that can have other values, or with the number of `Credits` for which a student registers.

Variables and, as a result, data, can be *independent* or *dependent*. The **Birth Date** of a person is independent of any other attribute but the value of his or her **Age** is decided by both the **Birth Date** and the **Current Date**. Dependent attributes are also called **derived** attributes.

☞ See Chapter 1 for a discussion of information, information systems, and their building blocks.

Previously, we described data as the building blocks of information. The object-oriented approach treats the information *system* as an organized interaction among objects. From such a viewpoint, variables are not free-floating entities, but containers that represent object **attributes** or pass values between objects as *parameters* inside *messages*. (As we shall see later, adopting this approach has a deep impact on data modeling and database design.)

Messages passed between *virtual* objects are digital and transitory: They disappear after they have completed their tasks. Messages passed between real objects, however, are objects themselves that the information system and, consequently, its data management system must track: payments, orders, treatments, etc. This, in turn, divides *entity objects* into two relative categories: *independent* and **transactional**.

Independent entity objects stand on their own: doctors, patients, managers, employees, etc., all have independent identities regardless of how they relate or interact with other entities. A check, however, needs a payer, a payee, and a bank, and a treatment needs both a doctor and a patient. In other words, a transactional object exists only because two or more independent objects have conducted a transaction. In *relational* data modeling, which we will explore later in this chapter, attributes of transactional objects point towards independent objects and define the *relationships* between these objects.

Data Management

☞ A *communication* system that carries data without regard for its persistence must not be mistaken for an *information* system, even though no information system can function without a communication system.

> Data management is storing and organizing data in a manner that can satisfy the needs of the information system and its applications.

Data management is the bedrock of most information systems. No civilization has been able to function without efficient record keeping. Tax, tribute, and accounting records are the oldest and the best-known examples, but any organized society or economy needs and demands a much vaster variety of records, from birth certificates to school transcripts, from marriage certificates to land deeds, from death certificates to court rulings, and so on.

Together with information systems, data management has gone through several radical changes through millennia of human history. The mission of data management, however, has remained essentially the same: Keep data safe but findable. Expectations, of course, have been transformed by technology. Where once only a royal court could keep an archive of clay tablets and an adequate bureaucracy to manage it, today anyone with a computer and an Internet connection is annoyed if the expected data is not readily available online. The data that we *cannot* find on-demand is fast becoming an exception.

Data management forms a *distinct* system within an information system. By system (or subsystem), we mean an organized collection of elements that work together to perform a task. By "distinct" we mean that although data management is an integral part of the information system, it has elements, organization, problems, and requirements that are different from other building blocks of the system such as communication, user interface, and processing. To understand data management, we must understand its own specific issues and components.

The Database

> A database is an organized collection of data.

Data are always abstract and virtual, regardless of whether it is recorded as Chinese characters, Arabic numerals, the Roman alphabet, or binary digits. To be stored, however, data must be stored on a physical device: stone, clay, papyrus, paper, magnetically charged particles on a disc, or optically readable "pits" on a CD or DVD.

A stored collection of data is called a database, although the term has many synonyms, near-synonyms, and related terms: data bank, archive, data store, library, etc. (The term "database" was only coined around 1946.) Because a database straddles both the virtual and the real worlds, its exact definition fluctuates between logical and physical. A collection of data that is *physically* cohesive is called a database, even though the relations between actual data may be weak or mostly arbitrary. More and more, however, a database is defined as a *logically* related collection of data. If such a collection resides on separate physical devices, it is called a **distributed** database. If, however, several collections share one physical space, the collection of databases is often termed a **server**.

The storage of data is never an end unto itself. A data management system must be able to carry out the following operations:

❶ *Create:*   accept *new* data and create entries in the database.
❷ *Retrieve:*   *find* and *read* the data that the information system and its users require.
❸ *Update:*   allow existing data to be *changed*.
❹ *Delete:*   permit unneeded data to be *removed*.

☞ These four operations are often referred to as **CRUD**: **C**reate, **R**etrieve, **U**pdate, and **D**elete.

Therefore, a database must be organized in a way that serves these purposes as best as possible. In designing the data management component of an information system, the *organization* of the database is the *most critical task* because it affects not a single application but the whole system, and it has consequences that extend far beyond the present into the future.

It is considerably easier and less costly to reengineer or replace an existing application than to redesign an existing database. A database is the most hard-to-replace *asset* of an information system, and an enterprise cannot afford to reorganize or discard such an asset with every turn and half-turn of technology. (Can a bank wipe out records of all customer accounts and start anew? Can a modern bank suspend all ATM and online activities to reorganize its database, even for a short while?)

How a data management system accomplishes the four tasks described depends, first and foremost, on technology. We must remember that data management belongs to the *solution space* in which the characteristics of the product, or solution, are defined by the technology that is either available or can be built on the foundations of what is available. On the other hand, we should also remember that *how* we use the available technology is not a foregone conclusion and the ingenuity of designers can provide solutions to problems that at first glance seem intractable.

Paper is the longest-running database technology in history. Yet the transition from inefficient scrolls to the codex, or book, format took a long time, even though the basic technology is the same. The use of hanging folders and various schemes and techniques for indexing paper is even more recent.

In this book and in most other current textbooks and technical literature, the term "database" refers mainly to digital collections of **structured** data. Theories, techniques, products, and applications for managing such databases are now quite mature and the designer can draw on numerous *patterns* and precedents to develop efficient and elegant solutions.

As seems to be inevitable, any technology that reaches maturity is suddenly confronted by challenges for which it has no ready-made answers. As a result of the rapid, worldwide adoption of the Internet and high-speed connections, the very concept of database is experiencing a radical transformation. The database technology must now cope with challenges presented by the Web: unstructured, qualitative, and streaming data.

Data management technology and methodologies *will* meet these challenges, but the answer to "exactly how?" is yet to be settled. Some solid design patterns must emerge before data management for the unruly cyberspace can be taught in a systematic way. New solutions, however, do not mean that the management of structured data will become obsolete. On the contrary, structured databases will remain pivotal to all human enterprises.

Interface & Language

> A database has an interface that is distinct from other components of the information systems. A specialized language is required to access this interface.

It is worth repeating that *interface* and *encapsulation* are the most important object-oriented concepts. Interface exposes the services of an object and encapsulation hides how these services are performed. It does not matter whether the object is small or big, or whether it is simple, composite, or complex. Similarly, it does not matter whether the services are actually done by the object itself, or whether each of them is delegated, behind the interface, to other objects.

In most information systems, ancient as well as modern, data management constitutes a distinct, large, and complex component. This component is, or must be, independent from any application that may use its services. Applications can request services from the interface of the data management subsystem, but they play no part in how these services are carried out. Furthermore, they must use a specialized *language* to communicate with the subsystem.

In the previous chapter we explained that the user interface must interpret messages passed between the problem domain and the solution domain. Often the same need for interpretation arises when two sub-domains must communicate. In a real-world business, the purchasing department must fill out forms in the "language" of the accounting department so that the latter may authorize the requested expenditure. In the communication between an application and the data management component of an information system, three set of entities must cooperate:

☞ See the sequence diagrams in Chapters 11 and 12.

❶ The **persistence layer** of the application. In previous diagrams for design, we often used a "placeholder" object (labeled **:persistence**) to represent the persistence layer. This layer, however, is a collection of *boundary* objects, instances of classes that mediate between an application or the entire information system and the outside entities. (A user interface is the most distinct and easy-to-recognize "boundary.") The number, the services, and the exact design of persistence classes depends on the requirements of the application system and the technology that it employs, but persistence objects have one clear function: They must translate application requests for data operations into a language that is understandable to the data management system.

❷ **Drivers** that carry messages and data between the application and the database. These drivers are managed by the operating system, not by specific applications or information systems. The level of the intervention by the drivers in the exchange of messages between the application and the database management systems varies with technology. In some cases, the persistence layer composes messages in a language that is understood by the driver, but not by the data management system. The driver then translates the message into a dialect that makes sense to the specific database manager. In other cases, the intervention is minimal and the driver functions as a simple carrier.

❸ The **database management system** that is responsible for storing data, maintaining it, and carrying out the requests of the application. (See this topic later in the chapter.)

System design involves both ends of the communication: the persistence layer *and* the database services. The distinction between the two, however, must be remembered at all times:

> **The persistence layer is *not* the same as the database component and the former must use a language that the latter understands.**

We will talk more about the interfaces and the languages of data management later in this chapter.

Integrity & Security

> A data management system must guard data against unintentional errors and intentional sabotage or theft.

Data is an *asset*, sometimes a priceless one, and must therefore be guarded. Anybody who has fallen victim to identity theft (and the number of such victims is increasing rapidly) knows how precious data can be. Theft and sabotage, however, provide only one set of threats to data. Defective design and human error can cause as much havoc as breaches of security. Computers do break down (physically) and crash (virtually) but, more often than not, when you are told that your vanished airline reservation or your $10,000 phone bill were caused by "computer errors," you should suspect bad database design or a design that allows human errors to go unnoticed.

Security is a highly specialized and technology-dependent field. Data integrity, on the other hand, is the domain of design, of both the user interface *and* the database. We can achieve a high level of data integrity by following design guidelines, by learning from established patterns, and by avoiding cutting corners.

The Database Management System (DBMS)

> Database management systems are products that encapsulate and carry out the responsibilities of data management.

The services of a data management system are too sensitive, too complex, and too specialized to be reinvented with each application or with each single information system. The resources needed to develop a full-scale, robust, and flexible data management system exceed what a single project or most enterprises can afford. Furthermore, a data management system must provide rock-solid reliability and, like operating systems, such trustworthiness requires multiple cycles of development and the corrective input of millions of users. At the same time, the services that a data management system must provide form patterns that are common enough to be packaged into a commercial product.

The emergence of DBMSs as commercial products came about very gradually. The first electronic computers, those based on vacuum tubes, had no persistence storage. Later, computers were outfitted with electronic punched card readers, providing them with paper-based data storage. Early magnetic storage was simply a reflection of punched card "records" in a different medium.

The introduction of the file system, made possible by innovations in hardware and software—random-access magnetic disc and the operating system as an entity independent of applications—provided an incremental change that, in the long run, made database management systems possible, though not immediately.

☞ Information *automation* did not start with electronic computers, and the history of punched cards starts in the 19th century. See Chapter 1.

Sequential Access

> Sequential access is a method in which data is grouped in records that are stored and retrieved serially from beginning to end.

Prior to DBMSs, data was the *private* property of an application. By "private" we mean exactly that: The meaning of a data item, and the relationship between data, was hidden from any entity other than the application that produced the data or consumed it. Furthermore, the only available data management tool consisted of organizing data into files of sequential records, regardless of whether the physical storage was punched cards, reel-to-reel tapes, or magnetic discs.

A "record" is a data structure in which one data element starts from a fixed position and occupies a fixed length that can accommodate the largest possible value belonging to the same "field." For example, a person's last name in an employee records collection, or "file," can start from position 31 and continue through position 55. If a last name is less than 25 characters in length, then the remaining spaces are left blank.

To find a data item that happened to be on the 1000th record, the application had to process the preceding 999 records first. Consequently, processing data into information was slow and cumbersome and data was treated as a *tactical* asset rather than a *strategic* one.

Variations of sequential data files are still used for storing data, including "delimited" files where fields are separated by a specific character such as a comma or a combination of characters. They are used, however, not as the main repositories of data but mostly for keeping private application information or as temporary holding bins for exchanging a set of data between applications. Gradually, though, both functions are migrating to XML (Extensible Markup Language).

ISAM: Precursor to DBMSs

> The Indexed Sequential Access Method (ISAM) improved the performance of data operations by storing indices or "keys" to data records.

☞ You should not confuse ISAM with indexing in general. Indexing data has indeed come a long way since ISAM. The variety and the complexity of current indexing technology is such that even discussing the highlights will seriously derail our discussion about database design. You can find good theoretical literature about various indexing techniques such as B-Tree, but the actual implementations are trade secrets. Fortunately, the indexing technologies offered by commercial DBMSs are so mature that you have only to learn how to *use* them, not how to create them.

The shortcomings of sequential access were easy for everybody to see. As often happens in the history of technology, the road towards sophisticated database management systems started with an idea that in retrospect seems rather obvious. In the 1960s, somebody asked a simple question: Books have indexes that allow you to find key items quickly; why not do the same thing for data records? For example, say that positions 60 to 70 of each employee data record holds the `Social Security Number` of an employee. When each record is written, we can store the value of the field and the record number in a separate but smaller record in a separate but much smaller file. To find an employee by the Social Security Number, we do not need to read the entire employee file but, instead, can process the records in the index file, find the entry with the right number, take the "key" to the full record, and quickly retrieve it.

This method, of course, is the most primitive way to index data, and does not address other important issues such as how to insert records between existing records and how to remove selected records *without* having to rewrite the entire set. Soon computer manufacturers started to address these and other issues with a series of acronymic offerings: Virtual Storage Access Method (VSAM), Keyed Storage Access Method (KSAM), Basic Direct Access Method (BDAM), Queued Sequential Access Method (QSAM), and many more designations ending with "access method." (We said "computer manufacturers" and not "software companies" for a simple reason: Computer companies sold you both hardware and software—the operating system, utilities, and language compilers—as a "bundle." It took many years of antitrust litigations, changes in technology, and parallel changes in the marketplace to separate hardware and software.)

With the incremental refinement to the organization and the accessibility of data storage, however, something else—something *qualitatively* more important—started to happen: the separation between applications and data management systems. The utilities that gradually took over the management of data required more information about what they were charged with managing: identifiers or names for the fields in the record, the type of each field, and its size, at a minimum. In other words, they demanded what today we call **metadata**, or *data about data*. Once such information left the confines of individual applications it became possible for data to become a shared resource, at least theoretically.

Early DBMSs

> Early database management systems required the applications to know the physical layout of data.

☞ Another contribution of CODASYL was COBOL (Common Business-Oriented Language), the first computer language that was verbose and English-like.

In late 1960s and early 1970s, data management came closer to becoming a complete system in its own right. Instead of incremental improvements, conceptual models for managing data were put forward. The two most prominent ones were:

- *The Network Model.* Proposed by CODASYL (short for **Co**nference on **Da**ta **Sy**stems **L**anguages, an organization founded in 1957 by the U.S. Department of Defense), this model was based on the following definition of a database: ❶ a database is a collection of files; ❷ a file is an ordered collection of entries; ❸ an entry consists of key or keys and data.
- *The Hierarchical Model.* In the hierarchical model, data records are organized as *master* and *detail* collections.

Based on these models or hybrids and adaptations, many actual database management systems were developed. All, however, required the client application to have an intimate knowledge of the *physical* organization of data. Moreover, they lacked a query or data-definition language, and applications had to use low-level functions by sending cryptic messages.

[Campbell-Kelly 2003, 42]

Again, these products were offered for specific mainframe computers, not as independent market products. One of the most notable successes of this generation was SABRE, the first real-time airline reservation system jointly built by IBM and American Airlines. (The project started in 1953, before IBM even had a computer on the market, and was not completed until 1964.) New development projects for such database management systems are unlikely, but you may still come across them if an enterprise has kept a "legacy" system.

The Relational Database Management System (RDBMS)

> By hiding the physical structure of data, the relational model presents a logical view of the database organization and provides the basis for using a high-level language for database management.

[Codd 1970, 377]

☞ "Data bank," though seldom used today, is a synonym for "database."

When Codd's paper was written, personal computers were still a few years away and the most advanced device for communicating with the computer was a "terminal," i.e., a monitor and a keyboard attached to a mainframe.

☞ **SQL** is often pronounced "sequel," because the original name was Structured *English* Query Language. For legal reasons, however, IBM changed the name.

Some authors point out that SQL is now a name, not an acronym. In other words, it does not stand for anything but itself.

The foundation of modern database management systems was laid down in 1970 by one theoretical paper and one man, E. F. Codd, who at the time was a researcher at IBM. Titled *A Relational Model of Data for Large Shared Data Banks*, it put forward a simple but elegant and momentous proposition:

> Future users of large data banks must be protected from having to know how data is organized in machine (the internal representation) . . . **Activities of users** at terminals **and most application programs should remain unaffected when the internal representation of data is changed** and even when some aspects of the external representation are changed. Changes in data presentation will often be needed as a result of changes in query, update and report traffic and natural growth in the types of stored information.
>
> The relational view (or model) of data . . . provides a means of **describing data with its natural structure** only—that is, **without superimposing any additional structure for machine representation purposes**. Accordingly, it provides a basis for a high level data language which will yield maximal independence between programs on the one hand and machine representation and organization of data on the other. [Emphasis added.]

Relational databases—Oracle, SQL Server, DB2, Sybase, etc.—are so established and pervasive that it might come as a surprise to know that for a long time it was considered an interesting but rather impractical idea. Even IBM, where Codd worked, was reluctant to abandon IMS, a hierarchical DBMS that it considered to be its strategic product. However, it was IBM that, by introducing SQL and a product called SQL/DS in 1980, made relational database management a serious and, in the end, winning contender in the marketplace.

SQL popularly stands for **Structured Query Language**, but it is used for *all* database communications and operations, not just queries. Though each database vendor markets its own extended version, SQL is based on ANSI (American National

Standards Institute) standards. The first standard was published in 1986 and, since then, it has been updated every few years.

Since the relational model underlies the most mature and the most solid databases in the marketplace, topics in this chapter focus largely on design for relational database management systems.

Object-Oriented Database Management Systems

> An object-oriented database management system (OODBMS) aims to make persistence transparent to object-oriented languages.

Relational database management systems were conceived and matured before object-oriented technology became the *de facto* standard for software development. This means that persistence—storing the "state" of objects in a database—requires mapping between attributes of the objects and the organization of the database (as we shall explore later in this chapter).

It is logical to expect that this divide between development languages and database management systems should be bridged to enhance productivity by removing the need to translate objects into other data structures, and to make software more robust by reducing complexity. It is logical and is eagerly sought after by software developers, but it is still a work in progress.

The first reason for the slow adoption of OODBMSs is, of course, due to the existing base of relational databases. As we argued, data has become a strategic asset for most enterprises and, therefore, databases cannot be discarded or changed simply because a newer and (perhaps) better technology has arrived.

The second reason is that although object-oriented technology dominates *new* software development, there exists a very large number of functioning and mission-critical applications that are *not* object-oriented but must be maintained. The *advertised* strength of an OODBMS is that it seamlessly integrates with object-oriented languages: It lets an object manager instantiate the object from the database with the same ease that you instantiate an object in memory. The same (theoretical) strength, however, can be a weakness. You may embed SQL statements in almost any language (including COBOL) to communicate with an RDBMS, whereas the "seamlessness" would leave such languages helpless. Various propositions for an object-data definition language have been put forward, but none has gained wide recognition.

☞ For a definition of **transaction processing**, see the "Procedural Integrity Assurance" section later in this chapter.

There are also technical and theoretical reasons: performance (or *perceived* performance), issues of transaction processing, and lack of widely accepted standards. The con and the pro sides are still vigorously defending their own positions and attacking those of their opponents, but such heated debates, by themselves, might persuade many businesses to wait until the dust has settled.

Nevertheless, database management systems *will* move forward, especially since the Web and the avalanche of unstructured data have brought forward issues that the relational model (or any other model for *structured* data) cannot easily address.

Another solution to bridging the divide between the object-oriented and relational models is **object-relational mapping** (ORM). An ORM software functions as a layer that mediates between the application and the relational database. Through this layer, the application sees the database as an extension of the virtual object space, whereas the RDBMS responds to messages (SQL or driver-dependent) that it knows how to process.

ORM has had a measure of success greater than pure object-oriented database management systems because the enterprise does not have to restart everything from zero. RDBMS sources, such as Oracle, have integrated ORM features in their products and third-party software vendors have developed products that work with multiple DBMSs. It seems like a win-win situation, but the reality is not so simple. Lack of standards and performance issues hamper ORM as well as OODBMSs, but there is another factor at work that is equally a problem: Many actual databases are not well-designed, and putting an object-oriented layer on top of them only accentuates their defects.

Desktop Database Management Systems

> Desktop databases management system emphasize ease of use.

Before the late 1970s and early 1980s, computers were seen and imagined only as extremely expensive and large systems that were to serve large enterprises with deep pockets, or slightly smaller businesses that were willing to "time-share." Databases, therefore, were designed to serve the same masters, not individuals. Personal computers, however, changed the landscape by creating a slowly increasing but eventually *vast* demand for *personalized* tools and application, including databases.

Like their mainframe siblings, but usually one step behind, desktop databases have evolved from indexed files to full-fledged relational models. The emphasis, however, has been on user-friendliness and ease of use, with varying degrees of success. PC users do not have the time or the resources to struggle with the complexities of design and/or installation and their needs are seldom as sophisticated as those of an enterprise.

The more recent batches of desktop DBMSs, such as Desktop SQL Server (Microsoft), use the same engines as the enterprise versions, but are packaged differently with a more helpful interface.

Desktop databases, from simple to sophisticated, have been a boon to productivity, to individuals as well as to small businesses who could not afford large, customized systems, and to neglected departments in larger enterprises who could not get satisfactory services from their own internal IT resources. Their legacy, however, is a mixed blessing. Companies that have grown, or that now can afford dedicated database servers and networks, must somehow integrate such databases with those of the enterprise, a task fraught with difficulties since their design is not usually very professional or reflects a narrow focus on a narrow slice of time and activity.

3. THE RELATIONAL MODEL

The most succinct description of relational databases is the one that we previously quoted from E. F. Codd: "The relational view (or model) of data . . . provides a means of describing data with its natural structure only—that is, without superimposing any additional structure for machine representation purposes." However, what exactly is this "natural structure"?

First of all, the term "natural" should not be taken literally—data organizations are human artifacts, not natural phenomena—but as a metaphor for "logical" as described repeatedly in this book: a model that describes the solution as independent from technology as possible. With such a definition, it is possible to arrive at more than one "natural" organization for data, as object-oriented database management systems are doing.

As we said, however, the relational model is the most mature and prevalent model of data organization. To design a specific database, we must first familiarize ourselves with the basic concepts of the relational model.

Tables

A table is the basic organizational unit of a relational database.

☞ In the relational terminology, a table is also called a *relation;* hence the term "relational."

☞ Storage in a computer is composed of files. The distinction between "table" and "file" highlights the distinction between the logical and the physical: A table may reside in one file or in several files, and one file may contain many tables—as is the case in most relational DBMSs.

☞ As is usually the case with mundane things, people can become passionate about naming preferences. We have normally used plural names such as **Orders** or **Customers** since a table is a *collection* of entities (unlike a class which is an abstraction). Others may argue—convincingly—that the name of the table must be singular. Some others, usually database

A table is a rectangular arrangement of data, composed of columns and rows. A column is also referred to as an **attribute**, a row as a *tuple*, and their intersection as a **cell**.

- *Column.* An attribute in the relational terminology is similar to an object-oriented attribute: It defines characteristics such as **Last Name**, **First Name**, and **Birth Date**. It has a name that must be unique within the table namespace and identifies the data type of the values that belong to it. It also imposes **constraints** on the range of data that might be assigned to it.

- *Row.* A row is a collection of data for a specific entity as defined by columns. It is similar to an instance of a class in the objected-oriented terminology and like an object has a unique identity, except that where an object's unique identity can be implicit, a row's identity must be explicitly defined as the value of a column or a set of columns. (See the following "The Primary Key" section.)

Nowadays, this layout seems so natural that one may wonder why it has to be described at all. As we shall point out more than once in this topic, the relational model was shaped in contrast to the theories and practices of the 1960s. A deck of punched cards or a similar sequential file did not always consist of data about the same *type* of entities. For example, to process data about orders from customers, each set of **Order** records were preceded by one **Customer** record (or card), and if orders related to various departments, then a **Department** record might precede batches of **customer order records**, and so on. As a result, the data did not necessarily line up vertically. The **Customer** record held *"fields,"* such as **Customer ID** and **Address**, that were different than those on an **Order** record, such as **Item** and **Quantity**. To be distinguished by the processing application, the records (or cards) were "punched" with an identifier, such as a **1** for the **Customer** record and a **2** for the **Order** record.

The relational view adopted a terminology that was consciously different from its predecessors because it wanted to emphasize conceptual differences: "table" instead of "file," "row" or "tuple" instead of "record," and "attribute" or "column" instead of "field." In the relational model, each *vertical* division or column represents one, and only one, type of data, and the *horizontal* division, or row, refers to *same* class of entities across the table. If one row represents a **Customer Order**, then all rows refer to orders, not to another entity such as **Customer** or **Department**. If one attribute represents the **Quantity** of the order, then every corresponding attribute on every row must represent quantity and nothing else.

Within the namespace of the database, a table must have a *unique name* that identifies its contents: **Patients**, **Treatments**, **Books**, etc. Depending on the DBMS, the name can be simple or include other attributes such as the owner's ID

Figure 13.2
**Tables: The
Basic Units of a
Relational
Database**

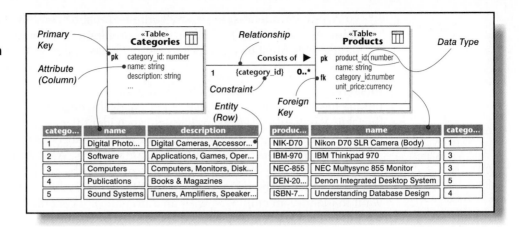

administrators (DBAs), prefer to add a unique prefix to both the table name and its attributes to separate "native" attributes from "foreign" keys (discussed later)— **patPatients**, for instance, and then **patLastName**, **patFirstName**, etc. Pick your own naming scheme because it really is not *that* critical. What *is* critical is *consistency*.

☞ Some databases might allow you to create a table *without* a primary key. Avoid this temptation as it can lead to trouble.

☞ A key that consists of more than one column is called a **composite key**. The columns that compose a key need not be adjacent or of the same data type.

(in which case **John.Patient**, where John is the table owner, is different from **Jane.Patient**, and both are unique). Each column name must also be unique, but only within the namespace of the table. For instance, a table may not have *two* **First Name** columns, but the table **Patients** and the table **Doctors** both may have a **First Name** attribute—exactly like naming attributes in classes.

The Primary Key

> The primary key is an attribute or a set of attributes whose values uniquely identify a row.

An attribute describes metadata: the column's name, its data type, its range of allowable values ("domain"), etc. The actual data are grouped in rows. In a relational database, rows are not in any *logical* order. (Even if they were, finding a row based on its location requires that the user know the row number beforehand—an impractical condition.) Besides, the number of rows is usually in constant fluctuation: rows are deleted and added. How are we, then, to identify a row?

A relational row represents an entity, similar to an object in the object-oriented model, and each entity in the table must be unique. To ensure uniqueness, each table must have a primary key that is composed of a column or a set of columns whose values *uniquely* identify a row. (In other words, no two rows in the same table can have the same primary key. For instance, in an **Employees** table, **Social Security No** can be assigned as the primary key since no two persons can have the same number. Or, for a **Shoe Inventory** table, we might assign the combination of **Shoe ID**, **Size**, and **Color** as the primary key.)

Sometimes creating a unique identifier from values of actual attributes is impossible, inconvenient, or undesirable:

- A bank customer might have multiple accounts with the banks. As a result, any data that is unique about the customer cannot uniquely identify the account.
- A patient is brought into the emergency room of a hospital. Even if we assume that the patient has a Social Security Number (not a safe assumption as the patient might be a foreign tourist), the patient might be unconscious and might lack an ID. The hospital, however, must provide medical services and must uniquely identify the recipient of the service.

- To ensure uniqueness, too many columns must be combined or some columns are too big. This is especially problematic when the primary key of one table must be used as a foreign key (see the next section) of another table.

In such cases, we can ask the DBMS to assign a unique value for each row. This unique identifier is a number that is automatically generated as rows are added to the table. We should be very familiar with such identifiers: account numbers (bank or otherwise), employee IDs, product identification numbers, etc.

Unique constraints are similar to primary keys. Also known as **alternate** or **candidate keys**, they ensure that the value of a **cell** (the point that a column meets a row) is unique for the table, regardless of the primary key. For example, we might want to identify an employee with an automatically generated **Employee ID**, but we might also want to ensure that the **Social Security No** is not duplicated anywhere.

Both primary and alternate keys must have unique names, for example **PK_Employee** for the primary key and **AK_SS_NO** for the alternate. (**PK** stands for "primary key" and **AK** for "alternate key.") Notice that the DBMS treats a column and a key as two different (although related) entities, even if the key is made up of only one column. Therefore, the names cannot be the same.

Columns whose values compose the primary key cannot be left blank (or **null**). Remember that "null" indicates a lack of information. Null is not "empty" as in an empty bottle, it is not N/A (not applicable), and it is not zero. Therefore, if the **Gender** column is included in the primary key, the value for each row *must* be **M** or **F** (or any other range of numeric or character values that we may assign to such a column).

☞ Keys and indexing should not be confused. The DBMS indexes primary and alternate keys for fast retrieval, but you may index many types of data. Why not index *every* column? Because the price in terms of storage and updating time would cancel any advantage and, most probably, would seriously harm the performance overall.

The Foreign Key

> The foreign key is an attribute in one table whose value must match the value of a primary or an alternate key in a different table.

[Groff 1999, 59]

The relational model rejects explicit pointers such as master/slave or parent/child relationships of hierarchical databases. Theoretically, entities in table rows do not *belong* to any other entity. But "relations" do exist and they are identified by foreign keys, where the value of one attribute in one table *must* match the value of a primary or alternate key in another table. For instance, the foreign key **FK_Author** identifies the relation of a book in the **Books** table to a writer in the **Authors** table. (The name of a foreign key must be unique and, conventionally, begins with an **FK** prefix.)

Unlike primary keys, foreign keys do not necessarily identify a row uniquely. Also, a table might have no foreign keys or might have many: In the context of Walden Hospital's information system, **Countries** has no foreign key, while **Appointments** must have at least *two* foreign keys, one relating it to **Patients** and the other to the **Medical Services** table.

☞ As we said, if the primary key of a table is a composite of too many columns, it might be a good idea to consider an automatically generated unique identifier for referencing. You can then keep the composite key as an alternate key.

Like primary keys, a foreign key can be a composite key *if* the primary key in the other table is a composite itself. Also, foreign keys can participate in a primary key: The primary key of the **Appointments** table, for example, can be composed from the primary key of **Patients** and the primary key of **Medical Services** plus the appointment's own **Date** and **Time**.

☞ Whether the value of a foreign key can be optional or not depends on the choices that you make during design. Likewise, the default behavior of DBMS depends on the particular product.

Unlike primary keys, foreign keys can be *optional*. This means that a row may accept a null value ("no data") where a foreign key is concerned. Where is such a situation desirable? Not for **Appointments**, as an appointment *must* relate to a **Patient** row, and not for **Books**, as a book must relate to a row in the **Authors** table. But consider a **Payments** table that records payments for purchases. Payments may be rendered in cash, by check, or by credit card. Necessarily, the table has a foreign key that relates it to the **Credit Cards** table. Some customers might pay by credit card, while others may choose cash or check. When the payment is *not* by credit card, therefore, the foreign key is allowed to remain null since it relates to nothing.

The foreign key should not be viewed as an "ownership" relationship, but rather as a *reference* or *dependency*. The table whose foreign key relies on the values in another table is called the *referencing* table, while the second one is known as the *referenced* table.

In the next section we further explore foreign keys in the context of data integrity.

Data Integrity

A relational database management system protects data integrity at four levels: column, row, inter-table, and procedural.

We must reiterate, before anything else, that data integrity and data security are not the same. Security includes access (physical and virtual), backup, and recovery, while data integrity, in the context of a database management system, is about consistency, accuracy, and correctness:

- The data management system is mostly responsible for *consistency*: agreement and logical coherence among data items.
- People and procedures have the highest responsibility for *correctness*: avoiding errors in data that is given to the information system and, ultimately, to the data management system.
- *Accuracy* is the responsibility of both: the information system must receive precise data, but the data management system must preserve accuracy throughout the operations that it performs.

The relational model presents a certain view and a certain organization of data—as we described. The data integrity mechanisms of relational database managements reflect the relational view and organization. Some of the mechanisms, such as primary and foreign keys, are almost transparent since they are, basically, part of the database organization: You design them *into* the database when you design the tables and define their relationships. Others need more conscious and explicit decisions.

One very important point: If any data integrity rule can be established equally well in both the database and the application, choose the database. Databases stay longer than applications and the same database usually serves multiple applications. Besides, the rules in the database are more transparent and easier to verify than those in applications.

Attribute Integrity

Attribute integrity is ensured by type definition, constraints, and foreign keys.

The term "**constraint**" simply means restriction. A constraint ensures that data meets certain criteria. The following constraints guard the integrity of data in columns:

- *Type.* Whatever tool you might use in creating a table, you must define the *physical type* of each attribute (column). By doing so, you also establish a minimum integrity rule: Do not allow any value that is not of the specified type or subtype. The simplest example is when you define an attribute as **Date**: trying to store anything but dates in cells that belong to this column will trigger an error. The accuracy, however, can be more refined: depending on the specific DBMS, a numeric type can be integer (whole numbers), currency (two decimal points only), float (for scientific numbers), and so on. For character strings, you can limit the size or define a pattern that the string must adhere to.

When you define the characteristics of an attribute, two other options are closely related to type:

- ■ *Null:* Can the cell be left without data? For example, in creating an entity (or row) for the **Appointment** table, **Appointment Date** *must* be specified whereas **Special Instructions** can be disregarded because it is not required.
- ■ *Default Value:* If no data for a cell is given, should the cell be assigned a default value? For instance, you can instruct the database to default the **Sales Date** column to today's date *unless* the operator overrides it. (Needless to say, a column with a default value cannot be "null.")

[Viera 2000, 205]

☞ In design, it is never assured that the terminology used in a general-purpose book (such as this) will agree with the implementations of technology. Implementations of the relational model, and SQL, are many and varied. What is more confusing is that the same term is sometimes used in exact opposition to its use in another DBMS.

[Groff 1999, 382]

- *Domain & Check Constraints.* As we stated, the **domain** is a set of allowable values for a given attribute: days of the week, months of the year, etc. The domain is independent of individual tables and, as a result, can be *reused* and applied to different columns in different tables. In effect, by declaring a domain you are creating your own data type.

Check constraints are, conceptually, the same as domains. The difference is that check constraints are declared for individual tables *but* are not restricted to individual columns: They can validate one column in relation to another column or a combination of columns (provided they are in the *same* table). For example, you can specify that the **Ship Date** cannot be earlier than the **Order Date**.

- *Unique Constraints.* The primary key and alternate keys ensure that the value in a single cell, or the combination of values in several cells, is unique for the *table*. We discussed these two in the previous topic.

- *Assertions.* Assertion constraints are similar to check constraints, but go beyond single attributes or single tables. For example, you can "assert" that the total **Order Amount** for a customer cannot exceed the **Credit Limit**, even though the credit limit is in one table (**Customers**, perhaps) and the orders belong to another (**Order Details**).

- *Foreign Key.* Foreign keys not only define the relationships between the tables and the entities that belong to them, but also constrain what values can and cannot be accepted by a column, or a set of columns, that compose a foreign key in the referencing table. In an **Orders** table, the values that can be assigned to **Customer ID** and **Product ID** are restricted to those that can be found in corresponding columns in the **Customers** and **Products** tables.

Entity Integrity

> Entity integrity is assured by the primary key.

Each row of a table represents one—and only one—entity that must be unique within the table space. This uniqueness is assured by the primary key. Relational database management systems automatically guard against any duplication of primary key value(s). Otherwise, we cannot be sure which row represents the real-world entity. Even if entities appear to be exact replicas, a unique key must be assigned to the row, like the serial numbers on banknotes, which *must* be exact copies of each other in any other respect.

Referential Integrity

> Referential integrity is safeguarding inter-table references established by foreign keys.

The dependency of a foreign key is **bi-directional**, though it may not appear so at first glance: A row in the **Books** table needs a row in the **Authors** table, but not *vice versa*. However, when you establish a primary/foreign relation between tables, the database management system would not (or should not) allow you to remove a row from the referenced table, or change its unique identity (the primary key) if a row in the referencing table is related to that row. Thus, if "Hemingway" has a row in the **Authors** table, then you cannot, by default, delete it if the **Books** table has an entry for *A Farewell to Arms*.

Referential integrity is the enforcement of references established between tables. If the referential integrity breaks, a relational database becomes a collection of disparate, and often incomprehensible, data: An order for the customer number **2800091** for 3 units of product number **002935** at an unknown price is hardly useful.

Referential integrity does *not* mean that the DBMS interprets it in only one way. On the contrary, you can set **cascading rules** that tell the system what to do when the referential integrity is affected. For example, if an application tries to delete a row from the **Authors** table, you can instruct the database management system to delete all referencing rows from the **Books** table as well. On the other hand, you may prevent any deletion from the **Customers** file if any row in the **Orders** table references the row that the user wants to delete.

Cascading rules affect the updating of both referencing and referenced entities as well. Should the system allow the primary key of the referenced entity to be changed? If so, then the change must cascade into other tables where the primary key is used as a foreign key. Or should we be able to change the foreign key? For example, if we decide that, after all, *War and Peace* was written by Tolstoy and not by Oscar Wilde, can we change the reference in the **Books** table without having to create a new entry? (The primary key in the **Books** table, in turn, might be a foreign key to other tables, such as **Orders**. Therefore, the problems can cascade as well.)

☞ When referential integrity breaks, it creates **orphaned** rows: *referencing* entities that have lost their *referenced* entities.

Some DBMSs, notably on the desktop, might allow the designer to bypass referential integrity, while others may allow the database administrator to suspend referential integrity, temporarily, for loading bulk data. Referential integrity, however, should never be taken lightly.

Procedural Integrity

> Triggers, stored procedures, and transaction processing assure data integrity when and where the relationships among entities are complex.

The integrity mechanisms previously discussed are called *declarative* because the rules are simply declared: They are more or less like a questionnaire that you might fill out, and *unlike* an essay or a term paper. When declarative rules are not enough, however, relational database management systems offer other mechanisms that are *procedural*:

A procedure is a named sequence of programming statements, variously called a function, a method, a routine, or a subroutine.

The ability to process procedural code is what makes a DBMS more than an enhanced database and a system in its own right. By using procedural language (see the following "SQL" section), the database designer can handle situations that are far too complex for declarative directives.

The procedural mechanisms fall into three categories: triggers, stored procedures, and transaction processing. We will discuss the first two later, but we should clarify one thing here: These mechanisms are not mutually exclusive and do communicate with each other.

Transaction processing needs clarification as well. Any kind of exchange—ideas, merchandise, money, etc.—can be called a transaction. In the context of database management, however, it has a very specific and technical meaning:

A transaction is a set of database operations that must succeed as a set. If one operation fails, then the whole transaction fails.

You may correctly define every table, every primary key, every foreign key, and every other constraint, but you might not be able to guarantee data integrity under complex conditions where the *business logic* cannot be reduced to the formal structure of the database, regardless of its sophisticated design.

- When you place an order with an online bookseller, a minimum number of steps must be taken to place the order successfully. First the information system must create an order in the **Orders** table (assuming that you already have an account). Then, for each book title, it must decrease the quantity on hand for an entry in the **Inventory** table and add the title and quantity to your order. After all titles have been processed, it must add up the total amount that you must pay and verify your credit card. As the last step, it must create entries in the **Work Orders** table so that the people responsible for shipping the books would actually do so.

- While you are ordering your favorite best-seller book, a few other customers are ordering the same title, but they click on the **Order Now** button a fraction of a second or so after you. Unbeknownst to all customers, only one copy of the book remains in inventory. If your credit card is verified, then that one copy is assigned to you and others must be asked whether a delay is acceptable because the title is backordered. But *before* the system tries to verify your credit card, the quantity on hand has already been decremented. In other words, the accuracy of the quantity is questionable: The book has been promised to you, but not until the credit card clears.

In these cases, and many like them, structural integrity does not handle the issue effectively: The DBMS simply does not know what such business rules require. It is the responsibility of database users (i.e., applications) to instruct the DBMS as to how to ensure data integrity. To do so, the application can issue the following commands to the database management system:

❶ *Begin Transaction:* Treat the database operations that follow as *one* transaction.
❷ *Rollback Transaction:* Cancel all operations performed after "begin transaction" because an exception (an error) occurred; in other words, return the state of the database to what it was *before* the transaction was started.
❸ *Commit Transaction:* Make all operations after the "begin transaction" command permanent. The transaction was successful and is now complete.

When the DBMS starts the transaction, it also *locks* the tables that might cause "dirty" reads or writes: queries that return inaccurate data and update requests that should not be performed until the current transaction is complete (or is rolled back). For more complex scenarios, industrial-strength DBMSs offer *nested* transaction processing, when one transaction can take place within another one.

SQL

SQL is the primary language for communication with relational database management systems.

[Codd, 1970]

☞ DBMS vendors also provide developers with proprietary and platform-specific tools and "drivers" for enhancing performance. No two are alike and a change in technology makes them obsolete fast. The business must weigh the boost to performance against the proprietary nature of the tools.

The original proposal for the relational model envisioned "a high-level data language which will yield maximal **independence** between programs on the one hand and machine representation and organization of data on the other." The features of the language itself, however, were not specified.

SQL, as we related before, originated from IBM, was gradually accepted by the marketplace, and became a *de facto* standard. In the 1980s, first the American National Standards Institute (ANSI) and then the International Standards Organization (ISO) adopted SQL as an official standard.

The dominant relational DBMSs in the marketplace comply, more or less, with a version of the standards, but each has its own "dialect," with extensions that sometimes genuinely serve a distinct purpose and sometimes are only different to preserve "backward compatibility" with the previous versions of the same DBMS. As a result, although an expert in Oracle's SQL (called PL/SQL) can adapt to—and work with—Microsoft's or Sybase's dialect (called Transact-SQL), the code cannot be transported from one DBMS to another without modifications.

In its most basic form, SQL is really a high-level language and can be readily understood. Figure 13.3 illustrates a simple SQL statement that retrieves selected attributes from a set of entities from the **Patients** table.

A query, however, is only one of the functions of SQL. Every operation of an RDBMS can be controlled through SQL:

[Groff 1999, 5]

- *Data Definition.* Define the structure of the database, including attributes, constraints, tables, and the relationships among items in the database.
- *Query.* Retrieve data from the database. The data that is retrieved can be atomic (a single item) or can be organized into sets. It can include calculated

Figure 13.3
SQL: The Language for Managing an RDBMS

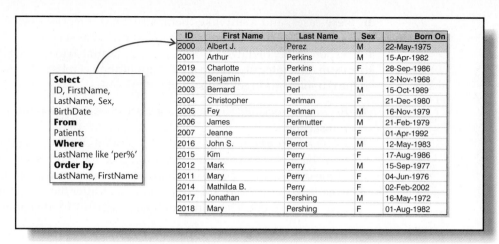

In this illustration, SQL is used to return a set of data from the **Patients** table based on a criteria for the **LastName** attribute. The function of SQL, however, is not limited to query, but covers the full range of database and data management operations.

(This is the same SQL statement that was used in Figure 12.2 in the previous chapter.)

☞ This book does not aim to teach SQL. The snippets of code that appear next to illustrations are only meant to give a general idea of how SQL works.

items, that is, data items that do not exist in the database but are *derived* from items in one or more columns, in one or more tables. In every case, the returned items also carry the data types by which they are defined in the database.

- *Data Operations.* Allow users to manipulate data by adding new data, and deleting or updating data that are already stored.
- *Security & Privileges.* Allow database administrators to specify who may access the database and what operations the users may perform on what tables and/or on what columns.
- *Multi-User Coordination.* Allows multiple users to access the database without interfering with each other.
- *Data Integrity.* Allows designers to specify how data integrity is to be guarded.

In retrieving, updating, or deleting data, SQL works on *sets* or groups of items that have some relation to each other. For example, in Figure 13.1, we are asking the DBMS to retrieve patients whose last name starts with "per." For more complicated tasks, SQL offers many functions and operators, some standard and some proprietary.

SQL is so entrenched in the world of database management systems that it is difficult to imagine data management without it. As we mentioned, however, new technologies have expanded our definitions of data and have presented SQL with new challenges. As a result, both standard bodies and vendors are trying to outfit SQL with new extensions and tools. These include:

- *SQL/OLB:* Object Language Binding to bind SQL and object-oriented platforms for Java development.
- *SQL/MED:* Management of External Data to access legacy and non-structured data.
- *SQL/OLAP:* On-Line Analytical Processing for high-level data analysis.

Views

A view is a virtual table that represents a selected set of attributes from one or more tables.

The relational model aims to hide the physical organization of the database by offering a logical view of data. Views present the next step in the same direction: They hide the complexities of the *logical* view by providing customized *virtual tables*.

The tables in a relational database are designed and optimized to ensure reliability, integrity, and performance by, among other things, removing redundancy. (See the "Data Normalization" section later in this chapter.) Such a structure may be "logical," but it is not necessarily "natural" or intuitive: When we pick up a book at the bookstore, we expect to find the title, the author(s), the publisher, and the price right on the cover. We do not expect to see codes that direct us to other documents to find the relevant information.

Figure 13.4 illustrates how we can use virtual tables to present a real-world view of data *without* undermining the logical organization of the database. The data about book titles are stored in three tables that correspond to domain objects **Author**, **Publisher**, and **Title**. (The fourth table, **TitleAuthor**, does not have an exact counterpart in the object-oriented view of the world. We shall talk about such tables later.) The view **vuTitleProfile** consolidates the data in which we are interested in one virtual table. From outside the database, this view is indistinguishable from an actual table: We may query it as we query any other table. Since a view does not alter the organization of the database, we can create as many views as we need: one for accounting, a second for marketing, a third for inventory, and so on.

In an object-oriented context, a view can be described as separating the *interface* from *implementation*: The consumer of the database services is isolated from the real source of data. Even if the logical organization of the database is altered, the functioning of the applications that use the views is not disrupted as long as the views are amended as well. For example, it may become necessary for the enterprise to create a **Prices** table that stores various price categories for books: a cover price (the existing one), a price for students, a price for institutions such as libraries, bulk price, and so on. As a result, the **Price** attribute is migrated from **Titles** to the new table. Without a view, existing applications must be changed immediately as well, or else they would break. If, however, the applications are using **vuTitleProfile**, they will remain functional because the view can be updated to find the cover price in the new table. New views, then, can be created to present the new organization of the database to its users.

In some aspects, virtual tables are different from actual tables. First, they have no keys, neither primary nor foreign. Second, they are often not updatable. The updatability of a view is decided both by its structure and the brand of DBMS. For example, you cannot add a row to **vuTitleProfile** because (among other things) it exposes none of the primary keys for its underlying table. In any case, update operations—add, change, and delete—should be done through stored procedures.

Stored Procedures

[Groff 1999, 682]

A stored procedure is a named set of SQL statements that provides the capability of performing database-related tasks from within the database itself.

Figure 13.4
Views: Hide
Complexity by
Virtual Tables

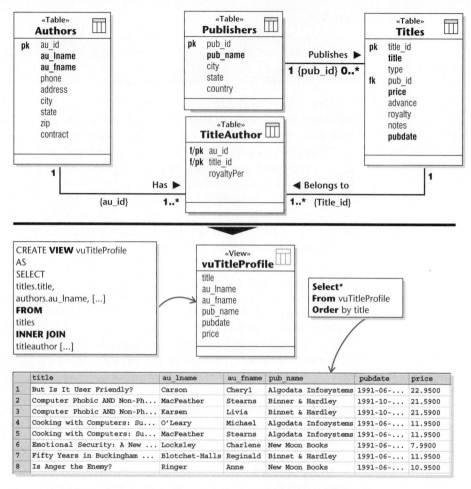

From outside **vuTitleProfile** looks like a real table (with certain limitations in updating). Views not only hide complexity, but protect the users of the database from changes in the schema.

(This example was created from **Pubs**; a sample database that comes with Microsoft's SQL Server. For an explanation of the diagram, see the "Modeling the Relational Database" section in this chapter.)

☞ SQL is the *dominant* language for stored procedures. Vendors of development languages such as Java or C# are feeling their way towards incorporating stored procedures within their own platforms.

Stored procedures are the ultimate method to *encapsulate* the database: hide its internal workings and complexity and expose only the functionality that its users need. In this respect, stored procedures are very similar to public *methods* that objects provide to the outside world.

Figure 13.5 illustrates the concept of a stored procedure as it applies to a **Cancel Order** use case for an online vendor of books, music, movies, etc. Canceling an order is not a one-step action but a *transaction*: a set of database operations, an abridged version of which appears in the illustration. If any step is ignored or fails, the integrity of data would be compromised: Inventory quantities may not be adjusted correctly or the work order for the shipping department may not be canceled, in which case the order would be shipped regardless of everything else.

A mission-critical information system is dependent on many such sensitive use cases where any defect in data integrity can do considerable harm. Stored

Figure 13.5
Stored
Procedures:
Encapsulate
Database
Operations
Inside
the Database

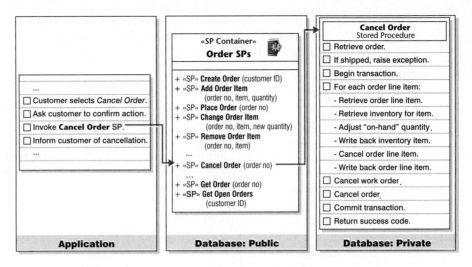

Stored procedures are essential for both the reliability and the security of the database. (See the "Data Integrity" section earlier in this chapter for transaction processing.) The actual name for "SP Container," a grouping of stored procedures, depends on the specific database.
[Naiburg 2001, 129–130]

procedures provide an effective mechanism for ensuring data integrity in **one place**: No matter how many applications, or how many versions of the same application, allow the user to **Cancel Order**, the *same* stored procedure carries out the service. Even if an stored procedure does not function correctly, the errors are far easier to detect and rectify if they are encapsulated in a stored procedure than in various applications.

Moreover, stored procedures provide a relational DBMS with an object-oriented *interface*. In Figure 13.5, stored procedures that relate to orders are modeled as the operations of a class, **Order SPs**. We have stereotyped the class as **«SP Container»** to identify it as a *package* of stored procedures. (The term "package" is product-specific and belongs to Oracle. The actual organization of stored procedures differs from product to product.) Like any other object, a package provides the outside world with services, the exact workings of which are hidden.

In addition to an object-oriented interface, stored procedures provide two other benefits that are no less crucial:

- *Performance.*   In any networked information system, the DBMS has its own server or servers. Each communication between an application and the database consumes network resources. Consequently, the performance decreases as the number of discrete steps within a transaction increases. By consolidating database operations in one "method" or stored procedure within the database, the degradation that results from network traffic and translation layers between the database and applications is avoided.
- *Security.*   Stored procedures can have security settings that are different from their underlying data structure. Therefore, users can have access to a stored procedure *without* having access to the tables on which the stored procedure operates. This point may not seem that important in theory,

but in practice it is crucial: By having access to tables, it is far easier to inflict damage to data, intentionally or inadvertently, than can be done through stored procedures.

[Groff 1999, 683] The stored procedure language (SPL) is usually a customized variant of SQL, different from DBMS to DBMS. Recently, however, both software development platforms and DBMSs have been drawing closer together by allowing the developer to write stored procedures in programming languages such as Java or C#. In any case, an SPL must provide the following capabilities: conditional execution (**IF . . . THEN . . . ELSE**), looping (executing a block of code **UNTIL** a condition is met or **WHILE** a condition is true), block structure (so that a set of statements can appear as a single statement), named variables, and, as we said, named procedures.

Like users and applications outside the database, stored procedures can call other stored procedures or use views.

Triggers

> A trigger is a procedure that is executed when the contents of a table change.

Triggers are very similar to stored procedures, except that they are *completely hidden* from the outside world. Like a stored procedure, a trigger can rely on procedural language to carry out complex operations; unlike a stored procedure, a trigger cannot be invoked by database users, but is executed automatically in response to one of the following events.

- **Insert**, when a new entity (row) is added to the table.
- **Delete**, when an existing entity is removed from the table.
- **Update**, when the value on an attribute (column) for a specific entity is changed.

Triggers are transparent to database users and cannot be bypassed, no matter what security clearance the user enjoys. For instance, we can convert our example for the stored procedure in Figure 13.5 to a trigger that, in response to setting the status of an order to **Canceled**, takes *all* or *some* of the specified steps.

Triggers and stored procedures are not always interchangeable. Triggers cannot be used to retrieve data "on demand." On the other hand, a stored procedure cannot control changes that occur outside of its domain: If a user (or application) changes the status of an entity within the **Orders** table without invoking the stored procedures, data integrity may be adversely affected without an automatic trigger. Therefore, the security model should be carefully crafted to correspond with how stored procedures and triggers are used.

In general, triggers are *data-centric* while stored procedures are *goal-oriented*. A trigger is invoked by a single action on a single item (entity or attribute), even if it results in changes to a set of tables. A stored procedure, on the contrary, is like a use case: It follows a scenario to achieve a goal that is identified by its name.

Triggers are often used when the standard **referential integrity** of the DBMS proves inadequate to the task. (The specifics depend on the DBMS and the table design.) A task, however, for which triggers *must* be used is *auditing*: keeping track of changes to the database. For example, if you have a **Price** table for stocks, you might want to track not only the current price of an item, but also its ups and downs during a certain period: a day, a week, a year, and so on. A trigger that is attached to the **UPDATE** event of **Price** can accomplish this task by inserting a row into the **Price History** table each time the current price is changed.

Triggers can become burdensome as the database grows more complex. Since, by their nature, triggers break apart business rules to accommodate them within **INSERT**, **DELETE**, and **UPDATE** events for single tables, it might become difficult to understand what they accomplish together and in relation to each other. In other words, we might end up with a lot of trees, but with no forest.

Data Normalization

[Muller 1999, 30]

> "Normalization is the process of establishing an optimal table structure based on the internal data dependencies."

[Dutka 1989, 3]

Data normalization is a set of guidelines, techniques, and concepts that allow us to

- identify logical relationships among attributes,
- combine these attributes to form relations (or tables), and
- combine tables in a schema to form a database.

A table can belong to one of seven *normalized forms*, or states. We will discuss the first three forms, which are essential for a well-designed *relational* database. First, however, we must point out that for those familiar with object-oriented concepts, data normalization ideas and guidelines may appear somehow irrelevant or even confusing. Let us explain.

The structural model of a database is called a **schema**. Creating a relational database schema from the artifacts of an object-oriented analysis and design is relatively straightforward. (See the "Mapping to Relational Databases" section later in this chapter.) We say "relatively" because ❶ object-oriented worldview and relational models are *not* perfect matches and ❷ the relational model predates object orientation and, therefore, presents guidelines and concepts that often address a (hopefully) bygone world with its chaotic practices of schema design. Nevertheless, sometimes it is necessary to examine these concepts carefully because:

☞ Not everybody would agree that there are as few as (or as many as) seven normal forms. The first three, those that we explore, were proposed by E. F. Codd. The others are too specialized for a general-purpose book such as this. If, however, you want to become an expert in relational database design, then you must study them. (See the "Suggested Readings" section at the end of this chapter.)

- Databases, as we said, usually have a longer lifespan than the applications that use them. It is very likely that you will come across relational databases that are not very well optimized. Understanding relational concepts will help you to handle issues that arise from such under-optimizations.
- Mapping objects to a relational database will become a more effective and streamlined process if relational concepts are understood *in their own terms*.
- Application designers must cooperate with database administrators and designers to create a good database. Since relational DBMSs are dominant almost everywhere, application designers and DBAs could easily become engaged in fruitless arguments if they cannot understand each other.

To understand data normalization, you must first imagine a world where object-oriented technology and concepts do not exist and where few rules exist for *logically* organizing data.

The First Normal Form

> A table is in the first normal form if it contains no repeating groups.

☞ The term often used to describe the single value in a cell is "***atomic***" [or "elementary"; that is, the value of an attribute for a single entity must not be divisible to other values (or atoms)]. The problem is that "atomic" varies from case to case and, frequently, is in the eyes of the beholder. For example, is an address an "atomic" value, or is it a "molecule" that can be further deconstructed into street address, city, state, etc.? As everybody has experienced, it depends: sometimes the apartment (or suite) number is presented as a separate field and sometimes it is not. The question that must be answered is this: Is the value atomic *enough*? In other words, do we need (or might need) further subdivisions?

To organize data into a table that is in the first normal form is nothing more than creating a table that conforms to the basic relational model: rows that represent one kind of entity, and columns that represent attributes of those entities. If data is not organized as such, then it is not a "relation."

It is useful, however, to restate the same concept from a slightly different viewpoint: A table is in first normal form if ❶ its attributes are single valued and ❷ the number of attributes (or columns) is fixed. In Figure 13.6, we see two organizations of the same data. The top part is not normalized: One "record" about the publisher precedes one or more records about authors (or is it about books?), and the pattern repeats itself. (It looks more like a report than a unit of a database.)

In the course of this book, we learned to view the world (or at least the problem domain) in an object-oriented manner. Therefore, we can rather easily distinguish three classes in the top part of Figure 13.6: **Publisher**, **Author**, and **Book**. Who would organize data in a such an "illogical" way? That answer is that, before relational databases, almost everybody did. As we mentioned before, the technology of punched cards, prior to file systems using random-access storage, could not process data in any other way. Data consisted of sequential records that were read through from beginning to end, and sequential files essentially mimicked the organization of punched cards.

The bottom part of Figure 13.6 takes the first step towards "normalizing" the data by defining two tables—the minimum necessary, since a table cannot have a

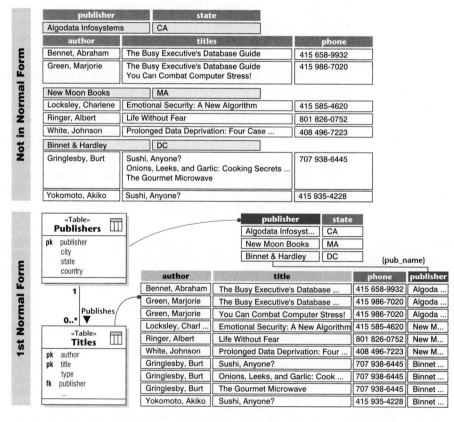

Figure 13.6 First Normal Form: Single-Valued, Fixed Attributes

In a table in the first normal form, the number of columns and the position of each column is fixed and does not change from row to row.

variable number of columns: **publisher** and **state** in one row, for example, **author**, **title**, and **phone** in another. Furthermore, each row must represent one—and only one—entity. As a result, each book must have its own row, and because rows must be unique, we need a combination of **author** and **title** to build a primary key for the **Titles** table, otherwise we would end up with replicated rows since a book may have more than one author (as you can see in the example).

The Second Normal Form

A table is in second normal form if the table is in first normal form and every non-key attribute is *fully* dependent on the *entire* primary key.

In most cases, the first normal form (or 1NF, for short) is woefully inadequate. In Figure 13.6, performing any database operation on the **Titles** table is problematic:

- To *change* or correct the name of an author or a book, we might have to change the values in multiple rows.
- To *add* (insert) one book into the table, we have to insert multiple rows if the book is a collaboration.
- To *delete* a book, we must find and remove *all* rows for the book. Referential integrity ("cascading" deletes) is of no help because each row in the table is an entity independent of another row. (Of course, you can set cascading rules to delete *all* books by a publisher if the publisher is removed. But publisher is in another table.)
- To *retrieve* information about one book, regardless of its author or authors, you might have to read multiple rows, and if the data in multiple rows do not match each other, you do not know which one to believe.

On top of it all, we have a lot of useless redundancy even if all data is correct and consistent. (As you can imagine, if a business needs to track books, authors, and publishers, the number of attributes that it must know about each entity is much higher than that in our illustrations.) To reduce redundancy and rationalize database operations, we must move our data to the second normal form (or 2NF). This normal form requires a high degree of both *decomposition* and *synthesis*: separating related attributes from unrelated ones and re-forming them into new tables.

In second normal form, attributes are about one thing, and one thing only. In a **Books** (or **Titles**) table that conforms to 2NF, we do not have an attribute that represents a book (such as **title**) and another attribute that describes something about the author (like **phone**) but is unrelated to the book itself.

How do we ensure that a table conforms to the second normal form? By verifying that every *non-key* attribute is *functionally dependent* on the *whole primary key*, and not just parts of it. Functional dependency, a term widely used in discussing normalization, simply means an attribute that is a "function" of another attribute. For example, **birth date** (February 2, 1882) is a function of **author** (James Joyce) and **publication date** (1916) is a function of the book's **title** (*A Portrait of the Artist as a Young Man*). If the second attribute changes so does the dependent attribute.

The **Titles** table that resulted from organizing data into the first normal form does *not* satisfy this requirement. To find the phone number of an author, it is

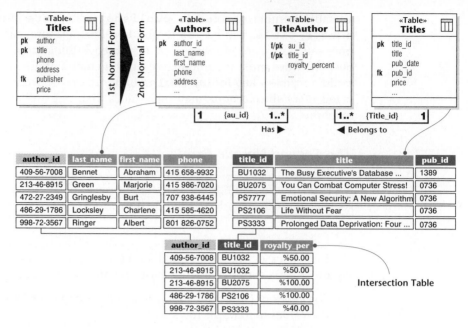

**Figure 13.7
Second Normal Form: Every Non-key Attribute Depends on the Entire Primary Key**

This normal form is the most important step towards removing redundancy.

not enough to know the identity of the author, but you must also know the identity of a book written by that author. Conversely, to find the publication date of a book, you must know both the identity of the book *and* its author (or one of its authors).

Figure 13.7 illustrates how the **Titles** table is converted from 1NF to 2NF. By "decomposition" (analysis), we have concluded that the attributes of the table are functionally dependent on three distinct entities: the book (or title), the author (or authors), and the publisher. We had already composed (or "synthesized") attributes relating to the publishers into a **Publishers** table that now identifies every book with only a foreign key. The remaining attributes are reorganized into two tables: **Authors** and **Titles**. The second table may have the same name as the one in first normal form, but it is not the same as it no longer contains any non-key attributes that describes authors. (We will discuss the third table, **TitleAuthor**, in the upcoming section "The Many-to-Many Knot.")

Figure 13.7 also illustrates another feature that is often necessary for normalization: addition of unique and stable identifiers to entities. In the real world (the world of objects, one might say), entities have identities regardless of whether their identity is expressed by a formal identifier or not. You recognize your regular mail carrier without knowing the mail carrier's Social Security Number or name, and you recognize your favorite shirt without assigning it a unique identifier. In the virtual world of a DBMS, however, *implicit* identifiers are useless: entities must have an *explicit* unique identifier, or primary key.

Sometimes a meaningful attribute of an entity can serve well as a unique identifier within certain limits: the name of a state, for example. In most cases, however, a meaningful identifier is ill-equipped to function as the primary key. The most important reason is that meaningful attributes are subject to error, change, or correction, and meaningful data change even when least expected: In 1989, the country of Burma changed its name to Myanmar. Considering that, in a relational database, primary keys frequently function as foreign keys in other tables, a change in identifiers can cause cascading problems. (A large, meaningful identifier such as a book's title can also take a lot of space.)

Again, for somebody steeped in object-oriented concepts, the second normal form seems mostly obvious: the phone number of a **Doctor** is simply not associated with a **Patient**. The exception is the intersection table (**TitleAuthor** table in Figure 13.7), which we will discuss in a later section.

The Third Normal Form

> A table is in third normal form if the table is in second normal form and no non-key attribute is dependent on another non-key attribute.

In a table that conforms to the third normal form (3NF), there are no transitive dependencies. A *transitive dependency* is a type of functional dependency in which the value in a *non-key* field is determined by the value in another *non-key* field.

In Figure 13.8, the attribute **sales_total** depends on the whole primary key (**title_id**), but its value is also dependent on two attributes: **price** and **ytd_sales** (year-to-date sales). If the price changes, and as the number of copies sold during the year increases, the value of **sales_total** changes as well, and this change is *not* dependent on the primary key. In object-oriented terms, **sales_total** is a **derived attribute**, and derived attributes must not be persisted (saved or stored)

The table also suffers from a symptom of weak design that is, unfortunately, very common: the tendency to disguise *aggregation* as an elementary attribute. The **ytd_sales** column is the total number of copies sold during the *year* and, therefore, is an aggregation. As we stated before, values in a normalized table must be as "atomic" as possible.

The requirement to know the sales figures for a year is quite reasonable. In fact, the **Title** (or the **Book**) class can have—legitimately—a **ytd_sales** attribute that returns the total by adding up all individual sales for a year. This does not mean that the actual aggregate number should be persisted to a table. What is more, keeping the sales price and the sales quantity as attributes of the **Titles** table can easily lead

Figure 13.8
Third Normal Form: Non-key Attributes Are Not Dependent on Non-key Attributes

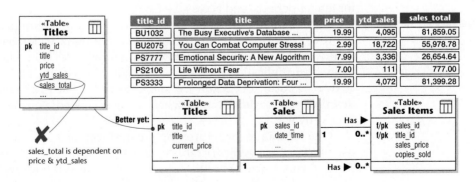

In this normal form, derived attributes such as totals are removed.

to ambiguity and inaccuracy. Is the value of **price** applicable to the whole year? And if today is January 1, what year are we looking at? The year appears to be a "hidden" attribute—an assumption—that is not explicitly identified and is therefore subject to speculation.

A better design, as Figure 13.8 illustrates, is to persist book sales as they happen. When the sales clerk rings a sale at the cash register, the application asks the DBMS to create a row for that specific sale and one row for each item (or book) sold. The DBMS inserts a row in the **Sales** table that has attributes such as date and time and the ID of the sales register. It also generates a meaningless but unique identifier, **sales_id**, that is used as the primary key for the **Sales** table and as a foreign key for each item sold. From this data, applications can generate many kinds of reports that would have been impossible with the previous organization of data: sales by date, by quarter, or by year; sales by a specific book or by author; sales by sales person or store, etc.

What about the **sales_price** in the **Sales Items** table? Are we not creating a redundancy that would be harmful to data integrity? The answer is no, on the contrary, we are preserving data integrity: **sales_price** originates from the **current_price** in the (reorganized) **Titles** table, but it is an attribute of the item sold, not an attribute of **Titles**.

Denormalization

> Denormalization might become necessary due to logical considerations, technological constraints, and performance degradation.

You must have noticed that more normalization means more tables. A database might conform to the best design guidelines and end up with dismal performance because there are too many rows in too many tables. A stock trading and tracking system can create millions of rows in a few days, and the number of tables in our Walden's information system, if it is really and fully implemented, can top several hundred.

Even in a moderately normalized database, retrieving any meaningful information would require the participation (or "*joining*") of many tables. Too many joins of large tables eventually decreases the performance to a level that it becomes unacceptable. Moreover, technological improvements—faster CPUs, faster storage devices with more capacity, DBMSs with better algorithms for indexing—are always offset, very soon, by user expectations: more data, new types of data, accumulated for longer periods, and accessible faster.

Denormalization is one (but only one) of the techniques that can be used to improve performance. For example, in a normalized database, an **Order Items** table would hold only **product code**, a foreign key that relates it to the **Products** table. If an application (or a stored procedure) needs the product description, it joins **Order Items** to **Products** and retrieves **description**. By duplicating the description in **Order Items** when a row is created, you can reduce the number of "joins" by one.

One technique for improving the performance of retrieval and reporting is to use *working* or *aggregate* tables: something that we told you *not* to do under the third normal form. The difference is that these tables are "extras" and do not affect the basic normalized schema. They are updated at regular intervals but

☞ **Sales** and **Sales Items** are also good examples of **transactional objects** that we mentioned before. Such objects do not exist independently, but result from the transaction between two objects. **Treatment** is another example: For a **Treatment** to exist, a **Patient** must interact with a **Doctor**.

[Halpin 2001, 643–644]

not in "real time." For example, at the closing of each day, a process can update the **Book Sales by Day** and **Store Sales by Day** (or by an other period) tables in which sales figures are aggregated. (There are many variations on this theme.)

Design, as we keep repeating, is always a compromise. By gaining an advantage, you might lose another one. By denormalizing, you make retrieval faster but insertion slower. The advisability of the trade-off depends on the ratio of retrieval to other database operations.

In any case, normalization should always take the context into account. (That is to say, it must follow common sense.) In a highly normalized database, addresses would be an aggregation of tables for the **Street Addresses**, **Cities**, **Postal Codes**, and **States** (and perhaps **Countries**). This schema has many advantages for a large marketing or mail-order business. For one thing, if the postal code is known to the operator, entering city or state becomes unnecessary and entry errors are reduced. For a local hospital, this schema is overkill.

Also, dedicating one row to one "big" item such as a car or a battleship is reasonable, but creating one thousand rows for one thousand pencils or paper clips in the inventory is not. In the latter case, the sane choice is to assign an aggregate column for the total number of pencils, instead of following the rules of third normal form to absurdity.

Intersection Tables

An intersection table represents the relationship between two different entities.

In Figure 13.7 (second normal form), the **TitleAuthor** table does not correspond to a single entity of any kind. Instead, it shows the association between a single author, who may have written many books, and a single book, which might have multiple authors. Such a table is called an **intersection** or a *junction* table since it represents where two or more entities come into contact.

Intersection tables are also where you see a noticeable divergence between the object-oriented and the relational model. These tables are *not* objects or even shadows of objects by any other name, but signify various *relationships* among objects or entities. In a database, the relationships between persisted entities *must* be likewise persisted as data.

Another name for such a table is a *resolution* table, since it helps us to solve some of the more intractable issues in the relational model. Among them are the many-to-many relationships and self-referencing relationships.

The Many-to-Many Knot

Many-to-many relationships must be converted to one-to-many relationships through *intersection* tables.

☞ See Chapter 8 for a description of **multiplicity**.

In most of our examples for the class diagram, the multiplicity of the source class (the one that describes the relationship) has been one, while the target class's multiplicity has varied. This is a reflection of the actual state of affairs. In some cases, however, you may end up with a "many-to-many" relationship—a relationship that presents no problem to the object-oriented theory but is problematic for the relational model.

☞ The **Classes** table is an example in which the primary key of an intersection is composed of more than two foreign keys. The **course_id**, however, indicates *inheritance*, not association. (See the "Mapping to Relational Databases" section later in this chapter.)

To solve the problem for a relational database, the many-to-many relationship must somehow be transformed into a relationship that is one-to-many. Intersection tables provide a *pattern*, or the core of a solution, for handling the problem, as is illustrated in Figure 13.7, where the **TitleAuthor** table changes the many-to-many relationship between authors and book into a one-to-many association.

Intersection tables usually—but not always—exhibit the following features:

- The primary key is composed entirely of foreign keys since a row in such a table does not have an identity by itself but relies on "participating" entities.
- The number of entities that provide the foreign keys is usually two.
- The number of *non-key* attributes is either nil or very low. If there are non-key attributes, they must follow rules for second and third normal forms: The non-key attribute must be functionally dependent on the entire primary key and only on the primary key.

Intersections are *not* always highly abstract relationships with no counterparts in the real world or the problem domain. Sometimes the many-to-many problem that surfaces during database design is due to a failure in *conceptual modeling* or *domain analysis*. As Figure 13.9 illustrates, the analyst may hand the designer a model in which the relationship between the **Teacher** and the **Student** is many-to-many: A teacher instructs many students and a student has many teachers. A close scrutiny, however, reveals that analysis has missed a major link in the chain: One teacher teaches one or more classes and one student participates in one or more classes. Thus, the **Class** class is the "natural" intersection that solves the many-to-many problem even *before* the time for database design arrives.

Self-Referencing Relationships

> A self-referencing relationship occurs when two or more entities of the same kind are related.

In the relational model, the relationships between tables are "flat": A foreign key signifies a relationship *in general*, not a specialized relationship such as ownership or hierarchy. These relationships, however, exist in the real world and the database design must accommodate them.

Figure 13.9 The "Natural" Many-to-Many: When the Intersection Exists in the Problem Domain

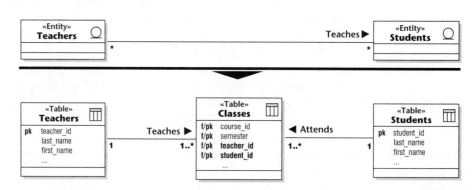

Relational databases cannot handle many-to-many relationships. Sometimes, however, the solution is right in the problem domain.

☞ The multiplicity in the "solution by intersection" may appear confusing because it is different from "the problem" and the "single-table" solution. The reason is that in a single-table solution, an employee exists regardless of whether the employee reports to anybody or supervises anybody. In the intersection table, if the employee does not supervise others, the employee does not appear as the **reports_to** foreign key (hence the **0..*** multiplicity on **Supervises** association), and if the employee does not report *to* anybody, then the employee does not appear as **emp_id** (hence the **0..1** multiplicity on the **Reports to** association).

In the real world—aptly called the problem domain in system analysis—we come across repeating problems, or patterns, such as organizational charts, directory structures, or chains of command in which entities of the same kind (employees, directories, or military personnel) have some kind of relationship with each other, often hierarchical. To design a solution for these recurring problems, the relational model offers two options: self-referencing tables and intersection tables.

We previously explained the intersection table. A self-referencing table is one in which the value of the *primary* key for one row can become the value of a *foreign* key in *another* row. It is a concept that can easily confuse us if a two-dimensional model (such as the one in the top part of Figure 13.10) is our only guideline. It may appear that the same entity, or object, is referring to *itself* (or "is chasing its own tail"). But it is more easily understood if we can imagine the same model in three dimensions, where a thread or a line (the foreign key) attaches one entity to another.

Figure 13.10 illustrates how this kind of relationship is modeled. As a class diagram, the only way to represent the relationship is to associate the class with itself: Many employees (or no employee) can report to one other employee. The table stereotypes provide two logical designs for the same conceptual class. In the first design, the same table represents the "reports to" relationship: The value of **emp_id** (primary key) for one employee can become the value of the **reports_to** (foreign key) of multiple employees. If an employee does not report to anyone, then the value of **reports_to** for that employee remains **null** (or "nothing"). If nobody reports *to* an employee, then the value of **emp_id** for that employee does not appear in any instance of **reports_to**.

In the second design, **reports_to** is removed to an intersection table and is combined with **emp_id** to form the primary key. If an employee does not report to anyone, then no row for that employee exists in the table.

A self-referencing table is acceptable (but only acceptable) if we are certain that the multiplicity between entities will remain one-to-one or one-to-many. If the multiplicity becomes many-to-many, then intersection tables provide the only solution. (In addition, allowing null values in key columns is considered by many to be a design weakness.)

Figure 13.10 Self-Reference: When the Same Kind of Entities Are Related

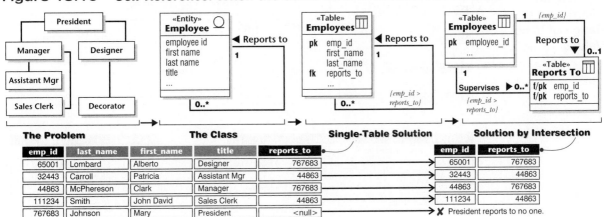

Intersection tables provide an effective solution to the problem of self-referencing tables.

Lookup Tables

> Lookup tables represent a range of valid values.

In database design, you will encounter the term "lookup table" repeatedly. Almost any table that has a foreign key in another table can be (and has been) called a lookup table: **Products** when entering **Order Items**, **States** when entering **Addresses**, etc. In short, the term often describes *how* a table is used, not *what* it is.

Here, however, we use the term narrowly: a lookup table defines and, often, describes a set of valid values for a given attribute. Earlier in this chapter, we defined "**domain**"—as used in data management—in the exact same terms. Rows in a lookup table do *not* correspond to entities (or objects), but represent a range of values for a *single* attribute in another table, enforced through a foreign key.

Figure 13.11 illustrates the concept in a simplified form. A questionnaire asks respondents to express their opinions on tax policy by selecting one of five options: no opinion, agree, strongly agree, disagree, and strongly disagree. The questionnaires may be presented online or on paper that is then scanned into the system. The responses are anonymous; therefore, each filled questionnaire is identified by an automatically generated number and stored in the **Responses** table.

The selection of each option for a question on the questionnaire results in a number in **Responses**: **0** for "no opinion," **1** for "strongly agree," and so on. Note that the **response** attribute in the table is actually a foreign key that constrains the values to rows in the **Response Range** table. If the application tries to assign a value to the **response** attribute that does not agree with the values of the primary key in the **Response Range** table, the DBMS raises an error.

A lookup table such as **Response Range** provides two additional benefits. First, it provides descriptions for *categorical* data items that are meaningless without descriptions. (As we explained earlier in this chapter, categorical

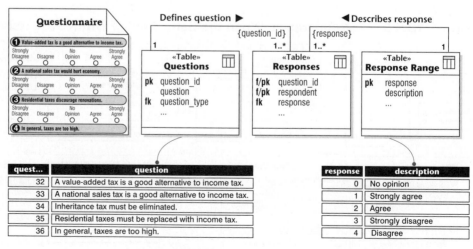

Figure 13.11 Lookup Tables: Identifying a Range of Valid Values

This is a simplified illustration of the scenario since it is likely that various groups of questions would have different ranges. (Hence the foreign key **question_type** in the **Questions** table.)

☞ The relationship between a lookup table and the attribute that it constrains is also known as **many-to-one** (*not* one-to-many), since many rows relate to just one column.

data are those that are meaningful only within a set: "hot," "cold," "freezing," etc.) Second, they are user-maintainable and, depending on the particulars of the situation, do not require changes to the database schema for changes to the range of values.

As beneficial as lookup tables are, one should not go to extremes in using them. A simple **YES/NO** attribute does not need a lookup table, and the total number of columns in a database is always a consideration.

Modeling the Relational Database

> The main modeling tool for modeling a relational database is the entity-relationship diagram.

The simplest form to use to represent a relation (table) is a function. The table's name is the name of the function (all caps), attributes are the arguments, primary keys are underlined (or double-underlined if alternate keys exist), and foreign keys are in italics:

> - TITLES (<u>title_id</u>, title, type, *pub_id*, price, pubdate, . . .)
> - AUTHORS (<u>author_id</u>, last_name, first_name, phone, . . .)
> - PUBLISHERS (<u>pub_id</u>, name, city, state, country, . . .)
> - TITLEAUTHOR (<u>*title_id*</u>, <u>*author_id*</u>, royalty_percent, . . .)

Such notation is quite useful if we are discussing individual tables within a textual narrative. The full modeling of a relational database's schema, however, requires the entity-relationship diagram (ERD). The name of the diagram is self-explanatory, but it is important to note that the emphasis of the diagram is on *entities* rather than on *tables*: It is really the entities that have attributes and relate to each other, even through they are represented as tables.

ERD is the most widely used tool for relational data modeling. Database development tools, whether independent or integrated into the DBMS, offer ERD for both forward and backward engineering: alterations to the diagram are automatically implemented in the database and changes to the database are immediately viewable in the ERD.

☞ Two notations for ERD are popular: Barker notation, put forward by Richard Barker in 1990, was originally adopted by Oracle. (Oracle now uses UML.) Information Engineering (IE) notation was promoted by James Martin and is supported by many tools. (But even for this single notation, no standard exists.)

[Halpin 2001, 316, 327]

Unlike UML diagrams, however, ERD does not have a unified notation. There are several notations in use, and the choice depends on the preferences of the vendor and/or the author. Fortunately, UML can handle the task efficiently: We have used UML throughout this chapter to illustrate our database examples.

Figure 13.12 shows two *physical* ER diagrams, each in a different notation. The right side of the diagram illustrates the four "books" tables in a notation that is proprietary to the Microsoft SQL Server. (See the "Second Normal Form" section earlier in this chapter for a UML version of the same diagram.) The attributes are identified by their "real" data types. Furthermore, any changes to the diagram will change the underlying tables and their relationships.

On the left side of the illustration is an ERD of four of Walden Hospital's tables in UML notation. By now, this diagram should be very familiar. Some explanation, however, will help in understanding the particulars:

- The ER diagram in UML is an adaptation of the *class diagram*. Tables correspond to classes in that they work as templates for entities: A row must provide

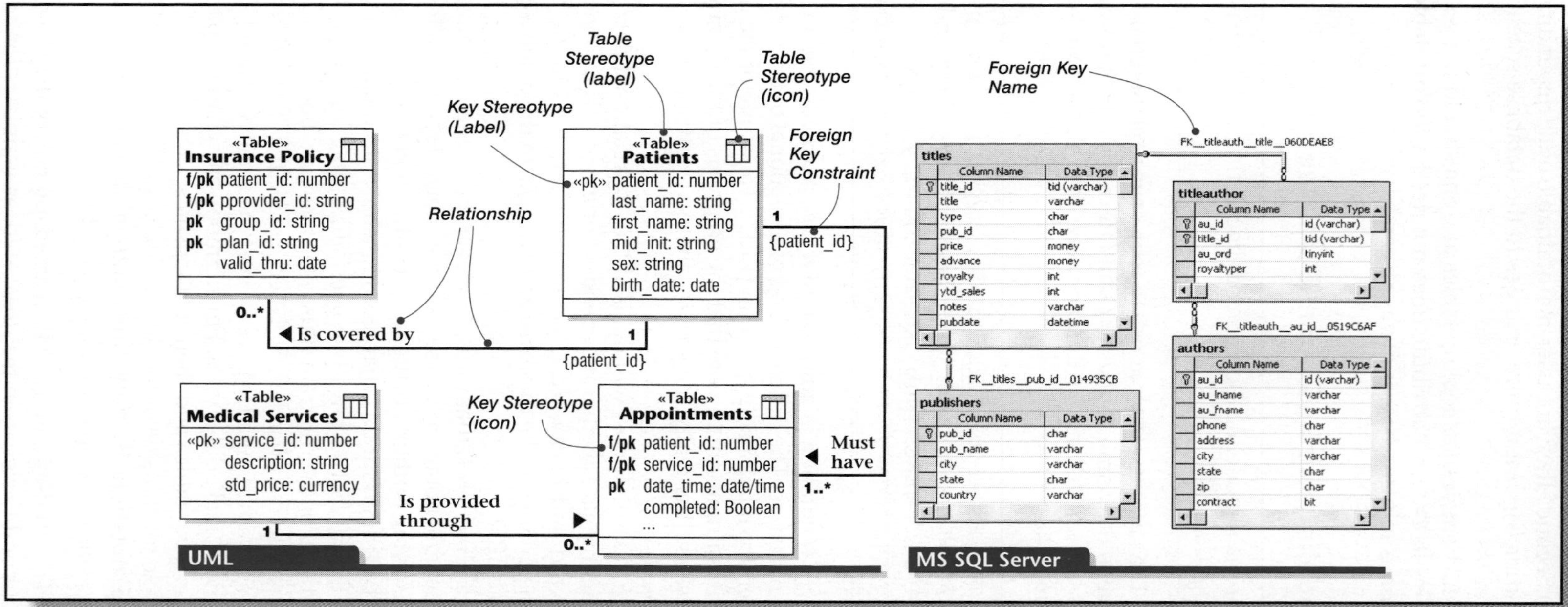

Figure 13.12 Entity-Relationship Diagram: One Model with Many Notations

values for the attributes that the table defines. However, tables are not instantiated the way classes are: In one database, every database operation—create, retrieve, update, or delete—works on the table itself, not on an "instance" of it. In another respect, and in a limited manner, tables can be compared to collection objects: They are collections of entities that are of the same kind.

- Tables have attributes, but not operations. Triggers (see the "Triggers" section earlier in this chapter) give the table a measure of dynamism, but triggers are private, not public. On the other hand, a collection of stored procedures is composed of operations, but lacks attributes. We must not overlook the fact that in working with a relational database, we are not working with virtual objects in an application, but with a database management *system.*

☞ See Chapter 10 for a discussion of **stereotypes** and other UML **extension mechanisms**.

- To distinguish an ER diagram from a normal class diagram, we should use *stereotypes* to prevent confusion. As Figure 13.12 and prior illustrations show, we should identify class boxes with stereotypes for «**Table**», «**View**», or «**SP Container**». (We can use a label for the stereotype, an icon, or both.) *All* modeling elements in UML can be stereotyped, including attributes and operations: «PK» for Primary Key, «FK» for Foreign Key, «SP» for Stored Procedure, or anything else.
- The association lines between boxes represent **foreign keys**, not any other object-oriented relationship such as aggregation or generalization. (See the "Mapping to the Relational Database" section later in this chapter.) It is a good practice to identify the foreign key on the association line with the UML notation for **constraint**: **{patient_id}**, for example, or **{author_id}**. If the name of the primary key in the first table does not correspond to the name of the foreign key in the second table, we can use the ">" symbol to denote the name change. For example, **{emp_id > reports_to}** means the primary key attribute is named **emp_id**, while the foreign key attribute is labeled **{reports_to}**. (See Figure 13.13).
- *Multiplicity* should always be specified. The UML's association line, by itself, is a simple line and does not indicate multiplicity. (Most other ERD notations indicate multiplicity by the shape of the line.)
- Other "*adornments*" such as a *direction arrow* and a *description* are very helpful in an ER diagram. Relationships between tables are mono-directional: from the table whose primary key provides the value, to the table whose foreign key accepts the value. Unfortunately, sometimes, coming up with a description for one direction is more difficult than for the other direction. If so, leave the description out. A model should make things easier to understand, not more difficult.
- Use any and all UML *extension mechanisms* that help you with the ER diagram. For example, even association lines can be specialized through stereotyping: The «**Optional**» stereotype means that the foreign key is optional and can remain "null." (Note, however, that such a stereotyped relationship is very different from **0..*** multiplicity. In an «**Optional**» relationship, a row may exist whose foreign key value is **NULL**. In a non-optional **0..*** multiplicity, if the row *does* exist, then the foreign key must have a valid value.)

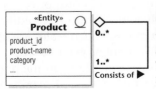

Figure 13.13
Self-Referencing Aggregation

This pattern, with many-to-many multiplicity, is very common and must be solved through an intersection table in the database.

4. Designing Persistence

Persistence design consists of two tasks: ❶ designing the database itself, and ❷ designing how the applications are to communicate with the database management system. In the preceding sections, we explored most of the basic concepts that are required to accomplish the first task. What remains is to view them, more strictly, from an object-oriented viewpoint and fill in some gaps.

The second task, relating applications, involves the design of a **persistence layer**, a logical component of the information system that mediates between applications and the DBMS.

Mapping to Relational Databases

> Mapping to a relational database is the application of relational and normalization rules to classes and their relationships.

Our discussion of the relational model started with its point of origin, when data and databases were not based on firm theoretical grounds. We should now move forward to the present, to the object-oriented era, and look at the relational model from our own vantage point.

Data, as we said, are values of attributes and, from an object-oriented viewpoint, variables are either attributes of objects or belong to the messages that the objects exchange with each other and with the outside world. If we have acquired an adequate grasp of both the relational and object-oriented models, then mapping one to another should not prove a difficult task.

We said "mapping one to another" because the mapping is not unidirectional: After you have created the database, the persistence layer must turn persisted data back into objects when required. And it is very likely that you will have to work with databases *not* designed by object-oriented designers.

The following are the general steps that should be followed to transform an object-oriented model into a relational one.

Classes

[Muller 1999, 343]

> Entity classes form the overwhelming majority of tables.

In the analysis section of this book, we focused on classes that result from analyzing the problem domain, classes such as **Patient**, **Invoice**, **Payment**, or **Appointment** that have, more or less, counterparts in the real world. The primary purpose of a database is to persist and safeguard the "state" of objects that are instantiated from these **entity** classes.

☞ See Chapters 10 through 12 for design classes and examples of control and boundary classes.

Design classes, introduced in this section, are usually not candidates for persistence. It is not necessary to save the "state" of *control* and *boundary* classes such as use case managers and forms. There are exceptions, of course. Many applications "remember" your recent actions—documents you have edited, for example—and allow you to change and save "user options." Such tables are different from application to application and their structure cannot be generalized.

It is worthwhile to emphasize the word "data" in the database. Tables do not have operations, *only attributes*. Therefore, if a class has only operations, it does not

☞ As we mentioned, naming tables can follow two equally persuasive but opposing guidelines. The first is that a table's name, like a class, must be singular since it represents individual entities. The other is that tables are collections of entities and, therefore, must have a plural name. We have followed the second approach to distinguish classes from tables. Both are, however, equally valid.

☞ We should reiterate that sometimes, for various reasons, we have to store data, such as totals, that are *not* normalized. In fact, a considerable part of **data warehousing** theory and practice is about how best to *de*normalize data for fast and reliable retrieval. The point is that denormalized data must be kept in tables that are separate from normalized tables. It is quite legitimate for a **Book** object to have a **year-to-date-sales** attribute, but wrong for a table that persists the data for a book title.

need a table. And it should not: Tables are only collections of data and need not have a behavior. When the application reconstructs objects from the data, then the objects will have their behavior back—very much like an application that recreates a movie from data on a DVD.

The list that results from selecting class candidates suggests one table per one class: a **Patients** table for the **Patient** class, a **Products** table for the **Product** class, a **Books** table for the **Book** class, etc. But this is likely to change as we go further.

Attributes

> Class attributes become table attributes (or columns).

The term "attribute" is shared between object-oriented and relational models, which should make the mental mapping more convenient. We must only remember that in the database, attributes refer to columns.

Logical database design does not need to specify physical data types. At some point, however, you must assign physical types to both sides of the equation and, frequently, physical types of object-oriented languages do not match those of the database. For example, the language might have a **Currency** type to handle reliable calculations where money is involved, but the database might lack such a type, or *vice versa*. To resolve such issues, application designers must work with database administrators, and many problems can be handled through stored procedures or the persistence layer.

As the rules for the third normal form (3NF) specify, **derived**, *dependent*, or *aggregate* attributes are not persisted. (Aggregate attributes are those that, like **year-to-date-sales**, return totals, averages, etc.) As a result, if the class is composed of only such attributes, it is deselected because it has nothing to persist.

The Primary Key

> A table must have a primary key.

A virtual object needs no *explicit* identifier: When a class is instantiated, the platform or the runtime environment keeps "pointers" to the instance that is safe until the object is destroyed. If you have a set of **Appointment** instances in the application, you can "loop" through them until you find the right one, regardless of whether the appointment has a unique identifier or not. As an entity in the table, however, the **Appointment** entity *must* have an explicit unique identifier.

The are two methods to assign a primary key. The first is to find an attribute or a set of attributes whose combined value makes an instance explicitly unique. You must, however, be confident that the candidate attributes ❶ always have a value because a primary key cannot be "null," and ❷ the attributes are not subject to (frequent) changes.

In a society where automation is widespread and is spreading even more, it is likely that some authority has already provided us with unique identifiers: stock symbols, Social Security Numbers, e-mail addresses, etc. These identifiers, however, must be used with caution. What if you are tracking the company in another market or in another country where its identifier is different? What if the emergency patient is comatose and has no ID, or is not American? What if the e-mail address changes?

Sometimes, the combination of attributes that are to compose the primary key is too long. A long primary key degrades the performance of the DBMS and is more likely to change. (A long primary key is also inconvenient to enter by hand.)

If your analysis of class attributes cannot identify an appropriate primary key, then you can ask the DBMS to create one for you. Such a (table) attribute is called an *identity column* and holds numbers that are usually created automatically. We are all familiar with such numbers: the myriad of account numbers that a person acquires when dealing with banks, online retailers, and phone companies (among others).

Selecting an "identity column" as the primary key is both convenient and inconvenient for the same reason: It is not likely to change because it is meaningless. *Because* of it, you must make a change to your classes: The ID must be added to the class; otherwise, the communication with the database will be disrupted. The application instantiates a class from the data in the database, but the database would not be able to save changes if the object lacks the identifier.

Repeating Attributes

Repeating attributes must be separated into tables.

In UML modeling, a class may have attributes that consist of repeating groups. An **Author** class can have a **books** attribute that lists all the books written by an author. (The notation for such an attribute is the name with an asterisk to its right to denote multiplicity—**books***, for example.) A diligent analysis frequently reveals that such repeating items are actually domain objects (a book certainly is) and deserve their own classes. Regardless of the reason, however, an object-oriented model allows repeating attributes and a relational model does not. Therefore, as was pointed out under "The First Normal Form," repeating attributes must be given their own tables.

Such a table must have its own primary key (unique identifier). Its relationship with the table that corresponds to the original class is established through a foreign key, as in any association.

Associations

Associations are mapped by primary-foreign key pairs.

Association is a structural relationship that defines the link between objects of one class with the objects of another class. To map this link to the database, the primary key of one table must become a foreign key in another table. (Like the primary key, a foreign key results in the addition of one more attribute to the *class*.) But which table must provide the primary key and which table must have the foreign key?

The answer depends on which class *defines* the other class. The **Patient** class defines the **Appointment** class. The **Author** class defines the **Book** class. Therefore, the **Patients** and the **Authors** tables provide the primary keys, while the **Appointments** and the **Books** tables "consume" it by providing the foreign keys. On the other hand, the **Country** class is *not* defined by **Patient** and, consequently, it is the **Countries** table that provides the primary key for the foreign key in the **Patients** table.

In this regard, the interface of the class might be misleading. If you look at the "Patient & Its Associations" class diagram in Chapter 8, you will notice that most of the classes (or rather objects) that are associated with **Patient** are exposed as attributes of the `Patient` class, as though it is *this* class that refers to associate classes and not the other way around. In the relational structure, it is often different: It is tables such as `Insurance Policies` and `Treatments` that must "know" about `Patients` through their foreign keys.

Multiple associations are identified by multiple foreign keys. `Treatments` must have foreign keys for the patient, the provider of the treatment, and the service (at least). In turn, the primary key of `Treatments` becomes one of the foreign keys in `Patient Billings`.

Multiplicity

> Multiplicity is mapped through foreign keys.

Except for many-to-many relationships, mapping class multiplicity to the relational model is straightforward:

- **One-to-one** multiplicity (1 to 1) is enforced by making the foreign key unique and *non*-optional (or required). In effect, a one-to-one relationship creates a second unique identifier, or an **alternate** key.
- **One-to-many** multiplicity (1 to 1..*) is enforced by making the foreign key *non*-unique but also non-optional. This includes multiplicities such as 1..3, 5..9, 10, and so on. In such cases, however, we must be aware that the standard RDBMS mechanisms will not work. Instead, we must rely on triggers and stored procedures to ensure that only a limited number of rows point towards only one entity in the defining table. (See the related topic in this chapter.)
- **Zero** on the source side (such as 0..1 to 1..*) is enforced by making the foreign key *optional*. In other words, the source table does *not* define the target table. For example, the author of a book may be unknown.
- **Zero** on the target side (such as 1 to 0..1 or 1 to 0..*) may appear like the previous case, but it is not: It does not mean an optional foreign key (one that can be left as **Null**), but the fact that no row may exist for a specific key value. If one does exist, however, a valid value is required. For example, a patient *must* have at least one appointment to be considered a patient, even if the appointment is later canceled. (At least that is the business rule that was stipulated.) On the contrary, a patient need not receive any treatments. But if the patient does receive a treatment, the `patient-id` foreign key in the `Treatments` table cannot be **Null**.
- **Many-to-many** multiplicity must be implemented through **intersection tables**, as we previously described. A row in an intersection table is defined by a primary key that is composed of foreign keys; therefore, the foreign keys cannot be "optional." On the other hand, the row is not required at all. As a result, if a certain number of rows *must* exist, the rules must be enforced through triggers and/or stored procedures, as the normal mechanisms of the database cannot enforce them.

Aggregation

> To map to a relational database, aggregation must be flattened into association.

The relational model is *flat*: Tables do not own each other and are not composed of each other. This means that aggregation and composition relationships must be changed to association to map to tables. The task is not complicated: The table for the aggregate class provides the primary key, the tables for aggregating classes implement the foreign keys, and the multiplicity stays the same. If an **Entertainment System** class consists of a **Sound System** and a **Video System**, the **Entertainment Systems** table provides the value for foreign keys in the other two tables. In turn, the **Sound System** table supplies the value for foreign keys in **Speakers**, **Tuners**, etc.

You should always, however, be on the lookout for **many-to-many** multiplicity, which often occurs with aggregation. With this kind of multiplicity, the solution is always an **intersection table**. In the student-teacher example that we explored before, a (school) **Class** object is really an aggregation of **Student** and **Teacher**. (See Figure 13.14.) Students may register for more than one class, and teachers may also teach more than one class. A one-column foreign key in **Students** or **Teachers** would not work.

A **self-referencing relationship** also occurs frequently with aggregation. (See Figure 13.13.) In the example for the entertainment system, the arrangement is problematic and wasteful—both in object-oriented and relational terms: It is an open-ended arrangement that forces us to add a class or a table for every product such as a DVD player, tape recorder, and so on. A better solution, in the object-oriented space, is to have one class, **Product**, that has a one-to-many aggregate relationship with itself. The solution for the database, as we discussed before, can be a self-referencing table (primary-foreign keys in the same table) or an intersection table (the preferred method).

Open-ended (or multi-level) aggregation is a well-known pattern when a business requires one of the following:

- *Bill of Material or Work Order.* A computer manufacturer offers many models, with options, that you can select and order online. Each computer has a motherboard, a chassis, a monitor, disk drives, etc. In turn, a motherboard has memory banks, a CPU, communication boards, and so on. Most components consist of other components and, what is more, they can be mixed and matched: The same product can participate in more than one aggregation.
- *Asset Management.* An enterprise may have many buildings, buildings may have many rooms, and rooms may house furniture and computers, but these items can be moved to other rooms or other buildings.

Inheritance

> In the inheritance chain, only classes with non-derived attributes are selected for mapping.

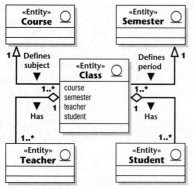

Figure 13.14
Inheritance and Aggregation

Class is an aggregate of **Student** and **Teacher**, but it also inherits features from **Course** and **Semester**. In the database, the relationships are mapped to the **Classes** table by one foreign key for each relationship.

Inheritance in an object-oriented space is a very important, and sometimes complicated, mechanism, but the rule for mapping *superclasses* and *subclasses* to a relational database is the same as for all other classes: If instances of a class do not have attributes, the values of which must be persisted, a corresponding table in the database is not required. If it does, then the table for the superclass provides the primary key, which is reflected in the table for the subclass as a foreign key.

Multiple inheritance follows the same rule: one primary-foreign key pair for each inheritance chain. (Many object-oriented languages do not allow multiple inheritance. Therefore, the issue may not arise at all.) Our example for (school) classes is interesting because **Class** is both an aggregate class and a subclass with *multiple* inheritance. (See Figure 13.14.) **Class** inherits its subject (Physics 201, for example) from **Course**, and its duration from **Semester**, but it is also an aggregate class that consists of **Teacher** and **Student**. In the database, the **Classes** table has four foreign keys: two for inheritance and two for aggregation.

The Persistence Layer

> The persistence layer is a set of components that manage the communication between the application and the DBMS.

If you read object-oriented literature extensively, you are likely to come across a guideline that, basically, tells you that objects must be responsible for their own database operations. This is well-meaning and politically correct advice, but it is misguided. (See the "Misguided Object Orientation" sidebar.) Undoubtedly, the spirit of object-orientation considers it a duty of objects to carry out their own responsibilities. The question is: Is it the right responsibility for the object? To arrive at the correct answer, we must consider the following points:

- Communication with a database is *complicated*: connect to the database, reestablish connection if lost, release the connection when the job is done, translate application messages to a format that is understandable by the DBMS, translate back query results to a format that can be understood by the application objects, switch between data sources if necessary, know the structure of the database, resolve security and privilege issues, and so on and so forth. Building such a complex functionality into individual objects is counterproductive. The spirit of object-orientation also guides us to manage complexity by specialization. "Divide and conquer," as we noted before.
- The *interface* of an object must not be confused with its private *functionality*. Even if an object has operations for CRUD (create, retrieve, update, and delete), it does not mean that the object itself must be responsible for carrying out such operations. An object can offer many services, but delegate *all* of them to other objects.
- An object cannot instantiate itself. To instantiate an object, another object must call a *constructor* method that often requires a set of values (ID, name, etc.). If these values are in the database (and frequently they are), then we would be trapped in a vicious circle: The object must retrieve data to instantiate, but it cannot instantiate because it cannot retrieve data.
- In any serious information system, data management requires **transaction processing**. (See the related topic earlier in this chapter.) This means that database operations cannot be left to individual objects, but must span a set of objects. If you look at our example for stored procedures earlier in this chapter, you will

notice that telling an **Order Item** object to "save yourself"—regardless of every other object and regardless of the required sequence of events—can wreak havoc with the core business of the enterprise.

Operations that require interaction with the database must be undertaken by two sets of objects: *control* objects that know when and how to request a service, and a specialized category of *boundary* objects that handle communication with the database. The latter objects are known, collectively, as the **persistence layer**.

☞ See Chapters 10 and 11 for a discussion of control and boundary objects.

The persistence layer is an architectural component that is basically *conceptual*, meaning that the same concept can be translated into different logical and physical designs, depending on the experience and the preferences of the designer and on technological considerations.

In the models in the previous chapters on application design, the focus of our discussions was on control, flow, and user interface. Therefore, we used simple "placeholder" objects to represent the persistence layer. The class diagram in Figure 13.15 depicts a persistence class, **Order Persistence**, that is responsible for managing database operations for instances of two entity (business) classes, **Order** and **Order Item**. (The illustration does not show other design classes for user interface, flow, and control that would be necessary in an application.)

Order Persistence is the only class that is responsible for "knowing" the DBMS and the complexities of the database schema. For example, when the **Place Order** method (that handles *new* orders) is invoked, the **Order Persistence** takes the following steps: connects to the database, starts a transaction, collects "persistable" data from the **Order** instance, sends a request to the DBMS to create a row in the **Orders** table (by composing an SQL statement or invoking a stored procedure), gets the new **order id** from the database, relays **order id** to the **Order** object, for each **Order Item** conducts a similar set of operations and, if everything goes well, commits the transaction and informs the application of success. (If something goes wrong, it rolls back the transaction and relays the problem to the application.)

The **Search Items** operation is no less complex. A modest set of search criteria may result in a wide variety of SQL statements or in calls to various stored procedures. Each statement or call, in turn, requires an intimate knowledge of the structure and/or the interface of the database. In fact, if the complexity of the search goes beyond a certain point, **Order Persistence** may have to delegate it to yet another

**Figure 13.15
Persistence
Objects:
Specialized for
Handling
Database
Operations**

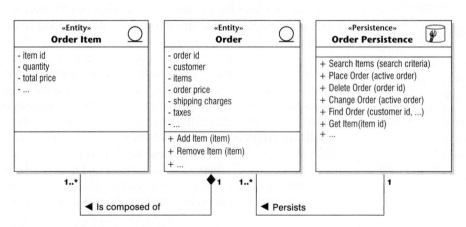

By delegating database operations to persistence objects, entity objects retain their simplicity and clarity.

object. (See the illustration for "Complex Search" in Chapter 11, an abridged version of the **DVD Search** page in Amazon.com.)

Another advantage of persistence objects is *isolation*: protecting entity objects and other components of the application from changes in the database. To generalize:

Entity objects should not be made responsible for tasks that are closely linked to technology, neither should design objects overstep the bounds of technology for which they are specialized.

For example, the enterprise may decide to switch from one DBMS to another. If database operations are encapsulated in one layer that is composed of specialized classes, then making changes to that layer would be enough to implement the switch, thus avoiding the need to perform surgery on entity or other objects. In our example in Figure 13.15, **Order** and **Order Items** are not affected, in any way, by whether the information system relies on Oracle, SQL Server, DB2, or even a Web service. These objects are only responsible for what they must be responsible for: orders, customers, items, taxes, etc. (And if you "normalize" them by factoring out derived attributes, they are rather simple—which is good.)

Serialization

Serialization is encoding the values of an object's attributes into a sequential stream.

When you complete a questionnaire for employment or for your medical history, you are "serializing" yourself, or rather your "state," from a specific perspective. This serialized portrait of you can be archived for later reference or can be transmitted to others to reconstruct your profile and make a decision: grant you a job or recommend a medical treatment.

This is what serialization is about: persisting the state—the overall condition—of an object in a sequential stream that can be used to reconstruct the state of an object later. When the application wants to save an object to the database, it must first serialize the object and transmit the resulting stream to the database. Then, when it wants to reconstruct the object, it must *de-serialize* it from data in the database.

Serialization streams take many formats: text strings, SQL strings, delimited files, etc. Until fairly recently, there was neither a standard nor a great market demand for such a standard: information systems and applications lived within inward-looking settlements that found no need to communicate with each other. As long as the language of a format was understandable within one enclosed community, it was good enough.

The onslaught of the Internet and the Web has changed the landscape. Communicating with dissimilar systems across the Web has become a necessity with compelling benefits and, since exchanging data is the primary purpose of this communication, settling on a standard (or a set of standards) has turned into an urgent necessity as well.

This role has been settled on **XML** (Extensible Markup Language). XML is *not* a language in the conventional sense—such as French for human communication or Java for computer programming—but a *markup* language: a syntax for encoding data that explains how the content of the stream is to be understood.

Figure 13.16 presents an XML sample that encodes data about an order, its line items, and the products to which the order items refer. Even though the code is more or less human readable, its purpose is transmitting data between machines, not between people. By de-serializing the stream, a different system,

Figure 13.16   Serialization: A Mechanism for Transporting Values

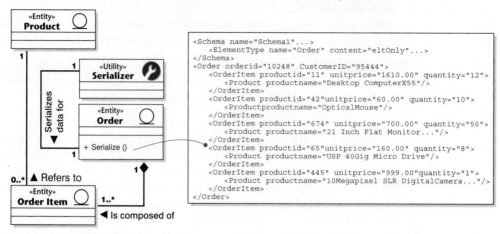

In this example, the state of **Order** objects is serialized into an XML stream. Serialized streams, however, are not limited to XML.

built on a different technology, can reconstruct the **Order**, **Order Item**, and **Product** objects, perhaps for issuing invoices.

XML is also *extensible*, meaning that its vocabulary can be extended to accommodate new requirements. In the same illustration, for example, the first few lines are a mini-dictionary (much abridged in our sample) describing the "schema" of the XML document. The same extensibility has allowed XML to be combined with other languages—both markup and procedural. SQL/XML is a merger with SQL and XHTML is a W3C (World-Wide Web Consortium) standard that combines XML with Hypertext Markup Language, the presentation language of the Web.

XML can accommodate both structured and unstructured data, and this capability makes it an attractive tool for Web applications. Major development tools and major DBMSs, such as Oracle and SQL Server, support XML, but in varying degrees and in varying formats, which makes some aspects of the "standards" a work in progress. This is to be expected, however: XML is hoped to be the ultimate data carrier, handling every kind of structured and unstructured data. (And since the market demands it, the vendors have shown a high degree of cooperation and flexibility to arrive at standards.)

XML or not, serialization is something that has to be done. The question is: Which component of the application should be responsible for performing the task? There is no *de facto* standard, but a few equally good patterns exist. Figure 13.16 presents one pattern: objects do their own serializing because they know best what they "know." In our example, the **Order** object serializes its own state *and* the state of the **Order Item** objects that compose it (including the product name from the **Product** object from which an order item is descended). Since serialization is somehow technology-dependent, the actual task is done by a utility object, **Serializer**, which is told by **Order** what to serialize through a set of messages. (If the serialization format or technology changes, we would have to modify the **Serializer** class, but not the order class.)

One shortcoming of this pattern is that individual entity objects are self-centered: They know about themselves, but not others. If a collection of orders is to be serialized—not a rare situation—then it is better to assign the responsibility to a collection object, **Orders** for example, to a life cycle object, **Order Manager** perhaps, or the persistence object, **Order Persistence** (which we introduced previously).

5. DELIVERABLES

In a sizable development project, the design of the database and the design of the persistence layer are seldom done by the same person or even the same team. Application developers must satisfy application requirements by designing boundary classes (the **persistence layer**), while database designers must produce **entity-relationship diagrams** that model the schema of the database.

Both groups must work closely together. There are, however, two potential stumbling blocks. The first is both conceptual and technological: Software developers think in terms of objects, while database designers tend to focus on data management and its technological requirements. The second stumbling block results from a divergence in goals: Application developers are concerned with the performance and the features of the application under development, while database designers need to concentrate on the more abstract—but bigger—picture of the whole information system and the enterprise.

This need for effective communication between unlike groups increases the need for modeling in database design. Although stored procedures and views can cushion the effects of later corrections to the database schema, they cannot protect the application from *all* disruptions due to defective design. Especially for database design, a minimum amount of upfront modeling can prevent severe problems later.

6. WRAP UP

☑ **Data and data management**

Data are values of variables. Variables, as the name implies, are containers, the value of which change. In an object-oriented context, variables are either attributes of objects or parameters in messages that they exchange with each other or with the outside world.

Data are abstract values, but they can be classified in relation to each other and to their contexts. Data can be either quantitative or qualitative, discrete or continuous, categorical or non-categorical, ordinal or nominal, structured or unstructured, independent or dependent (or derived). An automated information system can process only quantitative and discrete data. This means that qualitative or continuous data must be associated with values that are quantitative and discrete before they can be processed by such a system.

Data management is a crucial subsystem of most information systems. Its main task is storing and organizing data in a manner that satisfies the needs of the information system as a whole and the applications individually.

☑ **Database management systems**

A database is an organized collection of data and a database management system (DBMS) is a system that administers such a collection *for* the information system. At the very least, a DBMS must be able to carry out the following operations: create new entries in the database, retrieve (find and read) data as required by the applications, update (change) existing entries, and delete unwanted data.

An advanced DBMS, however, must do more than these basic operations; it must present an interface that encapsulates (hides) its internal structure, it must offer a high-level language for data management, and it must safeguard the integrity and the security of data.

☑ **The relational model and its major components**

The most successful DBMS model in present-day information systems is the relational model that was introduced before object-oriented technologies. A relational DBMS, by hiding the physical structure of data, presents a logical view of the database organization and provides the basis for using a high-level language for database management.

In the relational model, a **table** is the basic organizational unit for data. A table is a rectangular and flat arrangement of data, composed of **attributes** or columns, and **entities** or rows. The intersection of a column and a row is known as a **cell**. A **primary key** is an attribute or a set of attributes whose values uniquely identify a row. In addition, an entity may have other unique identifiers known as **alternate** or **candidate keys**.

The relationship between entities in different tables is established through **foreign keys**. The foreign key is an attribute in one table, the value of which must match the value of a primary or an alternate key in another table. Unlike primary keys, foreign keys are not required and do not, necessarily, identify a row uniquely. Like primary keys, a foreign key can be a composite, consisting of more than one attribute.

☑ **Database mechanisms that safeguard data integrity**

In the context of data management, data integrity is about consistency, correctness, and accuracy. A relational DBMS protects data integrity at four levels: **column** (or attribute), **row** (or entity), **inter-table**, and **procedural**.

Attribute integrity is ensured by *type definition*, by **foreign keys**, and by **constraints**. This last one consists of **domain** and **check** constraints. A domain is a set of allowable values for a given attribute. Check constraints are conceptually the same as domains but, unlike domains, apply to individual tables, whereas domains are reusable. **Assertions** are rules that go beyond single attributes or single tables.

Entity integrity is assured by the primary key: One, and only one, entity within a table can be identified by a specific value (or combination of values) in the primary key. Inter-table integrity is called **referential integrity** and is implemented by enforcing the constraints of foreign keys. Dependency between tables, established through foreign keys, is bi-directional and the designer can control the behavior of referential integrity by setting **cascading rules**.

Procedural integrity is used when the relationships among entities are too complex for the other mechanisms. The main tools of procedural integrity are **triggers**, **stored procedures**, and **transaction processing**. A transaction is a set of database operations that must succeed as a set: If one operation fails, then the whole transaction must be "rolled back."

☑ **SQL**

SQL is the primary language for communication with relational DBMSs. It allows the designer to create tables, enables users and applications to perform CRUD (create, retrieve, update, and delete) operations, permits database administrators to specify security and privileges, coordinates multi-user operations, and provides the designers with tools to ensure data integrity.

☑ **Encapsulating data management: views, stored procedures and triggers**

Encapsulation and information hiding are the hallmarks of an object-oriented approach: An entity must offer its services through a public *interface* but keep its inner workings private. The advantage of the relational model over its predecessors—exposing a logical view of data instead of physical one—serves object-orientation well, but it is not sufficient. Data management is not merely about data organization and maintenance, but also about data security, data integrity, enforcing business rules, and providing data-related services for various applications of the information system.

Three mechanisms in modern database management systems provide tools that we can employ to encapsulate data services, to enforce business rules, and to protect data security and integrity: views, stored procedures, and triggers.

A **view** is a *virtual table* that represents a selected set of attributes from one or more tables. Views can be used to hide the complexities of the logical view by providing "perspectives" that are tailored to various requirements *without* affecting or exposing the underlying structure of the database.

A **stored procedure** is a *named* set of (predominantly SQL) statements that allow data-related tasks to be performed from within the database itself. Stored procedures are similar to *methods* that objects provide to the outside world: They hide the complexity of operations and expose only the functionality that the users of the database need.

A trigger is a procedure that is executed when data within a table is altered through adding, deleting, or changing entities. Triggers are similar to stored procedures, except that they are completely *hidden*. Since no user or no application can bypass triggers, they also provide an effective mechanism for ensuring data integrity. (*Because* they are hidden, however, they can create an invisible tangle.)

☑ **The concept and the rules of data normalization**

Data normalization is a set of guidelines, techniques, and concepts to fine-tune a relational database by establishing logical relationships among attributes and tables and by removing redundancies that impede effective data management and harm data integrity. They are several normalized "forms" that a table can belong to, three of which are essential for a well-designed **schema** (as the structural model of a database is called).

A table is in first normal form (**1NF**) if it contains no repeating groups. It is in second normal form (**2NF**) if it is in first normal form and every non-key attribute is *fully* dependent on the *entire* primary key. Finally, a table is in third normal form (**3NF**) if it is in second normal form and no non-key attribute is dependent on another non-key attribute.

Normalization, however, should not be applied blindly. Several factors, including logical considerations, technological constraints, and performance issues may require the designer to denormalize certain attributes or tables.

☑ **Intersection tables and the issues they address**

An intersection table represents the relationship between two different entities. In an object-oriented space, objects can have **many-to-many** relationships with each other—regardless of whether they are instances of the same class (self-referencing) or not. In the relational model, this is not possible.

In a relational database, many-to-many relationships must be converted to one-to-many relationships through intersection tables. In an intersection table, the primary key is usually composed of foreign keys, provided by entities whose relationship is embodied in the table. Besides, the number of *non-key* attributes are often limited.

A **self-referencing relationship** occurs when two or more entities of the same kind are related. If the relationship is one-to-one or one-to-many, the issue can be resolved by establishing a foreign key from the primary key of the same table. Still, the intersection table is the preferred method.

☑ **Lookup tables**

A lookup table defines and, often, describes a set of valid values for a given attribute. Rows in a lookup table do *not* correspond to entities (or objects), but represent a range of values for a *single* attribute in another table, enforced through a foreign key. Lookup tables also can provide descriptions for categorical data items that are meaningless without descriptions. Optionally, they can be maintained by users.

☑ **The entity-relationship diagram (ERD)**

The entity-relationship diagram is the primary tool for modeling a relational database. As the name implies, an ERD presents the properties of entities and the inter-relationships. Unlike UML diagrams, however, ERD does not have a unified notation. UML, fortunately, provides an efficient mechanism that can be used to depict entity-relationship and many other diagrams: *stereotyping*, or the specialization of modeling elements. Through stereotyping, *class diagrams* can model the schema of a database: attributes, tables, primary and foreign keys, multiplicity, relationships, and stored procedures.

☑ **Mapping to relational databases**

Mapping objects to a relational database is the application of relational and normalization rules to classes and their relationships. The process of analyzing and designing an object-oriented information system should result in classes that already have the essential structural format that we need for mapping to an RDBMS: attributes that are fused with an entity. What remains is, mostly, converting the relationships among classes—association, multiplicity, inheritance, aggregation, and composition—into primary-foreign key pairs or, where it is warranted, into intersection tables.

☑ **Persistence layer & serialization**

Database management systems are complex subsystems of the information system. Communication with them requires specialized knowledge of the DBMS and the schema, or the structure, of the database. The persistence layer is a set of components that manages the interaction between the application and the DBMS. In a well-designed application, only *boundary* objects that are specialized for handling persistence should be allowed to communicate with the database.

Persistence—saving the state of objects—requires serialization, encoding data into a sequential stream. This stream can then be communicated to the database or to other clients, and can be *de-serialized* later to reconstruct objects. A serialized stream can take many formats, including **XML**, which is fast becoming the standard and can manage both structured and unstructured data.

7. KEY CONCEPTS

1NF (First Normal Form).   A table is in first normal form if it contains no repeating groups.

2NF (Second Normal Form).   A table is in second normal form if the table is in first normal form and every non-key attribute is *fully* dependent on the *entire* primary key.

3NF (Third Normal Form).   A table is in third normal form if the table is in second normal form and no non-key attribute is dependent on another non-key attribute.

Alternate Key. A key that uniquely identifies an entity (**row**) in a table, other than the one chosen as the **primary key**. An alternate key may be simple (one **attribute**) or **composite** (multiple attributes). Alternate keys are also known as **candidate keys**.

Assertion. Similar to a **check constraint** but can take into account multiple columns in multiple tables.

Attribute. In a relational database, defines the characteristics of a table **column**.

Attribute, Derived. An attribute, the value of which is derived from another attribute, called **determinant**. Derived attributes are (usually) not persisted.

Attribute, Determinant. An attribute, the value of which determines the value of another attribute, called **derived**.

Candidate Key. See **Alternate Key**.

Cascading Rules. Specify how database operations that affect a primary key are "cascaded" to (or affect) related entities through foreign keys.

Cell. The intersection of a **row** and a **column** in a table.

Check Constraint. A range of allowable values for a specific column in a specific table. Unlike **domains**, check constraints cannot be reused.

Column. The vertical organization of a **table**. A column is also referred to as an **attribute**. All data under a column must have the same characteristics.

Composite Key. Any key—**primary**, **foreign**, or **alternate**—that is composed of more than one attribute.

Constraint. Limit put on the allowable values for a column by data type, by foreign keys, and/or by **domains**.

CRUD. An acronym referring to operations that can be performed on data: **C**reate, **R**etrieve, **U**pdate, and **D**elete.

Data. Values of a **variable**. Data can be facts or assumptions.

Data, Analog. Data that results from measuring physical, real-world quantities. Automated information systems must **sample** analog data into **digital** data before they can process it.

Data, Categorical. Data that has significance only within the context of a set.

Data, Continuous. A stream of values that gradually change into each other with no discernable breaks between them. Automated information systems must rely on **sampling** to process continuous data.

Data, Digital. Data that is expressed in digits, suitable for processing by automated information systems. Digital data in modern computers are *binary*, composed of zeros and ones.

Data, Discrete. A finite set of values that are distinct from each other.

Data, Nominal. Data that does not follow an obvious order, such as gender. See also **Data, Ordinal**.

Data, Non-Categorical. Data that is meaningful by itself, without having to compare it with other values in a set.

Data, Ordinal. Data that belong to an *ordered* set, such as school grades. See also **Data, Nominal**.

Data, Qualitative. Data that cannot be measured, unless a measurable value is assigned to it. Value judgments such as "good," "bad," or "excellent" are qualitative data.

Data, Quantitative. Data that can be measured.

Data, Structured. Data with a predictable organization, as opposed to **unstructured** data.

Data, Unstructured. Data with an unpredictable organization, as opposed to **structured** data.

Data Definition Language (DDL). A language, such as **SQL**, that defines the structure of the database, including attributes, tables, and their relationships.

Data Integrity. Keeping data in a state that ensures consistency, correctness, and accuracy.

Data Management. Storing and organizing data in a manner that can satisfy the needs of the information systems and its components.

Data Manipulation Language. A specialized language, such as **SQL**, for communicating with the **DBMS** and performing data operations.

Data Normalization. The "process of establishing an optimal table structure based on the internal data dependencies." There are several levels of normalization. (See also **1NF**, **2NF**, and **3NF**.)

Data Type. The type of data that a column can accept, such as numeric, date, Boolean, or string. Physical data types depend on the specific DBMSs.

Database. An organized collection of data.

Database, Distributed. A database that is logically unified, but physically resides on more than one device.

Database, Server. ❶ A collection of databases that share one physical space. ❷ A dedicated computer for a DBMS.

Database Drivers. Specialized applications, or utilities, that carry and/or translate messages between applications and the database management system.

DBMS. Database Management System. A product that encapsulates and carries out the responsibilities of data management. A DBMS is a subsystem of the information system, but has a strong identity.

DBMS, Hierarchical. A model in which data records are organized as "master" or "detail" collections.

DBMS, The Network Model. A model in which the database is a collection of files, a file is an ordered collection of entries, and entries consist of keys and data.

DBMS, Object-Oriented. A DBMS model that aims to make persistence transparent to object-oriented languages.

DBMS, Relational. A model that hides the physical structure of data, represents a logical view of the database organization, and provides the basis for using a high-level language for database management. In a relational database, data are organized as **tables** (or *relations*).

Denormalization. A process that reverses **data normalization**. It may be necessary due to technological constraints, performance degradation, or other considerations.

Domain. In database management, the allowable range of values for an attribute. A domain is a kind of **constraint** that can be *reused* since it is not tied to any specific table or column.

Entity. In the relational model, a specific "thing"—an object, an event, or even a relationship—for which data is stored in **rows**.

Entity-Relationship Diagram (ERD). The primary tool for modeling the schema of a relational database. It has many notations but fits comfortably with UML as a "stereotyped" class diagram.

Foreign Key. An **attribute** in one table, the value of which must match the value of the **primary** or the **alternate** key in a different table. Unlike primary or alternate keys, a foreign key can be *optional*, meaning that its value can be **null**.

Indexed Sequential Access Method (ISAM). A **sequential access method** in which the performance of data operations is improved by storing indices or "keys" to data records.

Intersection Table. Represents the relationship between two different entities (or tables). Also called a *junction* or *resolution* table. Intersection tables are used to solve issues arising from **self-referencing tables** and **many-to-many relationships**.

Lookup Table. A table that represents a range of valid values, usually with descriptions, for a specific attribute in another table. The target attribute is defined as a foreign key that refers back to the primary key of the lookup table.

Many-to-Many Relationship. A relationship between two tables when many entities in one table can relate to many entities in the other table. Such a relationship must be resolved through **intersection tables**.

Many-to-One Relationship. Actually the same as a **one-to-many relationship**, but used to specifically describe the relationship between one attribute and a **lookup table**.

Metadata. Data about data. Metadata describe not the **variable** itself, but the characteristics of data that the variable may contain.

Null. Represents a *lack* of data. Nothing. Null must not be confused with zero.

Object-Relational Mapping (ORM). A software layer that mediates between object-oriented languages and relational DBMSs.

One-to-Many Relationship. A relationship where one entity in a table is related to many entities in another table.

One-to-One Relationship. A relationship where one row in a table is related only to one row in another table.

Persistence. Saving the **state** of objects to a "persistent" form, usually to a database.

Persistence Layer. A set of components or boundary objects that manage the interaction between the application and the database.

Primary Key. An **attribute** or a set of attributes, the value of which uniquely identifies a **row**.

Procedural Integrity. Assuring complex data integrity requirements through procedural code. **Triggers**, **stored procedures**, and **transaction processing** are the various forms that procedural integrity can take.

Procedure. A named sequence of programming statements. Also called *function*, *method*, *routine*, or *subroutine*.

Query. The request, in a high-level language such as **SQL**, issued to the database for retrieving data. The data returned by the database is called *query results* or the *result set*.

Referential Integrity. Safeguarding inter-table references established through foreign keys.

Row. The horizontal organization of data in a **table**, also known as a *tuple*. A row is a collection of data for a specific **entity** as defined by **columns**.

Sampling. Selection of values from a stream of data. The higher the sampling rate, the more accurate is the data.

Schema. The structural model of a database.

Self-Referencing Relationship. Occurs when two or more entities of the same kind are related. Such a relationship is sometimes implemented by creating a foreign key from the primary key in the *same* table. **Intersection tables**, however, provide a better structure.

Sequential Access Method (SAM). A method in which data is grouped in records that are stored and retrieved serially.

Serialization. Encoding data into a sequential stream.

SQL. Commonly interpreted as Structured Query Language, the primary language for communicating with relational database management systems.

State. The aggregation of values for the independent attributes of a particular object at a specific point in time.

Stored Procedure. A named set of **SQL** statements that provides the capability of performing database-related tasks from within the database itself.

Table. The basic organizational unit of a relational database. A table consists of horizontal **rows** and vertical **columns** (or **attributes**).

Transaction. A set of database operations that must succeed as a set.

Transaction Processing. Controlling the flow of a **transaction** by issuing the following commands: begin transaction, rollback transaction (some action failed), and commit transaction (everything succeeded).

Transactional Object. An entity object that occurs as a result of a transaction between two independent objects.

Trigger. A procedure executed as a result of a database event (insert, delete, or update).

Variable. Something the value of which is subject to change. Object attributes are variable, as are parameters (or arguments) exchanged between objects. The value of an *independent* variable does not depend on the value of other variables, while the value of a *dependent* variable changes if the value of some other variable is altered. (See also **Attribute, Determinant**.)

Variable, Derived. A variable the value of which is calculated from the values of other variables.

View. A virtual table that represents a selected set of attributes from one or more tables. Views lack keys and their updatability depends on the query that creates them.

XML. Extensible Markup Language. A language widely used for the **serialization** of data.

8. CONFUSING CONCEPTS

Domain. In system analysis and design, domain means a space where similar rules apply. In database design, however, it means a range of allowable values. In this sense, domain is a **constraint**.

Field. Field is a general-purpose term, used extensively with many varied meanings. In database design, it is synonymous with **attribute**, even though the relational model discourages its use to distinguish itself from earlier database management models.

9. REVIEW QUESTIONS

1. Distinguish the following data as discrete or continuous. Explain why.

   a. Temperature.
   b. Speed.
   c. Number of orders.
   d. Age.
   e. Weight.
   f. Price.
   g. Count.

2. Distinguish the following data as qualitative and quantitative. Explain why.

   a. Social Security Number.
   b. Zip Code.
   c. Degree of job satisfaction.
   d. Price.
   e. Age.
   f. Effectiveness.
   g. Compatibility.

3. Compare distributed databases to database servers.
4. What does "integrity" mean in the context of data management?

5. Provide examples for sequential access, both real and virtual.
6. Briefly explain the main differences among hierarchical, network, and relational databases.
7. Describe object-relational mapping. What are the required steps?
8. Describe primary and foreign keys. How do they differ?
9. How is the concept of encapsulation applied to database management?
10. Describe triggers. Discuss their advantages and disadvantages.
11. Explain the difference between physical and logical schemas.
12. Discuss why, in a relational database, first normal form is necessary. Is it sufficient to reduce redundancy? Why?
13. How do we map inheritance to a relational database? Describe the roles of primary and foreign keys in mapping.

10. EXERCISES

The following exercises apply to each of the four narratives introduced in Chapter 4: *The* Sportz *Magazine*, *The Car Dealership*, *The Pizza Shop*, and *The Real Estate Agency*.

❶ For any of these case studies identify *persistent classes*. Select one that you have worked on more thoroughly because, to design the database, you will need all the information about the system that you can get.

❷ Identify **intersection tables**—if any. Hint: Intersection tables usually result from many-to-many relationships between objects.

❸ Identify **lookup tables**—if any.

❹ If you have discovered **self-referencing** classes, decide how to map them to the database. (If you do not remember, read the relevant part of the chapter again.)

❺ Create one or more **entity-relationship diagrams** for all the tables that you have identified in the exercises above. (Never overcrowd individual diagrams.) Are there any *design classes* among those that must be persisted? Why (yes or no)?

11. RESEARCH PROJECTS & TEAMWORK

❶ Research a relational DBMS product and an object-oriented DBMS product. Compare their features in a short paper. Can you find the installed base of each product? If one is more popular than the other, why?

❷ Review classes that have resulted from the analysis and design of the online registration system for Walden Medical College (Chapter 4). Determine which objects belonging to which classes must be **persisted**. ("Persist," as you know by now, means saving the state of an object.) Define *detail attributes*, the values of which must be saved to the database—for example, first name, last name, address, etc., for the **Student** object. In a team session, compare your findings and elaborations. Why some classes and not the others?

☞ You can select any of the scenarios that, up to now, you have been working on. However, confirm the selection both with your team and your instructor. By comparing and contrasting various solutions to the same problem, you will appreciate the challenge of design more deeply.

❸ Map the *same* classes that you identified in the previous exercise to a *relational model*. (Usually you will end up with more tables than classes, especially when **intersection tables** are required or classes are **self-referencing**.) Present your design as an **entity-relationship diagram**. In a team session, compare and discuss the diagrams created by individual team members. If problems in mapping prove daunting, see if you can find the answer on the Web—before asking the instructor.

❹ *Capacity planning* for the database is a subject that we did not discuss in this chapter, largely because it is an *engineering* problem and to a great degree depends on specific technologies. However, in terms of storage, some designs are more wasteful than others. Review entity-relationship diagrams created by the team and discuss which one saves more space. (One factor: The higher the chances of missing data in a column are, the more likely it is that space would be wasted.) Remember, however, that efficient use of space is only one factor.

12. SUGGESTED READINGS

Books on database design, even very good books, are many. Due to the very specialized nature of database design and the prevalence of relational databases, however, the majority of the books are either about relational database design and SQL, or focus on one specific DBMS such as Oracle, SQL Server, and other commercial products.

Early UML literature mostly ignored persistence and database design. Fortunately, this omission is being remedied. *Database Design for Smarties: Using UML for Data Modeling* by **Robert J. Muller** (Morgan Kaufmann, San Francisco, 1999) is a comprehensive book that guides the reader through the most important concepts of database design as they relate to object orientation and the Unified Modeling Language. What makes the

book especially recommendable is its critical approach: The writer is not satisfied with echoing existing conventional wisdom or, worse, commercial hype.

UML for Database Design by **Eric J. Naiburg** and Robert A. Maksimchuk (Addison-Wesley, Boston, 2001) is a slimmer, more introductory treatment of UML and database design, though every concept in the book is supported by detailed diagrams.

Information Modeling and Relational Database: From Conceptual Analysis to Logical Design by **Terry Halpin** (Morgan Kaufmann, San Francisco, 2001) is an exhaustive book that is highly technical and focuses on object-oriented modeling, but does not shortchange the reader on the treatment of relational concepts.

Chapter

14

Patterns

1. OVERVIEW

A pattern provides the core of the solution to a problem. This chapter discusses patterns in general and presents examples that apply to different activities of software development.

- ☑ Inception
- ☑ Requirements Discovery
- ☐ Development
  - ☑ Analysis
  - ☐ Design
    - ☑ The Design Challenge
    - ☑ Application Design
    - ☐ **Patterns** ◀
    - ☐ Components & Reuse
    - ☐ Architecture
  - ☐ Implementation

Chapter Topics

- ➤ Concepts of pattern and pattern language.
- ➤ Design patterns.
- ➤ Analysis patterns.
- ➤ Modeling patterns.
- ➤ Anti-patterns.

Introduction

There is one theme to which this book has often returned: Solving problems involves not a *pair* but a *trio* of components—problem, solution-as-method (or how), and solution-as-answer (or what). In the previous chapters on design, we presented an object-oriented methodology on *how* to arrive at solutions. In a real development project, depending on the complexity of the problems that the information system must solve, designing the solution can be long, arduous, risky, expensive, and frustrating. But what if somebody, somewhere, has encountered the same problem or problems and can suggest solutions that would save you time and resources? In other words, what if you could bypass most of the solution-as-method and arrive, quickly, at solution-as-answer?

Nobody, of course, can hand you a blueprint for the entire design of your project: Some components of a system may resemble each other, but the whole is usually different. They can, however, tell you about their ways of solving problems that are similar to the ones that you might encounter. This idea is the essence of **patterns**: the understanding that many problems, or their components, are repeated and therefore can be handled by similar solutions.

The idea of learning from others is nothing new and is a built-in feature of being human. What differentiates this kind of learning from a firsthand experience is how effectively and how clearly the source can express and communicate the knowledge. Anecdotes and memoirs are great as a source of wisdom, but they are not sufficient to serve as references or guidelines for designing the nuts and bolts of a product. Learning from patterns requires a **pattern language**, a formal way to convey—as exactly as possible—what the pattern signifies, what the context is, what the solution involves, and what the consequences are.

We cannot learn every pattern by studying a chapter, a book, or even a series of books. Even in one discipline, such as software development, the number of potential patterns is vast. Patterns exist that nobody has written about, and patterns will emerge when we tackle problems that nobody wanted to solve before. Furthermore, the same repeating problem can give rise to multiple solutions, all equally valid but more appropriate to one context or to one kind of architecture than to others.

In this chapter, we aim to provide a general idea about patterns, with a few examples for various categories that relate to software development. Memorizing all patterns is like memorizing a dictionary or an encyclopedia: We can attempt it, of course, but it is not the best use of one's resources.

2. INTRODUCING PATTERNS

> A pattern is the *core* of the solution to a problem that occurs repeatedly in an environment.

In any profession that requires finding solutions, certain problems occur repeatedly:

- *Painting:* how to render the texture of a shiny fabric.
- *Car Manufacturing:* how to use the *same* machinery to "stamp" different body parts: left door, right door, left fender, right fender, etc., for different car models.
- *Agriculture:* how to restore nutrients to the soil without using chemical fertilizers.

- *Military:* how to move soldiers, equipment, and machinery across rivers of different widths and depths under battle conditions.
- *Architecture:* how to place kitchens and bathrooms in an apartment complex so that plumbing will take the minimum amount of space.
- *Software Design:* how to manage the creation, the lifetime, and the destruction of a large number of sibling objects in an application.

Each sphere of activity, or domain, has to cope with such repeating problems for which, gradually, one or more "standard" solutions gain acceptance. For instance, the solution to the problem that we cited for architecture is to "cluster" the plumbing: design the bathroom next to the kitchen and build adjacent apartments as mirror images of each other so that the kitchen-bathroom cluster of one apartment is next to the cluster of the other apartment.

Such problem-solution pairs are called **patterns**. In fact, to a considerable degree, the qualities that we praise as "expertise" and "experience" in an expert are the ability to recognize patterns and draw upon solutions that have worked in the past.

Patterns are neither methodologies nor recipes. Methodologies paint the development process in broad brushstrokes and stay clear of specific problems (though specific problems might be used as examples). Recipes or cookbooks, on the other hand, are about specific problems: We might make small adjustments, but the recipe assumes that its instructions, in detail, are fairly correct. Patterns are in a class of their own:

[Alexander 1977, x]

Each pattern describes a problem that occurs over and over again in our environment, and then describes the core of the solution to that problem, in such a way that **you can use this solution a million times over, without ever doing it the same way twice**.

Patterns also hold the promise of *reuse*, not in the conventional sense (which we will discuss in the next chapter), but in the sense that they allow us to reuse past experience to mold present solutions.

The Background

> Patterns are old. A systematic way to describe patterns and their consequences is new.

Since time immemorial, people have adopted and adapted solutions found by other people. Figure 14.1 represents two architectural patterns that are so successful that they have dominated the building of large spaces for thousands of years. We can find numerous other examples for patterns in the history of human activities, from hunting to pottery and from shipbuilding to medicine. Such adaptations, however, were not usually called patterns (except when used as a synonym for "model," as in "dress pattern"), and no systematic way existed to describe them.

In 1977, Christopher Alexander, an architect, and his coauthors published *A Pattern Language: Towns, Buildings, Construction*. Rather than focusing on narrow technical or aesthetic considerations, the book explored hundreds of patterns that define the relationships among people and their architectural habitats: the themes that, for good or for bad, are repeatedly adopted by people or builders.

**Figure 14.1
Pattern: Core
of the Solution
to a Recurring
Problem**

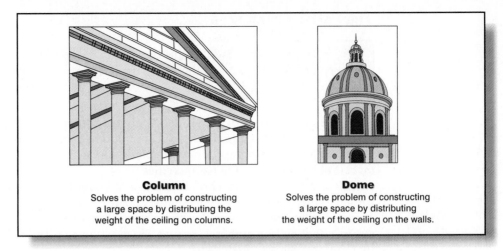

Column
Solves the problem of constructing
a large space by distributing the
weight of the ceiling on columns.

Dome
Solves the problem of constructing
a large space by distributing
the weight of the ceiling on the walls.

You can discover patterns in every field of human activity.

As it turned out, Alexander's greatest impact was not on architecture but on *software* architecture or, to be more precise, on object-oriented design. A systematic analysis and presentation of patterns requires distinct entities that only an object-oriented framework can provide.

Application of patterns to software design, both in theory and practice, started in the late 1970s and early 1980s. One of the first was the **Model-View-Controller** (MVC), an architectural pattern that separates the application into three logical components: data model, user interface, and control logic. (The general idea, if not the terminology, should be familiar to you by now.) The pattern, developed at Xerox's Palo Alto Research Center (PARC), was the foundation of the modern graphical user interface (GUI).

During the 1980s and early 1990s, many pioneers contributed to a growing awareness of patterns. One was Peter Coad, who in the article "Object-Oriented Patterns" offered certain guidelines and examples for identifying and adapting software patterns:

[Coad 1992, 153]

An object-oriented pattern is an abstraction of a doublet, triplet, or other small grouping of classes that is likely to be helpful again and again in object-oriented development.

Patterns are found by trial-and-error and by observation. By building many object-oriented models and by observing many applications of the lowest-level building blocks and the relationships established between them, one can find patterns.

What turned patterns into a serious subject in software development was the publication of *Design Patterns: Elements of Reusable Object-Oriented Software*, by Erich Gamma *et al* in 1997. (It has become known as the "Gang of Four" book, a reference to the number of its authors.) This book offered a viable framework for identifying and defining patterns that apply to software design.

Since then the literature has grown constantly, with books that either expand on existing patterns or present new ones for new contexts such as analysis, enterprise architecture, modeling, etc.

The Pattern Language

Pattern language has two meanings: ❶ the language for systematizing and presenting patterns, and ❷ the language that patterns form in relationship to each other.

Christopher Alexander envisioned patterns themselves as the building blocks of a "language": Architectural patterns are "idioms" that, when combined into ever larger sentences, paragraphs, and chapters, can shape human habitats—buildings, blocks, neighborhoods, towns, and cities.

More relevant to software development is the language that must be used to present patterns clearly and coherently. Like use cases, patterns must be described in an essentially *literary form*. On this there is agreement, but it should come as no surprise that no two authors agree on the exact format. The following is a template that presents the essential ideas:

☞ The pattern template and the previous example of many-to-many relationships are adapted or quoted from:

[Evitts 2000, 190–195 & 109–111]

• *Name.*   A name for the pattern. Following the lead of Gamma, many authors assign names that are easy to remember but sometimes hard to understand: "Flyweight," "Singleton," or "Memento," for example. Others may use more descriptive names such as "Many-To-Many Class Trio." Each pattern might also have *aliases* or other names.

(We discussed the *many-to-many relationships* in the last chapter. See that chapter for the related entity-relationship diagram and Figure 14.2 for an abstract version of the class diagram. Examples quoted for the following headings refer to the same pattern.)

• *Problem.*   What problem is this pattern to resolve?

"How to model the relationship between two classes that have many-to-many associations to each other."

• *Context.*   What environment does the pattern need to be successful? What technology or architecture is required? Explaining the context is of crucial importance to the application of patterns.

"Modeling classes using the UML during system design."

Figure 14.2
The Class Trio: A Pattern for Solving Many-to-Many Relationships

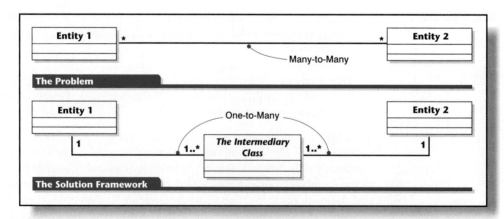

This illustration represents the same pattern that was used in the previous chapter to reconcile student-teacher multiplicity. Here, however, the pattern is expressed in abstract and domain-independent terms.

- *Forces.* What forces create the problem? How are they affected by the application of the pattern? Example:

  - "Many-to-many relationships occur often in the real world.
  - "It can be difficult to implement many-to-many associations in some object-oriented programming languages.
  - "Many-to-many relationships have no direct implementation in relational database systems in which they may have to be persisted.
  - "Direct many-to-many associations between classes can't describe anything more meaningful than a reference to another class: associations don't have attributes or behavior . . . "

- *Solution.* What should be done to solve the problem?

"Transform the many-to-many association between two classes into a trio of classes by creating an intermediary class with two one-to-many relationships . . . "

- *Example.* An example of the pattern. If the context is language-specific, then the example might include code as well.

"A teacher might teach many students and a student might have many teachers." (See the previous chapter for a detailed example.)

- *Participants.* What classes or objects participate in the pattern?

"Two classes that have a many-to-many association and the intermediary class that changes the association to one-to-many."

- *Resulting Context & Consequences.* What is the new context as a result of applying the pattern?

"A UML model with two classes linked by an intermediary class that has a one-to-many relationship to each of the first two classes. The resulting trio of classes will match the relational model, be easier to implement, and provide a richer way to capture the details of the relationship."

- *Discussion.* An overall view of everything about the pattern.

"Many-to-many relationships look deceptively simple to the modeler and even seem to make intuitive sense: Many people have accounts at many banks. . . . Fortunately, the solution that makes sense in an object-oriented environment is also the proven one that worked in the relational world . . .

"This allows attributes and methods to be added to the relationship. . . . The multiplicity can be tweaked on either side of the intermediary class to more precisely define the exact nature of the relationship . . . "

You will see other headings such as Classification, Intent, Sample Code, Related Patterns, etc., depending on the author and the context.

☞ The examples in this chapter are quoted from other authors, meaning that we have not introduced new patterns of our own. In presenting patterns, authors follow different templates that are difficult to reconcile. In addition, the purpose of this chapter is to provide a general introduction to patterns and their variations, not a detailed catalogue for development. Therefore, the examples are explained by a simple narrative, not a structured template.

The Risks

> Patterns must be used only with a thorough understanding of the problem, the context, and the consequences of applying the pattern.

Patterns are one of the greatest best hopes for software development, but beware: they have become fashionable and anything fashionable carries risks. With an ever faster pace, books, articles, and Web pages on patterns are appearing and applicants for system design or programming positions are interviewed on their knowledge of patterns.

The *first risk* is the quality of literature. As of this writing, most books on patterns have been of high quality (though sometimes difficult to read). As the popularity of patterns increases, lower quality literature is bound to appear. Demand always creates supply, but not always the best supply. (Fortunately, the Web often supplies fast critical feedback.)

The *second risk* comes from designers and developers themselves: There is a tendency to apply a tool as soon as possible if it is sufficiently promising or fashionable, even if the tool and its consequences are not adequately understood. When we learn an interesting pattern, we might be tempted to force it on a context that does not suit the pattern.

The *third risk* originates from the nature of patterns: You can use a pattern without a deep knowledge of its theoretical foundations. It is both a strength and a weakness: It saves a considerable amount of time and resources because you do not have to discover the solution yourself, but it can backfire disastrously if the problem domain is misunderstood.

Patterns are generalizations of the solutions that have worked in a certain context (or seem to have worked), but the method or the methodology behind them is not self-evident. In addition, patterns are not engineering models, so a seemingly minor change in the context or the requirements of the new solution can wreak havoc—directly or indirectly.

Patterns usually see the situation as a problem-solution pair, meaning that the "solution-as-method" is bypassed. If the problem and the solution are simple, an *experienced* person can grasp the method. If both are complex, we cannot be sure about the method. So it is always a good idea to analyze the pattern and try to figure out "why" besides "how." (This, also, is the function of the "Discussion" section in the pattern template that we introduced previously.)

Also, always remember that if a problem has any solution, it is likely that it will have more than one. Sometimes one solution is not inherently better than another, but is more appropriate because of other factors, including—but not limited to—existing infrastructure, cost, maintainability, and so on.

3. DESIGN PATTERNS

Any activity in software development can benefit from patterns, but the most well-known and elaborated are design patterns because, as we have mentioned, design lends itself neither to pure theory nor to the cookbook approach.

Design patterns are usually classified based on the type of problems that they address. Among them:

[Gamma 1997, 81]
- **Creational Patterns** abstract the process of instantiating (or creating) objects. "They help make a system independent of how objects are created, composed, and represented. . . . [A] creational pattern will delegate instantiation to another object."
- **Structural Patterns** define how the building blocks of an object-oriented system—classes and/or objects—can be combined to form larger structures.

- **Behavioral Patterns** address the communication and the assignment of responsibilities among objects. "These patterns characterize complex control flow that's difficult to follow at run-time."
- **Data Access Patterns** propose frameworks for handling issues of communication between the object space (the application) and the data space (the database). The object-relational mapping that we explored in the previous chapter is such a pattern.
- **Architectural Patterns** focus on the organization and the responsibilities of major components within the information system. (In the chapter on architecture, we will discuss some architectural patterns.)

Design patterns are not always easy to understand. We next present two examples that are relatively easy.

Factory Method

> The Factory Method pattern defines an interface for creating objects, but delegates the actual responsibility for selecting the class and instantiating the object to a subclass.

A full-service bank offers many account types: checking, savings, revolving credit, credit card, money market, etc. An ATM must allow the customer to manage all accounts, even though each account type follows a different logic: a savings account bears interest while a revolving credit account charges interest, the balance on a checking account shows the amount that the bank owes the customer while for a credit card the reverse is true, and so on. In addition, the bank may introduce new services that, as of yet, do not exist.

An ATM is merely one of the many components of a bank's information system. Any change, including the addition of a new account type, may require changes to the whole system, not only one component of it. It is in the bank's interest to design its information system in a way that minimizes the rippling effects of a change—as much as possible.

An ATM usually provides the customer with a list of accounts from which the customer may choose. The ATM then displays an account detail screen and allows the customer to perform operations such as withdrawal, deposit, and transfer. Though various account types share an interface, the operations that they implement are *polymorphic*, meaning that what happens when the customer invokes a method depends on the specific account *subclass*: withdrawing funds from a checking account only changes the balance, while withdrawing from a revolving credit account signals the information system to start charging interest on the account.

Consequently, the ATM application cannot instantiate a general-purpose **Account** object, but must create a **Savings Account**, a **Checking Account**, a **Credit Card Account**, etc. This means that the application is *tightly coupled* to account subclasses: It must recognize account types and must be changed each time a new service is introduced. Since, as we said, an ATM is not the sole application in the bank's information system, all components across the system that instantiate accounts must be updated as well. Needless to say, this is not the kind of redundancy that anybody welcomes.

In this context, and many like it, the best solution is to *decouple*, or separate, the *creation* (or instantiation) of the object from its *consumption*. The *Factory Method* pattern provides a way to implement this solution. As Figure 14.3 illustrates, instead

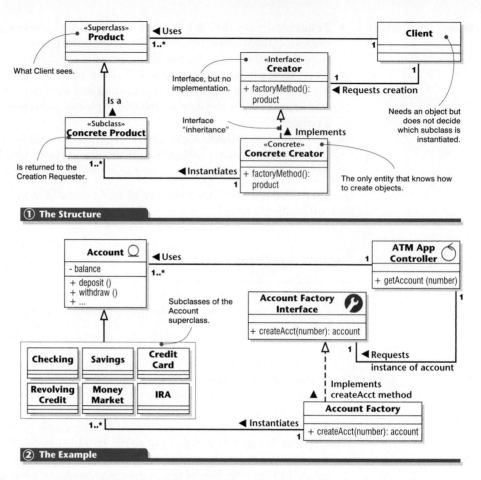

**Figure 14.3
The Factory
Method: A
Creational
Pattern**

① **The Structure**

② **The Example**

By implementing the Factory Method pattern, the application is isolated and protected from variations in the subclasses of a superclass. In this example, the bank can introduce new types of accounts without having to change the control objects.

☞ We will discuss *interfaces* in more detail in the next chapter. Here, it will suffice to say that an interface is a "public persona" that can be played by unrelated objects; a kind of inheritance in which subclasses inherit the public responsibilities of a class, but not the implementation.

of the consumer, a third object is responsible for instantiating objects. As long as all accounts are sub-classed from the **Account** class, the consumer (called the *client* in this context) need not know which subclass is actually instantiated. Figure 14.3 has two parts. Part one is an *abstract* model of the structure necessary to implement the pattern:

- **Client** is the class that "consumes" the object but has been isolated (or decoupled) from the creation of objects. It sends its requests for object creation to:
- **Creator**, an abstract or an **«interface»** class that offers a **factoryMethod** operation for instantiating objects.

   To provide another level of isolation in the structure, however, the **Creator** class itself is only an interface. The **factoryMethod** operation is actually implemented by:

- **Concrete Creator**, which is the only class that knows which subclasses must be instantiated and how to instantiate them. Since this class is application-independent, it can work with any application that requires its services. After selecting the appropriate subclass and instantiating it, **Concrete Creator** returns:

☞ You may be wondering why the **Creator** (interface) class is necessary at all. Why not dispense with it and use **Concrete Creator** directly? The answer is that you *can*, but you better not: Another level of isolation may be more work but it also allows more flexibility in handling future changes to the *concrete* class. An interface works like a layer of insulation in a building or shock absorbers in a car.

[Gamma 1995, 139]

- **Concrete Product**, or the actual subclass that now can be returned to the client who requested it. All **Concrete Product** objects must be subclasses of one class:
- **Product**, the interface of which is recognized (or "known") by the **client** object, regardless of which subclass is actually instantiated.

The second part of Figure 14.3 illustrates how the Factory Method pattern can be applied to concrete modeling in the specific context of a banking information system: **ATM App Controller** (an application control object) sends a request to the **createAcct** method of **Account Factory Interface** to instantiate an account. The request is actually handled by **Account Factory**, which is an implementation of the "interface." Based on the account number, **Account Factory** creates the appropriate subclass instance for the **Account** superclass.

Notice, however, that patterns are **domain-independent**. The Factory Method pattern can be used in designing solutions for numerous problem domains: anywhere that consumers of subclasses must be protected and isolated from their variations (in document management, for example).

The Object Adapter

> The Object Adapter converts "the interface of a class into another interface that the clients expect. Adapter lets classes work together that couldn't otherwise because of incompatible interfaces."

☞ See Chapter 13 for an introduction to the *persistence layer*.

Imagine that Walden Medical Center has outsourced the development of its information system to your firm. Furthermore, imagine that Walden agrees that you can sell your software to other hospitals, provided it gets a deep discount. You visit promising hospitals and medical centers and persuade them to consider your product. Many are enthusiastic, but there is one point on which they will not compromise: their choice of database management systems.

Hospital management applications are very data-intensive. Consequently, designing one application per one database brand is out of the question. Furthermore, DBMSs are upgraded every couple of years and every feature of the new version is not necessarily backward-compatible. Obviously, you need a flexible persistence layer to cope with various DBMS brands and versions.

For this problem, and many like it, the Object Adapter pattern offers a solution that is based on a sound object-oriented concept: isolate the provider of the service from its consumer by using an *adapter*. By using this technique, there is no need to change either the provider or the consumer, but only the adapter. (See Figure 14.4.) The idea works exactly as it does in the real world. When we travel to a country with a different electrical current and/or electrical outlets, we do not reengineer our electronic equipment, but simply buy an adapter. As a bonus, the adapter may include functionality that neither the provider nor the consumer of the service offers by themselves—surge suppresser, for example.

Like an electrical adapter, an object adapter may adapt to one service provider or more. What is required is that the adapter object or objects must offer the client (or the consumer) a "standard" *interface* to protect them from changes in the provider.

The potential for benefiting from the Object Adapter pattern is vast. Use the pattern when

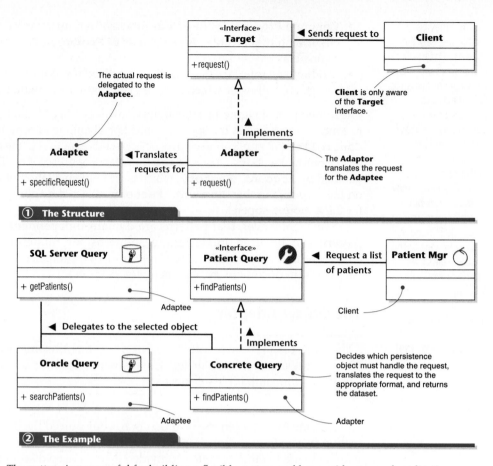

Figure 14.4
**The Object
Adapter: A
Structural
Pattern**

The pattern is very useful for building a flexible system and has a wide range of applications.

[Gamma 1997, 140]

- "you want to use an existing class, and its interface does not match the one you need.
- "you want to create a reusable class that cooperates with unrelated or unforeseen classes, that is, classes that don't necessarily have compatible interfaces.
- "you need to use several existing subclasses, but it's impossible to adapt their interfaces by subclassing every one. An object adapter can adapt the interface of its parent class."

4. ANALYSIS PATTERNS

In software development, design patterns appeared first and are the most popular. Like any other activity that involves solving problems, however, analysis can also benefit from the application of patterns.

In practice—and sometimes in theory as well—analysis has played an inferior role to design. As long as applications were relatively simple, weakness of analysis could be corrected by paying a modest price during design and implementation.

Information systems, however, have become much more ambitious and, as a result, compensating for weak analysis has also become much more difficult and costly.

Measurement & Historical Mapping

☞ The examples for analysis patterns are adapted from:

> Measurement and Historical Mapping patterns integrate bulk data gathering into an objected-oriented conceptual model.

[Fowler 1997, 41–42 & 303–305]

Analysts frequently ignore certain objects in the problem domain either because domain experts have no name for them or because they appear to be "excessive" for analysis. Some of the classes that we introduced in conceptual modeling for Walden Medical Center, such as **Address**, **Phone**, **Insurance Policy**, and **Credit Card**, might be judged by some to properly belong to the "solution domain," or design. (See Chapter 8.) Instead, they might argue, it is enough to specify a repeating attribute (such as **address[0..*]**), and leave it to the designer to decide how to handle the problem.

This argument has some merit, but for the *presentation* of models, not for analysis as a whole. As we saw in Chapter 8 on structural modeling, a class like **Patient** can easily acquire many collaborating classes, and including all of them in *one* class diagram might make the diagram too confusing to understand. In such a case, we can resort to *shorthand* modeling for individual diagrams.

On the other hand, analysis (and domain analysis) *must* define the entities within the problem domain as accurately as possible. Analysis and design are not separated by a wall and both activities are iterative, but if something is important to the problem domain, it is the task of analysis to identify it:

[Fowler 1997, 41]

> Modeling quantities as attributes may be useful for a single hospital department that collects a couple of dozen measurements for each in-patient visit. However, when we look across all areas of medicine, we find thousands of potential measurements that could be made on one person. Defining an attribute for each measurement would mean that one person could have thousands of operations—an untenably complex interface. One solution is to consider all the various things that can be measured (height, weight, blood glucose level, and so on) as objects and to introduce the object type phenomenon type. . . . A person would then have many measurements, each assigning a quantity to a specific phenomenon type. The person would now have only one attribute for all measurements, and the complexity of dealing with the measurements would be shifted to querying thousands of instances of measurement and phenomenon type. We could now add further attributes to the measurement to record such things as who did it, when it was done, and so on.

Like all patterns, the principles of the Measurement pattern (Figure 14.5) can be applied to many problem domains. As Fowler writes, **"If a type has many, many similar associations, make all of these associations objects of a new type."**

In the same problem domain, in a hospital like Walden, for example, old measurements are *not* discarded as soon as new ones are made. Often, the hospital must keep a *history* of measurements to track how patients respond to treatment and/or medication:

[Fowler 1997, 303]

> [Virtual objects] do not just represent objects that exist in the real world; they often represent the **memories of objects** that once existed but have

Figure 14.5
**Measurement
and Historical
Mapping: Two
Analysis
Patterns**

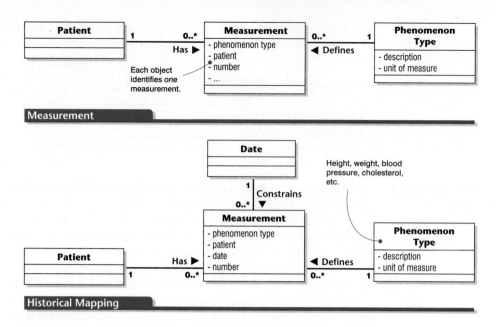

These two patterns are examples of what analysis must discover, but are usually and wrongly left to design.

since disappeared. Using objects to represent memories is perfectly acceptable—memory of existence is often as real to people as the existence itself—but it is important to be able to tell the difference.

The Historic Mapping pattern solves this problem by turning the attribute(s) that we must track into a separate class, and by constraining the class with a historical identifier—date, time, period, etc. (In our example in Figure 14.5 measurement is already a class by itself.) The entity object, **Patient**, retains its *unique* identity, but now the information system has acquired a "memory" and remembers the changing data about the entity. By using this pattern, we can track entities across time as well as space.

These two patterns have wide-ranging applications in many problem domains that must gather massive amounts of data and/or keep an audit trail of the data that they gather. Besides hospitals, banks and stock markets are two prominent examples.

5. MODELING PATTERNS

Analysis patterns are concerned with the problem domain. Design patterns address the issues of the solution space. Modeling is neither the problem nor the product that solves the problem, but a "solution-as-method," a means to an end, not an end by itself. Modeling "domain," however, has its own problems. For example:

- How to accurately represent the problem domain, regardless of the solution.
- How to be understandable to very different audiences: clients, domain experts, analysts, designers, and coders.

- How to keep control of modeling "inventory" so that the models stay up-to-date and are easy to find.
- How to be effective at both ends of the modeling spectrum: general views that identify the scope and detailed views that can be used as engineering blueprints.

Sooner or later, we come across patterns in any domain that present us with problems.

Dynamic Object Types

☞ This example for modeling patterns is adapted from:

[Evitts 2000, 107–108]

> Dynamic object types are those that must change type to represent "different but similar things at different times."

The class diagram in Figure 14.6 seems very mundane: employees of a restaurant are subclassed into various types such as waiter, manager, bartender, and so on. Each subclass, as we have learned by now, inherits the attributes and the operations of the superclass but specializes them where necessary.

Nevertheless, despite the appearances, a subtle problem exists that a static view of the relationship between classes cannot convey. Unless a new type of employee must be added, the class diagram stays the same. Instances of subclasses, however, are another story: An object can change roles over time, either temporarily or permanently. For example, a receptionist can "play" waiter when there are not enough waiters (temporary) or can be promoted to manager (permanent). Even a manager would lend a hand from time to time. In other words, the **Employee** entity remains the same but might move from subclass to subclass.

How do we model this kind of dynamic behavior? By using *constraints*, one of the extension mechanisms of UML. (See Chapter 10.) In Figure 14.6 the **{Overlapping}** constraint indicates the dynamic nature of instances. In all, UML has four *standard* constraints for "advanced" inheritance relationships:

[Booch 1999, 142–143]

- *Complete.* "Specifies that all children in the generalization have been specified in the model (although some may be elided in the diagram) and no additional children are permitted."

Figure 14.6 Dynamic Object Types: A Modeling Pattern

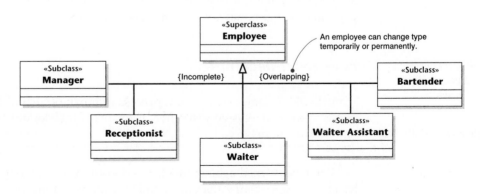

The class diagram does not need to change over time, but instances do change roles.

- *Incomplete.* "Specifies that not all children in the generalization have been specified . . . and that additional children are permitted." Our example in Figure 14.6 is **{Incomplete}** since kitchen and cooking staff were not included.
- *Disjoint.* "Specifies that objects of the parent may have no more than one of the children as a type."
- *Overlapping.* "Specifies that objects of the parent may have more than one of the children as a type." (These last two constraints were originally defined for *multiple* inheritance, but **{Overlapping}** can also be used for scenarios similar to the one we just described.)

☞ **Interface inheritance** is one of the mechanisms by which an object can play multiple roles. We will discuss this subject in the next chapter.

Figure 14.6 is a conceptual model and describes the problem domain. It also provides a very good reason for the problem that we posed before—"How to accurately represent the problem domain, regardless of the solution"—because designing or implementing it is not straightforward. No mainstream object-oriented technology or language can accommodate this model "as is" and all the known workarounds leave something to be desired.

6. ANTI-PATTERNS

On the reverse side of patterns is the concept of anti-patterns: the core of the solutions that do *not* work. Whereas patterns consist of problem-solution pairs, an anti-pattern is a pair of two solutions: the first solution—the one that leads to failure—is called the *problematic solution*; the second is referred to as the *refactored solution*. "The refactored solution is a commonly occurring method in which the [anti-pattern] can be resolved and reengineered" to prevent failure and increase the chances of success.

[Brown 1998, 16]

Design patterns, as indicated by their designation, focus on design problems. Anti-patterns, however, cover a vast territory, from gathering requirements to the management and the organization of the development process, from design to coding. Anti-patterns can be discovered in any aspect of software development, human or technological.

Anti-patterns do not necessarily start as problematic solutions. Frequently, they are solutions that have worked in the past but which become problematic because the context and the forces that affect the problem-solution pair change, but the changes are not taken into account. Previously, in discussing the risks of relying on patterns, we stated that you ignore the *methodology* of finding solutions at your own peril: You might know that some solution works, but if you don't know *why* it works you *will* be caught unawares when it doesn't work.

☞ The example for anti-patterns is adapted from:

[Brown 1998, 97–102]

Functional Decomposition

> Functional decomposition is the process of breaking down the functionality of a system into successively smaller tasks and subtasks until we reach the most atomic functions.

We have warned against functional decomposition before. But is it really such a terrible transgression? After all, "atomic functions"—functions that do one thing and one thing only—do exist and any complex system eventually consists of such functions.

Functional decomposition was *not* an invalid technique when procedural programming was the only available choice: The application started from a "main" entry point and then branched into ever smaller procedures until some function did something useful. In its context, functional decomposition was helpful because it prevented "super-functions," a seemingly endless expanse of code that even its writer could not decipher after a short while. (The so-called "spaghetti code" was one result of unreasonably long code segments.)

Procedural development and procedural technologies, however, proved inadequate in the face of increasingly complex demands on software. Object-oriented methodology and technology do not deny that software must perform functions to be of any use, but view functions as services that objects provide—the same way as in the real world where functions are carried out by something or somebody.

Use cases can be viewed as some kind of large-grained "functions." The anti-pattern occurs when the functionality is broken down, or "decomposed," successively into very small-grained functions which are *then* mapped to classes that are really nothing more than collections or "modules" of function. (This is one of the reasons why we advised against composing use cases that try to enumerate every possible action or exception.)

Figure 14.7 illustrates one possible, although extreme, shape that functional decomposition might take when applied to the **Patient Management** component of Walden's information system. In the top section, "Problematic Solution," you see a class diagram of the subsystem as functions that it must perform. Each class represents an

Figure 14.7 Functional Decomposition: An Anti-Pattern

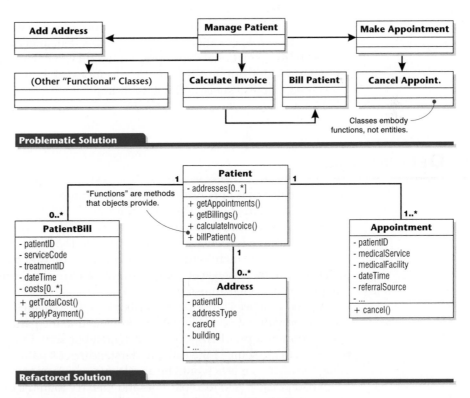

Functional mechanism works well with "structured programming" methodology but becomes problematic when applied to an object-oriented context.

arbitrary level of functionality: **Make Appointment**, for example, corresponds to a use case by the same name, while others, such as **Add Address**, belong to a more detailed level. The name of one class, **Manage Patient**, corresponds to the entire subsystem.

The bottom section, "Refactored Solution," represents a class diagram that must be very familiar to you: an *object*-oriented view of the same functionality. **Bill Patient**, for example, is still there, but it is now an operation of the **Patient** class that must collaborate with another class, **BillPatient**, to perform the service. (As you should know by now, the actual structure is more complex than what this example shows, even as a conceptual model.)

[Brown 1998, 98]

Like all anti-patterns, functional decomposition can be identified by symptoms and consequences:

- Classes are identified by functional names such as **Display Table** or **Calculate Invoice**. In object-oriented design, you arrive at control or boundary classes, such as **Appointment Mgr**, that are essentially functional, but entity classes like **Patient**, **Appointment**, or **Invoice** are abstractions of objects or "things," not merely their functionality. (Object-oriented development starts with analysis, not design.)
- Classes that result from functional decomposition usually lack attributes that are exposed through methods. In other words, attributes remain inaccessible to the outside world.
- The public interface of the class has only one operation.
- Object-oriented concepts and mechanisms such as inheritance, polymorphism, aggregation, or composition are absent.
- The structure and the flow of the system is difficult or impossible to model and/or document.
- The possibility of reuse does not exist, since functional decomposition is basically an "application analysis," not a system analysis. Components that result from functional decomposition might serve one application well (temporarily), but not a system. Applications are how an information system is used, not its essence and not its entirety.

7. Deliverables

Applying patterns is not an activity separate from others in the development process, but an integral part of each. Therefore, there are no "deliverables" for patterns *per se.*

As you encounter problems in analysis or design, you can consult patterns to find solutions that have worked in the past. Good sources on the Web and new books are appearing at an increasing pace, but how can you find the right one? Memorizing patterns is not the best use of your time and pattern names are not very helpful (even though they are often amusing).

A good practice is to glance over books and Web sites and read the snippets of text that provide a description for the problem that the pattern aims to solve. Then, if you encounter a problem, you might remember something about the pattern and refer back to the source for a fuller understanding. (A pattern to find patterns *without* going through long lists would be a welcome achievement.)

A bad practice is to read patterns and then try to find a case, any case, where you can apply it. Patterns are abstractions of experience, but we need experience to use them wisely and effectively.

8. Wrap Up

Concepts of pattern and pattern language

A pattern is the *core* of the solution to a problem that occurs repeatedly in an environment. Patterns are neither methodologies nor recipes. Methodologies paint the development process in broad brushstrokes and stay clear of specific problems. Recipes or cookbooks, on the other hand, are about very specific problems.

"Each pattern describes a problem that occurs over and over again in our environment, and then describes the core of the solution to that problem, in such a way that you can use this solution a million times over, without ever doing it the same way twice." [Alexander 1977.]

Patterns are old. A systematic way to describe patterns and their consequences, however, is new. Pattern language has two meanings: ❶ the language for systematizing and presenting patterns, and ❷ the language that patterns form in relationship to each other.

Like use cases, patterns must be described in an essentially literary form. No standard format for defining patterns exists. Any pattern template, however, should reflect a set of ideas that are essential to the proper understanding of the pattern:

- **Problem.** What problem the pattern aims to resolve.
- **Context.** The environment, the technology, or the architecture that is required to make the proposed solution successful.
- **Forces.** What forces create the problem and how they are affected by the application of the pattern.
- **Example.** An example of the pattern, including code, diagrams, etc., if applicable.
- **Participants.** A description of classes or objects that participate in the pattern.
- **Resulting Context & Consequences.** An explanation of the *new* context that results from the application of the pattern.
- **Discussion.** An overall discussion of the pattern.

Patterns must be used only with a thorough understanding of the problem, the context, and the consequences of applying the pattern. Patterns are presented as ready-made solutions. If the context that underlies the pattern is not properly understood or the context changes, the proposed solution might instead create more problems.

☑ **Design patterns**

Any activity in software development can benefit from patterns, but the most well-known and elaborated are design patterns. Design patterns are usually classified based on the type of the problems that they address. They include creational, structural, behavioral, data access, and architectural patterns.

☑ **Analysis patterns**

Design patterns appeared first and are the most popular. Like any other activity that involves solving problems, however, analysis can also benefit from the application of patterns.

☑ **Modeling patterns**

Modeling patterns relates neither to the problem domain nor to the "solution-as-answer," but to modeling that is a component of methodology or "solution-as-method."

☑ **Anti-patterns**   **[Brown 1998, 16]**

Whereas patterns consist of problem-solution pairs, an anti-pattern is a pair of two solutions: The first solution—the one that leads to failure—is called the *problematic solution*; the second is referred to as the *refactored solution*. "The refactored solution is a commonly occurring method in which the [anti-pattern] can be resolved and reengineered" to prevent failure and increase the chances of success.

9. Key Concepts

Anti-Pattern. The core of solutions that do *not* work. Whereas patterns consist of problem-solution pairs, an anti-pattern is a pair of two solutions: The first solution—the one that does not work—is called the *problematic solution*; the second is referred to as the *refactored solution*.

Pattern. The core of the solution to a problem that occurs repeatedly in an environment. Any area of activity that involves problem solving can benefit from patterns. In software development, these areas include analysis, design, and modeling.

Pattern Language. ❶ The language for systematizing and presenting patterns, and ❷ the language that patterns form in relationship to each other. Like use cases, patterns must be described in an essentially literary form. See also **Pattern Template**.

Pattern Template.   A template for defining and describing the essential points about a pattern such as name, the problem that it aims to resolve, the context of the problem, the forces that create the problem, the solution, the classes or objects that participate in the problem-solution pair, the consequences of applying the pattern, and a general discussion.

Patterns, Architectural.   Patterns that focus on the organization and the responsibilities of major components within the information system.

Patterns, Behavioral.   Patterns that address the communication and the assignment of responsibilities among objects.

Patterns, Creational.   Patterns that abstract the process of instantiating or creating objects.

Patterns, Data Access.   Patterns that propose frameworks for handling issues of communication between the application and the database.

Patterns, Structural.   Patterns that define how classes and/or objects can be combined to form larger structures or components.

10. REVIEW QUESTIONS

1. Define patterns, methodologies, and recipes and give an example for each.
2. How do patterns relate to reuse?
3. What activities in software development can benefit from applying patterns?
4. How can you ensure that a pattern provides the correct solution for your problem?
5. How do architectural patterns differ from structural patterns? Provide examples.
6. The Object Adapter pattern has great potential for design. Provide examples.
7. Explain the difference between design, analysis, and patterns.
8. Define dynamic object types. Besides the example in this chapter, can you think of other situations where we would encounter them?
9. Define anti-patterns, functional decomposition and the relationship between them.
10. What are some of symptoms of Functional Decompositions?

11. EXERCISES

The following exercises apply to each of the four narratives introduced in Chapter 4: *The* Sportz *Magazine, The Car Dealership, The Pizza Shop,* and *The Real Estate Agency.*

❶ Of all the patterns that you can find in books and on Web sites, we introduced just a handful. Of these, however, can you find one that applies to more than one of the given scenarios? Remember: Since patterns address recurring problems within a certain context, find similar problems to find the pattern. Create a diagram for *each* solution based on the pattern that you discover.

❷ Under *Analysis Patterns* we introduced "Measurement & Historical Mapping." Can you find a problem in any of the scenarios that this pattern can solve? (You may find more than one.) Create a diagram for it. Use Figure 14.5 as a guide.

12. RESEARCH PROJECTS & TEAMWORK

❶ Due to space limitations, we did not present our sample patterns in the **"pattern language"** that we introduced early in this chapter. As a team, select one of the patterns. Then, individually, try to present the selected pattern by using the *"template"* in this chapter. (Come up with your own formatting.) In a team session, compare, contrast, and discuss the results. Remember that you can add or subtract template fields, but you should be able to justify it. (Perhaps you can come up with an improved template. This is how better things appear!)

❷ Visit Web sites that discuss patterns. (The list is long.) Write a short paper on topics that you find interesting but that were not discussed in this chapter. Are there dissenting voices?

The literature on patterns is expanding rapidly, but the most referenced book on *design* patterns continues to be *Design Patterns: Elements of Reusable Object Oriented Software* by **Erich Gamma** et al. (Addison-Wesley, 1997). As the first comprehensive book on patterns in software design (it was originally published in 1994), it set a framework that others have generally followed. The catalog of the patterns that the writers present have not lost their relevance, in spite of the passage of time. The book, however, should not be casually approached: You must acquire an adequate background in design before you can benefit from it. Fortunately, many other books and Web sites offer extensive discussions on the patterns in the book.

For a more down-to-earth but exhaustive treatment of design patterns, you can refer to *Head First Design Patterns* by **Eric Freeman** et al. (O'Reilly, 2004). The book may appear *too* user-friendly to some, but it does not shrink from discussing, step-by-step, patterns that are difficult to grasp and are often misunderstood.

On *analysis* and *architectural* patterns, two books by **Martin Fowler** stand out: *Analysis Pattern: Reusable Object Models* (Addison-Wesley, 1997) and *Patterns of Enterprise Application Architecture* (Addison-Wesley, 2003). Like most other books on patterns, they are not easy to read, but you can find in them many original and valuable ideas. (We wish that more analysts and software architects would read, or at least consult, them.)

Communication with the database is often oversimplified in books on object-oriented design (as we mentioned in the last chapter). A professional book such as *Data Access Patterns* by **Clifton Nock** (Addison-Wesley, 2004) is therefore very welcome. It discusses patterns that may not be very ostentatious, but are essential when dealing with the nuts and bolts of interaction with the database.

You will not find much on *modeling* patterns but, fortunately, we can recommend one book very highly: *A UML Pattern Language* by **Paul Evitts** (Macmillan Technical Publishing, 2000). Its writing style is very intelligible and, as a bonus, it offers an informative discussion on patterns in general, the origins of patterns, and the pattern language. As a result, we also recommend it as an introductory book on patterns.

Anti-patterns deserve as much study as patterns but, as you would expect, advertising failures is not a very popular pursuit. *Anti-Patterns: Refactoring Software, Architectures, and Projects in Crisis* by **William H. Brown** and his coauthors (Wiley, 1998) discusses some of the most common anti-patterns in software development with an expert knowledge. *Pitfalls of Objected-Oriented Development* by **Bruce F. Webster** (M&T Books, 1995) was written before the market popularity of patterns, but it is as systematic as any pattern book hopes to be. The topics are relevant, concise, and useful.

Chapter

15

Components & Reuse

1. OVERVIEW

The concept of reuse covers a vast territory, from patterns that provide us with the successful results of past experience, to ready-made building blocks that often do not require us to know anything about their internal workings. Two of the major reuse concepts, components and inheritance, are discussed in this chapter.

- ☑ Inception
- ☑ Requirements Discovery
- ☐ Development
  - ☑ Analysis
  - ☐ Design
    - ☑ The Design Challenge
    - ☑ Application Design
    - ☑ Patterns
    - ☐ **Components & Reuse** ⬅
    - ☐ Architecture
  - ☐ Implementation

Chapter Topics

- ➤ Areas of reuse.
- ➤ Implementation inheritance.
- ➤ Interface inheritance.
- ➤ Emulating inheritance by composition.
- ➤ Components.
- ➤ Modeling components.
- ➤ Component-based development.

516

Reuse can apply to any activity in development, from analysis to design and implementation.

Introduction

The development of most complex products has two features in common. First, such products are built not as monolithic objects but from distinct parts that are developed independently. Second, neither the parts nor the techniques to build and assemble them are entirely new. These characteristics apply even when the methodology and/or the product are justifiably called "revolutionary."

Like science, technology is incremental. This incremental nature applies both to tangibles such as material and parts and to intangibles such as techniques and experience. Complex or revolutionary products are made possible only when the availability of what they require, be it tangible or intangible, achieves a critical mass.

This observation, however true, does not serve any practical purpose *until* you view it from the opposite angle and ask: What would result from a product development that does not share these characteristics? Aside from handicrafts and works of art, the result would be a product that might be exciting or prove a crucial concept, but is likely to be unreliable, low in quality, limited in features, too expensive, too difficult to maintain, or even too dangerous to use.

A new class of products, of course, is not born with all the trappings of an established one. The first automobiles were not the products of a streamlined assembly line, they were not constructed from well-tested parts available from a multitude of sources, and they were not built by an army of trained workers and technicians. The first piece of software only had to perform a very simple task to be extremely exciting to its creators who were witnessing a historical moment. At some point, however, the development of a product must cross a threshold that turns it from a profitable hobby or experimentation into industrial production. In other words, the development must turn to components and reuse.

2. AREAS OF REUSE

> Reuse can apply to any product, experience, and expertise that is required in development.

Reinventing the wheel: this idiom symbolizes an idiotic or wasteful venture. Nevertheless, reinventing the wheel has been the norm in software development rather than the exception. Things, fortunately, have been improving steadily, if slowly.

One culprit for this slow adoption of reuse has been the unbroken record of broken promises: Overenthusiastic promoters have sold many methodologies, products, and/or tools as ensuring "reuse without pain." The fact, however, is that reuse cannot be achieved as an afterthought or as a by-product of the normal course of development. Both the production of reusable "things" and their consumption need rigorous planning in excess of what is required for building applications. On the other hand, the rewards can compensate for the effort many times over.

Reuse is not limited to one concept or one methodology, but can embrace any method or artifact in software development. The following are among the most important:

- *Components.* The most obvious, the most reliable, and the most effective mechanism for reuse is the component. (See the "Components" section later in this chapter.) Well-defined and well-designed components have one distinct advantage over any type of reuse: They come as packages or black boxes and are largely foolproof. This advantage, though, does not obviate the need for other kinds of reuse.

- *Patterns.* We discussed patterns in the previous chapter. Patterns encapsulate experience in solving problems and, consequently, can be labeled as *"experience reuse."* Unlike components, they are not ready to use, but must be adapted to the specific problems at hand—an advantage if the required solution is similar to another solution but is not its replica.

- *Inheritance.* With object-oriented technology, both the workings of a class (its **implementation**) or only its **interface** can be inherited by another class. (As you shall see, the two are not the same thing.) For example, if you write a **Person** class that calculates the age of the person from his or her birth date, then its subclass, **Patient**, would be able to do the same by simply inheriting the implementation of **Person**.

[Basiura 2001, 18]

- *Web Services.* A Web service is a service that provides platform-independent application logic to consumers across the Web via standard protocols. Web services can be seen as the adaptation of components and distributed computing to the World Wide Web. (We will discuss Web services further in the next chapter.)

- *Method Reuse.* The purpose of this book, and many others on software development, is to make methods and techniques (or methodology) reusable. The difference between methodology and patterns is that while a pattern provides the outline of a solution, a methodology provides the guidelines for *discovering* the solution.

- *Refactoring.* Refactoring is refining and improving the analysis and design artifacts or the coding of a system *without* changing their behavior. Reuse is not the only result of refactoring, but by removing duplication and (unnecessary) redundancy, refactoring contributes to reuse. (See Chapter 7 for one area of refactoring. We will not discuss refactoring in relation to implementation and coding as it falls outside the scope of this book.)

**Figure 15.2
Solution by
Reuse**

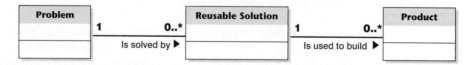

A problem can have many reusable solutions (provided it has any solution at all), while many products can use the same solution.

- *Source Code Reuse.* For very good reasons, this method of "reuse" is widely discouraged. If programmers find themselves engaged in repeated cut-and-paste operations, something is definitely wrong. Instead, they should consider refactoring and, perhaps, redesigning classes.

In one case, however, source code reuse is legitimate: solving problems by adapting solutions from "cookbooks." These how-to books (and their equivalents on the Web) constitute the overwhelming majority of literature on information technology. They might not offer groundbreaking ideas, and they might become obsolete with the next version of the technology that they cover, but they can provide designers and programmers with valuable advice and time-saving tips and examples. Often, since they are practical-minded, they can explain difficult concepts with a clarity that usually escapes more academic publications.

- *Templates.* Some vendors, including vendors of development platforms such as Java and Microsoft .Net, offer products that combine the various kinds of reuse into a *framework* or **templates** that can be customized for specific needs.

By breaking complexity into manageable units, the object-oriented technology and methodology are "reuse-friendly," but object orientation does not automatically ensure reusability or successful reusability. As we stated, reuse must be aimed at on purpose and with planning.

3. INHERITANCE REUSE

Inheritance is one of the basic concepts of object orientation: An object can be a specialized type of another object. By itself, this concept is theoretically significant but not very helpful if it cannot be put into practice. We know that **Dog** is a special kind of **Mammal**, similar to other mammals in most aspects but different in the rest. How is this knowledge of use in building an application or an information system?

Inheritance is not only a concept, but also a *mechanism* in object-oriented technology. If you have a **Mammal** class, you do not have to design the dog from scratch, but can reuse the **Mammal** class to arrive at the **Dog** class by adding or changing the necessary attributes and operations. And, once you have the **Dog** class, you can reuse it to create a **German Shepherd** class.

As a mechanism, inheritance is constrained by technology. What you can do with inheritance, and how you can do it, depends on the specific technology that you are using.

Implementation Inheritance

> Implementation inheritance is a mechanism by which a subclass can reuse, extend, or override the attributes and the operations of its parent.

The concept of inheritance is an abstraction: A child inherits attributes and operations, in whole or in part, from its parent or parents. *How* this occurs is not specified by the concept, for two reasons. The first is that the abstract idea covers dissimilar concrete situations. A colt makes no effort to inherit the characteristics of a horse. On the other hand, a car may inherit most of its properties from a general concept of the "car," but it is not really born of a parent car.

The second reason is that, from outside, the "how" does not matter. You can recognize and ride both a horse and a car without having to concern yourself with matters of parenthood or inheritance (except that you might prefer a horse that inherits its strength and agility from thoroughbreds and a car that "inherits" its brand from BMW). From inside, however, the "how" of inheritance matters greatly. You cannot build a horse like a car or bread a car like a horse.

Implementation inheritance, or *subclassing*, is a kind of inheritance in which the child, called the *subclass*, inherits not only the features but also the *functionality* of its parent, called the *superclass* or the *base class*. If the parent can draw a circle, so can the child *without* any extra effort.

Figure 15.3 presents a visual example of implementation inheritance. A textbox is one of the most widely used visual controls in the user interface. It is a simple editor that displays and accepts text. It is so simple, in fact, that it may appear unsophisticated. Creating a textbox from scratch, however, is anything *but* simple. Fortunately, all development tools include at least one kind of textbox, so you do not have to reinvent this control by yourself.

The basic textbox, however, is very generalized. With few limitations, it accepts every kind of input and displays any kind of text without interpretation or intervention. It treats an amount the same way that it treats a telephone number or a line of poetry. This general applicability is usually what makes the textbox such a pervading presence, but imagine that your application deals with finance and has exacting requirements regarding the entry and the display of amounts. For example, it might require that negative numbers be displayed in red, or that users not be able to enter more than two digits to the right of the decimal point.

Without inheritance, your choices are not ideal. The worst choice is to repeat the code that satisfies the requirements wherever it is needed. Another choice is to create your own textbox from scratch, an expensive and time-consuming option that also requires an expertise very different from that which is required to create a financial application. Yet another option is to refactor the functionality into a helper or utility class that is perhaps the best possible choice without inheritance but runs counter to the principle of encapsulation by exposing what should be hidden. (The last option may run into technical limitations and is usually more expensive in terms of development and execution resources.)

Figure 15.3 Implementation Inheritance: A Mechanism to Reuse, Extend, and Override Existing Functionality

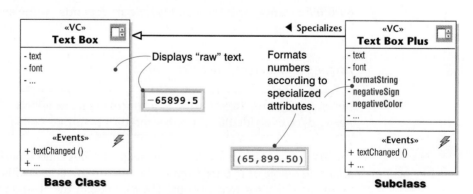

As an example, this is a very simple case, but describes the mechanism visually. Inheritance, however, can apply to any type of class, visual or nonvisual, entity or design, simple or complex.

The example in Figure 15.3 uses implementation inheritance to create a **Text Box Plus** class that encapsulates all the required functionality: It applies a different color to negative numbers, allows the consumer to specify the negative sign (simple dash or parentheses), formats the output appropriately, edits the input to filter out nonnumeric entries, and so on. The only thing that the developer has to do to reuse the **Text Box** class is to tell the development platform that the **Text Box Plus** class is a subclass of the former. Nothing has to be repeated.

Reuse, however, is not the same as copying. If **Text Box Plus** is exactly the same as **Text Box**, then inheritance has been an exercise in futility. Specialization is done for a purpose that takes one or both of the following forms:

- *Extension.* The subclass may add attributes and/or operations that do not exist in the superclass. In our example, **Text Box Plus** has attributes such as **formatString** and **negativeSign** that are necessary for its specialized role.
- *Overriding.* The subclass may change, limit, or block the implementation of a service offered by its parent. For example, an **Account** class may have a **calculateInterest** operation. Its subclasses, however, would most certainly change how the interest on the account is calculated: **Savings Account** would calculate it based on a fixed interest rate, **Money Market Account** would use a variable rate, and a **Checking Account** would disable it since checking accounts do not pay interest.

☞ As we mentioned in the chapter on structural modeling, a **protected** attribute or operation is identified by a pound sign (#) and is visible only to subclasses of a superclass. (Depending on the specific technology, the terminology or the visibility may be slightly different.)

Alternately, the designer of the **Account** class may have provided for these variations by defining the **calculateInterest** operation as *protected* so it would be visible only to its children. In this case, the subclasses would not have to override the operation completely: They can pass the required parameters, such as interest rate, to the base class to calculate the appropriate interest. This means that the base class can provide *specialized* services for its offspring.

Overriding is the basic mechanism for the concept of *polymorphism*, when the *same* message to the children of a superclass can produce different results. One popular example of polymorphism is the **Shape** class, whose subclasses such as **Circle**, **Square**, **Polygon**, etc., would produce different shapes by executing the same message, **drawShape**.

Two warnings about implementation inheritance are in order. The first is that, unlike in the real world, the link between the parent and the child is not disconnected once the child is born. This lasting connection is a double-edged sword. On the one hand, for example, if the parent of multiple subclasses can draw a circle but the circle is defective, then we can "teach" the parent to draw a better circle and all the children will immediately draw better circles too. On the other hand, it results in *tight coupling*, where any disruption to the behavior of the parent(s) would ripple down the inheritance chain.

The second warning concerns a *potential* problem that may be called the *hierarchical maze*. Since a subclass, in turn, can become the parent of other classes, the inheritance chain can go many levels deep. If this deep hierarchy is not managed well, or is *too* deep, discovering and fixing defects will become a Herculean task, especially if *multiple* inheritance is used.

Nevertheless, the inheritance mechanism is one of the best, most cost-effective, and most powerful features of object-oriented technologies, and the advantages usually outweigh the shortcomings. It should be used judiciously, intelligently, and with farsighted planning. But this is true of any methodology or technology.

Interface Inheritance

> Interface inheritance is a mechanism by which multiple classes share one interface but implement that interface independently of each other or of the parent class.

Every class or object has an interface—the sum of the services that it provides to the outside world. As a result of encapsulation, the interface is the only place where interaction with an object is possible. If, however, we take abstraction one step further and completely separate the "what" from the "how," we arrive at interface as an *independent* concept.

Interface as independent from implementation is a concept that is very familiar to us by our everyday experience. A waiter in a restaurant is not really an instance of a **Waiter** class. He or she does not inherit "waiting" properties from his or her parents and is not created by applying a **Waiter** cookie cutter to some substance. A waiter is someone who performs, or "implements," the responsibilities of waiting on customers. In other words, a waiter is an object that inherits a **Waiter** class's *interface*.

Unlike the implementation inheritance where the subclass inherits both the interface and the functionality of its parent for specialization, the purpose of interface inheritance is to arrive at a subclass that looks *exactly* like its parent but performs the services its own way.

Figure 15.4 represents one example of when interface inheritance is needed and how it can be used. An investment portfolio is often a composite of financial instruments such as stocks, bonds, or derivatives. The value of a portfolio can change rapidly and radically with market fluctuations. Therefore, the question of "what is the *current* value of a certain portfolio or its specific components?" is of utmost importance to investors as well as to managers who must keep the right balance among various financial instruments.

Financial instruments, however, are very different from each other. Neither their public services nor their internal workings can be meaningfully abstracted into one class. Even various derivatives that we have represented by one class for the sake of illustration are very dissimilar in their attributes. In short, the value of each type of financial instrument must be calculated in its own way.

To make this evaluation possible, the financial instruments in Figure 15.4 inherit an interface, **IFinancialInstrument**. (In normal language, read it as **Financial Instrument**: It is customary to start the name of an interface class with an "I.") The interface class has no implementation and, as a result, it falls to **Stock**, **Bond**, and **Derivative** classes to actually implement the **value** attribute (or any other member of the interface class). Each class, then, would calculate its own value differently.

☞ This example closely relates to the "Adapter" pattern that we discussed in the last chapter.

As the same figure shows, the subclasses keep their own attributes and operations, and they can be viewed as **Stock**, **Bond**, etc., without losing their individual identity. But if a client chooses to view them as **IFinancialInstrument**, the client would see only those attributes and operations specified by the **IFinancialInstrument** interface. As we said, the point about interface inheritance is to be able to treat different classes as one.

One Class, Multiple Interfaces

> A class can implement multiple interfaces, shared with other classes or exclusively its own.

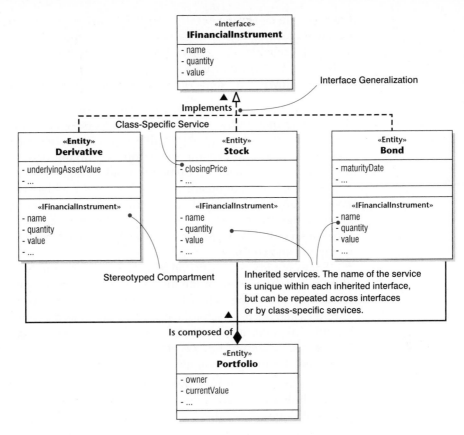

Figure 15.4
Interface Inheritance: Same Services, Different Implementation

In interface inheritance, a subclass is responsible for implementing each and every attribute and/or operation of the superclass.

☞ Janus, the Roman god of doors and gateways, was always shown with two faces: one face towards the beginning, the other towards the end. Like Janus, objects can have more than one face.

One interface allows many objects to appear as one. By implementing multiple interfaces, one object can be "reused" as several objects. Each interface may be shared with other objects or, as we shall illustrate later, may be used solely by only one object.

In the real world, objects may have multiple interfaces. One of the best-known examples is the Swiss army knife, but there are many other examples: reversible coats; radio-alarm clocks; seaplanes, ever-increasing combinations of mobile phones, cameras, pagers, Web browsers, and handheld game machines; etc. Most of us, too, implement multiple interfaces at the same time or across time: student, teacher, son, mother, boss, employee, and so on.

The same holds true for virtual objects, for essentially the same reason: **reuse** or *multiple use* of the same basic entity. Like a hand drill that can be fitted with various accessories for different uses—polishing, tightening screws, drilling—a virtual object can serve different purposes.

However, a question may arise: Since the limitations of the real world do not apply to a virtual world, why should we trouble ourselves with adding interfaces to the same object when we can create brand new objects, each for a distinct purpose?

True, but a virtual world has its own limitations. It might appear that virtual objects can be created easily and cheaply, but appearances are misleading: The interface can be simple, but the implementation can be extremely complicated and expensive. A clock's interface is very simple, but it took humanity a long time to arrive at a reliable mechanical clock, and a precise chronometer was not invented until the 18th century.

The following are some of the reasons for creating multiple interfaces:

☞ For a discussion of domain concepts and enterprise-wide consolidation of those concepts, see Chapter 5.

- *Complexity of the Services.*   An ever-increasing number of companies are discovering that, in the long run, an enterprise-wide analysis is beneficial to their needs. But the interface of objects that result from such a wide-ranging analysis and consolidation might become too complex. Having one object behind its multiple manifestations can result in tremendous advantages in terms of consistency, maintenance, enforcement of business rules, business intelligence, etc. A large information system, however, is composed of many subsystems developed by separate teams. Even though the requirements of different subsystems overlap—hence the advantages of an enterprise-wide domain analysis—one interface for all can become overwhelming and confusing.

For example, the production of a car is far from simple and needs the contribution of numerous groups, from the inception of the idea and market research to technical research, prototyping, safety tests, factory retooling, inventory, sales, etc. The list of attributes and operations for the class **Car** can indeed become very long. By constructing multiple interfaces over the *same* object—**MarketingCar**, **EngineeringCar**, **SalesCar**, **AccountingCar**, etc.—we can use the same **Car** "engine" but let each team view it from its own angle.

- *Security.*   In a hospital's information system, such as Walden's, we may need to hide the patient's financial data and credit card information from the hospital staff who do not need to know them. Even though the development team(s) for nonfinancial applications can be instructed to follow security guidelines, a large information system has numerous objects and even more attributes and operations. Therefore, it is best to secure the information at the source, whenever possible.

- *Multiple Functionality.*   Like a Swiss army knife, an object may genuinely perform more than one function. And, again like a Swiss army knife, it is usually "service" objects that acquire multiple interfaces for this reason, not business objects.

✍ The exact mechanism for accommodating changes to the interface is technology-dependent.

- *Growth & Change.*   As the business grows and changes, some objects may acquire new responsibilities. As we argued, an interface is a **contract** that must not be broken and cannot be changed without the agreement of its stakeholders. If the old interface cannot accommodate new expectations, then a new contract—an additional interface—has to be drawn up and the old one should be left in peace.

We cannot overemphasize the importance of understanding interface as *independent* from implementation. If you study object-oriented design long enough, you will come across some version of following advice repeatedly:

[Gamma 1997, 17]   **Program to an interface, not an implementation.**

Separating interface from implementation is what makes polymorphism possible and provides the foundation for component reuse (as well shall see later). It also reduces implementation dependencies between subsystems and makes the system, as a whole, more flexible.

Figure 15.5
Multiple Interfaces to Manage Complexity, Security, and Change

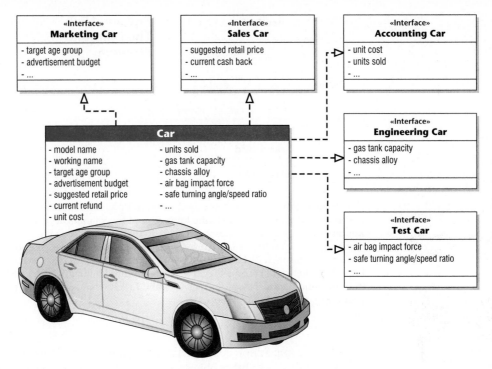

By implementing multiple interfaces, one object can appear as several.

Emulating Inheritance by Composition

Single and multiple inheritance can be emulated through composition.

☞ A detailed discussion of the pros and cons of inheritance, and especially those of multiple inheritance, would take us to a specialized domain that is outside the scope of this book. As an example, see the sidebar titled "The Diamond Problem." We are in neither opposing camp, but believe that "it depends."

Multiple *implementation* inheritance is a well-established concept. Many popular development platforms, however, do not support it. The reasons are not only technological, but result from logical and conceptual issues. In fact, even single inheritance is often a target of objections. For example, inheritance is often called "white-box reuse" that by exposing a subclass to the details of its parent's implementation "breaks encapsulation."

Fortunately, the *concept* of inheritance can be applied without the *mechanism* of inheritance, regardless of whether or not the technology supports multiple inheritance. This alternative consists of emulating inheritance through *object composition*.

Most man-made objects in the real world that we (and others) have cited as examples of multiple inheritance—Swiss army knife, seaplane, camera cell phone, etc.—are actually composite objects. On the other hand, animals or plants that have a pair of parents can be considered examples of "true" inheritance. Both, nevertheless, embody the same concept: The child object is "a kind of" its parents.

The composition approach is also called *black-box reuse* since the internal details of a class are not exposed to subclasses.

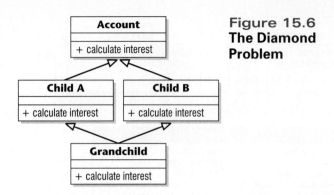

**Figure 15.6
The Diamond
Problem**

One of the logical problems associated with multiple inheritance is called, in its simplest form, the "diamond problem" (due to the form created by generalization lines). In this example, the **Account** class has two subclasses that are, in turn, inherited by the class **Grandchild**. The issue that arises is this: Is the **calculate interest** operation of the **Grandchild** inherited through **Child A** or through **Child B**? By increasing the number of parents and/or grandparents, the logical tangle would become bigger as well. Popular languages such as Java or C# do not support multiple inheritance. Others, such as C++ and Eiffel, which do support multiple inheritance, offer propriety solutions to the issue.

Object composition is defined dynamically at run-time through objects acquiring references to other objects. Composition requires objects to respect each others' interfaces, which in turn requires carefully designed interfaces that don't stop you from using one object with many others. . . . Because objects are accessed solely through their interfaces, we don't break encapsulation. Any object can be replaced at run-time by another as long as it has the same type. Moreover, because an object's implementation will be written in terms of object interfaces, there are substantially fewer implementation dependencies.

Object composition has another effect on system design. Favoring object composition over class inheritance helps you keep each class encapsulated and focused on one task. Your classes and class hierarchies will remain small and will be less likely to grow into unmanageable monsters. On the other hand, a design based on object composition will have more objects (if fewer classes) and the system's behavior will depend on their relationships instead of being defined in one class.

[Gamma 1997, 19]

Figure 15.7 is an example of emulating inheritance through composition, very similar to a Swiss army knife. The **Draw** class provides services such as draw line, draw circle, and so on. Instead of inheriting these services from multiple parents, it *delegates* the services to objects that compose it. The internal workings of composing objects remain private to those objects.

Reuse by composition is *dynamic*. How a service is performed is decided by the object, and the object only, not by its parent or parents. The **Draw** class can change how it responds to messages based on its own logic. If a service has to be changed or a new service is required, nothing in the inheritance chain has to be changed, because there is no inheritance chain.

Reuse by composition must rely on *abstract interfaces* to be effective. An abstract interface hides the internal composition of a composite object and allows the object to change its behavior without adversely affecting its clients.

The composition approach to reuse has its own disadvantages. First, it takes more coding. Instantiation of composing objects and delegations are not handled by

Figure 15.7
Reuse by
Composition:
Emulating
Inheritance
Dynamically

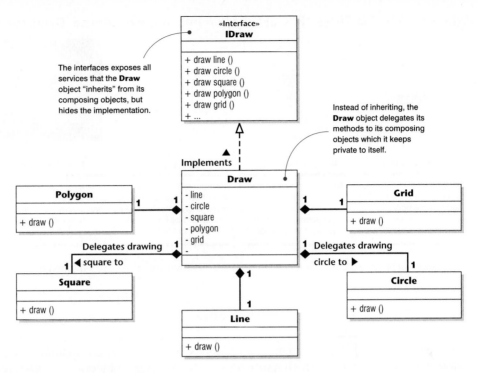

The **Draw** object reuses the services of many other objects, but the implementation is completely hidden behind the **IDraw** interface.

the runtime environment and must be specifically coded. (On the other hand, this is exactly how the logical problems of multiple inheritance are avoided.) Second, understanding the structure of the application becomes more difficult: The user might see the Swiss army knife as one convenient unit, but the developer has to understand the corkscrew, the knife, the bottle opener, etc., separately and in combination. However, flexible reuse has a price, and if you need it you must pay the price.

4. Components

Component-based products are quite familiar to us. They are everywhere: from the lowly household entertainment system to the high-flying Boeing jetliner. You may not have the means to assemble a Boeing 747 in your backyard, but you can put together a powerful computer from mail-order parts in your spare time with the simplest tools.

Building products from replaceable, interchangeable, reusable, and well-tested components has proven to be the most effective method to assure quality, make products more customizable, and, last but not least, reduce costs through economy of scale.

In software development, however, the benefits of component-based development have been late and slow in coming. Until fairly recently, the common method for developing software was *vertical*: build everything from start to finish in one project. Component-based development, on the other hand, is mostly *horizontal*: assemble software from independent units that are limited in scope but are well-defined, can be replaced, and, given the right functionality, can be recombined into more than one application and in more than one context.

Figure 15.8 The Three "R"s of Components: Replace, Reuse, Recombine

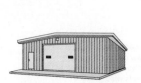		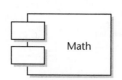		
Prefabs & Kits	**Manufacturing**	**Software**	**Electronics**	**Chemicals**
A wide range of products, from household items to houses, are offered as ready-to-assemble component kits.	Modern manufacturing relies on interchangeable and standard components for both quality and low cost.	Components allow every type of software to perform increasingly complex tasks that would be impossible without them.	The magic of electronic products depends on the creative use of complex but self-contained components.	By combining a limited number of atoms, both nature and man have produced an amazing array of chemical substances.

Components can be replaced and/or reused in products, but they can also be recombined in new ways.

Defining Components

☞ The term "component" is derived from the present participle of the Latin verb *componere*, which means "to put together." To wit, a thing that is used to compose another thing is a component.

> A component is a relatively independent, encapsulated, and replaceable unit of software that provides services specified by one or more interfaces.

Like many other concepts in system analysis and design, the definition of component depends on the definer and the context. One reason is that the term "component" is a general-purpose one: an element that is a constituent part of a system or a compound entity. Such a general definition, of course, applies to many things: atoms in a molecule, molecules in a chemical compound, chemical compounds in a cell, and so on.

Furthermore, although the term "component" is often used alongside "reuse," a component is not necessarily a *reusable* component. A custom-made dining table is made up of components but the reusability of its parts is not planned or probable. Building products out of components has advantages that are not limited to reuse and any description that overlooks this point would be incomplete.

The meaning of "component" is bound to retain some ambiguity but, in the context of software, the following properties help to clarify the concept:

• *A component is a binary and relatively independent entity.* We write software in a language that is human-readable, even though we must be trained to understand it. At some point this human-readable text must be converted to a *binary* language that can be understood and executed by the computer platform. A component is a binary unit, not a block of text:

☞ The binary code is either **compiled** or **interpreted**. The compiled code is directly understood by the operating system while the interpreted code is translated by an "interpreter" or "runtime library" each time it is executed. If a component is written in interpreted language, such as Java or C#, it needs support libraries to execute.

Being a binary entity, a component is not language-specific. It is, however, platform-specific. For example, the machine code that runs on an Intel Pentium will not run on a Motorola chip, an RISC chip, or any other chip that wasn't specifically designed to be binary-compatible with a Pentium. So a component is built for a designated target platform. The platform also identifies which operating system the component is built for. Just because a component executes Pentium machine code doesn't mean it will run on any operating system running on a Pentium machine.

[Faison 2002, xii]

A component is independent because it does not rely on its "client"—another component or an application—to perform its services. It is *relatively* independent because, at the very least, a component relies on the services of its underlying platform or, perhaps, on other components.

• *A component's interface is separate from its implementation.*   Even though most modern languages are object-oriented, the language used to create a component and its internal structure are irrelevant. A component is identified by one or more interfaces that, as we have stated before, act as **contracts** between the component and its clients.

A big difference between a component and any other software unit is that its interface cannot be "local": The interface must be recognized as valid by the operating system, the runtime environment, or both. What does this mean?

Like with objects, communication with components is conducted by exchanging messages. For components, however, the language and protocols of communication are more strict and formalized since a component must be able to communicate with *any* entity that uses the platform. This language can be roughly compared to shorthand: In your diary, you might use symbols that are understood only by you; a court stenographer, on the other hand, must record the court proceedings in a *standard* shorthand.

Each platform usually has a proprietary **interface definition language** (IDL) that defines how the interface of a component must be structured and what kinds of variables it can support. In the early days of software components, you had to explicitly use this language to create an interface. Fortunately, more modern development tools have made this task transparent to the developers: When you "compile" a component, the development platform, behind the scene, takes care of the necessary details (or tells you that something does not comply with the protocols).

The strict rules governing communication with components confers one great advantage to software development: It makes reuse of components possible. If the interface of a component complies with the requirements of the platform, then *any* application or component on that platform can use it.

• *A component is replaceable.*   Regardless of whether or not a component has been designed for reuse, it must be replaceable. Replacing the leg of a customized table might be more expensive or less convenient than replacing the tire of your car that was designed for reuse, but the principle is the same: If it cannot be replaced, it is *not* a component. (Again, we must differentiate between the term "component" in its general sense, that is, a synonym for "part," "element," etc., and the same term as it is understood by the software industry.)

The ability to replace components means that they can be upgraded or repaired *without* adverse effects on the entities that use them. (Unfortunately, this assertion is more theoretical than actual: Computer users have many stories about upgrading some piece of software that then wreaked havoc with the normal workings of other software.)

Software components are not applications but they help applications in various ways. Consequently, users would not normally recognize components as independent entities. There are, however, exceptions. Modern desktop operating systems allow users to select system-level services by selecting components. For example, the user can select a "default" printer from a list of installed printers. (See Figure 15.9.) What the user actually selects is a special kind of component called a **device driver**. In this case, the "device" is a printer and, as a result, the list consists of "printer drivers."

Printer drivers manage a large number of devices whose features and internal workings are dissimilar. Some have color; some don't. Some are laser, while others are inkjet. Some may even perform tasks that are not, strictly speaking, printing, such

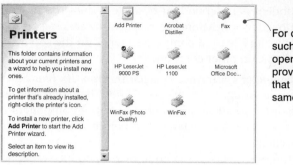

Figure 15.9
**System
Components:
Reusing
Common
Services**

Operating systems, such as Windows or Mac, free the applications from implementing common tasks by providing system-level components.

as sending faxes. None of these variations, however, need be the concern of any application that runs on a specific platform, because they all have the *same* interface. It is the printer vendors that must provide components that strictly conform to the interface specified and supported by the operating system.

This ability to select system services is so common today that it might seem to be a natural state of affairs. This is not the case: When the first personal computers appeared on the mass market, applications had to provide *internal* support for printers. Consequently, the compatibility between your favorite printer and your favorite word processor was not a foregone conclusion. In turn, vendors of print-intensive applications had to invest heavily in supporting a growing and unending list of printers. With system-level components both hardware and software vendors are freed from inventing the same wheel over and over.

Components vs. Objects

[Faison 2002, xiii]

Conceptually, components and objects are very close. So close, in fact, that it is easy to confuse them. Let us summarize what we have said from this viewpoint.

Nowadays, components are overwhelmingly created by using object-oriented languages, but this not necessary: If any entity implements an interface that follows the rules of the platform, it is a component. The component might be composed of one object, many objects, or no objects at all. (You might even create a component by using the zeros and the ones of machine language, though it would be akin to emptying the ocean by employing a household bucket.)

The other important distinction is the binary nature of components. In other words, components are *language-neutral*, while objects are language-dependent. If you create classes in one development platform (such as Java) you cannot import them, or their instances, into another platform (such as VS.Net) *as they are*. On a specific platform, however, components are ready to use by any client, be it an application or another component.

Functional & Extra-Functional Properties

[Crnkovic 2002]

A component usually has two sets of properties:

- **Functional** properties are those services for which the component was created and are exposed through one or more interfaces. The rules governing these interfaces are well-defined by the underlying platform.
- **Extra-functional** properties, or *component specifications*, describe the component itself: version number, copyright, performance, security, etc. Often, there

are no standards governing these specifications. For example, the version number may be missing or, if it exists, may be numerical or textual.

Modeling Components

☞ Though by now you should be thoroughly familiar with **stereotyping**, here we repeat the essence of the concept: Stereotyping is a mechanism for extending and specializing *modeling* elements through icons and/or labels.

> Components can be modeled both from the outside or from the inside.

In modeling classes, we needed only one shape to present the class: a black box. What goes inside the class is a matter of implementation, not modeling. Components, on the other hand, are often composed of classes or even other components. Therefore, modeling a component depends on whether you want to view it from the inside or from the outside.

Component as Black Box

Figure 15.10 presents three ways to model a component from the outside. The component is a "print engine" that can be used by any application on the same platform

Figure 15.10 Component from Outside: Modeling the Services

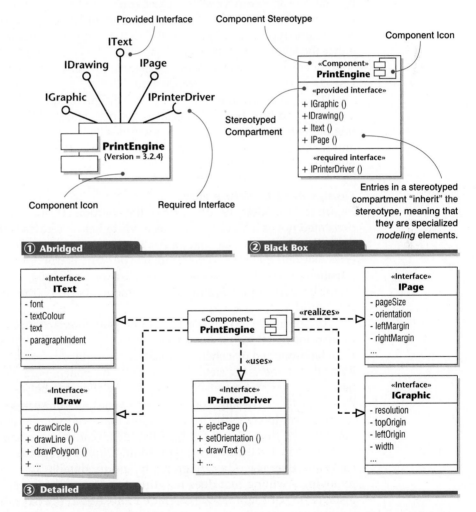

Depending on the level of detail that you require, components can be modeled as simple icons, black boxes, or class diagrams.

[Chonoles 2003,
327–330]

to print text and graphics on a printer. Your choice of models will depend on the level of detail that you may require. Regardless of the detail level, they all rely on the UML mechanism of stereotyping.

The first diagram is the most abridged one: a component icon with interfaces that it supports or requires. The standard UML icon for components is a box with two tabs—more or less like a plug—with the name of the component and, perhaps, tagged values inside. (The version number in our example is a "tagged value.") Each interface that the component provides is identified by its name (that usually starts with an "I") and a circle-tipped line that connects it to the component icon. If the component *requires* the services of an interface in its environment, then the connecting line ends in a half circle. In this case, the component requires that the platform provide it with another component that implements the services of a printer driver. (Earlier, we used printer drivers to illustrate components that are *not* hidden from users.)

The second diagram represents the component as a familiar "black box," very much like a class except that it does not contain attributes and operations but interfaces. The top compartment is stereotyped as **«provided interface»** and the bottom one as **«required interface»**. (Note that when you stereotype a compartment, all elements within the compartment "inherit" the stereotype; i.e., they are of the same type.) The black box itself is stereotyped as **«component»**. You may use either the label or the icon (which, as we said, is a standard UML icon), or both. You should, however, use at least one of them to prevent confusion: The box does not represent a normal class, but a component.

The third diagram is the most detailed. The component has been shrunk back to a stereotyped box, but the interfaces are presented in detail. A dashed inheritance line, stereotyped as **«realizes»**, identifies the relationship between the component and its interfaces, while a dashed arrowed line, stereotyped as **«uses»**, connects it with the interfaces that it needs.

Component as White Box

Figure 15.11 models the structure of the component from inside. The component is presented not as a black box but as a **white box** that reveals its inner structure. The model inside the box, labeled **PrintEngine** and stereotyped as **«Component»**, is a class diagram that should be familiar. The same is true for the "interface" notations outside the box. The new element consists of small boxes, or **ports**, that are placed on the borders. A port is a point of interaction between the component and the outside world.

An "incoming" port is one that connects an interface supported by the component to an inside class by a **«delegates»** arrow. Since interfaces lack implementation, they must be supported by concrete classes that actually do something. An "outgoing" port is one that connects the elements inside the component with interfaces that the component requires from the outside world. The relationship between the inside classes and the outgoing port usually consists of **«delegates»** or **«uses»** connections.

Some components are more complex than our example, and some are less. But as you can infer from Figure 15.11, adding detail can easily exhaust the space inside any one box. If such a threat exists, you should limit the representation of classes to their icons and then use other diagrams to specify details. You may even go further by removing anything that does not directly relate to the purpose of the diagram. For instance, in our example, we can hide **Line**, **Square**, **Polygon**, and **Circle** classes since they are available only through the **Draw** class. The composition of the **Draw** class can be delegated to another diagram like the one in Figure 15.7.

Figure 15.11
Component
from Inside:
Modeling the
Structure

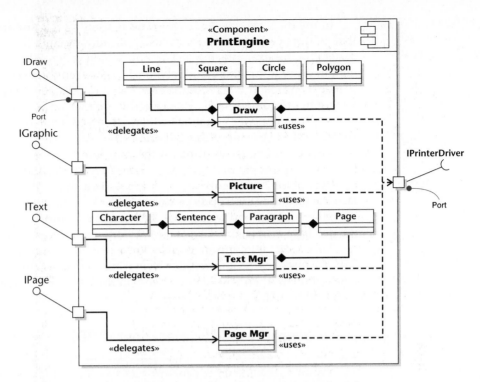

Ports are the points of interaction between the outside and the inside of the component.

The Component Diagram

The relationships *between* components are modeled through the **component diagram**, using the same tools that we previously described. Figure 15.12 presents the same component, **PrintEngine**, that we used in our previous examples, but in the context of its relationship with other components in the information system of a company that, among other things, has a **Sales** application. (For UML, *all* binary units are components; therefore, the **Sales** application is a component as well.)

Figure 15.12
The Component
Diagram:
Modeling the
Relationships
between
Components

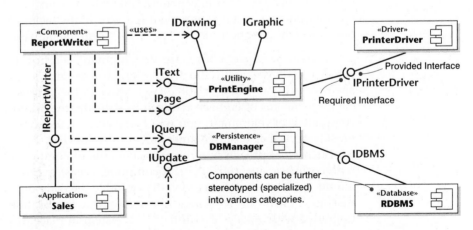

Components offer services *only* through interfaces. If a component depends on the services of another component, the relationship is shown as "ball and socket."

In the diagram, the **PrintEngine** is used by the **ReportWriter** component that, in turn, can be used by various applications within the company's information system. In this example, the **Sales** application *requires* the **ReportWriter** component in order to function. The relationship between the two is shown as a "ball and socket" connection where **ReportWriter** provides the **IReportWriter** interface for use by consumers such as **Sales**. (Notice that since all elements within the diagram are components, you may further stereotype them into finer-grained categories such as «**Utility**» or «**Persistence**».)

ReportWriter uses three of the four interfaces provided by **PrintEngine**. (It does not print pictures so it has no need for **IGraphic**.) It also uses the **IQuery** interface of the **DBManager** component. **Sales** shares the use of the **IQuery** interface but also uses the **IUpdate** interface of the same component since it both reads from the database and writes to it. **DBManager**, in turn, depends on the interface of the database management system to perform its services.

This kind of diagram is also known as a *wiring diagram* since it shows how the pieces of the information system are "wired together." If the components are large-grained, then it would become an *architectural diagram*. (We will discuss architecture in the next chapter.)

Component-Based Development (CBD)

> Component-based development has two meanings: ❶ developing components, and ❷ developing information systems and applications by assembling components.

Components are architectural entities and, as such, the methodology to select and/or assemble them relates to architecture. Nowadays, the praise for component-based software architecture is almost universal. But how do you arrive at components? What does it take to develop components? What price do we have to pay to benefit from them?

The technology to support components is relatively advanced. All modern platforms—be it at the level of the operating system or the development platform such as Java or .Net—are "wired" for components. The support and the features that they offer may not follow the same model or might be uneven but, as far as technology goes, the environment is very component-friendly. Many factors *beyond* technology, however, affect the adoption and the success of a component-based development:

• *Use vs. Reuse.* Software development is labor-intensive and, therefore, expensive. Consequently, the promise of reuse, regardless of the actual outcome, has always had an almost irresistible fascination for businesses. As a result, the value of components has often been reduced to their degree of reusability. In literature on component development, you will come across guidelines such as "a component must be reused at least five times" to be worth developing.

Such an approach ignores other benefits of components: *clarity* of purpose, *replaceability*, and *flexibility*. A component *must* expose its services through an interface, and it is far easier to verify or judge the component through this interface than to confirm the workings of a monolithic application. A component can be upgraded with *minimal* disruption to a system in place. (Do not believe, however, anybody who claims there will be *no* disruptions whatsoever.) And it is far easier to add or remove services in a component-based system or application.

This does not mean that the more parts an information system (or any other product) has, the better it is. It does, however, mean that a monolithic application is more fragile than a component-based one. If a component can be reused, so much the better. But reuse is not the only criteria:

One essential purpose of component-based architecture is to manage complexity.

• *Design vs. Domain Components.* The overwhelming majority of the off-the-shelf components in the marketplace are design components. A design component is one that solves a problem in building the *solution*. It might be as relatively simple as a visual control such as a dropdown list or as complex as an RDBMS. Domain components, on the other hand, are those that are specific to the problem domain. For example, a component called **BankAccount** would encapsulate all objects required for managing bank accounts and would provide interfaces that allow its "clients" to use its functionality in a consistent and comprehensive way.

As we have seen, design often follows **patterns** that can be highly generalized because they are *domain-independent*: a "selector" such as a dropdown can display any list regardless of the content and an RDBMS can manage any kind of data that can be mapped to a relational model.

Domain concepts cannot be as effectively generalized as design concepts. The reasons are varied. First, business objects and processes are not standardized: A **Customer** object does not have the same attributes and operations even in the same industry, such as banking, let alone across different sectors. Furthermore, it is exactly the differentiation between business processes that gives one company a competitive advantage over another. The moment a business process becomes "standard"—that is, is adopted across an industry—somebody breaks the standard to gain an edge.

Where external pressures, such as regulations, have forced standardization, ready-made software *is* available (even though it might be offered as an entire application instead of as components). General ledger software is one example; credit card verification for sales is another.

Second, domain objects and processes cannot be easily isolated from each other and packaged separately. The functionality of the **Patient** class is intertwined with that of **Appointment**, which in turn brings in **Medical Service**, **Medical Staff**, and so on. The cutoff point to create a "relatively independent" component is difficult to figure out.

It is no accident that even design components in the marketplace mostly address the *boundaries* of the application, that is, the user interface and the data management. The space between, the "middleware" where flow and control takes place and many business rules are enforced, is largely underrepresented in the component market. This means that the burden of developing domain components generally falls on the in-house development team. And it is not an easy burden to carry.

• *Buy vs. Build.* It is invariably cheaper to buy *reusable* components and very expensive to develop them. Software vendors can afford to invest heavily in developing components because they hope to recoup the expense in the marketplace. Businesses who develop software for in-house use, with few exceptions, cannot afford to do so. Besides, you can spend tens of millions of dollars to create an in-house data management system, but it is unlikely that the resulting product would compare favorably with a battle-tested DBMS from established vendors, even if it has some interesting or clever features.

On the other hand, using an off-the-shelf component means that the continued health of your system is now dependent on the continued health of the outside vendor and its ability to provide timely updates. With the approach of the year 2000,

☞ At the same time, monolithic applications were in no way better off. Whereas most commercial components and database management systems were updated in a timely manner, monolithic applications invariably had to be opened up or rewritten completely.

businesses had to scramble to cope with the so-called "millennium bug": not a "bug" in conventional terms, but the fact that most date-related components could not handle a four-digit year. If the vendor of such a component had gone out of business, or was not agile enough, then the business was out of luck and had to undertake a major renovation project.

Relying on components from outside sources involves risks that must be taken into account, although such risks are not limited to software development and apply to most industries. To counter risk-averseness on the part of their clients, some software vendors provide their clients with the source code for their components (sometimes for an additional fee).

• *Methodology.* To the degree that software shops follow any methodology, that methodology is unlikely to be optimal for component development. Object-oriented analysis and design is an ideal starting point, but it is not enough for developing components or developing *with* components. Again, we must emphasize the distinction between design components and domain components.

Design components are seldom conceived by analyzing a specific problem domain or business. Instead, the idea for them emerges gradually by noticing patterns through using and designing *solutions*: a database management system that unloads the repeated tasks of the data management from individual applications or a visual control that presents a long list more effectively than a textbox.

By nature, design components must be highly generalized to work with many kinds of solutions. At the same time, this requirement creates a seeming paradox:

A reusable component must be combined with other components to be of any use. It must be developed, however, as though it is the final product.

In other words, you cannot look to any *specific* solution to create a reusable design component. How such a component is used is basically unpredictable.

Domain components, on the other hand, are usually planned to work within *specific* solutions: If you conceive of them *after* the solution is built, it is already too late. If, through gathering requirements and domain analysis, you are forewarned that multiple applications within the same information system require the same functionality, you must plan ahead for a component or components that encapsulate that functionality.

This approach has two effects on the methodology, one negative and one positive. On the negative side, your allotted time for iterative refinement of requirements and product specifications shrinks because, at the very least, the interface of the component must be stabilized for the development of dependent components to proceed. (Remember that in building domain components, we are not usually aiming for mass-market generalization.)

On the plus side, multiple teams can work ***in parallel*** on design and implementation. This methodology requires a high level of discipline and effective project management. For complex systems, however, component-based development might hold the only realistic chance of success *even if components are not reusable.*

Testing Components

Components must be tested both independently and within the framework in which they will be used.

Testing of software is an extensive subject in its own right. Testing components, however, requires a methodology that goes beyond the framework of test parameters.

If we consider components as parts that go into building something bigger (and not merely as binary entities), then we have to test them both independently and in the context of the whole.

As building blocks, components often cannot complete a useful task by themselves, in the same manner that many parts of manufactured goods are only meaningful within their target assembly. For testing such components, the best and the most common way is to use a *test harness*, an application that focuses exclusively (or as exclusively as possible) on the component at hand. In addition to other benefits of component-based development, the "test harness" approach is the closest that software testing can come to the workings of a scientific laboratory: It removes as many extraneous variables as possible from the experiment.

It is not enough, however, for a component to pass this kind of test to get a seal of approval. Combining components frequently reveals shortcomings in individual components. The first set of shortcomings originate from incompatibilities: A car tire might pass every test by itself and yet it might not fit the target car. The second set results from the introduction of new variables and forces that the test harness *intentionally* keeps out: The breakaway foam that damaged the protective tiles of the shuttle Columbia (and resulted in its disintegration on reentry in 2003) was such an unexpected variable.

Sometimes a component, such as a database management system, cannot be tested in its entirety through a simple test harness. On the other hand, such a mega-component is most likely a composition of smaller components, each of which would (or should) have been tested independently. In addition, the behavior of big components can be grouped into distinct sets that can be tested through independent test harnesses. (Experience shows, however, that as components grow more complicated, a certain number of engineering defects are inevitable. The point of testing is not to do the impossible and account for every unknown variable, but to reduce them.)

If you are developing a reusable component for *commercial use*, then testing "in context" becomes more important but also more difficult as *you have no control over how and where the component will be used*. (This is why many architects and developers stay away from the "Release 1.0" of any component, hoping that by "Release 1.x" less prudent users will have reduced the number of bugs.)

Test harnesses are essentially throwaway applications. Software vendors mostly understand their necessity and consider them a necessary expense. Developers for in-house software are usually not so lucky: The clients do not see the point of "wasting" resources on something that will be discarded soon, and no amount of persuasion is likely to turn them around. For this reason, and others like it, the best hope for component "manufacturing" lies with vendors whose primary business is software.

5. DELIVERABLES

Design decisions and artifacts that concern components and reuse arrive from two opposite directions. The first direction is architectural: Deciding on the architecture also determines ❶ the large-grained components from which the system will be assembled, ❷ which components must be built, and ❸ which components must be purchased from outside sources.

The other direction is the generalization and the refactoring that occurs as development moves forward. We discover common attributes and behaviors among disparate entities that can be refactored into components. We are also likely to discover that entities that we thought were similar are, in reality, not similar at all, cannot be connected through inheritance, and cannot be generalized into components. In effect, the experience that comes from this direction acts as a "reality check" for architectural ideas.

A component diagram is the obvious artifact for components, but a component-based development affects the organization of the whole project:

> **In component-based development, delivery of components forms a set of major milestones.**

In a component-based system, each component must have its own *independent* delivery process and event. Such an approach would make the estimated date for the delivery of the *final* product more realistic and attainable.

6. WRAP UP

☑ **Areas of reuse**

Reuse, where possible, has two major benefits: It makes the product less costly because the same solution does not have to be reinvented repeatedly, and it makes the product more reliable since a reusable element is tested in different contexts.

Reuse is not limited to one aspect of the development or the product. **Components** are the most reliable and effective mechanism for reuse since they provide "black boxes" that can be assembled with no change. **Patterns** encapsulate experience in solving problems and, consequently, can be labeled as "experience reuse." **Inheritance** is an object-oriented technology that allows the descendents of a class to reuse its behavior, with or without modifications. **Web services** can be described as "components on the Web": They provide services across the Internet or intranets and the consumers can ignore *how* the services are rendered. The aim of *methodology* is to reuse abstract ideas as guidelines for *discovering* solutions on your own. **Refactoring** is the consolidation of analysis, design, or implementation artifacts to eliminate useless redundancy. **Source code reuse** is usually discouraged but can be valuable in providing examples for learning. Finally, development frameworks provide **templates**, bare skeletons that can be expanded into full solutions.

☑ **Implementation inheritance**

Inheritance is one of the basic concepts of object orientation: An object can be a specialized type of another object. Inheritance, however, is also a *mechanism*. The first type of this mechanism is **implementation inheritance**, also called *subclassing*, by which a subclass (or "child") can reuse, extend, or override the attributes and the operations of its parent *without* starting from scratch.

The subclass may change, limit, or block the implementation of a service offered by its parent.

This is called **overriding**. It may also add attributes and/or operations that do not exist in the superclass. This is called **extension**.

☑ **Interface inheritance**

The second type of inheritance is interface inheritance. It is a mechanism by which multiple classes share one interface but implement that interface independently of each other or of the parent class. Unlike the implementation inheritance where the subclass inherits both the interface and the functionality of its parent for specialization, the purpose of interface inheritance is to arrive at a subclass that looks *exactly* like its parent but performs the services its own way.

Besides sharing an interface with other classes, a class might implement *multiple* interfaces, regardless of whether any of the interfaces are shared with others. Multiple interfaces may become necessary for many reasons, including complexity of the services that one class may offer, security to ensure that other entities see only what they are allowed to see, multiple functionality, and change when the class must offer new services but must keep the existing "contracts" in place.

☑ **Emulating inheritance by composition**

Multiple *implementation* inheritance is a well-established concept. Many popular development platforms, however, do not support it. The reasons are usually not only technological, but also logical. Single and multiple inheritance, however, can be emulated through composition. In fact, many prefer composition to inheritance regardless of whether or not the technology supports inheritance.

The composition approach is also called *black-box reuse* since the internal details of a class are not exposed to subclasses. Reuse by composition is *dynamic*. How a service is performed is decided by the object at runtime, and by the object only, not by its parent or parents.

Reuse by composition must rely on *abstract interfaces* to be workable. An abstract interface hides the internal composition of a composite object and allows the object to change its behavior without adversely affecting its clients.

☑ **Components**

A component is a relatively independent, encapsulated, and replaceable unit of software that provides services specified by one or more interfaces. Even though a component is not necessarily reusable, it is the ideal method for creating flexible systems.

Although anything that goes into building something bigger can be called a "component," *software* components must have certain properties to qualify for the term: ❶ a component is a binary and relatively independent entity, ❷ a component's interface is separate from its implementation, and ❸ a component is replaceable.

Components are not the same as objects. A component might be composed of one object, many objects, or no objects at all. The other important difference is the binary nature of components: components are language-neutral, while objects are language-dependent.

A component usually has two set of properties: *functional*, or what the component does, and *extra-functional*, which describes the component itself. While the rules governing the first set are well-defined by the underlying platforms, the second set usually does not enjoy a standard definition.

☑ **Modeling components**

The standard UML icon is a box with two tabs, similar to a plug. Components, however, can also be represented by "stereotyped" boxes. A component can be modeled both as a *black box* that hides its internal structure, and as a *white box* that exposes that structure.

In black box modeling, we represent the interfaces that the component supports as lines that end in a circle. The outside world can interact with the component *only* through these interfaces. In turn, if the component requires an *external* interface in its environment, the requirement is shown as a line ending in a half-circle. This arrangement is often called *"ball & socket"* as the interface provided by one component must fit into the "socket" provided by its "client."

In white box modeling, the internal structure of the component is shown as a diagram inside the stereotyped box that represents the component. The communication between entities inside the box and

outside entities takes place through **ports**, shown as small boxes that are situated on the borders of the component box. An "incoming" port *delegates* a provided interface to an object, or another component, inside the component. An "outgoing" port conveys requests by internal entities to the required interface of an outside component.

The **component diagram** models the interactions *between* components. Since one component may support multiple interfaces and each interface has an independent "connector," the component diagram shows the use of each interface separately. Component diagrams are also known as *wiring diagrams* since they show how different parts of the system are "wired" together.

☑ **Component-based development (CBD)**

The term "component-based development" applies both to development *with* components and the development *of* components. In either case, the required methodology goes beyond the traditional analysis, design, implementation, and testing activities and involves packaging, integrating, versioning, and creating installation programs.

The technology for supporting components is mature, but other factors influence its success and adoption, including issues such as usability vs. reusability, the difficulties of developing "domain" components as opposed to "design" components, the respective advantages and disadvantages of building components versus buying them, and the optimization of methodology.

Component-based development also impacts project management. Milestones should include delivery of components and the dependencies between components must be taken into account. On the plus side, CBD allows multiple development teams to work *in parallel*, something without which large and complex development projects have no realistic chance of success in an acceptable timeframe.

Testing components also imposes requirements beyond the normal parameters of testing. Components must be tested both independently and within the framework in which they will be used. To come as close to laboratory conditions as possible, a component is usually first tested through a *"test harness,"* an application whose only purpose is to verify the component in an environment that is as isolated from unwanted interferences as possible. However, each new combination of components, including the assembly of the final product, requires an independent set of tests for two reasons: assuring compatibility *between* components and accounting for unforeseen factors and forces that the combination inevitably introduces into the context.

7. Key Concepts

Black Box Modeling. In the context of components, modeling that represents a component as a simple icon or a box that specifies its interface(s) without exposing its internal structure. See also **White Box Modeling**.

Client. An entity that uses the services of a component. See also **Provider**.

Component. A relatively independent, encapsulated, and replaceable unit of software that provides services specified by one or more interfaces. *Software* components share certain properties: ❶ a component is a binary and relatively independent entity, ❷ a component's interface is separate from its implementation, and ❸ a component is replaceable. Components are *language-neutral*, whereas classes (and objects) are language-dependent. They are, however, platform-dependent.

Component-Based Development (CBD). ❶ Developing components, and ❷ developing information systems and applications by assembling components.

Component Diagram. A standard UML diagram that models the relationships between components through their interfaces.

Composition. In the context of reuse, object composition can be used instead of inheritance, either to overcome logical problems or to compensate for the lack of support for multiple inheritance in specific technologies (which includes the majority of popular languages). Object composition is dynamic, meaning that the behavior of the "composed" object is decided at runtime and does not affect the implementation of composing objects. Like **interface inheritance**, composition must rely on abstract interfaces to encapsulate its services. The composition approach is also called *black-box reuse* since the internal details of a class are not exposed to subclasses.

Extension. In the context of implementation inheritance, the concept that a subclass may add attributes and/or operations that do not exist in the superclass. See also **Overriding**.

Implementation Inheritance. A mechanism by which a subclass (or child) can reuse, extend, or override the attributes and the operations of its parent (or superclass). Also known as *subclassing*, the child does not have to implement any method unless it wants to change it: If the parent can do anything, so can the child *without* any extra effort. See also **Interface Inheritance**.

Inheritance. An object-oriented concept stating that the children of a class inherit its properties. Inheritance *mechanism* is how this concept is implemented in a specific technology. There are two inheritance mechanisms: **implementation inheritance** and **interface inheritance**.

Interface. The sum of services offered by a class. All classes have interfaces, but an interface can be abstract and independent of implementation, meaning that the class to which the interface belongs can be "empty."

Interface Inheritance. A mechanism by which multiple classes share one interface but implement that interface independently of each other or of the parent class. Unlike the **implementation inheritance** where the subclass inherits both the interface and the functionality of its parent for specialization, the purpose of interface inheritance is to arrive at a subclass that looks *exactly* like its parent but performs the services its own way. Interface inheritance is the foundation for polymorphism. One class can implement multiple interfaces, shared with other classes or exclusively its own.

Overriding. In the context of **implementation inheritance**, the concept that a subclass may change, limit, or block the implementation of a service offered by its parent. See also **Extension**.

Pattern. Reuse of experience as an abstract problem-solution pair, formulated in a "pattern language" that can be applied to problems that occur repeatedly in a given context.

Port. The point of interaction between the internal entities of a component and the outside world. The port can be either "incoming," for an interface provided by the component, or "outgoing," for an interface that the component requires from its environment.

Provider. A component that provides services to its **clients**.

Refactoring. Refining and improving artifacts of analysis, design, and implementation *without* changing their behavior. Refactoring contributes to reuse by removing duplication and unnecessary redundancies.

Reuse. Concepts, methods, mechanisms, components, and all other tangibles or intangibles that allow us to build new solutions based on existing ones. Reuse can apply to any product, experience, and expertise that is required in development.

Reuse, Method. Applying guidelines that enable us to *discover* solutions.

Reuse, Source Code. Reusing existing code in the text format. Counterproductive if used instead of other reuse mechanisms, but productive if used for learning from examples and adapting solutions to the problem at hand.

Template. A reusable framework offered through a development platform that can be modified and/or extended for the task at hand.

Web Service. A service that provides platform-independent application logic to consumers across the Web via standard protocols.

White Box Modeling. In the context of components, a box that reveals the internal structure of a component. The communication between internal entities and the outside world is conducted through **ports**. See also **Black Box Modeling**.

8. Review Questions

1. Explain the significance of components in the context of object-oriented development.
2. How does component-based development help reuse?
3. Why can patterns be labeled "experienced reuse"?
4. How does the concept of inheritance relate to component-based development?
5. Compare horizontal and vertical software system developments. Which one makes use of components?
6. Describe multiple interfaces and explain why or when they are needed.
7. Compare and contrast components to objects.
8. Describe the differences between "black box" and "white box" component modeling.
9. Describe situations in which an organization should buy rather than build software components.
10. How should we test components?

9. Exercises

The following exercises apply to each of the four narratives introduced in Chapter 4: *The* Sportz *Magazine, The Car Dealership, The Pizza Shop,* and *The Real Estate Agency.*

❶ For one of the scenarios above, find candidates for **implementation inheritance**. Draw one or more diagrams to represent your findings.

❷ For the same scenario, select classes that work better with **interface inheritance**. Create a diagram and explain why this kind of inheritance makes more sense for this class set.

❸ Find candidates for *multiple inheritance* in any of the scenarios.

❹ Suggest possible **components** for one of the cases. Present these components from *inside* and *outside*.

10. Research Projects & Teamwork

❶ The chances are high that as an analyst or a designer you will be asked to *reverse engineer* an existing system. The reasons vary: a legacy system has to be upgraded, but not much is known about its (bad) design; or the business wants to imitate a more successful competitor.

As a team, select an online music store. Individually, study it and decide what *major components* are needed for such a site.

Draw simple component diagrams—not very detailed, identifying only major functions. In a team session, compare your conclusions.

❷ Continue with reverse engineering. Which entities inside the information system for the online music store can benefit from **inheritance**—implementation, interface, or composition? Draw diagrams and discuss them in a team session.

11. Suggested Readings

A good introductory book on components is *UML Components: A Simple Process for Specifying Component Software* by **John Chessman** and John Daniels (Addison-Wesley, 2001). It is, as stated in the preface, "a practical and technical book." It does not stray into theoretical fine points, nor into the complexities of specific technologies.

When it comes to actually building components, however, knowing the ins and outs of specific technologies is indispensable. There are many books on creating components with Java or .Net, but the Web sites of technology vendors, such as Sun or Microsoft, also provide good resources.

The discussion of components is ongoing and very lively. Many issues of *Communications of the ACM* provide cutting-edge articles about components and component-based development.

One of the most comprehensive books on components is *Component Software: Beyond Object-Oriented Programming, Second Edition* by **Clemens Szyperski** (Addison-Wesley, 2002). At more than 600 pages, it provides an extensive discussion of every aspect of components, component-related technologies, and component-based development. As a result, it cannot be approached casually.

Chapter 16

Architecture

1. Overview

The design of the solution cannot proceed from the parts to the whole. Before we can build the nuts and bolts of the solution, and before we can fasten them together, we must make architectural decisions and conceive of the overall framework that connects and organizes the pieces. The architecture of the information system is composed of not one but several overlapping frameworks that must cooperate to make the system work. An introduction to these frameworks and other architectural concepts and patterns is the subject of this last chapter on design.

- ☑ Inception
- ☑ Requirements Discovery
- ☐ Development
  - ☑ Analysis
  - ☐ Design
    - ☑ The Design Challenge
    - ☑ Application Design
    - ☑ Patterns
    - ☑ Components & Reuse
    - ☐ **Architecture** ⬅
  - ☐ Implementation

Chapter Topics

➤ An introduction to architecture and architectural elements.

➤ Methodology, patterns, and architectural views.

➤ The relationship of engineering to architecture.

➤ The significance of coupling to architecture.

- ➤ Architectural modeling and UML.
- ➤ Technology architecture.
- ➤ Architecture of components and applications.
- ➤ Service-oriented architecture and Web services.
- ➤ Data management architecture.
- ➤ Workflow architecture.
- ➤ Architectural patterns and the layering pattern.

Introduction

We describe new activities, new phenomena, or new discoveries by adopting and adapting *existing* terminologies. Buildings are among the earliest products of organized human activity to create something complex; therefore, it is to be expected that the term "architecture" should be applied to many human artifacts besides buildings, including software applications and information systems.

The application of "architecture" to software is both helpful and problematic. As we shall see in this chapter, an architectural approach towards system development helps us to organize and view the final product methodically, following guidelines that are generally solid and familiar to participants in the development process. On the other hand, the term carries a hint of something cast in stone—a sort of monument, an essentially stable and even unchanging or unchangeable edifice. The fact is that software architecture is more similar to the "architecture" of a baseball game in which periods of relative calm are punctured by bursts of activity to which all players must quickly adjust and react—or lose the game. In other words, information system architecture is not only about structure, but also about how readily this structure can morph in response to changes in the environment or the requirements.

What, then, is information system architecture? We will provide more formal and extensive answers shortly. Here, however, let us briefly examine the place of architecture in the context of the development process.

It may not appear so at the first glance, but both analysis and design must start from the "big picture." The term "analysis" literally means breaking something down to its components, but the goal of analysis in system development is to arrive at a *conceptual model* of the solution *as a whole*, even though we construct this model from units that result from "breaking down" the requirements within the context of the *problem domain*.

The mission of design is to create a *concrete solution* out of the conceptual model but, to succeed, it cannot randomly select the individual artifacts of analysis and transform them into engineering blueprints. Why? Because the building blocks of the solution must work within the *solution domain* as a whole, a domain with *its own* artifacts, organization, and relationships that do not have exact counterparts—or any counterparts at all—in the problem domain. In other words, design must formulate a *vision* of the solution *as a whole* before building the individual components of the final product.

Architecture is both the *definition* and the *embodiment* of this vision. It must also be the starting point for design: An improvised architecture would be a problematic and unreliable architecture, even if it is composed of the best and most reliable components.

As we stated in the introductory chapter on design, however, we cannot form a *concrete* vision of the whole unless we are familiar with what building blocks are available *or* possible. This is why we organized this section in the opposite direction of the "big picture": first, fine-grained design objects for flow, user interface,

Figure 16.1   Information System Architecture: Not One, But Many

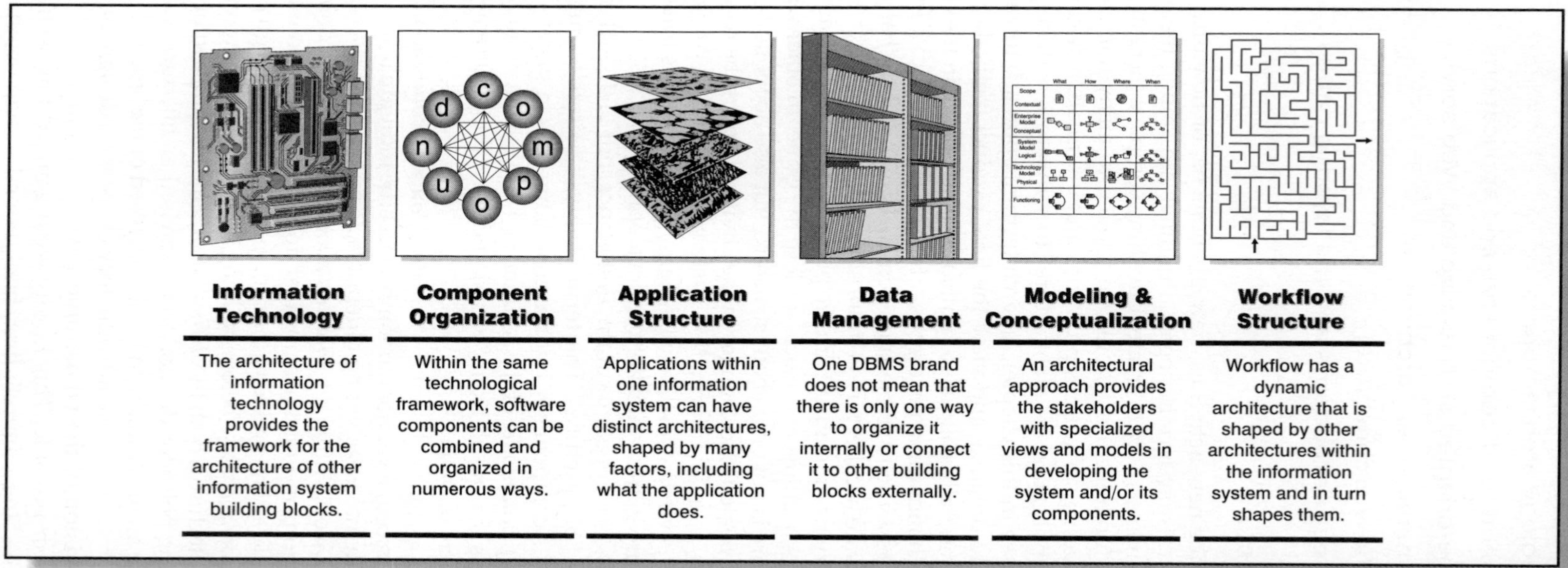

Information Technology	Component Organization	Application Structure	Data Management	Modeling & Conceptualization	Workflow Structure
The architecture of information technology provides the framework for the architecture of other information system building blocks.	Within the same technological framework, software components can be combined and organized in numerous ways.	Applications within one information system can have distinct architectures, shaped by many factors, including what the application does.	One DBMS brand does not mean that there is only one way to organize it internally or connect it to other building blocks externally.	An architectural approach provides the stakeholders with specialized views and models in developing the system and/or its components.	Workflow has a dynamic architecture that is shaped by other architectures within the information system and in turn shapes them.

Within the framework of technology and theory, the major building blocks of the information system can be viewed or organized in a vast variety of ways.

and data management; then patterns that allow us to pull back from the nuts and bolts and to view repeating relationships among them; and, finally, components that are architectural entities, meaning that they are organized together to create the architecture.

2. ARCHITECTURAL CONCEPTS

Almost everybody agrees that architecture is important. Beyond this, however, the agreement on what architecture is breaks down. As with everything else, there are differences on how architecture is viewed. Another reason, however, is that architecture affects almost everything in both the product itself and how the product is developed. As a result, it can be described in many ways that are different but not necessarily contradictory. Therefore, even though we present a definition of architecture, the best way to form an idea about architecture is to understand "architectural concepts," concepts that are frequently encountered whenever architecture is discussed.

Defining Architecture

☞ The *ANSI/IEEE* standard "1471–2000" defines architecture as "the fundamental organization of a system, embodied in its components, their relationships to each other and the environment, and the principles governing its design and evolution."

Architecture is ❶ the organization of a system's major components and the relationships of these components to each other and to the whole, and ❷ how such an organization and/or its development is viewed or modeled.

The first definition applies to the ***product itself***—that is, any product with sufficient complexity and sophistication. An automobile has an architecture: the chassis holds the body of the car and the engine, the axles transfer the movement from the engine to the wheels that in turn, together with the axles, support the chassis, and so on. Different types of automobiles implement the same architectural principles differently. The same observation—variety within the same architectural principles—is true for buildings, airplanes, applications, and information systems.

The second definition applies to the ***development approach*** and characterizes how the product is viewed and/or modeled throughout the stages of its development life cycle: conceptual, logical, physical, implementation, and deployment. Depending on the author and methodology, architectural views are described differently: owner's view, architect's drawings, architect's plans, contractor's plan, and so on. The basic concept, however, is the same: Information systems and applications have an architecture and their development should follow an architectural approach.

☞ Some have said that defining architecture as "the high-level organization of the system" is too general and too vague to be controversial and, in effect, if it cannot be controversial, then it cannot be helpful either. We disagree.

The most important point about architecture is that there must *be* an architecture and such

Architecture—any architecture for any product—must take into account certain principles at which we arrive through knowledge and experience. This assertion does not mean that ❶ all architecture is the same or ❷ you cannot experiment with architecture and/or improve it. It means, simply, that you cannot begin design with ignorance of architecture, or a dismissive view of it.

Architecture of an information system is where what is commonly called "creativity" reaches its highest form. In the same manner that a building can be utilitarian or luxury, ordinary or monumental, robust or unstable, the same architectural principles can lead to a variety of information systems and applications.

a plain definition is crucial in driving the message home.

You are likely to encounter quite a few unconventional or sophisticated definitions for software architecture. Some are interesting, some are worthy of serious consideration, some are adequately controversial, and some are simply too long by trying to cover every base. By all means, study them and discuss them at length, but do not let them confuse the issue: Design must start from a high-level view.

[White 1997]

Furthermore, architecture "is concerned not only with structure and behavior but with usage, functionality, performance, resilience, reuse, comprehensibility, economic and technological constraints and trade-offs, and aesthetics." [Booch 1999, 61] This list is no exaggeration: In its various aspects, architecture embodies most of the most fundamental concepts about software design.

How does architecture relate to design in general?

There are two general phases of design formulation that can be distinguished: (1) architectural design and (2) detailed design. Architectural design occurs immediately after requirements analysis and before detailed design. An architectural design is concerned with structural, functional, and behavioral issues of a system by modeling the problem and the outline solution. Structural issues that influence design decisions include organization and control structures; communication, synchronization, and data access protocols; physical distribution of functions of design elements; future developments, etc. . . .

Critical architectural design decisions are made in early stages of the software life cycle. These decisions have great repercussions in the evolution of a system. In addition, when changes are necessary it often happens that the structural decisions adopted do not accommodate the change. Software architecture defines the major computational elements of a system as a means to address these architectural-level decisions.

Architectural Elements

> An architecture is defined by the configuration of its elements—components, messages, and connectors.

[Fielding 2000]

By now, you should be familiar with both components and messages. We ended the discussion of components by declaring that **components** are architectural elements. We have also consistently stressed that the only way for objects and components to interact is by exchanging *messages*.

The new term here is "**connector**." The connectors are mechanisms through which components are connected together or communicate with each other. A message is (relatively) technology-independent, whereas connectors are technology-dependent but are independent of messages. Connectors work as conduits: They transfer messages between components regardless of what the message is. It is up to the component to reject the message, carry it out, or delegate it to another component.

In the physical foundation of the information system, connectors are very familiar: cables, wires, couplers, edge connectors, etc. The "messages" that they carry are electrical currents, analog or digital. Software connectors are virtual and, therefore, need a visualization of the specific technology. Each operating system or each development platform, such as Microsoft's .Net or Sun Microsystems' Enterprise Java Beans, defines its own protocols for the virtual wiring between components. Common Object Request Broker Architecture (CORBA) was proposed by the Object Management Group (OMG) as a standard to transcend platform dependency but its success was limited. Web services (see the "Service-Oriented Architecture" section later in this chapter) shows more promise as a universal standard for wiring of services and components because it has received the support of major players and development tool vendors (probably because they would be left out in the cold if they did not support it).

Various authors identify various entities as architectural elements. One of the more common is "*data*." We have excluded data from our definition not because data is not important but because in an object-oriented worldview, as we have stated repeatedly, data is not an independent entity. It is either the value of an object's attribute or the value of a variable that is embedded inside a message that passes between two objects.

Another term, though less common, is "**rationale**." To sum, "rationale" explains why elements are organized they way they are. We consider rationale to be of the utmost importance in development, but we do not think that it qualifies as a constituent element of architecture:

[Fielding 2000]

> As an illustration, consider what happens to a building if its blueprints and design plans are burned. Does the building immediately collapse? No, since the properties by which the walls sustain the weight of the roof remain intact. An architecture has, by design, a set of properties that allow it to meet or exceed the system requirements. Ignorance of those properties may lead to later changes which violate the architecture, just as the replacement of a load-bearing wall with a large window frame may violate the structural stability of a building. Thus, instead of rationale, our definition of software architecture includes architectural properties. Rationale explicates those properties, and lack of rationale may result in gradual decay or degradation of the architecture over time, but the rationale itself is not part of the architecture.

Let us not overlook the term "*configuration*" in the definition. An architecture is not merely a collection of its elements, but also *how* these elements are organized.

Patterns & Methodology

> Architecture as the actual organization of a system is a subject of patterns; architecture as a way to view the system or its development is an area of methodology.

☞ In the literature on software architecture, the term "**style**" is used extensively and frequently. Unfortunately, we could not find any definition that would be comprehensible, widely accepted, and satisfactory to us, all at the same time. The only common agreement (more or less) is a negative one: Unlike the style of artistic works, the style of software architecture does not refer to the *individual* expression. Our working definition is that **style is how a combination of architectural elements and patterns make a certain architecture different from, or similar to, other architectures**.

Seldom does an architecture appear from nowhere. Instead, successful solutions from the past are adapted, sometimes with incremental changes. When we talk about new or revolutionary architecture, we often are talking about new and revolutionary ways of combining existing *patterns* into a *style* that has distinctive characteristics. Another architecture might combine all or some of the same patterns in a different style.

We will discuss patterns in software architecture later in this chapter. The real world, however, provides numerous examples for the argument in the architecture of buildings. Domes and columns, the two architectural patterns that we discussed in Chapter 14, have been used throughout history to solve the same problem—how to support large ceilings—without downgrading the style of truly original architects.

In a nutshell, ❶ sound architectural decisions cannot be made without studying relevant architectural patterns, and ❷ the same architectural patterns do not mean the same architectural styles.

Architecture depends on many intangible qualities in the architect but, eventually, it is an artifact. As we have tirelessly argued in the previous chapters, there is usually more than one way to arrive at the same artifact, meaning that you must adopt a *methodology* over others.

Architecture is no exception, except that the term *"framework"* has more currency when architecture is concerned. The choice is not without significance. "Methodology" has come to imply a roadmap or a plan, while "framework" points more towards a structure within which a certain freedom of choice exists. Architectural frameworks usually avoid specifying processes and roadmaps. Instead, they aim to identify what is necessary or best ❶ to make an architecture take shape, and ❷ to make its meaning comprehensible to all stakeholders, from owners to builders.

With these two aims, it is only logical that *modeling* is the core element of all architectural frameworks. More than anything else, it is the models and the **views** that distinguish one framework from another.

Architectural Views

> An architectural view is a representation of the system that is shaped by four factors: what, who, when, and where.

In the chapter on methodology, we described modeling as follows:

> **Modeling is the systematic representation of the relevant features of a product or a system from particular perspectives.**

This definition is essentially architectural, even though what is represented might descend far deeper than the "grand view" of the system. The difference between a model and an architectural view is that the latter may consist of one model or several. Views may also share models.

Let us describe the four factors that must be taken into account when creating an architectural view:

• *What.* This factor seems the simplest, but appearances are deceptive. Unlike engineering blueprints (see the following "Engineering" section), an architectural view must have a wide scope. But what is a wide scope? The proper scope of an architectural view is wide open to subjective interpretation. The blueprint of a bolt may not appear high-level, but for a manufacturer of bolts it is a good architectural view. A one-page sketch of an aircraft carrier is assuredly high-level and indispensable to the Navy, but it is hardly enough to satisfactorily explain its architecture. In other words, the "what" depends on the complexity of the product and its components. If a product is worthy of being considered for "architecture," chances are high that it has more than one "what."

Furthermore, any artifact can be abstracted, or modeled, from different aspects. Even a building that is viewed mostly in terms of structure is a multilayered entity, both vertically and horizontally: the basement, the stories, the façade, the walls, the plumbing, the wiring, etc. An information system and its building blocks have both structure and dynamism. In other words, the "what" can be *behavioral*, *structural*, or *dynamic*.

• *Who.* A development project has different kinds of *stakeholders*, "people who have key roles in, or concerns about, the system: for example, as users, developers, or managers. Different stakeholders with different roles in the system will have different *concerns*. Stakeholders can be individuals, teams, or organizations."

features (in design), but they are *not* the same. Concern is simply an area of interest.

In our example of the online merchant, the management interest is focused on the "workflow architecture," while developers are interested in structural modeling. (See "The Architecture of The Information System" later in this chapter.)

Different concerns means that they are interested in different representations, regardless of whether or not they can understand the models meant for another class of stakeholders. The management of a company that wants to sell merchandise online is not interested in the architecture of the database (and most probably would find entity-relationship diagrams both irrelevant and difficult to comprehend), while the developers cannot function without it.

- *When.* Development is iterative but undoubtedly there is a big difference between when the idea of a house occurs to somebody and when the electricians must have blueprints and instructions to install the wirings and the electrical fixtures. In short, an architectural view must reflect whether the representation is *conceptual*, *logical*, or *physical* and whether it concerns *implementation* or *deployment*.

- *Where.* In real-world products, understanding the "where," the *viewpoint* or the *perspective* of a model, is easy. We can represent the "north view" of a building or the "front view" of a TV set without agonizing over our choices. Choosing the perspective for the architecture of a virtual product is somewhat more difficult.

One choice, in terms of selecting a perspective, is to give more prominence to one component over others. As we demonstrated in the chapter on structural modeling, the same class, `Patient`, can be represented from various perspectives: as a conceptual class, as the central figure in a network of associations, as the hub of collaboration, or as an aggregation. A similar approach would work for large-grained entities or components and packages as well.

☞ Some architectural frameworks use a set of factors that include "what," "who," etc. The meanings, however, are not necessarily the same.

The second choice relates to the dynamic nature of the information system. Whereas most concerns about a real-world building apply to its structure, software applications have a flow. (In fact, the primary mission of the structure of an information system is to support its flow.) This flow can be represented from various perspectives by selecting the appropriate modeling tool: a sequence diagram represents the entities as a space-time matrix of messages, a statechart diagram follows the story of one entity, and an activity diagram can be used to represent the workflow (among other things).

We cannot always find formal modeling tools to put together views that are necessary to address stakeholders' concerns. An example is reliability. An experienced eye might be able to detect whether a certain structure or flow is reliable or not, but it cannot be modeled directly. In such cases, you would have to represent the "view" as a textual narrative, a graph, a comparison chart, or whatever else gets the job done.

Engineering

> Engineering is the application of architectural concepts to the building of the actual product.

Programmers, developers, and computer science graduates are sometimes called "software engineers." At one time or another, almost anybody involved in developing software has been called an "engineer." The term is used so loosely that it has almost lost meaning and respectability.

The story of how this muddled interpretation came about is largely outside the boundaries of this book, but it is representative of repeated, periodic attempts to convince software buyers that what they are buying is solidly reliable because it conforms to a certain magical idea or a certain magical technology:

[Blum 1992, 11]

> Software engineering first emerged as a popular term of a 1968 NATO [the North Atlantic Treaty Organization] conference. . . . The juxtaposition of software and engineering was intended to be provocative. The digital computer was less than a quarter century old, and already we were facing a "software crisis." First we had invented computer programming and then we taught people to write programs. The next task was the development of large systems that were reliable, delivered on schedule, and within budget. As with every technological advancement, our aspirations were at the boundary of what we could do successfully. As it turned out, we were not very good at building large systems on time and without overruns. Consequently, software engineering emerged as the organizing force to overcome the barriers that threatened our progress.

This was in 1968, and the "software crisis," in one form or another, is still around. Adopting respectable terms by itself has not transformed software development into a disciplined discipline. Engineering, however, is a valid concept—*if* applied with more constraint and less as an advertising or marketing slogan.

Above all, it is essential to recognize the *scope* of engineering—what the term excludes as well as what it includes. Engineering is not architecture, though an engineer might be an architect. (Great, visionary, renowned architects, on the other hand, can be inept engineers—as is demonstrated by many famous, but structurally unsound, monuments.) Engineering is not programming, though a programmer might be an engineer. Domain analysis is not part of engineering, even though the engineer's job is to ensure that the physical solution fits the problem domain.

To engineer is to **understand** the conceptual solution, to **participate** actively in outlining the logical solution, and to **devise** the physical solution *in essential details*. These responsibilities require a thorough understanding of the technology and its myriad of effects. Whereas architecture must work with highly abstract concepts, engineering must decide how these concepts can be translated into concrete artifacts. Architecture can dream; engineering must turn dreams into reality. Architecture can conceive of a machine that orbits the globe and returns to earth; engineering must come up with material and alloys that will withstand the cold of space and the heat of reentry into the atmosphere. The architect can propose the high-level structure of a failsafe e-commerce system; the engineer must put forward the best combination of a DBMS, communication hardware and software, a development platform, and the operating system that is able to support such a system.

A result of this distinction between architecture and engineering is something that is sometimes overlooked or downplayed:

Architectural views and models must have a wide scope and a high-level view; engineering blueprints and models must be detailed.

Engineering is a vital link in the chain of software development; it is not, however, the only link or the whole chain.

Architecture as Composition

> When you think "architecture" you must think "composition."

Architectural decisions are not isolated from the overall direction of development, from how the problem domain is analyzed and how individual components are conceived. Successful thinking about architecture requires the right frame of mind:

[Ommering 2002]

Software developers traditionally start from a (single) system specification. They decompose the system into subsystems, the subsystems into components . . . and then implement the components and integrate them into subsystems and ultimately the system.

We want components to be combined in multiple ways into subsystems, and subsystems in multiple ways into systems. In other words, we want composition rather than decomposition , or a graph rather than a tree as design hierarchy.

One fundamental difference is that in a decomposition approach it does not matter where a certain feature is implemented, as long as it is implemented somewhere in the system. In a composition approach this does matter, since some components may be present in other systems, while others may not be included.

So, developers have to start thinking in terms of components that can be clicked together in different ways to obtain different sets of functionality . . .

Coupling

> Coupling is the extent of dependency among components of a system.

A car is mostly a *loosely coupled* structure. Were it not so, you would not be able to change the tires or replace engine parts. A building, on the other hand, is basically a *tightly coupled* structure. The foundation and the weight-bearing walls can be replaced only (if at all) at great cost.

Coupling describes how components depend on each other's services. This dependency, however, is relative: Coupling does not usually fall on one extreme or another, but somewhere between the two. A car's chassis is "tightly coupled" while most buildings have walls and façades that can be changed.

Coupling is not exclusively about replaceable components. In the chapter on database and persistence, we explained that before the relational model, the applications had to know the physical layout of data in order to use it. Relational databases not only hide the physical layout by exposing a logical structure, but also add "metadata" that describes the data itself. Compared to the previous databases, consumers of relational databases are less dependent, or have a looser coupling to, the services of the DBMS.

As the probability for change increases, so does the desirability of loose coupling. An information system is constantly subject to change, by forces inside and outside of the enterprise. Therefore, it needs an architecture that is as loosely coupled as possible.

Like many politically correct ideas, loose coupling has received a great amount of verbal praise but less than ideal support in theory or in practice. There are no comprehensive taxonomies (classification of principles) about coupling, though some authors have made valiant efforts. To be fair, the technological foundations were inadequate.

☞ See Chapter 9 for an introduction to events.

Now that we are more familiar with both UML and object orientation, let us explain two more things about events.

❶ UML does not have a special notation for events to distinguish them from "normal" messages. You can, of course, use a **stereotype** such as **«event»** or **«signal»** on the direction arrow to identify events.

❷ In introducing design, we emphasized that nothing happens in an application unless an object performs it. In object-oriented platforms and languages such as Java or C#, events themselves are really objects that function as messengers for another object. For this reason, such a messenger object is sometimes called a "**delegate**." A "*delegate*" is a dynamic sibling to "**connectors**," described in this chapter under "Architectural Elements."

[Gamma 1997, 139]

Two developments have changed, and are changing, the situation. The first is object orientation (both the concepts and the technology) and its logical outgrowth, the components. The second is the increasing popularity and the spread of Web services. (See the "Service-Oriented Architecture" section later in this chapter.)

Many factors that affect coupling are too specialized for a discussion here. However, among the mechanisms that we have explored in this book, four can play significant roles in reducing dependencies:

- *Events.* In discussing dynamic modeling, we introduced the concept of events and said that any action by an object that interrupts the existing condition of one or more other objects is an event. Among event types, we identified *signal* events, such as public announcements in a train station or the ringing of the phone, as significant because they are *asynchronous* and often *anonymous*.

"Asynchronous" signifies that the action that *triggers* the event is outside the space and/or time frame of the message recipient. In simpler terms, "asynchronous" means that you do not have to *wait* for the phone to ring, but can go about your business. In other words, you are not "tightly coupled" to the phone.

"Anonymous" means that the message is a "broadcast," not a "narrowcast," since it is received by any object that subscribes to the service, like a program on cable TV. The sender of the message does not have to know the identity of the recipients.

Not every communication can take the form of signal events, nor is it desirable that they do so. But when it *is* possible and appropriate, then it should be used as it sharply reduces dependency. Signal events are extensively used in modern computers and operating systems to maximize efficiency.

- *Abstract Interfaces.* We elaborated on the significance of interfaces from various perspectives until we arrived at the concept of "abstract" interfaces. (See Chapter 15.) An abstract interface does not belong to a specific class of objects but can be assumed by any object that can perform the services that the interface promises to provide. The "waiter" interface can be worn by any individual who can satisfy the demands of "waiting."

It is not difficult to see why working with abstract interfaces would reduce dependency. Architecture, as we said (and will say again), is more pattern-based than rule-based. In the chapter on patterns, we introduced you to the **Factory Method** pattern that defines an *interface* for creating objects, but delegates the actual responsibility for selecting the class and instantiating the object to a subclass. There are many more patterns that decouple objects by using interfaces.

- *Components.* Components and Web services (which we will describe later in this chapter) are usually more advertised for their role in reuse than for their other attributes. But, as we explained, a "component's interface is separate from its implementation." This makes the component replaceable and reduces coupling, regardless of whether the component is reusable or not.

- *Adapters.* Another pattern that we described in Chapter 14 was the **Object Adapter** pattern, which converts "the interface of a class into another interface that the clients expect," allowing classes to "work together that couldn't otherwise because of incompatible interfaces."

The example that we gave—that of working with different database management systems—is only one of the numerous situations where an object adapter can bring down costs and increase flexibility by reducing *friction* (another term for coupling).

If loose coupling is so good, then why not design everything, every time, in a loosely coupled manner? The first answer is that it is not *always* better. The chassis of a car would be weaker if it were screwed together. In software, for every layer of interaction that we add, we pay a price in performance, computing resources, maintenance, and, sometimes, security. Furthermore, if we raise the virtues of loose coupling to absurd levels, then we are apt to conclude that *no* coupling must the be the best. No dependency, of course, means no interaction: If people and systems do not interact, then the question of coupling is moot.

The second answer relates to technology. Technology usually creates a need for something before providing the capability to satisfy it. Nobody expected the monolithic but relatively small applications of the mainframe era, circa 1960s, to communicate in real time with any other application, let alone with another system. But then people started to ask for more features, which meant more complexity. Until then, the issue of coupling was both irrelevant and unsolvable.

The third answer is simply money. Upfront, a more sophisticated design is more expensive than a less sophisticated one. The advantages of loose coupling are only recognized with the passage of time as the pressures for change mount and the real costs for cutting corners begin to reveal themselves. Design is always a compromise, but the correct choices can only be made if you know what you are compromising.

☝ Loose coupling cannot be achieved without using components, but we should not confuse the two concepts. Steel beams and pillars are the structural components of many houses, but they are tightly coupled when the construction is done.

Architecture & UML

> UML's notations, standard diagrams, and extensibility mechanisms provide a well-rounded toolbox for expressing architectural views.

☞ Many authors use the term "**architectural description**" to refer to modeling, documenting, and analyzing architectural modeling and decisions. In this book, we have used the term "modeling" to represent the same activities. Both terms, however, are valid.

Architectural views are independent from both the process of development and modeling languages. Therefore, many notations have the potential to represent the views, as long as they are similarly process-independent. UML provides a set of tools that serve architectural descriptions well.

UML symbols and notations are few and simple, but extensible. (See Chapter 10 for an introduction to UML extension mechanisms.) Various architectural frameworks classify views and viewpoints differently, but UML can satisfy the modeling needs of most frameworks as far as formal diagrams are concerned. We must, however, pay attention to some important points about the relationship between architecture and UML.

• *UML's worldview is object-oriented.* UML is process-independent but paradigm-dependent. The theoretical framework of UML is an **object-oriented** one. UML diagrams are generally built on object-oriented foundations: objects, their abstractions, their interactions, their interfaces, encapsulation, and so on. Therefore, if an architectural framework considers "data" and "functions" as two separate entities, reconciling the taxonomy of such a framework and UML would not be easy. Of course, such a framework would not be compatible with object orientation in general.

• *Architecture is not a conceptual island.* Some authors define architecture as "everything." It is not, of course, but it does *affect* everything: The significance of the same architectural element changes when it is incorporated into different architectural patterns.

Architecture is about the organization of architectural elements, but this organization *is constrained by other interests*, forces, and viewpoints: project management, performance, security, etc. These viewpoints are *independent* disciplines that have their own modeling and description tools. For example, project management uses Gantt charts and network diagrams that are not related to UML. Nevertheless, they are viewpoints that have indisputable interests in the architecture. "For these cases, it is perhaps more efficient to use existing techniques than to recast them in the UML."

• *View integration remains a challenge.* In introducing views, we said that a view is shaped by "what, who, when, and where." For even a medium-sized architecture, the combination of these four elements can result in an overwhelming number of models. The challenge is twofold: ❶ how to keep these models in sync and ❷ how to clearly represent which path the flow of models takes from summary to detailed and back.

UML offers two standard relationships for managing this challenge. The **«trace»** stereotype over a dependency arrow represents a *historical* dependency between two models. That is, it indicates that the first model (a class, package, component, use case, etc.) is derived from the second model or is a new version of the second model. The **«refine»** stereotype indicates that one model is more or less abstract than the second one. Both stereotypes can be "chained," resulting in hierarchies. (See Figure 16.2.)

Figure 16.2   UML View Management: «trace» and «refine» Relationships

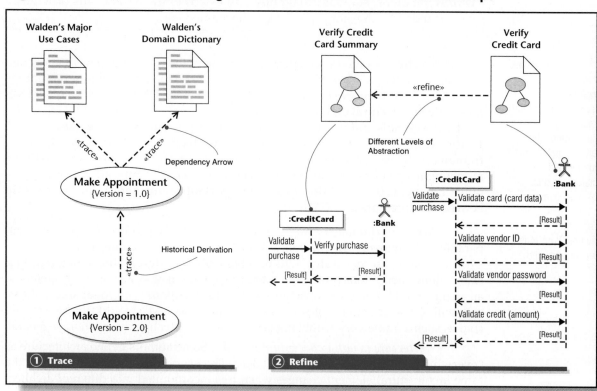

This figure merely illustrates the concepts. How these mechanisms are implemented, or whether they are implemented at all, depends on the modeling tool.

(For a full-sized view of sequence diagrams, see Chapter 9, Dynamic Modeling.)

The effectiveness of these two mechanisms depends on how specific development and modeling tools implement them. A good implementation would allow you to navigate up and down the **«trace»** and **«refine»** chains by clicking on the thumbnails representing models.

These two mechanisms, however, address only the "when" and the "what" of the architectural view. UML does not effectively address the "who" and the "where." (See "Architectural Views" earlier in this chapter.) For example, a complex use case might require several sequence diagrams in design because one very big diagram would be confusing to teams with different responsibilities in development: user interface, database, flow, entity classes, and so on. These diagrams would not be derivatives of each other; nor would they belong to different levels of abstractions. They are, simply, the *same* model seen from different viewpoints or perspectives.

- *Diagrams are only one component of architectural views.* Architectural views can be composed of many types of models. For example, use cases are the crucial component of behavioral modeling. Storyboarding is one of the more effective tools for designing the user interface. Therefore, regardless of what UML can or cannot do, no graphical notation—or any kind of notation for that matter—can satisfy the diverse needs of architectural views.

3. The Architecture of the Information System

> The architecture of a modern information system is a heterogeneous and cooperative architecture.

Architecture of the information system is not the same as "software architecture" for the very simple reason that an information system is more than software. (See Figure 16.1.) Furthermore, software itself is not all the same thing. Besides being virtual, a device driver is very different from a tax application, which in turn is unlike a database management system or an image editor. Such different entities cannot, and should not, have the same architecture.

Nevertheless, an information system does have an architecture. This architecture, however, is not like the architecture of a building, with clear outlines, a readily recognizable style, and relative stability. If an information system is built from scratch (which seldom happens) its architects may design it to start as a sharply defined entity, but this state of affairs would not last long.

The architecture of an information system is a *dynamic* one. Its building blocks, from the technological framework and applications to the workflow, change constantly. More importantly, some of the new components require a radical "rewiring" of the architecture. This rewiring and reorganization of the information system, however, cannot be accomplished the same way that we replace buildings. Seldom can we tear down an information system completely and replace it with a brand new one. A variable portion of the existing structure *must* be kept in operation even if the new and the old were not designed to work smoothly together. To paraphrase another writer:

Building an information system is like building the raft while crossing the river.

Technology

☞ Do remember that technology is not limited to the *tools* of technology. As we stated in the Chapter 1: **Information technology is the know-how, methods, tools, and material used to support information systems**.

> Technology provides the primary framework for the architecture of information systems.

A set of forces compete and cooperate to change the architecture of an information system far beyond the vision of the original architects. The architecture of an information system is made possible and is constrained by the information technology. Hence, technology is the primary force of architectural change.

The effects of technology are both direct and indirect. A successful technology has a "ripple effect" that is either not foreseen when it is introduced or is understood only dimly. First, we "discover" that a new technology, created in the hope of solving a specific set of problems, holds the promise of solving *other* problems. Then we set out to create the missing pieces that would allow the technology to realize its perceived potential. In turn, some of these new pieces create ripple effects of their own, and so on.

The Internet is a perfect example. The mission of DARPA (Defense Advanced Research Projects Agency), which in 1969 introduced ARPANET, the parent to the Internet, was highly challenging but rather clear-cut: create a network of computers that would continue to function even if a nuclear attack wipes parts of it out. The vast majority of legitimate and illegitimate activities that the Internet now offers were not even a gleam in its inventors' eyes.

The story of the evolution of information system architecture is more a story of integration and expansion rather than one of replacement. New technologies have allowed new architectural frameworks to include and expand existing ones.

The following is not a history of how computer technology has evolved, but a snapshot of architectures that the evolution of technology has made possible.

The Centralized Architecture

☞ Reports of the death of the mainframe are greatly exaggerated. Very powerful and expensive computers will always exist for the simple reason that the need for raw computing power will never go away. The difference is that the mainframes are no longer required for mundane tasks such as accounting, but are used in tasks such as simulating nuclear explosions.
The "new" mainframes and supercomputers are often fully integrated into a network as "nodes," albeit very powerful nodes.

> In a centralized architecture, all services depend on one computer system.

Centralized architecture does not mean that *all* services are performed by one computer or one processor. It does mean, however, that without the "center" the system will not work. The single computer system might delegate peripheral tasks to various processors, both inside and outside the computer, but it retains control of the services that make the system function.

The centralized architecture is often exclusively associated with "mainframes." In turn, a mainframe is often exclusively associated with those early computers that were very large, very expensive, and very isolated. Both impressions are misguided.

☞ This snapshot of the architecture of information technology—its history and its concepts—is almost cartoon-like in its simplicity. Our

The main error is confusing application architecture with the architecture of information system *technology*. It is true that early computers had monolithic application structures and had little or no contact with other computers. The centralized architecture, however, has not stopped with mainframe computers. Many home computers have a centralized architecture: The "system" stops if the computer stops, even though the operating system and desktop applications are component-based and modular, and even though such computers are often connected to the Internet.

intention, however, is only to provide pointers towards the frameworks within which software development takes place. There are numerous topics in the information technology that we had to leave out.

As we said before, the evolution of information technology has been more a process of expansion and absorption than one of replacement. For example, **peer-to-peer** networking (which has featured prominently in court battles between the entertainment industry and file-swappers) is a virtual "server-less" networking.

Another example that shows how an older concept can take advantage of a new technology is the **virtual private network** (VPN). VPN makes it possible to create a virtual WAN over the backbone of the Internet, secure *and* private.

☞ Here we are (mostly) talking about technology. There is an organizational aspect to "centralization" that makes the mainframe-only era utterly different from ours. See the "Workflow" section later in this chapter.

For early mainframes, the centralized architecture was a historical and technological necessity. Computers could cost millions of dollars and required a small army of technicians, operators, and data-entry people to run them, although they were not nearly as powerful as many of today's handheld devices. Not many companies were able to afford multiple computers, nor did they feel a pressing need to do so, as expectations were low. The day-to-day operation of the enterprise did *not* depend on computers.

The Distributed Architecture

In a distributed architecture, two or more computers on a network cooperate to perform services.

Phones were born as a network: A single phone that cannot be connected to at least one other phone is a useless object. A computer, on the other hand, can be useful all by itself. As a result, networking computers needed a leap of imagination and the convergence of several forces to appear and grow.

A major force, as we mentioned before, was the U.S. government's need for a fail-safe command-and-control system. The other force was the tide of rising expectations: The most obvious candidates for automation such as payroll and basic accounting were in hand and businesses were ready for more. "More," however, meant trusting more sophisticated and mission-critical tasks to automation, and this goal needed something different from a centralized architecture that depended on a single but expensive mainframe.

Networks did not appear with microprocessors, but microprocessors provided the technological momentum that eventually made networks a common presence in business. Again, defense and space programs were instrumental in launching a technology that quickly found an eager market in civilian life.

Distributed architecture took shape only gradually. LANs (Local Area Network) and WANs (Wide Area Networks) were first used for *file sharing*, not for hosting a distributed software architecture. In file sharing, the computers on the network, or "nodes," do not cooperate to perform tasks, but make their storage available to each other. Users can access data or run programs that are located on other computers.

The **client-server architecture** (CSA) was made possible by the evolution of networks and provided the real break from centralized architecture. In the CSA model, one or more *servers* provide services (hence the designation) that are consumed by the *client* computers. In addition to file sharing, these services include, but are not limited to:

- *Security.* A logical grouping of computers that share the same security rules is called a *domain*. (This is yet another definition for the term "domain.") The computer responsible for enforcing security across this logical grouping is usually called the **domain server**.
- *Database.* Databases are the strategic assets of enterprise information systems. Three factors have made dedicated database servers an absolute necessity: security, integrity, and performance. Modern database management systems are so resource-intensive that even if we could disregard security and integrity, most client computers could not be used for the DBMS anyhow.

Furthermore, a logical database can physically reside on multiple servers or storage devices, although it might appear as one database to its clients. *Mirroring* is often used to create a real-time image of the database as transactions occur. In turn, these mirror images can reside on far-flung computers and storage devices.

- *Application.*   The term "application server" has more than one meaning. The more obvious one is that the server is dedicated to executing certain applications that usually require minimal or no user intervention. (Printing invoices for a large utility company is one example.) The second one is more recent: An application server is a server that provides the core services of the application. In this definition, one or more servers hosts the "**middleware**," a collection of components that embody the application logic and business rules, minus the database and the user interface. (How many and what types of business rules should be in the middleware is subject to intense arguments.)

- *Web.*   A Web server is responsible for managing a Web site and providing the Internet client with the requested content. The detailed list of what a Web server must do depends on the site's type and the choices of the architect who can delegate some services to other servers in the network. If the site is a high-traffic one, identically configured Web servers can be combined into a *server farm* (or "cluster"). Through *load balancing*, servers in the "farm" can satisfy a set of requests.

- *Utility.*   Servers can be dedicated to any common service: printing, communication, storage, etc. A cable company, for example, has servers to provide "on-demand" movies.

The distributed architecture is often associated with terms, such as *three-tier* or *n-tier* architecture, that describe the *physical* organization of the information system rather than that of the technology, though the boundaries between the two are never clearly marked: When you hear or use the term "distributed architecture," you must be aware that it can convey more than one meaning. (For this reason, we will use the term "distributed components" to distinguish the concepts, although we continue to use "distributed architecture" when the distinction is not crucial.)

Components & Applications

> The organization of components is constrained by the architecture of technology but is not dictated by it.

Components and applications operate *within the box* that is defined by information technology. A specific technological framework, however, does not lead to a uniform architecture inside its boundaries. Without a network, components cannot be distributed across multiple computers, but the network does not prevent anybody from writing a monolithic application. On the other hand, applications on a stand-alone desktop computer are seldom, if ever, monolithic. Even the simplest applications rely on the services and the common libraries provided by the operating system.

We have previously discussed components and applications but, before going any further, let us discuss their relationships in terms of architecture. In Chapter 15, we defined a component as a "relatively independent, encapsulated, and replaceable unit of software that provides services specified by one or more interfaces." By this definition any binary file with at least one interface is a component, *including* an application which has been traditionally defined as an "executable" that performs a specific task such as word processing, accounting, and so on.

To understand the subtle differences between the organization of components and application architecture, we need to define the term "application" somehow differently:

> **An application is a *logical* grouping of components that cooperate to perform a specific task.**

In this definition, an application is not a special *type* of component, but a logical grouping of components. Therefore, a component or a set of components can potentially participate in multiple applications (although, in practice, certain components, including the "executable," would only participate in one). In fact, this is how modern applications are organized across the spectrum, from handheld devices and desktop computers to servers and supercomputers.

In this case, does it make sense to talk about the architecture of components and application architecture as separate concepts? Isn't the application architecture decided by how components are organized? The answer is that it not only makes sense to distinguish between the two, but it is crucial to do so. The point to remember is that while how components are organized is eventually *physical*, the architecture of an application remains *logical* and can be mapped to various physical configurations of components.

What does this mean in practice? Building the application from clearly defined *logical* components makes it not only more flexible but also more *scalable* since the physical mapping can take advantage of available resources with little or no need to redesign or recode the application.

Monolithic Applications

<table>
<tr><td>A monolithic application is a self-contained component that does not rely on other components and cannot be reused, in part or in whole, by other applications.</td></tr>
</table>

☞ The first commercially successful computer with an operating system was IBM's System/360. Though the concept was not exclusively IBM's, the company made a huge investment to make the concept workable.

Truly monolithic applications had a very short shelf life. When the computers did not have operating systems, every application had to build everything from scratch. With the introduction of operating systems in the 1960s, common functionality started to migrate from individual applications towards reusable "libraries."

This migration happened very gradually. The market was both small and fragmented since each hardware manufacturer had its own operating system and often a different operating system for each model. As a result, the client had to live with whatever reusability and functionality the manufacturer offered in standard libraries. Later on, some manufacturers opened up their libraries to change and expansion by clients who were seldom able to produce, or even conceive of, commercial-grade software.

☞ The most conspicuous exception to the separation of hardware and software has been Apple. Eventually, however, even Apple decided to switch to a more mass-market microprocessor.

The introduction of personal computers in the late 1970s and early 1980s was the start of a sea change in the modularization of software. ("Modular" was, and to some degree still is, a generalized synonym for component-based software.) The emergence of a mass market for software and the consolidation of operating systems into a few brands, mostly independent of hardware manufacturers, laid the foundation for a change in the architecture of applications.

@ An application composed of multiple components, like most desktop applications, is not necessarily a "distributed" application but simply a "multi-component" application.

A distributed application must be multi-component, but the reverse is not true.

☞ Whatever the future holds, we cannot deny that the vision behind the "thin clients" can be fascinating for enterprises that look back in longing to the simpler times of the centralized mainframe-only era. Up to now, however, thin clients have not taken the market by storm. But perhaps they are ahead of their time and things will eventually go their way.

☞ In terms of performance, there is a *hierarchy* among messages and this hierarchy will continue regardless of speed gains by technology. Without getting into technical details (which are not the same on different platforms), we can classify the messages, or "*calls*," into three groups: ❶ "in-process" calls that take place within the private space of the application within the local computer are the fastest; ❷ "out-of-process" calls that take

Nevertheless, in the early days of PCs, operating systems did not offer a solid platform for modularization. (No wonder, since they were mostly scaled down and stripped down adaptations of mainframe or minicomputer operating systems.) For example, in the mid-1980s, if you purchased a printer, you had to make sure that your favorite word processor supported it; otherwise you were out of luck since printing was handled by applications, not by operating systems. (As a result, most printers offered a no-frills "emulation" of the most popular and supported printer.)

Today, if we call an application "monolithic," we do not mean that it is *completely* self-contained. At the very least, an application would use the services of operating systems that have come a very long way since the 1960s or even the 1980s. "Monolithic," however, continues to a be a proper description for applications that can be compared to a thick novel composed of a single sentence.

Distributed Components

> A distributed software architecture is one in which software components cooperate and interact across a network to perform services.

In theory, distributing components to separate nodes makes perfect sense. Powerful servers are relatively cheap, so it follows that if you can dedicate one server to a service or set of services, you can increase performance dramatically and decrease the difficulties of installation and keeping the components up-to-date since you have to install only one copy of a component.

An offshoot of this theoretical argument has been what is known as "**thin clients**." In a completely distributed system, the sole remaining task for a client would be to manage the user interface. In effect, the workstation would have to be able to host a browser but not much more. As a result, the enterprise can save an unimaginable amount of money by doing away with "fat clients." Eventually, everybody would be better off because they can use "thin clients" to access a full range of applications and services on the Internet that vendors would offer for relatively modest fees (or no fee at all, since advertisers would reimburse them).

In practice, the landscape is much more complex and the results are mixed. What is technologically possible is not necessarily the best way. In other words, just because you *can* do something does not mean that you *should* do it. (Unfortunately, that is exactly what many architects have done.)

Components and subsystems that are *not* application-specific—database management systems, print servers, Web servers—have worked rather well on dedicated nodes. Distribution of application-specific components, however, has not been as successful.

The main reason is that when you distribute objects, you *always* pay an added price for the communication and the interaction among them. If the number of messages passed between components exceeds a certain limit, the traffic on the network suffers, regardless of how efficient and fast the nodes are.

Some designers opt to create distributed components out of classes: the **Patient** class would be made into a component that sits on a dedicated server, the **Appointment** class gets another server, and so on. The biggest problem with this approach is that a well-designed class is both fine-grained itself and has a fine-grained interface: Operations and attributes are as atomic as possible. As you saw in the previous chapters, the number of objects and messages increase exponentially in design. (Our examples were just examples. In a real application the number of classes

place between processes on the *same* computer are slower; and ❸ "remote calls" that are exchanged with other computers are the slowest. Imagine this hierarchy as messages exchanged within an apartment, within apartments inside a building, and between the building and the outside world.

☞ See Chapter 15 for a discussion of abstract interfaces. As we explained, the relationship between classes and interfaces is not one-to-one. One interface can represent a cluster of classes, several classes may share one interface, and one class can present multiple interfaces.

[Fowler 2003, 87–91]

☞ Fowler, only half-jokingly, states that if the choice is between object distribution and selling your ancestors into slavery, "sell your favorite grandma first if you possibly can."

can become overwhelming.) An application has both flow and state. To keep the flow on course and to manage the integrity of the state, a great number of messages have to be exchanged. This exchange can rapidly degrade the performance of not only the application but the network as a whole.

To overcome this obstacle, some designers reverse the class-definition process by coarse-graining them: Some classes are combined and methods are expanded to cover multiple attributes and operations. The outcome is that, often, by looking at the resulting classes, you cannot figure out what they are about. (To be fair, often voices of authority, in the form of how-to books and vendor Web sites, encourage this approach.)

Do we mean to say that distributing components is a failure? No, but it is not a cure for everything either. Using the distributed architecture effectively needs careful analysis and planning:

- The automatic class-to-component approach is a disaster. Just don't do it.
- The best candidate for distribution is a component that can be characterized as a *subsystem*, regardless of the number of classes. For example, a DBMS is a subsystem of the information system.

  In such a component, **the ratio of external to internal messages must be very low**. This means that the component performs complex tasks internally but has a relatively simple interface. As a result, the number of "remote calls" are low.
- If, after every consideration, you need coarse-grained classes and methods, do not discard valid object-oriented practices, but use *interfaces* instead of disfiguring classes. Using interfaces is always a good idea, but here it would also save you from creating distorted structural units that, among other things, would lock you into a certain technological architecture.

Distributing is not the only way to harness the power of multiple servers on the network. *Clustering* and *load-balancing*, which we mentioned before, provide solid alternatives to component distribution. In a cluster, a copy of the application is placed on each server, and if one node is busy the client request goes to the next node. In addition, the failure of one node would not bring down the system, whereas if a component is only one node, the failure of the node can take out the whole system in a chain reaction. ("For want of a nail the shoe was lost. For want of a shoe the horse was lost. For want of a horse the rider was lost . . . ")

Service-Oriented Architecture (SOA)

> SOA aims to compose applications from platform-independent services of virtual components.

☞ You will not find a widely accepted definition for SOA. For the moment, consider ours as a working definition or, rather, as a description.

Service-oriented architecture is one of the greatest hopes (and, inevitably, one of the greatest hypes) that has followed the success of the Internet, even though, strictly speaking, it is not tied to the Internet structure itself.

SOA envisions an application as a very loosely coupled cooperation between services that can be rendered and consumed transparently across a network, regardless of specific platforms that the nodes implement. In effect, an application would be composed of virtual components rather than physical ones.

What is a virtual component? When we create a component on a specific platform, its interface is *abstract* but it is a *concrete* entity, a binary file. Furthermore, the

☞ See Chapter 15 for a discussion of interface definition language and other issues concerning components.

interface may be abstract, but the IDL (interface definition language) and the protocols for communicating with the component are very much proprietary: A component created according to Enterprise Java Beans (EJB) specification would not interact with a component created through Microsoft's .Net platform. A virtual component is a component that ❶ relieves its consumers from the issues of its physical identity, and ❷ complies with universally accepted standards instead of following proprietary protocols.

The keyword here is "universally accepted standards" and, even though some proponents of SOA like to keep the concept abstract from specifics, the choice has generally come down to **Web services**, a set of standards (and upcoming standards) approved by the W3C (World-Wide Web Consortium) and supported by the major players in software and business. Depending on the viewpoint, the term "Web service" has been defined variously. Our definition here derives from how we described SOA:

☞ "Web Services Architecture," URL: http://www.w3.org/TR/ws-arch/

For an introduction to XML (Extensible Markup Language), see Chapter 13.

A Web service is a virtual component that offers its services via standard Web protocols.

XML (Extensible Markup Language) is the language of Web service messages. Without going deep into the jungle of acronyms and tech-speak, Web services also rely on the following concepts, technologies, and protocols:

- *Service Provider.* The entity that owns and publishes the service.
- *Service Requester.* The consumer of the service.
- *Service Broker.* The entity that connects the provider to the requester through a registry (See UDDI below.) The role of the service broker, however, is a matter of dispute since the provider can supply the registry as well.
- *SOAP.* The protocol that provides the framework for exchanging XML messages across the Internet by using HTTP (Hypertext Transport Protocol).
- *UDDI.* (Universal Description, Discovery, and Integration). An XML-based registry that defines the Web service: information about the provider, classification of the service based on industrial categories, technical information about how the service should be used.
- *WSDL.* (Web Services Description Language). Comparable to the IDL of various platforms, WSDL describes the interface of the Web service.

Web services are no longer merely a set of specifications and concepts but are actually used in the field. For example:

- **Amazon.com,** which owes its existence and prosperity to its innovative use of the Web, offers Web services that ❶ allow other vendors to offer their merchandise through the company's site, and ❷ allow the same vendors to offer Amazon's merchandise on their own Web sites. (Both sides, of course, get a cut from selling each others' wares.) Neither side needs to know anything about the technologies used by the other side internally.
- **eBay**, another successful Web business, offers Web services for searching, bidding, and creating auctions.
- **FedEx** and **UPS** offer Web services for tracking packages. Note that we are talking about the integration of this service into *automated* applications owned by outsiders, not about a visit to FedEx's Web site that offers the same service, manually, to individuals.
- Through the Web services of Microsoft's *MapPoint* you can integrate sophisticated maps into your own application without keeping an inventory of maps.

As new businesses adopt Web services, the specifications and the technologies are revised to keep up with new demands.

All this is very well, but what are the shortcomings of Web services? Web services are *stateless*: Once a request from a client (the consumer of the service) is performed, the server does not remember the client. The server has no idea of a "flow" or session and, as a result, every request is treated as though it is a new one. This has advantages: The server can serve a large number of clients and is not coupled to them. The downside is that it becomes the responsibility of the client to keep the "state" and remember how everything is sequenced. This task is not difficult but it is a very different model from "normal" applications where every object is responsible for tracking its own state.

☞ Being "*stateless*" is an attribute of all connections on the Web. See Chapter 11 for a discussion on how Web applications keep state.

One result of this statelessness is the lack of a *transaction model*. A transaction is a set of database operations that must succeed as a set. If one operation fails, then the whole transaction fails. With Web services, it is again the responsibility of the client to ensure transaction processing and pass the result to the Web service only if it is confident that everything is correct.

☞ See Chapter 13 for a discussion on **transactions**.

Other issues are essentially the same ones that we had with distributed components, plus the fact that XML is a text-based language, not a binary one: Translating XML messages back and forth to platform-specific binary messages further degrades performance. Here, however, we prefer to use the term "compromise" rather than "shortcoming." The reason is that Web services allow two utterly different systems to communicate and exchange services, something that otherwise would be impossible or would cost a lot because the solutions would be proprietary.

Something that cannot be justified is the urge felt by certain developers to implement any hot new technology indiscriminately. Some development shops have revamped their *internal* information systems to change all services into Web services, promising management that this will make interoperability and reuse a snap. When this happens, the "compromises" label should revert back to "shortcomings."

Data Management

> We usually buy a DBMS to build an information system, but we must still make crucial architectural decisions on how to use it.

It is difficult to imagine that somebody today would decide to create a database management system from the ground up as part of building an information system or writing an application. DBMSs are so complex that very few companies compete in the marketplace. As new opportunities arise—openings such as the "open source" movement and the interest in object-oriented databases—new contenders appear to fight an uphill battle against established vendors. As a result, the choice of the DBMS is a "buy" decision.

This leaves fewer architectural decisions in your hand, but the remaining decisions are nevertheless important:

- The design of the database, which we discussed in Chapter 13, is constrained by *the brand and the type* of the DBMS. A relational DBMS has different design requirements than an object-oriented one, and even relational database management systems are different in how you can organize security, users, roles, tables, and stored procedures—decisions that must be made at the "macro" or architectural level.

- Applications must communicate with the database. Who conducts this communication is architectural. We must design *persistence*, and the macro-structure of persistence can take many shapes. There are many design patterns that address this issue.
- If a business is geographically dispersed, you might *have* to use a **distributed database** architecture. Communication lines are becoming more reliable and a virtual private network (or VPN) can harness the flexibility of the Internet to improve the reliability of business networks, but for some businesses, such as airlines, the continuity of database operations is vital. Distributed databases, however, have huge issues, such as synchronization, that dwarf the problems that you encounter in dealing with distributed components.
- Increasingly, writing an application or creating an information system does not start from a blank page. You have to *integrate* a varying number of existing elements, including *disparate databases* that, as *strategic* business assets, you cannot simply discard. Whether this situation is due to mergers or other reasons, you are left with a serious architectural challenge. The issues are not only technological but are also shaped by the particulars of the situation. You can champion converting all databases into one, but can you ensure that the business is not disrupted? Should you a create a database or a layer of components that "front" for other databases, allowing existing applications to continue working while new ones are built?
- A situation similar to the same problem is **data warehousing**. We have not discussed data warehousing in this book because it is a highly specialized field in data management. In a nutshell, data warehousing is used when the intention is not the creation of a new system to replace others or the integration of an existing system, but when a large amount of data from disparate sources must be made accessible in a uniform format for analysis, reporting, and decision support systems (or DSSs). To describe what is necessary to design a data warehouse, we must say that "all bets are off." We are not implying that many good, solid, and useful patterns, methods, concepts, rules, and books on data warehousing do not exist, but that the variations in technology and data relationship are so high that the architect must work very hard to arrive at the right decisions.

☞ In Chapter 14 we illustrated the "Object Adapter" pattern by mapping it to a **Query** object that, transparent to the application, switches among different database management systems. This pattern, and a number of others, can help you to solve problems such as the previous one (disparate databases). One important challenge, however, persists: what to do with *existing* applications that do not have such built-in flexibility. Retrofitting applications cannot be taken lightly.

Modeling & Conceptualization

> Modeling and conceptualization are integral to the process of architecture.

A building would stand or fall regardless of whether or not a building plan or an architectural drawing exists, but you would stare in disbelief if somebody claimed that the Empire State Building was constructed with no plans whatsoever.

Not all buildings are the Empire State Building: Humans dwell and work in makeshift shacks, as well as modest, or at least more modest, structures. The degree of modeling and conceptualization required depends on the complexity of the artifact. On the other hand, people who build ramshackle cabins are unlikely to hire a professional architect.

We have dwelt extensively on the basic concepts and rationales for architectural modeling and architectural views. Here, let us reiterate that designing an information system is a highly abstract task: The requirements and the outcome cannot be understood without adequate means to visualize and describe them.

In a sense, the architects of the Empire State Building had it easier than the architects of a complex information system: Their creation was not subject to constant and fundamental changes.

Workflow

> Workflow influences the architecture of the information system and is, in turn, influenced by the architecture of information technology.

In "The Centralized Architecture" section earlier in this chapter we argued that this architecture did *not* disappear with the dominance of mainframe computers. Then how can we explain the lasting impression that centralization was a hallmark of the mainframe's bygone era? To be sure, one reason is that there were no other choices besides centralized computing. The stronger reason, however, comes from an almost subconscious association: "data processing" was the responsibility of a very centralized workflow architecture. The very expensive mainframe was housed in an almost sanctified glass enclosure that was accessible to only a select few. Data (paper) entered the enclosure, was processed, and came out as information (paper again). The great mass of users were mostly supplicants and were allowed no interference.

The relation between the organization of the workflow and information technology has always been bidirectional: Each influences the other and drives it forward (or backwards, if social resistance or inertia is strong enough).

Long-term social consequences of automation are not a subject of this book and architects are not hired to analyze such trends, but a keen architect must take into account how the workflow and the human organization will affect the new system and *vice versa*. Is the workflow envisioned by the client's (those who set the requirements) rationale and makes the best use of the system, or is it distorted because the client does not know better or does not want to do better? Will the organization be able to support the resulting workflow and the requirements of the new system? What organizational changes are necessary for the new system or will follow its introduction?

We have argued that modeling and conceptualization are an integral part of architecture as an approach. Workflow architecture is no exception and like other components of the information system, it needs more than one kind of modeling from more than one viewpoint. Also, the *scope* of workflow modeling is elusive since the effects of automation spread in concentric circles even to people who do not interact directly with the information system.

Our focus, however, is on the architecture of the information system and the workflow that is embodied by its applications. From this point of view, the workflow architecture can be modeled with tools that should be familiar by now:

❶ *Context Diagram.* Offers a snapshot or what user classes (or actors) do with the system and what the system does for them. (See Chapter 6 for a discussion on, and an example of, the context diagram.)

❷ *Use Case Diagram.* Provides a more detailed and dynamic view of how "units of workflow" relate to each other and to actors. (For use diagrams, see Chapter 7.)

❸ *Use Case.* Provides a detailed, step-by-step description of a unit of workflow as embodied by the behavior of the system and its interaction with actors. (Besides Chapters 6 and 7, also see Chapter 5, which explores the foundations of use cases.)

❹ *Activity Diagram.* Can be used to model business and system activities with complicated logical flows. (For examples of activity diagrams, see Chapter 9.) An activity diagram is not level-bound: It can present a high-level view or a detailed one.

The last item, the activity diagram, is also a very flexible tool for **Business Process Modeling** (BPM), which aims to represent a wider view of the workflow, one that is not limited to interactions with the information system. BPM is not a methodology or technology, but a framework of techniques and concepts, and does not have a unified notation. The Object Management Group's BPMN (Business Process Modeling Notation) is one of the better-known modeling languages for BPM and is very similar to UML notations used in the activity diagram. One of the differences is that BPMN has a specific notation for "data" that is not represented as an independent entity by UML. We believe that by using its extension mechanisms, especially stereotyping, UML can satisfy most diagramming needs of BPM.

4. ARCHITECTURAL PATTERNS

Architecture is essentially a pattern-driven activity.

☞ Chapter 14 discusses patterns and provides examples for them.

We said that architecture is more pattern-based than rule-based. This means that although a certain pattern for designing an architecture may apply to the majority of situations and therefore comes close to becoming a "rule," no architectural guideline can be applied with disregard for the actual situation.

What is more, since an information system is an aggregation of several subsystems, no single pattern or guideline is likely to apply to all subsystems. Usually, when software development and architectural patterns are discussed together, the term should be taken to mean "software patterns" or "application patterns." However, the patterns that we apply to various subsystems usually overlap. For example, if we want to use a "client-server" pattern to structure our software applications, it can work only if the technological framework of our information system is organized as a "client-server" network. Contrary to appearances, this not a foregone conclusion, because the exact same technology can be organized along the lines of a "peer-to-peer" pattern, or the application can be structured in a way that takes no notice of the client-server architecture of the network.

Since architecture is pattern-based, no rule book can make you an architect. You must study patterns and precedence and modify them to fit your context. And, although we have discussed patterns rather extensively before, a refresher observation or two would not be out of place:

[Fowler 2003, 10]

A key part of patterns is that they are rooted in practice. You find patterns by looking at what people do, observing things that work, and then looking for the "core of the solution." It isn't an easy process, but once you've found some good patterns they become a valuable thing. . . . You don't need to read . . . all of any patterns book to find it useful. You just need to read enough to have a sense of what the patterns are, what problems they solve, and how they solve them. You don't need to know all the details but just enough so that if you run into one of the problems you can find the pattern in the book. Only then do you need to really understand the pattern in depth.

Once you need the pattern, you have to figure out how to apply it to your circumstances. A key thing about patterns is that you can never just apply the solution blindly, which is why pattern tools have been miserable failures. I like to say that patterns are "half-baked," meaning that you always have to finish them off in the oven of your own project. . . . You see the same solution many times over, but it's never exactly the same.

Many architectural patterns do not appear as "architectural" at first glance, but as any other design pattern. The Layering pattern that we discuss next is obviously architectural, but the Object Adapter that we introduced in Chapter 14 may appear as too fine-grained to apply to architecture. However, if you reexamine our example—the application of the pattern to the communication with the database management system—you may discover that an application usually contains numerous such objects.

> **If any design pattern creates a pattern of its own, namely that it is repeated within a certain context, it should be considered at an architectural level and as an architectural pattern.**

The Layering Pattern

> A layer is a collection of components that provide similar services or that are highly dependent on each other for performing their services.

☞ **"Layer"** and **"tier"** are synonyms; therefore, using one for the other is usually acceptable. However, "tier" has a more hierarchical and "horizontal" connotation, whereas a layer can be vertical as well as horizontal. For example, you can "scrape layers of paint" from an over-painted wall, but you don't scrape "tiers of paint." As we shall see, we need both the horizontal and the vertical forms of the layers.

Layering is one of the most common patterns used in software architecture. It can even be labeled a "super-pattern" since it has many variations and one can easily imagine more variations.

The basic idea is simple: To manage a complex architecture, aggregate components that perform the same kind of services, plus the components that support them, into distinct layers. In such a structure, *horizontal* layers embody a hierarchy: The lower layer supports the upper layer and the upper layer relies on the services of the lower one. If done correctly, a lower layer has no dependency on the upper one. For example, in a rather simplified three-layer structure, the data management layer (the bottom-most layer) satisfies requests by the application logic (the middle layer), but requests no services from this layer. In turn, the presentation layer or the user interface (the topmost layer) relies on the services of the middle layer.

The layering pattern is not limited to application design, though our focus in this short introduction is on applications. When applied to the *physical* architecture of the information technology components, the layer is usually called a **tier**. As a result, we can have a two-tier, a three-tier, or even an *n-tier* architecture.

Gains & Losses

> Layering brings great advantages, but requires some compromises as well.

Layering is not merely an abstract "style" but makes the architecture both more robust and more flexible:

- As with smaller components, we must first "*scope*" a layer, meaning that we have to decide exactly what services a certain layer (and *only* that layer) must perform. This is no trivial task, but once done its development can be assigned to designers and developers who are more familiar with, or more *specialized* in, those services. For example, people responsible for designing and implementing the "persistence" layer do not have to worry about the intricacies of designing and coding the user interface of a Web application.
- *Testing* is more reliable and problems can be spotted more easily. If the communication with the database does not go well, we know where we should start looking. Even if the problem is not within the layer itself, it will provide us with useful clues because we know how the lines of communication are structured and where they will lead us.
- *Replace, Reuse, Recombine:* the "Three 'R's" that we assigned to components apply to layers as well. If you have carefully scoped your persistence layer, you have a better chance of saving the layers above from disruption when the persistence layer needs to be fixed or replaced. If several applications share the same database, then we can design the persistence layer in such a way that it can be reused by those applications or recombined with other specialized components or layers.

With all its advantages, and like everything else in design, the layered architecture is a compromise:

[Fowler 2003, 17–18]

- Some changes might ripple across all layers. For example, if we add a single attribute to the **Patient** class, then the database and every layer that works with this class must be altered.
- If (but only *if*) layers are implemented as physical components, then performance penalty can become an issue.

The Variations

> The interpretations of the layering pattern depend on the constraints of technology, theoretical leanings, and the particulars of the task.

As we said, the layering architecture, which appeared with the client-server architecture, has many variations and has evolved during the years. Some of the variations are due to the nature of the particular system or application. For example, an application that does not interact with human users does not need a user interface layer. (There are many such applications that in older times were called "batch jobs" because you could schedule them to be executed in batches and no further human intervention was necessary.) Other variations are due to differences in "philosophy" and/or technology. (Sometimes the same exact layer is identified by different names in the works of different authors.)

☞ Kyle Brown et al., 2003. *Enterprise Java Programming with IBM WebSphere, Second Edition.* IBM Press.

The "classic" layered architecture has three layers: presentation (user interface), logic (control and flow), and data source (persistence). Other schemes have more, not less. For example, an author writing on Java technology suggests five layers: presentation, controller/mediator (flow and control), domain (entity objects), data mapping (a "mediator" between the previous layers and the data source), and data source.

The Conceptual Layers

> We must identify and understand layers conceptually before designing or implementing a layered architecture.

Figure 16.3 provides another variation on the theme. In our *conceptual* scheme, layers can be **both horizontal and vertical.** (This is why we prefer to keep the term "tier" for the technological framework.) As we explained, a horizontal layer depends on the one below, but not on the one above it. Vertical layers, on the other hand, run across all horizontal layers, control them, sometimes use their services, and, most importantly, connect the layers together:

❶ *User Interface.* Horizontal. The user interface or the "presentation" layer holds all objects that are responsible for interaction with the user. This includes not only visible objects such as forms, Web pages, and their subdivisions, but also actions. The interaction with the user may include certain actions, such as editing (constraining) user input, that are strictly speaking "rules," but excluding them would result in a "shaky" user interface. For example, if the user inputs a string of characters in a field that is for "birth date," the user interface must catch the

Figure 16.3 Layering: An Architectural Pattern

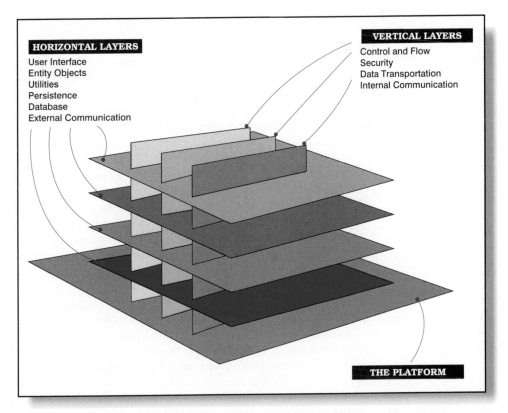

This is a conceptual view of layering. The concrete partitioning of layers and components depends, to a large degree, on the architecture of information technology and the choices made by the architect.

error, even though the defense against such an error should run as deep as the database itself. This is especially important for Web applications since a round-trip to the server (Web site) is inconvenient. (See Chapter 12.)

❷ *Entity Objects.* Horizontal. Entity classes are those classes that correspond to "business" or "domain" objects: **Patient**, **Invoice**, **Student**, and so on. They usually result from analysis, even though some are refined or broken into more than one class during design. Entity classes are usually *persisted*, that is, their state is saved. (Entity classes are discussed throughout the book, not in any one specific chapter. Nevertheless, see Chapter 10 for a discussion on the relationship between entity and design classes. Also see Chapter 13, which describes how the "state" of entity objects are stored.)

❸ *Utilities.* Horizontal. "Helper" or "service" classes that are neither "entity" nor "control." They are often "functional." For example, both Java and .Net platforms have a **Math** class that provides mathematical functions. However, even though these classes are functional, they do not result from the "functional decomposition" that we have warned about. These are "libraries" that provide specialized services to the components of the solution. For instance, a **Loan** object (which is not a result of "functional decomposition") might ask **Math** to perform calculations, but the responsibility of the **calculateInterest** method and all the information about the loan remains with the **Loan** object. Many utility classes either come with the development platform or can be purchased as component libraries (e.g., for charting) from third parties. In these cases, you are not responsible for partitioning them, but you will find that for most any application you have to write your own utility classes as well.

❹ *Persistence.* Horizontal. Objects in this layer mediate between the application and the database management system. This layer should hide the complexities of the database from the application and act as a buffer that, as much as possible, protects the application from changes in the database. (Persistence is extensively discussed in Chapter 13.)

❺ *Database.* Horizontal. You do not usually create a database management system as part of writing an application, but it *is* an independent layer. What is more, the structure of the database is yours, not the vendor's, and stored procedures can enforce a large number of business rules. In other words, the database participates in the application, even if application developers are not directly involved in its design. (Database and database management systems are discussed in Chapter 13.)

❻ *External Communication.* Horizontal. The purpose of this layer, or even the very need for it, depends on what we mean by "external communication." An appropriate example is an application that must use FTP (File Transfer Protocol) to send and/or receive files over the Internet, must convert what is received into a format understandable by the local information system, and must do the reverse for outgoing data.

❼ *Control & Flow.* Vertical. This layer runs across all other layers. It directs the flow of the application, marshals services for various objects ("introduces" them to each other), and enforces certain business rules (but not necessarily all). The control and flow objects form the essential vertical column that holds the application together. (See Chapter 11 for examples.)

❽ *Security.* Vertical. Strictly speaking, security is part of the control and flow layer. The need for it depends on the complexity of security requirements. Whether or not you decide to have such a layer, it is always useful to think of it as a distinct conceptual entity. The horror stories about identity and data thefts that are appearing with increasing frequency in the news media should help to concentrate your mind. You should also note that security is not only about prevention, but about *auditing* as well. Some users have legitimate privileges that they might abuse. Therefore, sometimes, interactions must be tracked even if there is no security breach as such. (Refer to Chapter 11 for simple examples of security.)

⑨ **Data Transportation.** Vertical. Objects interact by exchanging messages. Sometimes messages are simple, with only a few variables. At the other extreme, objects might need to send or receive "bulk" data. For instance, when we want to see a list of patients, the list must travel all the way from the database to the user interface. In an object-oriented environment, as we have said, no action takes place and no task is carried out unless an object or a set of objects do it. All full-featured development platforms provide one or more classes that can carry large amounts of data. One of the most prominent is the *dataset* that carries structured data in a tabular format. (See Chapter 11 for a discussion of datasets.)

⑩ **Internal Communication.** Vertical. The mechanisms that carry messages between objects are provided by the platform (the operating system or the development platform), and their wirings are largely transparent to developers. In certain instances, you might need to expand these mechanisms by building your own internal communication channels.

The application might require one or more of these layers. Conversely, in certain applications, a set of components might be so important as to require its own layer.

All these layers rely on the platform, both hardware and software. Were we to model the platform, we would see that it is made up of layers as well: device drivers that connect the physical world to the virtual one, file and storage systems, presentation "engines," etc.

Design & Implementation

> The relationship between conceptual, logical, and physical layers is not necessarily one-to-one.

The layers that we described are conceptual, meaning that the structure of most applications, but by no means all, can be layered in this manner. The moment that we step from concept into design, however, we have to adapt our concepts to the technology: first to the general framework (logical), then to the specifics (physical). In this transition, the actual layering is very likely to change.

The first and most important reason is that we might set boundaries that are conceptually sharp but in reality are not so well-defined. One controversial area consists of "*business rules*," and we must explain the problem with more than a couple of sentences. The basic question, however, is short: Where should the business rules be enforced?

The answers to this question have depended on both the technology and the methodology (or the lack of it). If you are improvising as you go along, then there is no pattern for where things take place. Since most *ad hoc* development usually starts with the user interface, it is the user interface that is saddled with all responsibilities.

Other, more reasoned, answers usually revolve around the latest technological innovation. Since commercial database management systems were the first highly reliable components of the information system to appear, the "stored procedure" solution is the oldest one. Then came dedicated "rules engines." A more recent answer, with the appearance of "application servers," is that the "middleware" must be responsible for enforcing business rules, and nothing else.

The truth is that ❶ a lot of times there is no general agreement on what a "business rule" is, and ❷ those that we can agree upon clearly fall into different categories that obviously do not belong to a single layer: facts, inferences, action enablers, constraints, computations, etc. (See Chapter 5 for an introduction to the taxonomy of business rules.) Discussions with the proponents of one or another "single solution" to the enforcement of business rules such as the "middleware" option can easily degenerate into a circular logic: If it is a business rule it must go to the middleware; what cannot or should not go into the middleware is not a business rule.

A conceptual layer called "business rules" is acceptable, but it is unwise to try to actually convert it to a single physical layer called, for example, a "rule engine." "Referential integrity," for example, clearly must be enforced by the DBMS. (Unless, of course, referential integrity is disqualified as a business rule.)

The second reason is technology. A database or a file system is a separate layer, even if the database or the file operations of your application are miniscule. On the other hand, particular configurations and technologies might make extensive layering difficult, meaningless, or expensive in terms of performance.

The third reason is money. Creating a more elegant and/or flexible architecture always costs more "upfront" money than a less elegant and/or flexible one. Budgetary constraints or deadlines, however, are other elements in the "design compromise" with which you will have to deal.

Layering is a useful pattern, not a sacred rule. In the final analysis, when and how to layer is up to the architect, who must weigh many complex factors. Nevertheless, *conceptual* layering is always useful, regardless of whether it is implemented as physical layers or not. At the very least, it is an incentive to clearly define what *kind* of responsibilities your classes must have. On the whole, this is no small thing.

5. DELIVERABLES

In the previous chapter, we mentioned that components are architectural entities. Many of the architectural artifacts and relationships can be effectively represented by the same modeling tools that we used for components.

Architecture, however, runs across all development and although the architect is not necessarily the creator of most models and views, he or she has the responsibility of organizing and presenting them. How views are organized are influenced by the architectural framework that is adopted (or adapted) by the architect.

One way to organize models, favored by the creators of UML, is known as *4+1*. (See Figure 16.4.) In this framework, there are four views that are interconnected by one view, the *use case view*. Of the four, two are logical—the *design view* and the *process view*—and two are physical—the *implementation view* and the *deployment view*. (We will discuss implementation and deployment in the next chapter.)

What should be done to create these views? In the following we quote the guidelines at length.

☞ All emphasis is ours.

- *Specify a **use case view** of the system, encompassing the use cases that describe the behavior of the system as seen by its end users, analysts, and testers. Apply*

Figure 16.4
4+1: A Framework for Organizing Architectural Views

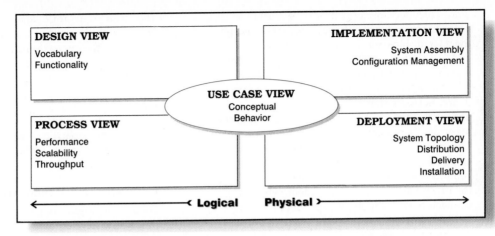

DESIGN VIEW	IMPLEMENTATION VIEW
Vocabulary	System Assembly
Functionality	Configuration Management

USE CASE VIEW
Conceptual
Behavior

PROCESS VIEW	DEPLOYMENT VIEW
Performance	System Topology
Scalability	Distribution
Throughput	Delivery
	Installation

< Logical   Physical >

This framework, favored by the creators of UML, is one of the simpler frameworks.

[Booch 1999, 425]

use case diagrams to model static aspects, and interaction diagrams, statechart diagrams, and activity diagrams to model the dynamic aspects.

- *Specify a **design view** of the system, encompassing the classes, interfaces, and collaborations that form the vocabulary of the problem and its solution. Apply class diagrams and object diagrams to model static aspects, and interaction diagrams, statechart diagrams, and activity diagrams to model the dynamic aspects.*

- *Specify a **process view** of the system, encompassing the threads and processes that form the system's concurrency and synchronization mechanisms. Apply the same diagrams as for the design view, but with a focus on active classes and objects that represent threads and processes.*

- *Specify an **implementation view** of the system, encompassing the components that are used to assemble and release the physical system. Apply component diagrams to model static aspects, and interaction diagrams, statechart diagrams, and activity diagrams to model the dynamic aspects.*

- *Specify a **deployment view** of the system, encompassing the nodes that form the system's hardware topology on which the system executes. Apply deployment diagrams to model static aspects, and interaction diagrams, statechart diagrams, and activity diagrams to model dynamic aspects.*

- *Model the **architectural patterns** and **design patterns** that shape each of these models using collaborations.*

6. WRAP UP

☑ **An introduction to architecture and architectural elements**

Architectural decisions are the most important design decisions; that is, they decide the most important aspects of the solution. To understand architecture, we must first gain a good knowledge of the nuts and bolts of the solution, but the design of the product must start with architecture because

it is the architecture that decides the fate of every nut and every bolt.

The importance of architecture, however, works against a clear definition since various definitions might view it from widely different viewpoints without even contradicting each other. What is more, the term *architecture* can apply to both the *actual* product and an *abstraction* of it. In other words, architecture can be seen as ❶ the organization of a system's major components and the relationships of these component's to each other and to the whole, or ❷ how such an organization and/or its development is viewed or modeled.

An architecture is defined by the configuration of **architectural elements**: components, messages, and connectors. We have studied components and messages. "**Connector**," however, is a new term. The connectors are mechanisms through which components are connected together or communicate with each other. A message is (relatively) technology-independent, whereas connectors are technology-dependent but are independent of messages. Connectors work as conduits for messages.

☑ **Methodology, patterns, and architectural views**

Architecture as the actual organization of a system is a subject of patterns; architecture as a way to view the system or its development is an area of methodology.

How an architecture combines or uses patterns is called its **style**. Another architecture might combine all or some of the same patterns in a different style. In other words, style is how a combination of architectural elements and patterns make a certain architecture different from, or similar to, other architectures.

In discussing architecture, the term "*framework*" has more currency than "methodology" because "methodology" has come to imply a roadmap or a plan, while "framework" points more towards a structure within which a certain freedom of choice exists. Architectural frameworks usually avoid specifying processes and roadmaps. Instead, they aim to identify what is necessary or best ❶ to make an architecture take shape, and ❷ to make its meaning comprehensible to all stakeholders, from owners to builders.

The main tools in this mission are usually called **architectural views**. An architectural view is a representation of the system that is shaped by four factors: what, who, when, and where. By "representation" we mean modeling in a very broad sense, as the systematic representation of the relevant features of a product or a system from particular perspectives. The difference between a model and an architectural view is that the latter may consist of one model or several. Views may also share models.

The "*what*" of the view may appear simple, but it is not: For each view, depending on other factors, we must *select* what to show because no model can show everything. Furthermore, the "what" can be behavioral, structural, or dynamic.

The "*who*" is about stakeholders of the system, people with different concerns. For example, the concern of the owners is primarily what the system does, while the users want to know about how the system interacts with *them*. "*When*" indicates the timeframe *within* development that the view represents: analysis (conceptual), design (logical or physical), implementation, or deployment. Finally, "*where*" expresses the viewpoint or perspective, the "angle" from which the view represents the product.

☑ **The relationship of engineering to architecture**

For a while, engineering was seen as the Holy Grail of software development: If we could apply engineering principles to software, then "the software crisis" would be over. That time is past and the mantle has been passed to architecture. However, if we can break through the hype, past and present, we will find that software engineering is a valid concept if our expectations are adjusted somewhat: Engineering is the application of architectural concepts to the building of the actual product.

To engineer is to understand the conceptual solution, to participate actively in outlining the logical solution, and to devise the physical solution *in essential details*.

☑ **The significance of coupling to architecture**

Architecture is about composition. When we think about architecture, we must think about how things are connected, not what we will end up with if we decompose the structure. Coupling is the extent of dependency among the components from which the system is composed. Generally, a *loosely coupled* system has advantages over a *tightly coupled* one, but other factors such as structural strength, performance, maintenance, and cost should be taken into account as well.

To loosen coupling in software, we can use certain mechanisms that we have discussed in previous chapters: signal events, abstract interfaces, component-based architecture, and patterns such as the "Object Adapter."

☑ **Architectural modeling and UML**

Architectural views need "descriptions" and models that are not provided by UML. Plus, architectural views are independent from both the process of development and modeling languages. UML's standard diagrams and extensibility mechanisms, however, can satisfy many of their *visual* demands. The only exception is when or where a framework is *not* object-oriented; for example, when a framework considers "data" and "function" as separate concepts.

An important issue in architectural modeling is *view management*: how to keep the models that result from the selection of "what," "who," "where," and "when" connected and in sync. UML offers two stereotyped relationships for view management: «**trace**», which indicates historical dependency between models, and «**refine**», which shows a model as a less abstract version of another one. These two mechanisms, however, only address the "when" and the "what" of the architectural view. UML does not effectively address the "who" and the "where."

☑ **Technology architecture**

The architecture of an information system is an aggregation of the architectures of its components. Therefore, it must be characterized as a heterogeneous and cooperative architecture, not as a centralized one.

A set of forces compete and cooperate to change the architecture of an information system during its lifetime. The architecture of an information system is made possible and constrained by the information technology.

Centralized architecture predates other technological architectures since computers, unlike telephones, do not need a network of their kind to perform their basic tasks. In a centralized architecture, all services depend on one computer system. When networks did not exist, this architecture was the only available choice, but centralized computing has not disappeared. Among others, most desktop computers used in homes can be considered as centralized.

In a **distributed architecture**, two or more computers on a network cooperate to perform services. Distributed architecture took shape only gradually. LANs (Local Area Network) and WANs (Wide Area Networks) were first used for *file sharing*, not for hosting a distributed software architecture.

The **client-server architecture** (CSA) was made possible by the evolution of networks and provided the real break from centralized architecture. In the CSA model, one or more *servers* provide services that are consumed by the *client* computers. Database management, Web hosting, and application services are the most prominent tasks usually performed by dedicated servers, but the list includes other services as well. Distributed *network* architecture must not be mistaken with distributed *software* architecture.

☑ **Architecture of components and applications**

The architecture of software or the organization of components is constrained by the architecture of technology but is not dictated by it.

An application can be defined as a *logical* grouping of components that cooperate to perform a specific task. While how components are organized is eventually *physical*, the architecture of an application remains *logical* and can be mapped to various physical configurations of components.

A monolithic application is a self-contained component that does not rely on other components and cannot be reused, in part or in whole, by other applications. No modern application is truly monolithic as it must rely on the services of the operating system. Still, the label can be applied to applications that consist of only one component.

In a **distributed software architecture**, software components cooperate and interact across a network to perform services. (However, an application composed of multiple components, like most desktop applications, is not necessarily a "distributed" application, but simply a "multi-component" application.) In theory, distributing components across servers enhances performance and reduces installation issues. In practice, the distribution of application-specific components, as opposed to general-purpose subsystems such as the database management system, has not been very successful. We must not undertake a distributed software architecture just because the technology "is there." A viable alternative to this approach is "clustering" and "load-balancing."

☑ **Service-oriented architecture and Web services**

Service-oriented architecture (SOA) aims to compose applications from platform-independent services of **virtual components**. SOA envisions an application as a very loosely coupled cooperation between services that can be rendered and consumed transparently across a network, regardless of specific platforms that the nodes implement.

A virtual component is a component that ❶ relieves its consumers from the issues of its physical identity, and ❷ complies with universally accepted standards instead of following proprietary protocols. The technology choice for "virtual components" has generally come down to **Web services**. A Web service is a virtual component that offers its services via standard Web protocols.

The adoption of Web services is gaining momentum. It offers one great benefit: It allows utterly disparate systems to communicate with each other over the existing Internet by using standard Web protocols. However, besides performance penalties associated with any distributed scheme, Web services are *stateless*. As a result, it is the responsibility of the clients to keep state and ensure the integrity of **transactions**.

☑ **Data management architecture**

We usually buy a DBMS to build an information system, but we must still make crucial architectural decisions on how to use it. Nowadays, because of its complexity, a database management system is always a separate subsystem. Some business models require that the database itself be physically distributed. Distributed databases, however, have huge issues, such as synchronization, that dwarf the problems that you encounter in dealing with distributed components.

Another area in which the data management architecture presents us with challenges is **data warehousing**. In a nutshell, data warehousing is used when the intention is not the creation of a new system or integration of an existing system, but when a large amount of data from disparate sources must be made accessible in a uniform format for analysis, reporting, and decision support systems.

☑ **Workflow architecture**

Workflow influences the architecture of the information system and is, in turn, influenced by the architecture of information technology. A keen architect must take into account how the workflow and the human organization would affect the new system and *vice versa*. Does the workflow envisioned by the clients' rationale make the best use of the system, or is it distorted because the client does not know better or does not want to do better? Will the organization be able to support the resulting workflow and the requirements of the new system? What organizational changes are necessary for the new system or will follow its introduction?

Like other components of the information system, workflow architecture needs more than one kind of modeling from more than one viewpoint. Also, the *scope* of workflow modeling is elusive since the effects of automation spread in concentric circles, even to people who do not interact directly with the information system

☑ **Architectural patterns and the layering pattern**

Architecture is essentially a pattern-driven activity. This means that although a certain pattern for designing an architecture may apply to the majority of situations and therefore comes close to becoming a "rule," no architectural guideline can be applied with disregard for the actual situation. What is more, since an information system is an aggregation of several subsystems, usually no single pattern or guideline can apply to all subsystems.

Layering is one of the most common patterns used in software architecture. A layer is a collection of components that provide similar services or that are highly dependent on each other for performing their services. The basic idea is simple: To manage a complex architecture, aggregate components that perform the same kind of services, plus the components that support them, into distinct layers. In such a structure, *horizontal* layers embody a hierarchy: The lower layer supports the upper layer and the upper layer relies on the services of the lower one.

Layers can be both horizontal and *vertical*. Vertical layers run across all horizontal layers, control them, sometimes use their services, and, most importantly, connect the layers together.

The relationship between conceptual, logical, and physical layers is not necessarily one-to-one. For a number of reasons, a conceptual layer might not become a logical or a physical layer. (A physical layer on a separate server is called a **tier**; hence the terms "two-tier," "three tier," and "n-tier.") Nevertheless, *conceptual* layering is always useful, regardless of whether it is implemented as physical layers or not. At the very least, it is an incentive to clearly define what *kinds* of responsibilities your classes must have.

---

7. KEY CONCEPTS

Application.   From an architectural viewpoint, a logical grouping of components that cooperate to perform a specific task. Conventionally, only the "executable" part is called an "application," but an "executable" is often only the "switch" that turns the application on.

Application, Monolithic.   A self-contained component that does not rely on other components and cannot be reused, in part or in whole, by other applications. In practice, almost all modern applications rely on the services of the operating system, although "monolithic" continues to be a proper description for applications that consist of only one component.

Application Server.   A server on the network that is ❶ dedicated to executing certain applications or ❷ provides the core services of the application embodied in the "**middleware**."

Architecture.   ❶ The arrangement of a system's components and the relationship of these components to each other and to the whole. ❷ The view or views of such an arrangement and relationships. The first definition applies to the *product itself*, while the second definition applies to the *development approach* and characterizes how the product is viewed and/or modeled throughout the stages of its development life cycle.

Architecture, Centralized. In a centralized architecture, all services depend on one computer system.

Architecture, Components. How the components of an information system, including **applications**, are organized or interact. The architecture of components may or may not follow the distributed architecture of the information technology.

Architecture, Distributed. When computers on a network cooperate to perform services. Variations include *file sharing*, **client-server**, and **peer-to-peer**. Distributed architecture may or may not be reflected in how software components are "partitioned" or distributed. See also **Components, Distributed**.

Architectural Elements. Components, messages, and **connectors** whose configuration defines the architecture.

Architectural Pattern. Any pattern that applies or affects the architecture of the system. Can apply to large-grained components of the system, such as **layers**, or can apply to many small-grained objects that make it an architectural solution.

Architecture, Information System. The architecture of a modern information system is a heterogeneous and cooperative architecture. It is an aggregation of the architectures of its subsystems.

Architecture, Technology. Provides the framework for the architecture of the information system. Within the technological framework, the architecture of other components of the information system may be possible or not possible but, within these limitations, the technological framework does not force us to choose a particular architecture.

Architecture, Workflow. The dynamic organization of work and people to achieve specific goals. Includes how people's interaction with the information system and its applications is organized.

Client-Server Architecture (CSA). A **distributed architecture** in which a number of computers on the network are "servers" (perform services) and the rest are "clients." Depending on the *physical* configuration of the software, a specific CSA is called two-tier, three-tier, or n-tier (for many **tiers**).

Cluster. A set of computers on a network that are configured with the same exact software. Through "load-balancing," each server is activated if its sibling is overwhelmed with service requests from the clients. Often used to manage Web sites with a high number of requests (in which case it is also referred to as a "Web farm"), but can be used with any application with a potentially large number of clients.

Component, Virtual. A component whose physical presence and location is irrelevant to the client to which it provide services and which adheres to platform-independent standards and protocols. A **Web service** is a virtual component.

Components, Distributed. A distributed software architecture in which software components cooperate and interact across a network to perform services. Must be distinguished from the general term, **distributed architecture**, that can apply to the technological framework as well.

Connector. An **architectural element**. A mechanism through which components are connected together or communicate with each other. Unlike messages that are (relatively) technology-independent, connectors are technology-dependent but (relatively) independent of messages.

Coupling. Defines the extent of dependency among components of the system. Architecturally, a "loosely coupled" architecture is more flexible than a "tightly coupled" one, but flexibility comes at a price, both monetary and otherwise, that must be taken into account in designing the "couplings" of a system.

Database, Distributed. An architecture that is distributed on separate servers.

Data Warehousing. A system that integrates data from disparate databases and data sources for reporting and analysis.

Domain Server. A network server that is responsible for enforcing security rules on a logical grouping of computers (or the "domain").

Engineering. The application of architectural concepts to the building of the actual product.

Layer. In software architecture, a collection of components that provide similar services or which are highly dependent on each other for performing their services. A physical layer on a separate server is called a **tier**. Physically, a layer is a large-grained component. A layer can be conceptual, logical, or physical. A "horizontal" layer provides services to the one above, but relies on the one below. A "vertical" layer runs across horizontal layers and connects or controls them.

Layering Pattern. A pattern for organizing an application in separate layers.

Middleware. A collection of components that embody the application logic, but not the user interface or the database. The middleware is often deployed on its own **application server**.

Peer-To-Peer. A type of distributed computing in which computers on a network (or a "virtual network") equally contribute to performing tasks or take turns in becoming "servers" or "clients."

Rationale, Architectural. The reason that explains why architectural elements are organized the way they are. Some architectural *frameworks* consider rationale as a constituent of **architectural views**.

«refine». A stereotyped relationship in UML modeling that shows one model "refines" or is less abstract than another model.

Service-Oriented Architecture (SOA). An architecture that aims to compose applications from platform-independent services of virtual components. The virtual components are usually **Web services** although, theoretically, other types of virtual components can take part.

Service Broker. In the context of **Web services**, the entity that connects the *Web provider* to the *Web requesters* through a registry. See also **UDDI**.

Service Provider. In the context of **Web services**, the entity that owns and publishes the service.

Service Requester. In the context of **Web services**, the consumer of the service. Also called "client."

SOAP. The protocol that provides the framework for exchanging XML messages across the Internet by using HTTP. It is a building block of **Web services**. The original acronym stood for "Simple Object Access Protocol," but now SOAP is merely an acronym without a description (like SQL).

State. The condition of an object or an application at a certain point in life. For an application, a specific point in its flow. Web applications and **Web services** are "stateless," meaning that every request is treated as a new one.

Style, Architectural. The specific manner in which an architecture uses *patterns* or combines them. Many architectures may use the same patterns but end up with different styles.

Thin Client. A computer whose sole responsibility is to render the user interface and accept user input. Such a computer depends on the network and a **distributed architecture** for the execution of applications.

Tier. A *physical* software **layer**, installed on its own server. Usually described by the number of its tiers (two-tier, three-tier, or n-tier), such an application is dependent on the **distributed architecture** of the information technology.

Transaction. A set of database operations that must succeed or fail as a whole. **Web services** lack a transaction model.

«Trace». A stereotyped relationship in UML modeling that shows one model is a "historical derivation" from another model.

View, Architectural. A representation of the architecture that is shaped by four factors: what, who, when, and where. "What" consists both of the **architectural elements** and their behavioral, structural, *or* dynamic aspects. "Who" defines the stakeholder. "When" defines the development phase for the view: conceptual (analysis), concrete design (logical or physical), implementation, or deployment. "Where" refers to the viewpoint or perspective.

Virtual Private Network (VPN). A network that is not physically independent from the Internet (or any other large network) but appears to its users as a self-contained and secure network.

UDDI. Universal Description, Discovery & Integration. An XML-based registry that defines a **Web service**.

Web Server. A server on the network that is responsible for managing a Web site and providing the Internet client with the requested content. To increase capacity and performance, Web servers are often combined into "server farms" that operate through "load balancing."

Web Service. A *virtual component* that offers its services via standard Web protocols. Web services are the building blocks of **service-oriented architecture** (SOA) although, in theory, SOA may use other types of virtual components in addition, or instead of, Web services.

WDSL. Web Services Description Language. Describes the interface of the Web service. An IDL (interface definition language) for **Web services**.

XML. Extensible Markup Language. A language widely used for the serialization of data. Used in **Web services**.

8. CONFUSING CONCEPTS

Distributed Computing, Hardware & Software. An information system is integrated with its computing platform, regardless of whether this platform is a single computer, a network of computers, or the Internet. A distributed *software* architecture must rely on a distributed hardware architecture, but the first does not necessarily follow the second. Even if an information system or an application is composed of independent components, the architecture does not automatically become a "distributed" one because *all* components can be on the same computer. Of course, if an application is all one piece, or "monolithic," it can never become distributed.

Tier & Layer. A tier is a physical layer that is executed from a separate server. The reverse, however, is not a "given": A physical layer is a large-grained component, not necessarily a tier. In other words, an application that is composed of multiple components does not automatically become a two-tier, three-tier, or n-tier application. Tiers are hierarchical and horizontal, while a layer, conceptually at least, can be vertical as well.

9. REVIEW QUESTIONS

1. Architecture is defined from two perspectives: the product itself and the development of the product. Compare the two definitions.
2. How does architecture relate to design?
3. How and why does the architecture of the information system differ from software architecture?
4. What is the relationship of technology to the information system architecture?
5. Provide an example of centralized information system architecture.
6. Define distributed information system architecture and provide an example.
7. What is service-oriented architecture? How does SOA help the flexibility of an information system?
8. Provide examples of Web services and discuss the contribution of Web services to the efficiency of information systems.
9. Compare and explain vertical and horizontal layers in application architecture.
10. Discuss how we should handle "business rules" in the architecture of an information system.

10. RESEARCH PROJECTS & TEAMWORK

❶ There are quite a few new (or not so new) architectural concepts that we did not have enough room even to introduce. One of them is *mashup*: creating a virtual workspace by mixing independent applications *within* a single Web page *and* by the user. One of the more successful platforms for mashup is provided by Google. (The platform even allows nonprogrammers to create simple "gadgets.")

Research this topic on the Web and present the results in a team meeting. Is mashup a viable architectural approach for business? How can it help architecture to be more *loosely coupled*? What effects could it have on the methodologies for developing software?

Organize your findings and submit them to your instructor.

❷ Like any other topic in software development, architecture (or even the need for it) is controversial. Visit Web sites on software architecture and try to answer the following questions:

- Which new concepts in architecture are currently "hot"?
- Which are the most controversial? Gather a few "pros" and "cons."
- Which concepts are the most *in*comprehensible?

Gather your research into a "team findings" and submit it to your instructor.

11. SUGGESTED READINGS

Almost every topic associated with software and its development has been discussed under "architecture." (The same was true for "software engineering" when the term was more fashionable.) We, however, have a stricter view of architecture's boundaries and our suggested readings reflect this view.

This chapter does not even scratch the surface of architecture. For a proper introduction, we suggest *Software Architect Bootcamp* by **Raphael Malveau** and Thomas J. Mowbray (Prentice Hall PTR, 2001). The book discusses various approaches to architecture and related activities at length, and still manages to be useful.

As we said, design patterns can become architectural patterns if they are repeated enough across the solution. Therefore, the suggested readings for patterns in Chapter 14 apply here as well. For patterns that directly impact the architecture, refer to *Patterns of Enterprise Application Architecture* by **Martin Fowler** et al. (Addison-Wesley, 2003). As with other design catalogues, this book is not light reading and you must have gained some professional experience in design.

Software Architecture in Practice, Second Edition by **Len Bass**, Paul Clemens, and Rick Kazman (Addison-Wesley, 2003) is, true to its title, more about the practice of architecture. When you become a hands-on architect, remember this book.

One of the best-known architectural frameworks is **Zachman's** framework, named after J. A. Zachman, a researcher at IBM. In 1987, in the *IBM System Journal*, he published an article titled "A Framework for Information Systems Architecture" in which he put forward the concept of architectural views and for which, deservedly, he became well-known. It still deserves reading as it lays out a clear and persuasive case for following an architectural approach to software development.

Zachman's idea of architectural views are well established now and even frameworks that do not follow his system of classification use the concept. Meanwhile, many books and papers have expanded Zachman's framework. One of the more recent and detailed ones is *Enterprise Architecture Using the Zachman Framework* by **Carol O'Rourke** et al. (Thomson Course Technology, 2003). The book is comprehensive, readable, and will considerably add to your knowledge about architecture.

You should be aware that the Zachman's framework is *not* object-oriented. Some have made valiant efforts to reconcile it with object-orientation, but as long as "what" (data) and "how" (functions) separate Zachman's architectural views, we doubt that such efforts will achieve real success.

This book is not devoted to architecture and the history of software architecture is mostly outside its scope, but we believe it is an injustice that writings that have laid the foundations of innovative technological thinking are frequently overshadowed by the same trends that they have helped to unleash. **David Parnas** is a pioneer in both object orientation and software architecture, and *Software Fundamentals: Collected Papers by David L. Parnas* (Addison-Wesley, 2001) is a worthwhile reading in its own right. A quotation from the author provides the reason:

> I would advise students to pay more attention to the fundamental ideas rather than the latest technology. The technology will be out of date before they graduate. Fundamental ideas never get out of date.

Chapter 17

Implementation

1. OVERVIEW

The process of development starts with gathering requirements and analysis, and continues with design. It is concluded by implementation, a range of activities including programming, testing, deployment, and maintenance. This chapter provides a short introduction to these activities.

- ☑ Inception
- ☑ Requirements Discovery
- ☐ Development
    - ☑ Analysis
    - ☑ Design
    - ☐ **Implementation** ⬅

Chapter Topics

- ➤ Coding.
- ➤ Programming languages and tools.
- ➤ Coding standards and code review.
- ➤ Testing and its variations.
- ➤ Deployment and the deployment diagram.
- ➤ User training.
- ➤ Maintenance.

Introduction

The purpose of analysis and design is to create not models but a product. Implementation is a set of activities that transform the abstract concepts of analysis and the detailed specifications of design into an actual product that people use.

Implementation is the last activity of the system development life cycle. It often overlaps with other activities of the development life cycle and is highly complex and iterative by itself. The primary purpose of implementation is to deliver an operational system that meets the needs of the users of the system.

Implementation starts with coding and **programming**. It includes **testing** that is conducted both in parallel to programming and at its conclusion, and **deployment** that consists of installation, configuration, and user training. **Maintenance** is often necessary after deployment and, depending on the reasons, may require a full cycle of development, including analysis and design.

Since this book is not about implementation and programming, this chapter can provide you with only a very brief glimpse of what is involved, and what is involved is vast and complicated and constantly changes with the technology. After a short discussion about programming tools, we also introduce the **deployment diagram**, the last major tool in UML, which models the relationships between software components and computing "nodes" such as servers, workstations, networks, etc.

2. CODING

> Code is the brick and the mortar of a software product. High-quality software cannot result from low-quality code.

In the beginning, software development was coding and nothing but coding. As software and expectations from software grew more complex, this narrow approach started to result in unreliable products. Nowadays, regardless of specific methodologies, coding is viewed as *part* of software development, not its whole. Nevertheless, we must not overlook the very important fact that coding is the ultimate realization of the solution: No code means no software.

Coding follows and depends on physical design. In turn, coding might force the physical design to change if it shows that certain design concepts are defective, missing, or ignorant of technological realities. (It is too easy to design something that looks perfect on paper but fails in reality.) This relationship between design and coding has a number of implications:

- The more accurate the design is, the less complicated coding becomes. Design, especially physical modeling, strictly defines the services that an object must provide and, as a result, creates a precise scope for coding.
- Errors in design are more costly to correct than errors in coding. The primary reason is that erroneous code is often more localized than defective design. Remember encapsulation: An object uses another object's services by sending messages to the methods that are provided through the latter object's interface. If the design of the interface is defective, it negatively affects every other object that communicates with that interface.
- No design is perfect. Some design defects are not predictable and can be discovered only through coding and testing (which, in turn, is not possible without coding). Corrective actions to design that are necessitated by coding and testing might be simple or complex, but they are unavoidable.

As important as analysis and design are, coding should not be taken for granted. Programming is a specialized skill and, notwithstanding the eternal wishes of

Figure 17.1 Coding: Transforming Design into Software

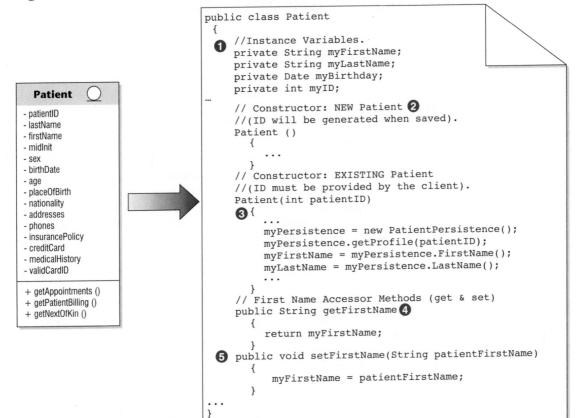

Patient ◯

- patientID
- lastName
- firstName
- midInit
- sex
- birthDate
- age
- placeOfBirth
- nationality
- addresses
- phones
- insurancePolicy
- creditCard
- medicalHistory
- validCardID

+ getAppointments ()
+ getPatientBilling ()
+ getNextOfKin ()

```java
public class Patient
{
    //Instance Variables.          ❶
    private String myFirstName;
    private String myLastName;
    private Date myBirthday;
    private int myID;

    // Constructor: NEW Patient    ❷
    //(ID will be generated when saved).
    Patient ()
    {
        ...
    }
    // Constructor: EXISTING Patient
    //(ID must be provided by the client).
    Patient(int patientID)
    ❸ {
        ...
        myPersistence = new PatientPersistence();
        myPersistence.getProfile(patientID);
        myFirstName = myPersistence.FirstName();
        myLastName = myPersistence.LastName();
        ...
    }
    // First Name Accessor Methods (get & set)
    public String getFirstName ❹
    {
        return myFirstName;
    }
    ❺ public void setFirstName(String patientFirstName)
    {
        myFirstName = patientFirstName;
    }
    ...
}
```

Above right is only a fraction of the code necessary to implement the Patient class on the left.

1. Variables that the object uses to store what it "knows." These include, but are not limited to, the attributes. "Date" and "String" are actually Java classes, the instances of which are used as variables.

2. The 1st constructor method.

This particular method has no arguments and, therefore, is used to instantiate a new patient.

3. The 2nd constructor method instantiates a patient that already exists in the database. (It is also an example of "overloading" methods.) The Patient object immediately creates another object that retrieves its "state" from the database.

4. This "get" method exposes one of the attributes to the outside world. Without such accessor methods, other objects cannot access to private variables.

5. The "set" method allows outside objects to change the value of a private attribute. Here, through code, the object can control the input value.

This (very) partial example is in Java, but the basic structure is shared by most object-oriented languages. Beyond that, however, the same class can be coded in a variety of ways. Handling of exceptions (or "error checking," not shown here) is a critical part of any code but can take many shapes depending on the preferences of the architect, the designer, and/or the programmer or the type of the exception.

(The numbered notes refer to topics that we have previously discussed in design chapters.)

business for interchangeability of workers, programmers are *not* created equal. Neither are programming tools, platforms, or practices.

The Choice of the Language

> The choice of the programming language depends on many factors, among which technical excellence is only one.

In most cases, how a programming language is selected is similar to how a human language is selected: You use it because that is what you know or because that is what somebody else with whom you have to work knows. There is nothing inherently wrong with this picture. Language is a means of communication, be it with humans or machines. It is only after you have mastered the basics of the language that you can communicate effectively. In other words, the efficiency of using a language to solve a problem has a proportionate relationship to the efficiency of using the language itself.

Programming languages are both easier and more difficult than human languages. On the one hand, the concepts that programming languages express are more limited than those that human languages must handle. On the other hand, the syntax of programming languages is much more strict and demanding and some of the concepts that the languages must handle are highly abstract and/or relate to entities or operations in the virtual world that cannot be readily compared to those in the real world.

As we said in the last chapter, engineering is how the architectural concepts are implemented and, properly speaking, the choice of the programming language is a task for the engineer who must work with the architects and the designers to create the physical design. In practice, the freedom of the engineer in choosing the programming language is sharply limited by the following factors:

- *Proprietary Languages & Dialects.* Certain products with which you *must* work can be programmed only (or mostly) in a proprietary language. For example, it is a given in most situations that you buy a commercial database management system such as Oracle or MS SQL Server. The first uses PL/SQL and the second, Transact SQL. Both languages are variations of some version of standard SQL but their differences are *not* negligible.

  If you are developing Web applications, you must include Web browsers in this category as well. Short of writing your own proprietary browser, you must work in the language (or rather langua*ges*) that a specific browser understands. Whatever you choose for your database management system and whatever language you select for implementing your objects, the behavior of the browser can be controlled only by its own version of HTML, JavaScript, XML, etc.

- *Existing Environment.* Seldom does an engineer start with a clean slate and choose a language solely based on its merits. We are not at the start of the computer revolution and the enterprises that have the resources to develop software, whether for in-house use or for the marketplace, have an investment in the past. This past consists of both humans and the software that the enterprise has accumulated over time.

  Enterprises have attempted to counter the "human inertia" by hiring consultants or outsourcing, but even if the new consultants or the "out" sources are technically qualified, they must start to learn the domain concepts from scratch. What is more, existing software cannot be discarded simply because new tools are better or seem better.

The choice of a language has both covert and overt costs that must be taken into account. Architecture and logical modeling are not as technology-independent as the theory might lead you to believe. Architects and designers usually come from programming backgrounds and have affinities to specific languages and technological paradigms. (A joke has it that people will stop using COBOL when the last COBOL programmer departs for programming heaven.)

- *Heterogeneous Architecture.*   Having to use proprietary languages is one result of the heterogeneous architecture that we discussed in the previous chapter. An information system is composed of many components, and the language that works for one component may not work for another or may not be available for it.

    The most important component of any information system is the platform or the operating system. Although software development is not often seen as programming the operating system, many administration tasks need a language that directly communicates with it. The languages used for these purposes are frequently *scripting* languages such as PERL or VB Script that lack the sophistication of Java or C#, but there is seldom any other practical alternative as the "scripts" must be maintained on the fly by the staff who are professionals in administrating systems but not in software development.

- *The Development Methodology.*   We cannot meaningfully map the artifacts of an object-oriented analysis and design to a procedural language and *vice versa*. Regardless of other factors, the language must support the concepts that lie at the foundation of the development methodologies. (If no language supports such fundamental concepts, then the methodology should not have been used for actual development.)

- *Bias.*   Some programming shops have very strong sentiments about certain companies. One shop would never buy the products of a particular company while the other would not consider any product as legitimate if it is not made by the same company.

    Another bias is a perverted sense of language loyalty. A certain language is sometimes considered "soft" and "not for *real* programmers," while another might be labeled as "wasteful" because it requires too much typing.

None of these factors means that the engineer has no freedom at all. This freedom, however, comes in cycles. Languages reflect a technological framework and when the technological framework changes, the resistance to the new fades away.

Programming Tools

> Programming requires multiple tools to achieve its goals. Integrated development environments aim to create one command center for conducting all or most programming activities.

[American Heritage 1996]

"Code" is a "system of symbols and rules used to represent instructions to a computer." This simple definition hides a large set of activities, tasks, and tools that are necessary to make "programming" a reliable and productive discipline. The most important items in the set are:

☞ Early computers were directly programmed by entering binary code

- *Source Code Editors.*   A source code editor is a text editor designed specifically for creating and editing code by programmers. It may be a stand-alone application or a built-in component in an integrated development environment (or IDE, see the information following this list). Source code editors have features specifically

through switches that were set to OFF (zero) or ON (one). Therefore, no translation was necessary.

As you can imagine, such an approach severely limits the volume of code. (Add to it the fact that those computers did not have permanent memories to store the programs.) But expectations were very low and the programs were mostly mathematical formulas.

designed to simplify and speed up the input of source code: syntax highlighting, auto-competition, context-sensitive help, etc. These editors may also provide a quick way to run a compiler, interpreter, debugger, or other programs related to the software development process.

Most text editors can be used to edit source code. (In the early days, punch cards were the only available tool for programming as they were the sole means of communicating with the computer.) However, if they do not enhance, automate, or altogether ease the editing of code, then they are simply "editors" and not "source code editors."

- *Compilers & Interpreters.* Instructions written in languages such as C++, Java, C#, and Visual Basic may seem cryptic to nonprogrammers but are nevertheless human-readable. Computers, however, understand a binary code of **1**s and **0**s. As a result, some intermediary must translate the code to the language of the computer. Such intermediary applications fall into four categories.

❶ *Assemblers.* Assemblers expect the code to have a one-to-one relationship to the machine language. For example, in the assembly language, you cannot simply say "**A** = **B** + **C**", but must go through all the steps that the CPU (central processing unit) must take to accomplish the task: specify the memory address of **B**, transfer the value of that memory location to a "register" in the CPU, specify the memory address of **C** and transfer *its* value to another "register," instruct the CPU to add the two values into another register, and, lastly, specify the memory address of **A** and store the result in that location.

Assembly languages are the oldest group of programming languages and, as cumbersome as they appear now, represented a giant leap over programming in machine code by replacing the machine code with mnemonics and symbols. Even now, assembly languages are sometimes used to test new chips, to extract the last ounce of performance from the computer, or to teach computer science students how a digital computer actually works.

❷ *Compilers.* Compilers translate the human-readable code in high-level languages into machine languages *without* requiring the programmer to know how the computer works. To put it differently, the programmer has only to know how to state the problem in the symbols and the syntax of a language such as FORTRAN or C++ and the compiler then "compiles" all the machine-language instructions that it requires. The output of the compiler is an "executable" program that can directly talk to the machine and thus no longer needs a translator.

❸ *Interpreters.* Interpreters are similar to compilers except that they execute the instructions each and every time the program is run and do not store the translation as an executable. In essence, interpreters are applications that execute other applications that exist as source code. Visual Basic, in its early versions, was one of the better-known interpreted languages. All scripting languages, including JavaScript that is widely used on Web pages, are interpreted.

❹ *Virtual Machines.* Virtual machines essentially work like interpreters, but are more complex and comprehensive. The idea behind virtual machines is **platform independence**: Since the applications are written for a *virtual* machine and not a real one, then (in theory at least) applications can run on any platform that supports the virtual machine.

In some instances, virtual machines, like compilers, store an "intermediate" code and execute this "virtual assembly" instead of the source code. Sun Microsystems' Java and Microsoft's Visual Studio .Net (C#, VB, etc.) are virtual machines. (Java, however, has been transported to more platforms than Visual Studio languages.)

- *Debuggers & Testers.* Syntax errors are detected by code editors, but other errors need more specialized and sophisticated tools. A debugger allows you to examine the program from *inside*: look into the variables and inspect the flow as the code is being executed, alter the value of variables, and, sometimes, go back and forth in the flow. Testers, on the hand, examine the application from *outside*, often from the viewpoint of the user, and report inconsistencies.

☞ See Chapter 16 for a discussion of architectural views and their relationship to modeling.

- *Builders & Linkers.* Regardless of whether the code is interpreted or compiled, source code modules do not necessarily correspond to the binary modules that can be executed. Builders create required binary modules and linkers, as the term implies, connect them together.

- *Modelers.* All the models that we have discussed in this book can be easily created with pencil and paper. Besides, there are many good tools for creating UML diagrams. A more logical solution, however, is to integrate modeling with programming: forward-engineer code from models and reverse-engineer models from code. The track record of integrated tools in this respect is somehow uneven, especially if you take the support for architectural views into account as well. Fortunately, the picture is getting better and some "add-in" applications have done a relatively good (but not perfect) job.

- *Resource Editors.* Even the simplest user interface is no longer limited to text. Users have come to expect icons, pictures, sound, and even animation and video. Such components are *not* code and the traditional source code editors are unable to manage them. Resource editors are responsible for managing non-code building blocks of the software, including alternate texts for multilingual applications. (Equipping an application with multilingual capabilities is known as "localization.")

- *Installers.* The computer on which you write the code has everything that is needed to run the code. Software, however, must be installed on the users' machines and, more often than not, these machines lack the support system and the libraries required to execute the applications. An installer is an application that ❶ gathers the necessary modules into a package for installation on a target machine and ❷ allows the user to customize the installation.

- *Revision Controllers.* An information system is usually coded by multiple programmers and the code is usually revised many times. It is easy to lose track of the valid code and difficult to prevent programmers from undoing each other's work or from working on incompatible versions of the same code module. Tracking source code versions and preventing "cross editing" is the task of one category of revision controllers.

Revision control software, however, is used to maintain documentation and configuration files as well as the source code. In theory, revision control can be applied to any type of stored information or data. In practice, however, the more sophisticated techniques and tools for revision control have seldom been used outside software development. Some of the more advanced revision control tools offer many other facilities and allow deeper integration with other tools and software engineering processes.

The previous list is in no way comprehensive and the short descriptions cannot convey all the complexities of these tools. For example, a moderate-size application might have somewhere between thousands to a few hundred thousand lines of code. Considering the high number of class libraries that come with the development platform and the numerous variables and methods that that are accumulated during coding, a "minimal" code editor is clearly inadequate. A modern editor must be able to present the programmer with the list of variables and class members, provide context-sensitive help, suggest full words for partial ones (a feature known as "auto-completion"), highlight errors and keywords, hide or reveal sections of code, map the parameters of database stored procedures to methods, etc.

Bringing together all or most of these tools is the goal and the promise of *integrated development environments*, or IDEs. Microsoft's Visual Study (Figure 17.2), Sun Microsystems' Java Studio Creator, and Oracle's JDeveloper are some of the popular integrated development environments.

Coding Standards

> Coding standards are essential to teamwork, understanding the code, debugging, and maintenance.

Figure 17.2 Integrated Development Environment: The Command Center for Programming Tools and Activities

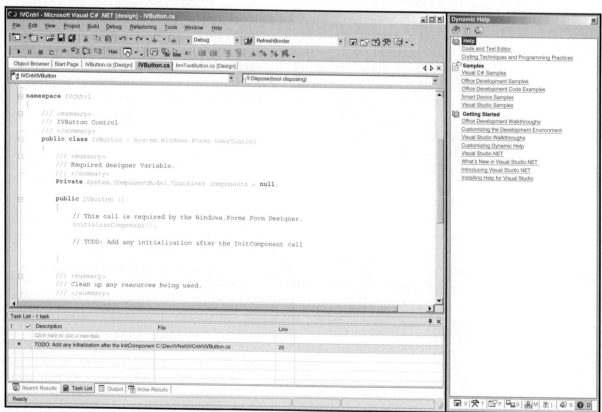

This example, from Microsoft's Visual Studio 2003, shows the start of coding for a visual control, a button.

Different people tend to write code differently. Code written by 10 different developers will most likely show 10 different coding styles. The primary reason for adopting a set of coding standards is to make it easier for developers to read and understand each other's code. Although peer review is not pervasive, almost everyone has to maintain, or at least step through, code written by someone else. A small difference in coding style can make a big difference in the speed of reading and understanding the code.

In the rush to get an application out the door or to meet a deadline, it is easy to neglect good style and readability. Factors such as naming conventions and code consistency are taught in any good computer science curriculum, but are quickly pushed to the back burner when a developer is put under pressure to show results.

☞ See "Code Conventions for the Java Programming Language." URL: http://java.sun.com/docs/codeconv/index.html. For "80 percent" read "a large percentage." Such statistics are difficult to verify or disprove.

The development manager, however, must manage the delicate balance between meeting deadlines and producing quality code. Coding standards help to maintain the quality and, ultimately, reduce the cost of development. According to Sun Microsystems' research, 80 percent of the lifetime cost of a software is spent on maintenance, and hardly any software is maintained for its whole life by its original author.

The second reason for adopting coding standards is to prevent bugs. Good coding standards can make it less likely that bugs will creep into the code, and if the standards can be applied as the code is written, the savings will be considerable. For example, the development environment does not care if you name a variable **AB** and another one **BA**, but if you follow such a naming approach, assigning values to the wrong variable should be a foregone conclusion.

Code Review

> Code review is an important but often neglected activity.

☞ "Extreme Programming," an "agile" method that we introduced in Chapter 3, suggests that code review should become part of the process of coding through "pair programming." The usefulness of this approach is far from universally accepted as it means an ever-present source of distraction for the programmer.

Coding requires deep concentration and focus and, consequently, is often a solitary activity. This necessity can have a few unfortunate side effects: ❶ A defect may go unnoticed even though the same programmer might notice the same defect in somebody else's code, ❷ enforcing standards is left to individual programmers, ❸ the less experienced programmers cannot benefit from the work of the more experienced ones, and ❹ the programmers can become trapped in their own little corner of the project.

Code review can ease these problems but is often neglected. The fault lies equally with management and the programmers themselves: Code review takes time and planning and, as a result, costs money, and the programmers might be too proud or too self-conscious to expose their code to public scrutiny. But, without a shadow of a doubt, ignoring code review can cost more money and cause more embarrassment down the road.

Code review cannot work in an amphitheater. The optimal number of participants in the review can vary, but more than six should be avoided, If they have to talk at a louder than normal conversational level, then there are too many people. The team should meet at more or less regular intervals. If face-to-face meetings are not possible, then the interaction can take place online through virtual private networks or intranets: What is lost in terms of immediacy and intimacy can be compensated by more measured reviews and time for thinking.

There are two types of code review: *walkthrough* and *inspection*. Walkthrough is less formal and essentially consists of going over the lists of questions and/or possible defects provided by the participants. Inspection, on the other hand, is more formal and consists of going over code line-by-line. Participants use checklists to identify potential problems, provide reports of defects that they have detected, and suggest solutions. The use of each method depends on the size and complexity of the project.

Code review can find some errors *before* the product or a component of the product is ready for testing and, as such, is a cheaper tool for quality assurance.

There are situations in which you should *stop reviewing*. For example, incomplete or contradictory analysis and defective design can push the programmers to compensate by filling the blanks without solid information or guidance. In such a case, the problems should be sent back for further analysis or design.

Nevertheless, it is wise to conduct reviews "early and often" to save time and money. As coding progresses, early defects can be buried under later defects and can become more difficult to discover.

3. Testing

> Testing is the last defense in assuring software quality.

If quality assurance is not built into the *process* of product development, then a final testing will not save the product. Nevertheless, we cannot skip testing, final or otherwise. Testing allows us to verify the quality of the product or its components in a systematic manner, requirement by requirement and feature by feature. And if the conditions of testing are realistic enough, we might discover *unexpected* problems and solve them *before* the product is deployed.

Before discussing testing processes and techniques, we should go over some of its basic concepts. Software testing is running the software to verify that it functions correctly. Testing always aims to improve the quality of what is being tested. The simplest description of testing is comparing "what is" with "what ought to be."

Often, software testing is described as either "defect detection" or "reliability estimation." While both descriptions have some truth in them, they are also problematic. The problem of defining software testing as "defect detection" is that testing can only suggest the presence of flaws, not their absence, *unless* the test scenario can include them as well. The problem of defining it as "reliability estimation" is that the *input* for selecting test cases may be flawed, not the software.

Whatever the exact definition, finding "**bugs**" is included in everybody's expectations from testing. What is a bug, then? In simplest terms:

A bug is a flaw in the development of the software that causes a discrepancy between the expected result of an operation and the actual result.

A bug can result from *all* activities that take place to develop and deploy software: gathering requirements, analysis, design, installation, configuration, and database management. It might also be something that is at odds with what the customer expects, regardless of what the requirements have specified.

Software testing must provide answers to two important questions:

- *Validation:*   Are we building the right product? The purpose of validation is to ensure that the system has implemented all requirements, so that each function can be traced back to a particular business requirement.

- *Verification:* Are we building the product right? Verification is similar to validation, except that is does not go all the way back to the business requirements, but to the requirements of the activity immediately before the present one. For example: Does logical modeling correspond to the conceptual model? Or: does physical modeling satisfy the demands of the logical model? And so on.

Levels of Testing

> Software must be tested for each phase of implementation and deployment.

No single test can validate or verify the quality of a piece of software. The details of what tests should be conducted before a software can be declared "ready" depends on the methodology, the testing tools, and, last but not least, the architecture of the system. In general, however, we can identify the following categories:

- *Unit Testing.* "Unit" is the smallest piece of code that has an identity. In object-oriented languages, this unit is a class. In "structured" languages, this unit is a function.

Unit testing does not mean that we can test a class (or a function) in isolation from others. As you must have gathered by now, classes often use the services of other classes and, therefore, are dependent on them. The point of unit testing is to have a small test program, usually called a "test harness," that focuses on the smallest possible collection of classes.

The test harness invokes each method in the class and if the method has parameters, allows the programmer (or the tester) to enter various values for the same variable.

The tactic to follow is to first test classes that have no dependencies on other classes, then the circle around them that are dependent *only* on those classes, and so on. As you can imagine, unit testing can start simple, but if the software is complex enough it cannot remain simple, or even possible.

- *Component Testing.* We have strongly recommended component-based development before. (See Chapter 15.) Here, we must emphasize its significance in testing. Component testing is *not* a replacement for unit testing, but follows a similar tactic and should start when unit testing stops. Whereas unit testing can become cumbersome at a high level of complexity, a component must hide class-level complexities behind clearly defined and mission-oriented interfaces.

One definition of component is a binary piece of software that is physically separate from other pieces. In the context of component-based development, however, our definition is somewhat different: "A component is a relatively independent, encapsulated, and replaceable unit of software that provides services specified by one or more interfaces." This is the relevant definition for component testing.

Component testing, of course, is contingent upon a component-based architecture. If the whole application is composed of one component, that is, if the application is "monolithic," component testing becomes meaningless.

Components can be dependent on other components, and often are. The rule is the dependencies must always be one-way: If component **B** is dependent on component **A**, then component **A** cannot be dependent on component **B**. If such a *circular dependency* exists, then something in design has gone wrong and the test results are not helpful or dependable.

- *Integration Testing.* Integration testing is really a continuation of component testing, and there is no firm dividing line between the two. However, whereas in component testing the focus is on individual components, in integration testing every component has to be tested again once a *new* component is integrated into the whole.

- *System Testing.* System testing is conducted when *all* components of a system or subsystem are in place. In effect, system testing is a kind of "dress rehearsal" before the system is shown to the paying clients.

System testing is usually long in duration, as every feature must be tested. It can be frustrating as well if previous levels of testing have been ignored or have not been thorough. But it can also reveal problems that *cannot* be detected by the previous test. These problems essentially revolve around one question: Does the product satisfy requirements? Even if the software passes every previous test with high marks, it can fail here.

- *Acceptance Testing.* Acceptance testing can be described in a short statement: A product passes acceptance testing when the people who have paid for its development accept it. If the product is for in-house use or is custom software, then the process is rather straightforward: You receive the "test results" by demonstrating the software to the clients and/or by letting them use it for a while. Nevertheless, complications can arise: Who defines the level of the acceptance testing? Who creates the test scripts? Who executes the tests? What is the "pass/fail" criteria for the acceptance test? When and how do we get paid?

Acceptance testing for mass-market software is more complicated: If you release the software to the market and wait to get feedback, the "test" will most probably fail. What you have to do, in essence, is to "invent" the client before releasing the software. There are two methods for achieving this goal:

- *Usability Study.* You hire people to play the client by using the software. The "actors" must be relatively qualified for testing the software and should be given a free hand, but you can help them by providing general test scripts or pointing out features that you would like them to test.
- *Beta Release.* Beta release works on a voluntary basis: People will invest time on a pre-release software if they are excited about its promises. Of course, you can always encourage them further by other incentives. For example, you can sell them the final product at a reduced price if they return "bug reports" or provide you with feedback.

Testing & Object Orientation

> Object orientation can reduce bugs, but not automatically. It can even produce its own kind of unwanted side effects.

Through encapsulation and information hiding, object-oriented technology can reduce defects that result from exposing variables to free-for-all access. In addition, by packaging services into the distinct interfaces, it creates entities that are more "testable" than shapeless expanses of functions. In short, object orientation creates units that are responsible for what they know and what they do and, as a result, can be held accountable.

Careless design and faulty implementation, however, can wreak havoc with any tool, and object-oriented technology is no exception. Unfortunately, object orientation also creates its own *special* chances for committing bugs or raising barriers to effective testing:

- As we said, *encapsulation* prevents bugs that result from global data scoping. On the other hand, by hiding the inner workings of the objects, testing can only discover errors, not necessarily *why* they happen. To put it differently, encapsulation is both a blessing and a curse: It hides complexity but complexity can hide errors.

  There is no magic formula to avoid this predicament, but one technique is always helpful: *delegation*. If one function is too complex or too long, delegate some of the work to other, simpler functions. And if a class is too complex or too long, delegate some of the work to other classes. In the second case more care must be taken, but in neither case is the public interface of the class changed.

  Code review, which we previously discussed, is a good process for finding what is "too long" or "too complex" because the code is reviewed by programmers other than the author of the code who, hopefully, can judge it from a useful distance.

- A deep *inheritance* hierarchy can create complexities of its own. Inheritance is a very powerful mechanism for reuse. Programmers also find it very convenient to use: If you find a class that offers most of the services that you want, you can inherit and extend it to a new class, and if later you find out that the new class needs a couple of services for another task, you can create a newer one by inheriting and extending it, and so on. In no time, the chain of inheritance can become very long and if you find a bug, you have to go back and forth to find the source. The same is true for *polymorphism*, the ability of class descendants to respond differently to the same message.

- Objects interact by sending messages, as we have repeatedly emphasized. Some messages can be sent at any time but, often, they must follow a sequence. A very simple example is when you work with a `Circle` object: You must invoke the `draw` method before you can call the `move` method. *Message sequencing*, however, can become too complex for the reliable testing of all possible combinations.

Object-oriented technology gives you good tools for making a reliable product. It does not relieve anybody from the responsibility for good design and good programming.

4. DEPLOYMENT

> Deployment covers *all* activities that make the software available for use.

The deployment process covers many interrelated activities that prepare the software for users to use. Software can be deployed at the users' site, at the development site, or at both. Since each software is different the details of each activity cannot be exactly defined, but they can be categorized as follows:

- *Release.* Release includes all the operations to prepare a system for assembly and transfer to the customer site. Therefore, it must determine the resources required to operate at the customer site and collect information for carrying out the subsequent activities of the deployment process.

- *Installation.* Installation is usually done, partially or totally, by specialized applications, called *installers*. For mass-market software, such as a word processor, the installer must be able to guide the user through each and every step of the process and automate most of the tasks for installation. For vertical market software and enterprise tools and applications, a minimum level of technical know-how on the customer's part is usually required, but the vendor must still provide the necessary tools and guidelines.
- *Updating.* Updating is the process of installing a new version of the software. It can be considered, usually, as a less complex installation since many of the needed components have already been installed. Sometimes, however, updating can be *more* complex. For example, if the format of the database has changed, the updating process must unload the old data first, change the database, and reload the data.
- *Adaptation.* Adaptation is also a process that modifies a previously installed software but is different from updating in that the adaptations are triggered by local events at the customer site, not because the software developer has changed anything.

The Deployment Diagram

[Booch 1999, 408]

> The deployment diagram is used "to visualize the static aspect of the physical nodes and their relationships and to specify their details for construction."

[Booch 1999, 408]

The deployment diagram is the last major tool in the toolbox of UML. This diagram is not specifically about hardware, but about how the software is configured *in relation to* the hardware:

☞ Emphasis added.

> The UML is primarily focused on facilities for visualizing, specifying, constructing, and documenting *software artifacts*, but it is also designed to address hardware artifacts. This is not to say that UML is a general-purpose hardware description language. . . . Rather, UML is designed to model many of the hardware aspects of a system sufficient for a *software engineer* to specify the platform on which the system's software executes and for a systems engineer to manage the system's hardware/software boundary. In the UML, you use class diagrams and component diagrams to manage to reason about the structure of your software. You use sequence diagrams, collaboration diagrams, statechart diagrams, and activity diagrams to specify the behavior of your software. At the edge of your system's software and hardware, you use the deployment diagram to reason about the topology of processors and devices on which your software executes.

[Booch 1999, 464]

The deployment diagram is a **structural diagram**. It is very similar to class and component diagrams, except that it depicts the relationship between **nodes**:

A node is a "physical element that exists at run time and that represents a computational resource, generally having at least some memory and, often times, processing capability."

(Figure 17.3) illustrates one possible deployment of Walden Medical Center's information system. The diagram assumes that the information system supports two sets of applications: one Web-based for the outside world, the other client/server for

Figure 17.3   The Deployment Diagram: The Runtime Configuration of Nodes and Software Components

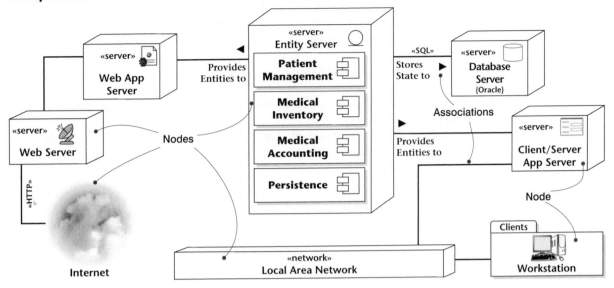

You can use all the extension mechanism of UML, such as stereotyping and dependency, with the deployment diagram.

use inside the hospital. Both sets share the same entity classes and the same database. Application flow, however, is split between two servers. (To keep it simple, we have not included all subsystems and have not shown *all* common components between Web and client/server applications.)

Let us explain the deployment diagram through this example:

- The *cubes*, or the three-dimensional boxes, represent nodes. A node can be a "unit of computing" or a set of such units: a server, a workstation, a disk drive, a LAN (Local Area Network), or even the whole of the Internet.
- Like other elements of the UML, nodes can *stereotyped*. As we explained before, stereotyping can be done through a label such as **<<server>>**; by using an icon, such as a cloud for the Internet; or by combining both, such as the elongated box for the **<<network>>**. (The cube itself is actually a *standard* UML stereotype.)
- The *relationship* between nodes is represented by standard UML connections. In our example, we have used association but, if necessary, you can use any other connection such as dependency, generalization, or aggregation. The purpose of the deployment diagram, of course, is *not* purely hardware configuration, but it can accommodate situations where you want to show the hardware organization in more detail.

☞ See Chapter 10 for a discussion on *packaging, stereotyping* and UML *extension* mechanisms.

- Unlike classes, but like components, nodes can be represented as both *black boxes* and *white boxes*. In (Figure 17.3), the **Entity Server** is shown as a white box that contains software components common to both Web and client/server applications. Other nodes have been represented as black boxes but, if necessary, we can reveal their insides as well.
- We can use all UML *extension mechanisms* in deployment diagrams. For example, we have constrained the database server as **{Oracle}**.

- One node, **Clients**, is represented as a *package*. Client workstations are not of the same type (or "class") and, therefore, a package provides a better representation.
- In one important aspect, the deployment diagram is very different from a class diagram: the deployment diagram can be *instantiated*. This means that it can represent instances of nodes, not just their "classes." For example, if our database is distributed, we can show each database server individually. In this case, we use the object naming convention of an object name (optional), followed by a colon, followed by the class name: **ny:DatabaseServer**, **ca:DatabaseServer**, etc.

  Note that an "instantiated" deployment diagram can be too large to be useful. If instantiations are necessary, first create an abstract diagram and then create a set of partial instances.

Deployment diagrams are not always necessary. If the application runs on only one computing device and does not manage specialized hardware, then they are not really needed. On the other hand, if the software is designed to manage hardware that is not handled by the operating system, then it is likely to need deployment diagrams.

The deployment diagram is most useful when a system is ready to be deployed, but it should be started well before that. The deployment can have a marked impact on the software architecture and *vice versa* (as we discussed in the previous chapter). Therefore, it is best that software and hardware architects should cooperate in advance of the actual deployment. The deployment diagram affects not only the work of system engineers *downstream*, but should be coordinated with the software architecture *upstream*.

User Training

> Use cases provide effective templates for user training. One kind of training, however, cannot fit every situation.

People use applications to do something, even if that "something" is pure entertainment. As we said many chapters ago, "a use case details the interaction of an actor with a system to accomplish a goal of value to the actor." An application is the realization of use cases that share a mission and the core of "user training" is to show the user how to navigate the flow of use cases.

The idea of "user training" must be integrated into the development itself. If we wait for the deployment to start thinking about it, then it is too late. Beyond this general observation, however, the exact nature of training depends on what, who, and where.

- *What.* Automation has infiltrated or taken over so many activities that it is absurd to assume that training for one kind of application can be useful for another. Operating a nuclear power plant or a jetfighter does not lend itself to learning by trial and error in the real setting. Similarly, using an image editor such as Adobe Photoshop has a completely different logic than buying merchandise from a Web-based application: The first application cannot make assumptions about your workflow, while the second one must leave no doubt whatsoever about the course of actions that you must make to order something.

- *Who.* "Who" is more complicated than "what," but at the same time it is dependent on it. Whether the application is simple or complex, we have to know if its users will be relative experts, relative novices, or both.

Experts would benefit from *ease-of-use* while novices would need *ease-of-learning*. Not only are the two not the same, but in many cases they are incompatible. If the task is complex, an easy-to-learn application can take more time and more navigation than an expert can tolerate. On the other hand, if a complex task is presented in an easy-to-use manner, the novice may find it overwhelming. Furthermore, many users of mass-market software begin as novices but become experts at some point in time. The same easy-to-learn flow would soon become a difficult-to-use feature for them.

It is, of course, possible to design a software that serves both groups and those in-between, but not always, and not cheaply. Automation can make a workflow easier, but not necessarily the concepts behind the workflow.

- *Where.* The approach must also be different between *in-house* software and applications for the *mass market*. An in-house development usually involves the eventual users and, if necessary, the enterprise can force them to attend lectures and seminars or read documentation. That is to say, you have a truly "captive audience." For the mass market, on the other hand, you must *captivate* the audience. The mass market is open to competition and if the users do not like your ease-of-use or your ease-of-learning, they will go to the competitors. That is why certain vendors offer two versions of the same product. For example, Adobe sells one version of its flagship Photoshop for experts and another (at lower price) to the general public.

To create the right blend for training users, we have the following tools at our disposal:

- *The User Interface.* The first and most important tool for user training is the application itself. Nothing helps users better than a streamlined, logical, and well-designed user interface.

Use cases, through enumeration of steps and sub-steps, normal or alternate, provide the framework for training: how to register a patient, how to withdraw cash from an ATM, how to draw a circle, how to shoot down the enemy's starship, and so on. Design maps the concepts of behavioral modeling into a model of the user interface and it is through the user interface that the "problem domain" (the users) interacts with the "solution domain" (the information system). In effect, the task of "user training" starts long before any software and, consequently, any user exists.

The design of the user interface must not stop with the visual controls that satisfy the minimal requirements of the use case. Graphical user interfaces (GUIs), including Web browsers, enable the designer to offer a wide variety of help and directions to the user: "bubble help" when the mouse hovers over a visual control, messages in a message panel when the same action occurs, context-sensitive help triggered by a function key, and other methods that allow the user to get "snippets" of help without leaving the form or the page.

To overcome the frequent incompatibilities between "ease-of-use" and "ease-of-learning," most popular applications allow the user interface to be customized. Buttons can be added to the toolbar or removed from it, shortcut keys can be assigned to specific actions and existing ones can be changed, certain toolboxes can be displayed or hidden, and so on. Undoubtedly, a successful strategy for customization results from years of user feedback, *usability studies*, and a high level of expenditure. Lower-budget applications, however, can benefit from ready-made components for user customization. Not every application, of course, can be customized extensively.

- *Wizards.* Wizards are a special *kind* of user interface. Instead of assuming that you know what is needed, a wizard guides you through a task step by individual step. Forms (or Web pages) presented by wizards have a minimal number of visual controls to satisfy the requirements of a single step.

In Chapter 12 on the user interface, we illustrated the concept of storyboarding with an example from Walden's Patient Management system: **Register Patient**. If you look at that example, you will see that most everything needed for registration is concentrated on one form. A wizard, by contrast, would first present you with a form for finding the patient, then another form for entering contact information, then a third form for insurance, and so on. Through buttons such as **Previous** and **Next**, the wizard would allow you to go back and forth in the flow, but would not let you skip a required step.

Wizards are good for novices, but if you use it a number of times you may find it tedious and time-consuming. The remedy is to provide users with an alternate approach and let them select whichever fits their level of expertise. This, however, makes the application more expensive and more difficult to maintain.

- *Online Help.* Nowadays, you expect every application to provide you with immediate help when you press a function key on desktop applications or click a link on a Web page. This is called *context-sensitive* help, meaning that it displays information that directly relates to the task at hand: to the particular flow, form, or field with which you are working. A *good* online help, however, is structured in a way that allows you to explore the context of the "task at hand" by going from particular to general and back. (Not a simple proposition, by any means.)

Online help should also be organized in a way that allows the user to read the topics from the beginning to the end, select topics from a table of contents, and find topics through searching by keywords.

- *User Guides & Tutorials.* There should be no marked differences between the contents of online help and printed user guides. In fact, the trend has been towards online help or digital documentation at the expense of printed versions. This trend has more than one reason: paper documentation is expensive, takes physical space, is costly to store and inconvenient to move, can become outdated faster if the software is updated frequently, can delay the introduction of the software, and, last but not least, cannot be downloaded through the Internet. About the only reason that remains for printed documentation is prestige: Software that comes with thick documentation looks more serious.

Tutorials appear in two forms that are often combined: instruction manuals or interactive lessons. An instruction manual, printed or digital, presents step-by-step lessons that you must read and then follow on the actual software. An interactive tutorial uses an "imitation" of the software or the software itself to guide you through. (Some applications, such as Microsoft Excel, can be programmed to allow a certain degree of interactive learning.)

To a large degree, the value and the format of the tutorial depend on the nature of the application. For an enterprise application that embodies a specific workflow, such as Walden's Patient Management, a straight instruction manual is good enough. For a general-purpose application, such as Photoshop, an interactive approach can be more effective for novice users. In fact, such applications have created a thriving aftermarket for tutorials.

- *Simulators.* Simulators are different from tutorials in that they do not guide you through the application but allow you to experiment with its workings without serious consequence. Like games, you can always restart the simulation even if your plane has crashed.

Simulators are complex applications in their own right and, as a result, are very expensive to develop. In certain situations, however, there is no safe alternative for training the users. A real nuclear reactor is not the right context for learning its control programs.

- *Workshops, Classes & Webcasts.* In-house development can (or should be able to) count on the participation of users through workshops. Workshops offer two benefits to the users: They get the software that they want and they are trained in the process as well. Obviously, mass-market software is developed differently. Even if the vendor brings in sample users to participate in the development or launches a "beta" program to receive feedback, a great number of users would be left out.

Classes, whether for teaching in-house software or mass-market applications, have the same advantages and disadvantages as other kinds of classes: they are focused but of short duration, students can learn by asking relevant questions or can derail the discussions by posing irrelevant questions, the interest and the commitment of the teacher or the students can be low or high. This is why classes always need the support of other training tools as well.

Webcasts ("Web Broadcasts") can make classes or lectures available on a more permanent basis and for a wider audience. Webcasts can be "canned" (recorded) or live, and combined with "chat rooms" for interaction with the instructor or among students. On the whole, the innovative potential of the Web and the Internet for teaching and training is yet to be exhausted.

Change & Maintenance

> Change is inevitable; therefore, we must expect it.

Even if a software is perfect, the world is not a perfect place. It changes and the software that serves it must change as well. But software is never perfect to begin with. To build any kind of software the creators must go through a process of abstraction, and abstraction, by definition, leaves something out.

Some schools of thought suggest that there is no essential difference between development and change management, known as "maintenance." Certain kinds of maintenance share most activities with development, but the two are *not* the same. Once a software is deployed to users, a host of new problems appear. Sometimes the problem is backward compatibility: Individuals and enterprises have a great investment in databases, files, and documents that were managed with the old version, as inadequate as that version might have been. At other times, the problem is continuity: The operation of air traffic controllers cannot be interrupted for the installation of a new software. A new software might be able to start with a clean slate; a deployed software enjoys no such luxury.

The term "software maintenance" has established itself firmly, although it is not quite accurate: Unlike a building or a car, software does not degrade through time and use. Whatever term we use, maintenance (or upgrade) becomes necessary for a variety of reasons, including:

- *Engineering Defects.*   Analysis and design are correct, but either the system has "bugs" or the platform has proved unreliable.
- *Analysis & Design Defects.*   A software might fall victim to incomplete or defective analysis or bad design (and many do). In fact, a very high number of "bugs" are *not* really engineering defects, but result from the failure to do what we have tried to describe in this book.
- *Obsolescence.*   Anything and everything in the world of computers becomes obsolete, sooner or later. A payroll application written in assembler, coded on punch cards, and executed on an IBM/360 mainframe was at some point in time the summit of technological progress and the envy of those who could not afford it, but is now almost an archaeological curiosity. Organizations, however, must try to survive technological change and need new software.
- *Change of Requirements.*   A software might do what it does faithfully and reliably, but at some point we might want it to do things differently—even if only slightly so: regulations change, the workflow changes, companies merge, and so on.
- *Competition & the Evolution of Expectations.*   In this regard, software is little different from any other product: New technologies create expectations that had not existed before and vendors seek a competitive edge by adding new features that, sometimes, nobody had requested but which quickly become necessities.

To sum up, software should never be designed under the illusion that it can be perfect and will never change. Preparing for change is neither easy nor always possible, but the methodologies and the practices that we have explored throughout this book—robust domain analysis, modeling, flexible architecture, and component-based development—can serve as shock absorbers to change, both wanted and unwanted.

5. DELIVERABLES

Software development moves not sequentially, but on parallel tracks until the tracks converge when the software is released to the customer or the market. We have said, often enough, that object-oriented analysis and design is iterative. Implementation, or specifically coding and testing, is even more iterative, both in relation to design and within itself.

The final deliverables of implementation are easy to identify: components that are packaged for installation. What takes place between design models and compiled code depends on the quality of analysis and design and on the quality and the organization of programmers.

To program a component, you create a "project" within an integrated development environment. (Depending on the technology or the vendor, the "project" may also be called "workspace," "solution," or something else.) You also "register" the project with your revision control application. You then add classes to the project or use the modeling component of the IDE to create "skeleton" code for them.

Many IDEs allow you to work on more than one project at one time. This ability has two main advantages: ❶ development of components can proceed in parallel and ❷ you can create your test applications (or "test harnesses") alongside the component.

Even small applications are usually coded by a team of programmers. It is the task of the revision control program to ensure that ❶ only one programmer can work on a source code module at any given time and ❷ previous versions are saved and changes can be undone if necessary. Note that a source code "module" corresponds to a physical file and can contain more than one class. On the other hand, the IDE might accommodate "partial classes," which means the code for one class can be dispersed among multiple physical files and multiple programmers can work on it simultaneously.

IDEs also offer built-in debuggers. As we said, debuggers verify the code from *inside*. Using the debugger, the programmer verifies the syntax and can inspect the variables as the code is executed. Some IDEs even allow the programmer to change the value of a variable "on the fly" to test the reliability of code with a range of values.

The code is released back to the version control application when the programmer believes that the code is stable enough to be integrated into the project as a whole. However, in the meantime, *other* programmers have been working on the other parts of the project and the new code, as stable as it might appear, might not work with what they have changed, added, or removed, in which case, the code must go through another iteration.

At some point, a component is ready to be "compiled" (transformed into binary code). Tactics for how to proceed with the binary component vary. In any case, it is always necessary to test the component in the binary format.

As often happens, programmers discover inconsistencies or errors in the design. Well-intentioned but misguided programmers might try to solve these problems by themselves and sometimes do it well but, at the very least, design problems must be discussed with the team and, if necessary, the design must be revised. Classes do not exist in a vacuum but must work with other classes, and if two programmers interpret and code the same design differently, the integrity and the reliability of the whole component is harmed.

Code reviews offer a reliable method for preventing such problems—and others—as we have mentioned.

System testing must be conducted when all components are compiled and tested, individually and in relation to each other. The exact nature of system testing (and acceptance testing) depends on the product and on testing tools. Test results, however, must be documented and verifiable.

6. WRAP UP

☑ **Coding**

Coding is the realization of analysis and design: No code means no software. On the other hand, coding without robust analysis and design cannot lead to quality software. Both sides of the equation are equally important.

The more accurate the design is, the less complicated coding will become. Errors in design are more costly to correct than errors in coding, but no design is perfect. Some design defects are not predictable and can be discovered only through coding and testing. As important as analysis and design are, coding should not be taken for granted. High-quality software cannot result from low-quality code.

☑ **Programming languages & tools**

Although the programming language should technically be of high quality, the choice of the programming language depends on many factors. For components such as database management systems, you must often use the language or the dialect that they require. If you create Web applications, you cannot ignore the languages that browsers require. Sometimes the existing framework and available resources constrain the freedom of choice for the programming language. Furthermore, the methodology that you follow for development must be translatable to the programming language.

Programming requires multiple tools to achieve its goals. Integrated development environments aim to create one command center for conducting all or most programming activities.

Not all development platforms offer or need all possible programming tools, but a general list of such tools includes compilers or interpreters, virtual machines that are similar to interpreters but offer a whole environment, debuggers and testers, builders and linkers, modelers, resource editors, installers, and revision controllers.

☑ **Coding standards & code review**

For teamwork, debugging, and maintenance, coding standards are of the utmost importance. The primary reason for adopting a set of coding standards is to make it easier for developers to read and understand each other's code.

Code review is often neglected but, among other things, it is a major tool for enforcing standards. There are two types of code review: *walkthrough* and *inspection*. Walkthrough is less formal and essentially consists of going over the lists of questions and/or possible defects provided by the participants. Inspection, on the other hand, is more formal and consists of going over code line-by-line.

☑ **Testing & its variations**

Quality assurance must be built into the process of product development, but testing is the last line of defense against defects. Testing, however, is not a single activity: Software must be tested for each phase of implementation and deployment.

Unit testing is testing the smallest piece of software with an identity. In object-oriented technology, unit testing applies to individual classes that, however, must be tested along with the other classes that they depend on.

A component is a relatively independent, encapsulated, and replaceable unit of software that provides services specified by one or more interfaces. *Component testing* is only meaningful if the software's architecture is component-based. It does not replace unit testing, but extends it.

Integration testing is a continuation of component testing but verifies how the components work in relation to each other, and every component has to be tested again once a *new* component is integrated into the whole.

System testing is conducted when *all* components of a system or subsystem are in place. A product passes *acceptance testing* when the people who have paid for its development accept it.

Object-oriented analysis, design, and technology can reduce bugs, but not automatically. It can even produce its own kind of unwanted side effects: *encapsulation* makes testing the inner workings of an object more difficult, *inheritance* can create complex inheritance trees, and *message sequencing* can make systematic examinations of messages confusing.

☑ **Deployment & the deployment diagram**

Deployment covers *all* activities that make the software available for use. These activities include release, installation, updating, and adaptation.

The deployment diagram, the last major UML tool, is used "to visualize the static aspect of the physical nodes and their relationships and to specify their details for construction." This diagram is not specifically about hardware, but about how the software is configured *in relation to* hardware.

The deployment diagram is a structural diagram that depicts the relationship between **nodes**. A node is a "physical element that exists at run time and that represents a computational resource, generally having at least some memory and, often times, processing capability." You can use stereotyping and other UML extension mechanisms with the deployment diagram.

In one important aspect, the deployment diagram is very different from a class diagram: The deployment diagram can be *instantiated*. This means that it can represent instances of nodes, not just their "classes."

☑ **User training**

People use applications to perform tasks. These tasks are modeled through use cases and, therefore, use cases provide effective templates for user training. However, one kind of training is not enough; nor can it fit every situation. The exact nature of training depends on *what* the user is to be trained for, *who* the user is, and *where* the training is to take place.

The primary tool for user training is the *user interface*, its design, its flow, and the tools that it can exploit to help and guide the user. A *wizard* employs a user interface that guides the users, step-by-step, through simple forms or pages. However, it can be time-consuming and annoying to experienced users.

Online help, context-sensitive or otherwise, is nowadays expected from all applications. Online help should be organized in a way that allows the user to read the topics from the beginning to the end, select topics from a table of contents, and find topics through searching by keywords. Training can also benefit from *user guides* and *tutorials*. Tutorials can be interactive applications in their own right, but not every kind of application lends itself to interactive tutorials.

If trial-and-error is not an option in learning to operate an information system or an application, then it must be taught through *simulators*. Creating a simulator is often an expensive undertaking, but it must be done when the mission of the system demands it.

User training can be rounded up by *classes* and workshops. However, whereas the users of in-house software and vertical applications can be required to attend workshops and classes before or after deployment, classes for mass-market applications form an *after*market.

Increasingly, the potential of the Web is being used for training through *Webcasts*, chat rooms, and online courses.

☑ **Maintenance**

Software should never be designed under the illusion that it can be perfect and will never change. "Maintenance" may not be a term that is really appropriate for software, but what it implies is unavoidable: Things change and software that is already in use must be fixed, upgraded, or replaced. Maintenance becomes necessary for a variety of reasons, including engineering defects, failures in analysis and design, obsolescence, change of requirements and expectations, and competition.

7. KEY CONCEPTS

Adaptation. Modifying a previously installed software to work with changes in the target (customer) system.

Assembler. An application that converts "assembly code" into machine language. Assembly code is a set of symbols that have a one-to-one relationship to the operations of the CPU (central processing unit).

Bug. A flaw in the development of the software that causes a discrepancy between the expected result of an operation and the actual result.

Builders & Linkers. Applications that create binary modules and connect them as physical files. They might be integrated into the **compiler** or the **interpreter**.

Code Review. Must be regularly conducted to ensure that **coding standards** are followed, programming defects are reduced, less experienced programmers learn from the more experienced ones, and programmers become familiar with the areas in which they have *not* worked. Two types of code review are *walkthrough* and *inspection*. Walkthrough is less formal and essentially consists of going over the lists of questions and/or possible defects provided by the participants. Inspection, on the other hand, is more formal and consists of going over code line-by-line.

Coding. Converting design models and concepts into code written in a **programming language**. "Code" is a "system of symbols and rules used to represent instructions to a computer."

Coding Standards. Guidelines for composing code, from naming variables to adding comments and the structuring of instructions.

Compiler. Translates the human-readable code in a high-level **programming language** into machine languages *without* requiring the programmer to know how the computer works.

Debugger. A programming tool that allows the programmer to examine the code from *inside*. See also **Tester**.

Deployment. All activities that make software available for use. Includes **release**, **installation**, **updating**, and **adaptation**.

Deployment Diagram. A UML diagram used "to visualize the static aspect of the physical nodes and their relationships and to specify their details for construction." See also **node**.

Installation. ❶ Gathering the necessary modules into a package for installation on a target machine and ❷ guiding the user to customize the installation.

Interpreter. Similar to a **compiler**, except that it executes the instructions each and every time a program is run and does not store the translation as an executable.

Maintenance. Changing or replacing software due to the following factors: engineering defects, analysis and design failures, obsolescence, change of requirements, the evolution of expectations, and competition.

Modeler. An application that allows its users to create analysis and design models. Certain modelers can forward-engineer models into code and backward-engineer code into models.

Node. A computing device in the **deployment diagram**. A node is a "physical element that exists at run time and that represents a computational resource, generally having at least some memory and, often times, processing capability."

Programming. A set of activities that include **coding**, **debugging**, and **testing** with the ultimate goal of creating binary *components* or "programs" that can be executed by the computer or a **virtual machine**.

Programming Language. "Any artificial language that can be used to define a sequence of instructions that can ultimately be processed and **[American Heritage** executed by the computer. **1996]** Defining what is or is not a programming language can be tricky, but general usage implies that the translation process—from the source code expressed using the programming language to the machine code that the computer needs to work with—be automated by means of another program, such as a compiler."

Release. All operations necessary to prepare a system for transfer to the customer site or publishing to the market.

Resource Editor. An application that manages non-code resources, such as multilingual texts, pictures, and videos, used in programming.

Revision Controller. An application that tracks and controls revisions to code and other kinds of documents. Essential to team development and programming.

Source Code Editor. A text editor designed specifically for creating and editing code by programmers. It may be a stand-alone application or a built-in component in an *integrated development environment* (IDE).

Tester. An application that verifies the working of the software from *outside*. See also **debugger**.

Testing. A process with two goals: *validation*—are we building the right product?—and *verification*—are we building the product right? Software must be tested for each phase of implementation and deployment. Different types of testing include unit testing, component testing, integration testing, system testing, and acceptance testing.

Updating. The process of installing a new version of the software.

User Training. Any activity or artifact—classes, online help, tutorials, etc.—that helps the users to work with an information system or an application. User training must be tailored to "who," "what," and "where."

Virtual Machine. A complex and comprehensive **interpreter** that mimics a whole computer system. Virtual machines are, at least theoretically, platform independent.

8. REVIEW QUESTIONS

1. When can we, or should we, start implementation?
2. What are the major activities of implementation? How do they relate to each other?
3. Some might say that coding is not as important as analysis or design since programming errors can be identified and corrected easily. Do you agree with this statement? Why?
4. Do we need coding standards even if they make no difference to the functionality of software?
5. Compare and contrast assemblers, compilers, interpreters, and virtual machines.
6. Is technological excellence enough for choosing a programming language?
7. What roles do code review and testing play in quality assurance? Compare and contrast.
8. Why do we need different *levels* of testing? Can't we just test the finished software?
9. Does object-oriented technology help or hinder testing?
10. Is the development life cycle over with deployment?

9. RESEARCH PROJECTS & TEAMWORK

❶ Conduct research on the most popular *development* languages and *platforms*. (There are not that many.) Find out what the proponents of one say *against* the other. Gather the findings of team members and submit them to your instructor.

❷ Select a software with which all team members are familiar. Individually, create a list of **bugs** and annoying features that you have encountered in using the software.

What are the possible reasons—defective design or insufficient testing? Consolidate your lists and your answers.

❸ Select a software and study its *"help"* documents—printed, digital, or online. What are their shortcomings? How can they be improved? How can the design of the software itself be improved to *lessen* the dependence on documentation?

10. SUGGESTED READINGS

For *any* topic or subtopic in this chapter, especially programming and languages, you will find more books than the combined total for the majority of subjects in the previous chapters (or so it appears). Implementation is not all about coding and technology, the same way that building a bridge is not exclusively about civil engineering. Computer science, however, is as essential to writing software as engineering is to building bridges and other structures.

A deservedly popular book on computer science is *Computer Science: An Overview, 7th Edition* (Addison-Wesley, 2003) by **J. Glenn Brookshear**. One such book, of course, cannot cover in detail a subject as extensive as this one, but as an overview it achieves its goal. What is more, the book often provides a historical perspective that is sorely needed but is frequently missing from books on computer science.

A number of books that we suggested previously have chapters on various topics of implementation. Sometimes, a suggested book is packaged as a guide to programming in this or that language but is actually more than that (which is why we are suggesting them in a book on analysis and design).

REFERENCES

[Alexander 1977] Alexander, Christopher, Sara Ishikawa, and Murray Silverstein, 1977. *Pattern Language: Towns, Buildings, Construction.* New York: Oxford University Press.

[Alhir 1998] Alhir, Sinan Si, 1998. *UML in a Nutshell.* Sebastopol, CA: O'Reilly.

[American Heritage 1996] *The American Heritage® Dictionary of the English Language,* Third Edition, 1996. Houghton Mifflin Company.

[Arlow 2004] Arlow, Jim, and Ila Neustadt, 2004. *Enterprise Patterns and MDA: Building Better Software with Archetype Patterns and UML.* Boston: Addison-Wesley.

[Armour 2001] Armour, Frank, and Granville Miller, 2001. *Advanced Use Case Modeling: Software Systems.* Boston: Addison-Wesley.

[Arrington 2003] Arrington, C. T., and Sayed H. Rayhan, 2003. *Enterprise Java with UML.* New York: Wiley.

[Ashrafi 1995] Ashrafi, Noushin, Hessam Ashrafi, and Jean-Pierre Kuilboer, "ISO-9000-3: Guidelines for Software Quality," *Information Systems Management,* Summer 1995.

[Avison 2003] Avison, David E., and G. Fitzgerald, "Where Now for Development Methodologies?" *Communications of the ACM,* Vol. 46, No. 1 (January 2003).

[Avison 1995] Avison, David E., and G. Fitzgerald, 1995. *Information Systems Development: Methodologies, Techniques and Tools, 2nd Edition.* London: McGraw-Hill Book Company.

[Awalt 2004] Awalt, Don, and Rick McUmber, "Secrets of Great Architects," *Microsoft Architects Journal,* Vol. 3 (July 2004).

[Bahrami 1999] Bharami, Ali, 1999. *Object-Oriented Systems Development: Using the Unified Modeling Language.* Boston: Irwin McGraw-Hill.

[Basiura 2001] Basiura, Russ, Mike Batongbacal, Brandon Bphling, Mike Clark, Andreas Eide, Robert Eisenberg, Brian Loesgen, Christopher L. Miller, Matthew Reynold, Bill Sempf, and Srinivasa Sivakumar, 2001. *Professional ASP.NET Web Services.* Birmingham, UK: Wrox Press.

[Bass 2003] Bass, Len, Paul Clements, and Rick Kazman, 2003. *Software Architecture in Practice, Second Edition.* Boston: Addison-Wesley.

[Beck 2000] Beck, Kent, 2000. *Extreme Programming Explained.* Boston: Addison-Wesley.

[Bennet 2002] Bennett, Simon, Steve McRobb, and Ray Farmer, 2002. *Object-Oriented Systems Analysis and Design Using UML.* Englewood Cliffs, NJ: Prentice Hall.

[Bittner 2002] Bittner, Kurt, and Ian Spence, 2002. *Use Case Modeling.* Boston: Addison-Wesley.

[Blum 1992] Blum, Bruce I., 1992. *Software Engineering: A Holistic View.* New York: Oxford University Press.

[Booch 1999] Booch, Grady, James Rumbaugh, and Ivar Jacobson, 1999. *The Unified Modeling Language User Guide.* Boston: Addison-Wesley.

[Booch 1994] Booch, Grady, 1994. *Object-Oriented Analysis and Design with Applications, Second Edition.* Redwood City, CA: The Benjamin/Cummings Publishing Company, Inc.

[Brooks 1995] Brooks, Frederick P., Jr., 1995. *The Mythical Man-Month: Essays on Software Engineering.* Reading, MA: Addison-Wesley Publishing Company.

[Brookshear 2003] Brookshear, J. Glenn, 2003. *Computer Science: An Overview: 7th Edition.* Reading, MA: Addison-Wesley Publishing Company.

[Brown 2001] Brown, Kyle, Gary Craig, Greg Hester, Jaime Niswonger, David Pitt, and Russell Stinehour, 2001. *Enterprise Java Programming with IBM WebSphere.* Upper Saddle River, NJ: Pearson Education.

[Brown 1998] Brown, William H., Raphael C. Malveau, Hays W. "Skip" McCormick III, and Thomas J. Mowbray, 1998. *Anti-Patterns: Refactoring Software, Architectures, and Projects in Crisis.* New York: Wiley.

[Campbell-Kelly 2003] Campbell-Kelly, Martin, 2003. *From Airline Reservations to Sonic the Hedgehog: A History of the Software Industry.* Cambridge, MA: The MIT Press.

[Chapin 2002] Donald Chapin, "What's the Business in Business Rules?" *Business Rules Journal,* Vol. 3, No. 10 (October 2002). URL: http://www.BRCommunity.com/a2002/b119.html.

[Chessman 2001] Chessman, John, and John Daniels, 2001. *UML Components: A Simple Process for Specifying Component-Based Software,* 2001. Boston: Addison-Wesley.

[Chiera 1938] Chiera, Edward, 1938. *They Wrote on Clay.* Chicago: The University of Chicago Press. (Copyright Renewed 1966)

[Chisholm 2002] Malcolm Chisholm, "The Black Box Problem," *Business Rules Journal*, Vol. 3, No. 3 (March 2002). URL: http://www.BRCommunity.com/a2002/b100.html.

[Chonoles 2003] Chonoles, Michael Jesse, and James A. Schardt, 2003. *UML 2 for Dummies*. Indianapolis, IN: Wiley Publishing, Inc.

[Clark 2001] Clark, Andy, 2001. *Mindware: An Introduction to the Philosophy of Cognitive Science*. New York: Oxford University Press.

[Coad 1997] Coad, Peter, Mark Mayfield, and David North, 1997. *Object Models: Strategies, Patterns, and Applications, 2nd Edition*. Upper Saddle River, NJ: Prentice Hall.

[Coad 1992] Coad, Peter, "Object-Oriented Patterns," *Communications of the ACM*, Vol. 35, No. 9 (September 1992).

[Cockburn 2002] Cockburn, Alistair, 2002. *Agile Software Development*. Boston: Addison-Wesley.

[Cockburn 2001] Cockburn, Alistair, 2001. *Writing Effective Use Cases*. Boston: Addison-Wesley.

[Codd 1979] Codd, E. F., "Extending the Data Base Relational Model to Capture More Meaning," *ACM Transactions on Database Systems*, Vol. 4, No. 4 (December 1979), 397–434.

[Codd 1970] Codd, E. F., "A Relational Model of Data for Large Shared Data Banks," *Communications of ACM*, Vol. 13, No. 6 (June 1970), 377–387.

[Conallen 2003] Conallen, Jim, 2003. *Building Web Applications with UML, Second Edition*. Boston: Addison-Wesley.

[Cook 1996] Cook, Melissa, 1996. *Building Enterprise Information Architecture: Reengineering Information Systems*. Upper Saddle River, NJ: Prentice Hall.

[Cooper 1995] Cooper, Alan, 1995. *About Face: The Essentials of User Interface Design*. Foster City, CA: IDG Books.

[Cooper 2003] Cooper, James W., 2003. *C# Design Patterns: A Tutorial*. Boston: Addison-Wesley

[Coplien 1997] Coplien, James O., 1997. "Domain Analysis and Patterns," Bell Labs. URL: http://users.rcn.com/jcoplien/oopsla/OopslaDomainPatterns-1.html.

[Crnkovic 2002] Crnkovic, Ivica, Brahim Hnich, Torsten Jonsson, and Zeynep Kiziltan, "Specification, Implementation, and Deployment of Components," *Communications of ACM*, Vol. 45, No. 10 (October 2002).

[D'Souza 1999] D'Souza, Desmond Francis, and Cameron Wills, 1999. *Objects, Components, and Frameworks with UML: The Catalysis Approach*. Boston: Addison-Wesley.

[Dutka 1989] Dutka, Alan F., and Howard H. Hanson, 1989. *Fundamentals of Data Normalization*. Reading, MA: Addison-Wesley.

[Evitts 2000] Evitts, Paul, 2000. *A UML Pattern Language*. Indianapolis: Macmillan Technical Publishing (MTP).

[Faison 2002] Faison, Ted, 2002. *Component-Based Development with Visual C#*. New York: M&T Books (Wily).

[Fielding 2000] Fielding, Roy Thomas, 2000. *Architectural Styles and the Design of Network-Based Software Architecture*. Doctoral Dissertation. University of California, Irvin. URL: http://www.ics.uci.edu/~fielding/pubs/dissertation.

[Fowler 2003] Fowler, Martin, 2003. *Patterns of Enterprise Application Architecture*. Boston: Addison-Wesley.

[Fowler 2000a] Fowler, Martin, with Kendall Scott, 2000. *UML Distilled, Second Edition: A Brief Guide to the Standard Modeling Language*. Boston: Addison-Wesley.

[Fowler 2000b] Fowler, Martin, 2000. *Refactoring: Improving the Design of Existing Code*. Boston: Addison-Wesley.

[Fowler 1997] Fowler, Martin, 1997. *Analysis Pattern: Reusable Object Models*. Boston: Addison-Wesley.

[Freeman 2004] Freeman, Eric, and Elisabeth Freeman with Kathy Sierra and Bert Bates, 2004. *Head First Design Patterns*. Sebastopol, CA: O'Reilly.

[Gamma 1997] Gamma, Erich, Richard Helm, Ralph Johnson, and John Vlissides, 1997. *Design Patterns: Elements of Reusable Object Oriented Software*. Reading, MA: Addison-Wesley.

[Glass 2002] Glass, Robert L., 2002. *Facts and Fallacies of Software Engineering*. Boston: Addison-Wesley.

[Goldfedder 2002] Goldfedder, Brandon, 2002. *The Joy of Patterns: Using Patterns for Enterprise Development*. Boston: Addison-Wesley.

[Graham 2001] Graham, Ian, Alan O'Callaghan, and Alan Cameron Wills, 2001. *Object-Oriented Methods: Principles & Practice, Third Edition*. Boston: Addison-Wesley.

[Groff 1999] Groff, James R., and Paul N. Weinberg, 1999. *SQL: The Complete Reference*. Berkeley: Osborne/McGraw-Hill.

[Haggerty 2000] Neville Haggerty, 2000. "Modeling Business Rules Using the UML and CASE," Business Rules Community. URL: http://www.brcommunity.com/cgi-bin/x.pl/features/b016.html.

[Halpin 2001] Halpin, Terry, 2001. *Information Modeling and Relational Databases: From Conceptual Analysis to*

Logical Design, Using ORM with ER and UML. San Fransisco: Morgan Kaufmann Publishers.

[Harmon 2000] Harmon, Paul, Michael Rosen, and Michael Guttman, 2000. *Developing E-Business Systems and Architectures: A Manager's Guide.* San Francisco, CA: Morgan Kaufmann.

[Hilliard 1999] Hilliard, Rich, 1999. "Using the UML for Architectural Description," *UML 99: Proceedings of Second International Conference on the Unified Modeling Language.* New York: Springer-Verlag.

[Jackson 2001] Jackson, Michael, 2001. *Problem Frames: Analyzing and Structuring Software Development Problems.* Harlow, England: Addison-Wesley.

[Jackson 1995] Jackson, Michael, 1995. *Software-Requirements and Specifications: A Lexicon of Practice, Principles and Prejudices.* Harlow, England: Addison-Wesley.

[Jacobson 1999] Jacobson, Ivar, Grady Booch, and James Rumbaugh, 1999. *The Unified Software Development Process.* Boston: Addison-Wesley.

[Jacobson 1995] Jacobson, Ivar, Maria Ericsson, and Agneta Jacobson, 1995. *The Object Advantage: Business Process Reengineering With Object Technology.* Wokingham, England: Addison-Wesley.

[Jacobson 1992] Jacobson, Ivar, Magnus Christerson, Patrik Jonsson, and Gunnar Övergaard, 1992. *Object-Oriented Software Engineering: A Use Case Driven Approach.* Harlow, England: Addison-Wesley.

[Johnson 2000] Johnson, Jeff, 2000. *GUI Bloopers: Don'ts and Do's for Software Developers and Web Designers.* San Fransisco: Morgan Kaufmann Publishers.

[Kean 2001] Kean, Liz, 2001. "Domain Engineering and Domain Analysis," Carnegie Mellon University: The Software Engineering Institute (SEI). URL: http://www.sei.cmu.edu/str/descriptions/deda_body.html.

[Kendall 1999] Kendall, Kenneth E., and Julie E. Kendall, 1999. *Systems Analysis and Design,* Fourth Edition. Upper Saddle River, NJ: Prentice Hall.

[Kleppe 2003] Kleppe, Anneke, Jos Warmer, and Wim Bast, 2003. *MDA Explained, The Model Driven Architecture: Practice and Promise.* Boston: Addison-Wesley.

[Kulak 2000] Kulak, Daryl, and Eamonn Guiney, 2000. *Use Cases: Requirements in Context.* New York: ACM Press.

[Landay 1996] Landay, James A., and Brad A. Myers. "Sketching Storyboards to Illustrate Interface Behaviors," Electrical Engineering and Computer Sciences, University of California at Berkeley. URL: http://www.cs.berkeley.edu/~landay/research/publications/CHI96/short_storyboard.html.

[Leffingwell 2000] Leffingwell, Dean, and Don Widrig, 2000. *Managing Software Requirements: A Unified Approach.* Boston: Addison-Wesley.

[Lin 2002] Nelson Lin, "Alternatives for Rule-based Application Development," *Business Rules Journal,* Vol. 3, No. 10 (October 2002). URL: http://www.BRCommunity.com/a2002/n007.html.

[MacDonald 2002] MacDonald, Mathew, 2002. *User Interfaces in C#: Windows Forms and Custom Controls.* New York: APress (Springer-Verlag, New York, Inc.).

[Malveau 2001] Malveau, Raphel, and Thomas J. Mowbray, 2001. *Software Architect Bootcamp.* Upper Saddle River, NJ: Prentice Hall.

[Martin 1996] Martin, James, and James J. Odell, 1996. *Object-Oriented Methods: Pragmatic Considerations.* Upper Saddle River, NJ: Prentice Hall.

[Martin 1995] Martin, James and James J. Odell, 1995. *Object-Oriented Methods: A Foundation.* Upper Saddle River, NJ: Prentice Hall.

[Mayhew 1992] Mayhew, Deborah, J., 1992. *Principles and Guidelines in Software User Interface.* Englewood Cliffs, NJ: Prentice Hall.

[McBreen 2002] McBreen, Pete, 2002. *Software Craftsmanship: The New Imperative.* Boston: Addison-Wesley.

[McClure 1997] McClure, Carma, 1997. *Software Reuse Techniques: Adding Reuse to the System Development Process.* Upper Saddle River, NJ: Prentice Hall.

[McConnel 1996] McConnel, Steve, 1996. *Rapid Development: Taming Wild Software Schedules.* Redmond, WA: Microsoft Press.

[Muller 1999] Muller, Robert J., 1999. *Database Design for Smarties: Using UML for Data Modeling.* San Fransisco: Morgan Kaufmann Publishers, Inc.

[Muller 1997] Muller, Pierre-Alain, 1997. *Instant UML.* Birmingham, UK: Wrox Press.

[Naiburg 2001] Naiburg, Eric J., and Robert A. MaksimChuk, 2001. *UML for Database Design.* Boston: Addison-Wesley.

[Neighbors 1981] J. Neighbors, 1981. *Software Construction Using Components.* Ph.D. Thesis. Irvine: Department of Information and Computer Science, University of California.

[Nock 2004] Nock, Clifton, 2004. *Data Access Patterns: Database Interactions in Object-Oriented Applications.* Boston: Addison-Wesley.

[Norman 2005] Norman, Jeremy M. 2005. *From Gutenberg to the Internet: A Sourcebook on the History of Information Technology.* Novato, CA: Historyofscience.com.

[Norman 2004] Norman, Donald A. 2004. *Emotional Design: Why We Love (or Hate) Everyday Things.* New York: Basic Books.

[Norman 2002] Norman, Donald A. 2002. *The Design of Everyday Things.* New York: Basic Books

[Ommering, 2002] Ommering, Rob van, 2002. "Building Product Populations with Software Components," *International Conference on Software Engineering: Proceedings of the 24th International Conference on Software Engineering.* ACM, 2002. URL: http://portal.acm.org.

[Orfali, 1997] Orfali, Robert, and Dan Harkey, 1997. *Client/Server Programming with Java and CORBA.* New York: John Wiley & Sons, Inc.

[O'Rourke 2003] O'Rourke, Carol, Neal Fishman, and Warren Selkow, 2003. *Enterprise Architecture Using the Zachman Framework.* Boston: Course Technology.

[Parnas 2001] Parnas, David L., 2001. *Software Fundamentals: Collected Papers by David L. Parnas.* Boston: Addison-Wesley.

[Petroski 2003] Petroski, Henry, 2003. *Why There Is No Perfect Design.* New York: Vintage Books.

[Petroski 1985] Petroski, Henry, 1985. *To Engineer Is Human: The Role of Failure in Successful Design.* New York: St. Martin Press.

[Prieto-Diaz 1990] Prieto-Diaz, Rubén, "Domain Analysis: An Introduction," *Software Engineering Notes*, 15–2, April 1990. URL: http://www.cs.jmu.edu.

[Ravichandran 2003] Ravichandran, T, and Marcus A. Rothenberger, "Software Reuse Strategies And Component Markets," *Communications of the ACM*, Vol. 46, No. 8. (August 2003).

[Reeder 2001] Judi Reeder, 2001. "Templates for Capturing Business Rules," Business Rules Community. URL: http://www.brcommunity.com/cgi-bin/x.pl/features/b056.html.

[Robertson 1999] Robertson, Suzanne, and James Robertson, 1999. *Mastering the Requirements Process.* Harlow, England: Addison-Wesley.

[Rosenberg 1999] Rosenberg, Doug, and Kendall Scott, 1999. *Use Case Driven Object Modeling with UML: A Practical Approach.* Boston: Addison-Wesley.

[Royce 1998] Royce, Walker, 1998. *Software Project Management: A Unified Framework.* Boston: Addison-Wesley.

[Schneider 2001] Schneider, Geri, and Jason P. Winters, 2001. *Applying Use Cases, Second Edition: A Practical Guide.* Boston: Addison-Wesley.

[Shneiderman 1986] Shneiderman, B., 1986. *Designing the User Interface: Strategies for Effective Human-Computer Interaction.* Reading, MA: Addison-Wesley.

[Shoemaker 2004] Shoemaker, Martin L., 2004. *UML Applied: A .Net Perspective.* New York: APress (Springer-Verlag, New York, Inc.)

[Smith 1986] Smith, Sidney L., and Jane Mosier, 1986. "Guidelines for Designing User Interface Software," Report ESD-TR-86-278, Electronic System Division, MITRE Corporation, Bedford, MA. URL: http://hcibib.org/sam/.

[Sparks 2001] Sparks, Geoffrey, 2001. "Database Modelling in UML," Methods & Tools e-newsletter. URL: http://www.martinig.ch/mt/index.html.

[Spolsky 2001] Spolsky, Joel, 2001. *User Interface Design for Programmers.* New York: APress (Springer-Verlag, New York, Inc.).

[Starr 2004] Starr, Paul, 2004. *The Creation of the Media: Political Origins of Modern Communications.* New York: Basic Books.

[Stephens 2003] Stephens, Matt, and Doug Rosenberg, 2003. *Extreme Programming Refactored: The Case Against XP.* New York: APress (Springer-Verlag, New York, Inc.).

[Strum 1999] Strum, Jake, 1999. *VB6 UML: Design and Development.* Birmingham, UK: Wrox Press Ltd.

[Szyperski 2002] Szyperski, Clemens, 2002. *Component Software: Beyond Object-Oriented Programming, Second Edition.* Boston: Addison-Wesley.

[Taylor 1998] Taylor, David A., 1998. *Object Technology, A Manager's Guide: Second Edition.* Boston: Addison-Wesley.

[Tenner 1996] Tenner, Edward, 1996. *Why Things Bite Back.* New York: Vintage Books.

[Togaf 2002] Open Group Architecture Forum (TOGAF), 2002. "Developing Architecture View," The Open Group. URL: http://www.opengroup.org/architecture.

[Urman 2002] Urman, Scott, 2002. *Oracle 9i PL/SQL Programming.* New York: Oracle Press, McGraw-Hill/Osborne.

[Van Gigch 1991] Van Gigch, John P., 1991. *System Design Modeling and Metamodeling (The Language of Science).* New York: Plenum Pub Corp.

[Van Slyke 2003] Van Slyke, Craig , and France Bélanger, 2003. *E-Business Technologies: Supporting the Net-Enhanced Organization.* New York: John Wiley & Sons, Inc.

[Viera 2000] Viera, Robert, 2000. *Professional SQL Server Programming.* Birmingham, UK: Wrox Press Ltd.

[Vitharana 2003] Vitharana, Padmal, "Risks and Challenges of Component-Based Software Development," *Communications of the ACM*, Vol. 46, No. 8 (August 2003).

[Wampler 2002] Wampler, B. E., 2002. *The Essence of Object-Oriented Programming with JAVA and UML*. Boston: Addison-Wesley.

[Webster 1995] Webster, Bruce F., 1995. *Pitfalls of Objected-Oriented Development*. New York: M&T Books.

[Weisfeld 2000] Weisfeld, Matt, 2000. *The Object-Oriented Thought Process: The Authoritative Solution*.Indianapolis, IN: Sams Publishing.

[White 1997] White, S. A., and C. Lemus, 1997. "The Software Architecture Process," University of Houston-Clear Lake. URL: http://nas.cl.uh.edu/whites/webpapers.dir/ETCE97pap.pdf.

[Wiegers 2003] Karl E. Wiegers, 2003. Managing *Software Requirements*. Redmond, WA: Microsoft Press.

[Wirfs-Brock 2003] Wirfs-Brock, Rebecca, and Alan McKean, 2003. *Object Design: Roles, Responsibilities, and Collaborations*. Boston: Addison-Wesley.

[Wysocki 2000] Wysocki, Robert K., Robert Beck Jr., and David B. Crane, 2000. *Effective Prject Management, Second Edition*. New York: John Wiley & Sons, Inc.

[Yourdon 1994] Yourdon, Edward, 1994. *Object-Oriented System Design: An Integrated Approach*. Upper Saddle River, NJ: Prentice Hall.

[Zachman 1987] Zachman, J. A., "A Framework for Information System Architecture," *IBM Systems Journal*, Vol. 26, No. 3 (1987).

INDEX

Page numbers with f indicate figures; those with t indicate tables.

A

Abstract class, 41–42, 41f
Abstractions, 34
 class as, 251, 252, 295
 classification and, 33, 50
 generalization and, 283, 283f
 hierarchical, 35
 inheritance and, 519
 interface and, 256, 526–527
 methodology and, 56–57
 modeling and, level of, 78
 parallel, 35
 process of, 197–198, 197f, 198t
 use case steps and, 217
Abstract units, 295
Acceptance testing, 74, 592
Accessor methods, 305, 387,
  388–389
Accessor operations, 304–305
Accounting firms, 15
Acme International, 5, 5f, 6
Action enablers, 171
Activity diagrams, 238, 326, 327f
 building blocks of, 240t
 deliverables and, 243, 328
 flow chart and, 47
 logical flow and, 238, 239f, 319
 swimlane and, 326
 synchronization bar and, 326
 use case and, 238, 244
 workflow and, 566
Activity thread (path), 87, 96
Actor generalization, 223, 243, 244
 abstract actors and, 224
 children, 231–232, 244
 concrete actors and, 224
 multi-levels of, 224
 parent actors (super-use case),
  231, 244
 specialization and, 224, 243
 sub-roles, 224
 super-roles, 223, 223f, 224
 system's response to, 217–218
Actor instance, 312, 314
Actors, 188
 abstract, 224
 business, 212–213
 class and, traits shared by, 314
 concrete, 224, 231
 discovering, process of abstraction
  and, 197–198, 197f, 198t
 prominent, identifying, 196–198
 qualifications of
 as a role, 187–188
 specialized, 224

supporting (or secondary), 188, 190,
  213, 213f, 214
use case and, 187–188, 187f
Actors, primary, 187, 191, 212
 delineating use cases and, 235
 extend relationship and, 226
 include relationship and, 227–228
 vs. initiator of use cases, 212
 multiple, 213
 as stakeholders, 214
 supporting actors and, 213, 213f
Actor system, 212–213
Adaptation, 594
Adapters, 505–506, 506f, 552–553
Ad hoc, 65, 94, 96
Adornments, 355–356, 356f
Aggregates, 281–282, 472–473, 481
Aggregation
 composition and, 40, 281–282,
  281f, 282f
 elementary attributes and, 471
 inheritance and, 484f
 many-to-many multiplicity and, 484
 of objects, 40, 40f, 51
 open-ended, 484
 relationships, 51
 self-referencing, 479, 479f, 484, 484f
Agile methodologies, 72, 93, 95, 96
Alexander, Christopher, 498–499, 500
Algorithm, 17
Alternate flow, 297t, 316, 316t
Alternate key, 456, 458, 483
Alternate messages, 313
Amazon.com, 17, 562
American Airlines, 451
Analog data, 444
Analysis patterns, 506–508, 508f
Anecdotes, 56
Anonymous messages, 308
ANSI (American National Standards
  Institute), 451–452
Anti-patterns, 510–512, 511f
Application flow, 371
 control and, 379, 381, 381f, 382f, 383
 dataset and, 378–379, 380f
 life cycle object and, 375,
  377–378, 377f
 object of, 374–375, 376f
 use case, magnifying, 371–374,
  372–373f
Applications, 13–14
 components of, major, 370f
 control of, 370–371
 definition of, 369
 state of, 390, 391f, 392–393
 vs. systems, 14

web, 390, 391f, 392–393
 see also Architectural components and
  applications
Application server, 558
Architect's view, 48
Architectural components and
  applications, 558–559
 coupling and, architectural, 552
 distributed components, 560–561
 distributed, 560–561
 monolithic applications, 559–560
 SOA, 561–563
 virtual, 561–562
Architectural design, 64, 81, 95
Architectural diagrams, 534
Architectural elements, 546–547
Architectural enterprise, 14
Architectural frameworks, 548
 4 + 1, 548, 572–573, 573f
 technology and, 555, 556–557, 558
 UML and, 553
 views and viewpoints and, 553, 555
Architectural patterns, 498–499, 499f,
  503, 566–567
 see also Layering patterns
Architectural rationale, 547
Architectural style, 547
Architectural views, 548–549, 553, 555
Architecture, 96, 545–546
 architectural views and, 548–549
 centralized, 555, 556–557, 558
 as composition, 550–551
 connectors and, 546, 552
 coupling and, 551–553
 course building blocks and, 250
 defining, 545–546
 deliverables and, 572–573, 572f
 design concepts and, 347
 elements of architecture and, 546–547
 engineering and, 549–550
 maintainability and, 108
 patterns and methodology of, 547–548
 UML and, 553–555
 unbalanced, 68
 see also Distributed architecture
Architecture of information systems, 555
 data management and, 563–564
 modeling and conceptualization and,
  564–565
 vs. software architecture, 555
 workflow and, 565–566
 see also Architectural components and
  applications
Arguments. *See* Parameters
Artifact, 77, 95
Artificial intelligence (AI) systems, 17